The King of God's Kingdom
A Solution to the Puzzle of Jesus

The King of God's Kingdom

A Solution to the Puzzle of Jesus

David Seccombe

PATERNOSTER PRESS

Copyright © 2002 David Seccombe
George Whitefield College
PO Box 64
Muizenberg 7950
South Africa
Phone: +27 21 7881652
Fax: +27 21 7881662
email: dseccombe@gwc.ac.za

First published in 2002 by Paternoster Press

08 07 06 05 04 03 02   7 6 5 4 3 2 1

Paternoster Press is an imprint of Authentic Media,
P.O. Box 300, Carlisle, Cumbria, CA3 0QS, UK
and
P.O. Box 1047, Waynesboro, GA 30830-2047, USA

Website: www.paternoster-publishing.com

British Library Cataloguing in Publication Data
A catalogue record for this book is available from the British Library

ISBN 1-84227-075-3

Cover Design by FourNineZero
Typeset by WestKey Ltd, Falmouth, Cornwall
Printed and bound in Great Britain by Biddles Ltd, *www.biddles.co.uk*

Contents

Abbreviations   *x*

Introduction   *xi*

Chapter 1 Dead Or Alive?   **1**
  Christianity is Different   1
  The Earliest Christian Preaching   4
  Two Thousand Years of Resurrection Debate   5
  What Kind of Evidence?   13

Chapter 2 Evidence   **17**
  The Empty Tomb   17
  The Testimony of Witnesses   23

Chapter 3 The Resurrection Story In   **33**
The Four Gospels
  Evidence From the Four Gospels   33
  When Were the Gospels Written?   36
  What does Mark Tell Us?   45
  What do we Learn from Luke and Acts?   49
  Does Matthew Add Anything New?   54
  What Else Does John Say?   60
  Is the Evidence Sufficient?   64

Chapter 4 The Prophet And The King   **70**
The Appearance of John   70
Was John a Political Revolutionary?   73
How did John see Himself?   75
A National Crisis   78
The Coming One   80
Repentance and Baptism   82
Jesus is Baptized   88
The King–Messiah   90
Jesus is Appointed King–Messiah   96
The Gospel Writers' View of Jesus' Baptism   100
A Critical Moment   103

Chapter 5 The Enemy   **108**
Alone in the Desert   108
Satan   115
Temptation   120

Chapter 6 Becoming Known   **136**
The Gospel of John and the Story of Jesus   136
Early Experiences   141
Pointers to a New Age   147
Baptizing in Judaea   150

Chapter 7 Herald Of God's Kingdom   **155**
In Nazareth   156
The Kingdom of God Debate   166
The Source of Jesus' Kingdom Understanding   178
Jesus' Contemporaries and the Kingdom   186
The Gospeller   191

Chapter 8 Capernaum By The Sea   **200**
Capernaum   200
Socio-Economic Pointers   206
A Day in the Life of Jesus of Nazareth   211
Authority   219

Chapter 9 All The King's Men **229**
Kingdom and People 229
The First Followers 230
Sinners 233
Celebration 240
Many Disciples 243
The Twelve 247
The Sermon on the Mount 249
Kingdom Living 261
Jesus' 'Ethical System' 264
The Kingdom and Possessions 265
Perplexing Questions 270

Chapter 10 Miracle Worker **277**
A Contradiction 277
Miracles 279
Other First-Century Wonder-Workers 284
Jesus the Miracle Worker 289
Demon Possession 295
Jesus and Evil Spirits 301
Did Jesus Really Do These Things? 306
Signs of the Kingdom 310

Chapter 11 Parables Of Divine Strategy **319**
Parable Maker 319
Seeds of the Kingdom 323
Interpreting Parables 326
Parable of the Sower 329
Harvest 333
God's Empire 339
A Hidden Kingdom 341
A Compromised Kingdom 342
Jesus' Strategy 345
The Mysteries of the Kingdom 348
A Ministry of the Word 351

Chapter 12 Opposition **357**
   Many Enemies   357
   Two Great Issues   359
   The Pharisees   362
   Lord of the Sabbath   370
   God's Commandments and Human Traditions   378
   Marriage and Divorce   382
   Real Defilement   385
   The Commandments and the Kingdom   387
   Conclusion   390

Chapter 13 Who Is This Man? **398**
   Expanding the Mission   398
   Jesus' Road Team   399
   The Mission of the Twelve   400
   Herod Hears   406
   The Feeding of the Five Thousand   410
   Departure from Galilee   413
   A Story of Human Struggle   416
   Who is He?   422
   A Suffering Messiah   428

Chapter 14 Last Chance **440**
   Final Months in Galilee   440
   Decision to Die   446
   Result of the Mission in Galilee   447
   Proclaiming the Kingdom to Judaea   452
   The Journey to Jerusalem   459
   The Power and the Glory   463
   Why Must Jesus Die?   467
   The Disciples and the Cross   473
   And After Three Days Rise   475

Chapter 15 The Coming Of The King **483**
   The Raising of Lazarus   483
   Jesus Becomes an Outlaw   488

Return to Jerusalem 491
The Kingdom is Delayed 493
The Disillusioned Disciple 499
Royal Procession 501
The Temple 506
Jesus in the Temple 509

Chapter 16 Day Of Judgement **520**
Official Reaction 520
The Last Meal 521
Gethsemane 532
The Judgement of the Jews 537
The Judgement of Rome 543
The Charge Against Jesus 546
The Judgement of the World 551
The Last Battle 553
Burial 559

Chapter 17 The Future **568**
Journey's End? 568
Beyond the Tomb 571
Who Was He? 572
The Question of the Future 576
What if Israel had Accepted Jesus? 578
Jesus' Predictions 581
Did Jesus Predict the Time of His Coming? 591
Final Solution 597
The Mission and Achievement of Jesus 601

Bibliography 606
Scripture Index 621
Ancient Sources Index 634
Author Index 636
Subject Index 641

Abbreviations

ANF   *The Anti-Nicene Fathers,* various editors (Edinburgh: T&T Clark; Grand Rapids: Eerdmans, 1979 onwards)

DJD   *Discoveries in the Judaean Desert,* eds. D. Barthélemy et al. (Oxford: Oxford University Press, 1955 onwards)

NDIEC   *New Documents Illustrating Early Christianity,* ed. G.H.R. Horsley (Sydney: Macquarie University, 1976 onwards)

NPNF   *The Nicene and Post Nicene Fathers* 1st and 2nd series, various editors (Grand Rapids: Eerdmans, 1978 onwards)

OCD   *The Oxford Classical Dictionary,* ed. S. Hornblower & A. Spawforth (Oxford University Press, 1996[3])

SB   H.L. Strack & P. Billerbeck, *Kommentar zum neuen Testament aus Talmud und Midrasch* (München: C.H. Beck, 1926–1961)

TDNT   *Theological Dictionary of the New Testament,* ed. G. Kittel (Grand Rapids: Eerdmans, 1964–1976)

Introduction

With the dawn of a third millennium important questions demand answers. What kind of man launched the faith we know as Christianity? Did he do so deliberately, or by accident? What was his vision of the future? Was and is it a realistic, tenable vision? Is Christianity consistent with his vision? Is the church the sum total of his vision, or did he intend more? Is Christianity and the legacy of Jesus a blessing or a curse? Such issues crowd upon us as we try to evaluate the life of the man whose birth marks the commencement of our millennial system.

At the most superficial level it is easy to argue that Jesus has proved to be the most influential person who ever lived. Yet the new millennium finds many wishing for a post-Christian age, for a world society which has outgrown religious differences, as it has outgrown racial and other differentiations. John Lennon's oft-played song 'Imagine' hits the mark. But what if 'nothing to die for,' meant nothing to live for. A utopia of well-fed, comfortable consumers was an option Jesus rejected with the words, 'Human beings shall not live by bread alone, but …' This 'but' signalled his own vision for what he called 'the Kingdom of God.' In part this book is an attempt to uncover and understand that vision.

At the outset of the Christian era Jesus announced the coming of a new age, and those who believed him played a big part in shaping the last two thousand years. They have never had the field to themselves; there has always been conflict with other dreams for the future. Nevertheless, the modern world with its hospitals and hospices, schools and universities, legal, labour, and welfare systems, has been shaped in large measure by their struggles.

Will the followers of Jesus continue to be shapers? The last year of the second millennium marked the end of two centuries of Christian penetration into Africa. Christianity has become the dominant faith of most countries of South, East, Central and West Africa. In the same years it has spread into China, India, South East Asia, the Pacific, Australasia, Korea and many former non-Christian lands. Christianity's advances in Africa and Asia in the past century have so far outstripped the decline in the west that the missiologist Patrick Johnstone says 'we are living in the time of the largest ingathering of people into the Kingdom of God that the world has ever seen.'[1] What Christianity's future will be in the third millennium remains to be seen.

Christianity's Great Enemy

Christianity's greatest problem has always been the enemy within: its adherents' ignorance of Jesus' original vision. An African Christian leader has described Christianity there as 'an enormous lake – one inch deep.' Impoverished understanding is the major cause of Christian decline, whether it takes the African form of syncretistic mergers with other belief systems, or the western one of bored disdain for its apparent irrelevance.

This ignorance begins with lack of knowledge about Jesus, and in no small measure stems from the two hundred year troubled history of attempts to write his life. When the four gospels stood to people's minds as revelation from God, there was hardly need for anything further to explicate the man. But the end of the eighteenth century saw the collapse of this consensus. The discovery of ancient gospel manuscripts containing readings at variance with the received text sowed the seeds of doubt. Radical rewritings of the Jesus story, portraying him as a political revolutionary, suggested the gospels were not telling the whole truth. A growing belief in the impossibility of miracles fed the suspicion. Further attempts to reconstruct his life foundered on the different order of events in the four gospels. And there were aspects of Jesus' teaching that were felt to be downright offensive. Listen to D.F. Strauss' comments on Jesus' claim that he would return after his death:

> Such a thing as he has here prophesied of himself cannot happen to a man. If he prophesied the like of himself and expected it, then to us he is a fanatic (Schwärmer); if he uttered it of himself without any real conviction, then he was a braggart and a deceiver.[2]

The Search for the Real Jesus

Once it entered popular thinking that the gospels had got it wrong, an excited rush to discover the real Jesus began. What emerged from a myriad of studies, however, was no consensus, but a Babel of contradictions. Albert Schweitzer, a nineteenth-century German scholar, classified the thousands of lives of Jesus of his day into rationalist, traditional, fictitious, mythological, liberal, and eschatological categories. A Jesus emerged to fit every philosophy – Marxist, capitalist, liberal, Essene and mystic – giving rise to the jibe that life-of-Jesus scholars were like people peering down a deep well, trying to see the face at the bottom and seeing only their own reflections.

This confusion had two roots. First, if the historical Jesus was radically different to that which the gospels present, anyone could select what they regarded as historical and render a truer portrait. Second, the instinct then running deep in western culture, that whatever else Jesus was, he was the ideal human being, easily controlled what scholars would accept as historical. They selected what agreed with their ideal of humanity and rejected what did not: leading to the Jesus-in-our-own-image syndrome.

Late Twentieth-Century Trends

The trend of Jesus research in the past fifty years has been to seek to identify sayings and events in the gospels that can be confidently affirmed as historical, and to erect a history of Jesus on this hopefully reliable foundation. This essentially Cartesian approach suspends faith – either because we do not believe, or because we wish to go through the exercise of determining how much of our belief can be demonstrated beyond reasonable doubt – and seeks to determine how much of the gospel tradition can be proven reliable by processes of historical testing. It is also interesting to see if any of it can be disproven. However, the logic which expects a truer history of Jesus to be erected on the basis of material which passes the scholars' bar of reasonable proof, than that which the gospel writers have given is flawed.[3] The proof of this is the rush of studies since the 1970s portraying Jesus as: political revolutionary, charismatic wonder-worker, man of the Spirit, peasant Cynic, comic savant, Essene renegade, grass-roots social reformer, aspiring divine viceroy, and more. What is one to do with the bulk of gospel material which does not fit such images and cannot be historically verified, but which also cannot be disproven. 'What cannot be proven to have happened, did not necessarily not happen.'[4] Histories based on a fraction of the available testimony, and consequently open to massive subjectivity, are unlikely to be reliable. Could one write a history of Julius Caesar, or anyone in the ancient world, if all the evidence which could not be proven true was disallowed?

A Canonically-Based Life of Jesus

The present study proceeds on the working hypothesis that the gospel writers were reasonable, honest men telling the story in their own way and for their own purpose, but basically as they knew it to be. The approach is canonically based[5] in that it takes the traditional four-fold canon of the gospels as reliable unless disproven. I am aware this is a huge assumption, and invite my reader, if he or she does not share it, to regard it as an hypothesis to be tested. It is based on my long familiarity with the gospels and the experience of having discovered them again and again to be correct on a disputed point. A huge amount of painstaking study of the gospels has taken place over the past two centuries, much of it with the aim of discrediting them. But this has not been the effect; increasingly they have emerged not perhaps proven true, but at least proven credible.

We are helped (as well as hindered) by there being four gospels. If, despite the superficial conflicts, a coherent picture of Jesus and his mission emerges from the four, the assumption will be strengthened that they tell the story of a real person. If the study devolves into contradiction it will be a fair indication that the assumption is wrong.

The working hypothesis I have advanced obviously presupposes the possibility of miracles. Here too there has been a change in scholarly thinking in the last century. Many now accept that there is no scientific or philosophical reason to deny miracles in advance. The move from believing them possible to seeing them as a reality is an issue raised in historical form by the life of Jesus, and it will be dealt with in its place.

Why Write A History Of Jesus?

Only in the last two centuries has it been thought necessary to write histories of Jesus.[6] We have four gospels each of which gives, not so much an ordered history of Jesus and his ministry, as something more like a portrait. Each portrait is different, but they are unmistakably images of the one man. Taken separately or together 'the face' which emerges from the gospel writers' work is compelling to the point of creating and sustaining faith. A friend of mine in London ran a group for enquirers and doubters. They simply read through the Gospel of Luke, stopping when anyone wanted to question or discuss a point. As the weeks went on, one after another found themselves drawn to and believing in this Jesus who had previously been alien and unknown. Another friend in Western Australia was asked by a student from communist China if she would explain Christianity to her. My friend suggested that they read the Gospel of Mark together. The student became a Christian as a result.

So why try to write a history of Jesus? Am I not virtually trying to write a fifth gospel? In a sense I am, and believe it appropriate for every Christian to construct a personal account. Each of us, having seen Jesus in the manifold form in which he is presented in the New Testament, will want to synthesize what we have seen and found compelling. I do not mean that all should write books, but that each in their own medium of expression will want to make the attempt to render some kind of 'portrait.'[7] This, indeed, is how the four gospels originally came into being, and Christians ever since have been retelling the story in their own words, some through books, others through drama, and some over the back fence. My first intention, then, is simply to speak about the Jesus I find compelling. But there is another reason.

One of the reasons no one bothered to write a history of Jesus before the eighteenth century was that the gospels were regarded as truthful and adequate records; anything that could be written would only be a rehash of what was already there. Then Hermann Reimarus (an influential eighteenth-century scholar) sought to show that the gospel presentation of Jesus was false, and expose the fraud of Jesus' first disciples. Thus 'history' set itself in opposition to the gospels. We are heirs today of two centuries of sceptical scrutiny of the gospels. We simply cannot ignore the question of what really happened, and whether the 'face' which the gospels portray is a reasonable representation of Jesus of Nazareth, or perhaps something more akin to the imaginative fancies of modern day religious artists. My second intention, therefore, is to test a reconstruction of the history of Jesus' public ministry made on the basis of a confident regard for the integrity of the gospel sources. I will need to test its coherence, internal consistency, and agreement with our knowledge of the times, and show that it hangs together better than those reconstructions which in varying degrees dispute or ignore the witness of the gospels. And there is a third reason.

One of the attractions of the gospels to researchers is that they contain so many puzzles. At one level they are like a detective novel in the way they drop clues on every page. Yet they do not, like a novel, come to a neat conclusion which shows how everything fits together into a coherent picture. The ministry of Jesus is mysterious. He did and said many things which do not fit neatly into traditional Christian interpretation. Does this mean that Christians have not fully understood his quest? His disciples had a similar problem, and even Jesus spoke of 'the mystery of the kingdom of God.' One thing which suggests that the gospels are telling us about the real Jesus, and not just the beliefs of the early church, is that so much of what they relate raises questions which they do not attempt to answer. At the risk of stretching the metaphor, it is as though in a number of different portraits of a person some small scars are evident, though no one tells how they got there. Someone viewing these portraits cannot help asking how the subject came to have these scars. In the story of Jesus the 'scars' are many and they do not all relate to matters which are incidental. Why did Jesus seek baptism from John? Why did he undertake a forty day fast? Why did he then abandon fasting? Why did he baptize in the early part of his ministry and then cease? What did he mean that men of violence were seizing the kingdom? Why did he say the kingdom was present, and at other times imply it lay in the future? The list of not easily answered questions goes on.

The Importance to Christianity of the Life of Jesus

The message of the earliest Christians was a man – Jesus Christ – and their mission was to portray him so that others would be drawn to put their trust in him and be saved. Paul wrote to the Corinthians, 'We do not preach ourselves, but Jesus Christ as Lord, and ourselves as your servants for Jesus' sake' (2 Corinthians 4:5). He went on to say that the God who at creation said 'Let there be light' had now caused to shine in the darkness of human hearts 'the light of the knowledge of the glory of God in the face of Christ.' The glory of God had been revealed, and could still be seen 'in the face of Christ.' What did this mean, but that the beauty and excellence of the invisible God had become visible in the person of Jesus? As often as his story was told and his person portrayed, God's glory became visible, drawing men and women to trust and love him in a new way. Indeed, if the third and fourth chapters of 2 Corinthians are studied carefully it can be seen that entry into a life of relationship with God, and also the transforma- tion of the individual which takes place gradually within that relationship, comes about through seeing and contemplating the 'glory of God in the face of Christ.'

When I was in India I saw an artist's impression of the face of Jesus. Such art has never impressed me. If it were in the least bit important to have a visual image of Jesus, the New Testament would surely have left us some physical description of him. His actual appearance was evidently irrelevant to what the early

Christians meant by 'the face of Christ.' However, the owner of the picture called me closer and told me its story. It was the work of a Korean Christian who had been imprisoned during the Korean War. On close examination the picture consisted of Matthew's Gospel, painstakingly written out by hand so that a face with crown of thorns emerged from the lightening and darkening spacing of letters. The picture was something of a parable. If the first generation of Christians saw the glory of God in the Jesus they heard and saw and touched, for us today that vision is mediated through the four gospels.

But today, despite the accessibility of the gospels, the 'face' of Jesus is marred beyond recognition if it is visible at all. The first half of the twentieth century suffered a loss of confidence in the possibility of knowing anything much about the historical person of Jesus. This has filtered down through the churches to the general populace, creating widespread ignorance – still everywhere apparent – about Jesus' ministry and work. I recall hearing a Cambridge preacher tell his congregation that only four things could be known with any certainty about Jesus: that he was a Galilean, that he was born in Nazareth (that was what he said!), that he was baptized by John, and that he was crucified by the Romans. Someone at a university extension course I gave on the life of Jesus identified herself as a church person but added as her reason for attending, 'We don't hear much about Jesus in the church.'

Preachers of all persuasions find the gospels uncomfortable to work with, except where they lend themselves to preaching moral lessons. In one church I attended for several years, sermons on the gospels, when they featured at all, consisted of an explanation of why this or that passage did not contradict the doctrine of justification by faith, even though it appeared to. We were told what its message was not, but left stranded as to what its message actually was.

Personal

Doctoral studies on Jesus' teaching on wealth and poverty immersed me for three years in the literature of his world. I left the University of Cambridge desiring, if I ever had the opportunity, to attempt a life of Jesus. Six years' preaching reinforced this interest. The congregation I worked in experienced rapid growth. Every Sunday a significant number of new faces appeared, who often turned out to be people who had rarely if ever been to church before, but were wondering whether there is an answer in Christianity to the insecure, impersonal meaninglessness of modern life. They were not like the seekers of one hundred, or fifty or even twenty years ago. Their choice was not simply between 'church' and 'world'; they had a variety of religious and philosophical options from which to choose. One could not simply say 'The Bible says!' for there are other bibles. One could no longer say 'You should come to church!' for the church had been endlessly discredited in their eyes.

What could we show them? A warm and caring community, and perhaps counter for a time their loneliness and alienation? I was moved by the number of people appearing in church who had been hurt by others and were desperately searching for something genuinely human. Or one could present a Christian 'philosophy of life' and provide a satisfying 'worldview' to those who are confused about the meaning of life. In a congregation with a large number of students this was important and effective. Or we could present a Christian way of life to those who were sickened by the moral confusion around them. This was a special concern of many parents of young families. But at the base of anything we wished to declare as Christian, stands Jesus. He is the 'Lord' who calls the caring community into being, and sustains its caringness. He is the centre of a Christian philosophy of life. He is the authority and the motive for a Christian way of life. But is he true? The question of truth matters to people, and it should matter to them. Certainly there are those who are happy to lap up the benefits without inquiring into the basis, but many are not. There are also costs and demands, and who will face these unless they know that they stem from what is real and true. I was not happy just to give people a warm community, a satisfying view of life, and a health-giving moral outlook. I wanted to give Jesus Christ, for he is the source of these things and of much more. I often experienced the sadness of people appearing for a while and attaching themselves to this or that aspect of the church's life, but in the end leaving because they had not encountered him. I came to see that my most important task was to show people Jesus.

I found myself psychologically incapable, however, of preaching what I was not persuaded is true. I was aware of the huge amount of scholarly criticism of the gospel accounts of the life of Jesus that has taken place in the past two centuries, and that necessitated a great deal of questioning and re-examining on my own part. The biggest issue for me has always been, 'Does it add up?' Much in the gospel records has seemed at times not to. But increasingly it *has* added up, and it is this that I have wanted to share – with the kind of inquirers who kept appearing in my church, with other preachers, with those training for ministry, and with any who care to interest themselves in the life of the man who more than any other challenged this world to its foundations.

My chance came in 1986 when the church gave me a year's study leave. I spent a term lecturing on the life of Jesus at Union Biblical Seminary in Pune, India, and then read and wrote for eight months at the University of Tübingen, Germany. Renewed pastoral responsibilities prevented me bringing the work all the way to publication, but in 1993 I became Principal of George Whitefield College in Cape Town, South Africa, where I turned again to systematic teaching on Jesus and the gospels. In 1998 I spent a semester as a guest lecturer at Oak Hill Theological College in London, where I was able to revise the study and bring it close to publication.

An Emerging Thesis

The investigation did not commence with any particular thesis, but I soon realized the importance of identifying Jesus' intention. The twentieth century began with Albert Schweitzer's explosive ideas about Jesus' life-quest. The organ builder turned theologian reviewed the preceding century's attempts to understand the life of Jesus and developed radical conclusions of his own, whose shock waves reverberate into this millennium. At the turn of the last century he struck the death knell of Christianity – unless he can be fairly answered. The influence of this extraordinary thinker on my own work will be apparent. His question was a proper one, even if his answer was mistaken. The quest, the aim, the purpose, the intention of Jesus is the key to understanding him. What was it that drove Jesus forward and made him do the things he did? A proper understanding of his preaching of the kingdom of God will provide the answer. Despite his shocking conclusions, Schweitzer forced scholarship to look at Jesus' message against the thought background of his own times. The so-called 'third quest for the historical Jesus' has resumed Schweitzer's inquiry with an increasing consensus that for Jesus the kingdom of God meant some kind of real historical restoration of Israel. My own study moves in the same direction.

But if Jesus' kingdom was a new age that was tangible and near, what became of it? Approaches which conclude that Jesus meant something more than a spiritual kingdom collide with its non-appearance, and must then wrestle with the implications of a deluded Jesus. The thesis that unfolds in this study is that Jesus did indeed announce the breaking in of a concrete new age of restoration for Israel (and the world). Enjoyment of it, however, was always conditional on acceptance of him. From early in his ministry he also warned of a dreadful alternative – a national catastrophe – if his call was ignored. It was this which eventuated – in the way he predicted. The kingdom retreated, but only in its final consummate form. Its authority and power were paradoxically established by Jesus' death, at the very moment of its rejection and apparent defeat. The kingdom lives and grows hidden and often unrecognized in the world. It awaits its ultimate unveiling.

I have called what I have written a 'life of Jesus.' Strictly speaking it is not so, for I have not concerned myself with the stories of Jesus' birth and early life. They are not unimportant, but they did not feature in his ministry, nor much in the impact he made on the people of his day. I have therefore focused attention on the two to three years of Jesus' public ministry which was of paramount concern to the gospel writers. I begin the inquiry at the third day after his death, for that, in a way, is where he entered world history. I then move back to the ministry of John the Baptist to trace the story forward. Following the lead of the gospels I have at times presented the story chronologically, at times thematically. At the end I return to the questions of truth and hope.

Notes

[1] P. Johnstone, *Operation World,* 25.

[2] D.F. Strauss, *Leben Jesu für das deutsche Volk bearbeitet* (1864), 236. Translation from G.R. Beasley-Murray, *Jesus and the Future*, 21.

[3] I have argued this at length in D. Seccombe, 'A New Approach to the Life of Jesus', 533–538.

[4] A rough translation of a comment I read somewhere in a work of Heinz Schürmann.

[5] ibid., 525–548.

[6] Although there was interest in the subject much earlier. For example, in AD 150–160 Tatian compiled a running narrative of the four gospels known as the *Diatessaron*. It became the standard text of the gospels in the Syriac-speaking churches until the fifth century.

[7] R.T. France subtitled his book, *The Man they Crucified*, 'A Portrait of Jesus'.

Chapter 1

Dead Or Alive?

Christianity is Different

It is doubtful there would be any such thing today as Christianity apart from the belief that Jesus came alive again after he was killed: 'there would be no gospel, not one account, no letter in the New Testament, no faith, no church, no worship, no prayer in Christendom to this day without the message of the resurrection of Christ.'[1] Admittedly, there are millions of Buddhists in the world and no one claims that Buddha's body did not decompose naturally after he died. Muhammad too lived and died, and that is the last that was seen of him in this world. Yet the followers of his religion today number hundreds of millions. Why should it be different with Jesus? Of course, Buddhists do not think that their founder is dead, nor do Muslims; the Buddha has won through to the final state of fusion with everything that is, Muhammad is in heaven. Why should it not be the same for Christians? Could they not follow a Jesus who lived and died and (we might assume) went to heaven? Certainly they could, but it would not be Christianity as it has been believed and lived until now.

For Christianity began with the apostle Peter's announcement in Jerusalem that Jesus of Nazareth, publicly executed seven weeks before, had been raised from his tomb by God, and so conquered death in a way that opened a door of hope to all who would trust in him. The early Christians invited people to a personal relationship with a living Jesus, which would culminate in their sharing in a similar coming-out-of-the-tomb experience. This was the faith which went out from Jerusalem, which is the creed of the Christian church, and which makes Christianity alarmingly vulnerable to questions about what really happened.

Buddha reached Nirvana! Yes, but does anyone know whether he really did, or even whether Nirvana is real? It is a question of believing. Many people in the west are now drawn to Buddhism because it appeals to them as a satisfying philosophy of life; unfortunately there is no question of there being any way to know whether or not it is true.

Muhammad reached heaven, and so will those who believe in him! Yes, but again we must ask how one can be sure; and once more it seems to be a matter of believing. The Koran says so, and you either believe it or you don't. It seems to be a matter of predisposition (if it is not a matter of birth): if it attracts you as a way of life then you will believe it. The words of the Koran were given to Muhammad by God – Muhammad said so! There is no question of testing his claim; you either believe it or you don't.

With Jesus it is different. From the beginning he was followed because something remarkable *happened* that seemed to prove that he really did come from God. His teachings and the claims he made about himself were put to the final test and did not fail. Not much more than thirty-six hours after he died his tomb was empty and all sorts of people were meeting him again, talking with him and eating with him.

For a religion to hold water it must do at least three things well: it must give a straight answer to the question of whether God is real, and it must have something sensible and hopeful to say about the mess the world is in. But it must be more than just beliefs; there are too many alternatives – I cannot base my life on something I would *like* to be true. So it must do a third thing; it must provide some foundation, some proof.

Christianity became the faith of hundreds, then thousands and millions because of the resurrection. True, it was not the resurrection alone; it was Jesus himself and what he taught and promised that drew people. But without the resurrection it is unlikely his way would ever have raised its head above those of the scores of other philosophers, teachers, revolutionaries and even miracle workers, who competed for followers in the first century.[2] Many modern reinterpretations of Jesus by people who do not think the resurrection took place neglect the fact that the early Christians followed him because of the resurrection, and there is no evidence that they followed him for any other reason. If it is objected that many followed him *before* his death, the evidence we have indicates that they followed him then because of his message about the kingdom, which in part was a message about resurrection, and demanded a resurrection to validate it.

For, as we shall see, Jesus did much more than teach timeless truths. He declared that through his efforts God would bring about a great transformation of the world – an ultimate resurrection into which he would lead the way. The resurrection of Jesus was thus seen as more than a demonstration of his authentic messiahship, it had the character of a preview of what was to come. He also said things about himself – his special relationship with God, his place in God's plan, and his right to people's allegiance, which invited ridicule if they could not be authenticated.

It should not be forgotten that Jesus' way was in conflict from the beginning with Judaism, a faith which commanded the allegiance of millions, and the respect of many more who were not Jews. This was the faith that all Jesus' earliest followers believed in wholeheartedly. It offered something worthwhile in both present and future, and was a faith with credible foundations. There is evidence that the question, 'Who is right, Jesus or our leaders?' troubled Jesus' first followers deeply until the day when the tomb was found empty and they talked to him and ate with him once again.[3] Could they have withstood the obvious inference that Jesus was mistaken, if he had never been seen again?

The Earliest Christian Preaching

When the first Christians called people to faith in Jesus, they hinged their message on the resurrection. When Peter first proclaimed to the Jews in Jerusalem that Jesus was the Lord Messiah, one third of his address was about the resurrection: God had raised Jesus up, he said, because it was impossible that death should hold him; this is what the Scriptures had foretold and this was how God exalted Jesus to the position of supreme ruler of Israel and the world (Acts 2:14–40).

When the apostle Paul was invited in Athens to lay his message before the Court of the Areopagus, he concluded his argument with the warning that Jesus would one day judge the world, and that God had given *proof*[4] of this to all people by raising him from the dead (Acts 17:22–32). Later we will consider the degree of proof intended. It is interesting to observe the reaction of these educated Greeks. They mocked the very idea of resurrection. What Paul said had happened to Jesus was very different to what many Greeks in those days believed about the immortality of the soul. It would not have been at all strange for them to hear that Jesus had died and his soul had been received by God. Many probably would have applauded. Socrates had died with such a hope.

But one problem with this belief lay in knowing what really happened once a person passed from the sphere of earthly life. Who could know for sure whether Socrates lived on, or whether the smoke from his funeral pyre was the end of everything, as the many Greeks who followed Epicurus believed? Who could know for sure what lay behind the veil of death without actually going there and coming back? But Paul was saying that God actually stood Jesus up again after he had been dead for three days (the Greek word *anistemi,* resurrect, means to stand someone up again). This was a claim which called for investigation. Something had happened in the physical world which might give an answer to the riddle of life and death. It must be said in the Court's favour that although some mocked, others asked that Paul might return so they could enquire into the matter further.

It is clear from these and other New Testament examples, both that the early Christians were willing to demonstrate the truth of their belief in Jesus, and also that their proof had to do with the reality of the resurrection.[5] Once that was demonstrated everything else followed. This willingness to argue on the basis of historical events which are open to independent investigation is one of the unique features of Christianity. No other religion in the ancient world did this; few religions or philosophies since that time have dared to do it.[6] This is both the strength and the vulnerability of Christianity: it concerns itself with the question of its own truthfulness, and does not ask that it be believed for any other reason than that it is the truth. It invites people to consider its claims critically and allows itself to be dismissed if it is found not to be true. And it knows that if Jesus did not rise from the dead it is *not* true; it is founded on a lie. This is the appropriate place, then, to cast a quick eye over how belief in the resurrection has fared since it made its debut nearly two thousand years ago.

Two Thousand Years of Resurrection Debate

The First Century

A quick read of the speeches in Acts will show how much to the fore were proclamation of and argument about the resurrection.[7] That this is not simply a hobbyhorse of Luke's can be seen by comparison with the rest of the New Testament. Paul, for example, can remind the Thessalonians of how they began to be Christians:

you turned to God from idols to serve the living and true God,
and to wait for his Son from heaven, *whom he raised from the dead* –
Jesus, who rescues us from the coming judgement (anger/wrath).

(1 Thessalonians 1:9–10)

The pivotal place of Jesus' resurrection in the structure of the
apostolic gospel is evident. It had happened, and could only be
explained as an act of God. So it is not surprising to read of Paul's
mission to Thessalonica, that 'he reasoned with them from the
Scriptures, explaining and proving that the Christ had to suffer
and rise from the dead' (Acts 17:3). Matthew also indicates
something of the debate that was going on between Jews and
Christians over the resurrection at the time he wrote his gospel
(28:15). And this debate continued for centuries.

Centuries of Controversy

Justin Martyr (AD 100–165) in his *Dialogue with Trypho the Jew,*
charged that the Jews had 'sent chosen and ordained men
throughout all the world to proclaim that a godless and lawless
heresy had sprung up from one Jesus, a Galilean deceiver, whom
we crucified, but his disciples stole him by night from the tomb,
where he was laid when unfastened from the cross, and now
deceive men by asserting that he has risen from the dead and
ascended into heaven.'[8] Justin also wrote a book defending
Christianity's resurrection beliefs to Greeks who regarded flesh
as inherently corrupt and irredeemable.[9]

Later in the second century, perhaps partly in response to
Justin, the pagan philosopher Celsus wrote his *True Doctrine,*
debunking Christianity and the resurrection, and calling forth a
point by point reply in the third century from the famous
Alexandrian Christian teacher, Origen.[10] In the fifth century, the
continuing controversy is seen in Augustine's remarks:

There is no article of the Christian faith which has encountered such contradiction as that of the resurrection of the flesh … On the immortality of the soul many Greek philosophers have disputed at great length, and in many books they have left it written that the soul is immortal: when they come to the resurrection of the flesh, they doubt not indeed, but they most openly deny it, declaring it to be absolutely impossible that the earthly flesh can ascend into heaven.[11]

Thus at various points in the early centuries we hear the ongoing debate, until, we suppose, Christianity became so well established, that the need for spirited defence of this foundational belief lessened and intellectual energy turned elsewhere.

The Attack is Renewed

Attention was rudely called back to the resurrection by the publication in 1777 and 1778 of two anonymous essays titled 'On the Resurrection Narrative' and 'On the Intention of Jesus and his Teaching'.[12] The author, revealed long after his death to be Hermann Samuel Reimarus, a Professor of Hebrew at the University of Hamburg, ruthlessly detailed what he saw as the contradictions and improbabilities of the gospel resurrection narratives and argued that Jesus' disciples removed his body from the tomb and invented the story that he had been raised.

Few have followed Reimarus to his extreme conclusion, but the new question mark he raised over Jesus and his resurrection has continued to provoke discussion to the present. The nineteenth century saw the writing of literally thousands of 'lives' of Jesus, some of which in the name of rationality tended to see the gospels as honestly mistaken in depicting miracles when in fact nothing had taken place to disturb the order of nature. H.E.G. Paulus, for example, had Jesus fainting on the cross and appearing alive to his disciples before he succumbed to his wounds and died.[13]

Other 'fictional' lives (they did not see themselves this way, of course) quarried clues from the gospels and wove from them imaginative tales of deception and intrigue. K.F. Bahrdt, for example, imagined Jesus as part of an Essene plot to change the crude beliefs of the Jews. Needing a front man, who would appear to have risen from the dead and would therefore have great credibility, members of the brotherhood persuaded Jesus to provoke execution and feign death. He was then removed from the cross and delivered to his tomb, where skilled physicians were waiting to revive him. He lived on for many years as part of the brotherhood.[14]

The influence of the rationalists' naturalistic explanations and 'fictional' accounts is still to be encountered at the end of the twentieth century. A sensationalist popular book based on an alleged conspiracy surrounding the Turin Shroud appeared in 1992, claiming that Jesus was drugged with opium and later recovered from his wounds with the help of the aloe-packed shroud which had been provided by Essene helpers.[15] An Australian Qumran scholar, Barbara Thiering, known for her theory that Jesus was a key figure in the Essene community at Qumran, claims to have discovered a secret message encoded in the gospels and Acts that tells the real history of the Christian movement. According to Thiering, Jesus, Simon Magus and Judas Iscariot were crucified together at Qumran. Jesus was forced by the pain to drink snake poison provided by a rival priest and lost consciousness. The three, two of them with legs broken, were sealed in a tomb to die, but were secretly attended by community members with special medicines and brought out alive. Jesus lived on as the secret head of his movement until after AD 64.[16] With the best will in the world this belongs in the category of fiction and owes more to Bahrdt than to any alleged code within the gospels. Is it not strange that the gospels nowhere even allude to the Essenes; and the Scrolls have no clear reference to Jesus or Christianity, yet each is supposed to be about the other? Is it conceivable that Jesus remained in hiding for over thirty years, directing a movement whose followers were dying for their belief in his resurrection, without any indication of the truth emerging until it is found in a secret code two thousand years later?

Is the Resurrection a Myth?

Another approach, called 'mythological' by Schweitzer, was pioneered by the Tübingen philosopher–theologian D.F. Strauss, in a study of the life of Jesus published in 1835. Following Reimarus' lead, Strauss did a thorough 'deconstruction' of the gospels, exploiting every possible inconsistency and improbability to prove them historically indefensible. Faced then with the question of what happened after Jesus' crucifixion, Strauss is clear. 'The proposition: a dead man has returned to life, is composed of two such contradictory elements, that whenever it is attempted to maintain the one, the other threatens to disappear. If he has really returned to life, it is natural to conclude that he was not wholly dead; if he was really dead, it is difficult to believe that he has really become living.'[17] He is not impressed by arguments that Jesus survived the cross, so is 'induced to doubt the reality of the resurrection' (never having entertained it as a possibility anyway!). The evidence points away from a deliberate fraud on the disciples' part, so Strauss concludes that they must have become convinced by experiences of a psychological nature that Jesus was alive. Once they thought he was risen they invested the story with messianic glory by adding more and more supernatural (mythological) colour.

Strauss' influence has been considerable. One direction the debate took in the twentieth century was to treat the New Testament's stories of the resurrection as the mythological packaging of the first Christians' faith that something ultimate for human existence had happened in the death of Jesus.[18] Another saw them as the results of powerful psychological or spiritual experiences of Jesus' ongoing influence. Willi Marxsen's, *The Resurrection of Jesus of Nazareth* is the classic recent study along these latter lines; Göttingen professor, Gerd Lüdemann, is presently arguing a similar case and has brought the nature of the resurrection into the popular eye once more in Europe.[19]

It should be noticed that 'mythological' interpretations of the resurrection effectively remove it from the threat of the historian. It becomes an idea rather than an event, a matter of preference whether I believe it – of existential decision, as Bultmann would have it. This flight from history was characteristic of the first half of the twentieth century. After Schweitzer the writing of lives of Jesus fell into disrespect and the quest for some more reliable basis for faith than historical judgements about his earthly ministry intensified. Some wished simply to assert it in disdain of historical argument (e.g. Karl Barth[20]), but with a consequent weakening and decline of Christianity.

It is now more than two centuries since the quest for an alternative, naturalistic explanation of the resurrection tradition began. It continues unabated, as we have seen. This is, in part, a reaction to the fact that many in the churches continue to be convinced by the witness of the New Testament and faith in a literal resurrection. So much so, that the Christian church, which once was seen to be on its way to decline and death, has a larger and more widespread membership than ever before in its history.[21]

Resurrection Comeback

The resurrection stories have always had their defenders. In 1866 Brooke Foss Westcott, Cambridge Regius Professor of Divinity and later Bishop of Durham, provided a succinct common-sense defence of the historical resurrection for the English-speaking world. After the Second World War generations of English-speaking students were introduced to historical arguments for the resurrection through Norman Anderson's *Evidence for the Resurrection*[22] and John Stott's *Basic Christianity*. Anderson was Professor of Oriental Laws and Director of the Institute of Advanced Legal Studies at the University of London, Stott a prominent London Anglican preacher. Though relatively slight, these two books launched students in many countries into a movement confidently affirming the Christian faith which is still to be felt in much of the world.

In 1968 Cambridge professor C.F.D. Moule, introducing a collection of essays on the resurrection by German theologians, noted a greater readiness in English scholarship to see the resurrection as an 'objective' event (one that caused the disciples' faith, rather than was caused by it), and put forward a number of considerations of his own in support of an actual bodily rising.[23]

In Germany, Wolfhardt Pannenberg, a professor of Theology at the University of Munich, went against the stream of German scholarship in championing a real resurrection.[24] The resurrection, he argued, was God's historic and historical affirmation of Jesus' ministry and claims. No less against the stream was another German defence of Jesus' resurrection in 1977, but this time from one who described himself as a 'faithful Jew' and did not believe that Jesus is Israel's Messiah. Nevertheless, says Pinchas Lapide, the evidence is clear that Jesus rose and therefore must have been a very good man who is definitely part of God's plan for the Gentiles. 'In regard to the future resurrection of the dead, I am and remain a Pharisee. Concerning the resurrection of Jesus on Easter Sunday, I was for decades a Sadducee. I am no longer a Sadducee.'[25]

In 1984 the attention of people in Britain was focussed on the nature of the resurrection when David Jenkins, amidst protests, was consecrated Bishop of Durham in York. He was well known for his view that the resurrection was a purely spiritual come-back; he dismissed the notion of bodily resurrection as 'a conjuring trick with bones.' Three days after the consecration York Minster was struck by lightning. The interest of the media was understandable.

Murray Harris, who had already written on the subject of resurrection, responded to the bishop's views with a popular booklet and later with a fuller study.[26]

In 1985 two American philosophers, Antony Flew and Gary Habermas debated the issue of whether Jesus rose from death before an adjudicating panel of five philosophers and five debate judges at Liberty University.[27] In 1989 the American scholar William Lane Craig produced a major positive assessment of the New Testament evidence.[28] On the other side, several books from the pen of John Dominic Crossan, co-chairman of the Jesus Seminar, have appeared during the nineties, presenting the view that Jesus was buried by his executioners in a shallow grave and probably eaten by dogs ('horror is history').[29] The resurrection stories are explained as a vision of Paul, and fictitious pastiches of wishful thinking and prophecy recast as history. In 1996 an inter-disciplinary 'Resurrection Summit' took place in New York with nineteen prominent scholars representing various opinions.[30] The resurrection debate is thus assured of continuing into the third millennium.

It would be naïve to think that this argument will be settled in the public arena. Too much is at stake in the realm of commitment, behaviour and worldview. People simply have to make up their own minds. This inadequate sounding of a gigantic ongoing discussion makes it clear that there is evidence to consider; Christianity tells no one to suspend their critical faculties and just believe. The debate also pinpoints the two vital questions: what kind of resurrection does the New Testament speak of, and how strong is the evidence for it having happened?

What Kind of Evidence?

We have already noted the desire of some to find the basis of faith in something more secure than a historical judgement about Jesus' resurrection. Surely if God is revealing himself in Christ it should be enough to preach him and call people to faith. Alternatively, if the resurrection is truly God's act it should be enough to preach it and God will impress it upon the heart as true. There is truth here, but it is not the whole truth. For if God is revealing himself in Christ, it is in Christ crucified and risen. And if I am indifferent to the question of whether he died and rose, whatever faith I may think I have will bear little relation to that of the first Christians. When the early Christians preached the resurrection and called people to faith on its account, they sought to demonstrate its truth. It is certainly not the case that all that is required to make a Christian is a convincing argument for the resurrection. Nevertheless, if Christianity is unable to mount a reasonable justification for viewing this pivotal event as real, can anyone be expected to pay attention to its message?

There are in the world today a surprising number of people who claim to believe in Jesus as a result of some sort of personal encounter with him. Some would jump from this to affirm personal spiritual experience as the only 'proof' needed. However, not everyone can lay claim to such an experience, and even those who can are often the first to say they need a more solid and factual basis for their faith than an experience which with time may have faded in their memory, and may be uncomfortably open to being explained away as psychological. It is also very dissatisfying for the believer to have nothing more to tell someone who is inquiring about Christian belief than their own personal experience, not to mention how frustrating it is for the enquirer. The glory of Christianity is that it stands on more than one leg. Those on the journey to faith need to be able to examine something objective and real, and the question of whether Jesus lived again is their obvious first port of call. This is particularly so in the west, where we live with a generation which has been taught to believe that the Christian faith has nothing objective and 'provable' to stand on, and that everything in the realm of 'faith' is a matter of believing whatever you will. It is difficult to believe on the basis of someone else's personal experiences, no matter how impressive they may be, and even those who have come to faith on some other basis than the demonstration of the truth of Christianity find the need to study the concrete evidence of its foundation, to confirm what they have believed, to interpret their experiences and to give them a fact-based assurance when their personal experience of life is making them doubt the realities which Jesus proclaimed.

The objective evidence of Jesus' resurrection is first and foremost the witness of those who saw him alive after he had died and who told their stories. In the second place, it is the circumstantial evidence of details connected with the resurrection event and the consequences which radiated from it. The most notable piece of circumstantial evidence is, of course, the empty tomb, so to that we shall turn first.

Notes

[1] G. Bornkamm, *Jesus of Nazareth*, 181.

[2] N.T. Wright, *Jesus and the Victory of God*, 110 makes the same point.

[3] Mark 9:11, e.g., shows how seriously the disciples listened to the arguments of the Jewish scribes.

[4] *pistin pareschon* – 'furnish proof'.

[5] In 1 Thess. 1:9–10 we can see behind the new stance of the community the outline of the message that was preached to them. Everything hinged on the claim that God raised Jesus from the dead. Also see Rom. 1:4; 1 Cor. 15.

[6] Under the challenge of Christianity, Mormonism sought to give evidence of its truth claim by appeal to the witnesses who allegedly saw the golden plates from which Joseph Smith allegedly translated the Book of Mormon.

[7] Acts 2:24–32; 3:14–15; 4:10; 5:31–32; 10:40–41; 13:30–37; 17:3,18, 31–32; 23:6; 24:15; 26:23.

[8] Justin Martyr, *Dialogue with Trypho the Jew*, 108. See *ANF* 1.253.

[9] The surviving fragments are available in English translation in *ANF* 1.294–299.

[10] Origen, *Against Celsus*. For an English text see *ANF* 4.395–669.

[11] Augustine, *Expositions on the Psalms*, 89.32.

[12] English translation in Reimarus, *Reimarus: Fragments*, 153–210.

[13] H.E.G. Paulus, *Das Leben Jesu als Grundlage einer reinen Geschichte Urchristentums*. For description and discussion of Paulus' thinking see Schweitzer, *The Quest of the Historical Jesus*, chapter 5. And Fuller, *Easter Faith and History*, 38–39.

[14] For a summary and discussion of Bahrdt's views see Schweitzer, *Quest*, 38–44.

[15] H. Kersten & E.R. Gruber, *The Jesus Conspiracy*.

[16] B. Thiering, *Jesus and the Riddle of the Dead Sea Scrolls*.

[14] D.F. Strauss, *The Life of Jesus Critically Examined*, 735–736.

[18] E.g., 'In fact, faith in the resurrection is nothing other than faith in the cross as the salvation event, as the cross of Christ'. R. Bultmann, 'The New Testament and Mythology: The Problem of Demythologizing the New Testament Proclamation', 39.

[19] Lüdemann thinks the disciples became convinced of Jesus' resurrection by a succession of visions which are explainable from their psychological condition after the crucifixion, e.g. Peter's guilt over his betrayal of Jesus. G. Lüdemann, *What Really Happened to Jesus*; *The Resurrection of Jesus*.

[20] See the discussion of the Barth–Bultmann debate in Fuller, *Easter Faith*, 8–111.

[21] Johnstone, *Operation World* , 25. Most of the statistics on which this judgement is based are from churches which believe in Christ's bodily resurrection.

[22] Published in 1950, this was only a booklet. He followed it with *Christianity: The Witness of History* (1969) and *A Lawyer among the Theologians* (1973).

[23] C.F.D. Moule (ed.), *The Significance of the Message of the Resurrection for Faith in Jesus Christ*.

[24] W. Pannenberg, *Jesus: God and Man*, 53–114; idem, 'Did Jesus Really Rise from the Dead?', 102–117.

[25] P. Lapide, *The Resurrection of Jesus*, 125.

[26] M. Harris, *Easter in Durham*; idem, *From Grave to Glory*. See also his earlier *Raised Immortal: Resurrection and Immortality in the New Testament*.

[27] G.R. Habermas & A.G.N. Flew, *Did Jesus Rise from the Dead?*

[28] W.L. Craig, *Assessing the New Testament Evidence for the Historicity of the Resurrection of Jesus*.

[29] E.g., J.D. Crossan, *Who Killed Jesus?* 188. For a critique see W.L. Craig, 'John Dominic Crossan on the Resurrection of Jesus', 249–271.

[30] The Summit's papers have been published in S.T. Davis, D. Kendall & G. O'Collins (eds.), *The Resurrection*.

Chapter 2

Evidence

The Empty Tomb

A Circumstantial Detail?

I begin with the empty tomb, conscious of the fact that many today object to such importance being placed on a circumstantial detail. It is true that in itself the empty tomb is but a detail. It is not a part of the faith, nor something which of itself is preached, and it does not establish the truth of the resurrection. Nevertheless it is not unimportant. Many a murderer has been convicted, and many an innocent person acquitted, on the basis of a circumstantial detail which in itself seemed totally insignificant. The importance of the empty tomb lies more in the case against Christianity. If it was *not* empty, then Jesus could not have been raised in the way the early Christians claimed. From the beginning it has been recognized that if Jesus' body remained in its tomb, or if it was taken elsewhere and there decomposed in the way of all human remains, the central pillar of Christian belief is removed and very little will remain in the rubble of the edifice that collapses around it.

A Modern Preoccupation?

It is frequently claimed, however, that argument about the empty tomb is a modern preoccupation, and that there is no evidence of concern about it in the earliest Christian thinking: Paul does not mention it in his famous summary of the church's resurrection tradition (1 Corinthians 15:1–8), it does not figure in the early preaching recorded in Acts and there is no mention of it in the New Testament letters. The first Christians preached that Jesus was raised from the dead, but they did not connect this with the emptiness of Jesus' tomb. Therefore, some see the idea of an empty tomb as something which must have entered into Christian thinking and into the gospel records at a later stage when arguments over whether Jesus had been born as a real man with a real body arose. To resolve this controversy, it is argued, certain Christians invented the story of the empty tomb and it became so popular that it found its way into all four gospels.[1]

A Unanimous Tradition

The evidence that Jesus' tomb was empty from the Sunday after his death must begin with the four gospels. I shall say more about the details when I consider each individually; for the present it is enough to observe that all four agree on the emptiness of the tomb, as does the apocryphal Gospel of Peter.[2] There are no ancient sources which deny or question the empty tomb. Even the Jews argued about how the tomb became empty, not whether it was empty.

A further indication of the empty tomb accounts' authenticity is the discovery of the tomb by women. The role of women as the first witnesses of the resurrection was a problem for early Christianity. Had the empty tomb been an imaginative creation, its author would hardly have selected women as its discoverers. Yet it is the uniform witness of the gospels that this was in fact the case.

Did Paul Think the Tomb was Empty?

Here the controversial text is Paul's statement to the Corinthians

> I delivered to you … what I also received … that Christ died for
> our sins … and that he was interred and that he was raised on the
> third day (1 Corinthians 15:3–4)

Some argue that his juxtaposition of 'was interred … and raised'
clearly implies a belief that Jesus' body was buried and was
raised.[3] Others will not concede this and point to 15:44 as
evidence that Paul did not think that what was raised was the
same body as was buried. The assertion that Christ was raised
on the third day suffers a similar fate. To some it is evidence of a
historical happening associated with the discovery of the empty
tomb on the third day, but for others it simply denotes the
beginning of appearances which may have had nothing to do
with the buried body of Jesus. To resolve this impasse it is
necessary to look elsewhere in Paul's writings.

A glance at Romans 8:10–11 makes clear how Paul thought of
the rising of Jesus. The God who through the power of the Holy
Spirit raised Jesus from the dead will one day (at the final
resurrection) raise our *mortal bodies* from death. He contrasts
the raising of our mortal bodies with our present spiritual
experience, where our spirits are alive but our bodies are dying.
This shows that Paul distinguished between 'spiritual' and
'bodily' and saw Jesus' rising in the second category. It also
exhibits the resurrection of Jesus' body not just as a historical
curiosity, but as the guarantee of the future. Indeed, Paul then
proceeds to locate the Christian's resurrection (he calls it 'the
redemption of our bodies') in the context of a liberation of
the whole world from its bondage to decay. This renders
intelligible his calling Christ's resurrection 'the first fruits of those
who have fallen asleep' (1 Corinthians 15:20, 23). Paul's moral
exhortation in 1 Corinthians 6:13–14 on the importance of the
body also clarifies his understanding that it was the physical body

of Christ that was raised: 'The body is not meant for immorality but for the Lord and the Lord for the body. And God raised the Lord and will also raise us up by his power.' This last sentence is irrelevant if it does not refer to Jesus' *body*. We must conclude, then, that Paul's resurrection terminology (*egegertai*: was raised; *anastasis*: resurrection) means resurrection of the body, which is what we would expect from one educated in a Jewish milieu, and a Pharisee at that. The Jewish concept of resurrection is that the whole person, body included, is reconstituted and walks again.[4] While it could possibly be argued that bodily resurrection was irrelevant to Paul's own vision of Christ on the road to Damascus and that by proclaiming him as resurrected he only accommodated his message to the understanding of the Jews, it is ludicrous that he should do so to the Greeks, for whom the thought of bodily resurrection was offensive and only worthy of mockery. Yet *resurrection* was as much at the heart of Paul's gospel to Greeks as it was to Jews.

The Empty Tomb in Early Christian Preaching

We must now challenge the view that the empty tomb does not figure in Acts or in very early Christian preaching. In fact it features in Peter's Pentecost address, the very first recorded Christian sermon (Acts 2:14–41). To begin with Peter asserts that, 'God raised Jesus up having loosed the cords of death, because it was not possible that death should hold him.' To place that in a framework of Old Testament understanding, he quotes a psalm of David which talks about God saving someone's mortal body: 'Moreover my flesh also shall dwell in hope, because you will not leave my soul in Hades, neither will you give your Holy One to see corruption' (Psalm 16:9–10). Next Peter argues that because everyone knows that King David died and was buried and that his remains decomposed in the normal manner, the psalm cannot refer to him, but must look forward to his future son. It was common knowledge that God had promised King David a descendant (the Messiah) who would finally rule over Israel for ever. David must therefore have been prophesying the resurrection of the Messiah.

> Brothers I may say to you without fear of contradiction of the patriarch David, that he both died and was buried, and his tomb is with us to this day. Being therefore a prophet, and knowing that God had sworn with an oath to him that one of his descendants would sit upon his throne, he, foreseeing it, spoke of the resurrection of the Christ, that he was neither left in Hades, nor did his flesh see corruption. (Acts 2:29–31)

This argument only works if everyone in Peter's audience already knew that Jesus' tomb was empty. Peter as good as invites them to go and examine, not Jesus' tomb, but the tomb of King David, to see that it still contains his bodily remains. If Jesus' remains were still in existence there would be no argument. We see here that Peter did not *announce* the empty tomb; his speech *assumed* that it was common knowledge. What he explained, with the help of the Old Testament, was its significance.

The Pentecost Sermon is thus solid evidence from the very beginning of Christianity of the notorious fact of the empty tomb. It is also evidence of how Peter thought of the resurrection of Jesus. God had reversed the death process and had returned Jesus with his body to a new life in which decay and corruption no longer exercised power over him. This makes clear that when the first Christians spoke of Jesus' resurrection, they did not mean that his body was simply returned to the old form of flesh and blood, decay-bound existence. He had broken through death and was alive in a new way. Nevertheless, his whole person, body included was involved in this historic and historical breakthrough. A transformation had taken place of Jesus' dead mortal body into a living immortal body.

Some object that the Pentecost Sermon is more representative of the thinking of Luke and the preoccupations of his day than a faithful record of Peter's address, but the very absence of any explicit mention of the empty tomb is the clearest indication that this is not so. If Luke were putting words into Peter's mouth to answer the problems of his own time, he would surely have drawn attention to the emptiness of the tomb. It is altogether too subtle to suppose he let it hang as an implication for the sake of an authentic-sounding speech. Peter does not answer the question of later decades, but the question of the earliest weeks of Christianity – what is the *meaning* of this empty tomb? In doing so he provides us with powerful circumstantial evidence of what the original state of affairs was. This goes a long way to explaining why three thousand people accepted baptism in the name of the living Lord Jesus Christ on that very occasion (Acts 2:41). Such a scale of response can only mean that people were well aware of the outward facts of the case, and only needed the scriptural interpretation to convince them that Jesus really was the Christ whom God had raised from the dead.

In his now classic defence of the real resurrection, Frank Morison made a number of useful observations about the early days of the Christian movement. He notes that public proclamation of Jesus' resurrection only seven weeks after his execution must have occasioned great controversy. The authorities would have been forced into self-defence, and their most effective defence would have been to produce Jesus' body. Evidently they could not. He also points out that the movement's early growth was not in Galilee, but in Jerusalem where Jesus had died and been buried; that it grew at the rate it did can only be explained if it was common knowledge that the tomb was empty: 'By the very irony of fate the disciples were committed to prosecuting their campaign within a quarter of an hour's walk of the place in which, if their contention was false, the mouldering remains of their great leader lay.'[5]

It is difficult to conclude otherwise than that it was public knowledge in Jerusalem in the weeks following Jesus' death and burial that his body was no longer in its place.[6] There are, of course, various possibilities as to what happened to it, the most obvious being that it was taken by his disciples. Morison regards this as a psychological impossibility and will discuss it no further; even Strauss considers it inconsistent with the later behaviour of the disciples. Nevertheless, it was certainly canvassed by some of the early opponents of Christianity, and was the basis of Reimarus' attack on the integrity of the Christian movement, so we will return to it later.

The Testimony of Witnesses

What is to be made of the various witnesses who allegedly saw Jesus alive after he was dead? There are two levels of testimony: that of the eye-witnesses, who for the most part did not write down what they saw, and the secondary witnesses, who collected and wrote down the experience of others. We will take the evidence as well as we can, in chronological order, dealing with any discrepancies which occur as they arise.

About twenty years after the events we are investigating, Paul wrote to the Corinthian believers, some of whom were beginning to doubt whether there was any resurrection to look forward to in the future. He answered them very simply, that Jesus' resurrection guaranteed that of all his followers, and was the foundation of the Christian gospel which they had believed.

> For I delivered to you first of all what I also received,
> that Christ died for our sins according to the Scriptures
> and that he was buried,
> and that he has been raised on the third day according to the Scriptures
> and that he appeared to Cephas [Peter],
> then to the Twelve

then he appeared to more than five hundred brothers at once
of whom most are still around, though some have fallen asleep;
then he appeared to James, then to all the apostles;
and last of all as to one born at the wrong time
he appeared also to me. (1 Corinthians 15:3–8)

Although this was written in the mid fifties (from Ephesus), it
should at once be noted that it records what Paul received as the
original Christian message and had himself been preaching it for
more than twenty years. For the most part it is second-hand
witness; it relates what others saw. At one point, however, it claims
to be eye-witness testimony: Paul himself has seen Jesus alive. Let
us consider the value of Paul's first-hand testimony.

The Witness of Paul

Though it speaks of an appearance of the risen Jesus which was
later and somewhat different to the other appearances, the
testimony of Paul is compelling. No one disputes that he wrote
1 Corinthians, and that here and elsewhere he claims to have
seen the resurrected Jesus. So we are dealing with a first-hand
report of someone who actually claims to have seen Jesus alive.
We also have Luke's second-hand reports of the same event
(Acts 9; 22; 26). And we are in a position to study the actual
effect of this appearance on Paul's life over a long period of
time. It is well known that before his conversion, which he
attributes solely to this meeting with Jesus, he was in bitter
opposition to the Christian movement. He saw it as a serious
threat to the Jewish religion which had been handed down
from Moses. Afterwards we find him as the chief witness of the
fact that Jesus really was the Messiah, and that, far from being
subversive of Judaism, 'the Way'[7] is its true continuation and
fulfilment.

Unique Qualifications

Paul was unique in early Christianity. He was a student of Gamaliel I, the leading rabbi of his day. In Jewish tradition there is a chain of succession of great rabbis leading from Ezra through Hillel and Shammai to Gamaliel I, and on into the second century.[8] If he had not become a follower of Jesus, Paul might well have been part of this succession. Indeed, if the intellect he displays in his letters, and the energy he gave to his mission are anything to go by, Saul of Tarsus, would probably be ranked by Jews today as one of their very great rabbis. As a Christian, he was qualified to be the expert witness able to give authoritative judgement on the question of whether Christianity represented a departure from the historic path of Moses and the prophets. His judgement was that there was a clear line of continuity from Abraham and Moses to the resurrection of the Messiah Jesus.[9] It was all part of God's ongoing action to save the world.

Paul was also a man of rank and education in the wider sphere; he understood both Greco–Roman and Jewish worlds. In the course of his mission he had opportunity to proclaim and argue his faith in the risen Jesus not only in multitudes of market places and synagogues across the Mediterranean world, but also in the philosophers' Court of the Areopagus in Athens (Acts 17:16ff.), before the Jewish supreme court (the Sanhedrin, Acts 22:30ff.), in the court of the Roman Proconsul in Caesarea Maritima (Acts 24:1ff.), before the Jewish King Agrippa II (Acts 25:13ff.), and probably before the court of the Emperor Nero in Rome. He carried his testimony consistent to the end and sealed it with his blood, executed according to tradition during the latter part of the reign of Nero (AD 54–68).[10]

Did Paul have a Vision?

On his own testimony, Paul's conversion was occasioned by the appearance to him of the risen Jesus. It has sometimes been suggested that Paul's experience was of a visionary nature and therefore not evidence of a *real* resurrection. We need not quarrel with terming his encounter a 'vision'; he does so himself (Acts 26:19). Luke's descriptions speak of an intense light and a voice, with the emphasis falling on the voice; Jesus identified himself to Paul and they conversed. The question is whether the vision came from outside or from inside of Paul's psyche, whether the risen Christ spoke to him or he spoke to himself. Many writers have felt they had a sufficient insight into Paul's psychology to be able to explain the vision from within: his fanatical zeal for Judaism, his persecution of the Christians, his witness of the steadfast testimony of Stephen, his subsequent single-minded enthusiasm for the Christian cause, his later visions – all of these, so they say, mark a personality likely to have been turned by an internally generated vision.[11]

However, the objectivity of the vision is vouched for in Luke's reports by the brightness and noise, both of which were witnessed by Paul's companions (though they did not hear any actual words), and Ananias' independent vision, which led him to seek Paul out, heal him, and convey a message from Jesus, complimentary to that which Paul had already received. Paul was evidently not a lone witness to the authenticity of his experience.

Certain other things are also clear. To begin with, the experience was sufficient to convince Paul of Jesus' bodily resurrection and constitute him as Jesus' devoted follower for life. Secondly, though no stranger to visions (cf. 2 Corinthians 12:1–9), Paul describes this event in quite different terms. Thirdly, Paul speaks of it as the last of a series of appearances and nowhere intimates that such a thing could or should happen again to him or anyone else. Fourthly, it constituted Paul an apostle along with the other apostles – thus he appears to place his experience on a level with theirs in its effect, though he notes his own case as special. This should caution us against claiming all the earlier appearances were of the same character as his. 'As though to one abnormally born' is an attempt to render the Greek *ektroma*, which usually means an abortion. It carries the notion of birth (Paul's birth as a Christian and an apostle), but an unnatural and violent one (on the Damascus Road he was jerked from being the foremost opponent of Christianity to its foremost exponent), at an unnatural time. Paul evidently thought that resurrection appearances belonged properly only to the period immediately after Easter.

The debate over Paul's experience will go on. Some will interpret early Christian history as a fundamental divergence from Jesus, seeing Paul and his vision at the place of departure. Yet there is plenty of evidence to affirm Paul's own view of it – an encounter with the risen Jesus – an interpretation which, despite all the controversy that surrounded his ministry even in his lifetime, was acknowledged by the other leaders of the early church.[12]

Individuals and Groups who saw Jesus Alive

Besides being an expert on things Jewish, Paul was also in a position to be extremely well informed about the historical origins of Christianity. We learn from one of his letters that three years after his conversion he went to Jerusalem and spent a fortnight with Peter. Also at this time he made the acquaintance of Jesus' brother James (Galatians 1:18–19). So his report that Jesus appeared to Peter and James does not rest simply on church hearsay; he knew these men personally. In his many travels to and fro it is hard to think that he would not have had ample opportunity to speak to others of 'the twelve', 'the apostles' (whoever they may have been), and the five hundred who saw Jesus all at one time. Some of these had died, but most, he knew, were still alive, so he may well have had recent contact with some of them.

Peter

Paul gives pride of place to Peter as first witness of Jesus'
resurrection. It is one of the puzzles of the New Testament that
we are nowhere told anything about this encounter except that
it happened. Luke is the only other writer who mentions it, and
he supplies the information that it took place on the 'third day',
the Sunday on which Jesus first began to appear. We will speak
more of this when we come to the records of the gospel writers.
Peter is reported to have seen Jesus on other occasions in
company with the other disciples, but it seems to have been this
first and astonishing encounter (since he had most shamefully
denied all knowledge of Jesus a short time before) between
himself and Jesus alone, that helped establish his undisputed
leadership in the early church.

We are fortunate to possess Peter's own personal testimony
to the effect which finding Jesus alive again had upon him.[13] He
began his first letter, 'Blessed be the God and Father of our
Lord Jesus Christ, by whose great mercy we have been born
again to a living hope by the resurrection of Jesus Christ from
the dead' (1 Peter 1:3). We may imagine this reflects his own
personal experience of renewal from the defeat and shame of
his cowardly denial. It was an objective meeting with the raised
Jesus which brought about his subjective 'rebirth' from despair
and disgrace to new and living hope. The latter would not have
come to be without the former.

We can follow enough of Peter's later life to see that he too
carried his witness to the risen Messiah to the end of his life.
According to early tradition he died by crucifixion in Rome in
the time of the emperor Nero.[14] One of the significant
characteristics of Peter's life is that he did not try to hang on to
his position as leader of the early church, but surrendered it
to James and set out as a missionary to tell the Jews who
lived outside of Israel what he had witnessed and knew to be
true. This is hardly the action of someone driven by any other

motive than a conviction of the truth and urgency of his resurrection gospel.

James

The case of James is almost as compelling as that of Paul, for he
too first features in Christian history as a critic of Jesus (John
7:5). It is understandable that a blood brother could have been
suspicious and kept his distance from the early movement. He is
not mentioned by name, but was no doubt one of the brothers
of Jesus gathered with the disciples and Jesus' mother in
Jerusalem shortly after Easter (Acts 1:14). We do not know
exactly when and how Jesus encountered him and assured him
that he really was the Messiah; what we do learn from various
sources is the direction of his life from that time forward. In his
one surviving letter he calls himself 'James, a slave of God and of
the Lord Jesus Christ' (James 1:1): a strange way to speak of a
brother! By the end of the forties he had taken over Peter's
position as leader of the church in Jerusalem, where he achieved
a reputation amongst Jews and Christians alike for holiness of
life. With such respect was he held, that, according to Josephus,
the Jewish High Priest Ananus was deposed from office for
instigating his execution in AD 62.[15]

Multiple Witnesses

Paul also mentions appearances of Jesus to at least three different
groups. Apart from the appearance to 'the twelve', which is
probably that which Luke and John record on the first Sunday
night, these cannot with confidence be identified with those
which the gospel writers recount. What can be said is that by
the mid fifties there were a considerable number of people who
were identified as belonging to different groups which claimed
to have seen Jesus alive after his death. Peter, James, Paul, the
twelve (though James the son of Zebedee had been killed,

Acts 12:2), a larger group called 'the apostles' (they may have
been the seventy-two whom Jesus sent out to proclaim the
kingdom in Galilee and Judaea, Luke 10:1ff.), and a group of
five hundred.

It is the existence of these groups of witnesses which makes it
difficult to dismiss the resurrection appearances as hallucinations
of some kind. It also helps explain the remarkably rapid
expansion of Christianity, which must largely be attributed to the
vigour and confidence of these witnesses. The impressiveness of
their achievement is part of what led the Jewish scholar Pinchas
Lapide to the conclusion that Jesus must indeed have been raised
from the dead.

> How was it possible that his disciples, who in no way excelled in
> intelligence, eloquence or strength of faith, after the shattering
> fiasco of Golgotha, could begin their victorious missionary drive
> – a drive which left all their pre-Easter successes in the shadows?
> The answer of the apostles was short and unambiguous: the
> resurrection of Jesus from the dead.[16]

We have now seen how central and indispensable to early
Christianity was the resurrection, and how strong is the
evidence for the circumstance of the empty tomb. The report in
1 Corinthians has opened up the first decades of the Christian
movement as a time in which many claimed to have seen Jesus
alive again after his terrible death on the cross. What do the four
gospels contribute to our enquiry?

Notes

[1] E.g., P. Carnley, *The Structure of Resurrection Belief* , 52ff. Carnley's ultimate
conclusion is that Jesus' resurrection is something which was inferred from the
early Christians' experience of the Holy Spirit; the empty tomb and the stories
of physical appearances were created to meet theological and apologetic needs.
Such theories betray as much theological bias as they claim to discover in the

early Christians. They divide the witness of the New Testament against itself in order to come to a 'historical' conclusion (belief in the resurrection of Jesus' body was no part of earliest Christianity), which then becomes a needed theological conclusion: it is of no importance today to believe that Jesus bodily 'stood up again'.

² Part of a Gospel of Peter was discovered in the tomb of a monk from the eighth- to twelfth-century. Most scholars regard it as second century or later. J.D. Crossan, *The Cross that Spoke: The Origins of the Passion Narrative*, however, has reconstructed from it an alleged primitive gospel, which he thinks is older than the four canonical gospels. This then becomes part of his rewriting of Christian origins. A flimsy basis indeed, when even his so-called 'Cross Gospel' tells of an empty tomb. For a recent discussion of the relationship of the Gospel of Peter to the canonical gospels see A. Kirk, 'Examining Priorities: Another Look at the Gospel of Peter's Relationship to the New Testament Gospels', 572–595.

³ E.g., C.F.D. Moule, *Resurrection*, 7f.

⁴ Cf. Psalm 16; Isaiah 53; Ezekiel 37; Daniel 12:2.

⁵ F. Morison, *Who Moved the Stone?*, 181–182. Strauss (*Life*, 743) saw that the short time between the crucifixion and Pentecost was fatal to his theory that the disciples became convinced of the resurrection when they returned to Galilee where there was no dead body to remind them of its impossibility. He gratuitously discounts the Pentecost tradition, therefore, and has the public preaching begin much later when there was no danger of the body's appearance.

⁶ A recent historian states that 'if we apply the same sort of criteria that we would apply to any other ancient literary sources, then the evidence is firm and plausible enough to necessitate the conclusion that the tomb was indeed found empty' (M. Grant, *Jesus*, 176). Cf. Pannenberg, *Jesus*, 74–75.

⁷ The original name of the Christian movement, given by its own followers, was 'the Way', or 'the Way of the Lord' (Acts 9:2; 18:25, 26; 19:9, 23; 22:4; 24:14, 22). This name identified their movement with the ongoing plan of God, from which the Jews who refused to believe in Jesus had turned aside (Isaiah 30:21; 35:8; 40:3; Mark 1:3).

⁸ *Mishnah Aboth* 1:1–16.

⁹ See Acts 9:20; 13:16ff.; 24:10ff.; 26:1ff., etc.

¹⁰ For a summary of the evidence relating to Paul's execution see F.F. Bruce, *New Testament History*, 348.

¹¹ A.N. Wilson, *Jesus*, 23–43, is a recent example of this approach.

[12] See Galatians 2:1–10; 2 Peter 3:15–16; Acts 10–11; 15.

[13] Many dispute Peter's authorship of 1 Peter, but the grounds are inconclusive. Scholars who defend the possibility of Peter's authorship include J.N.D. Kelly, *A Commentary on the Epistles of Peter and of Jude*, 26–34; J.A.T. Robinson, *Redating the New Testament*, 150–169. J.R. Michaels, *1 Peter*, lv–lxvii, thinks it was written by Peter at an old age; E. Selwyn, *The First Epistle of Peter*, 7–38; B. Reicke, *The Epistle of James, Peter & Jude*, 69–71, by Silvanus as author writing under Peter's authority; ; and E. Best, *1 Peter*, 49–63, a member of a Petrine school writing in the name of his recently deceased master. The lack of decisive evidence, which makes it easy to create hypotheses, makes it wise to accept the letter's own designation (acknowledging that Silvanus had a role in the writing), which was evidently accepted by the recipient congregations and never questioned by the early church. It should not be forgotten that the letter was couriered to these congregations by someone of stature (probably Silvanus) who would have had full knowledge of its provenance.

[14] Bruce, *History*, 381–388.

[15] Josephus, *History*, 20:200–203.

[16] P. Lapide, *Auferstehung: Ein Judisches Glaubensarlebnis*, 35 (my translation); also *Resurrection*, 69.

Chapter 3

The Resurrection Story In The Four Gospels

Evidence From the Four Gospels

Some see the gospels as honest records of actual events, others as fanciful elaborations of originally reliable traditions. Some take one gospel as more reliable than the others, build a historical picture from it, and judge the others accordingly, others take what they see to be probable elements from all the gospels and dismiss others as 'legendary', 'mythological' or 'apologetic'. It is not as easy as it once was to justify singling out one gospel as more reliable than the others, and this is especially the case in their resurrection accounts. Although at many points there is obvious interdependence, particularly amongst the first three gospels, when it comes to the accounts of the resurrection they are at their most independent. The best approach is to follow each account where it leads, recognizing the possibility that different writers may have had different sources of information at their disposal; indeed each may have had access to people with living memory of the events. We must also take account of literary and theological factors, since each writer had different problems and issues to address, and applied different techniques to achieve their ends. Once we have a clear picture of what each gospel writer is saying and why, we can 'compare notes' and see what emerges in the way of a historical picture.

Are the Gospels Harmonizable?

It has become almost a dogma of modern New Testament research that the gospel accounts of the resurrection cannot be harmonized, to the point that it is felt ill-considered even to try. This makes it impossible to approach the question of history, since historical knowledge is chiefly gained by a process of criti-cal harmonization. In any attempt to reconstruct the past – and this is as true of ancient history as it is for a court of law trying someone for murder – all the testimony, reports, depositions and circumstantial details are first set out. Then a picture is sought which agrees with all the data. The harmonization of multiple reports of an event is usually the path to a clearer picture. Seldom is all the data without real or apparent contradictions. One or all of the reports may contain false information. There may be complexities in the event or inadequacies in the reports which make it difficult to get at the truth. Yet even here it is the disagreements or disharmonies which allow us to pinpoint the problem areas and perhaps unmask a false report, or correct a false interpretation or assumption.

There is such a thing as forced harmonization, and it is this that has made it a dirty word for some. Christians have an obvious interest in the integrity of the gospels and the truth of the resur-rection, and have sometimes resorted to silly harmonizations which do nothing to further their cause. There is wisdom in the remark with which Vincent Taylor prefaced his chapter on the resurrection:

> Well meant attempts to harmonize the narratives by the aid of ingenious, but not convincing, speculations, only serve to bring historical criticism into disrepute, and it is wise neither to attempt them nor to entertain them.[1]

Yet it is quite another matter to claim that the resurrection accounts are *incapable* of harmonization, for this implies that some or all of them are hopelessly erroneous, or that they are something other than accounts of real events. Paradoxically, in seeking to close the process of historical inquiry, this line of thought incites the very attempts at harmonization it deplores. In one such attempt John Wenham ably demonstrated that the four gospel accounts are indeed capable of reasonable reconciliation.[2] He has made a defensible reconstruction of a sequence of events which could have given rise to such diverse accounts. His reconstruction is not necessarily entirely correct (he does not claim this), but it does show that a series of events can give rise, when retold from various points of view, to the sort of variety we find in the four gospels.[3]

It is good that people go on trying as best they can to piece together the information to form a coherent picture. Whether negatively, through seeing that their solution does not work, or positively, through seeing that it does, the cause of truth is advanced. It is not essential to belief in the reality of the resurrection that we know the exact sequence of events of the first few days. But it is important to know that there *was* a sequence, and that the message which each gospel writer brings is based on fact and not on his own or his community's imagination. Such harmony as emerges from my own consideration of the gospels will be the reader's task to assess.

Presuppositions

In examining something like the resurrection, it is difficult to avoid presuppositions. There is a 'watershed' of belief. Some will give the gospel writers the benefit of the doubt, others will exploit any doubts to discredit them. That is as it must be. I make no apology for beginning with the assumption that the writers may be treated as honest reporters until proven otherwise, but it is important to listen to the arguments of those who start from a different point to see whether there is real basis for their scepticism. It is by examining very different hypotheses arising from varied starting points that we can see which best fits the evidence.

When Were the Gospels Written?

Any historical assessment of the resurrection narratives demands that something be said about the authors of the gospels and the time and order in which they wrote. The Gospel of Mark is regarded by most scholars as the earliest of the gospels,[4] often said to have been written about AD 64 – the time of Nero's well known persecution of Christians. This date is then used as a benchmark for the other gospels. Luke and Matthew appear to be dependent on Mark and are therefore given dates somewhere in the next thirty years.

The Problem in Dating Gospels

Mark may well reflect some concern about persecution, and it is understandable that scholars would be drawn to the best known official persecution of Christians as an explanation for this. However, Jesus was crucified, John the Baptist beheaded, Stephen stoned – and Jesus had warned that following him would always be risky. A concern about persecution could fit any time in the first century, there is no hard evidence requiring a mid sixties date for Mark. Thus different scholars have placed Mark in the forties, fifties, sixties and seventies. There is no obvious fact within the gospel which decides matters one way or the other. Mark, then, is a poor standard for any dating scheme. So are Matthew and John, and so would Luke be if it stood alone. For all the gospel writers tell the story of things that happened in the years AD 28–30, and if they also reflect happenings in their own time of writing, they do it indirectly, indistinctly and only 'as in a glass darkly'.

A Benchmark for Dating

Luke, however, wrote a companion volume on the story of the early church, and here we find something solid on which to base a dating. Part of Acts is autobiographical: the author joined Paul's missionary party at Troas and crossed with him to Philippi sometime in AD 53. He did not accompany Paul away from Philippi, but picked up with the party at the same place six years later and travelled with Paul to Jerusalem and later to Rome (Acts 16:11–18; 20:5ff.).

It has been objected that too much should not be based on the 'we sections' of Acts, since they may have been added from someone's travel diary. But any sensible author, incorporating into a narrative a source written in the first person, would specify who they were quoting, or recast it in the third person. Luke clearly intended that we understand him to have been present. If it is suggested that he were not – that he propounded a deliberate fiction – one wonders why he left himself out of so much of the rest of the story, especially 16:40–20:5.

We can be confident then that the author of Luke–Acts was one of Paul's travelling partners, present with him for the last four years of his recorded ministry. In addition to writing the gospel, he told the story of the spread of Christianity, and particularly of Paul's role up to the second year of his imprisonment in Rome (AD 62). He could have written this account any time between AD 62 and the end of his life, but there are several factors which make it clear that he published not long after the conclusion of his story. Six events of considerable importance to early Christianity took place in the ten years following the end of the story in Acts: Paul's trial, Nero's persecution, Peter's death, Paul's death, Nero's death (AD 68) and the Jewish–Roman war which culminated in the fall of Jerusalem and the destruction of the temple in AD 70. Every one of these is relevant to the story and themes of Acts, yet none of them is mentioned. The absence of any reference to Paul's trial is particularly glaring, for the whole book moves to this climax, as he testifies before the Areopagus, the Jews in Jerusalem, the Sanhedrin, the procurator Felix, his successor Festus, the Jewish king Agrippa II, and then appeals to Caesar. It is hard to credit Luke ending his story at this point, whichever way the trial may have gone. It appears he must have finished writing when Paul was still under house arrest, in AD 62 or shortly after.

The one 'fact' which is alleged to tell against this is Luke's knowledge of the fall of Jerusalem. In various places in the Gospel Jesus speaks of Jerusalem's destruction in a way, it is said, that betrays knowledge of the event after it has happened. In Luke 21:20–24, for example, Jesus predicts that Jerusalem will be surrounded by armies and trodden down, and that Jews will be led away captive among the nations. The description is more explicit than Mark's and is thought to betray Luke putting words into Jesus' mouth to describe what Luke knew to have taken place.

However, C.H. Dodd's counter-argument is now well accepted. Jesus' descriptions of Jerusalem's fall utilize imagery from Old Testament accounts of the Babylonian destruction of Jerusalem, with none of the tell-tale characteristics of the AD 70 Roman holocaust (Josephus graphically portrayed Jewish factions fighting each other inside the besieged city, cannibalism and mass crucifixions). [5] Add to this, that nowhere in Acts does Luke speak of or allude to Jerusalem's fall or the destruction of the Temple. If he felt the need to place knowledge of these events in Jesus' mouth, why not in the mouth of Peter or Stephen or Paul? Next to the resurrection the fall of Jerusalem was sensational vindication of Christian claims, and even if he had decided to curtail his story it would be extraordinary for him not to draw his readers' attention to its significance, actually if it had happened. Obviously it had not.

A feature of Luke's Gospel supports the conclusion that he wrote in the early sixties. The first two chapters provide us with an attractive portrayal of ordinary pious Jews waiting for the advent of the Messiah – at least it is attractive to us. In reality they appear to have been expecting a political revolution. The songs of Mary ('he has put down the mighty from their thrones', Luke 1:52) and Zechariah ('that we should be saved from our enemies', Luke 1:74) are so explicitly revolutionary that Paul Winter suggests they may have originally been Maccabaean war songs. Such a framing of the Christian story could have done nothing but damage to Luke's cause, were he writing between AD 65 and the eighties, when acute memory of the war perhaps abated. Militant revolutionary activity gathered pace in Israel from about AD 64, when Gessius Florus arrived as procurator. War broke out two years later and lasted until AD 70. The scandal, the shame and the anti-Jewish feelings it provoked must have gone on for at least another ten years. Luke even calls one of Jesus' followers a zealot, unthinkable in the years AD 65–80, since it was the Zealots who were the chief belligerents. Before AD 64, however, all this could have been quite innocent.

The issues which Acts addresses – the acceptance of Gentiles into the Christian movement, their reception without circumcision, the rightness of Jews sharing table fellowship with Gentiles, the legitimacy of the Pauline mission – are all issues of the forties, fifties and sixties when Christianity was predominantly a Jewish movement pushing out to the Gentile world.[6] It is difficult to think that it could have been like this after the war.

We may be confident, then, that Acts was written between AD 62 and 64, and the Gospel of Luke shortly before.[7] It is safe to suppose that Luke was quarrying material for both on his journey to Jerusalem and in the two and a half years that Paul was imprisoned in Caesarea.

In the prologue to his Gospel, Luke tells us that others had written before him. One of his sources was Mark, another a document also utilized by Matthew, designated today as Q.[8] Mark and Q must therefore have been in existence by the late fifties. Although this is not the date given Mark by most scholars, it does not conflict with any of the evidence and has its supporters.[9]

Who Wrote the Gospels?

It was once a truism of biblical scholarship that the four gospels were anonymous writings to which the names Matthew, Mark, Luke and John were attached sometime in the second century. Scholars felt, therefore, that they had a free hand to apply their detective skills to identifying the real authors. In fact it is far from certain that the gospels ever circulated without their author's names. There are no anonymous ancient texts of the gospels and there are no texts which claim any other authorship than the four names known to us. Nor do the church fathers suggest any such names. Martin Hengel has pointed out that a book without its author's name was as much an oddity and cause for suspicion in the ancient world as it is today. As for the author's not being named in the actual text of the books, Hengel notes the obvious, that they seldom are in modern books either. The author's name is generally found outside the book proper, on a title page.[10] Adolf Harnack, who argued that the standardized titles 'According to' Matthew, Mark, Luke and John, found on the gospels from the second century, must be the work of whoever first put the four together, is clear nevertheless that these would have replaced the original titles, 'for these works must have born titles'.[11] The author's name is the readers' guide to how reliable they are to judge the book's content. When we consider that two of the names – Mark and Luke – were relatively obscure people who were not apostles, the impression that we are dealing with reality is strengthened.

We do not begin, therefore, with a blank slate. There is a *prima facie* case for regarding the gospels as the works of Matthew, Mark, Luke and John: four known figures in the first generation of Jesus' followers. We should certainly gather all the other evidence and consider any indications which may speak against these ascriptions, but not be too hasty in overturning opinions which appear to have been undisputed in the years when there was far greater access to the relevant facts.

Who Was Mark?

Mark (John Mark) was the son of Mary, the owner of one of the large houses where the Jerusalem Christians met in the early days (Acts 12:12). He was a cousin of Barnabas who was prominent among the first generation of Jerusalem Christians, and who was sent out to investigate the acceptance of Christianity by Gentiles in Syrian Antioch. When Barnabas and Paul set out from Antioch on their first missionary journey, they took Mark along 'as *hyperetes* (servant)' (Acts 13:5). He may have been more than a bag-carrier. A *hyperetes* could be any kind of helper, but with the status that goes with being the personal attendant of someone of rank. The word is used of priests as servants of God, public officials and military officers. Most telling for its meaning here is that Luke uses it to describe the synagogue official who had charge of the scripture scrolls in the synagogue (Luke 4:20), and of those who provided him with material and prototypes for the writing of his gospel (Luke 1:2). One of these, we know, was Mark. It has been suggested that Mark had some role in studying the Scriptures, and in particular the prophecies about Jesus.[12] This is possible, but it may also be that Mark had the special task of providing the gospel story to help the newly formed churches sustain their ongoing Christian life.[13] It is hard to see how they could have survived for long without some access to the teachings and life story of Jesus. Luke introduces Mark not, as one would expect, when the party is constituted and sent out, but in the context of their preaching the word of God in the synagogues of Salamis. Mark, as the son of a wealthy Levite family, may well have had scribal training, equipping him with the skills of writing and producing manuscripts. He had had close contact with the apostles and disciples since the very first days after Jesus' resurrection, perhaps even before. He may already have had a working relationship with Peter. Papias, a bishop of Hierapolis in the early second century, says that he heard it from the apostle John, that Mark was Peter's 'interpreter'. This may describe an educated personal assistant, trained in scribal technique, who promulgated his master's teaching.[14] Papias is generally understood to refer to a much later association between Peter and Mark, but it may well be that he also had these early days in mind. If it was Mark's task to provide for newly established churches, some account of Jesus' life and teaching – orally or in writing – and if he utilized Peter's stories to do this, we can understand how his gospel originated, and see how serious it was when Mark abandoned the mission in Pamphylia (Acts 13:13; 15:37–41). This is a hypothetical reconstruction, but it makes sense of the information we have.

Though Paul refused to take Mark on his next journey and replaced him with Silas, he is later found in company with Peter (1 Peter 5:13) and finally back in association with Paul (2 Timothy 4:11). The written gospel may have been developing under Mark's hand in this period. It was available to Luke in close to the form known to us by the late fifties. The connection between Mark's Gospel and Peter, attested by several early Christian writers,[15] and the fact that it was the first of its kind, explains its authority in the first century, and why Matthew and Luke incorporated it almost in full into their own gospels.

It is not difficult to see why Luke and Matthew would have wanted to expand Mark. It contains no information about Jesus' birth and early years, very little of his teaching and no accounts of resurrection appearances. Each in his own way has produced a much improved teaching tool for the churches he was working with. Had it not been for the connection with Peter, the Gospel of Mark, like Q, might have ceased to be produced and fallen into oblivion.

When were Matthew and John Written?

We do not know when Matthew wrote his gospel, though there are indications of a date prior to AD 70, when the temple was still standing and when the Sadducees were still a force to be reckoned with.[16]

That the Fourth Gospel was written by the apostle John, son of Zebedee, one of the inner three of Jesus' disciples, is solidly attested by the church fathers and implied in the gospel itself. It mentions its author not by name but as 'the beloved disciple' who was in the place closest to Jesus at the last supper, entered the High Priest's courtyard the night of Jesus' arrest, watched at his crucifixion, took charge of Jesus' mother, saw the empty tomb, was first to recognize Jesus by the Sea of Galilee, and followed Peter and Jesus as they talked of Peter's future ministry.[17]

Martin Hengel, in a detailed study of the authorship of the Fourth Gospel, ruled out the son of Zebedee as a possible author because he could not square the gospel's sophistication, its Jerusalem outlook, and its author's Jerusalem contacts with a Galilean fisherman. Nevertheless, the considerable evidence drives him to conclude that the real author was from Jerusalem, was the beloved disciple, and was also named John: later confusion with the son of Zebedee is understandable.[18] Either way we are dealing with an apostolic eyewitness. But the Fourth Gospel is the work of one of the three great minds (with Jesus and Paul) that dominated first century Christianity. It is extremely unlikely that his identity would have been lost or confused by the early second century, especially considering that he was known to Papias and Polycarp.

How we date John depends on how we view the last chapter. Is it an original part of the gospel or a later addition? Chapters 1–20 could be placed anytime in John's life after Mark was written (I am of the opinion that John deliberately set out to complement Mark). The last chapter, however, is concerned to correct a widespread misapprehension that Jesus' return would be before John's death. It is at this point that the author explicitly touches events not in the time of Jesus, and it is here we get a clue to dating. It suggests a time later in the century when most of the other apostles had died. Some think chapter 21 was written shortly after John's death by his disciples and appended to his gospel. Yet its style and themes tie it closely to the gospel. A later editor would be unlikely to continue the reference to 'the disciple whom Jesus loved', and rather refer to him by name. This curiously indirect way John has of referring to himself may be the habit of one deeply influenced by having heard his master refer to himself in the third person, as 'Son of man', and overwhelmingly appreciative of the love he experienced from Jesus. To say of himself 'We know that his testimony is true' (John 21:24) would not have been unnatural for one who had heard his master say, 'We speak of what we know and bear witness to what we have seen' (John 3:11), and who knew there were those who could corroborate his witness. Thus I see the gospel as a work of the later period of the apostle's life, but for how long he worked on it, and whether there was an earlier edition without the epilogue, I cannot judge.[19]

In terms of historical witness, then, we have four writings belonging to the generation of Jesus' immediate followers. Two (John and Matthew) written by original disciples, one (Mark) written in close dependence upon Peter by a disciple who was present in Jerusalem in the earliest days of Christian preaching, and the other (Luke) by an associate of Paul who had contact with many of the original players and with members of Jesus' family, and who had ample opportunity to research the details of the story. There is also the tentatively reconstructed document Q, belonging to the period before AD 60. With regard to the resurrection, we have four patently independent accounts. We will examine them in their probable order of appearance, to see what each adds to our knowledge of what happened on that fateful Sunday.

What Does Mark Tell Us? (Mark 16)

The surprising thing about Mark's account of the resurrection is that it tells us so little. After the Sabbath, on Saturday evening, Mary Magdalene, Mary the mother of James and Salome bought spices to anoint Jesus' body, and very early on the Sunday morning they came to the tomb, wondering as they did, who would remove the stone for them. Looking up they saw that it had already been rolled away. Entering the tomb they saw a young man dressed in white who told them not to be afraid, that Jesus of Nazareth had been raised. They were to go and tell the disciples *and Peter* that Jesus would go before them into Galilee: they would see him there. The women fled from the tomb trembling with fear and told nothing to anyone.

So abrupt is the ending that various ancient copyists took it upon themselves to write a better conclusion. These can be found in the footnotes of some Bibles. The absence of anything after verse 8 in the most ancient manuscripts and the very different style of the Greek of the conclusions shows that they came from a later time.

Thus Mark has hardly given us an account of the resurrection at all. He tells us nothing of any appearances to anyone. This can be explained if we suppose that he never intended to write the resurrection story, but only an account of Jesus' ministry and death. This would be understandable if he was writing for people who he knew were already familiar with the stories of the resurrection. We have seen that the *fact* of the resurrection was the centre of Christian preaching. We have also seen Paul's enumeration of those who had seen the risen Jesus. It stands to reason that the *fact* was accompanied by the *story*. Mark apparently wrote for people whose knowledge of this was adequate, and sought to fill in the not so well-known 'beginning of the gospel' (Mark 1:1) – the actual story of Jesus' ministry.[20] Thus he brought his gospel to a close with the angel's dramatic announcement that Jesus was alive, and the note of the women's holy fear.

If we ask whether Mark tells us anything we do not already know from the earlier sources, the answer is that he adds the story of the women's discovery of the empty tomb. Simply because it is there in all four of the gospels it has generally been overlooked that Mark is our first witness for this story.[21] This could be significant in terms of what he wants positively to convey. It stands to reason that if he omitted almost everything, there could be special significance in what he did include.

Why doesn't Paul mention the Women?

In any reconstruction of the first Easter events, the women's discovery of the empty tomb finds a firm place.[22] It is curious, then, that the women are not mentioned by Paul in his rehearsal of the resurrection witnesses; nor are they alluded to anywhere in Acts, indeed anywhere in the New Testament outside the gospels. This raises the suspicion that for some reason these first witnesses did not rate much of a mention in the early preaching of the resurrection. Possible reasons for this are not hard to find. The testimony of women was not allowed in Jewish courts, so their witness would not have served well in the arguments that must have taken place. Celsus, in the second century, mocked this aspect of Christianity:

> While he was alive he did not help himself, but after death he rose again and showed the marks of his punishment and how his hands had been pierced. But who saw this? A hysterical female as you say, and perhaps some other one of those who were deluded by the same sorcery.[23]

Even in the New Testament we see how easily the women could be eclipsed in the telling of the Easter story. The men walking to Emmaus say to the stranger who has joined them, 'Certain of our women surprised us: coming early to the tomb, and not finding his body, they came *saying* they had *even* seen a *vision* of angels saying that he was alive' (Luke 24:22f.). Later, when the travellers return to tell the disciples that they have seen the Lord, they are met with the announcement, 'The Lord has *really* risen and has appeared to Simon (Peter)' (Luke 24:34). The italics are mine, but the disbelief which greeted the women's story is plain to see; it is not until Jesus appears to Peter that the women are believed. At the beginning the women's witness was not accepted, and by the end of the first day it was obsolete. The shape of the public resurrection gospel would henceforth be: 'He appeared to Peter …'

Was Mark setting the Record Straight?

This being so, it looks as though Mark may have been doing something to set the record straight, and if Peter stood behind his gospel it is understandable why. Throughout Mark Peter is portrayed as an anti-hero. His portrait is drawn 'warts and all'. The gospel can be read in part as a very honest testimony to a painfully slow coming to the light. It would be perfectly in character with this to hear Peter saying, 'Contrary to what many think, I was not the first to learn that Jesus was alive.' It would no doubt suit this theory better if Mark had given us a story of Jesus' actually appearing to the women, but given the limited purpose of his gospel the point still stands.

We need to realize that all the gospel writers were under constraints of space. They probably wrote on scrolls which were limited in length, and expensive. Each copy had to be handwritten by a professional scribe. If they wanted their gospels to be copied and read they had to be extremely careful about length. They were not writing for the Emperor's library like Josephus. Judged according to this consideration their achievement was enormous; they managed to compress into the space of a short pamphlet material that has fed the world for two thousand years, and which has exhausted the efforts of many a great intellect. The restrictions pressed upon them the need to be extraordinarily selective of their material, as well as various literary devices which we shall note when we come to them. Mark is about half the length of Matthew and Luke; the author no doubt thought hard about what he could allow himself and stay affordable to his readers. It has been pointed out that Mark is considerably lower down the literary-cultural scale than Matthew and Luke,[24] and this may have had an economic aspect as well. For Mark to have launched into an account of resurrection appearances may have put him beyond the bounds of his project.

The strange ending of Mark in which the women say nothing to anyone (having just been told to tell the disciples) may have been motivated in part by the author's desire to preserve the impression that the early preaching emanated not from the women but from the men. He hardly intended to imply that the women were disobedient in not speaking, nor that their silence was for ever. The purpose is rather to note the tremendous impression made on them. Trembling, astonishment and fear (not the same word he uses of their initial fear of the young man) are reactions of those who are in the presence of a holy revelation. So they were first to find the tomb empty, but the resurrection gospel did not go forth from them.

If this is near the truth, Mark's introduction of the women was historically motivated. He was simply following Peter in setting the record straight. The women had no value for the preaching of the gospel, perhaps even a negative value. The resurrection story contains more than can be accounted for by its use in preaching and apologetics. This says a great deal about how Jesus valued these women, who had followed him in life and stood by him through his ordeal.

So, Peter's witness, coming to us from Mark, gives us interestingly not the story of his own meeting with Jesus, but the story of the women. His lead was followed by the other gospel writers and the women's discovery of the empty tomb has now become probably the best known part of the story of Easter Day.

What do we Learn From Luke and Acts? (Luke 24; Acts 1:1–11)

Read the resurrection accounts in Luke 24 and Acts 1 and you will be struck by how little Luke gives us compared with the wealth that Paul's summary indicates was available. He tells us how, early on the Sunday morning, a group of women found the tomb empty and were told by two men in shining clothes that Jesus was alive. They told the apostles but were not believed. That afternoon two men encountered Jesus on the road to Emmaus. They journeyed together and then shared a meal, during which Jesus revealed himself to them and then disappeared. They returned to break the news to the gathered disciples only to learn that he had already appeared to Peter. Then Jesus appeared to the whole group, spoke to them of the scriptural necessity of his death and resurrection, and ordered them to stay in Jerusalem. Leading them out to Bethany, he ascended into heaven. Luke gives the impression that Jesus' appearances all took place in Jerusalem on the first day, and if the record in his gospel were all he provided we would certainly conclude that he was in irreconcilable contradiction to Matthew and John, who describe appearances over a longer period of time. In Acts, however, he takes up the story again and makes clear that between the beginning and end of the events described in Luke 24 there was a forty day period of appearances. In other words, in the gospel he has condensed a long story into something much shorter, and even in Acts he is only telling part of the story for, while not ruling them out, he makes no mention of appearances in Galilee. Here we observe one of those space-saving literary devices mentioned earlier, which easily create the impression of contradiction if they are not recognized.

Luke's Special Interest in the Fulfilment of Scripture

Though Luke is working with a scroll (or scrolls) double the length of Mark, he is still forced to be selective. Three incidents are related, in each of which there is a clear expression of the *necessity* of Jesus' death and resurrection. The first occurs in the story of the women when the angel says to them, 'Don't you remember how he spoke to you when he was still in Galilee, saying that the Son of Man *must* be delivered up into the hands of sinful men, and be crucified, and the third day rise again' (Luke 24:6–7). The theme is repeated to the men on the road to Emmaus, where Jesus himself explains from the Scriptures that death and resurrection was the God-appointed destiny of his Messiah. Finally, when he appears to the group of disciples in the evening Jesus opens their minds to understand the Scriptures, and in particular the necessity of his death for the proclamation of repentance and forgiveness of sins to all the nations.

Luke's interest in this particular theme, and his predilection for the incidents in which it featured, is readily understood when we consider that one of the most offensive things about Christianity, both for Jews and Gentiles, was Jesus' shameful execution in a manner reserved for the worst class of criminal. High-born Romans or Greeks like Theophilus (Luke 1:3; Acts 1:1), if they were ever to take seriously Jesus' messianic claim, would need to be convinced both that someone executed in the due course of Roman law was innocent, and that his execution was a necessary part of God's plan. In the resurrection stories Luke continues his great theme of the ongoing progress of God's plan of salvation, highlighting the continuity between Old Testament promise, Jesus' life, death, resurrection and the preaching mission of the early church.

Were there Two Groups of Women?

In the details of the story of the women Luke speaks of larger numbers than does Mark. He mentions at least five and identifies one of them as Joanna, the wife of one of Herod's high officials (Luke 24:10). On the basis of this, Wenham makes an important suggestion which could reconcile many of the apparent contradictions in the resurrection stories: there were, he suggests, two separate parties of women who went to the tomb on the Sunday morning.[25] The presence of Joanna is certainly cause for thought. Mark's mention of the two Marys and Salome may well, as Wenham says, suggest the viewpoint of Peter who saw the departure of this group from the house in which he was staying. Luke had a definite interest in Joanna, probably because of her high position, which put her on a level with the kind of people for whom he was writing. Her double appearance in his gospel may also indicate that he had had some personal contact with her or people who knew of her. He certainly had a source of information from within the Herodian household.[26] Wenham suggests that the detail of the women preparing spices on Friday night, which seems to contradict Mark's statement that they did not buy the spices until after the sabbath (compare Luke 23:56 with Mark 16:1), came from Joanna and her party.[27] This would deal with the first of Hermann Reimarus' ten contradictions in the resurrection accounts.[28]

Was there One Angel or Two?

Another of Reimarus' 'contradictions' surfaces in Luke. Whereas Mark has only one man appear to the women, Luke has *two* in 'shining apparel'. Considering that Luke had Mark's Gospel before him, I can only think he mentioned two because he knew it to be a fact from his other sources, and recognized Mark's account as a simplification. Matthew on this point simply copied

Mark, and John independently confirms Luke's account. Whether it is to be seen as an irreconcilable contradiction depends on whether Mark is seen to be asserting that there was only one (and not two) men, or simply mentioning the one who spoke or for some other reason dominated the incident. If anything the conflict strengthens the overall historical case for the resurrection story, for if Luke were simply repeating and embellishing an essentially made up story he would hardly have introduced a deliberate contradiction. His independence of Mark at this point shows that he is also dealing with his own gathered information about the actual course of events.

The Emmaus story (Luke 24:13ff.) also contains hints of a separate source of information. It is often dismissed as a symbolic tale probably created by Luke himself, but if it were, it is strange that he identified one of the travellers by name. The naming of characters is not a strong feature of the gospel tradition. If he were story-telling I think Luke would have left them anonymous, or possibly given names to both of them. The naming of only one is evidence of some sort of interest in that particular person. It may have been that Luke actually got the story from Cleopas, or from someone who knew Cleopas, or that he received the story with Cleopas' name already firmly attached.[29]

Why is there no Description of Jesus, Meeting with Peter?

The Emmaus travellers return to tell the disciples in Jerusalem that they have been with the Lord, only to find that he has also appeared to Peter. Luke's is the first and only gospel which tells us that Jesus appeared on the first day to Peter, though in this he only confirms what we have already learned from Paul. It seems to have been well accepted amongst the first Christians that Peter was the first of the twelve to see the risen Jesus, though the story itself was apparently not told. If it had been, it would most certainly have been repeated in the apocryphal Gospel of

Peter, written in autobiographical form in Peter's name. This gospel jumps straight from Jesus' appearance to the women to his appearance to all the disciples at the lake of Galilee. We may imagine that the earlier meeting was very personal to Peter, another indication that there was more to the resurrection story than was useful for preaching or suitable for public consumption. It also indicates that the gospel writers were not inventors of stories. Had they been, they could hardly have passed up the opportunity of this one.

Was Jesus a Ghost?

Luke tells us that while they were still all gathered Jesus appeared among them and reassured their natural disbelief by showing them that he was neither ghost nor angel nor vision. In Tobit 12:19 the angel that accompanied Tobias in the form of a man reminded him that he had not seen him eat any food, and that what he had seen was therefore a vision. It was natural that the disciples should think they were seeing a ghost, as they did once before when Jesus walked to them on the sea (Mark 6:49; cf. Acts 12:15). Luke's story makes perfect sense in relation to the needs of the disciples at that time, and it is hardly necessary to import the controversies of a later generation to explain the stress it lays on the 'physicalness' of the resurrected Jesus. We will be safe in assuming that the teaching which Jesus then proceeds to give the disciples is part of what was given over the next six weeks (amplified in Acts 1). Luke concludes his gospel with Jesus departing (again amplified in Acts 1), the disciples returning to Jerusalem and praising God in the temple.

We may sum up Luke's contribution as evidence of a separate source for details about the women's discovery of the tomb; of an appearance to the Emmaus travellers indicating a source connected with Cleopas; further reference to Peter's meeting with Jesus; an account of a meeting with the twelve (also in Paul and John) in which Jesus reassured the disciples that he was truly himself; and a double account of his final departure from his disciples.

Does Matthew Add Anything New? (Matthew 28)

Matthew tells a dramatic story. On Sunday morning as the women set out for the tomb there is an earthquake, an angel descends and the guards at the tomb are stunned into immobility. The angel tells the women that Jesus is alive and sends them to break the news to the disciples that he will see them in Galilee. On their return the women are met by Jesus and worship him. He repeats that he will see the disciples in Galilee. In the meantime the guards report to the chief priests and are bribed to spread the story that Jesus' disciples stole his body while they slept. The eleven go to Galilee, Jesus meets them at the place appointed, declares his kingship and charges them with their mission.

It is only now, as we examine Matthew's account, that we find any follow-on to Mark's intimation that Jesus would appear in Galilee. He also adds two totally unexpected pieces of information to our picture of the resurrection: first that the tomb was guarded from Saturday to Sunday, and secondly that Jesus actually *appeared* to the women. To date we have not had the slightest hint of either of these. The appearance of Jesus to the women after they left the tomb could easily be dismissed as an invention of Matthew if it were not for the fact that it is independently mentioned by John. Otherwise the accounts of John and Matthew are so divergent that Wenham has reason to see here appearances to two separate groups of women, which Matthew has amalgamated in his simplified retelling of the story.

I can see no theological or apologetic reason why Matthew or anyone else would invent the story of the appearance to the women. He only records that it took place; Jesus seems to have told the women no more than the angels had already said. It appears that Matthew has included it mainly for historical reasons; he did not find it in Mark, but knew of it and perhaps had a particular personal relationship to the event.

Was the Tomb Guarded?

Matthew gives the story of the guard a lot of space, and it is not hard to see why. He, or the people for whom he wrote, were involved in an argument with Jews over what really happened to the body of Jesus. Just as no one writing about the resurrection today can overlook the current debate over whether Jesus' rising involved the standing up of his physical body, so Matthew was unable to write without reference to an important dispute of his day. The gospels were not just recording history for posterity, and therefore trying to include everything, they were addressing issues which were of particular importance at the time.

The story of the guards has been mercilessly slated by the critics. 'Surely one of the most extravagant inventions ... a Christian fabrication devised to counter the current Jewish assertion that Jesus was not raised from the dead', says one recent commentary.[30] Reimarus deals with it not as a contradiction (for it is nowhere else mentioned), but as an historically improbable 'fancy' intended to divert suspicion from the disciples.[31] In this judgement he has been followed by many commentators, though there are still some brave enough to rise to Matthew's defence.

What are the main objections to the story of the guard, other than that it is nowhere else mentioned? First, the priests could hardly have been expected to know that Jesus had spoken of rising from the dead, when the disciples themselves seemed so ignorant of the fact. Secondly, it is highly unlikely that the High Priests would go to Pilate on a Sabbath. Thirdly, the women would not be going to the tomb to anoint Jesus' body if they knew there was a guard on duty. And fourthly, guards who faced a possible death penalty for sleeping on duty would hardly be bribed to confess such a thing. We may add that the presence of guards, even if they were in catatonic shock, would interfere with the way Mark, Luke and John tell of the women's discovery of the tomb.

In favour of Matthew it has often been pointed out that the story contains so many oddities, which handicap its usefulness in Christian defence of the resurrection, that it could only be true. If the Christians were going to make up a story of the tomb being guarded, surely they would have had it guarded the whole time (as the second century Gospel of Peter has it) and not just from Saturday onwards. And surely they would not have suggested the guard was asleep. That would only play into the hands of those who suspected the disciples had stolen the body. Better to have had the guards executed after telling their story and not being believed (as in Acts 12:19), or to have invented an alibi for the disciples.[32]

The very fact that this story occurs in relation to a Jewish–Christian debate speaks in favour of its veracity. Least of all in a public argument can one afford to invent stories; they are too easily exposed with disastrous consequences for the whole case they are meant to support. To presume that Matthew or his source would invent such a tale to help their defence is to presume a naïvete that borders on imbecility.

Some very useful observations about the development of the argument which must underlie Matthew's story have been made by W.L. Craig.[33]

> First stage: Christians proclaim 'Jesus is risen.'
> Second stage: Jews reply 'His disciples stole the body.'
> Third stage: Christians say 'How could they? There was a guard at the tomb.'
> Fourth stage: Jews say 'But the guard admitted they went to sleep.'

> Fifth stage: Christians say 'But they were bribed to say that by the priests.'

Notice how much of the story came not from Matthew or the Christians but from the Jews. *They* accuse the disciples of stealing the body and *they* say the guard went to sleep. The argument itself, therefore, testifies first to the emptiness of the tomb (something which the Jews never disputed), secondly to the existence of the guard, and thirdly to the guards' confession that they went to sleep. Recalling our earlier discussion, it also testifies to the importance of the empty tomb both for Christians and Jews, not just with respect to theological questions about the reality of the incarnation, but regarding the very truth of the claim that Jesus had risen. Any attempt to cast doubt on the resurrection has to start here. And the most likely alternative to the Christian proclamation, as the Jews saw clearly, is that the disciples stole his body.

A number of things can be said about the 'improbabilities' of the story of the guard. To begin with, it was raised against Jesus at his trial that he had threatened to destroy the temple and in three days build another. The charge did not stick so there must have been discussion of what he had said and what he had meant. This could well have led to discussion of statements he had made about his rising from the dead on the third day. It is not surprising that such thoughts would not have returned until after the excitement of the execution had subsided, nor surprising that the High Priest might have wanted to take extra precautions with a crucified miracle-worker, many of whose followers were still in Jerusalem. The objection that the High Priest would never have gone to Pilate on a Sabbath shows a poor appreciation of the pragmatics of those who see them-selves charged with defending public order (and safeguarding their own actions); in any case they could well have sent their agents. To the objection that the guards would not condemn themselves for a bribe, it might be said that they would probably have been accused of sleeping on duty anyway; they would have had little choice but to accept any money offered to them and cooperate with their superiors. From the priests' point of view the whole thing was hollow, but what alternative did they have?

The problem of the consistency of the story with the other gospels may well be another by-product of the gospel writers' brevity. The earthquake may have been a local shaking accompanying the descent of the angel and the rolling back of the stone, which were witnessed by the guard, who then departed for the city prior to the arrival of the women.[34]

There is one other clue that may speak in favour of the presence of a guard at Jesus' tomb. For a long time the detail of the resurrection stories that most worried me was the fact that the women went to the tomb *alone*. It appears that some of them set out from the house where Peter and John were staying. Why, if they knew there was a heavy stone across the entrance of the tomb, did not one or two of the men go with them? And how did the women think they *might* be able to obtain access? The presence of the guard would answer both these questions: the men who still feared for their own safety would not have wanted to go to where they knew an armed guard was posted, and the women might have hoped, since their mission was only to anoint the body, that the guards would move the stone and let them in. Thus the evidence all points to the existence of a guard, and it is this more than anything else which makes it clear the disciples could not have stolen Jesus' body. Had they overpowered the guard, there would have been such a hunt for them that they would never have survived to make their public appearance at Pentecost.

Jerusalem or Galilee?

What are we to say to the apparent contradiction between the disciples being told to go to Galilee in Mark and Matthew, and receiving their initial sight of Jesus in Jerusalem according to Luke (and staying there for at least a week according to John)? C.F.D. Moule has suggested that Jesus' instruction to depart to Galilee is to be interpreted less as a command than as a reassurance that they need not be afraid to return home, for Jesus would appear there too.[35] Building on this suggestion, might it not be that Jesus' words were meant to counter the practical problem of large numbers of his followers milling around in Jerusalem. Many came up with him from Galilee to celebrate the Passover and would still have been in the city on the Sunday morning. Once the word was out that Jesus was alive again they would not have wanted to return to Galilee for fear of missing out on seeing him themselves. The message of Jesus and the angels could then have been both a command and an assurance, not just to the eleven but to all the Galilean disciples in Jerusalem who remained loyal to him. There is obviously no contradiction if Jesus then appeared to the eleven before they left, nor even if he kept them in the city until the end of the week.

For the majority of Jesus' Galilean disciples, their meeting with him probably took place in Galilee. This may be the meeting that Matthew describes on the mountain, it may be the appearance to the five hundred which Paul records, the two could be the same, or there could have been other meetings of which we know nothing. Matthew's selection of the mountain appearance was dictated by the words spoken on that occasion, which provided a perfect conclusion to his gospel. Jesus' messianic authority is declared and the apostles are commanded to disciple the nations, baptize in the threefold name and carry forward his teaching. They are assured of Jesus' day by day presence until the close of the age.

Matthew's contribution, then, is the information that from Saturday the tomb was watched by a detachment of soldiers who fled in fear early on Sunday morning, that Jesus himself appeared to a group of the women, directing his Galilean disciples to return home, and that he appeared to the eleven in Galilee.

What Else Does John Say? (John 20–21)

John's account is the most detailed and circumstantial of all the resurrection narratives. It bears the stamp of eyewitness testimony and helps to resolve many of the apparent conflicts in the other accounts.

The story begins in the early morning before dawn. Mary Magdalene arrives at the tomb and finds it open. Was she alone? John mentions no other, but when Mary reports to the disciples she says, '*We* don't know where they have laid him.' John too has simplified his story. There is no sighting of angels at this stage; Mary assumes the worst (she must at least have looked into the tomb) and runs to tell Peter and John that Jesus has been taken away. If Mary was accompanied by other women, and they were carrying materials (some of them expensive) for the work they intended to do, they may not all have returned together, especially not running, as John says of Mary. This would explain John's not mentioning any others. For the rest of his account Mary Magdalene may have been alone. The other gospels may describe what happened to the others, or they could be a conflation of several events.

Peter and 'the disciple Jesus loved' then come running to the tomb. The description of their race has every mark of coming from the memory of one of the runners. The 'beloved disciple' reaches the tomb first but hesitates to go in; Peter goes in. These details are quite pointless unless they be memories indelibly etched in the mind of the author.[36] John enters after Peter, sees the empty grave-clothes and believes. The author dissociates his believing from the Old Testament Scriptures, which he feels should have led him to faith. It was not, as it were, his faith in God which first caused his belief in the resurrection, but the mere shock of seeing the empty tomb and how it was arrayed. He quits the tomb believing that Jesus is alive yet still in confusion as to what it means.

What Happened to Mary?

Mary is left weeping outside the tomb. She seems to be alone, though it is not impossible that other women were with her. Looking into the tomb, she sees two angels who ask her why she is crying. She answers their question and, turning back, sees Jesus standing behind her. There is no way of reconciling this with what the other gospel writers say about the angel's announcement to the women, if it is the same women and the same appearance which they describe. It is Jesus who reveals that he is alive to Mary Magdalene; in the other stories angels make the announcement.

However, we have already noted that the other gospels may be describing the appearance of angels to the other women, and have included Mary Magdalene because she too encountered angels and in a general way was involved in the whole incident. Martin Hengel has argued that the way in which Mary Magdalene is always named first testifies to her undisputed primacy among the women in the early church, which is most naturally explained by her having been the first witness of the risen Jesus.[37] It may also point to a difference between her meeting with Jesus and that of the other women.

Mary does not recognize Jesus until he speaks; at first she assumes him to be the gardener and asks him the whereabouts of Jesus' body. Already in the numbness of bereavement, and now facing the shock of the missing body, she can think only of finding it and completing the work she came to do. Mary evidently has not recognized the two figures in the tomb as angels, though John is clear that is what they were. This may be the reason why Mark and Luke speak in their accounts not of *angels* but of *men*; that was the initial impression they made. Jesus then addresses her by name and she at last recognizes that he is alive and answers him in their native Aramaic.

John fills in for us in some detail the story of Jesus' appearance to Mary. The only story which compares with it for detail in the other gospels is Luke's account of the men on the road to Emmaus. C.H. Dodd comments, 'this *pericopé* has something indefinably first hand about it. It stands in any case alone. There is nothing quite like it in the gospels. Is there anything quite like it in all ancient literature?'[38]

Much has been made of the fact that Jesus now tells Mary not to touch him, whereas in Matthew we are told that the women took hold of Jesus' feet and worshipped him. The accounts probably relate to different groups of women, but quite apart from that, the reason Jesus spoke these words was likely that she had taken hold of his feet and was clinging to him. Mary needed to learn that although he was risen, he could not always be with her in a tangible form.

Doubt Resolved

At the end of the first day, as we saw in Luke, Jesus appears to the group of disciples. He proves himself fully alive, and speaks to them of the Holy Spirit and of their future mission. A week later he appears to them again, this time with Thomas present. Thomas' unbelief and the way in which Jesus brought him to faith evidently appealed to John as the perfect conclusion to his gospel. When Thomas is totally convinced that for Jesus the impossible has happened, he confesses him, 'My Lord and my God' – the conclusion John wishes every reader to draw from his gospel.

Will Jesus return before the Death of John?

We have already discussed John's epilogue. Like Matthew's story of the guard it answers a problem that had arisen in the church. John was getting old. People were saying that Jesus would come again before he died. Jesus himself had said so! But John knew that that was not what Jesus said, so he wrote to set the record straight. The very existence of this problem tells us something. People knew and treasured the words of Jesus, but in this case a wrong interpretation has been placed on one of them, which could cause big problems once John died. So John told the story of the occasion on which the words had been spoken and exactly what Jesus had said. He says it was the third time Jesus appeared to the whole group of his disciples. We must therefore assume that it took place prior to the mountain gathering that Matthew describes. Jesus revealed himself in a way which was a significant reminder of the days of their early call to be disciples, when they had also taken a miraculous catch of fish (Luke 5:1ff.). John is the first to realize that it is Jesus on the beach telling them where to fish, but true to form it is Peter who jumps out of the boat to get to Jesus as quickly as possible. Jesus has already begun to prepare breakfast and tells them to bring some of the fish they have caught. After they have breakfasted together Jesus speaks with Peter, establishing him as 'shepherd' of his sheep and indicating to him something about his eventual death. Peter then asks what will become of John, and Jesus answers him with the words which have been misquoted and misunderstood, '*If it is my will* that he should remain until I come, what is that to you? You follow me.' The story of the appearance by the lake gains credibility from the fact that it is secondary to John's purpose of putting the record straight about what Jesus had *not* said.

In addition to affirming the truth of his witness, the author left a signature on this story to be read by those who have eyes to see. How much ink has been spent trying to uncover the significance of those one hundred and fifty three fish that John tells us were taken in the net that day! It is the sum of the numbers from one to seventeen, said Augustine, and corresponds to the ten commandments and the seven gifts of the Holy Spirit. It is the total number of all the species of fish in the sea, said Jerome. It is the sum of the values of the letters of the Hebrew words meaning 'church of charity' and the fish represent disciples, said another. Its numbers add up to 'Ichth' a shortened form of the Greek word for 'fish' – expressing the unity of the great fish Jesus Christ with his little fishes drawn up from the wicked depths through apostolic endeavours led by Peter. And so on, *ad nauseam*.[39] But surely they are right who remind us that fishermen always count their catch, and note the condition of their nets. I have not yet forgotten the night my father came home from one of his usually fruitless beach-fishing expeditions with a fifty-two pound jewfish. I have not forgotten the weight of the fish; nor has he. John 21 was written by a fisherman.

Is The Evidence Sufficient?

On the day of Pentecost Jesus' disciples burst upon the world with the news that God had raised their master, body and all, from the dead, and exalted him to the place of highest authority in the universe. They preached it and they proved it. In the very city where he died they declared him alive, and the authorities were powerless to contradict them. All Jerusalem knew the grave was empty and many were convinced by the apostles' account of what had happened.

Three of the witnesses are accessible to us through the New Testament, Peter (Mark), John, and Paul. We have uncovered the existence of many more whose witness was available in early days and is available to us second hand: Mary Magdalene, the other women, Cleopas, James, the Twelve, many Galilean disciples, those who could give their attestation to John's Gospel. We may add to this the researches of Luke and the witness of Matthew. What each source reports has the appearance of being a small part of something larger and more complex. It is not important that we know all the details of what happened in those first and following days; some of it we can reconstruct, some we can only surmise, much is lost. It is right that historians go on trying to reconstitute the picture, but with the information we have they will always be tentative reconstructions. What is important is that we see that there is enough evidence on which to base a firm and honest judgement that Jesus really did live again. And therefore possibly still lives. But can there ever be enough evidence to support a conclusion as large and unlikely as a resurrection?

It is just at this point that we begin to be troubled by the argument of the eighteenth century Scottish philosopher, David Hume, who said that the occurrence of any miracle is so unlikely that no amount of evidence could ever be enough to prove it.

Two things should be said in response. First, when Paul addressed the philosophers in Athens and claimed that God had 'furnished proof (of a day of judgement) to all people by raising him from the dead,' he hardly intended to claim a rigorous demonstration of the philosophical or mathematical kind. He meant that God had done something real and public and left ample testimony to the fact. This testimony is not such that it cannot be gainsaid; most of Paul's audience mocked the possibility of a resurrection. Some, however, believed. Faced with Paul's testimony – and we have seen in 1 Corinthians 15 that he was capable of bringing much more than his own to the witness stand – a judgement was called for: to believe him or disbelieve. Witness is the backbone of Christian evidence, and we stand today in a position little different to those philosophers. They, of course, could cross-examine Paul. We are limited to a historical cross-examination of the surviving records. Yet even after two thousand years Christian faith is not an irrational step into the darkness of what you have no reason to believe; it is (in part) a reasonable judgement that what has been testified by witnesses is true. Secondly, to Hume a miracle was in defiance of everything that is usual and expected, and the amount of evidence needed to counterbalance such apparent 'impossibility' could never be enough. It is true that in most situations where a miracle is alleged, there is insufficient evidence to outweigh our natural scepticism. But suppose we were to come across a man whose words, actions and story brought us to the realization that resurrection *in his case* was the 'natural' thing to expect? By natural I do not mean non-miraculous, but that within the frame of reference which the events surrounding him have created such a miracle is to be expected.

Thus there is one all important piece of evidence, without which we would always have some residual doubt: the man himself, the Jesus whose life and work led him into this tomb, and possibly out again to new and undying life. Who was he? What was he like? What was he doing? Perhaps only when we have explored that story can we really make up our minds over whether this empty tomb means a new age, or must remain one of those forever mysterious question marks.

Notes

[1] V. Taylor, *The Life and Ministry of Jesus*, 222.

[2] J. Wenham, *Easter Enigma*.

[3] I do not, e.g., find his identification of Mary Magdalene with Mary of Bethany at all convincing. But, so far as I can see, disallowing this does not much effect his overall reconstruction.

[4] Mark has held the field as the first of the evangelists since the middle of the eighteenth century, when the 'two document hypothesis' began to be accepted as the best explanation of the similarities of the first three gospels. C.H. Weisse (*Die evangelische Geschichte kritsch und philosophisch gearbeitet*, 1838) is generally credited with first elaborating the theory that Mark was the earliest gospel, though in fact G.C. Storr, writing in defence of the inspiration of the NT had argued it before him. Weisse followed the accepted view that Mark was an

'epitomizer' until he noticed that the details Mark allegedly added were too insignificant to be explained in this way. The alternative was that he was the original; Matthew and Luke were the epitomizers. Mark's priority has been challenged by W.R. Farmer, *The Synoptic Problem*, who revived what is known as the Griesbach Hypothesis (after J.J. Griesbach), that Matthew wrote first, was copied by Luke, that Mark epitomized both, and that there was no document Q. Farmer has been followed by some, but the majority of scholars feel the evidence still weighs in Mark's favour. For more recent discussion see C.M. Tuckett, *The Revival of the Griesbach Hypothesis*; *Synoptic Studies*.

[5]   C.H. Dodd, 'The Fall of Jerusalem and the "Abomination of Desolation" ', 47–54.

[6]   See D. Seccombe, 'The New People of God', 366–70.

[7]   V.E. Vine ('The Purpose and Date of Acts', 45–48) thinks Acts was written to Jews and Christian Judaizers as an appeal for 'reconciliation as Paul draws near to his trial,' in the hope that they would close ranks and not disown Paul at this critical moment.

[8]   The existence of a written document Q is still debated, but appears to me the best explanation of the considerable quantity of non-Markan material shared by Matthew and Luke. It is hard to see how the common order in sequences of this material in Matthew and Luke could be the result of anything but a common source. Of course, it could be that Matthew used Luke (or vice versa, see R.H. Gundry, *Matthew*), but the complete dissimilarity of Matthew and Luke's birth and resurrection sections makes this unlikely. For an English account of Q see T.W. Manson, *The Sayings of Jesus*; more recently C.M. Tuckett, *Q and the History of Early Christianity*.

[9]   Supporters of a date for Mark in the fifties include D.A. Carson et al., *An Introduction to the New Testament*, 96–99) and E.E. Ellis, 'The Date and Provenance of Mark's Gospel', 801–815.

[10]   M. Hengel, *Studies in the Gospel of Mark*, 64–84.

[11]   A. Harnack, *The Origin of the New Testament*, 68.

[12]   C.S.C. Williams (*The Acts of the Apostles*, 156) thinks Luke uses *hyperetes* as an equivalent to the synagogue *Hazzan*, and suggests that Mark may have drawn up proofs of Jesus' messiahship from OT texts.

[13]   D. Seccombe, 'The Story of Jesus and the Missionary Strategy of Paul', 123–5.

[14]   R. Riesner (*Jesus als Lehrer*, 20–24, 63) cites Krizinger's conclusion that against the background of hellenistic rhetoric Peter's 'interpreter' meant that Mark was the person who officially instructed others in the teachings of Peter.

[15] The earliest statement is quoted by Eusebius in *Ecclesiastical History*, 3.39 from Papias' now lost *Interpretation of the Oracles of the Lord*. Also: Irenaeus, *Against Heresies*, 3.1.1 (AD 180); Tertullian, *Against Marcion*, 4.5 (AD 200); Eusebius *HE*, 2.15; 6.14 (quoting Clement of Alexandria, AD 200); *HE*, 6.25 (quoting Origen, AD 300). See the discussion of this evidence in Ellis, 'Date and Provenance', 804–806. Ellis argues that it all points to Mark having been written during Peter's lifetime.

[16] See Gundry, *Matthew*, 602–606.

[17] John 13:23; 18:15–16; 19:26–27, 35; 20:2–10; 21:7–24.

[18] M. Hengel, *The Johannine Question*. He also argues that the two sons of Zebedee were martyred too early for John to have authored the gospel (21, 158 n. 121).

[19] For further reading on the authorship and date of John see Carson et al., *Introduction*, 138–168.

[20] This point was made in an unpublished lecture by D.W.B. Robinson.

[21] E.L. Bode, *The First Easter Morning*, in a dissertation devoted entirely to the evangelists' treatment of the story of the women, completely overlooks the question of how they got into the story in the first place.

[22] See P. Perkins, *Resurrection,* 86.

[23] Origen, *Against Celsus*, 2:55.

[24] G.D. Kilpatrick, *The Origin of the Gospel According to St Matthew*, 124–125.

[25] Wenham, *Enigma*, 64ff.

[26] See pp. 435ff., n. 1, 13..

[27] Wenham, *Enigma*, 68f.

[28] Reimarus, *Fragments*, 177–179.

[29] Luke is not noted for introducing names into his stories; in one case he drops a name which Mark has supplied (Luke 18:35 = Mark 10:46; see D. Seccombe, *Possessions and the Poor in Luke–Acts*, 131, 174f.). He might have named Cleopas because he was a well-known person in the early church (his name may be a Graecized form of Clopas, an uncle of Jesus by marriage (John 19:25); see Wenham, *Enigma*, 37–39).

[30] F.W. Beare, *The Gospel According to Matthew*, 539.

[31] Reimarus, *Fragments*, 153–170.

[32] Suggested by G.M. Lee, 'The Guard at the Tomb', 169–175.

[33] W.L. Lane, 'Guard'.

[34] See Wenham, *Enigma*, 77f.

[35] Moule, *Resurrection*, 4–5.

[36] J.H. Bernard, *A Critical and Exegetical Commentary on the Gospel according to St John*, II. 660, says 'That the first disciple to note the presence of the grave-clothes in the tomb did not actually go into it first is not a matter that would seem worth noting, to any one except the man who himself refrained from entering. This strongly suggests that we are dealing with the narrative of an eye-witness.' See also J.A.T. Robinson, *The Priority of John*, 289–291.

[37] M. Hengel, 'Maria Magdalena und die Frauen als Zeugen', 243–256.

[38] C.H. Dodd, 'The Appearances of the Risen Christ', 115. Dodd mentions this 'feeling' again in *Historical Tradition in the Fourth Gospel*, 148, written when he was 80 years old.

[39] For some of the literature see J.A. Emerton, 'The 153 Fishes in John 21:11', 86–89; P.R. Ackroyd, 'Reply', 94; N.J. McEleney, '153 Great Fishes' (John 21:11), 411–417; J.A. Romeo, 'Gematria and John 21:11: The Children of God', 263–264; M. Rissi, 'Voll grosse Fische, hundertdreiundfünfzig (John 21:1–14)', 73–89; B. Grigsby, 'Gematria and John 21:11 – Another Look at Ezekiel 47:10', 177–178; O.T. Owen, 'One hundred and fifty three Fish', 52–54; J.M. Ross, 'One hundred and fifty three Fish', 357; P. Trudinger, 'The 153 Fishes: A Further Response and Further Suggestion', 11–12; K. Cardwell, 'The Fish on the Fire: John 21:9', 12–14.

Chapter 4

The Prophet And The King

The Appearance of John

Suppose we returned to Palestine early in AD 28 and tried to locate Jesus. The chances are that our investigations would prove fruitless. If we were to enquire in Sepphoris and Tiberias, the two most important cities in Galilee, it is doubtful if anyone would have heard of him – the same in Capernaum. In Jerusalem we would run into the same difficulties. Jesus of Nazareth? Not many Jerusalemites would have heard of *Nazareth*, let alone *Jesus* of Nazareth. And if we did chance to come across someone who had met him (for he had often been in Jerusalem), they would wonder *why* we wanted him; were there not plenty of good builders in Jerusalem? Should we chance to mention a famous preacher, I think their eyes would have lit up with sudden understanding and they would have hastened to tell us that it was not Jesus of Nazareth we sought, but John the Baptizer.[1] He could be found any day on the other side of the Jordan preaching to the crowds and baptizing.[2]

One of the extraordinary things about the Jesus story is how quickly it all happened. From the beginning of his ministry to its end was a mere three years, and yet he has affected the world more than any other in human history. Four years before his death and resurrection Jesus was a nobody, a small town builder, from a family with few connections and no wealth, and he was completely unknown in the arena of national affairs.

John the Baptizer, on the other hand, was a household name. There would have been few in Israel who did not have an opinion about him, although he too had only recently come into the public eye. Luke, the historian among the New Testament writers, sets the Baptist's ministry within a historical context which would have allowed his contemporaries to date John's appearance with exactitude:

> In the fifteenth year of the reign of Tiberius Caesar, Pontius Pilate being governor of Judaea, and Herod being tetrarch of Galilee, and his brother Philip tetrarch of the region of Ituraea and Trachonitis, and Lysanias tetrarch of Abilene, in the high-priesthood of Annas and Caiaphas, the word of God came to John the son of Zacharias in the wilderness. (Luke 3:1–2)

We, however, because of uncertainties about ancient calendars, are left in some doubt. Probably John made his debut late in AD 27, though some date it a year or two later.[3]

Luke believed John was a prophet; the word of God had come to him, just as it had to Moses, Elijah, Jeremiah and others before him. He was also recognized as such by his contemporaries.[4] That is one reason the crowds poured out to hear him and be baptized in the river. There had not been a recognized true prophet in Israel for over four hundred years and it was believed by many that the coming of a glorious new age would be characterized by the reappearance of prophecy in Israel.[5]

Perhaps it was the place where John appeared and the strange clothes he wore which first aroused the rumour that there was again a prophet in Israel. For he lived in the rough country and his activity was confined to wilderness places. He also wore the rough camel hair top and leather skirt which called to mind descriptions of prophets, particularly of Elijah (Mark 1:6; 2 Kings 1:8; Zechariah 13:4). It may have been pure curiosity which first drew people out to see John. Jesus was later to ask why they had gone, and suggest that it may at first have been to see a madman or a spirit-possessed ecstatic (Luke 7:24–26).[6]

John did no miracles (John 10:41). The people were confronted in the wilderness by 'a voice' decrying their sins and warning them of God's coming judgement. Preachers of sin and destruction often do not succeed in doing more than raising a smile. Only those who reach the conscience, causing people to see themselves as they really are, achieve a serious response. John evidently touched many hearts. His power as a preacher is recorded not only in the New Testament, but also by Josephus, a Jewish historian of the first century. Josephus had less information for the gospel period than for those before and after; nevertheless he knew of John, and his comments provide us with a strong bridge between the gospels and secular history.

Josephus tells how in AD 36 Herod Antipas lost an army in a border war with Aretas of Petra. The conflict was caused in part by bad feeling aroused when Antipas divorced Aretas' daughter and married his own half-brother's divorced wife, Herodias. John protested the illegality and impiety of this union and, according to Mark 6:16ff., lost his life for it. It was understandable that the people would see Aretas' victory and Herod's defeat as God's providential settling of the score.

> To some of the Jews the destruction of Herod's army seemed to be divine vengeance, and certainly a just vengeance, for his treatment of John, surnamed the Baptist. For Herod had put him to death though he was a good man and had exhorted the Jews to lead righteous lives, to practise justice towards their fellows and piety towards God, and so doing to join in baptism. In his view this was a necessary preliminary if baptism was to be acceptable to God. They must not employ it to gain pardon for whatever sins they had committed, but as a consecration of the body implying that the soul was already thoroughly cleansed by right behaviour. When others too joined the crowds about him, because they were aroused to the highest degree by his sermons, Herod

became alarmed. Eloquence that had so great an effect on mankind might lead to some form of sedition, for it looked as though they would be guided by John in everything that they did. Herod decided therefore that it would be much better to strike first and be rid of him before his work led to an uprising, than to wait for an upheaval, get involved in a difficult situation and see his mistake. Though John, because of Herod's suspicions, was brought in chains to Machaerus, the stronghold that we have previously mentioned, and there put to death, yet the verdict of the Jews was that the destruction visited upon Herod's army was a vindication of John, since God saw fit to inflict such a blow on Herod.[7]

Was John a Political Revolutionary?

Some have inferred from the nature of John's end that he was more of a political threat than either Josephus or Mark indicates. Certainly the tetrarch was worried that he might prove so. J.D. Crossan thinks the location of John's mission on the Peraean side of the Jordan was politically significant: John took the people out of the Holy Land and by baptizing them re-enacted Joshua's crossing of Jordan and sent them back home as 'a network of ticking time bombs to await the great denouement.'[8] Antipas had to take action. Crossan locates John within a pattern of such activity in the years leading up to the Jewish–Roman War: in the fifties a number of prophetic revolutionaries led their followers into the wilderness as prelude to an attempted takeover – one said the walls of Jerusalem would fall at his command. However, it is a fundamental error to explain John from events which took place twenty to thirty years after him, as though Antipas could know from events which had not yet happened the danger in what John was doing.

One can properly speak of a revolutionary purpose in the normal political sense only if there is an intention to call people to armed overthrow of the existing government. Since Josephus, Mark and Luke each independently represent a John whose message was directed towards national repentance; who neither incited the people to arms nor preached subversion, it is pure invention to make of him a revolutionary in the ordinary political sense.

However, in an ultimate sense one cannot deny that John's message had political implications. Matthew and Luke (Q) say that John announced the imminent arrival of the kingdom of God, an upheaval which must bring all human governments crashing down. John's demand that even the tetrarch repent would undoubtedly imply that his government, his person and his new bride would be swept away together if they continued in their sinful relationship. While Antipas may have been prepared to tolerate this as the ranting of a self-appointed prophet – he may even have feared to lay hands on him and compound his guilt – it is not surprising that Herodias was not. She may well have viewed John's great following, combined with his personal attack on herself, as a political threat and goaded Antipas into action.

Thus Josephus' explanation that Herod arrested John because he feared an uprising and Mark's moral explanation complement each other, and cohere with the public's blaming of Herod's later defeat upon his treatment of John, especially since it was his divorced wife's father who defeated him. It is a testimony to the magnetic power of John that even when he was a prisoner Herod listened to him and was perplexed by his teaching. Herod himself was happy to have John away from the people, but that was not enough for his offended wife; as Jezebel had nursed a personal grievance against Elijah, so Herodias was determined to do away with John, and when the opportunity came, she manipulated her husband to have John beheaded (Mark 6:17–29).

How did John see Himself?

Did John just consider himself a mover of people, as Josephus presents him? Jesus called him 'a prophet, and more than a prophet', as great a man as had ever lived (Luke 7:26–28), though his greatness in Jesus' eyes lay not so much in his abilities and courage, as in the critical role which God assigned him in the development of his plan of salvation. This was why Jesus could go on to say that the least in the kingdom of God (any one of his disciples) was greater than John; their's was to be an even more crucial role.

Many, who at the time of his ministry saw John as a prophet, also wondered whether he might be more than a prophet. For if the renewal of prophecy meant the nearness of the new age, then it might be that John was one of those special prophetic figures who was expected in the run up to the arrival of God's kingdom. It was a matter of some importance, since people sensed that momentous things were afoot; that was why they came out in such large numbers and with such excitement. How they understood John in relation to the coming age determined where they were themselves. Since the plan of God had already been revealed in the prophetic Scriptures, it was a matter of discovering where John fitted there. 'Elijah' was an obvious possibility. At the end of Malachi stands a passage which strongly influenced Jewish beliefs about how God would establish his kingdom.

> Behold, I will send you Elijah the prophet before the great and terrible day of the Lord comes. He will turn the heart of the fathers to the children, and the heart of the children to their fathers; lest I come and strike the earth with a curse. (Malachi 4:5–6)

There were reasons for expecting God's 'final solution' to come at a time of rebellion and lawlessness (e.g., Daniel 12:1, 10). However, many teachers wondered how the Messiah could save his people if he caught them at such a time. The answer to this problem was seen in Elijah's ministry: he would come just prior to the end and restore the people to obedience.

The author of the fourth gospel was probably once himself a disciple of John the Baptist (John 1:35–40). He recalls that a delegation was sent from the Pharisees in Jerusalem to check the Baptist's credentials (John 1:19–28). They asked him if he was the Messiah or Elijah or the Prophet, three figures who were expected to appear in relation to the new age. John denied being any of them, although Jesus himself later ascribed to him the role of Elijah. This is curious and must surely recall a genuine denial on the part of the Baptist. Early Christianity acknowledged him as 'Elijah' on Jesus' authority. Despite much that has been written, the fourth evangelist had no reason to represent him otherwise, for his portrait of John as the forerunner is positive throughout. It is true that John says 'he was not the light, but came to bear witness to the light' (1:8), but he also has Jesus say 'He was a burning and shining lamp, and you were willing to rejoice for a while in his light' (John 5:35). It must have been the Baptist himself who denied that he was Elijah.

It may be that he did not want to be saddled with some of the expectations which attached to the coming of Elijah. The scholars expected Elijah to solve all the party disputes about interpretation of the law, which threatened to split the nation, and also to put right the disordered situation of the official family registers. Because of all the wars, exiles and resettlements there was uncertainty about who were the Jews of pure blood, who were of the priestly families, and so on. Elijah would settle all these questions and reorganize the nation for its new glory under the rule of the King–Messiah.[9] John the Baptist showed no concern for such matters. Nor did he demand an exact and scrupulous observance of the law, which the Pharisees would have thought was what repentance entailed. Instead, he cut to the heart of the prophets' concern for justice and brotherly love, just as Jesus would later do. So he alienated many of the teachers, though he opened up the possibility of repentance to ordinary people who could not hope to succeed in keeping a law which had become so complex.

However, it is also probable that John did not think of himself as Elijah at all. He may have been influenced by the figure of the ancient Elijah, especially if he knew the prophecy that was given at his birth (Luke 1:17). He may even have imitated him in his dress and conduct.[10] Nevertheless, if *God* did not reveal to him that he was 'Elijah', it is doubtful that a man like John would have taken the title to himself. His essential humility is a feature of many of the descriptions we have of him.[11] In fact it was Jesus, sometime after John's death, who first declared that John had fulfilled the role of the promised Elijah. As late as the time of the transfiguration, Jesus' three closest disciples, one of whom had been a disciple of John, were quite unaware of it (Mark 9:11). The teachers were saying that Jesus could not be Messiah, since Elijah must come beforehand, and he had not yet come. The disciples were evidently troubled by this argument, as well they might be had they remembered John's denial. Only when Jesus explained to them that Elijah had indeed come in the person of John, even if he had gone unrecognized, were their doubts resolved.[12]

When those who had been sent to check on his credentials asked him to state who he was, if not Elijah, Prophet or Messiah, John answered that he was just a voice, 'I am a *voice* crying in the wilderness, "Make straight the way of the Lord", as Isaiah the prophet said' (John 1:23). The 'Voice' in Isaiah (40:1–11) was the one who was to prepare the way for God to come to his people. 'The Arm of the Lord' would then come and liberate Israel from the powers of the world which had repeatedly embroiled her in warfare and trodden her down. God would then rule his people by means of his 'Arm', caring for them as a shepherd cares for his sheep. Isaiah refers here to what is spoken of in many parts of the Old Testament: the coming of Messiah to restore Israel to her glorious position as God's people. In the Aramaic paraphrase of this chapter, which may well have been in use in John's day, the gospel herald is told to say to the cities of Judah, 'The kingdom of your God is revealed'.[13] This new age that John's contemporaries eagerly looked forward to was sometimes referred to as the kingdom of God.

Wonderful things were afoot, yet John saw his task as a humble one. He was not the Messiah, nor Elijah, nor even the herald who would announce the arrival of God, but the one who would prepare the way. His was the humble task of the voice, crying in the wilderness, seeking to build a level highway through Israel's national life that would allow God to save his people and not condemn them. Nevertheless, his identifying himself with this voice placed John's ministry in a clear relationship to the events which would quickly lead to the establishment of God's kingdom.

A National Crisis

John believed that God was about to bring the present wicked age to a conclusion. For Israel this would mean a confrontation with God in the form of a great judgement and final separation of the righteous and the wicked. The Jews were familiar enough with the idea of judgement. At points in their history God had acted against them with terrible severity: destroying Jerusalem, razing the temple, allowing the people to be led off into slavery. Albert Nolan thinks John foresaw a similar war with Rome which would bring immense destruction. The only way out was national repentance in the form of a great social revolution.[14] However, a close inspection of John's message reveals something much more discriminating and final: 'Every tree that does not bear good fruit will be cut down and cast into the fire;' the wheat would be brought into the granary and the chaff would be burned with fire (Luke 3:9, 17). These are descriptions of a last judgement in which God will make his decision on the destiny of every human being.

There is, accordingly, an individualism about the preaching of John. The old prophets for the most part warned of the fall of the whole nation, often holding out the possibility that God might relent if the nation were to turn. Here the judgement is inevitable; the only question is who will be destroyed and who rescued. There is no hint that whatever is about to happen might not happen if enough people would repent. This accounts in part for John's individualistic rite of baptism.

Yet for all the individualism of his message, John did preach to the nation.[15] Noting various points of similarity between John and the Dead Sea community at Qumran, some scholars have wondered whether John may have been influenced by or even grown up with this sect . However, at just this point of his appeal to the whole nation we see how different John was. The community at Qumran was a closed conventicle; only by the strictest process of initiation lasting more than two years could a person be 'converted to the truth' and enter into membership of the 'true' people of God.[16] The Pharisees too were a guild which guarded its membership, though we do not know what their entrance requirements were. There was teaching for ordinary people in the synagogues, of course, but the prominent teachers of the law were oriented more towards teaching small groups of enrolled disciples. John, however, like his forebear Elijah, wrestled with the soul of the nation. 'There came out to him Jerusalem and all Judaea, and all the region of Jordan' says Matthew (3:5). He addressed the populace, challenged the religious rulers and, as we have seen, even attacked the morals of the governor. John identified no righteous part or party within the nation and emerged from no identifiable group. He was the solitary 'voice' in the wilderness – the voice of God – crying to every individual in the nation to take stock and return before it was too late.

This appeal to the nation was not incidental. John was the forerunner of God's return to his people. That was a national matter. According to Malachi, God was sending Elijah to restore the people to righteousness, lest he should come 'to smite the earth with a curse' (Malachi 4:5f.). Salvation and judgement were bound up together, and if at the time of God's visitation, the nation was to be found in the state John knew it to be, what would it mean? To be sure, a remnant might be saved, but John must have hoped that an identifiable Israel and not just a band of survivors might be rescued from condemnation as a result of his ministry. That may be why he did not spare even the tetrarch (who was half Jewish).

The Coming One

All that stood between John's audience and the fiery judgement was the appearance of 'the coming one', whose task it would be to carry out the great separation. Whether that separation consisted of the removal of a few unfruitful trees or the destruction of the whole forest depended on what response the nation made to John's warning. According to John, 'the coming one' was already there, hidden somewhere amongst the people (John 1:26), waiting for God's moment to be revealed. When some suggested that it might be John himself, he strenuously denied it. His role was only preparatory and symbolic; the man of real power was yet to be revealed: 'I baptize you with water; but one mightier than I is coming. I am not worthy to unfasten his shoes. He will baptize you with the Holy Spirit and with fire. His fork is ready in his hand; he will winnow his threshing floor and gather the wheat into his granary; but the chaff he will burn with inextinguishable fire (Luke 3:16f.; Matthew 3:11f.).

What an extraordinary thing! Here is no Assyria or Babylon to act as God's chastising rod. Rather, a single man, wielding the winnowing fork of judgement, will destroy the wicked and gather the righteous into the coming kingdom. We can guess at how the people may have imagined this man. Those at Qumran were waiting for such a one and were already rehearsing their battle formations. They were the faithful remnant, they thought; the king would come to them first, reinforce them with legions of angels, and lead them on a campaign of conquest, first to exterminate the evildoers of Israel, and then to destroy God's enemies among the Gentile nations. As to how John imagined the 'coming one' executing his mission we are given no clue, except that it would be supernatural.

Corresponding to John's symbolic baptism there was to be a real baptism of the Holy Spirit and fire. These are the twin poles of Israel's prophetic expectation. Like the prophets before him, John saw them as part of one great outpouring of God: destruction on the wicked and God's Spirit on the righteous. Isaiah spoke of the Spirit being poured from on high at the same time as 'hailstones, when the forest comes down' (32:15–19); Joel looked to the day when God would 'pour out my Spirit on all flesh' at the same time as the moon turns to blood and 'the great and terrible day of the Lord comes' (2:28–32). According to Isaiah, the final outcome of this twin visitation would be a new age of justice, peace and prosperity. It is to this, no doubt, that John referred when he proclaimed that 'the kingdom of heaven is at hand' (Matthew 3:2).

The 'coming one' who would do all this was already in their midst. When he revealed himself the people would meet their Judge. How would they and the nation fare? Would Israel meet with its glorious destiny, or would God come only to 'smite the land with a curse'? The latter was a real and terrible possibility, for as John perceived it, most of his countrymen stood on the wrong side of the line. They may have comforted themselves that they were Israelites, children of Abraham, and probably no worse than the next person. If God was going to reject them he would have to knock out all the rest as well. He would hardly disqualify the whole nation from its inheritance. What then would become of his promises? To John that was a dangerous delusion. God had demonstrated in the past that he would not be held to ransom through his promises by a presumptuous and wicked people. He had wiped the nation out before.[17] God could raise children for Abraham from the stones and so fulfil his promises. The Lord would not build his kingdom of chaff and fruitless trees. There was only one sensible course: to return to God and to bear fruit worthy of repentance. The alternative was rejection from God's future world when the Coming One burned out all that was worthless and irredeemable (Luke 3:8–9).

Repentance and Baptism

John demanded that people repent and be baptized (Luke 3:3–6). God was interested in the state of people's hearts. Repentance was the only way in which things could be restored and a straight and level highway appear on which God could come to bless. In believing this John was not greatly out of step with his religious contemporaries. Pharisees despaired of the kingdom arriving unless the people first repented.[18] The Qumran community saw its own repentance as what marked it for salvation. Yet there was obviously something very different about John. Essenes, Pharisees and Sadducees had in common the belief in scrupulous fulfilment of the many commands of the law. The God-pleasing person was the one who succeeded in knowing and keeping the most commandments. But John's call for repentance was a call for a total return to God. He saw the people, not as guilty of breaking this or that commandment, but as being in total rebellion against God and indifferent to his claim on their lives. This was as true for the religious as it was for the irreligious. 'A nest of snakes' is what he called the crowds (Luke 3:7). In Matthew these words are addressed to the Pharisees and Sadducees (3:7). They posed as teachers of the way of God, but deceived themselves about their own righteousness; they were as far from God in their hearts as the tax-collectors. What everyone needed was a complete change of heart towards God.

Such an inward revolution could not be *performed* as a commandment. It involved a complete turn-around in a person's attitudes. This inward conversion, if it were real, would produce a new way of life, much as a healthy tree produces good fruit. But the conversion itself could hardly be performed as a single act, or even a succession of acts. It could only be agreed to, prayed for, and signified by some token. The thing itself was deep and spiritual, its reality would show itself clearly by the fruit it bore.

Why did John Baptize?

John's baptism was the way he provided for people to signify this inner revolution, or perhaps their desire for it, which is its first step. The main method employed by modern biblical researchers to help us understand the meaning of such a practice is to look for parallel rituals in the surrounding culture. The problem is that there is really no one like John in his own time (except Jesus). And as for his baptism, there were so many ritual washings practised by the Jews that it is hard to know whether John's should be explained in terms of one, all, or none of them. Judaism associates holiness with cleanliness, unholiness with defilement. There were many ways in which a person could be defiled and rendered unfit to associate freely with others or to engage in a religious activity like offering sacrifice. After touching a corpse, for example, or coming into contact with any kind of human discharge, a ritual wash was required to restore one's cleanness. This was part of everyday life in first century Israel. Members of the Dead Sea community took a daily bath before joining together to eat their main meal. The steps down into their baptismal cisterns have a ridge in the middle so the person coming down does not defile the one coming up. Thus it is difficult to imagine that John's baptism would not at least have been taken to signify cleansing, and therefore an original defilement. However, John's once and for all baptism, connected to his radical demand for a complete change of mind and life, does not find its full explanation here.

A practice known as proselyte baptism, described in the Mishnah and Talmud, would if it existed in the first century, throw an interesting light on John's baptism. Male and female converts to Judaism were initiated by a once and for all baptism; the males of course also underwent circumcision. If this was in John's mind, his baptism implied that the people had forfeited their claim to be the people of God and needed to be readmitted as though they were Gentiles. This would accord with his warning to the people not to count on being children of Abraham (Luke 3:8). It could also account for John's choice of the Jordan: the baptized would be entering the land anew. It would also have made John exceedingly controversial. However, the existence of proselyte baptism in the first century is still debated. With no reference to it in Philo and Josephus, many scholars are doubtful and think it must have begun after the fall of Jerusalem.[19]

A further possibility is suggested by a legend about Adam found in *The Life of Adam and Eve*, a Jewish book roughly contemporary with the New Testament. Adam says to Eve

> Stand in the water of the river [Tigris] for thirty-seven days. But I will spend forty days in the water of the Jordan. Perhaps the Lord will pity us … Adam walked to the Jordan River and stood on a stone up to his neck in water. (*Life of Adam and Eve* 6:2–7:2)

This is an interesting association of baptism, the Jordan and a plea for forgiveness. Other baptisms were not forms of contrition, nor were they associated with repentance. Since John's baptism was closely bound up with repentance it may also have been, like Adam's in this legend, a way of beseeching God for mercy.

However much light we may be able to throw onto the intended significance of John's baptism from the contemporary background, we should also be open to the possibility of something quite unprecedented. John cannot be explained just as a product of his environment simply because the most powerful formative influence in his life was the coming of the word of God which made him a prophet. We find in the prophets of the Old Testament an extraordinary originality which created a breach with the religious and social evolution of their times. Because they were under the influence of a word from *outside*, they became outsiders to their own generation (see, e.g., Amos 7:10–17). We may presume that John's baptism 'spoke' to his generation with all that its contemporary parallels might suggest of sin and defilement, of contrition and repentance, of cleansing and forgiveness and entry into God's true people. But primarily it will have gained its meaning from his message. It was the means he specified for people to admit the justice of God's judgement on their life, both individual and national. It was their admission that they had forfeited their right to membership of God's chosen people, and their plea that he nonetheless accept them. It was their 'Yes' to John's promise that the Messiah was coming soon, their plea for forgiveness and inclusion amongst his people in the kingdom of God. In short it was their public 'Amen' to his whole message and programme.

Did People Receive Forgiveness?

Did John's baptism also *confer* God's forgiveness? We might assume it did, since the gospels call it 'a baptism of repentance for (unto) forgiveness of sins'. But did it secure forgiveness there and then? Or was it the pledge of a forgiveness that would come later from the coming judge?[20] The question is more than academic, for John was explicit that his baptism was symbolic and preparatory; the real baptism of Spirit and fire would come with the Messiah (Matthew 3:11; Luke 3:16). One of the first things which raised the wrath of the religious establishment against Jesus was his presuming to declare people forgiven, yet there is no hint of any such outcry against John (Mark 2:1ff.). We must conclude, then, that John's baptism was not seen to result in forgiveness there and then, but to prepare one to be forgiven at the great judgement which would follow the arrival of the 'coming one'.[21] This, then, is one of the great differences between John and Jesus, which marks John as the forerunner and Jesus as the fulfiller. It also explains the radical difference between John and his disciples' way of life and that of Jesus and his. John called the people to a repentance which made sobriety and fasting an appropriate response. Jesus gave forgiveness and reunited strangers with their God; celebration was the appropriate reaction. It is interesting that Jesus speaks no word of disapproval about John on this issue, nor John of Jesus (Mark 2:18–20; Luke 7:31–35).

John's Ethical Demands

It was natural that people would ask John how they should live. He was calling them back to 'the *way* of the Lord'. In the Pharisaic system one set about pleasing God by keeping all his laws. To make sure this happened the 613 laws of the Old Testament were expanded with a bewildering number of additional rules to cover every situation imaginable at the time. The whole body of law was called *halachah* – 'walking'. Over a century later this was codified as the Mishnah. Repentance for Jews of John's day meant taking on oneself the 'yoke of the law', which in practice meant pursuing a more exact observance of *halachah*. But to the people's question John pointed in a different direction: 'The multitudes asked him saying, "What then must we do?" He answered them, "Let him who has two coats give to him who has none, and let him who has food do likewise" ' (Luke 3:10–11).

There is nothing in the law of Moses as searching and radical as this. Its origin may be Isaiah 58. In this chapter the people are fasting for God's deliverance and complaining because he does nothing to help them. God answers that the kind of fasting he wants to see is the cessation of injustice and the practice of real brotherly love:

Behold you fast for strife and contention and to hit with the fist of wickedness. You should not fast as you do this day if you would make your voice heard on high.

Is this the fast that I have chosen, the day for a man to afflict his soul? Is it to bow down his head like a rush, and to spread sackcloth and ashes under him? Will you call this a fast and an acceptable day of the Lord?

Is not this the fast that I have chosen: To loose the bonds of wickedness, to undo the bands of the yoke, and to let the oppressed go free, and that you break every yoke? Is it not to share your bread with the hungry, and to bring the homeless poor into your house? When you see the naked to give him clothes, and not to hide yourself from your own flesh.

Then shall your light break forth like the morning and your healing shall spring forth speedily. (Isaiah 58:4–8)

This passage tells us what God wants to see in people who are genuine about wanting him to rescue them. If they want his rescue, they will be busy in the rescue of others; it is unthinkable that they should pray for his kingdom to come when they themselves are helping to perpetuate the injustice and hardship that God's kingdom will undo. John preached an ethic which was appropriate to his conviction that God's kingdom was about to dawn. He did not direct the people to the static and timeless demands of the law, but to a dynamic way of life which should characterize people who are longing for and expecting God's arrival to put all things to rights.[22]

Two specific groups of people are recorded as coming to John, asking special direction for their lives.

Tax-collectors also came to be baptized, and they said to him, 'Master what must we do?' And he said, 'Extort no more than what is appointed to you.'

And soldiers also asked him saying, 'What about us, what must we do?' And he said to them, 'Don't extort money by violence or false accusation and be content with your wages.' (Luke 3:12–14)

This is remarkable. Soldiers and tax-collectors were the chief agents of oppression encountered by ordinary people yet John tells neither to quit their jobs. It is clear from this that he did not advocate revolt, though there were some in his day who did. He looked in another direction for the answer to injustice, and only demanded that instruments of the state should use their power responsibly, justly and compassionately. It is again in accord with Isaiah 58 that those who are looking towards the kingdom should cease their oppression and robbery, even when these are almost required in their profession. Luke may have brought these two special cases forward because when he was writing in the sixties revolutionary activity in Palestine was hotting up and would soon reach disease proportions; anyone who mentioned the kingdom of God could be suspected of having violent revolutionary aspirations. People might well have wondered whether John's intentions had been altogether peaceable. The examples are also significant for John's own time and showed his contemporaries that he would not be drawn into any revolution of human making; his eyes were towards God and what he would do supernaturally through the promised 'coming one'.

Today we remember John because of Jesus, though originally it was John who was famous, and Jesus completely unknown. The gospels tell us that the point at which the change about began was when Jesus came to John at the Jordan and requested to be baptized.

Jesus is Baptized

Even the ultra-sceptical admit that Jesus was baptized by John. It is rated as one of the undoubted facts of Jesus' life. This was one story the early church would never have invented. Yet the very unlikeliness of the account makes it inevitable that the business of understanding it will not be easy. The story itself is easily told. In Mark we find it in its briefest form:

Jesus came in those days from Nazareth in Galilee and was baptized in the Jordan by John. And immediately as he came out of the water he saw heaven opening and the Spirit as a dove coming down to him, and a voice came from heaven: 'You are my son, whom I love, in you I take delight.' (Mark 1:9–11)

The first question which leaps to the mind of all who are willing to grant that Jesus was at least an exceedingly good man, is why he would come amongst those who were confessing their sin and request baptism. Matthew, whose account is fuller than Mark's, makes it clear that this is not just a modern problem. He anticipates the question and tells us that though it troubled the Baptist, Jesus insisted (3:14–15). Jesus did not undertake his baptism lightly; his rather ponderous reply to John suggests that he knew it to be the right way forward for him. He too could see the incongruity, yet wanted to fulfil God's plan.

A number of suggestions have been given as to why Jesus wanted John to baptize him. Some have asserted, in a matter-of-fact way, that Jesus must have been conscious of sin and wanted forgiveness like everyone else. Christians have always believed this not to be the case. First, because at no other point does Jesus give the slightest indication of it – even here his answer to John acknowledges that there is something strange about his being baptized. Secondly, the great achievement of Jesus' life hinged on his being guiltless before God. And thirdly, the Christian's ultimate conviction that Jesus was God-become-man makes his sinning against God unthinkable. But all this is to run a long way ahead. Let us be content to leave whether Jesus was sinless as an open question for the present and explore other reasons he might have had for being baptized.

Some have thought that Jesus wanted to identify with John's movement. Certainly his coming to John had this effect. Yet he could have achieved the same result without going through baptism. Jesus might have come and joined John as a baptizer without himself being baptized, or he could have accepted the invitation to baptize John.

A long line of Christian interpretation reasons that if Jesus was not repenting of his own sins, he must in some way have been associating himself with the sins of others, or perhaps with their judgement. Certainly his baptism associated him with sinners. He may or may not have seen himself 'standing in' for other people, but it is conceivable that he felt a bond of unity with his people which made him unwilling to stand aside from their corporate guilt as a nation, and therefore made his standing with them in baptism appropriate. Further, his baptism associated him with the repentant community which awaited the gift of forgiveness and the outpouring of the Spirit, which the 'coming one' would dispense when he revealed himself and his kingdom.

The King–Messiah

Each of the first three gospels locates the beginning of Jesus' ministry at his baptism and suggests that it was there that God commissioned him as his Messiah. The Fourth Gospel does not disagree with this, though its focus is on the descent of the dove as the signal to the Baptist of Jesus' messianic identity.

Does 'Christ' Mean God?

Christians reading the gospels may fall into a difficulty at this point, which can confuse their understanding of the New Testament, especially the first three Gospels. With the prior conviction that Jesus is God incarnate, they assume that messiahship must be another way of talking about divinity. Since godhood must be eternal – past and future – the notion of Jesus *becoming* the Messiah does not fit, and so it is unconsciously rejected. With that rejection, however, much of what the gospels say becomes unintelligible. For they want to convince us that Jesus is the Messiah (or Christ), and also to show us how he became so. That is a very different thing to proving Jesus divine. John is explicit: 'These things are written that you may believe that Jesus is the Christ' (John 20:31). John clearly wishes us to see that Jesus is also truly God; that is why his gospel climaxes with Thomas' confession, 'My Lord and my God' (John 20:28). Nevertheless, this is something additional and distinct from messiahship. Mark's primary purpose is to demonstrate Jesus' messiahship, though he hints at something greater. Matthew and Luke also go further, but their main concern too is to prove that Jesus is the Messiah.

So what does it mean that Jesus is the Messiah? And what sense does it make to speak of him being commissioned as the Messiah at his baptism?

From Genesis to King David

The notion of a God-appointed human saviour emerges in Scripture as early as the story of Adam and Eve: the disgraced Eve was promised a 'seed' (whether an individual or a collective is unclear) who would bruise the serpent's head (Genesis 3:15). This promise accounts in part for Genesis' preoccupation with the particular line of descendants passing through Abraham and Jacob, and the protection of Sarah and other women in the story. When Jacob gives his final blessings to his sons, Judah is marked out as the family from which kings will descend until the coming of one who will rule the nations (Genesis 49:8–12). Jacob's prediction gives him the obscure name Shiloh, to which Ezekiel gives the sense 'the One to whom judgement belongs' (Ezekiel 21:27). It is not unlikely that John the Baptist's appellation, 'the coming one', which he appears to have used in preference to Messiah, is derived from these scriptures.

The notion of a future God-appointed ruler resurfaces at various points in the biblical saga, a notable example being the oracle of Balaam:

> I see his but not now;
> I behold him, but not near.
> A star will come out of Jacob;
> A sceptre will rise out of Israel. (Numbers 24:17)

However, the messianic idea emerged more clearly during the time of King David. David himself was anointed with oil by the prophet Samuel to be the God-appointed king of Israel (Messiah/Christ means 'anointed one'). Along with his anointing God gave David the gift of his Spirit to empower him for his task (1 Samuel 16:1–13). This in itself was nothing unique. Priests, prophets and kings were all anointed for their task. However, David was promised a descendant who would reign eternally as God's representative over his people. Because of his close relationship with God he would receive the title 'Son of God' (2 Samuel 7; 1 Chronicles 17). As with David, this Messiah would rescue God's people from their enemies, keep them in safety and plenty, and lead them in the ways of God.

Fundamental to the Messiah concept is that the future deliverer should be a human being and a descendant of David, that he should be specially appointed (anointed) by God as king of his people, that he should be endowed with the Holy Spirit for his task, that he should reign forever, and that his reign should extend from Israel to the Gentile nations. His special task is to drive evil from the world. Indeed, Israel's messianic hope is the Bible's answer both to the problems of evil and suffering, and to the problem of power and conflict among nations.

What the Prophets said about the Messiah

In the dark days of Israel's rebellion and gradual disintegration it was in large part the promise of this coming King and a future kingdom which kept hope alive and ensured Israel's survival. Isaiah contemplated the promise of the woman's seed and looked forward to the son who would be born to take the government upon his shoulders. Isaiah calls him the 'Root of Jesse' (David's father), who would judge and rule righteously, reunite the scattered exiles of Israel and draw the Gentile nations to himself (Isaiah 7–9, 11). Jeremiah calls him a 'Righteous Branch' of David's line – 'a King who will reign wisely and do what is just and right in the land' (Jeremiah 23:5). Ezekiel calls him David – 'I will place over them one shepherd, my servant David, and he will tend them … I the Lord will be their God, and my servant David will be prince among them' (Ezekiel 34:23–24). Daniel sees him in a vision as a human being (son of man) coming before God to receive all the peoples of the earth as an eternal kingdom (Daniel 7:13–14).

Between the Testaments

The desire for such a saviour continued long after the close of the Old Testament period, and was particularly strong in the century before Jesus. From a collection of psalms of the first century BC comes this description of the hoped for King:

> See, Lord, and raise up for them their king,
> the son of David, to rule over your servant Israel in the time known to you, O God.
> Undergird him with the strength to destroy the unrighteous rulers,
> to purge Jerusalem from Gentiles who trample her to destruction;

in wisdom and in righteousness to drive out the sinners from the
inheritance;
to smash the arrogance of sinners like a potter's jar ...
He will gather a holy people whom he will lead in righteousness;
and he will judge the tribes of the people that have been made
holy by the Lord their God ...
And he will be a righteous king over them, taught by God.
There will be no unrighteousness among them in his days,
for all shall be holy, and their king shall be the Lord Messiah.

(*Psalms of Solomon* 17:21–32)

In Jesus' Time

The Dead Sea Scrolls have brought to light a Jewish community
approximately contemporary with Jesus and it is interesting to
observe how intense was their hope for a coming deliverer – so
intense that they were already designing banners and rehearsing
battle formations for the great war against wicked peoples, into
which the King would lead them.

For our Sovereign is holy and the King of Glory is with us; the
host of his spirits is with our foot-soldiers and horsemen ...
Rise up O Hero! Lead off Thy captives O glorious One!
Gather up thy spoils O Author of mighty deeds! ...
Smite the nations Thine adversaries and devour flesh with Thy
sword!
Fill Thy land with glory and thine inheritance with blessing.

(The War Rule, 1QM19)[23]

Strange as such fervent expectancy seems to us, it would be a
mistake to think that it was untypical among the Jews; this is just
one expression of the longing of most for this coming King.

A further treasure of messianic belief is the translation-
paraphrases of the Old Testament, which were read in Aramaic
speaking synagogues. Though written some time after Jesus

they often preserve older traditions. These targums, as they are called, are full of hope for the coming of the one they call the King–Messiah. One example is typical of many explanatory additions which show how Jews before and after Jesus read their scriptures with hope in the coming King:

> And Rachel died, and was buried in the way to Ephrath, which is Bethlehem ... And Jacob proceeded and spread his tent beyond the tower of Eder, the place from whence, it is to be, the King Meshiha will be revealed at the end of days.
>
> (*Targum Jonathan Genesis* 35)

No better picture do we have of the hopes of ordinary Jewish people at the beginning of our era than what Luke gives us in the birth and infancy narratives of his gospel. Mary, Zechariah, the shepherds, Simeon, Anna – ordinary people expecting that one day, perhaps in their own lifetime, God would fulfil his promise to send a deliverer. Mary's response to the announcement that she is to bear the Messiah is to rejoice that God has remembered his promises to Israel by bringing forth the one who will mean the putting down from their thrones of Gentile rulers and the filling of the hungry (Israel) with good things (Luke 1:46–55). John the Baptist's father exults that God 'has raised up a horn of salvation for us in the house of his servant David ... Salvation from our enemies and from the hand of all that hate us ... to grant us that being delivered from the hands of our enemies might serve him without fear in holiness and righteousness all our days' (Luke 1:68–79).

In the early first century messianic hope spilled over from expectation into active rebellion. In the period of instability following the death of Herod the Great a number of rebels set themselves up as kings of the Jews. In quelling the resulting disturbances the Roman governor of Syria crucified two thousand of the leaders.[24] Herod the Great knew what he was doing when he took pre-emptive action to crush the rumour of a possible Messiah in the region of Bethlehem some years before. Thirty years later, in the time of Jesus and John, talk of a Messiah was still perilous.

Jesus is Appointed King–Messiah

Did Jesus see himself as the Messiah-to-be when he came to be baptized? Luke alone gives us any information about Jesus' youth, and then just one brief story (Luke 2:40ff.). It shows that at the outset of his teenage years Jesus had an unusually close relationship with his heavenly Father. Taken along with the birth stories, this reference to God as Father suggests that he was aware of a messianic destiny (though it does not mean that he thought he held the messianic office at that time). If so, we can see a further appropriateness in his baptism as an act of solidarity with his people: as king Jesus would have to carry a responsibility for them before God.

Whether Jesus presented himself for baptism simply as a member in solidarity with the rest of the nation, or as one who knew he was destined to be its leader, it was at this moment that God declared that he *would* be its ruler. This is the real significance of Jesus' baptism in the gospels, and its historicity cannot be lightly brushed aside. It is vouched for by his appearing to stand in an inferior position to John. The story would not easily have survived in Christian memory, let alone be exalted to a key place in Jesus' life, were it not both true and important for some reason. The most obvious reason is that it was something which was of great importance to Jesus (the words from heaven were addressed to him), and he communicated this to his disciples. This being so it is foolhardy to overlook what the first three gospels unanimously assert was its significance to Jesus. None of them says *why* he was baptized, but they all agree that God greeted it by designating him as the Servant–King of Israel: 'You are my son, the beloved one, in whom I am well-pleased' (Mark 1:11; Matthew 3:17; Luke 3:22).

For a Jew well versed in the Old Testament, as Jesus most surely was, these words were pregnant with meaning. They hark back to two important passages, the first messianic psalm and Isaiah's first description of 'the servant of the Lord'.

Psalm 2 speaks of the future Messiah–King of Israel, who is anointed to rule in Jerusalem, designated God's son, and promised ultimate political dominion over all the nations of the earth.

> The kings of the earth set themselves …
> against the Lord and against his anointed (Messiah) …
> Yet I have set my king upon my holy hill of Zion.
> I will tell of the decree of the Lord,
> He said to me, '*You are my son*;
> Today I have begotten you.
> Ask of me and I will give you the nations as your inheritance,
> And the uttermost parts of the earth as your possession.'
>
> (Psalm 2:2, 7–8)

There is no sense here of the Messiah needing to do anything; God declares him king and establishes him as ruler, not only of Israel but of every nation on earth. However, the Servant of the Lord, who features in a string of passages in Isaiah 42–55, has a very active role. God establishes the messianic kingdom through his efforts. Filled with the Spirit of God, he, quietly yet at the cost of great personal suffering, puts an end to evil in the world, brings home the scattered Israelites from their places of exile, and establishes the rule of God both in the land of Israel and to the ends of the earth.

> 'Behold my servant whom I uphold; my chosen *with whom my soul is well pleased*.
> I have put my spirit upon him; he shall bring judgement to the nations …
> he will not fail nor be discouraged until he has established judgement in the earth; and the islands will wait for his law …

> I the Lord have called you in righteousness and will hold your
> hand,
> and will give you for a covenant of the people, for a light to the
> nations;
> To open the eyes of the blind, to bring out the prisoners from the
> dungeon, and those that sit in darkness out of the prison house.'
>
> (Isaiah 42:1, 4, 6–7)

God's words to Jesus at his baptism declared him to be the King of Psalm 2, and his to be this Servant task. It is surely significant that all this happens at the moment Jesus takes his place alongside his fellow Israelites and affirms his solidarity with them in their impending judgement.

Jesus may well have grown up with the conviction that his destiny was to be the King–Messiah. If so, in one sense then he was the Messiah from his birth. Nevertheless, he was only a private citizen until the day God actually anointed him and appointed him to his messianic office, and this he did at his baptism.

What was John's Role in Jesus' Anointing?

Samuel was the anointer of David, and Elijah too was an anointer of kings (1 Samuel 10:1; 16:13; 1 Kings 19:15–16). Jesus' baptism and anointing also come through one who was recognized in Israel as a prophet. However, John was told that the one on whom he saw the Spirit descend and remain was the one who would baptize with the Holy Spirit and with fire. The prophet stood by, and it was God himself who performed the anointing, not with the symbolic medium of oil, but by a direct pouring out of his Spirit, made visible for John and for Jesus in the form of the dove.[25] John's task was discreetly to announce Jesus to the people and give his prophetic witness to God's choice of him (John 1:29–34). He does not appear to have proclaimed Jesus publicly. To have done so would have been very dangerous. But he did point Jesus out to those whose loyalty and discretion could be relied upon, and some of these became Jesus' first disciples.

Did John Know Jesus was the Messiah?

According to the Fourth Gospel, John the Baptist twice asserts that he did not know Jesus before the dove alighted on him during his baptism (John 1:29–34). On the surface this appears to contradict Matthew who implies that John knew Jesus before (3:13–14). Why else would he have been embarrassed to baptize him? We should probably understand John's double denial, then, to mean that he did not know before the baptism and the descent of the dove that Jesus *was the Messiah*. Jesus and John were distant relations (Luke 1:36) and John may have anticipated that some would think they had set things up to launch Jesus on a messianic career. He needed to state clearly that only through God's sign to him did he become aware that the 'coming one' whose way he was preparing, was none other than Jesus.

It might still be argued on the basis of Luke 1–2 that John should have known from his mother that Jesus was Messiah-designate. I can only think that thirty years is a long time. There may have been a number of messianic claimants in Jesus' and John's youth who would have sown confusion and created doubt about second hand reports, even in one's own family. High hopes for Jesus seem to have faded even among his immediate relations.

But, if John was totally unsuspecting that Jesus was the 'coming one', why did he baulk at baptizing him, as Matthew represents him doing? My own feeling is that John must have had some previous contact with Jesus and known him to be a man with an extraordinary relationship with God. We need not confuse ourselves here with talk of sinlessness. John's preaching was not, like some modern preaching, aimed at convincing people that if they have committed one sin, they are totally condemned. Rather, he was seeking to convict people that the whole direction of their lives was in guilty rebellion against God. It is understandable that faced with a man whom he knew from past experience to be very much in relationship with God, he might hesitate at the thought of baptizing him, and, conscious of the extent of his own guilt, request that Jesus baptize him. If this were so it is an indirect testimony to what was uniformly believed by the first Christians, that Jesus had never stepped out of the closest relationship with his Father. This could be true without John having any certain knowledge that Jesus was to be the coming Messiah.

The Gospel Writers' View of Jesus' Baptism

The descent of the Holy Spirit to remain upon Jesus and the words which came from the open heavens were the commissioning of Jesus the carpenter as the Messiah of God. Each of the gospels makes this clear in its own way and puts its own slant on it. Mark starts his story, 'the beginning of the gospel of Jesus *Christ*': John prepares the way, Jesus is baptized, God designates him as his Servant-Son and his messianic mission unfolds after a period alone in the wilderness (Mark 1:1–14). Matthew makes it clear in the prologue to his gospel that Jesus is the Christ. He shows Jesus' genealogy from King David, relates how he was greeted by the Magi as the future king of the Jews, and how King Herod recognized him as a threat to his own dynasty (Matthew 1, 2). It is the baptism which signals the start of Jesus' life's work. Luke also makes the identity of Jesus clear from the outset with his account of John's and Jesus' beginnings (Luke 1, 2), but again it is Jesus' baptism which marks the start of his work. Luke underlines the messianic character of the baptism by moving directly from it to a genealogy which places Jesus as a direct descendant of David (Luke 3:23–38). He also emphasizes how, from that point on, Jesus was driven and empowered by the Spirit of God (Luke 4:14). When Jesus preached at Nazareth he declared that the Spirit of the Lord was on him because *God had anointed him* (Luke 4:18). John does not describe the baptism itself, but has the Baptist testify, because of the descent of the dove, that Jesus is 'the Lamb of God who takes away the sin of the world' (John 1:29, 36) and 'the Son of God' (John 1:34).

The Son and the Lamb

Some have denied that the Baptist could have said these last two things about Jesus. Both statements sound like the theology of the later church being placed on his lips by the gospel writer. But this is not necessarily the case. It is well known to students of the Bible that the term *son of God* in the Old Testament can simply mean *the Messiah* and does not necessarily carry the idea of his being 'eternally begotten', or 'of the substance of God'. Israel was called the son of God because it was chosen by God to be in a special relationship with him (Exodus 4:22). Israel's Messiah was designated son of God because God promised to adopt him into special relationship (2 Samuel 7). In calling Jesus *the son of God* John the Baptist need be saying no more than if he were to call Jesus the *son of David*, that is, the Messiah. Indeed, this was how his disciples understood him at first (John 1:41, 45, 49). Thus our starting assumption as we journey forth into the gospels must be that 'son of God' has this very human meaning, although we will see that Jesus himself eventually forces us to something very much deeper.

What then of 'the Lamb of God who takes away the sin of the world?' Is this not the later church's doctrine of a dying saviour, grossly out of place on the lips of John the Baptist who envisaged Jesus' task primarily as judgement?[26] Again it is not necessarily so. In one of the Aramaic versions of Exodus there is a story told about the king of Egypt:

> And Pharaoh told that he being asleep had seen in his dream, and, behold, all the land of Egypt was placed in one scale of a balance, and a lamb, the young of a sheep, was in the other scale; and the scale with the lamb in it overweighed.[27]

The lamb, of course, is Moses, who single-handed rescued his people from slavery in Egypt. It is not at all strange, if John knew this story, that he would greet the 'coming one' as 'the lamb of God'.[28] Perhaps it was John the Baptist who originated the idea that Jesus' mission was to lead the new exodus.[29] As for his 'taking away the sin of the world', it should not be forgotten that atonement through sacrifice is not the only way of removing sin. The establishment of divine justice and even the fiery judgement of unrepentant evildoers are also part of the Old Testament programme for bringing into existence a sin-free world. The destruction of evildoers and salvation of the repentant which formed John's programme for the 'coming one' surely falls into the category of taking away the sin of the world.

However, we should not assume that because there is no record of it that John the Baptist was totally without expectation of some sort of future sacrificial atonement. The Qumran community anticipated that their saviour-king would 'make atonement for the sins of all the children of light'.[30] To be sure, they did not think that he would sacrifice himself, but that he would deal with sin *by* sacrifice was part of their programme because it was part of the Old Testament's programme (Deuteronomy 32:43; Daniel 9:24). John's vision ranges wider than their sectarian narrowness to encompass the whole world, but otherwise the expectation may be similar. If such ideas were entertained by Jews contemporary with John, it can hardly be maintained that they are anachronistic on his lips.

A Critical Moment

This chapter has rather suddenly become 'theological', and the reader may well feel they have been pulled forward too quickly into the belief world of the gospel writers. Some will be quite happy to accept their unanimous interpretation of Jesus' baptismal experience, others will hesitate at so easily introducing into a historical inquiry a voice from heaven and a commissioning from God. Jesus was certainly baptized by John; historically that is very sure. It is also clear that Jesus began his whirlwind ministry very shortly after his baptism. The inference that something dramatic happened at the time of his baptism is so strong that even scholars unwilling to allow anything supernatural into the story concede that Jesus must have had some life-changing spiritual experience at this time. It is not, in fact, necessary that we come to a conclusion about the exact nature of that experience at this stage. But it is good that we have in our minds the gospel writers' understanding of it; so that we can assess for ourselves as the story proceeds whether it is the best view of things, or not. The events at Jesus' baptism were, after all, private. Only Jesus heard the voice; only he and John saw the dove. Most people had to make up their minds about Jesus on the basis of other more public events, and even those who received John's testimony about Jesus also had to wait on things yet to come to know how far it was justified.

For Jesus' own point of view, there is abundant evidence from the time of his ministry that he saw himself as sent, commissioned, sealed and anointed.[31] The fact that his ministry began so suddenly after his baptism means that we should probably trace these convictions to the baptism, and recognize a strong presumption in favour of the one and only version that his early followers recorded of what actually happened there.

Whichever way we take it, it is clear that at the baptism of Jesus we stand at a crucial moment in human history. I began by saying that in three years Jesus achieved something which, judged even from the viewpoint of secular history, goes beyond anything that can be said of any other human being. Yet for most of his life he was completely unknown. His cousin John was a man of modest fame; he made it to the history books without the influence of Christianity. Yet John's real importance is that he introduced Jesus onto the stage of history. The builder of Nazareth comes to John and is baptized. At that point God designates him as the one who, in an outpouring of fire and the Holy Spirit, is to bring history as we know it to its conclusion and introduce the rule of God on earth. It would be fascinating to know what thoughts went through Jesus' mind at that moment, as he stood on the bank of the Jordan and wondered what he would do next.

Notes

[1] Riesner (*Lehrer*, 227) points out that the reaction of the people of Nazareth to Jesus preaching in their synagogue gives the impression that it was the first time they had heard him.

[2] The place of John's baptizing has not been positively identified. John places him at this time at Bethany beyond the Jordan. Origen in the third century knew of no such settlement on the east side of the Jordan. R. Riesner ('Bethany Beyond the Jordan', 29–63) has made a case for identifying this Bethany with Batanaea, a territory of Herod Philip north east of the Sea of Galilee. If this were true it would radically alter our picture of John's ministry. However there are strong reasons for thinking it is not so. The gospels associate John's ministry with the Jordan, from which the territory of Batanaea, a highland plateau (the OT Bashan), is far removed. Mark tells us that great crowds from Judaea and Jerusalem in particular came out to hear John (1:4f.), which would hardly have been the case if he was four or five days' journey away. Mark and Matthew are explicit that Jesus was baptized in the Jordan (Matthew 3:13; Mark 1:9).

[3] The difficulty arises from knowing how the reign of Tiberius was reckoned. J. Finegan (*Handbook of Biblical Chronology*, 259–273) gives 16 possible reckonings ranging from AD 26–30. Tiberius shared a co-regency with Augustus and became Emperor proper on 19 August AD 14. That year ended on 30 September. The fifteenth year therefore began on 1 October AD 27. We shall see that a date for the appearance of John of late AD 27 accommodates all the rest of the gospel data (the three Passovers in John, the crucifixion in AD 30 (so Robinson,

Priority, 155). H.W. Hoehner (*Chronological Aspects of the Life of Christ,* 29–37), arguing for an extra year in Jesus' ministry than is apparent in the gospels, places the crucifixion in AD 33 and opts therefore for AD 29 as the start of John's ministry.

[4] Mark 11:32. Josephus' account of John is consistent with this belief, *History,* 18.116–119.

[5] When Judas Maccabaeus came to rededicate the temple in 167 BC he solved the problem of what to do with the altar (which Antiochus had used for the sacrifice of a pig) by ordering that it be dismantled and its stones stored 'until there should come a prophet to give an answer concerning them' (1 Maccabees 4:42ff.).

[6] G. Theissen (*The Shadow of the Galilean,* 6) hints that 'a reed shaken by the wind' might be an allusion to Herod Antipas, who instead of having his own effigy on his coins had a reed. See D. Hendin, *Guide to Biblical Coins,* 67–69, for pictures of Antipas' coins. It is more likely that wind is an allusion to spirit and a 'reed shaken by the wind' someone who is not in control of his own behaviour, i.e. a madman or someone possessed by a spirit.

[7] Josephus, *History,* 18.116–119.

[8] J.D. Crossan, *Jesus: A Revolutionary Biography,* 43. Wright (*Victory,* 160) says 'anyone collecting people in the Jordan wilderness was symbolically saying: this is the new exodus'.

[9] See *Mishnah Eduyoth* 8:7. Also G.F. Moore, *Judaism,* 358–359; W.D. Davies, *The Setting of the Sermon on the Mount,* 50–51.

[10] J.P. Meier (*A Marginal Jew,* 2, 48–49) argues that John's clothing and food could be that of a desert nomad. I think Mark's description of John in 1:6 is meant to recall Elijah, but this does not mean the likeness was intended by John.

[11] E.g. Matthew 3:11, 14; John 1:20–23; 3:27–30.

[12] Matthew 11:14 may preserve a saying which belongs later than the story in which it is embedded, or it may simply not have been heeded at that early time.

[13] *Targum Isaiah* 40:9.

[14] A. Nolan, *Jesus Before Christianity,* 14–19.

[15] See B.F. Meyer, *The Aims of Jesus,* 117–118.

[16] 1QS 5.

[17] See Jeremiah 7.

[18] The *Assumption of Moses,* a work from early in the first century AD speaks of 'the day of repentance in the visitation wherewith the Lord will visit them in the consummation of the end of the days' (1:18).

[19] See C.H.H. Scobie, *John the Baptist,* 95–102.

[20] 1QH 6:8f. says 'You will purify and cleanse them of their sin, for all their deeds are in your truth'. This seems to envisage a future forgiveness for which the community members were being prepared.

[21] This is also the opinion of Meier, *Marginal Jew,* 55: 'If the water baptism of John conferred forgiveness of sins here and now, one wonders what exactly was left for the stronger one to do with his baptism of the Spirit.'

[22] Note that in Isaiah 58:12 there is mention of 'the repairer of the breach, the restorer of paths to dwell in'. In the Targum he becomes 'the restorer of the right way, the converter of the wicked to the law'. This may have helped draw this passage into the cluster of texts that were germinal to the Baptist's programme. In Sirach 48, Elijah is the one who will 'restore the tribes of Jacob', and Jesus too says that 'he restores all things'. See Seccombe, *Possessions*, 46–52, 182ff.

[23] The War Rule needs to be read in its entirety to get a feel of the fervour and urgency of messianic expectation at Qumran. Also see 4Q521 which mentions the Messiah by name; 4Q246 where he is called the 'Son Of God'; 4Q252 where he is the 'Messiah of Righteousness' and the 'Branch of David'; 11QMelchizedek which calls him Melchizedek ('King of Righteousness'). See R. Eisenman & M. Wise, *The Dead Sea Scrolls Uncovered*; G. Vermes, *The Dead Sea Scrolls in English*.

[24] Josephus describes the outbreaks of revolutionary violence which took place following Herod's death in *War*, 2.39–79; *History*, 17.250–298.

[25] A bird seems an appropriate symbol in light of Genesis 1's imagery of the Spirit brooding like a bird over the chaos. A dove might be thought to bring connotations of gentleness (Isaiah 42:1–3), or of salvation and covenant mercy (Genesis 8:8–11). Other than this there does not appear to be any history of symbolism employing the dove adequate to explain the representation here.

[26] Scobie (*John the Baptist*, 149–151) dismisses both 'Son of God' and 'Lamb of God' as possible utterances of the Baptist.

[27] *Targum of Palestine Exodus* 1; cf. *Testament of Joseph* 19.

[28] This gives substance to the conjecture that John's 'Lamb of God' could be a conquering Lamb such as we encounter in Revelation (e.g., 5:6). See C.H. Dodd, *The Interpretation of the Fourth Gospel*, 230–238.

[29] N.T. Wright (*The New Testament and the People of God*, e.g. 300–301) has shown that Jews of the first century saw themselves as still in exile and looked to the future partly in terms of a return analogous to Israel's escape from Egypt.

John's identification of himself as the 'Voice' of Isaiah 40 is consonant with this, so language which depicts the 'coming one' as a Moses-like figure is not incongruous.

[30] 11QMelchizedek.

[31] E.g. Mark 1:38; Luke 4:43; Mark 12:1–11; Luke 4:18; 7:19ff.; 10:16, 22; John 5:36; 6:27.

Chapter 5

The Enemy

Alone in the Desert

Was it obvious to Jesus from the moment of his baptism, how he would go about his God-given mission and what he would do first? To begin to answer this we must be clear what that mission was, at least to the extent that it has been revealed at this stage in the gospels.

At his baptism God designated Jesus as the Son who would rule as his king, and as the Servant who would establish his kingdom. The extent of this kingdom, we have seen, reached beyond Israel to the ends of the earth. If Jesus took this seriously, and we shall see that he did, the question of how he was to establish it must have loomed very large. John the Baptist had defined Jesus' mission as to baptize with the Holy Spirit and with fire. He was to bring the blessings of God's life-giving Spirit to the good seed which was to be gathered into the granary of God's kingdom, and to destroy the wicked with inextinguishable fire. That Jesus took even this last prescription seriously as part of his mission is to be seen in a passionate utterance of his later ministry: 'It was to cast fire upon the earth that I came, and what would I that it were already alight. But I have a baptism to be baptized with, and how I am hemmed in until it is completed. Do you think that I have appeared to give peace on the earth?' (Luke 12:49–51). It is plain, then, that Jesus had neither repudiated nor forgotten what was laid down for him at the beginning by the voice from heaven and the voice of the prophet. Yet how he would achieve his goal was evidently a matter of some complexity for him. Was this complexity clear from the beginning? We cannot say for sure, but it is highly suggestive that between his commissioning and his entry into public ministry, each of the first three gospels recounts Jesus spending an extended time alone in the wilderness.

Mark tells the story in two sentences (Mark 1:12–13). Matthew and Luke have much longer versions (Matthew 4:1–11; Luke 4:1–13), which are enough alike for us to be fairly certain that they both derive from the source Q. It is from this longer version that we learn that Jesus fasted during this forty day period, and the details of the temptations he faced. John has no account of this incident.

Fact or Fiction?

Jesus' wilderness ordeal is a curious story which bristles with difficulties, foremost among them the role played by the Devil. It is not surprising, therefore, that its historicity has come under attack. Some writers on the life of Jesus simply ignore it.[1] Yet, as E.P. Sanders admits (though he dismisses the details of the stories as 'mythological'), it is intrinsically likely that Jesus fasted and experienced temptation at the outset of his ministry.[2]

Admittedly, the story relates a situation and a dialogue to which there could have been no witness except Jesus himself. But is it not possible that Jesus spoke at some later time of the temptations he faced at the outset of his ministry, explaining them in terms of the Devil? Whatever we may think today, Satan was very much part of the thought world of first century Jews, and every strand of the gospel tradition bears witness to his prominence in Jesus' thinking. Jesus was, after all, an exorcist of note, and when accused on one occasion of casting out demons with the help of the Devil, he retorted that on the contrary, it was because he had bound this 'strong man', that he was able to plunder his kingdom (Mark 3:22–27). C.H. Dodd inferred from this saying that Jesus must have been conscious of some earlier victorious struggle with the Devil; the temptation story was thus likely to be authentic.[3]

A very adequate defence of the temptation stories has been made by the French theologian, Jacques Dupont, who among many other things points out that the temptation story is the work of a powerful personality with a profound understanding of the mission of Jesus and a remarkable poetic gift. Since its interpretation of his mission corresponds to what Jesus says on various other occasions, Jesus must be considered a very likely contender as author of the story. The profound and extensive use of Scripture also points as much or more to Jesus' authorship than to that of an early unknown Christian scholar. Dupont says that the problems which are often alleged to have given rise to the temptation story, namely Jesus' refusal to work signs and his failure to carry out the political programme expected of the Messiah, were really only problems up until the resurrection. From then on Christians proclaimed the resurrection as God's great sign, and declared that Jesus would soon come on the clouds of heaven to fulfil all the as yet unfulfilled 'political' parts of his messianic mission. The value of the temptation stories would therefore have been greatest before Easter.[4] In this Dupont supports T.W. Manson's suggestion that it would fit with the development of Jesus' relationship with his disciples if he had related his experience of temptation to them sometime after Peter's confession of him as Messiah.[5]

The nineteenth century is infamous for its attempts to write the history of Jesus in terms of his psychological development. Such attempts are now seldom made because there is just not enough material to enable a close correlation of the course of his ministry with the development of his inner convictions. To overlook this story of temptation, however, is to squander such precious insights as we do have, for not much more reason than that it gives such prominence to the Devil. Who would wish to discount the stories of Luther's inner struggles because he described them in terms of the Devil? Jesus' public career was triggered by whatever happened at his baptism; we have already seen that. Exorcism was a prominent part of Jesus' ministry. At various points along the way he spoke of an ongoing conflict with evil powers. Between baptism and ministry stands this story of fasting and ordeal at the hands of the Devil. It is critical that we seek to understand it if we wish to have any hope of understanding Jesus on his own terms.

Why the Wilderness?

Two questions leap immediately to the fore when we apply ourselves to understand the temptation stories: Why the wilderness? And why did Jesus fast? The gospels do not tell us, perhaps because it would have been obvious enough to the first readers.

Several times during his later ministry we are told that Jesus sought a place of solitude to pray, usually at times when he was under pressure of some kind, as when the people of Capernaum wanted him to remain in their town, or at a moment of decision, as when he was about to choose the twelve. It should not surprise us then, that immediately after his commissioning Jesus would seek to be alone. The wilderness offered itself, for looking west from the Jordan one sees only barren plains rising into rugged mountains, both devoid of any visible vegetation. The wilderness also had meaning. It was the place of Israel's birth, the place where Moses first met God in the fiery bush, and where he later took his people for their betrothal to Yahweh at the foot of Mt Sinai. The wilderness was Israel's place of getting to know the Lord and, significantly for our enquiry, the scene of their forty year testing. From out of the wilderness they came at the end of that generation, to cross the Jordan not far from where John was baptizing, and take possession of Canaan. Throughout Israel's turbulent history the wilderness was always there, reminding them of their beginning, of times of purity and failure, of God and of his covenant. And prophets declared that as the evil age rolled to its conclusion God would once more meet with his people in the wilderness and renew his love. As Israel's scriptures looked both back and forward, shaping the people's self-awareness, God's action in the wilderness stood centre-stage (e.g., Deuteronomy 8:15–16; 32:9–10; Psalm 78:40f., 52–54; Isaiah 40:3; Jeremiah 2:2; Hosea 2:14).

In view of all this it is not surprising that the Qumran community, seeking to renew their faith in Israel's God, should make their home in the wilderness, or that John the Baptist should have located his ministry on its edge. Following in his footsteps, it is no surprise to find Jesus drawn in that direction either, in the days following his messianic call. David himself had tasted the rigour of this very same wilderness prior to establishing his kingdom (Psalm 63:1).

We may guess that Jesus' chief motive in withdrawing to the wilderness was prayer; that went naturally with fasting, but if his intention was to meet with God, he ended up with something very different. Just as Israel after its commissioning as God's nation faced forty years testing in the wilderness, so for Jesus the wilderness became a place of satanic temptation.

Why did Jesus Fast?

Six weeks is a very long time to go without food, though longer fasts are known. On 5 May 1981 Bobby Sands died at the end of a sixty-six day hunger-strike. The Indian Christian Sahdu Sundar Singh sought to imitate Jesus' fast but fell into a coma before the end.[6] Such a fast on the part of Jesus demands an explanation, especially when we consider that there is no evidence that he ever fasted again, except perhaps on the night of his arrest.[7] To have continued for that time must have required iron determination, even if we need not insist that Jesus ate absolutely nothing.[8] There are occasional springs and pockets of vegetation in the Judaean wilderness. It may be that Jesus was just so totally preoccupied that he took no thought for food except the occasional offerings of the bush. Nevertheless, he must have become very hungry and the forty days must have had a particular significance for him.

For clues to this significance we are justified in looking to the Old Testament, since, as we shall see, it exercised from beginning to end a massive influence on how Jesus understood his task. He was doubtless familiar with the two occasions in which Moses spent forty days and nights on Mt Sinai with God, neither eating nor drinking (Exodus 24:18; 34:28), and with Elijah's forty day fast when he returned to the same mountain (1 Kings 19:8). These may have been Jesus' pattern.

More to the fore in the gospel writers' understanding, however, was the forty years that Israel spent in the Sinai wilderness before entering the promised land. Mark probably implies this by his juxtaposition of wilderness, forty days, and temptation (Mark 1:12f.). Matthew and Luke are explicit: to each of the Devil's temptations Jesus replies with a quotation from Deuteronomy, the book in which Moses reminds the people of God's dealings with them in the wilderness.

Did Jesus see a strong connection between what he was doing and Israel's wilderness experience? Since all the analogous elements appear to belong to the event itself, he must have. However, a connection in Jesus' mind with Israel's wanderings does not fully explain a forty day fast. Israel's time in the wilderness was not a period of sustained deprivation, though the people did undergo periods of hunger (and failed the test!). For the most part there was miraculous provision of manna, meat and water. Why might Jesus particularly have wished to fast?

In pre-exilic times the one formal fast of the year was the Day of Atonement,[9] but people were often driven to fast at other times by urgent situations where they needed to implore God's help, or at moments when their consciousness of sin and need of forgiveness became overwhelming. Often these two things were connected, as, for example, when the Ninevites declared a fast because of Jonah's warning that God was about to destroy their city (Jonah 3:5). Fasting became more institutionalized after the exile, and in Jesus' time Pharisees at least fasted two days every week. However, its meaning will not have changed much, and there was a periodic reminder of its function as the accompaniment of prayers for forgiveness and salvation in the Day of Atonement ceremonies when it was customary to 'afflict' oneself as sins were confessed and forgiveness sought.

We may be fairly confident that the sheer magnitude of the task that lay ahead of Jesus and his need of God's help was one factor driving him to prolonged fasting. It may be that he was also seeking further revelation from God.[10] However, Jesus has just come from John the Baptist so a clue to the meaning of his fast may be found in John's programme. John and his disciples fasted regularly. No doubt it belonged with his exposure of the nation's sin and his solemn warning that judgement was coming on all who failed to repent. 'A fasting of repentance for the forgiveness of sin' accords well with his baptism. It is interesting that Jewish legends had Adam seeking God's forgiveness after his expulsion from the garden by fasting for forty days up to his neck in the Jordan.[11] Could it be that just as Jesus joined in Israel's baptism, so he set himself to engage in a solemn fast of prayer for the nation's forgiveness? I shall argue later that Jesus' parable of the fig tree (Luke 13:6–9) depicts his own ministry to Israel. God comes to his vineyard and finds there a fruitless fig tree. He instructs the gardener to cut it down. We recall the Baptist's warning, 'The axe is already laid to the root of the trees; every tree that does not bear good fruit is cast into the fire' (Matthew 3:10). But now the gardener pleads for a stay of execution: 'Let it alone, sir, this year also, till I dig about it and put on manure. And if it bears fruit next year, well and good; but if not, you can cut it down.' It would suggest an explanation of the forty days if Jesus were fasting and praying for God to delay judgement on Israel. It would also explain the glaring discrepancy between what John proclaimed the 'coming one' would do and the actual shape of Jesus' ministry.

For Jesus has been told he is to be Israel's king. He is thus qualified to act on their behalf, and a symbolic reliving of their experience in the wilderness in the form of a penitential fast may well have commended itself to him. Isaiah's Servant of the Lord, with whom Jesus was also connected at his baptism, is also a representative or personification of Israel: 'He [God] said to me, You are my servant, Israel, in whom I will be glorified' (Isaiah 49:3). This particular servant was to be more truly Israel in God's eyes, a truer son and servant, than Israel itself. As such, he would fulfil the mission in which Israel had failed – bringing salvation to the ends of the earth (Genesis 12:3). It was possibly scriptures such as these which suggested to Jesus his course of action.

Having said all this, one can hardly claim that Old Testament and contemporary patterns, the Baptist movement included, fully explain Jesus' sojourn in the wilderness. There is something original and creative, derived either from Jesus himself of from the Spirit who drove him out, which makes the story unique in biblical literature, stamps it as authentic, and forbids us from thinking we have fully plumbed its depths.

Satan

It has been the experience of many saints that a season devoted to prayer and the enjoyment of God became a time of temptation. So it was with Jesus. The form of the story, however, prevents us from dealing with it merely as an account of Jesus' inner struggles. Satan is too prominent.

To many the Devil is nothing more than a figure from ancient mythology or a personalization of the forces of evil in the

individual and in the world.[12] The difficulty when it comes
to understanding the gospels is that Jesus seems to have seen his
life-struggle as a personal conflict with the one called Satan
(Adversary) in his native Aramaic, who in Greek is known as
Diabolos (Devil, Slanderer, Accuser, Adversary). Thus we cannot
begin to understand Jesus on his own terms without reference to
Satan. If we dismiss him at the outset as a myth, we prejudice our
inquiry into Jesus, judging him from the beginning to be one
who held an outmoded and untrue view of spiritual reality.[13] It
will be more fruitful to leave the question of Satan's real existence
open for now. If we are disposed to think there is a possibility that
Jesus may in truth have come from God, we should also hold out
the possibility that he had a better understanding of spiritual realities than does the anti-spiritual worldview of modernism. At the
very least, one can treat the Devil as an historian would; as a real
part of Jesus' thought-world.

Does the World Belong to Satan?

In the course of his attempts to seduce Jesus from his messianic
destiny, Satan makes the extraordinary claim that all the world's
kingdoms have been delivered up to him, and that he has the
right to dispose of them as he wills (Luke 4:6). Even more
surprisingly, Jesus does not dispute this. Indeed on several
occasions in the gospels he himself refers to Satan as 'the ruler of
this world' (John 12:31; 14:30; 16:11). This forces upon us the
question of who Jesus saw the Devil to be – what he thought
about Satan's role and the extent of his power. Is it true that the
world in some sense belongs to the Devil, and if so, how and in
what manner?

Jesus and his contemporaries believed in the Devil. Jewish
religious literature for two or three centuries before and after
Jesus abounds with references to him under a variety of names
and titles: Azazel, Mastema, Beliar, Belial, Beelzebul, Beelzebub. It

is a surprise to discover how little he figures in the Old Testament. Apart from the story of Adam and Eve's temptation where he is involved only by inference, Satan is encountered by name only three times. Once he incites David to carry out a census in Israel (1 Chronicles 21:1), then he stirs up trouble for Job (Job 1:6–12; 2:1–8), and finally he stands to accuse the high priest of the returned exiles (Zechariah 3:1–2). Later Jewish understanding was extrapolated from these references and a few other clues (like the hint of an angelic fall in Genesis 6:1–4).

Of first importance was Adam and Eve's encounter with the Devil. God created human beings to rule his creation (Genesis 1:26–28), a responsibility which began with their possession of the Garden of Eden. As they set about their work, they were accosted by the serpent who tempted them into rebellion against their Creator. What kind of being was it who so used the snake and dragged the human race into disgrace? It is a common understanding among Christians that it was an angel who at some time prior to creation became proud and made some move to usurp God's position as lord of the universe. As a result he was ejected from heaven and now exercises his hatred of God in spoiling creation and seeking the destruction of human beings. The basis for this understanding is found in two highly poetic oracles in Isaiah (14:12ff.) and Ezekiel (28:12ff.) and in a symbolic vision in Revelation (12:7ff.). It is an inadequate basis, however, since neither of the oracles speaks of Satan, but of the kings of Babylon and Tyre, and Revelation 12 speaks not of what happened before creation, but what happened at the coming of Jesus. Nor was this the view of Satan held by Jesus' contemporaries.

It makes much more sense of the dynamics of the biblical saga if Satan's envy is seen to be directed not at God but at humans, as a consequence of their being created to rule the universe. The Hebrew word *satan* meant an adversary or accuser before it ever came to denote a particular non-human individual. At the beginning of his reign Solomon was able to rejoice that the Lord had given him peace and that there was no adversary (*satan*) to trouble him (1 Kings 5:4). Later in his life *satans* in the form of Hadad the Edomite and Rezon of Zobah did arise to trouble him (1 Kings 11:14, 23, 25).[14] In every instance where we meet Satan in the canonical writings it is as an adversary or accuser of human beings. Elsewhere in Jewish literature, when Adam and Eve question the Devil about the reason for his enmity towards them he answers that when Adam was created in the image of God he refused to worship him as his superior and fell under the judgement of God.[15]

The intended extent of the sovereignty given to Adam's family develops as we move through Scripture. At the beginning it is over the animal and plant creation of which the Garden of Eden was a first instalment. Later the family of Israel is given the land of Canaan, which is also a promise of some sort of dominance over the whole world. Paul understood the promise to Abraham's descendants to include possession of the *kosmos* (Romans 4:13), which could mean the world or possibly the universe. Also according to Paul, the inheritance which Christ will share with his people is no less than 'all things' (Ephesians 1:10, 18–23). The understanding of many Jews at Jesus' time, and of the New Testament writings, is that humankind's dominion was ultimately to include rule even over the angelic realms (Hebrews 1–2; 1 Corinthians 6:3).[16]

Humanity's original primacy in the creation, and the projected extension of their authority to include the universe and the angels, makes Satan's activity towards the human race understandable. From the beginning his efforts have been directed not so much towards inflicting suffering as to putting particular people under duress and trial with the object of discrediting and disqualifying them from their inheritance. God appears to permit him this function of trying and testing. Once he succeeds in tempting a person, drawing him into sin, he then becomes his *accuser* before God, and God seems also to permit him this function. (The words *satan* and *diabolos* are both used of accusers and prosecutors in a court of law.)

In the story of the original fall, Satan enquires whether there is anything God has forbidden Adam and Eve to do, and uses this to incite doubt about God's goodness, and disobedience to his word. As a consequence they are disgraced in the eyes of heaven and barred from their inheritance (which included the tree of life). Though created for dominion, in acceding to the serpent's suggestions they surrendered true dominion to Satan. From that moment on they and their descendants will struggle to maintain what is left to them of their dominion over the earth, but as often as they submit to Satan's temptations they actually fulfil *his* will. It makes sense, therefore, for Satan to say that the kingdoms of the world have been delivered up to him – not by God, but by the human race to whom they were originally entrusted. The author of 1 John tells us that 'the whole world (*kosmos*) is in the power of the Evil One' (1 John 5:19). The word *kosmos* originally meant an intricately and beautifully worked piece of jewellery. By analogy it came to mean the world or the universe. In the Bible it denotes the organized interlocking system of cultures, governments, economies, worldviews, fashions and ideas which, because so much of its inspiration has come from satanic temptation, and because so often those who operate it have surrendered to his suggestions, is seen to be under the control of the Evil One.

Satan and Suffering

The book of Job explains how physical suffering can play a role in Satan's activity. Satan appears here to have some legitimate access to heaven, and is using it to further his hostility towards humanity. He accuses Job of being righteous only because of the generous way in which God treats him. If God were to take away his possessions and his health, he would curse God to his face. God accepts the challenge and permits Satan to take from Job his many blessings. It is significant for the story that Job never knows of this heavenly debate, though it is the cause of all his woes.

He only knows that God is trustworthy, and in his continuing trust and refusal to curse God he ultimately vindicates his confidence in him.

Job's story is not an isolated episode, it is intended as an explanation of certain forms of undeserved suffering. So it is not surprising to find Jews of a later period discerning the activity of Satan where the Scriptures made no mention of him. In the Babylonian Talmud Satan queries Abraham's loyalty just as he did Job's. God accepts the challenge and commands Abraham to sacrifice his beloved son.[17] The same pattern is indicated in the New Testament where Jesus says to Peter, 'Simon, Simon, behold, Satan asked for you, that he might sift you like wheat; but I have prayed concerning you that your faith might not fail' (Luke 22:31f.). A challenge to the genuineness of Peter's faith had been thrown down in heaven, which would now give rise to an unpleasant sequence of events. However Satan's efforts to undermine Peter were opposed by the intercession of Jesus, and he would ultimately emerge unharmed.

The question arising from this pattern is whether Jesus' ordeal in the wilderness should not be seen as the working out of some such satanic challenge to his faithfulness at the moment when God has commissioned him as the new head of the human race.

Temptation

Testing (temptation) is a major theme in the Bible. Gerhardsson makes the interesting point that the Bible never speaks of unbelievers or of Gentile nations being tempted, but only God's people, and God-believing individuals.[18] Gibson describes the Bible's notion of testing as 'being probed and proved, often through hardship and adversity, in order to determine the extent of one's worthiness to be entrusted with, or the degree of one's loyalty or devotion to, a given commission and its constraints.'[19] Adam and Eve were tested and failed. At the point of a new beginning Abraham was tested regarding his love for Isaac and his trust of God and was vindicated. At the point of another possible new beginning, the wilderness generation of Israelites was also tested, and like Adam lost its place. Something similar is hinted at with the High Priest of the returning exiles, though in his case it appears God intercedes to uphold him (Zechariah 3:1–2). In Job we have seen a thorough exploration of this aspect of human suffering. Jesus and Peter were tested, as were the whole band of disciples in the Garden of Gethsemane. The newly emerging Christian church would also experience trials (Acts 5:1ff.). In the Lord's Prayer (Luke 11:4) and in Gethsemane Jesus tells his disciples to pray that they will not fall into such testing (Mark 14:38). All this is Satan's attempt to discredit God's choice of humanity as ruler over his creation and the executor of his purposes. God allows Satan's challenge in order that human beings may ultimately triumph and his choice of them be justified. Humanity, for its part, generally has no inkling of this, though it is the cause of many vexations. It has always been a puzzle why God should have allowed the inspirer of so much evil and suffering to remain in existence, and also why human beings at times have had to suffer so much. On one occasion Job cries out in his agony,

> What is man, that you should make him great,
> and that you should set your heart upon him,
> and that you should visit him every morning
> and try him every moment?
> How long will you not look away from me,
> and let me alone till I swallow my spit. (Job 7:17–19)

He is perplexed that God should pay him so much attention; why can he not be allowed to die like any dog? He does not know that a struggle is going on in heaven, and that he is what is at stake. Why does God pay us humans so much attention, when at times it means such pain and suffering for a person or a nation?

The beginning of the answer lies in the Garden of Eden, where God does not immediately execute his warning of death against Adam, and does not destroy the serpent for what he has done. Instead God declares that, although the serpent has injured man and will injure him again, ultimately a seed of the woman will arise who will crush his head (Genesis 3:15). Thus, although it would have been quite possible for God to have annihilated the Devil at the beginning, it appears to be his plan to bear with Satan's activity until a *human being or human beings* (not God), should reverse the original defeat.

Both Mark and Luke in their accounts of the baptism and temptation give clear pointers to the fact that they saw a link between Jesus' temptations and the temptation of Adam. Mark does it with his comment that Jesus was 'with the wild beasts, and angels ministered to him' (Mark 1:13). I would certainly not rule out the contention that this recalls the peace which will rule between humans and the animal creation in the messianic age: the wild beasts are at peace with the Messiah and the angels are subject to him. But the description would also have evoked in Jews of the first century memories of the story of Adam and Eve. I have already referred to the Jewish book called *The Life of Adam and Eve.* It is impossible to overlook the many similar motifs in the two stories. I do not imagine the gospels were necessarily dependant on the book itself, but upon the body of tradition which in their day surrounded the Eden story. According to *The Life of Adam and Eve*

> Adam came to Jordan and he entered into the water ... even to the hairs of his head, while he made supplication to God and sent up prayers to him. And there the angels came together and all living creatures, wild and tame, and all birds that fly, and they surrounded Adam like a wall, praying to God for Adam.[20]

Luke makes the connection clear by bringing his genealogy of Jesus right down to 'Adam, the son of God' (Luke 3:38). He locates the genealogy between Jesus' baptism, where he is declared to be the Son of God, and the temptation, where this sonship is tested. Clearly the sonship of both Adam and Jesus is related to their appointment to rule the world, and their testing is an attempt to subvert this appointment.

Three particular temptations are specified in Matthew and Luke.[21] There may well have been others since both Mark and Luke characterize the whole of Jesus' time in the wilderness as a period of temptation. However, three stood out as of particular importance, the three things that tempted him most perhaps, that he later related to his disciples. Interpretations of the meaning of Jesus' temptations are legion, not surprising given the absence of explanation in the gospels. Yet it seems to me that we cannot abdicate a search for understanding; Jesus would not have shared this knowledge with his disciples and they would not have handed it on if it had not been important.

The temptations have been viewed as simple tests of Jesus' human obedience,[22] as temptations to prove his messiahship to himself,[23] as temptations to demonstrate it forcibly to others, as temptations to false methods of achieving his messianic goal, and as temptations to doubt the divinely ordered way of being the Messiah that was made plain to him at his baptism.[24] I am not sure there is much distinction between these last two. Whether Jesus had absolute clarity about the method of his mission from the moment of his baptism is not clear; the period in the wilderness may in part have been to determine it. Nevertheless, the Isaianic Servant role indicated by the voice from heaven must certainly have given him a lead, and anything which drew him in another direction would most surely have been temptation from his God-ordained path. On the other hand, the gospel writers have as yet given few clues about what this path is, happy to allow it to unfold with Jesus' ministry. There is good reason to think that Jesus was essentially struggling with false methods of achieving his messianic goal, without altogether ruling out some of these other suggestions.

Command These Stones to Become Bread

According to Matthew, Jesus' first temptation was that he turn stones into bread (4:2–4). For Gerhardsson the temptation Jesus faced here was the simple human one of giving in to his craving for food at an inappropriate time; what was being tested was his determination to love and obey God when his natural inclinations were dragging him in another direction.[25] This is good as far as it goes, but I think there has to be more to it. Both Matthew and Luke indicate that this temptation took place after the completion of the forty days. This hardly suggests that they saw any wrong in Jesus breaking his fast and eating. Was the issue whether he would follow the will of God, or the dictates of the Devil? Certainly it was *an* issue, but it would be a mistake to imagine that the Devil was obviously or visibly present to Jesus, any more than he is to us when we are tempted, or he was when he tempted Jesus through Peter. Temptation comes as a suggestion to the mind. Whether it is a good or evil suggestion, or whether its origin lies in ourselves or is a satanic inducement only becomes evident when we reflect on its *nature*. Jesus would have recognized the satanic origin of the temptation not because the Devil stood next to him in a dark cape, but from the evil nature of the suggestion.

Where then lay the evil? Did the Devil's 'if you are the Son of God' suggest an uncertainty on Jesus' part about whether he really was God's King? Was he being tempted to reassure himself? The contrary is surely the case; Jesus has just been commissioned by a voice from heaven. Both he and the Devil share the knowledge of his messiahship. Satan incites him to take action on that basis. There is no appeal to God to act on his behalf here; it is suggested that *he command* the stones. So the evil must lie in the act of utilizing power which is at his disposal by virtue of his messianic office. But what could be wrong with turning stones into bread? When Israel in the wilderness was hungry God sent supernatural bread to feed them. Jesus himself will later deem it appropriate to create bread for the five thousand. It seems forced to suggest that it was evil to do something for himself, which he would later properly do for others.[26] Indeed, in the strange incident of the fish with the coin in its mouth Jesus does employ the miraculous to his own aid (Matthew 17:24–27). The loaves of bread must have suggested to Jesus a larger temptation than the satisfaction of his own momentary hunger.

The Messiah's ultimate task was conquest: to free the world of evil and to rule it for God. How did Jesus propose to do this? He had fasted for a long time and was experiencing the driving force of hunger in a way the well-fed rarely do. At the same time he probably became increasingly aware of how hunger could be exploited. If he could create bread from stones, could he not win human hearts and rule them by offering the fulfilment of felt needs? One of the foremost methods of gaining and holding power in this world has always been to offer people more than your opposition. The Caesars maintained their power base in Rome only at the cost of regular free handouts of food to the citizens (the *annona*). One sees the same thing in democratic societies, where everything is subordinated to economic issues. Communism came to power in so many countries on the back of promises of land, food and justice. Being unable to produce these things from the stones, its power henceforth had to be held by force and the elimination of all opposition.

If Jesus had been willing to create bread by command, he would not only have been able to satisfy his own hunger, but also to win the adulation and loyalty of the people, who would follow whomever could best satisfy their needs. Needs are legion of course, for humanity is a hungry beast. We need food, but give us that, and we need other things: money, cars, sex, marriage, homes, children, jobs, status, power, entertainment, and so on. The one who can produce what they promise, and give what they will to whomever they want will have absolute power.

However, all these needs are witness to the fact that humanity's hunger is not ultimately satisfied by consuming the things it thinks it wants. Our constant hunger testifies to a deep lack of fulfilment that does not find its satisfaction in the things of this world. Jesus' reply to the Devil is thus totally appropriate. 'Human beings do not live by bread alone, but by every word proceeding from the mouth of God.' The word 'live' here does not mean existing as opposed to dying, but quality living as opposed to existing.[27] Jesus meant that humanity's ultimate fulfilment lies not in things, but in God and in his will for us declared in his word.

The evil latent in the Devil's suggestion, therefore, is that Jesus build his kingdom by supplying people's felt needs. If he had power to create bread he could, and there could be no safer way to dominion and adulation. But it would lack what is at the heart of God's kingdom: the love of God himself and trusting obedience to his ways. It would be the fulfilment of the secular humanist dream, but it would be Babylon. So Jesus refused the suggestion. He would not entertain the possibility of 'buying' his kingdom, nor use his miracle power indiscriminately to satisfy human desires. Later in his ministry Jesus did encounter a situation where he evidently considered it God's will that he create bread to satisfy the hunger of the crowds (John 6:10ff.). And the very problem, which, if I am correct, the first temptation highlights, rushed upon him. The crowds wanted him to do it again, and to be their king on the basis of constant provision. He fled from the popularity and acclaim which they subsequently tried to heap upon him, and when later they caught up with him in Capernaum, answered them in words that recall his reply to the Devil: 'You seek me not because you saw signs, but because you ate the loaves and were filled. Do not work for food which perishes, but for that which endures to eternal life.'

We will see as his ministry unfolds and Jesus publicizes the coming of God's kingdom that he unashamedly offers food for the hungry, but only in the consummated kingdom (Luke 6:20–25). What comes first is the offer of peace with God and a place in the kingdom through faith in the word of his Son (Luke 7:36–50; 10:22; 11:27–28).

Throw Yourself From the Temple

> Then the Devil took him to the holy city [Luke has *Jerusalem*] and placed him on the wing of the temple and said, 'If you are the Son of God throw yourself down, for it is written, He will command his angels concerning you and they will raise you with their hands lest you strike your foot on a stone.' Jesus said to him, 'You shall not tempt the Lord your God.' (Matthew 4:5–7)

Gerhardsson says that what is being tested here is whether Jesus loves God more than his own life. But the action the Devil suggested would be very inappropriate if it were, for Jesus was tempted to invent a situation in which he deliberately put his life at risk to test God's willingness to save it. This is more the action of someone who wants to demonstrate that his faith is greater than his fear of death, than of one tempted to value his own safety too highly. But I do not think Jesus was tempted here to prove his faith either, though that is a common enough temptation. I have a friend who was persuaded by his guru that if his faith were sufficient he could fly. To prove his faith he choked back his natural fear and launched himself from the top of a building. God did not respond, though his life was spared when a roof onto which he fell gave way and brought him down with only some broken bones. During his subsequent convalescence in a Christian hospital in Kathmandu he discovered real faith in Jesus.

Was Jesus' temptation, then, to test his new status as Son of God by trying God's willingness to send in angels to protect him?[28] If that were all it was, it seems odd that the action would be located specifically at the temple. Any cliff face would have sufficed, and there are many in the region traditionally associated with Jesus' wilderness ordeal. Someone who entertains a doubt about God's readiness to rescue them is unlikely to set up a test where there will be crowds to witness a failure.

It is the role of the temple in this temptation that leads me to think that we are again dealing with a possible strategy for Jesus' messianic career. We need not imagine that he was actually taken to Jerusalem and placed on the roof of the temple, nor that in the next temptation he was actually transported to the top of a high mountain. He was probably tempted as we all are, through the agency of the imagination. Unlike the first temptation, then, he was not here contemplating immediate action, but something he might do later; for the moment he was alone in the wilderness considering possibilities. The temple was the place of God's presence in the midst of his people, located in the city that was to be the Messiah's capital. It was the obvious place to demonstrate kingship. Indeed, there was an expectation amongst the Jews that the Messiah would come first to the temple and there proclaim his kingdom:

> Our Masters taught, When the king Messiah appears, he will come and stand on the roof of the Temple and will make a proclamation to Israel, saying, 'Poor ones, the day of your redemption is come. And if you do not believe me, behold my light which rises upon you, as it is said, *Arise shine for thy light is come, and the glory of the Lord is risen upon thee*.'[29]

Notice that the Jews expected the king to demonstrate his messiahship by doing something recognizably scriptural, in this case manifest his light in accordance with Isaiah 60:1. Jesus was tempted to appear on the roof of the temple and there in the sight of the people do a scriptural miracle. The Jews were particularly impressed by signs and wonders (1 Corinthians 1:22). One that could be attested from a prophetic messianic scripture (Psalm 91:11–12) would be particularly persuasive. The Jews of Qumran believed that when the Messiah came he would be accompanied by armies of angels.[30] Nothing could be better calculated to win the hearts of the Jews than a demonstration at the temple in which God proved his choice of Jesus by sending angels to his rescue. One might add that such a temptation might have been particularly persuasive for Jesus, since it suggested a course of action which appeared to have biblical sanction.

In this respect it is instructive to hear the Devil quoting scripture at Jesus, Jesus considering it an inappropriate scripture for the situation, and producing the right passage for the occasion. He shows himself not only a master of the content of scripture, but also of its interpretation and application. How much evil has been done in how many situations by an inappropriate application of a word of scripture!

Jesus answered that to do such a thing – to put pressure on God to fulfil his word our way and in our time – would be to put him to the test. This was something the Israelites had done repeatedly during their time in the wilderness. The Hebrew word *nissah* is used of partners in a covenant testing out whether each other are being faithful to the terms of their agreement. It was very appropriate that God should test his people, but an act of faithlessness for Israel to test God. One of the places of their wandering was named Massah ('Testing') in memory of their putting God to the test. They questioned, 'Is the Lord among us or not?' and drove him to perform a miracle to prove his care of them (Exodus 17:1–7; cf. Deuteronomy 6:16). It was an affront to the honour of God for people to dictate how he should serve them, expressing unbelief and suspicion of his reliability and love.[31]

Of course there could be various motives for putting God to the test. In Israel's case it was to manipulate him to provide water and food immediately. It could be to prove one's faith, to test God's faithfulness, to manipulate God to do something, or a combination of such motives. According to Josephus, a self-proclaimed prophet named Theudas convinced his followers that the Jordan would open at his command, presumably as a prelude to setting up the longed for kingdom.[32] The parallel to Jesus' temptation is striking. In the lead up to the Roman–Jewish war, putting God to the test reached disease proportions. Josephus gives a description of the times

Deceivers and imposters, under the pretence of divine inspiration fostering revolutionary changes, they persuaded the multitude to act like madmen, and led them out into the desert under the belief that God would give them tokens of deliverance.[33]

It looks as though these false prophets, whoever they may have been, were seeking to force God to bring in his kingdom by provoking a situation where he would have to intercede. During the course of the war the Jews at times did seemingly crazy things – continuing to fight in a hopeless military position, demonstrating their faith in a heroic way, fighting if necessary to the last man, always in hope of a last minute miracle.[34] Their behaviour is explained by their belief that by showing faith and putting themselves into a situation of extremity they could force God's hand to intervene on their behalf. The consequences were always tragic. God does not surrender to manipulation, no matter how well meant.

I suggest that the motive behind Jesus' temptation was (like Theudas') to create a display that would compel belief and win Israel's allegiance. Jesus' refusal of this temptation meant, first, his unwillingness to put God's readiness to come to his rescue to the test. It also represented his refusal to reverse the relationship of humanity to God and of son to Father. Jesus would not manipulate his Father through his promises, but trust him to fulfil them in his own way. Lastly, it was the rejection of a political option: Jesus would not use spectacular signs and wonders to win people's allegiance to his kingdom.

This would not be the only time this temptation surfaced. Repeatedly Jesus would be challenged to produce a sign to prove to his critics that he came from God. It is significant that Mark describes this in the language of testing/temptation and that Matthew and Luke follow him (Mark 8:11; Matthew 16:1; Luke 11:16). Jesus never seems to have doubted that angels were there to protect him if he were to ask for them. Even as he was arrested he assured his disciples that God would send him twelve legions of angels if he were to ask (Matthew 26:53). But that was not what his mission called for. As he was hoisted to the pinnacle of his cross Jesus would hear again the words 'If you are the Son of God,' this time from those who condemned him, taunting him to use his powers to save himself: 'Let him come down from the cross and we will believe in him' (Matthew 27:40, 42). As at the first Jesus refused the suggestion. He would let himself fall to his death, trusting that angels would indeed bear him up, but he would not put pressure on God as to the how or when.

All These Kingdoms Shall Be Yours

In the final temptation the Devil challenges Jesus directly with the issue which must have filled his thoughts during his period of fasting, the question of how the world could be won and ruled (Luke 4:5–8). There can be little doubt here that we are dealing with a temptation which is specific to his commissioning as the establisher of God's kingdom. The Son of God of the psalm alluded to at Jesus' baptism was to receive the earth as his possession; the kings of the nations were to kiss his feet (Psalm 2:8–11). The Servant in whom God is well pleased was to establish justice in the earth, to be a light to the nations, to bring God's salvation to the ends of the earth (Isaiah 42:4; 49:6). The Devil brought to Jesus' mind all the kingdoms of the world and their glory, promising to give them to him 'on a plate' if Jesus would worship before him. There is no mountain high enough for a view of all the kingdoms of the world, but such is the power of the human imagination that it can readily encompass such glory in a moment of time and desire it for its own.

The desire for dominion is understandable. In Jesus' case it was no sin; it was enjoined upon him. To wish to achieve it without tears would be an obvious temptation. That Satan might view the allegiance of the Messiah as his greatest triumph is also conceivable. The puzzle is how worship of Satan could have presented itself as a real temptation to Jesus. For I presume these were not play temptations. Again we should rid from our minds the thought that the Devil stood before Jesus in some quasi-material shape, asking him literally to bow in worship. What the gospels relay to us is Jesus' interpretation of his experience. Perhaps he saw just how easy it would be to win the kingdoms if he were to employ the armoury of evil tactics which have been used from time immemorial to achieve political power: lies, intrigue, false promises, fear, torture, propaganda, armies and weapons of war. I am only guessing, but it may be that he saw this road as tantamount to worship of Satan. Having said this, we need to confess ignorance of the dynamics of relationship between Jesus and Satan. Perhaps Satan did suggest what for himself was the irresistible temptation, homage from the King-elect, in return for all he had to offer. Perhaps he overplayed his hand. For Jesus to turn from God in so blatant a manner was unthinkable.

In declining the offer Jesus did not turn his back on dominion, he simply refused to take it from Satan's hand. Had he done so it would not have been the kingdom of *God* which he established, but a dictatorship, which, however benevolent, could only be held with the good will of the acknowledged ultimate satanic power. It would be the kingdom of Antichrist. But Jesus would have none of it. God was his lord, and it would be *God's* kingdom he would establish, in God's way.

What Jesus' positive strategy would be, now that he had turned his back on economic miracles, display miracles and direct alliance with evil will be seen as the rest of his story unfolds. At this point it may simply be observed that in refusing to buy popularity and power, in declining to put pressure on God to protect him, and in rejecting any form of collaboration with the one who claimed to hold sway over the world, he placed himself in an extraordinarily vulnerable position.

A Preliminary Victory

What then is the meaning of Jesus' episode in the wilds? Adam was put to the test and failed, and in a manner surrendered his sovereignty to the Devil. As often as his descendants follow the Devil's suggestions they ratify their first father's original decision. Any human who receives favour from God becomes in return the object of satanic attempts at undermining and disgrace. Although a few, by God's grace, have emerged victorious in isolated skirmishes, none of Adam's family has ever fully maintained their independence and loyalty to God in the face of this Adversary. Now Jesus, the son of David, the Israelite, the son of Adam, the son of God, has been anointed by the Holy Spirit and declared to be 'my beloved Son, in whom I am well pleased'. This is the man who is set to establish God's kingdom and rule his world. But first he must endure the Devil's attempts to defeat and disqualify him. It is the Spirit of God who drives him forward to this contest (Mark 1:12; Matthew 4:1; Luke 4:1), for, as the gospel writers have learned from Jesus, the Devil's defeat lies at the centre of God's plan to rescue and rule the world (Luke 10:18; 11:20; John 12:31–32). Jesus emerges from the battle victorious. Later he will say that he has bound 'the strong man' (Mark 3:27), that 'the ruler of this world' has no hold on him (John 14:30). But this is only a preliminary skirmish. The war is not yet won. Luke tells us that having finished every temptation the Devil departed from him until a more favourable moment (4:13). He will come again when the occasion is right with yet more powerful inducements.

Notes

[1] E.g., P. Pokorny ('The Temptation Stories and their Intention') thinks Mark's short version originated from the disciples' desire to give an apology for Jesus' ability to drive out demons and speak in the name of God, and that the Q version was the work of a learned scribe, intended to reject the Jewish notion of a political messiah. The episode is ignored by M. Goguel, *The Life of Jesus*; Bornkamm, *Jesus*; and Meyer, *Aims*.

[2] E.P. Sanders, *The Historical Figure of Jesus*, 112.

[3] C.H. Dodd, *The Founder of Christianity*, 124. Wright (*Victory*, 457–459) also argues backwards from the shape of Jesus' ministry to the likelihood of a temptation at its outset.

[4] J. Dupont, 'Tentations de Jésus au désert', 30–76. See also Taylor, *Life*, 52.

[5] T.W. Manson, *The Servant Messiah*, 55–56; cf. J. Jeremias, *The Parables of Jesus*, 123.

[6] Sundar Singh thought he had succeeded. He was carried out of the forest in a coma. It was subsequently demonstrated that he could not have fasted the whole forty days.

[7] One of the things which aroused curiosity about Jesus' ministry was his refusal to fast like the rest of the Jews and even the Baptist (Mark 2:18ff.; Luke 7:33ff.).

[8] It is not necessary to insist that Jesus' fast (Luke 4:2) was absolute for the entire forty days.

[9] Leviticus 16. See M. Harris, *Exodus and Exile: The Structure of Jewish Holidays*, 56–64; A.P. Bloch, *The Biblical and Historical Background of Jewish Customs and Ceremonies*, 163–180.

[10] F. Neugebauer (*Jesu Versuchung*, 35–37) shows that fasting was sometimes associated with seeking divine revelation and thinks this was Jesus' motive.

[11] *The Life of Adam and Eve*, 6. The book is thought to be first century. The legend it tells may be later. See J.H. Charlesworth, *The Old Testament Pseudepigrapha*, 2, 258–295.

[12] E.g., P. Pokorny, 'The Temptation Stories and their Intention', 127: 'Satan was obviously the personification of the almost mysterious fact of the misuse of the structures, traditions and ideas that become independent of men and often exert an almost personal pressure on them.'

[13] See R. Bultmann, *Jesus Christ and Mythology*, 15.

[14] Further references to general uses of the Hebrew word *satan* are Psalm 71:13; 109:6,20. For the related *sitnah* as enmity or accusation, see Genesis 26:21; Ezra 4:6.

[15] *Life of Adam and Eve*, 11–17 (Charlesworth, *Pseudepigrapha*, 2, 260–264).

[16] *The Life of Adam and Eve* shows this understanding was wider than the early church. See previous note.

[17] *Babylonian Talmud Sanhedrin* 89b. See the discussion in J.B. Gibson (*The Temptations of Jesus in Early Christianity*, 113–115), who sees this as a close parallel to Jesus' wilderness ordeal.

[18] B. Gerhardsson, *The Testing of God's Son*, 26.

[19] Gibson, *Temptations*, 56–57.

20 Slavonic *Life of Adam and Eve*, 36:4–37:1; cf. *Life of Adam and Eve*, 7–8 (Charlesworth, *Pseudepigrapha*, 2, 260f., Charles, *Pseudepigrapha*, 136). Also see V. Taylor, *The Gospel According to St Mark*, 164.

21 The order of the temptations does not appear to have been significant. Matthew and Luke vary the order, though presumably they had access to them in a single written source. One of them has obviously changed the order, though we can only guess which one, since there is no obvious theological reason operative in either case. It may be that the story was also known to one of them in a different order and he changed his source to agree with something more familiar.

22 Gerdherdsson, *Testing*.

23 G.P. Thompson, ' "Called – Proved – Obedient": A Study in the Baptism and Temptation Narratives of Matthew and Luke', 1–12.

24 Gibson, *Temptations*, 97–118.

25 Gerhardsson, *Testing*, 41–53. Also R.T. France, *Man*, 41; *Jesus and the Old Testament*, 50–53.

26 Neugebauer (*Versuchung*, 40–41) thinks the temptation was to use his miraculous powers to satisfy his own and his disciples' hunger.

27 The Greek words *zaomai* and *zoe* mean life understood in terms of its content and quality. In John they are used absolutely to mean 'eternal life'. In relation to Jesus' words to the Devil, John 5:24 is particularly interesting (cf. John 10:10; Luke 12:15; 15:24, 32). See also Seccombe, *Possessions*, 140f.

28 J.A.T. Robinson ('The Temptations') thinks all the temptations were directed at Jesus' uncertainty about his new status as Son of God, inducing him to put God to the test for a proof of this status.

29 *Pesikta Rabbati*, 36. The *Pesikta Rabbati* is relatively late, but this particular teaching is attributed to the Masters (the Tannaim) who were the earliest generations of rabbis before the production of the Mishnah (about AD 220). This tradition is therefore likely to reach back to the first century.

30 1QM 12; 11QMelchizedek.

31 These points are made by Gerhardsson, *Testing*, 28. Pages 25–35 contain an excellent treatment of the subject of temptation in the Old Testament.

32 Josephus, *History*, 20.97. Josephus places this event in the procuratorship of Cuspius Fadus, AD 44–46. If this is the same Theudas mentioned by Gamaliel (Acts 5:36) it may have happened earlier.

33 Josephus, *Jewish War*, 2.259.

34 Josephus, *Jewish War*, 6.285–287.

Chapter 6

Becoming Known

The Gospel of John and The Story of Jesus

After Jesus' commissioning at the Jordan and forty day ordeal in the wilderness, with its culmination in victory over every attempt to seduce him from his proper path, we expect to see some positive action in the direction of his new mission. Matthew, Mark and Luke signal Jesus' dramatic appearance in Galilee with an electrifying announcement.[1] The Fourth Gospel, however, is quite different. The move to Galilee which Mark mentions does not take place until well into the story (John 4:1–3, 43–45). In the meantime Jesus has made contact with some of those who are to become his disciples, has travelled to Galilee and back, launched a dramatic attack on the merchants in the Jerusalem temple, ministered in Jerusalem, and preached and baptized in Judaea.

Although it is possible to run the story as John presents it, together with that of Mark, many treatments of the life of Jesus, suspicious of John's historical accuracy, omit any ministry prior to the Galilean mission. This raises in acute and practical form the question of what weight we should give each gospel as we pursue what really happened in Jesus' life and ministry.

Until the nineteenth century the four gospels were, by and large, accorded equal worth – considered equally true. The obvious difference between John and the other three was attributed to their outlook and intention: according to Clement of Alexandria, the first three related the bodily facts, John gave the spiritual meaning.[2] But in 1832, in his lectures on the life of Jesus at the University of Berlin, Friedrich Schleiermacher declared the outline of Jesus' ministry in John and the synoptics to be irreconcilable. He gave historical preference to John on the grounds that he was an apostle where the others were not. Three years later this approach was stood on its head by David Friedrich Strauss who discounted John as an historical source because he considered it to be thoroughly dominated by a theological purpose. Another three years and the theory of Markan priority emerged. For the latter half of the nineteenth century Mark was regarded as the key to unravelling the history of Jesus. Matthew and Luke were used to supplement Mark's picture, and John, now believed to be the work of a second-century theologian, fell into disuse. This was tempered to some extent in the English speaking world by B.F. Westcott's defence of the apostle John's authorship of the Fourth Gospel.[3] Nevertheless, the prevailing scholarly mood at the beginning of the twentieth century was against John.

Much has happened in the last one hundred years, however, to modify this assessment. The discovery in Egypt of a fragment of John dated to early in the second century provided proof that the gospel had been written earlier, and therefore within the possible lifetime of a disciple of Jesus.[4] Similarities between the Fourth Gospel and the Dead Sea Scrolls (discovered in 1948) showed that the thought-forms and language of John, formerly thought to derive from the Greek-thinking world (unlikely therefore in the work of a Palestinian disciple of Jesus), are actually thoroughly first-century Jewish.[5] There now exist three schools of opinion about John. One continues to regard it as a work of theology with little historical worth, unrelated to a first generation disciple.[6] A second view thinks it had some connection with John or one of Jesus' Jerusalem disciples, perhaps the work of a school of John's disciples. It is therefore a mixture of valuable early historical data and later theological reflection.[7] A third school of thought accepts the gospel at face value as the work of a disciple of Jesus, who, though undeniably writing a book of great theological profundity, conveyed historical details of Jesus' ministry which he knew.[8] (I outlined my reasons for agreeing with this last line of thinking in chapter 3.)

The major source of suspicion about John's historical reliability is its degree of theological sophistication compared with the other gospels. Whereas the synoptics tend to convey stories and sayings with a minimum of intrusion on the part of the author, John's thought and style is everywhere discernible in his text. In an age when history and interpretation were seen to threaten each other this was fatal for the estimation of John's historical value. However, all history is now seen as a blending of fact and interpretation and all the gospels are recognized as theologically motivated. This means that each of them is written with a faith intention – an interest in the meaning and ultimate significance of what it records. It does not necessarily compromise their historical integrity, though it may influence the way that history is presented. The claim of the early Christians was that something had happened in history which was of ultimate significance in relation to God and his purpose for the world. In the gospels we are dealing with the interlocking of two dimensions: history and meaning. The presence of one does not necessarily compromise the other. There is also the dimension of the gospel writer's literary art, which can interfere, but does not need to, with the telling of what happened. We must be aware that all these elements are present and examine each part of the gospels as best we can with the knowledge and tools at our disposal.

Can any one source today legitimately be given priority over the others? That an eminent New Testament scholar could write a major book entitled *The Priority of John* shows how greatly thinking has changed.[9] It is unlikely that John is prior in the chronological sense. That honour surely belongs to Mark. But Mark's priority does not establish its historical superiority, even over Matthew and Luke, unless we supposed they knew nothing other than Mark. That can hardly be the case. They all belong to the generation when first hand memories of the events were accessible, as well as some written accounts. An eclectic approach to the sources seems wisest, utilizing all four gospels, with the realization that each is a synthesis of the historical, theological and literary. Where the history lies can only be discovered by entry as sensitively as possible into the intention and technique of each writer. Of course, it is necessary to begin somewhere, and the double baseline of Mark and John offers the most promising way forward, though it must be constantly subject to modification as the investigation proceeds. It may bother some readers that other starting positions and approaches to the sources are possible. They are. The ultimate test of one's starting point is the coherence and credibility of the picture that emerges.

John and Mark

According to John, Jesus met his first disciples at the Jordan after his baptism (John 1:35–51). For a time he continued his association with the Baptist, engaging in a similar ministry of preaching and baptizing (John 3:22ff.). Although this is nowhere mentioned in the first three gospels and many treatments of the life of Jesus omit it, others, and particularly English works of the twentieth century, have included it.[10] They do so, first, because it is intrinsically probable that Jesus would have spent time in association with the Baptist; secondly, because there is evidence independent of John that the twelve disciples reckoned their association with Jesus from the time of John's baptism;[11] and thirdly, because whatever is made of the Fourth Gospel as a whole, some of the details which it supplies of this early ministry are so insignificant from a theological point of view that they must surely be genuine reminiscences.[12]

But how are we to account for Mark's omission of this period? And how are we to account for John's omission of things as vital to the gospel record as Jesus' baptism and temptation? It is characteristic of all the gospels that they leave out far more than they include. This was inevitable considering the size of the scrolls to which they were limited and the scope of the events they were dealing with. Some of the techniques they utilized in the resurrection stories have already been discussed. It is not surprising that Mark should have stylized and simplified the course of Jesus' ministry in the interests of a clearer impression of what he saw as its essential progression. He was probably guided in this by the shape of early gospel preaching. When Peter first preached the gospel to the Gentile centurion Cornelius, his message had a story shape and contained a definite historical outline:

> You know the thing that happened throughout the whole land of the Jews, beginning from Galilee after the baptism which John preached: Jesus from Nazareth, how God anointed him with the Holy Spirit and power, how he went about doing good and healing all those who were oppressed by the devil, because God was with him. We are witnesses of all which he did in the country of the Jews and in Jerusalem. They even killed him, hanging him on a tree. God raised this man up and allowed him to be seen ... (Acts 10:37–40)

Here is the barest outline of the Jesus story. It shows that from the point of view of later preaching the movement began in Galilee after John's ministry and proceeded to crucifixion and resurrection in Jerusalem. The correspondence between this summary and the outline of Mark led Dodd to reject Schmidt's theory that Mark's framework was his own invention with no relation to history.[13] The shape of the early proclamation (*kerygma*) ignores the period of ministry John describes in Judaea and Jerusalem immediately after Jesus' association with the Baptist. Perhaps it was felt to have a different character to the Galilean and later Jerusalem ministry, or to be less significant. Why that may have been we shall see in due course.

John's gospel has an entirely different architectural plan to the other gospels. It consists of a series of events and discourses, most of them in Jerusalem, which build an impressive picture of Jesus and who he was. One consequence of John's focus on Jerusalem is that it is very difficult to pick out the shape of a distinctive Galilean mission, though there are indications that it is going on. It may even be that John intentionally steered clear of areas he knew were well covered by the other gospels, setting out to balance their portrait to some extent. John hardly builds on Mark as a literary source, but it is most improbable that he would have been unaware of it (or of Luke).[14] This could well account for what appears to be a studied omission of Jesus' baptism, temptation, and many other events related by the synoptic gospels, as well as his inclusion of a cycle of stories from an early Judaean ministry.

In describing this period I shall, for the moment, pass over important questions about possible contradictions between John and Mark, and the authenticity of Jesus' miracles. It is good that we first get a feel for how John has sketched this phase of Jesus' story. For he writes at more than one level, in a way that not only tells a story but hints at its meaning. Afterwards we can attend to whether John is correct about the real significance of the events at the beginning of Jesus' ministry.

Early Experiences (John 1:35–4:42)

Drawing Disciples (John 1:35–51)

Jesus' first two followers were originally disciples of the Baptist. One of them is Andrew, the other is unnamed. John the Baptist points Jesus out to them as the 'lamb of God' and they approach him. He takes them to where he is staying and they spend the rest of the day together. The details, including even the time of day, are so inconsequential that they must be personal reminiscences

(John 1:35–40). Andrew introduces his brother Peter, Jesus brings Philip, and Philip introduces Nathaniel. If the unnamed disciple was John the son of Zebedee, all five were Galileans: three of them, Andrew, Peter and Philip from the lakeside town of Bethsaida, John from Capernaum, and Nathaniel from Cana.

We feel the excitement of these men who have listened to John speak of a 'coming one' and now believe that Jesus is he. There is none of the political caution we noted with John the Baptist. Andrew announces to Simon, 'We have found the Messiah.' Philip describes him as 'the one Moses wrote about'. Nathaniel doubts, because he knows of no scriptural promise relating to Nazareth, but hails him as 'the Son of God, the king of Israel' once he experiences Jesus' supernatural knowledge. Three titles and a description all add up to a longing, that this be Israel's promised king.

The simplicity of the story is deceptive; there is a profound underlay, characteristic of John. To the disciples' tentative inquiry Jesus replies, 'Come and see.' To doubting Nathaniel Philip says, 'Come and see.' To his readers too the author wishes to say, 'Come and see.' Jesus replies to Nathaniel's enthusiasm in words that recall Jacob's dream (Genesis 28:10–17): 'You will see heaven opened, and the angels of God ascending and descending upon the son of man.' As God revealed to Jacob that his meeting place with human beings was Canaan, so now heaven and earth will meet in the person of Jesus. How this will happen is about to unfold. The new associates return to Galilee. There is no indication of why, and certainly no indication that Jesus had begun any systematic public ministry.

A Wedding in Cana (John 2:1–11)

Jesus' attendance at the wedding feast at Cana appears to be a private family invitation. He is not yet a public figure. The wine runs out and Jesus' mother calls on him for help. He protests, but proceeds nevertheless to give instructions to the servants, saving the occasion by transforming the contents of six stone jars, each holding over one hundred litres, into the finest wine. The gospel writer's interest in this story is threefold. It is the first miracle Jesus performed, it was significant for the development of the disciples' belief, and he saw the particular character of the miracle as a picture of what Jesus was about to do to the life of the Jewish people.

Passover in Jerusalem (John 2:13–22)

The arrival of Passover takes Jesus up to Jerusalem. It was customary for every Jew who could to make the pilgrimage at this time of the year to eat the Passover in the environs of the holy city. Jesus is offended at the temple being used for business purposes. Animals for the sacrificial cult were being sold, probably in the Court of the Gentiles, the area of the temple set apart for non-Jews to worship in. The attendance at feasts of foreigners, as well as Jews and proselytes from many countries gave rise to a considerable trade in various currencies. The temple tax was received around Passover time, and had to be paid in Tyrian coinage. Jesus could not have objected to this in principle; it was the use of his Father's house for it that offended him. With a makeshift whip he drove the animals out of the temple, poured out the money of the money changers and upended their tables. His disciples recognized in him the marks of a true *zealot*, a man passionate for the honour of God even to the point of violence.[15] To the Jews' natural demand for some sign to prove his authority for acting in this way, Jesus replies with a riddle: 'Destroy this temple and in three days I will raise it up again.' They protest that construction has been in progress for forty-six years; will he build it in three days? John leaves the incident hanging with the concluding remark that Jesus spoke of his body, though his disciples realized it only after his resurrection. Again the layers of ambiguity are typically

Johannine. Is Jesus really suggesting they destroy the temple to test his credentials? Or is he warning them that by continuing to treat the temple in this way they will bring about its certain destruction? If so, does this mean he is promising to raise a new temple beyond the conflagration? Does he think he will do it in three literal days? And what kind of temple will it be? All these questions are left to the Jews (and the reader) to ponder.

Conversation with a Pharisee (John 2:23–3:15)

Jesus receives some acclaim for his activities in Jerusalem at this Passover season. John records his unwillingness to put much store in such response; he did not count it real faith (John 2:23–25). As an example we are given the account of Jesus' conversation with a member of the Jewish high council (Sanhedrin). Nicodemus indicates a degree of belief in Jesus – he must come from God, for no one could do what he does unless God were with him – but Jesus tells him he has not begun to see the kingdom of God; he can neither see nor enter it until he has experienced a rebirth by the Spirit of God. The Spirit moves as it wills, seemingly placing this regeneration beyond the reach of human beings, but Jesus paradoxically adds that the son of man is to be lifted up, like Moses' brass serpent in the wilderness, so that whoever believes in him may have eternal life. John interrupts the story to reflect on God's love in sending a saviour to the world (John 3:16–21).

Jesus and his disciples then go to preach and baptize in Judaea. John the Baptist is also at work near Salim. When his disciples complain about the crowds who are forsaking him and going to Jesus he explains that his work is nearing its completion. His God-given task was to be the best man and introduce the groom; now that the bridegroom is here he must joyfully step back (John 3:22–30). Again the author adds his comments about the pre-eminence of the one who has come from heaven (3:31–36).

Encounter with a Samaritan Woman (John 4:1–43)

Finally in this preliminary phase, John tells us of Jesus' conversation with a Samaritan woman. The success of Jesus' baptizing mission has drawn hostile attention. He determines to move to Galilee. This relocation probably corresponds to the withdrawal into Galilee which Mark notes as due to the arrest of the Baptist (Mark 1:14). On the road he stops at a well near the foot of Mount Gerizim in Samaria. His disciples disappear into the town to buy food and Jesus is left in conversation with a woman. He offers her living water and draws her to recognize, first that he must be a prophet, and then that he is the Messiah. They dialogue together on the correct place for worship, a point of contention between Jews and Samaritans. The time is coming, Jesus declares, when worship will no longer be localized; God is seeking men and women who will worship him in spirit and truth. The disciples return as the woman departs to tell her countrymen that she has found the Messiah. Jesus has lost interest in eating. As the Samaritan villagers come forth to greet him he bids his disciples lift their eyes to the harvest. He spends two days there, and many believe because of what they hear.

A Historical Sequence?

The question that confronts us as we look back over this considerable section of John is how it relates to the history of Jesus' early months of ministry. We cannot unquestioningly assume that every incident happened in the sequence John describes, because there are so many cases in the gospels where material is gathered for topical rather than chronological reasons. Particularly problematic is the account of the cleansing of the temple which the other gospels locate in the last week before Jesus' crucifixion. Most scholars, radical and conservative, think that John has brought this story forward in the interests of his theological scheme.[16] It seems improbable that such a thing should have happened twice, and, because of the long-established preference for Mark's ordering of events, his placement of it has been accepted.

It is true that in John the story has a strong theological underlay. In line with the prologue's declaration that 'the Word became flesh and tabernacled amongst us' (1:14), Jesus hints at replacing the temple with his own body. Nevertheless, it is difficult to believe that John would carry out such a radical reshuffle just to emphasize this. It is conceivable that Mark might have made such a rearrangement, for he only records one visit of Jesus to Jerusalem, at the very end of his life, but John has the option of placing it in either location. Many things Jesus did are not specific to time and place and are used by the gospel writers in various contexts to build their portraits. The cleansing of the temple, in public, in Jerusalem, at Passover, is not like that. Its disturbance of the surrounding history, if it were misplaced, would be too great. For this and other reasons some scholars defend John's location of the story.[17]

In fact, this is one of the few incidents in the life of Jesus which is connected with a particular date, and it agrees with John's placing of the incident. 'For forty six years this temple has been under construction,' expostulate the Jews, 'and will you build it again in three days?' Herod the Great began his famous rebuilding project in 20 or 19 BC, so these words must have been spoken about AD 27 or 28, two or three years prior to the Passover of Jesus' death.[18] John's placing of this dramatic event, therefore, has a good claim to being historical. The possibility that there was a similar action in the temple two years later will be dealt with in due course.

A believable sequence for the preliminary stage of Jesus' ministry has emerged: Jesus makes contact with various early disciples, travels to Galilee to attend a wedding feast, returns for Passover and cleanses the temple. This results in a spurious following in Jerusalem, which he addresses typically in an inter-change with a well-disposed Pharisee. Jesus undertakes a preaching and baptizing mission in Judaea, and then journeys to Galilee through Samaria. The only incident that might belong elsewhere, given its thematic function in the narrative, is the Nicodemus dialogue, though there are indicators that it too belongs somewhere early in Jesus' ministry.[19]

Pointers to a New Age

John recorded this series of incidents not out of antiquarian interest, but because it added up to something significant about Jesus and his mission. He did not invent this significance, but conveyed what was implicit in what Jesus was doing. The wedding feast is curious. It hardly appears as a Jesus planned debut. He regards his mother's prompting as inappropriate and untimely. Nevertheless, he acts, and in addition to an impressive miracle creates a profound parable. Israel saw its plight in terms of a marital estrangement from its covenant God. In the coming messianic age God would return to marry his bride. It would be a time of celebration and wine in abundance.[20] John the Baptist saw the 'coming one' as the bridegroom, and Jesus spoke later of his coming in a similar way. He also used the figure of wine as an image of the new age.[21] Could it have been God's providen-tial appointment to unveil his king as the rescuer of a spoiled wedding feast in a Galilean village? Water intended for Jewish ritual washing – indicative of the age of law and promise – is transformed into the finest wine.[22] For Jesus as well as the gospel writer, then, the wedding feast at Cana proclaimed the coming of the new age when God would be reconciled to his people and the great wedding celebration would take place.

If Cana spoke of a new age, the temple incident spoke of a new temple. An event as public and dramatic as this demands our careful attention. E.P. Sanders rightly sees it as a key to understanding Jesus' programme. However, Sanders rejects the evangelists' presentation of it as a cleansing motivated by Jesus' moral outrage at what was going on in the temple, seeing it rather as a carefully staged prophetic demonstration of the destruction of the temple, implying its replacement by the promised new temple of the messianic age.[23] He is undoubtedly right to point to first century hopes of a new temple and the corresponding implications of Jesus' action, but is Sanders justified in rejecting the moral dimension of the demonstration? It is true that Jesus was not opposed to the temple and its sacrifices, true too that sacrifices and votive offerings required animals and money; trade was an unavoidable complement to the operation of the temple. However, to pretend that carrying out this business within the temple precincts was unobjectionable strains credulity. It was abhorrent to John and Mark (John 2:16; Mark 11:17); why would it not have been to Jesus?

If Jesus' cleansing of the temple was close to being his first public act, it is clear that we must try to understand it in relation to his association with John the Baptist. John's movement, which Jesus has now joined, was one of national repentance. What could be more natural after John's appeal for the people to repent and calling of the rulers to task for their scandalous conduct, than that someone in the movement should protest against abuses at the temple. Jesus understood John's ministry in terms of Malachi's prediction of a coming Elijah. Could he have overlooked Malachi's temple oracle?

> Behold, I will send my messenger, and he shall prepare the way before me, and the Lord whom you seek will suddenly come to his temple, the messenger of the covenant, in whom you delight … But who may abide the day of his coming and who shall stand when he appears? For he is like a refiner's fire, and like the washerman's soap. (Malachi 3:1–2)[24]

Did Jesus see himself as a purifier of Israel's worship? From his words about the Father seeking true worshippers (John 4:23–24) it would appear so, though the fact that he did not follow up his protest with demands for permanent reforms, his hint about building a new temple, and his indication to the Samaritan woman that worship in the new age would cease to be localized, all point to something infinitely more radical than a reform of current temple practices.

The focus of Jesus' exchange with Nicodemus is the need for a supernatural rebirth through the agency of the Holy Spirit if a person is to see or enter the kingdom of God. This occurs in relation to a note about Jesus' profound distrust of his would-be supporters, and the comment that he knew what human beings were really like. Thus, to the indication of a new age and a new temple we may add new people. Jesus' words to the Samaritan woman round this theme off with the promise of new worship and new worshippers (John 4:20–24). Wedding, wine, new temple, Spirit-renewed people, and transformed worshippers are all Old Testament motifs belonging to Israel's restoration and the the new age. Clearly John has selected these stories carefully, but he hardly invented the underlying theme. If this goes back to Jesus we have evidence of an exciting outlook at the commencement of his career which may in part answer our question about how he envisaged establishing his kingdom. Instead of a reign built on meeting people's desires, or over-whelming them with power, or through alliance with evil, Jesus foresaw a community of true spiritual worshippers brought into being by the miraculous working of the Holy Spirit, and forming in some manner around him the temple of the new age. Perhaps I am running too far ahead – I am conscious that talk of a *community* at this point is open to misinterpretation and that the exact relationship between Jesus, community and temple is unclear – nevertheless the indicators point in the direction of Israel's restoration and a new age.[25]

Baptizing in Judaea

John briefly notes that Jesus and his disciples spent time baptizing somewhere in the Judaean countryside, and that their activity drew such a response as to bring Jesus into tension with some of John's disciples and the Pharisees (John 3:22–4:2). The mention here of baptizing presents us with a clue for solving the puzzle we noted earlier, that John describes a considerable preliminary ministry in Jerusalem and Judaea, whereas, the synoptics and Peter depict Jesus' ministry proper beginning in Galilee. There is no hint in any of the gospels that any baptizing took place once the Galilean ministry began.

The Judaean and Galilean ministries shared in common: disciples, miracles, crowds of half-believers, and talk about the kingdom. Baptism and fasting dropped away once the Galilean ministry commenced, but something new appeared in its place: Jesus began to announce and celebrate the actual arrival of the kingdom of God. He proclaimed it in a way that implied it was so close as to be in some way present; its doors were open and entry could be immediate. There is no indication in John that while in Judaea and Jerusalem Jesus was saying much more than the Baptist: warning of impending judgement and baptizing into the promise of a place in the Messiah's kingdom.

There are also a number of indications in John that an important change was about to take place. The first of these comes from the lips of the Baptist. He refused to entertain jealousy at the success of Jesus' mission, and indicated to his disciples that he saw his own task as nearing completion, with Jesus' set to increase (John 3:23–30). He likened his relationship to Jesus as that of friend to a bridegroom: now that the bridegroom has come all attention must shift to him. It is significant that this image turns up later on the lips of Jesus in relation to the arrival of the messianic joy-time.

The second indication of change comes in Jesus' conversation with the Samaritan woman. To her question about the relative merits of worship at Jerusalem and Mt Gerizim, Jesus replied in favour of Jerusalem and the Jews. Nevertheless, a change was about to take place that would render such distinctions of place obsolete – the time was so near that Jesus hesitated between future and present tenses: 'Believe me woman, *the hour is coming* when neither in this mountain, nor in Jerusalem will you worship the Father … *But the hour is coming and now is* when the true worshippers will worship the Father in spirit and in truth. For the Father is seeking such worshippers' (John 4:21–23).

This is striking when we also consider Jesus's words to his mother at the wedding feast. 'My time has not yet come' indicates a sense of the prematurity of messianic activity at that time. But the sense of imminent arrival of a decisive epoch evident in his words to the Samaritan woman, is something we will meet again and again in the Galilean ministry, is hinted at. It suggests something had signalled Jesus that God's time had now come. Mark notes this at Jesus' entry into Galilee: 'The time is fulfilled and the kingdom of God is at hand' (Mark 1:15). One further saying indicates a change. When Jesus' disciples returned from a foraging expedition in the Samaritan town they were surprised that Jesus, hungry as they knew him to be, was not interested in food. He had more urgent things on his mind. 'My food is to do the will of the one who sent me and to complete his work. Don't you have a saying, There is yet four months and the harvest comes? Behold I say to you, lift up your eyes and see the fields: they are white for harvest' (John 4:34–35). Once again, this time with passion, Jesus indicates a new state of affairs. Others had laboured at the sowing and now the disciples were about to enter into a glorious harvest time.[26]

A New Ministry in Galilee

The traces are plain enough of an interesting preliminary period in Jerusalem and Judaea, with at least one trip to Galilee, and, on the journey of departure from Judaea, a short period of ministry in Samaria. It appears that Jesus identified with, and joined in the work John had begun, until he judged that the time was ripe for something new. Two practical considerations necessitated his move. One was Jesus's increased notoriety amongst the religious watchdogs in Jerusalem (John 4:1–3), the other Herod Antipas' arrest of John (Mark 1:14; Matthew 4:12). At first glance it is curious that Jesus should go to Galilee, for it was also part of Herod's territory. However, there is some indication that Herod may have been concentrating his attention at that time on Peraea.[27] The move to Galilee may have been to avoid a dangerous pincer movement between Herod's political sensitivities in his southern province and the religious sensitivities of the Jerusalem Jews. In Galilee, at least for the moment, Jesus would be less under the official eye. Perhaps he also sensed that Herod's removal of John was God's bringing to its appointed end the mission which John already sensed was drawing to a close. This was certainly the way the gospel writers saw it; the day of the bridegroom had arrived and the friend must fade into the background (John 3:29–30).

Notes

[1] Matthew 4:12–17; Mark 1:14–15; Luke 4:14–21.

[2] Eusebius, *Ecclesiastical History*, 6.14.7.

[3] B.F. Westcott, *The Gospel According to St John*.

[4] Known as p[52] this fragment of John 18 is held at the John Rylands University Library of Manchester and is probably the oldest known fragment of the NT.

[5] J.A.T. Robinson 'A New Look at the Fourth Gospel', 94–106.

[6] E.g., R. Bultmann, *The Gospel of John: A Commentary*.

[7] E.g., Dodd, *Historical Tradition*; R.E. Brown, *The Gospel According to John* and *The Community of the Beloved Disciple*.

[8] E.g., Robinson, *Priority*; Hengel, *Johannine Question*; L. Morris, *The Gospel According to John*.

[9] Robinson, *Priority*. The book was published shortly after his death.

[10] E.g., A.C. Headlam, *The Life and Teaching of Jesus the Christ*, 40, 153–155; W. Sanday, *Outlines of the Life of Christ*, 45–48; Taylor, *Life*, 55–57; Dodd, *Founder*, 124–125.

[11] Mark 1:14 implies a relationship between John and Jesus which necessitated a shift on Jesus' part when John was arrested. Acts 1:21f. indicates that the twelve reckoned their association with Jesus from the time of John's ministry.

[12] Dodd, *Historical Tradition*, 302–312; Robinson, *Priority*, 158ff.

[13] C.H. Dodd, 'The Framework of the Gospel Narrative'.

[14] R.H. Lightfoot's view (*St John's Gospel*, 31–32) that John wrote intentionally to supplement Mark (and the other gospels) makes good sense. It is difficult to think that John meant his gospel to stand alone as a complete account of Jesus' ministry without baptism, temptation, mission of the twelve, transfiguration, bread and wine sequence at the last supper, trial before Caiaphas, etc.

[15] The prototypical zealot was Phinehas (Numbers 25:1ff.).

[16] For a recent form of the argument from a passionate opponent of John's historicity, see M. Casey, *Is John's Gospel True?*, 4–14. For a view more sympathetic to John, see R.T. France, 'Chronological Aspects of Gospel Harmony', 40–43.

[17] J.A.T. Robinson, *Priority*, 127–131; ' "His Witness is True": A Test Case of the Johannine Claim', 455–460.

[18] See Josephus, *History*, 15.380; Robinson, *Priority*, 130f.; Brown, *John*, 115f. Hoehner (*Chronological Aspects*, 38ff.) thinks the Jews spoke only of the *sanctuary* whose remodelling was completed forty-six years previously. But if their intention was to point out *how long* the building had been standing they surely would not have gone back to Herod's remodelling, but to the original construction five hundred years previously. Finegan (*Biblical Chronology*, 276–280) calculates both possibilities and reaches AD 27 and 30 as possible dates of the saying. According to Josephus (*History*, 15.421) the sanctuary proper was built by the priests in eighteen months. Both Hoehner and Finegan reckon this time began in 20/19 BC, but this can hardly be so. Josephus gives the impression that work on the sanctuary began some time after the commencement of work on foundations, retaining walls, and gathering materials for the whole project.

[19] Nicodemus is mentioned three times in John, as though his story is well known to the gospel writer. In 19:39 he is described as the one who came to Jesus *at the first*. If the John 3 discourse belongs to the time when Jesus was active alongside the Baptist, the strange words '*We* speak of what *we* know … and you do not receive *our* witness' make good sense as a reference to Jesus and John.

[20] Isaiah 25:6–9; 50:1; 54:4–8; Hosea 1–3; Amos 9:13–15.

[21] John 3:29–30; Mark 2:19–20, 22.

[22] Isaiah 25:6 pictures the time of fulfilment as a banquet of aged and refined wine. The master of ceremonies' compliment to the groom, 'You have kept the best wine until last,' echoes this thought.

[23] E.P. Sanders, *Jesus and Judaism,* 61–119. Ezekiel 41–43 depicts an idealized temple for the new age. According to Targum Isaiah 53:5 (post Christian) the Messiah will build the temple (cf. Targum Zechariah 6:13).

[24] Commentators also point to Zechariah 14:21 where it is said there will be no trader in the house of the Lord in the last days.

[25] The Qumran community saw themselves as a temple of human beings. 4QFlor 1:6–7 (4Q174 3:6) says 'He has commanded that a sanctuary of men be built for himself, that there they may send up, like the smoke of incense, the works of the law.' Cf. 4Q511 35.2–3. (*DJD* VII, 237). Once Jesus' resurrected body comes to be seen as the beginning of the community of the new age (1 Corinthians 15:20) the connection of temple – new community – Jesus' resurrected body becomes clearer. This will be further developed below.

[26] This interpretation can only be maintained by treating the aorist *apesteila* (*apestalka* in some manuscripts) in John 4:38 ('I sent you to harvest that over which you have not laboured') as a prophetic aorist (cf. Luke 1:51–53; 10:18). Jesus certainly saw his Galilean ministry as a time of harvest (Matthew 9:37; Luke 10:2) however we may interpret the harvest parables. J.A.T. Robinson ('The "Others" of John 4:38', 61–66) suggests on the basis of Albright's identification of Ainon near Salem (John 3:23) with a place in Samaritan territory, that the others who did the sowing were John and his disciples.

[27] See H.W. Hoehner, *Herod Antipas,* 147. The fact that John was imprisoned and executed at the Machaerus Fortress in Peraea suggests Herod's attention to his southern frontier.

Chapter 7

Herald Of God's Kingdom

The arrival of the bridegroom is a dramatic moment, and so is harvest time. When Jesus mysteriously told the Samaritan woman 'The time is coming *and now is*,' he was indicating the arrival of something very significant on the divine calendar. When we leave the Gospel of John to pick up the beginning of Jesus' public ministry in Galilee the first thing we meet is another solemn time statement 'After the arrest of John, Jesus came into Galilee proclaiming the gospel of God, and saying, *The time is fulfilled* and the kingdom of God is at hand; repent and believe in the gospel' (Mark 1:14–15). It is this sense of the arrival of an all important day, of the clock having struck a decisive hour, that is the immediately discernible difference between Jesus' work with John in Judaea and his new ministry in Galilee.[1] This is powerfully underlined by a statement he made later in relation to their two ministries: 'The law and the prophets were until John; from then the kingdom of God is announced (*gospelled*) and everyone is forcing into it' (Luke 16:16; cf. Matthew 11:12–13). As Jesus saw it, a new age was breaking upon the world. The era of the law and the prophets came to its climax and close with John the Baptist. Now with Jesus' arrival in Galilee, the great hope which they had promised and longed for was appearing.[2] Matthew's gospel indicates the drama of the moment by linking Jesus' coming to Capernaum with Isaiah's promise to the lands of the north: 'The people sitting in darkness have seen a great light, and

to those sitting in the land under the shadow of death, light has
dawned for them' (Matthew 4:16 quoting Isaiah 9:2). We have
already noted an early rabbinic tradition that the Messiah's
coming would be recognized by his sending forth his light into
the land.[3] For Matthew the light came to Galilee with Jesus'
presence and preaching.

It is plain that one of the most significant things about Jesus'
early ministry in Galilee was his message. Mark and Matthew
summarize it as 'the kingdom of God (heaven) is at hand'.
However, when we, naturally, want to know something more
about this – how it sounded on Jesus' lips and in what terms he
preached it – we learn nothing from Mark and little obvious
from Matthew. Annoyingly, Mark gives us a fifteen word
summary of Jesus' central message, carries us all over Galilee
reminding us that proclaiming the gospel was his all important
task, but never once shows him actually doing it in his own
words.[4] For moderns, who are far removed from the thought
world of which the kingdom of God was a key part, this is
frustrating. And it is a relief to discover that Luke rectifies the
omission in an emphatic way.

In Nazareth (Luke 4:16–30)

Luke must have felt the lack in Mark, for in place of Mark's
summary he has placed an incident in which Jesus actually
proclaimed his gospel. This is his readers' first look at Jesus'
ministry. Jesus returned to Galilee from his time in the wilderness, full of the power of the Spirit of God. He taught in the
synagogues and achieved immediate fame (Luke 4:14f.). Then
we are taken to the synagogue in Nazareth to see what
happened in one particular town. Of course the place where
Jesus grew up was hardly typical, nor was it the first town to
hear him; Luke selected it because Jesus' message there was
typical, and because he had the story from a good source. In the

late fifties Luke had contact with Jesus' brother, James, who was either an eyewitness to what happened in Nazareth that day, or knew the story from others.[5] It was also of interest because Jesus' dialogue with the Nazarenes hinted at the possible transfer of his ministry to Gentiles if Israel refused it. The physical attack which this message provoked also foreshadowed the ultimate outcome of his mission.

Jesus was no stranger to this synagogue. He had spent most of his life in Nazareth and it was his custom to attend synagogue on the Sabbath. The synagogue was a familiar institution in every Jewish community where a quorum of at least ten members could be found. It was no doubt the place of much of his schooling, where he learned to read the Hebrew Scriptures and translate them into his native Aramaic, and where he was instructed in the laws and customs of his nation.[6] Already at the age of twelve Jesus had attracted attention in Jerusalem for his understanding of divinity (Luke 2:46–47). From the age of his *bar mitzvah* he would have taken his turn with the other men at the synagogue meetings, reading the scriptures aloud and leading the prayers.

The Synagogue Service

The synagogue service consisted of set recitations and prayers, readings from the Torah (the Pentateuch), the Haphtarah (the Prophets), the Targum (translation into Aramaic) and Psalms, a sermon based on the readings, and a blessing if a priest were present.[7] It is no surprise that the ruler of the synagogue in Nazareth should invite Jesus, a past member of the community who had already made a name for himself elsewhere, to read the Haphtarah and bring a message to the congregation.

Jesus stood in the accustomed manner and read the last of the songs of the 'servant of the Lord' from the scroll of Isaiah. He probably chose this reading himself, as a set lectionary of readings from the Prophets did not come into force in the synagogues until a later time. Considering what had happened to him at his baptism and how the voice had declared him to be theServant, it was a significant choice. He was permitted to read additional passages if he wished,[8] and added part of the passage we now identify as Isaiah 58.

> The Spirit of the Lord is upon me, because he has anointed me.
> He has sent me to 'evangelize' the poor (*ptochous*),
> to announce to captives their release, and sight to the blind;
> *to send forth the oppressed in a release;*
> to proclaim the acceptable year of the Lord.
> (Luke 4:18–19 from Isaiah 61:1–2; italics from Isaiah 58:6)

The fusion of Isaiah 61 and 58 is revealing. The passages are thematically connected, although this appears clearly only in the Hebrew original. The main reading is about the announcement of 'the year of favour of Yahweh' (Greek: 'the acceptable year of the Lord'), Isaiah 58 speaks of 'the day of favour of Yahweh'. The reader of the Haphtarah was allowed to prepare the way for his sermon by stringing together passages with similar or connected themes. The Rabbis called it 'pearl stringing'. In later times there was a rule that you could not go backwards through the Scriptures, but this is unlikely to have existed in Jesus' time.[9] The theme common to the two readings Jesus chose is jubilee, 'the year of favour of the Lord'.

Jubilee

The jubilee institution was part of Israel's ancient social legislation.[10] When God brought them into Canaan the land was divided and each family received its inheritance. God was the owner of the land and each family a tenant. Rent was paid in tithes, by caring for the needy, and in righteous behaviour. The land was to be passed down from generation to generation and the overall structure of God, land, tribe and family preserved.[11] Of course there were difficulties. A common one being when a family fell into debt and was unable to continue farming their land. Under the jubilee legislation land would revert to its traditional owners at the end of each forty nine year period. Thus land could only be leased for the period remaining until the next jubilee. Jewish slaves also went free in the year of jubilee, and debts were cancelled. The jubilee took its name from the great ram's horn (*jobel*) which was blown on the Day of Atonement at the end of the forty ninth year to announce the beginning of the jubilee. Commencing the jubilee on the Day of Atonement established a connection between God's forgiveness of the people's sins, the release of slaves, cancellation of debts, and the restoration of land to its proper owners. The fasting spoken of in Isaiah 58, which displeased God so much, was probably connected with the Day of Atonement, the one official pre-exilic fast day. The fast which God approves is 'to loose the bonds of wickedness, to undo the thongs of the yoke, to let the oppressed go free and to break every yoke'. 'This', says the prophet, is 'a day of favour of Yahweh', and Jesus associated it with the jubilee he declared in Nazareth.

It is not known for how long the jubilee lasted as a social phenomenon in Israel. In any case, after the invasions and deportations of the eighth and sixth centuries it became difficult to know which land belonged to whom, and the jubilee became impractical. It survived, however, as an expectation for the future. When God acted to restore the fortunes of his people it would take the form of a great jubilee. Sin would be forgiven, the people brought home from exile, all the oppressive powers destroyed, the land restored, and people would again receive their inheritance.

A remarkable document among the Dead Sea Scrolls (11QMelchizedek) strings together the very passage Jesus chose (Isaiah 61) with other passages relating to jubilee to spell out an exciting scenario for the future. The Qumran community, and no doubt many other Jews, divided history into jubilees (seven weeks of years). They understood the difficult prophecy in Daniel 9:24–27, in which seventy weeks are decreed before the establishment of God's kingdom, to mean that four hundred and ninety years (ten jubilees) would elapse between the rebuilding of Jerusalem after its destruction by the Babylonians and the coming of the Messiah (Melchizedek) to annihilate Satan, make atonement for sin, and liberate God's people from the oppression of the nations. Their reckoning put them near to the last generation, and although there is no evidence that they tried to predict the timing of these great convulsions in any exact way, their excited preparations for the last battles of divine vengeance show how near they imagined the end to be. If any of their understanding was shared by other Jews, and it most assuredly was, the theme of Jesus' reading would not have been unfamiliar to his listeners in Nazareth. We begin to understand the enormity of his next words.

Fulfilled Today

Jesus finished the reading and sat down. Every eye in the synagogue fixed itself upon him. His 'sermon' must have startled them with its brevity, for it was a bald statement: 'Today this scripture has been fulfilled in your ears.' With these words the reading was suddenly transformed from a prophecy about a messenger who would one day come to announce the jubilee of Israel's salvation, to the actual announcement made by the anointed messenger himself.

What exactly was Jesus saying? Was it release from spiritual bondage, forgiveness and inward enlightenment that he announced? Traditionally, this is the way it has been taken. However, in recent times there have been loud protests at this 'spiritualization' of Jesus' message. One American 'black theologian' asserts

Because most biblical scholars are the descendants of the advantaged class, it is to be expected that they would minimize Jesus' gospel of liberation for the poor by interpreting poverty as a spiritual condition unrelated to social and political phenomena … The poor are the oppressed and the afflicted, those who cannot defend themselves against the powerful. They are the least and the last, the hungry and the thirsty … It is important to point out that Jesus does not promise to include the poor in the Kingdom *along with* others who may be rich and learned. His promise is that the Kingdom belongs to the poor *alone*.[12]

Liberation theology also sees Jesus' Nazareth sermon as foundational to the political, if-needs-be violent, struggle to overthrow oppressive structures and uplift the oppressed classes. Others would not go so far as advocating violent action on Jesus' authority, but nonetheless see his statement as a call for social upheaval in the context of a simmering revolutionary movement in his day.[13] All three views miss the mark, I believe, and seriously underestimate the scope and magnitude of Jesus' meaning. For he announces no less than the total restoration of Israel's spiritual, social, political and economic life by a decisive act of God – beginning at the moment of his declaration.

Who are the Poor?

The terms of the announcement are worth pausing over. It is easy to read our own meanings into words and phrases that may have had a quite different feel to Jesus' hearers. 'The poor,' for example, to most westerners connotes third world peasants and perhaps the lowest classes in their own country. But the word *ptochos* normally means 'destitute', those who are unable to subsist without charitable assistance: people like Lazarus, the widow with her last farthing, the blind and lame. It is almost synonymous with beggar. The peasant majority of the first century were not seen as 'poor' in this sense, nor were Jesus and his disciples, who carried a money-bag and gave alms. If Jesus were proclaiming salvation to these poor it was to a very limited group.

But in fact the language of poverty had another reference. From the days of exile in Babylon Israel had seen herself as 'poor' in the sense that she was downtrodden, oppressed and in need of God's rescue no less than the destitute beggar. Isaiah had promised that God would save the poor, originally meaning the oppressed poor *within* Israel, but later the whole oppressed nation.[14] Seeing Israel as poor became so intrinsic to national self-understanding that sectarian groups like the Qumran community could seize the title and actually name themselves 'the Poor'.[15] When Jesus announced God's jubilee for the poor, the audience would have heard him addressing them: Israel in its desperate need of deliverance. But deliverance from what?

Rescue of the Captives

Curiously, the ill most emphasized in Jesus' reading is Israel's captivity. Since Babylon they had seldom been a free people. Roman occupation was the present manifestation of a captivity which began when the Assyrians overran the northern tribes in 721 BC, became complete when Babylon destroyed Jerusalem in 586 BC, and continued with successive occupations by Persians, Greeks and Romans. The Jews fervently believed that God would one day act to liberate them from this captivity; he had promised to. When Jesus said he had been sent to preach release to the captives, he would have been heard in these terms. However, many Jews saw their captivity on a bigger canvas even than this. Their political weakness was no accident; it was part of God's judgement on them for their rebellion against his covenant. He had delivered them into the hands of Belial (Satan) whose tyranny brought sickness, demon possession, corruption of their national leadership and all sorts of evils in addition to Gentile occupation.

A pre-Christian writing known as the *Testament of Dan* says, 'And there shall arise unto you from the tribe of Judah and Levi the salvation of the Lord; and he shall make war against Beliar, and execute an everlasting vengeance on our enemies; and the captivity he shall take from Beliar, the souls of the saints, and turn disobedient hearts to the Lord … and no longer shall Jerusalem endure desolation, nor Israel be led captive'.[16] Some listeners may have heard Jesus announcing release from Satan and the whole host of ills that came with him.

'Sight to the blind' sounds to modern readers like a medical miracle. To Jesus' listeners it could be this, but it had another meaning, especially in an Isaianic context. The Hebrew of Isaiah 61:1 promises opening the eyes not of the blind, but of *prisoners*. It predicts the coming home of Jews from Gentile nations which were characterized as dark dungeons. Israel was the place of light because it was the place of God's presence. Outside the borders of the holy land people dwelt in darkness. Coming home was release from a dark prison into the light. Jews in Jesus' time registered the anomaly that so many of their countrymen who had been dispersed at the times of great exiles had never returned. It is true that most of them stayed where they were out of choice, but still the future was perceived in terms of a great homecoming, so that Jesus' audience in Nazareth would have heard him announcing the return of the exiles from Gentile lands – as well as from under Gentile domination in their own land. 'Say to the prisoners, "Come forth", to those who are in darkness, "Appear" … Lo, these shall come from afar, and lo, these from the north and the west … For the Lord has comforted his people and will have compassion on his poor ones' (Isaiah 49:9, 12–13).

Thus Jesus declared nothing less than the long-awaited restoration of Israel: the end of Gentile domination, of satanic domination, the gathering of the dispersed exiles and the destruction of all oppressive structures – political, social, economic and spiritual – in an ultimate jubilee of divine forgiveness and reconciliation.[17] Is this what he referred to in

other places as the kingdom of God? In due course we shall see
that it was. For the moment we can see the error of limiting Jesus'
words to the spiritual or political or economic. The Jews were
more holistic in their thinking than this; Jesus' announcement
encompasses salvation in all its dimensions.

The Day of Vengeance

In ending the reading with a significant omission Jesus threw
even more emphasis onto this salvation–jubilee theme. In Isaiah
61:1 the messenger proclaims 'the acceptable year of the Lord *and
the day of vengeance of our God*'. Jesus omitted any reference to
judgement.[18] His theme was pure salvation, pure grace, and this is
startling when we compare him to Qumran and to John the
Baptist. The community at Qumran expected the coming king
to unleash the vengeance of God against his enemies. So did John.
The 'coming one' would burn the chaff with unquenchable fire;
the axe was already at the root of the tree. What has become of
the day of vengeance in Jesus' preaching? We should probably
connect its absence with his forty day fast, which I have suggested
involved a plea for mercy, or at least a postponement of the day of
reckoning.

A Time of Acceptance

The Nazarenes' first reaction to Jesus' message was favourable;
they were amazed at the words of grace that he spoke. They may
have been impressed by the *way* he spoke, but what astonished
them more was *what* he said. They knew themselves to be
members of the nation that was poor and captive and blind and
oppressed. Jesus was announcing that God's arms were wide open
in acceptance of every single person in the synagogue: rich, poor,
young, old, righteous and sinners. God's acceptance meant the

end of all evils, including their nation's captivity, and a new and glorious age of prosperity and peace *today*. These were gracious words indeed!

As the story unfolds, however, we see that although God was ready to accept them, they were not ready for him, at least not in the form which he was now approaching them. At first their reaction was a very understandable reference to Jesus' origins: 'Is not this Joseph's son?' This seems harmless enough (although in Mark's version it could be insulting),[19] but it expresses the beginning of a conflict in their minds between the ordinariness of the Jesus they know (or think they know) and the immensity of what he is declaring to them. Jesus understood the direction of the murmuring which broke out in the synagogue, and began to dialogue with their growing reaction. They would question why, if he had the authority he implied, he did not do something to improve his own situation: 'Physician heal yourself!' This was exactly the point of the first wilderness temptation. They also had some doubts about what they had heard, so they would challenge him to prove himself by doing in Nazareth some of the miracles they had heard about from Capernaum. This was the second temptation. Jesus always refused to do miracles to prove himself to sceptics, and Mark tells us that he did very few in Nazareth (Mark 6:5). Instead, he pointed to the perennial problem faced by God's prophets, that their own people would not accept them. So, as in the past, the prophet here would be forced by the hostility of his own people to turn to outsiders who would receive him as a messenger of God. Others would then become the benefactors of blessings that were intended by rights for his own people.

So the situation turned ugly. Jesus' own townsmen attempted to stone him. This means that as well as being intensely irritated by his words, they felt he had blasphemed against God. The duty of a community towards blasphemers was to stone them to death. One form of this punishment involved pushing the person from a high point to stun them, and then throwing stones at them until they were dead.[20] Jesus was taken forcibly to the top of the hill on which Nazareth is built, but escaped from them without being hurt. Some see this as a miracle; more likely it was an example of that personal force which one sees from time to time in Jesus, and occasionally in others. The angry mob, faced with the need for someone to act first, were paralysed, and Jesus was able to walk through their midst (compare John 18:6). According to Luke he went down to Capernaum, and Nazareth lost what could have meant great blessing.

The Kingdom of God Debate

Our excursion into Luke has confirmed what Mark tells us, that Jesus' proclamation in Galilee was about the arrival of a long-awaited time, the coming of a new era in human and divine affairs. Mark calls this new thing 'the kingdom of God', a term which Jesus himself used repeatedly. To understand it is the master key to unravelling Jesus' career.

It must be said at the outset that discovering what Jesus meant by the kingdom of God is not straight-forward. We could list the following alternative definitions, most of which are current. The kingdom of God is heaven. It is God's sovereign rule over all things. It is the church. It is God's rule in the hearts of his people. It is a transformed society in which God is known as Father and all people are brothers. It is a way of talking about God revealing himself powerfully. It is a liberated, egalitarian society where all oppressive structures have been destroyed. It is a thousand year Jewish kingdom which will appear before the final judgement. It is a transformed world ruled by the King-Messiah. Each of these definitions leads to a different Christianity. It is of supreme importance that we uncover *Jesus'* meaning of the term. So much of his teaching and action relates to it (perhaps it all does) that we will certainly fail to understand *him* if we don't.

A Political Kingdom?

The kingdom of God has been the subject of much discussion over the past two centuries. In 1778 Reimarus made the observation that Jesus himself never defined what he meant by the kingdom, and must therefore have been using a term that his hearers well understood. If we want to understand what Jesus meant, therefore, we need to go to the historical background and ask what Jesus' hearers *already* understood about the kingdom of God. According to Reimarus they had a very political understanding; they would have taken Jesus to mean that the Messiah was coming to free them from all their enemies and establish a kingdom centred on Jerusalem, in which Israel would rule the rest of the world. According to Reimarus, this was exactly what Jesus meant people to understand; he set about announcing this kingdom and worked towards getting himself accepted as Messiah. His cry of despair on the cross was his acknowledgement that he had failed.[21]

A Spiritual Kingdom?

Such a negative estimation of Jesus' purpose was obviously unacceptable to many who maintained that his intentions were spiritual, and his understanding of the kingdom of God non-political. Strauss (1835) acknowledged the force of Reimarus' argument, but noted that Jesus never formed a political party, nor sought secular power, even when he had opportunity to do so. Strauss resolved this seeming contradiction by supposing that Jesus removed the political notions connected with the kingdom idea to a supernatural world, which in Strauss' understanding was a mythical world.[22]

On this view, Jesus was in opposition to the Jews of his day precisely at the point of their understanding of the kingdom. They had a worldly notion of the kingdom; Jesus spiritualized it. This 'solution' has proved exceedingly influential in all sorts of Christian writing down to the present. Its problem is that nowhere in the gospels does Jesus either redefine the kingdom or appear to correct the Jews' understanding of it in any whole-sale way.

Gospel scholarship in the latter part of the nineteenth century was dominated by the 'liberal' concept of a 'universal moral kingdom' (Albrecht Ritschl).[23] Adolf von Harnack described this as discarding the 'husk' of crude beliefs Jesus inherited from the Jews and extracting the 'kernel' of his original thought: 'the rule of the holy God in the hearts of individuals'; the kingdom of God is 'God and the soul, the soul and its God.'[24] Jesus' intention was thus to found a new society of transformed individuals based on the timeless ethical and religious principles of the fatherhood of God and the brotherhood of humanity.

The End of the World or the Timeless Reign of God?

The violence done to the gospels by the liberal view, and the unnatural way it sought to 'save' Jesus from the beliefs of his day was bound to bring a reaction, and it came from Ritschl's own son-in-law, Johannes Weiss, a professor at Marburg. Weiss argued in 1892 that Jesus envisaged a dramatic intervention by God to establish a new material order of things and usher in a new age. Initially Jesus expected this to happen in his own lifetime, but later saw that it would not come until after his death. Jesus did not reject the political aspects of the kingdom, but believed that it was impious for people to seek to achieve them by their own means. The kingdom was to be a supernatural creation of God himself, without the help of human hands. Jesus' task was to prepare the people for the great moment by means of repentance. At the conclusion of his essay Weiss states categorically that 'The Kingdom of God as Jesus thought of it is never something subjective, inward, or spiritual, but is always the objective messianic Kingdom, which usually is pictured as a territory into which one enters, or as a land in which one has a share'.[25]

A few years later (1898) Gustav Dalman stated just as categorically that the kingdom of God should never be thought of spatially as a *realm*, but only as an *activity* of God. The word *kingdom* he replaced by *sovereignty* or *reign* (*Herrschaft*, *Gottesherrschaft*).[26] He maintained this on the basis of the term's usage in Hebrew and Aramaic (mostly rabbinical) sources. This has been followed ever since by those who maintain that Jesus preached a purely spiritual kingdom, since it easily allows a shift from an objective, historical 'something' to a mental experience.

Many ancient Jewish documents were discovered and published in the nineteenth century and the thought world of Jesus' contemporaries became better understood. In 1906 Albert Schweitzer accused Dalman of an anti-eschatological bias, and counter-argued that Jesus must be understood against the background of apocalyptic writings from the centuries before and after him, not against the more remote background of later rabbinic Judaism. Schweitzer agreed with Weiss that in proclaiming the kingdom of God Jesus was declaring the end of history as we know it, and announcing God's supernatural intervention to put all things to rights. By combining Weiss' conclusion about the nature of the kingdom with Reimarus' reconstruction of Jesus' intention, Schweitzer reached his own assessment that Jesus sincerely but mistakenly believed that God would intervene during his ministry to reveal him as the heavenly Son of man on the clouds of heaven, bringing normal history to an end and establishing a supernatural other-worldly kingdom.

Present or Future Kingdom?

The shock waves of Schweitzer's conclusions roll on into the twenty-first century. Christianity in any form known in the past could not continue if they stood. Some, like Rudolf Bultmann, accepted them and, following Schweitzer's own lead, pursued a radical reinterpretation of Christianity. The majority stuck with Dalman and the liberal notion of an inward spiritual kingdom. The first significant challenge to Schweitzer's understanding came from the Cambridge New Testament scholar C.H. Dodd, who in a book on the parables (1935) drew attention to what we have already noticed: Jesus' conviction that the kingdom of God *had arrived* and *was present* in his ministry. If it was a presently experienced reality, things could not be quite as Schweitzer claimed. Dodd suggested that the 'thoroughgoing eschatology' school was in effect proposing a compromise: in the face of sayings which declared the kingdom present, and others in which it was clearly future, 'they offered an interpretation which represented it as coming very, very soon'.[27] Dodd's solution depended on his reinterpreting Jesus' future-sounding kingdom sayings to remove any notion that there was more yet to come. This was no compromise, but a sell-out to one half of the data. It also entailed a serious loss of definition in what the kingdom is. If it is the reign of God breaking in and becoming present in the ministry of Jesus, but chiefly manifested in his death, what is left of Israel's glorious hope, of which it is also supposedly the fulfilment? Thus attempts to improve on Dodd were inevitable.

The names that dominated the next phase of thinking about the kingdom of God were Werner Georg Kümmel, Joachim Jeremias and George Eldon Ladd. All insisted that for Jesus the kingdom was both present and future. Kümmel (1945) explained the relationship in terms of the continuity of the person of Jesus: 'the encounter with the man Jesus in the present demands a decision which will be the determining factor for the eschatological verdict of Jesus when he comes as the Son of Man'.[28] His return as judge of the world makes 'the attitude of men to the earthly Jesus the criterion of the verdict of Jesus, the eschatological judge'.[29] Kümmel flatly states that Jesus was wrong in thinking that the time of fulfilment would be within his disciples' generation, but thinks it a matter of no great moment, since he did not say it often, and insisted elsewhere that the hour of his coming was unknown.[30] Acccording to Jeremias (1947), Jesus was unique in his time in teaching that the kingdom was 'dawning' in his ministry.[31] It is in the process of coming – present 'because the Saviour is already here',[32] but future because he is working towards a great consummation. Ladd (1964), following Dalman's lead, insisted that the kingdom of God must be understood as God's reign, not a realm. God began to rule on earth in a new way when Jesus came, and he will intervene to do so again at the time of Jesus' return. Because the kingdom means God's active rule it comprises judgement as well as salvation; Israel's judgement is therefore an aspect of the kingdom of God, of God ruling. Ladd did not accept that Jesus predicted his return within a generation.[33]

The Last Thirty Years

More recently thinking about the kingdom has gone along three main lines. Some writers – particularly those associated with the Jesus Seminar – have steered away from any notion of a future supernatural intervention, seeing Jesus not against a Jewish background, but as something akin to a wandering Greek philosopher. The kingdom of God is then a way of following God in the present which has consequent societal and political impact. According to Crossan the kingdom of God is 'people under divine rule', 'a kingdom of nobodies and undesirables in the here and now of the world'.[34] Marcus Borg, another fellow of the Jesus Seminar, understands the kingdom of God in terms of the present experience of the Spirit. 'For Jesus the language of the kingdom was a way of speaking about the power of the Spirit and the new life which it created. The coming of the kingdom is the coming of the Spirit, both into individual lives and into history itself.'[35] The Jesus Seminar has publicly stated its view that Jesus had a different view of the kingdom to his later followers and John the Baptist: 'Jesus conceived of God's rule as all around him, but difficult to discern. God was so real for him that he could not distinguish God's present activity from any future activity. He had a poetic sense of time in which the future and the present merged, simply melted together, in the intensity of his vision.'[36] One might be forgiven for wondering who has lost touch with the real world, Jesus or the Seminar? They admit the subtlety was lost on Jesus' followers. It is hard to take seriously any view that does not listen to the impact the announcement of the kingdom of God had on Jesus' very Jewish contemporaries, particularly if it posits radical discontinuities between Jesus and John the Baptist on the one side, and the early Christians on the other. It is clear in all the gospels that Jesus' followers flocked to him in expectation of something very big and exciting happening in the near future. If Jesus meant something entirely different, why did he use such a term which evoked such feelings? The Jesus Seminar proclaims the Achilles heel of its view when it votes a pink designation to all the sayings and parables in which the kingdom is represented as present (Jesus *probably* said these things), but a black designation for all the sayings in which the kingdom is seen as future (Jesus *never* said them). Such draconian picking and choosing from the gospel material cannot be expected to reach a true conclusion. The Jesus Seminar would have us believe they are the first to have ever understood Jesus.

The second approach explains Jesus' kingdom message against the background of first century Jewish revolutionary outbreaks. These were many, particularly at the death of Herod the Great, at the end of the reign of Archelaus, and at the time of the Roman–Jewish War. It is reasonable to inquire whether Jesus may not have been part of some movement of liberation or social reform. However, it will become increasingly clear as our own inquiry proceeds that his concerns were too focused upon the supernatural realm to be easily classified in this way.

The third stream is characterized by an increasing realization of the peculiarly Jewish character of Jesus' kingdom expectations. This hardly amounts to a new discovery; the essential Jewishness of Jesus' kingdom understanding goes back to Reimarus and Schweitzer and has always been part of any discussion of his aims. Nevertheless, it has often been perceived as a difficulty, and has tended to be de-emphasized in favour of a universal human vision of the future. George B. Caird[37] and Ben Meyer have sought to correct this. Meyer showed that in proclaiming the kingdom, or 'reign of God' as he consistently translates it, and in symbolic actions like choosing twelve disciples, Jesus announced the arrival of Israel's promised restoration.[38] This emphasis continues in the work of E.P. Sanders, who sees particular significance in Jesus' temple demonstration. Belief in a new temple was part of the restoration ideology of first-century Jews, so an implied or enacted threat to destroy the present temple, making way for a new one, was a significant prophetic action on the part of one who was proclaiming the 'soon' arrival of the great restoration. Sanders does not think Jesus saw the kingdom as present, only near.[39] N.T. Wright argues that in one manner, Jews in Jesus' day believed themselves to be still in exile. The return from Babylonian exile and the glorious future that, according to Isaiah and the other prophets, lay beyond it, had not yet really taken place. 'God's kingdom to the Jew in the village in the first half of the first century, meant the coming vindication of Israel, victory over the pagans, the eventual gift of peace, justice and prosperity.'[40] Israel under the Roman yoke still strained forward to the return from exile and God's return to his people. Jesus' kingdom preaching declared them arrived. Wright believes that the restoration expectations of Jesus' contemporaries have been misunderstood by many scholars because the surrealistic pictures of Jewish apocalyptic writing which appear to envisage heavenly struggles inaugurating a supernatural and other-worldly future are in fact symbolic portrayals of God's renewal and re-establishment of *this* world and its history. It is wrong, then, to see the kingdom as heaven, or as a realm beyond space and time; it is the new state of affairs in history and in the world, when God will have acted to fulfil his promises.[41]

There is no doubt that the discussions of the past century have brought us closer to the world of Jesus and his contemporaries. Since Jesus did not feel the need to define what he meant by the kingdom and nowhere seems to take fundamental issue with his disciples' view, we need to take this background very seriously. That Jesus, when he used the term kingdom of God, was 'deliberately evoking an entire story line that he and his hearers knew quite well',[42] namely the story of restoration, is surely correct. It is also clear that with his appearance in Galilee he saw the promised new age as somehow becoming present, at the same time as it remained in some sense a thing for the future.

Is the Kingdom of God an Activity or the New Age?

It is now necessary to take issue with the assertion that the Hebrew, Aramaic and Greek terms usually translated 'kingdom' (*mamlacah*, *malkuth*, *basileia*) mean 'reign' not 'realm'. Regardless of several protests that have been raised over the years,[43] this has become a virtual truism of New Testament scholarship, and has led to a great deal of unnecessary complication.

Dalman stated categorically, 'No doubt can be entertained that both in the Old Testament and in Jewish literature *malkuth* when applied to God, means always the "kingly rule" never the "kingdom" as if it were meant to suggest the territory governed by Him.'[44] Just as categorically on the other side Ernst Lohmeyer declared, 'I say Kingdom of God, not kingship of God, for, whatever the Aramaic may mean, the Greek word undoubtedly signifies something in time and space and not merely a divine function'.[45] I would wish to broaden the enquiry a little and ask about the general meaning of the term kingdom. Is it not suggestive that neither of the two secular uses of the word in the gospels has the meaning 'rule' or 'reign'? When Jesus says that kingdom will rise against kingdom he means something like a nation (Mark 13:8). Herod Antipas' extravagant offer to give Salome anything she should ask, 'to the half of my kingdom' (Mark 6:23), clearly has the meaning 'realm' – the sum total of the tetrarch's possessions. It is doubtful he is offering to give her half his authority and make her his co-ruler.

A further check reveals that in the Old Testament and later Jewish writings *malkuth* and *basileia* are indeed used of the reign or ruling of a king, but also of his territory,[46] his people,[47] of a nation that is ruled by a king,[48] of a monarchical system,[49] and of a government.[50] One single passage, 1 Maccabees 1:6–51, uses *basileia* with most of these senses:

> [6] So he summoned his most honoured officers, who had been brought up with him from youth, and divided his kingdom (territory?) among them while he was still alive.
>
> [10] From them came forth a sinful root, Antiochus Epiphanes, son of Antiochus the king; he had been a hostage in Rome. He began to reign in the one hundred and thirty-seventh year of the kingdom (rule) of the Greeks.
>
> [16] When Antiochus saw that his kingdom (reign) was established, he determined to become king of the land of Egypt, that he might reign over both kingdoms (nations, territories?).
>
> [41] Then the king wrote to his whole kingdom (people) that all should be one people
>
> [51] In such words he wrote to his whole kingdom (people). And he appointed inspectors over all the people and commanded the cities of Judah to offer sacrifice, city by city.

It is not always easy to be sure of the exact connotation; what is clear is that the word has a far greater semantic range than the simple activity of ruling. It appears to me foolish, therefore, to insist that God's kingdom can only mean his reign, particularly when it is also clear that only with difficulty can this meaning be made to fit many of Jesus' sayings. Consider the parable of the Mustard Seed as an example.

Like a Mustard Seed

> And he said, 'With what can we compare the kingdom of God, or
> what parable shall we use for it? It is like a grain of mustard seed,
> which, when sown upon the ground, is the smallest of all the
> seeds on earth; yet when it is sown it grows up and becomes
> greater than all the vegetables, and makes large branches, so that
> the birds of heaven can nest in its shade.' (Mark 4:30–31)

Jesus likens the kingdom of God to the great tree of
Nebuchadnezzar's dream, which pictured Nebuchadnezzar and
his empire affording nurture and protection to all the peoples
and nations of the world (Daniel 4:4–12). The image is also
used by Ezekiel to picture the greatness of Israel's king and
kingdom in the last days (Ezekiel 17:22–24). Jesus sees the
kingdom in its present manifestation as small, but destined to
become a mighty empire. It is difficult to see how God's act of
ruling could grow like this; it is the sphere over which he rules
which grows, the people and even ultimately the territory. In
mind is the restored world which results from God's activity, not
that activity itself.

Dalman himself distinguished various categories among Jesus'
kingdom sayings, for example 'an approaching dispensation' and
'an order of things'. But how is an approaching dispensation an
activity of ruling? One suspects the awkward fit is made easier for
him by the linguistic flexibility of the German word *Herrschaft*
which, like the English 'kingdom', can mean the total content of
a king's rule as well as the ruling itself. It is better to recognize, as
Billerbeck did long ago, that although in the rabbinical writings
'the kingdom of heaven or God' is always used to describe the
rule of God (*Gottesherrschaft*) over his people, so that to take on
oneself the yoke of the kingdom of heaven is to obey the Torah or
to recite the *Shema*', Jesus' use of kingdom of God is different,
describing God's eschatological gift (rather than his present
demand) and often denoting a realm (*Gottesreich*).[51]

Most Bible translators, in recognition of the possible range of meaning of *malkuth* and *basileia*, have stuck with 'kingdom' and its strong connotations of realm, as the best all round translation; it puts an unnatural strain on the text to consistently use 'reign' or 'sovereignty'.[52] It is unfortunate that the one aspect this fails to convey well is the dynamic action of ruling, so it is good to emphasize that *malkuth* and *basileia* probably have more of this connotation than the English 'kingdom'. But to insist that this is their only meaning is simply incorrect.

Indeed, even scholars who repeat Dalman's linguistically derived definition are forced, as they approach the question from the direction of Jesus' words and actions, to acknowledge a greater field of meaning, even the presence of a quasi-territorial sense in some of Jesus' thinking. Sanders speaks of 'the "sphere" (whether geographical, temporal or spiritual) where God exercises his power'.[53] Wright admits that Jesus' kingdom language evoked the sense of holy land, 'since Yahweh had promised this country to his people'.[54] Thus, although Dalman's linguistic conclusions have been almost universally accepted in the matter of actually interpreting the ministry of Jesus the eschatological interpretation (kingdom equals a new state of affairs in a new age) has held the field for the simple reason that it squares better with what Jesus himself actually says about the kingdom.

Kingdom as Community

Jesus' words to his disciples when they tried to prevent those with little children coming to him confirm the direction of our thinking. 'Let the little children come to me. Do not prevent them, for of such is the kingdom of God. Truly I say to you, whoever does not receive the kingdom of God as a little child shall never enter it' (Mark 10:14–15). Notice first that the kingdom consists both of children and those who receive it like children. Thus included in the concept of the kingdom are those who belong to it. It is hard to resist the impression that Jesus saw the kingdom, partly at least, as a community. It is then logical to speak as he does of entering it. But it is also something which one receives; something wonderful which it is possible to miss out on. Israel's promised inheritance naturally springs to mind. The children receive it, or at least the promise of it, by coming to the King and gaining his blessing. In none of this does God's sovereignty fit naturally as an explanation of his kingdom.

The Source of Jesus' Kingdom Understanding

There are several lines of approach to the puzzle of what Jesus meant by the kingdom. We tried to discern the shape of his thinking in his pre-Galilean ministry and saw his expectation that the great fulfilment of Israel's hopes was about to dawn. We have heard him in action in the Nazareth synagogue and compared what he said with Mark's summary description of his proclamation. Next we looked at the shape of the debate over the last two centuries and became more aware of some of the issues raised by his terminology. We conducted a very limited linguistic exploration of the possible meaning of Jesus' kingdom language. Several further approaches suggest themselves, which should provide confirmation or otherwise of the direction of our thinking so far, and will also deepen our appreciation of the significance of Jesus' message. First, we shall look at the Old Testament background to the idea of the kingdom. Secondly, we will see how the phrase was used by Jesus' contemporaries. Thirdly, the conceptually related idea of 'gospel' will be examined. And, finally, in the following chapters we shall see how our understanding coheres with the rest of Jesus' teaching and ministry.

The Jewish Scriptures

Jesus addressed his contemporaries with kingdom language, announcing something for which the Jews had long been hoping. It would be a mistake, however, to think he derived his understanding of the kingdom from contemporary ideas. At his baptism Jesus heard from the open heaven words of Israel's Bible. When he was clarifying the course of his mission in the wilderness he countered temptation with words of Scripture. At Nazareth he announced his programme with the words of Isaiah. A glance at any of the gospels, indeed, any layer of gospel tradition, reveals a man who saw the Jewish Scriptures – Law, Prophets and Writings – as the word of God. The teaching and understanding of his contemporaries had to measure up to this yardstick before it was acceptable. Jesus could say to the Pharisees, 'You have abandoned the commandment of God and are holding fast to human traditions' (Mark 7:8). We will be wise, then, to enquire whether the Old Testament Scriptures contain ideas which illuminate Jesus' announcement of the kingdom of God. To begin with, the Psalms use kingdom language to celebrate the everlasting sovereignty of God: 'Yahweh has established his throne in the heavens, and his kingdom rules over all' (Psalm 103:19); 'Your kingdom is an everlasting kingdom, and your dominion endures throughout all generations' (Psalm 145:13). God rules for ever over everything. He is God Almighty who made and upholds the universe. Nothing happens outside of his purpose and plan. This belief is fundamental to Old Testament faith. 'I form light and create darkness, I make well-being and create woe, I am Yahweh, who does all these things' (Isaiah 45:7). Jesus shared this conviction of the Old Testament. He told his disciples that even if they were killed it would not be outside of God's control. 'Are not two sparrows sold for a penny? And not one of them will fall to the ground without your Father's will. Even the hairs of your head are all numbered' (Matthew 10:29–30).

However, this cannot be Jesus' meaning when he speaks of the kingdom of God. For God's universal kingship is a constant, the kingdom Jesus spoke of *comes*; previously it was absent. To understand this we need to remember that, although God rules over everything, his sovereignty is actively and consciously resisted on earth. Human beings have joined in rebellion against the lordship of the Creator and he has responded by withdrawing the blessing in which they were to have lived. This creates a situation where God's kingship in the world is compromised, first by disobedience, and then by the consequent evil and suffering which stands contrary to the will of the good Creator (Lamentations 3:33).

For the most part the Old Testament is the story of God's action to re-establish his kingship and restore blessing to the world. This he begins to do through a family and then a particular nation with whom he chooses to enter into personal committed relationship. From the very first, when God covenanted with Abraham to make of him a great nation, bless his descendants, and be their God, the idea of this people as a kingdom over which he ruled was never far away.[55] At the moment that Israel was constituted as God's covenant nation he told them they were to be a kingdom of priests and a holy nation (Exodus 19:6). In other words, all of them were to stand in a peculiar relationship of closeness and service to God, and he would rule over them as king.[56] Their national constitution, drawn up for them at Sinai, was that of a kingdom: a people under a king in a land. By rescuing them as well as by creation God established his right to be their king, and was about to acquire a land for them.[57]

God's kingship over his people was expressed at the beginning through law, through his providing them a land, through his care of them, through judgement when they rebelled, and through acts of salvation when they cried to him for help. Judgement usually meant being overrun by foreign nations. Unlike the surrounding nations there was no human king in Israel for the first five hundred years of their existence. Salvation, when it was needed, was mediated by heroes (usually prophets) whom God raised up for the purpose.

The kingship of David opened a new era in the relationship of Israel with its God. Human kingship in Israel began properly with Saul, but he defied God and tried to rule the people without a corresponding submission of himself to God's law. In David God found a man 'after his own heart', who would rule *for* him, over his people. David and his descendants were appointed, therefore, to the permanent rule of God's people. To that end God covenanted with David to adopt one of his descendants as his own 'Son', and to allow him to build God's house, the temple. God promised to establish his kingdom (rule, dynasty, government?) forever. These promises became the foundation of Israel's national and messianic hope.[58]

> When your days are fulfilled to go to be with your fathers, I will raise up your offspring after you, one of your own sons, and I will establish his kingdom (*malkuth*). He shall build a house for me, and I will establish his throne for ever. I will be his father, and he shall be my son; I will not take my steadfast love from him, as I took it from him who was before you, but I will confirm him in my house and in my kingdom for ever and his throne shall be established for ever.
>
> (1 Chronicles 17:11–14; cf. 2 Samuel 7:12–16)

1 Chronicles 17 is more recent than 2 Samuel 7 and shows a marked development in its use of kingdom terminology. Though 2 Samuel 7 also envisages a dynasty and probably a sphere of rule, 1 Chronicles goes further in identifying this as *God's* kingdom and likening it to a house. The chronicler sees Israel (God, king, people and land) as God's kingdom. It would be nonsensical to speak of Solomon or the Messiah ruling in God's *sovereignty*.

Under David and Solomon Israel achieved political, economic and cultural greatness, such that it could be said that God had fulfilled his promises to Abraham and David (1 Kings 4:20–34).

In a manner of speaking the kingdom of God had come: the people dwelt together in a God-given land, enjoying blessing and dominance because they were ruled by God through a just, wise and obedient king, who maintained the God-given law and the sanctuary (temple) of God's presence in the midst of his people. The kingdom of David and Solomon was to provide a concrete model for expectations of Israel's future kingdom.[59]

However, Solomon turned away from God in his later years, and in the generations which followed the kingdom of Israel disintegrated religiously, politically, socially and economically. Civil war divided the country, north from south, into two kingdoms. Foreign idol-gods displaced or corrupted the worship of Yahweh. Injustice on a large scale impoverished sections of the population. The northern kingdom was conquered by the Assyrians and scattered into the surrounding countries. Finally, Judah itself fell to the armies of Babylon. Jerusalem was destroyed, the temple burned and the survivors carried into state-slavery in Babylon. Though the Persians later allowed them to return to Jerusalem and rebuild the temple, their situation was not greatly improved; they existed under the patronage of the Persian Empire and their king was no more than a local governor. At this point the rule of the kingly line of David ceased altogether. Things came to such a state that a prophet could say 'We have become as at the beginning, like those over whom you never ruled' (Isaiah 63:19).

It is one of the paradoxes of the history of this people, that the darker things became in the realm of *realpolitik* the brighter shone the expectation that God would do something to fulfil the promises he had made to their forefathers. The prophetic promise of God's intervention in world affairs developed in a variety of directions. The greatest problem was the sinful rebelliousness and guilt of Israel; they had proved themselves beyond the power of human reformation. Isaiah declared that God would atone for their guilt (Isaiah 1:18; 53:1ff.), Ezekiel that he would give them a new heart and put his Spirit within them

(Ezekiel 36:26f.), and Jeremiah that he would write his law upon their hearts (Jeremiah 31:31ff.).

Next would come the people's political restoration. Most of God's chosen ones lived in foreign lands, in darkness, away from God's lightening presence. God would bring them back into his presence, into the land, into the light, and unite them under one king, a prince of the house of David. This anointed one or Messiah would protect them against foreign aggression and also regulate their internal life so that peace, justice and harmony reigned within and without. Isaiah especially looks forward to a situation where not only would Israel be safe from her neighbours, but where, through the ministry of God's Servant, the nations themselves would convert to live under God's law and willingly submit to the leadership of his king. Some of the prophecies of Israel's dominance over the Gentiles seem crude and oppressive, but the ultimate picture is of a world at peace, where weapons of war have been forged into tools of agriculture, and where all people dwell in harmony under the kingship of God.[60]

There was no end to what the promised future would hold: the land would be rebuilt and become prosperous, disease would vanish and all would live to a ripe age. Death itself would be swallowed up, and the dead raised. God would come to dwell in the midst of his people in a new temple, out of which would flow a river of life-giving water, rejuvenating the wilderness and bringing life into the Dead Sea. What it all added up to was a new age in a renewed world (universe?), in which God and his people would dwell together in a new kingdom of harmony and righteousness.[61]

We will find references to and echoes of most of these ideas in the ministry and teaching of Jesus, but the part of the Old Testament which features most prominently in his words about himself and his kingdom is the book of Daniel. Significantly, it is here that the idea of the kingdom of God comes to its clearest Old Testament expression.[62]

Daniel is written against the background of the great world empires which one after another conquered and ruled Israel. In a number of prophetic dreams and inspired interpretations God reveals the political future of the nation. In Nebuchadnezzar's first dream four successive world empires are pictured as a great statue of gold, silver, bronze, and iron mixed with clay. A stone is cut out without human hands and smashes the statue's feet. The statue is broken up and blown away, and the stone grows to fill the whole earth. The meaning of the dream is that God will destroy the kingdoms of the world and set up an eternal kingdom of his own (Daniel 2:31–44).

In the best known of Daniel's dream-visions he sees the great sea (unstable humanity[63]) stirred by a tempest. Out of it rise four terrible beasts (kings or empires) which rule the earth with tyranny and cruelty. But in the end God sits for judgement. Dominion is taken away from the animal-rulers and given to 'one like a son of man' who comes on the clouds of heaven to be presented before God. To him, as representative of the saints of God, is given an eternal kingdom over all the nations of the world (Daniel 7:13–14).

It cannot be accidental that the name Jesus most often used to refer to himself, 'Son of Man', occurs here together with the language of kingdom. Being precise about the exact meaning of 'kingdom' in Daniel 7 is not easy. In the key verse, 7:14, it is used twice and could be either a synonym for dominion or the sphere of authority over which that dominion is exercised; probably its first occurrence means dominion, and its latter the total complex of king, his rule and that over which he rules.[64] In any case, what is plain is that a new state of affairs and a new age results from this award of authority. From now and for ever the whole world submits itself to the authority of this son of man and his people.[65]

If Jesus, even in part, took his understanding of the kingdom from Daniel some observations are in order. The kingdom Daniel describes is manifestly ruled by a human being. It is in fact nothing other than the messianic order we meet elsewhere in other dress. If Jesus termed it the kingdom of *God* it was because of God's ultimate ownership of it, because it was brought into being by God, because it perfectly conformed to and expressed God's will, and because he wanted to emphasize that relationship with God was its very core. But essential to it is that it involves the rule of a human being, and that it is Israel's kingdom, extended to embrace all the peoples of the world.[66]

In the light of this developing Old Testament story it seems artificial to apply an uncertain linguistic guillotine to Jesus' use of the term 'kingdom of God' – making him speak solely of the sovereignty of God. God would certainly exercise his sovereignty, but it would be with the specific objective of bringing his many promises to fulfilment, and it would result in a new spiritual, political, social and environmental state of affairs. There would be a new relationship with God, a faithful king, a new community, and a renewed world. Jesus has adopted as the central slogan of his ministry a term which, though not common in the Jewish Scriptures, nonetheless sums up the whole direction in which their history and revelation tends. 'The time is fulfilled and the kingdom of God is at hand' means that Israel's history and the promises of all her prophets are about to reach their goal.

The political dimension of all this is impossible to sidestep. Jesus from among other possibilities fixed on a political term. The kingdom of God is in part the biblical solution to the perennial problem of political power. The rule of the Messiah over a united world is the consummation of humanity's political nature and existence. Jesus, as an Old Testament believer amongst a nation of Old Testament believers, could not have used the term without intending to be understood in this ultimately political way. N.T. Wright is absolutely correct to insist that Jesus' listeners would have heard him announcing the end of their exile.[67] Moses had warned that rebellion would lead to exile and scattering. Restoration must begin with reconciliation to God, but this would entail the end of foreign domination and the return of the scattered people. It also meant a new king, a new order, a new temple, a new peace and a renewed environment. We shall now see that this understanding continued to be reflected in Jewish literature before, during and after the first century.

Jesus' Contemporaries and the Kingdom

The Jews went on developing their thinking after the last Old Testament book was written. In a wealth of literature from the second and first centuries BC and the first century AD we are able to see the variety of their reflections on how the promises that had been given them would reach fulfilment. The term 'kingdom of God' does not occur frequently enough for us to say it was a common way of speaking, though often enough to be sure it would have been recognized as a reference to the new age. *The Assumption of Moses*, a writing from about the time of Jesus, shows that the idea was certainly well established:

> And then His kingdom shall appear throughout all his creation,
> and then Satan shall be no more,
> and sorrow shall depart with him ...
> For the Most High will arise, the Eternal God alone,
> And he will appear to punish the Gentiles,
> Then you, O Israel, will be happy,
> and you shall mount upon the necks and wings of the eagle[68]

It is probable here that we should think of God's kingdom as his sovereign power, but its appearance obviously introduces a new state of affairs which is objective, historical and ultimately political. Satan would be banished from the world, along with all the evils and sorrows that his activity has entailed. Prominent among these was the Gentile (at that time Roman) control of Israel. The oppressed people would be liberated into happiness.

The idea of God's kingdom *appearing* in this passage is a clue to the importance of some other evidence, which, although coming from much later writings, is relevant to our understanding of Jesus' time. The targums (Aramaic paraphrases of the Old Testament) come, in their final written form, from a period several centuries removed from the New Testament, and we cannot assume that everything they say represents how Jews in Jesus' time thought. It is clear, however, that much of their tradition stems from an earlier time. In the case we are considering, we find the notion of the *appearance* of the kingdom of God several times in different targums, and it seems reasonable, considering the presence of similar ideas in *The Assumption of Moses* and in Jesus' preaching to suppose that on this point the targums reflect an early tradition.

> How beautiful upon the mountains of the land of Israel are the feet of the Messenger who announces peace, the Messenger of good, who announces salvation, who says to the congregation of Zion, The kingdom of your God has been revealed.[69]

In the Hebrew text of Isaiah, which this targum sets out to explain, the messenger says to Zion, 'Your God reigns.' The targum makes clear its view that what the messenger proclaims is not the timeless sovereignty of God, but the arrival of a brand new state of affairs through the intervention of God.[70] In this and similar targums what is envisaged is the coming of the Messiah, the rescue of Israel from foreign powers, the return of those who have been scattered from distant lands, and the perfecting of Jerusalem and the land of Israel. This new state of affairs will be eternal.

The targums and other contemporary literature are mostly ambiguous about whether the kingdom refers to the new state of affairs, or to the power of God that would bring it into being. Certainly the latter idea is always present, but the idea of a renewed Israel or of a messianic realm, is also never far away.[71] In Micah 4:7–8, for example, God's rule over his people is brought side by side with the restoration of the political kingdom of Israel: 'The Lord shall reign over them in Mount Zion from now until for ever … to you [Zion] the former kingdom shall come, the kingdom of the daughter of Zion.' The targum to this passage explains it in relation to the kingdom of God and also brings the Messiah into the picture:

> And the kingdom of the lord shall be revealed upon them in Mount Zion from now until for ever. And you, the Messiah of Israel, hidden from the sinners of the assembly of Zion, for you the future kingdom is coming. And the former dominion shall come to the kingdom of the assembly of Jerusalem.

We see here a striking running together of ideas of God's sovereignty, the Messiah's kingdom, and a new political future for Jerusalem. It seems artificial to limit the term 'kingdom' solely to the activity of God's ruling.

The Dead Sea Scrolls

We have had several occasions to mention the beliefs of the community that lived in Jesus' time on the north-west shore of the Dead Sea. Their rediscovered library, which contains their own and other writings, is the best source we have for knowing how at least some Jews at the time of Jesus were living and thinking. Believing that the end was not far away, this community had withdrawn from what they saw as a hopelessly corrupt society, purifying themselves in readiness for the coming Messiah. Actually they awaited two Messiahs, one a priest, the other the Davidic Prince who would liberate them. They aimed to be found prepared and ready to fight for him in the last great war against the forces of darkness. Though only a small band, with the help of the angel armies of God, and led by the prince whom God would send, they would ultimately triumph. The final victory would bring about the fulfilment of God's promises to Israel, and they would rule the world.

Their kings shall serve you and all your oppressors shall bow down before you; [they shall lick] the dust [of your feet]. Shout for joy [O daughters of] my people! Deck yourself with glorious jewels and rule over [the kingdoms of the nations! Sovereignty shall be to the Lord]. and everlasting dominion to Israel.[72]

When the new age arrived the High Priest was to be blessed with the words 'May you attend upon the service in the Temple of the Kingdom', and the Master of the Congregation was instructed to bless the Davidic Prince 'that he may establish the kingdom of His people for ever'.[73] Thus, although the exact expression 'kingdom of God' does not occur in the scrolls published to date, there are ideas and expressions so similar that Jesus' language must have been readily understood.

Ordinary Jews

The most nearly contemporary and relevant portrayals of the hope against which Jesus' announcement of the kingdom was first heard and interpreted are actually to be found in the New Testament itself, in the songs which greet the Messiah and his forerunner (Luke 1:46–55, 68–79). These songs testify to the expectation of ordinary Jews, that in sending a saviour God would deliver his people from the fear of their enemies, and set them up to serve him in righteousness and holiness in accordance with the many promises he had made through his prophets.[74] The fact that Luke records these songs, along with the stories of Simeon, the old man who was looking for the *comforting of Israel*, and Anna, the aged widow who spoke in the temple to those who were looking for *the redemption of Jerusalem* (Luke 2:25, 38), shows that such a starting point for our understanding of the kingdom of God is perfectly in line with where he wanted the readers of his gospel to begin.

A Real Restoration

Every path along which we have pursued the meaning of Jesus' kingdom proclamation has brought us to the same point: the Old Testament promise of restoration. Yet it is obvious to everyone that no Jewish political messianic kingdom resulted from the ministry of Jesus. Are we faced then with the choice of admitting that he was mistaken, or of transforming his kingdom into something non-material and non-worldly – claiming that he was totally out of step with the expectations of his contemporaries? We will continue to examine both sides of this dilemma as the story proceeds, but there is a third possibility which I believe will lead us in the end to the correct answer. Jesus may have understood the kingdom very much as his contemporaries did (I do not say *exactly* as they did), but have proclaimed it not as an *inevitability*, but as a *possibility*. Something may have happened subsequent to his initial announcement (even its appearance) which logically and properly *delayed* the full manifestation of the kingdom, in a way which was nevertheless totally in accord with his message.

What we have seen so far does not suggest Jesus disagreed radically with the Jews' basic idea of the future. Not that they all thought exactly alike. We know they did not. The Pharisees and the Sadducees differed over whether the new age would involve a resurrection of the dead, for example. Jesus said there would be. Apart from this his only disagreements over what the kingdom would be like are when he insisted that orders of precedence would be upended ('the first will be last' – Mark 10:31, 35–45), and when he declared that marriage would be obsolete (Mark 12:18–25). Nowhere in the gospels do we see him telling the Jews that their hopes for a material fulfilment of the Old Testament promises, even of their political aspirations, were misplaced. Where he did differ radically was on the question of *how* the kingdom would be brought into being. It is on this question of strategy that Jesus said and did so much that was different to common understandings of the kingdom's arrival. In a final exploration of the nature of the kingdom we will meet the first stage of Jesus' kingdom strategy.

The Gospeller

The first three gospels tell us that Jesus' main activity in the early days in Galilee was proclaiming the kingdom. At the beginning he preached mainly in the synagogues. Later he took to open air preaching. They describe his message as 'the gospel', and his activity as 'gospelling'. Familiarity with these terms and the common understanding that 'gospel' means 'good news' can easily anaesthetize us to the dramatic payload they carried at Jesus' time. In fact, in the Jewish realm at least, 'gospel' did not mean 'good news',[75] nor was it a common term in everyday speech.

In the Greek world gospel language (*euaggelion, euaggelizomai, euaggelistes*) had to do with the making of important announcements, particularly those of a political kind like accessions of emperors and victories in battle.[76] The 'evangelist' was the person who carried an important announcement; he was rewarded with a *euaggelion* (gospel). Only in later times, possibly under Christian influence, does this word come to mean the news itself. A gospel was never trivial news. A famous inscription found in the market place at Priene says, 'The birth of the god (Augustus Caesar) was for the world the beginning of gospels on his account.'[77] Here 'gospels' (*euaggelia*) probably refers to the sacrifices which were offered in celebration of the momentous announcement.

Hebrew (and Aramaic) has an equivalent set of terms. The Hebrew *mebassar* (Aramaic *mabassar*) was the courier who in the days before radio carried important messages (Hebrew *besorah*), probably on foot and perhaps across a considerable distance. It was a matter of great prestige to arrive with an important announcement, and large rewards were given. A race between two such 'gospellers', both wishing to be first to David with the news of Absalom's defeat, is recorded in 2 Samuel 18:19–33. When the watchman spots the first runner in the distance David realizes he is a courier: 'He carries gospel (*besorah*).' But the message could be good or bad. When the front runner is recognized as Ahimaaz, David is sure he must be carrying a good message: 'He is a good man and comes with a good *gospel*.'

A very particular use of this language, which was to become influential in forming the shape of Jewish expectations about the future, is found in the book of Isaiah. In the vision of God's return to his people in Isaiah 40, a courier (*mebasseret, euaggelizomenos*) is told to get up onto a high mountain and announce to Jerusalem and the cities of Judah the coming of God to rule over them. The idea is taken up again in Isaiah 52:7–8:

> How beautiful upon the mountains are the feet of the *mebasser*, who publishes peace, who *gospels* good, who publishes salvation, who says to Zion, 'Your God reigns.' Hark, your watchmen lift up their voice, together they sing for joy; for eye to eye they see the return of Yahweh to Zion.

The picture is not unlike David waiting for news of the outcome of the battle with Absalom, only here it is Jerusalem's watchmen waiting for the news of Yahweh's victory over their enemies, which will mean Israel's liberation. The courier arrives on the mountains of Judaea with the stupendous news that God is returning to be their king. I have produced a tortuous translation to make clear where gospel terms occur. The idea also occurs in Isaiah 61:1, the passage Jesus read at Nazareth. 'The Spirit of Yahweh is upon me, because he has anointed me to *gospel* (*lebasser, euaggelisasthai*) the poor.' The prophet looks forward to the day when a Spirit-anointed courier will arrive to announce God's great jubilee deliverance.

Thus basic gospel terminology became part of Israel's restoration language. The coming of the gospeller meant the arrival of the great deliverance, as a song from the century before Jesus makes clear:

Blow the trumpet in Zion to summon the saints,
Cause to be heard in Jerusalem the voice of the *Gospeller*;
For God has had pity on Israel in visiting them.
Stand on the height, O Jerusalem, and behold your children,
from the East and the West, gathered together by the Lord ...
Let the Lord do what he has spoken concerning Israel and
Jerusalem;
Let the Lord raise up Israel by his glorious name.[78]

The blowing of the trumpet and the voice of the gospeller meant
the arrival of God's salvation. It may even be that the trumpet
spoken of here is the *jobel* (ram's horn) that was to herald the start
of the year of jubilee.[79] For Jesus to say the Spirit of the Lord was
upon *him*, because God had anointed *him* to gospel the poor, was
to claim to be this end-time Gospeller, whose very words would
signal the breaking in of God's kingdom.

If Jesus saw himself as Isaiah's Gospeller,[80] a number of
important conclusions follow. To begin with we have one more
clear indication that he understood the kingdom of God to have
become present in his ministry. Secondly, we see that his presence
was part of the fulfilment. It is not just that he proclaimed the
coming or presence of the kingdom as a prophet or commentator
might. He, the announcer, is part of the fulfilment, for he is the
promised courier. More than this, we see how he began to make
the kingdom present. For in declaring Isaiah's words fulfilled
there and then in Nazareth, Jesus transformed what was a long-
range prediction of the coming of someone who would one day
announce the day of salvation, into the words of the announcer
himself. The words actualized what they announced.

Australia became part of the kingdom of England at the
moment Captain Arthur Philip ran up the English flag at Botany
Bay and solemnly claimed the land for King George III. In like
manner, Jesus inaugurates the kingdom of God by solemnly
announcing its arrival. It seems too simple, but that is how
kingdoms come. Of course, to announce a kingdom in the heart

of someone else's territory is sure to provoke a reaction, and we shall see that Jesus' claim did not go uncontested. For the moment it is enough to realize that Jesus saw himself as the eschatological herald: we learn why it was so important for him to preach. Part of the process of making the kingdom a reality was declaring it. Jesus was like the old-time herald, before the days of radio, television and mass-circulation newspapers, going through the land declaring that a new government was in power. The message the herald brought was called a gospel, in Jesus' case 'the gospel of God', for the new order which he proclaimed was the kingdom of God.

For the people who heard such an announcement there were two options: believe or disbelieve. If you believed, it was time to forsake old loyalties and declare allegiance to the new power. That is why Jesus followed his declaration with 'Repent and believe in the gospel' (Mark 1:15). If you disbelieved, you could oppose him, even kill him in the name of the old power. But if his message was true, such a course of action could have catastrophic consequences. In Nazareth Jesus had no need to issue any call for repentance. The announcement itself polarized people to turn angrily against him as a blasphemer. They tried to kill him. But according to Luke he escaped and went on his way, down from the hills to the Sea of Galilee, to Capernaum. In the next chapter we will take a look at the town that Jesus chose as his base. Then we will explore the impact Jesus and his message had on other Galileans.

Notes

[1] For an interesting description of the difference between Jesus and John see E. Linnemann, *The Parables of Jesus*, 38–39.

[2] The vast gulf Jesus saw between John and 'the least in the kingdom of God' (Luke 7:28) makes it clear that he saw John very much on the side of the law and the prophets. However, Jesus' high estimation of John ('among those born

of women no one is greater') indicates that he saw John as more than a prophet because John's ministry was so closely bound to his own. In this sense John almost participated in the 'fulfilment'.

[3] *Pesikta Rabbati* 36 is a sermon on 'the light of Messiah'.

[4] The form of the gospel after Jesus' resurrection and the dawn of the apostolic period was quite different to what it had been before. There is a sense in which the form of the gospel which Jesus announced was obsolete when Mark was writing. This may account for his apparent neglect.

[5] Some doubt the authenticity of this story, because Mark in his account of Jesus' time in Nazareth gives no indication of any violence (Mark 6:1–6). In favour of Luke it should be noted that: (1) The combination of Isaiah 61 and 58 in the reading points to Palestinian and not Hellenistic origins, for it is sensible only in the Hebrew text of Isaiah. (2) Luke would not have invented an attempt on Jesus' life by his own townsmen if it did not have some basis in fact. Such a story could hardly have helped the Christian cause. (3) Luke had access to James the brother of Jesus, who would have had knowledge of what had happened in Nazareth. (4) Mark may have omitted it because he felt that mentioning it would necessitate telling the whole story, which he had no reason to do.

[6] About AD 570 the Piacenza pilgrim was shown the place in the Nazareth synagogue where Jesus had learnt the alphabet. The synagogue may have been a later one, but the story attests the synagogue as the usual place of elementary education. On this and the probability of Jesus having received such an education, see Riesner, *Lehrer*, 129, 182, 228–231. Further on school and synagogue, see E. Schürer, *The History of the Jewish People in the Age of Jesus Christ*, II, 415–463. On the likelihood of a synagogue at Nazareth in Jesus' time see Riesner, *Lehrer*, 222f.

[7] Riesner, *Lehrer*, 137f.

[8] Seccombe, *Possessions*, 47.

[9] Ibid., 46ff.

[10] Leviticus 25:8–55.

[11] See C.J.H. Wright, *God's People in God's Land*, 3–65.

[12] J.H. Cone, *God of the Oppressed*, 78–79.

[13] J.H. Yoder (*The Politics of Jesus*, 34–77) thinks Jesus called for a literal jubilee – hence his emphasis on remission of debts. Differently, R.A. Horsley, *Jesus and the Spiral of Violence*, 251–255.

[14] In Isaiah 3:15 God identifies the poor who are being exploited by wealthy neighbours as his people and contends for them (also 10:2). The Messiah will

concern himself particularly with these poor (11:4). The new age will be an era of safety for the poor and weak (14:30). However 49:13 refers to the whole nation; its poverty consists of exile and Gentile domination (also 41:8–20). This identification of the poor with Israel is also to be found in Psalm 9:12, 18; 68:10; 149:4; Zechariah 11:7, 11 and is commonplace in later Jewish writings. Note that the Hebrew words *'ani* and *'anaw* are rendered in English as poor, afflicted, needy (sometimes humble); their reference is nearly always to an objective condition of deprivation.

[15] The community referred to itself as the *'ebyonim* (poor) and the poor of grace. Their experiences of persecution at the founding of the community formed the justification for this. In identifying themselves with the poor they made an exclusive claim to Israel's salvation. See Seccombe, *Possessions*, 41–43.

[16] *Testament of Dan* 5:10–13; cf. *Testament of Zebulun* 9:8; 11QMelchizedek.

[17] See Seccombe, *Possessions*, 24–43, 56–63, 67.

[18] J. Jeremias (*Jesus' Promise to the Nations*, 45) thinks it was Jesus' omission of 'the day of vengeance' (on Gentiles) that aroused the hostility of the synagogue against him.

[19] In Mark 6:3, 'son of Mary' was probably meant to imply illegitimacy.

[20] See the discussion in J. Blinzler, 'The Jewish Punishment of Stoning in the New Testament Period', 147–161.

[21] Reimarus, *Fragments*, 74–75, 123–128.

[22] Strauss, *Life*, 293–296.

[23] C. Marsh, *Albrecht Ritschl and the Problem of the Historical Jesus*, 85.

[24] A. von Harnack, *What is Christianity?*, 57, 58.

[25] J. Weiss, *Jesus' Proclamation of the Kingdom of God*, 133.

[26] G. Dalman, *The Words of Jesus*, 91–147.

[27] C.H. Dodd, *The Parables of the Kingdom*, 49.

[28] W.G. Kümmel, *Promise and Fulfilment*, 142.

[29] Ibid., 153.

[30] Ibid., 149ff.

[31] J. Jeremias, *New Testament Theology*, 108; also 96–108; 241–249; *Parables*, 115–124; 221–227.

[32] Ibid., 120.

[33] G.E. Ladd, *The Presence of the Future*, 122–148, 307, 321–323. The first edition of this work was published in 1964 as *Jesus and the Kingdom*.

[34] J.D. Crossan, *The Historical Jesus: The Life of a Mediterranean Jewish Peasant*, 266, 298.

[35] M.J. Borg, *Jesus: A New Vision*, 198.

[36] R.W. Funk, R.W. Hoover, et al., *The Five Gospels: The Search for the Authentic Words of Jesus*, 136–137.

[37] G.B. Caird, *Jesus and the Jewish Nation*.

[38] Meyer, *Aims*.

[39] Sanders, *Jesus and Judaism*, 61–119, 123–156; *Historical Figure*, 183–187, 253–262.

[40] Wright, *Victory*, 204.

[41] Wright, *People of God*, 280–299; *Victory*, 95–96. The this-worldly nature of the realities typified by apocalyptic symbolism is also argued for by T.F. Glasson, 'Schweitzer's Influence – Blessing or Bane?', 289–302.

[42] Wright, *Victory*, 199.

[43] H. Windisch ('Die Spruche von Eingehen in das Reich Gottes', 163–192) analysed the NT use of kingdom of God, particularly the way it is so often entered or inherited and concluded that the prototypes of holy land and cultic community lie behind it. S. Aalen (' "Reign" and "House" in the Kingdom of God in the Gospels', 215–240) argued that the kingdom 'is to be understood as a community, a house, an area where the goods of salvation are available and received.' See also E. Lohmeyer, *Lord of the Temple*, 62–91.

[44] Dalman, *Words of Jesus*, 94.

[45] Lohmeyer, *Lord of the Temple*, 63.

[46] Daniel 1:20; 5:11; 1 Maccabees 6:14; 10:33–34; 15:29; 2 Maccabees 9:25.

[47] There are a number of cases where the targums substitute 'kingdoms' for the Hebrew 'peoples' (e.g., *Targum Micah* 4:1; *Targum Zechariah* 8:22; 9:10).

[48] Isaiah 13:19; 47:5 and throughout; Jeremiah 1:10, 15 and throughout; Ezekiel 29:14–15; Daniel 4:17 (of the earth?); 6:7; 10:13; 11:2. For the Hebrew 'great mountain' of Zechariah 4:7 the targums have 'foolish kingdom' (*Targum Zechariah* 4:7); *Targum Amos* 9:8.

[49] Sirach 46:13.

[50] Psalm 102:22 (*mamlakoth*); 103:19; Daniel 2:44; 5:16 (?); 6:1. This usage is common in rabbinic sources where *malkuth* on its own often refers to the Roman government.

[51] SB, 1, 180–184.

[52] This strain is evident in Meyer's, *Aims*, which consistently uses 'sovereignty' instead of 'kingdom'.

[53] Sanders, *Jesus and Judaism*, 126.

[54] Wright, *Victory*, 206.

[55] In Genesis 14 Abraham is offered gifts by the king of Sodom. Accepting them would entail accepting his patronage, so Abraham refuses: 'I have

sworn to the Lord God Most High, the Possessor of heaven and earth that I would not take a thread or a sandal thong of anything that is yours'. Following Abraham's clear confession of allegiance to the kingdom of God (he also pays tithes to the priest of God Most High), God pledges him his protection and makes a covenant with him.

[56] Some think this means they were to be a nation where everyone exercised a priestly rule, but this is unlikely given that *mamlacah*, can equally mean 'a nation and its king' or 'rule'.

[57] The Song of Moses in Exodus 15 celebrates Yahweh's military prowess in defeating his enemies and rescuing his people. The song looks forward to his planting them in their own land where he will establish his sanctuary. The final line declares 'Yahweh will reign for ever and ever,' possibly an ascription of eternal sovereignty, but more likely in this context to mean God will reign as king over Israel.

[58] See Psalm 2; 72; 89; 110; Isaiah 11; Jeremiah 33:15ff.; Ezekiel 34.

[59] See, e.g., Psalm 72.

[60] E.g., Isaiah 9:1–7; 11:1–16; 49:1–13; 60:1ff.; Ezekiel 34:1ff.

[61] Amos 9:13ff.; Joel 3:18; Isaiah 65:17–25; 25:6ff.; Ezekiel 37:1ff.; 40:1ff.; 47:1ff.

[62] Alongside the kingdom predictions of Daniel, the mysterious prophecies of Balaam, the Gentile seer, should not be overlooked. Called by the king of Moab to curse the Israelites as they passed near his land on the way to Canaan, Balaam was seized by the Spirit of God and prophesied the rising of a king in Israel who would lead them to ultimate blessing in the world (Numbers 22–24). The influence of these predictions can be seen in the beliefs of Jews in Jesus' time.

[63] For the association of the sea with humanity see Psalm 65:7; Isaiah 17:12; 57:20; Ezekiel 26:3.

[64] In Daniel 7:23–24 'kingdom' has the sense of king plus rule plus what is ruled.

[65] Some interpret Daniel's son of man as a figure for the remnant of Israel, since in his interpretation of the vision Daniel says 'the kingdom and the dominion and the greatness of the kingdoms under the whole heaven shall be given to the saints of the Most High' (Daniel 7:27). Dominion may be awarded to the saints, however, through the glorification of their representative. The individual nature of the image 'son of man', its probable links with Jewish messianism, and the presence of messianic theology in Daniel 9:26, make it probable that it was meant in this way. Certainly Jesus took it of an individual, albeit a representative of many.

[66] Jesus could only have seen the kingdom as God's in the sense of God appearing and ruling directly, if he saw the Son of Man as no less than God himself.

[67] Wright, *Victory*, 204.

[68] *Assumption of Moses* 10.

[69] *Targum Isaiah* 52:7.

[70] E.g., *Targum Isaiah* 24:23; 40:9.

[71] 'The kingdom of God, the kingdom of the messiah, and the dominion of Israel (over the nations) belong together for the Targum.' J.J. Collins, 'The Kingdom of God in the Apocrypha and the Pseudepigrapha', 95.

[72] War Rule, 1QM 12:14–16. The square brackets indicate places where the text is damaged and the reading uncertain. Cf. 1QM 19:7–8. Vermes, *Scrolls in English*, 138.

[73] Blessings 1QSb (=1Q28b) 4:26; 5:21. Vermes, *Scrolls in English*, 269–270.

[74] For an exposition of the imagery of the Song of Mary, see Seccombe, *Possessions*, 70–83.

[75] In 1 Samuel 4:17 a 'gospeller' (*mebasser*) brings the news to Eli that the Ark has been captured and that his sons are dead.

[76] See *NDIEC*, 3, 10–15. In one papyrus such language is used to announce a marriage, but most of the other cases are important political events.

[77] See G.A. Deissmann, *Light from the Ancient East*, 366.

[78] *Psalms of Solomon* 11.

[79] Leviticus 25:9. See Charles, *Pseudepigrapha*, 643.

[80] For the conclusion to stand it is important to be sure that gospel language goes back to Jesus himself. Its frequency in most of the New Testament (except in the Johannine writings) raises the question of its origin. It occurs on the lips of Jesus, in addition to the Isaiah reading at Nazareth, in the Q saying of Matthew 11:5 (cf. Luke 7:22) with reference to Isaiah 61:1. Also Mark 13:10 (Matthew 24:14); Mark 14:9 (Matthew 26:13); Mark 8:35; 10:29; Luke 4:43; 16:16. Its occurrence in Jesus' sayings in Mark, Q, and Luke rules out its being the creation of any one of the evangelists. O. Betz ('Jesus' Gospel of the Kingdom', 68–74) argues for its dominical origin, pointing out that 'gospel' occurs in the targum to Isaiah 53:1 ('Who has believed this our gospel – *besorah*'?) in the circle of passages whose influence we have already seen.

Chapter 8

Capernaum By The Sea

Capernaum

> Skirting the lake of Gennessar, and also bearing that name, lies a
> region whose natural properties and beauty are very remarkable.
> There is not a plant which its fertile soil refuses to produce, and its
> cultivators in fact grow every species; the air is so well tempered
> that it suits the most opposite varieties. The walnut … palm trees
> … figs and olives … For not only has the country this surprising
> merit of producing such diverse fruits, but it also preserves them:
> for ten months without intermission it supplies those kings of
> fruits, the grape and the fig; the rest mature on the trees the whole
> year round. Besides being favoured by its genial air, the country is
> watered by a highly fertilizing spring, called by the inhabitants
> Capharnaum.[1]

Such is Josephus' description of the region to the north-west of
the Sea of Galilee which Jesus chose as home-base for his
mission. He left his home in Nazareth, according to Matthew,
and went to live in 'Capernaum-on-the-Sea' (Matthew 4:13).
Luke, as we have seen, takes us to Nazareth for a first look at the
Galilean ministry, but he makes it quite clear that Jesus had
already been at work in Capernaum, and his fame as a miracle-
worker had spread from there (Luke 4:14, 15, 23). Mark begins
his account of Jesus' ministry with a Sabbath day in Capernaum.

This was not his first visit; according to John he spent some days there after the wedding at Cana (John 2:12). Many Galileans had also seen him in action at the Passover in Jerusalem. Some of them must have come from Capernaum. John also says that Jesus' second Galilean miracle, though it was done in Cana, involved the healing of the son of a nobleman from Capernaum (John 4:45–54). It must therefore have taken place before this particular Sabbath day. Nevertheless, the sequence Mark relates has all the marks of a public beginning of ministry in Capernaum and Galilee. From then on Capernaum was home to Jesus: the place from which he went and to which he returned. Some think he had a house there, though it is more likely that he stayed in the house of Peter and Andrew and considered this his home (Mark 1:29; 2:1; Matthew 9:1).

What kind of place was Capernaum, and why did Jesus choose it as his base? We are fortunate that the ruins of Capernaum have been identified, so it is possible to form a picture of what it might have been like in the time of Jesus. The town is built on a strip of flat land about four hundred metres wide and one kilometre long between the hills and the sea. The ruins are dominated by the partly reconstructed synagogue, which probably covers the one which stood in Jesus' time. The spring which Josephus mentions (seven springs in fact) is actually about two kilometres from Capernaum, at a place called Tabgha. There is evidence that Tabgha was an industrial area belonging to Capernaum. Some of the water was probably sold to another nearby town and the rest used to drive mills and feed tanneries and potteries.[2] Many grain mills and olive presses made out of the black basalt rock found around the lake are still to be seen in the ruins of Capernaum and Chorazin. There must have been an industry in manufacturing these. Such a grain mill found at Masada suggests they were in demand far from the region of their origin. The palms which are still to be seen in the ruins bear witness to the suitability of the land for the cultivation of dates. The soil of the hillsides which overlook the town is rich, brown and volcanic. Nowadays it carries a patchwork of citrus orchards. In Jesus' day one would have seen figs, olives, grapes, nuts, wheat, barley and a good many other things. The odd climate on which Josephus remarks is a result of the Sea of Galilee's location in the Rift Valley, two hundred metres below sea level. This causes something of a greenhouse effect, pleasant in winter, oppressively hot and still in summer, but ideal for the ripening of fruit. As an agricultural area Capernaum was extremely well placed and was probably quite prosperous in the first century.

It had another advantage: the Sea of Galilee was well stocked with fish and was home to a prosperous fishing industry. Forty years after Jesus, Josephus was able to gather a fleet of 230 boats to make a mock attack on Tiberias, and not much later the lake saw a naval battle between Jews and Romans in which 6700 Jews died.[3] In 1986, when drought brought the level of the lake to an all time low, a nine metre fishing boat was discovered, imbedded in mud close to Migdal (Magdala, Tarichaeae). It has been dated between 100 BC and AD 67 and may well have been in use around the time of Jesus; its location suggests it may have gone down in the battle.[4] Close to Capernaum a number of warm springs emptied into the sea, attracting fish to be caught by the town's fishing fleet. Exploration of one part of Capernaum (now owned by the Greek Orthodox Church) has revealed a sea wall running for several hundred metres along the shore with a stone jetty where boats would have been moored.[5] Peter and Andrew came from Bethsaida at the top end of the lake, but worked in Capernaum in a fishing partnership with the sons of Zebedee. Fresh fish would have been sold as far afield as they could be transported, but there was also an industry in dried and pickled fish, which increased the number of markets, and even made export possible. Magdala, eight kilometres away from Capernaum, had a fish salting industry which gave the town its Greek name of Tarichaeae (*tarichos* = salt fish).

A great trade road from Mesopotamia and Damascus followed the shore of the lake for some distance and, three kilometres from Capernaum, turned away towards the Mediterranean coast on its way to Egypt.[6] A branch road continued along the lake, through Capernaum, to the border of Gaulanitis four kilometres away, and on into Herod Philip's territory. Capernaum was the home of the garrison which policed this border-crossing and protected the customs men who lived in the town.

Life under the Herods

Exciting work has been in progress for many years now attempting to piece together the social, political and economic circumstances of Galilee in Jesus' time. This is important because how we understand his words and actions depends on the situation we think he addressed. There has been a tendency to see the Galileans as predominantly poverty stricken peasants pushed to banditry and revolt by crushing taxation, and to imagine Jesus as offering some sort of solution. But this is far from the reality. The Galileans had memories of the horrors of civil strife. In the troubled period when Julius Caesar was extending his power to the east, and after his assassination, Galilee was in turmoil. First, a brigand chief named Ezekias terrorized the border areas of Galilee and Syria. He was defeated and executed by the young Herod in 47 BC.[7] A few years later, seeking to establish himself as king, Herod fought another successful campaign against Galilean revolutionaries and supporters of the last of the Hasmonaeans. The mopping up operation involved dislodging belligerents and their families who were hiding out in the caves of Arbela.[8]

Once Herod consolidated his power, opportunity for revolutionary activity was squashed; we hear of no serious uprising in the next thirty years. With Herod's death in 4 BC and uncertainty about the succession, a wave of revolution spread through Galilee and Judaea. In Sepphoris, the capital of Galilee, Judas, son of the

Ezekias Herod had rooted out years before, seized power. When the legions marched from Syria, Sepphoris was burned and its inhabitants sold into slavery. When the rest of the rebellion was crushed Varus had two thousand of the leaders crucified.[9] Anyone older than Jesus would have memories of the cost of rebellion. Herod Antipas received Galilee and Peraea in the division of his father's kingdom and ruled from 4 BC until AD 39. There were no major upheavals in Galilee in this time; indeed not until the outbreak of war with Rome in AD 66. Depictions of Galilee as a land simmering on the edge of revolt are far from reality. Bandits and revolutionaries holed up in the caves of Arbela are a serious anachronism in a sketch of Jesus' social background.[10] Herod would never have tolerated it; nor would his son. Our best guide to social conditions in Galilee in the twenties and thirties of the first century are the gospels.[11] They would surely have preserved hints of civil disruption on such a scale had it existed. Of course most of Galilee's Jews longed for freedom from Roman domination, and from the local rule of Antipas, but this was motivated more by national pride and religious convictions than by economic factors. While the two Herods were in power, and without a messianic leader, such hopes had to be kept in proportion – easier when life was prosperous.

The reigns of Herod and Herod Antipas were years of relative peace and prosperity. Taxes were heavy – when Herod died the Jews were quick to petition first Archelaus, and then Caesar for relief – but the burden should not be exaggerated. The land tax would have been at least 25% of produce; harbour taxes amounted to 2.5% of the value of goods transported; customs were also charged at borders, and perhaps at city gates. In addition to these were the customary Jewish tithes for the priests and the poor, and the annual temple tax paid by every Jewish male. Added together they would not have amounted to the taxes paid to modern states, though such a comparison means very little. Contrary to the impression given by many authors, there was no Roman taxation during this period.[12]

Herod's obligations to Rome related mainly to times of military emergency. The fact that people paid their taxes, and that Herod, and later Antipas, were able to carry out their impressive programmes of city building and public works is an indication of the prosperity of the period. It is true that under Herod the Great much Jewish tax went abroad into public benefactions to raise the king's prestige. Josephus concludes a catalogue of his foreign works with a rhetorical flourish: 'And that broad street in Syrian Antioch, once shunned on account of the mud – was it not he who paved its twenty furlongs with polished marble, and, as a protection from the rain, adorned it with a colonnade of equal length?'[13] But there was much government spending within the land that must have stimulated local economies. One thinks of the thousands who were employed on the temple from 20 BC until the early sixties. Eighteen thousand workmen were laid off at its completion, just prior to the great war with Rome – only to be re-employed paving Jerusalem with white marble.[14] The sight of a skilfully turned stone pipe section, tongued and grooved to fit into a continuous pipeline, remnant of a Herodian water system and now part of a house in Bethlehem is a reminder of the technological and industrial sophistication of the era. The magnificent aqueduct running along the coast to Caesarea, Caesarea's fine harbour, and the distinctive carved stones of Herodian building work at the temple mount and at Hebron, tell of a skilled and diversified work force and a degree of prosperity. Herod was not soft towards his subjects – rulers sought glory, not to provide welfare – yet even this striving for glory acted as a check on impoverishment, and rulers were well aware that over-taxation could lead to revolt. In times of great need, but also once as a magnanimous gesture, Herod reduced taxes.[15] In a case where famine was devastating his kingdom, he even cut up the gold and silver ornaments of his own palace to obtain grain from Egypt, with the result that the population was sustained and the land able to recover quickly.[16]

The Roman census undertaken by Quirinius, when Archelaus was exiled and Judaea and Samaria came under direct Roman rule, makes it clear that Galilee continued paying its taxes to Antipas; there was no additional Roman tax. That people continued to pay their tithes and the annual temple tax, and to travel to Jerusalem to make their free-will offerings at the temple, are not indications of a population suffering great distress. The wealth of the temple grew enormously during this period. We hear of no starving priests in the country – a sure symptom of economic distress when it happened, since the traditional Jewish offerings were easier to evade than those exacted by the government.

Socio-Economic Pointers

An easy and reliable way of gaining a feel for the society familiar to Jesus and his followers is to read the gospels with an eye to the incidentals – people's occupations, the commodities that indicate livelihoods, differences of social status, the things people do when they are not at work, money matters, and, of course, indicators of social and political distress. Such a survey is somewhat akin to going on an imaginary holiday to Jesus' Galilee and coming home to write an account of how people there live. You are experiencing a random sampling of people and their activities. There is much you will not have seen, but it is doubtful you would find a better way of getting a general picture.

What, then, were some of the occupations of Jesus' contemporaries – those we meet, and those we infer from some of the commodities we encounter? Impossible to overlook are those who worked the land: the sower who broadcast his seed in hope of a one hundred-fold increase, even if it turns out to be thirty. He may have owned a small family property with sons to work in his vineyard, or perhaps been the tenant of a larger landowner, or a share farmer, or the manager of a large estate. He may have been a subsistence farmer, or the grower of cash crops like wheat, barley, olives, grapes and figs. He may have needed to attend alone, with his sons, to ploughing, seeding, pruning, hoeing, harvesting, winnowing and crushing, but probably hired workers at busy times. Harvest was one time when labourers everywhere received wages and rejoiced together if the crop was good. There were also tasks best handled by specialists: working oxen, shepherding sheep and goats. On two occasions we meet pig herders, in one instance with a herd of two thousand.

As the farmer worked the soil, so the fishermen ploughed the lake. We encounter a two family partnership, along with their hired men, boats, nets and lines. Fish was eaten in Jerusalem, so there must have been preservers, transporters and merchants attached to this trade. And there were sparrow catchers; I do not know where else to mention them.

We turn to the tradesmen. There were house builders, the good ones digging deep and laying foundations on rock, though some were not so careful; Jesus came from a family of builders. Stonemasons were everywhere, shaping blocks, lintels, columns and beams for houses, palaces, synagogues and the temple; also sculpting millstones, olive presses, winepresses, rock tombs and monuments. And there were carpenters, sandal makers, winemakers, potters, spinners, weavers, fullers, and stoneware manufacturers.

Service providers were also to be found in the form of estate managers (stewards), household servants and slaves, scribes, lawyers, doctors and prostitutes. Business people and merchants too: absentee landlords, entrepreneurs, investors, money-lenders and money-changers, bankers, oil and grain merchants, sheep stealers, highwaymen, innkeepers, and even a pearl merchant. Government officials and public servants were also plentiful. We meet customs men, tax collectors, magistrates, bailiffs, court and prison officers and executioners. And alongside these the priests and Levites, public health officers, teachers, synagogue rulers and attendants, and temple workers and not forgetting the informal sector, the book writers, itinerant preachers and exorcists.

Just to consider this sampling of gospel encounters is to notice the absence of such obvious things as butchers, bakers and candlestick makers, all of whom must have been there. But we are seeking only for a feel of things.

Socially, we meet people ranging from a rich man who dressed in purple (imported from Tyre) and fine linen (Egypt) and feasted sumptuously every day, to the sick beggar dropped at his gate in the hope of scraps. In between were the many who probably had little surplus, but who made their way, and were able to travel to the festivals and enjoy an average life. Holiness-wise, there were the priestly elite and the self-appointed Pharisee guardians of their own and others' holiness. There were the ordinary law-abiding, temple-loving traditional Jews. And there were the tax-collectors, prostitutes, practitioners of unclean trades and lepers. In the household hierarchy were the rich property owner, the well-to-do estate manager, the peasant family, and the servants and slaves where they could be afforded. Widows, orphans, maimed, blind, sick and beggars belonged to the dependant class.

What were they doing when they were not at work? Jesus variously summed up what people did as 'eating and drinking, marrying and giving in marriage', and what they bothered themselves with as 'the cares of the world, the delight in riches and the desire for other things' and, not so flatteringly, 'dissipation and drunkenness, and the cares of this life.' Such descriptions did not come out of an era of economic hardship. We meet people fasting and feasting, attending synagogues and doing pilgrimage to Jerusalem. Children played in the market-place as those with pretensions swept by in long robes. The blind and maimed begged, as the day labourer waited in hope of a job. Sometimes there were not enough workers; a vintner visited the market several times to hire workers. People chatted and did business; someone pondered how to relieve a widow of the house that was way too big for her.

Water had to be drawn, grain ground (it took two to work a Galilean millstone), food cooked, cloth woven, clothes sewn, and hospitality extended. There was the round of dinner parties and banquets, births, circumcisions, funerals and weddings. Weddings required a wedding garment and shame on the groom who provided insufficient wine! Adultery was committed, divorces arranged, the sick and prisoners visited.

How did it balance up in drachmai and denarii? The hired hand got his denarius a day (ten litres of wheat or half a litre of olive oil for a denarius); Estate managers juggled business debts of 1000 denarii in olive oil and 2500 denarii in grain. Brothers quarrelled over their inheritance. Some women of independent means supported Jesus and his disciples on the road. When people travelled they carried food and money. Food was also bought along the way and they stayed in inns. In some places there were robbers hungry for the traveller's money. Most people payed taxes, but many still managed to save: a woman who had ten silver coins worried to distraction when one went missing (the silver mina was worth 100 denarii). The poor, maimed, blind and lame only lived by the generosity of others; they did not often get invitations to dinner parties. Jesus taught people not to hoard, but to share and lend, and not to seek redress when debts go unpaid. His disciples carried a money bag to meet their needs and gave alms to the poor. When he sent them out on a missionary journey he told them to take no gold, silver or copper, but to depend on God's miraculous provision. One of his disciples betrayed him to the authorities for thirty silver pieces, which ended up buying a field to bury strangers. Everyone dreamt of finding a treasure hidden in a field.

What possible indicators are there of serious civil unrest? On Pilate's orders some Galileans were massacred at the temple;

they must have been protesting about something. It was not uncommon for bandits to prey on travellers along the inhospitable Jerusalem to Jericho road. Barabbas committed murder in an insurrection in Jerusalem. Two outlaws were crucified with Jesus. Insufficient, I think, alongside the sheer ordinariness of the bigger picture, to conclude that Jesus worked in a situation of acute social distress. Which is not to say the atmosphere was not highly charged for other reasons. It was, as we shall see.

Due to its fertility Galilee was densely populated. There were two hundred and four settlements. Josephus reckoned the smallest village to have had a population of fifteen thousand – an exaggeration perhaps, but a pointer to a busy and prosperous region.[17] The gospels call Capernaum a *polis* indicating a substantial town, though not necessarily a city. Tiberias, the replacement capital of Galilee, was on the lake seventeen kilometres from Capernaum. The government-financed building work undertaken there must have been a considerable boost to the surrounding economies. Sepphoris, Galilee's largest city, was thirty kilometres away along the road through Magdala. The port city of Ptolemais (Acre) was twenty-five kilometres west. The great trading centre of Tyre was twenty-five kilometres north of Ptolemais. Jerusalem was one hundred and fifty kilometres south of Capernaum. The accessibility of these large centres must have been a stimulus to trade and production.[18] There is an ancient record that John the son of Zebedee supplied fish to the house of the High Priest in Jerusalem.[19] A modern writer comments on the whole country

> The soil and climate of Galilee make it by far the most fertile and productive region of the country, and its location as a hinterland to two thriving ports meant that its produce could be easily transported to lucrative markets. Galilee produced all the important agricultural items that were in demand in the ancient world.[20]

Jesus chose to make his home here in Capernaum, in a town of farmers and fishermen, tradespeople and tax collectors, soldiers and synagogue staff, and all the many others that a community with such a diverse economic and social base would carry. It was not the capital, nor even one of the biggest cities in Galilee. But unlike Nazareth, tucked away in the hills, it was a city in touch with the world.

A Day in the Life of Jesus of Nazareth (Mark 1:21–38)

Concern for exact chronology is not a mark of the gospels. Attempts to write a strict biography of Jesus have always foundered on this fact. Modern readers want events in order, so they can ponder the development of their subjects' thoughts and the build up of forces which takes place around them. We do not have the detail to write that kind of biography of Jesus. Yet the gospels do give us an extraordinary amount of information. Each evangelist draws his portrait of Jesus, using episodes, sayings and discourses in ways that may not be strictly chronological, but typical and perhaps even more illuminating than strict chronology. Papias said of Mark, that he wrote what Peter preached *faithfully and accurately, though not in order.*[21] We have already seen an example of how Luke did this in his placing of the Nazareth incident to illustrate Jesus' kingdom preaching. We will see it again and again in all of the gospels, and will be able to ponder the positive gains which are brought to us by their art, at the same time as we are careful not to read more into their ordering of events than the evidence justifies.

Mark's day in Capernaum, however, bears all the marks of being a remembered whole, told for the simple reason that it happened at the outset of Jesus' Galilean ministry.[22] It goes back, no doubt, to the preaching and reminiscences of Peter, who would have had a clear recollection of the day Jesus made his public debut in the town in which he would live and work. Luke carries it intact into his gospel; Matthew, for whatever reason omits the episode in the synagogue.

On the morning of the Sabbath Jesus went with his disciples to the synagogue service and taught. Following the service they went to the home of Peter and Andrew where Jesus healed Peter's mother-in-law and they spent the afternoon in quiet. In the evening, when the Sabbath came to an end and people could once more move about freely, crowds arrived at the door with their sick and Jesus healed them. Before daylight the following day Jesus went off alone to pray, and, when his disciples found him and urged him to return to where the crowds were waiting, he announced his intention to move on to preach in the neighbouring towns.

The Synagogue at Capernaum

The first thing a modern visitor to Capernaum sees is the ruin of the large white limestone synagogue which stands on a raised foundation amidst the rubble of the surrounding town. The positive identification of these ruins as Capernaum – the ruin was known to the Arabs as Tel Hum – was assisted by a remark of the pilgrim Egeria in AD 383, that to enter the synagogue in Capernaum it was necessary to go up many steps. It is the best preserved ruin of an ancient synagogue in Israel, and year by year more of it is being pieced together as missing parts are discovered and replaced. Its main central gallery was nine metres wide and twenty metres long, with raised galleries on either side for women and uncircumcised attenders. Authorities differ on when the present synagogue was built: some hold it to be late second or early third century, others fourth or fifth.[23] Whichever, it was probably built on the site of a previous synagogue made of black basalt, part of which lies beneath the present ruin.[24] The building of the earlier synagogue was funded by the commander of the local garrison (Luke 7:5), and must therefore have been quite new at the time Jesus attended it. Any Jewish man might be asked to be the preacher, that particular Sabbath in Capernaum it was Jesus.

First Impressions (Mark 1:21–28)

First impressions are important. It was Jesus' authority which struck the members of the synagogue that day.

> They were astounded at his teaching, for he taught them like someone who had authority, and not like the scribes. (Mark 1:22)

He had no formal rabbinical training, though like most Jewish men he would have had both an elementary education focused on reading the Scriptures, and life-long exposure to scriptural exposition and discussion by laymen and professionals. It is understandable they would have compared him with the professionals, since what struck them was the authority in his words and manner.

The Jewish scholars (scribes[25]) were very conscious of authority. Someone who taught in the synagogue was teaching the ways of God. God was the ultimate authority and he had spoken his mind to Israel at Sinai. The next authority, therefore, and in principle the ultimate accessible authority, was Moses and the Torah. Prophets had arisen from time to time in their history, speaking with an authoritative 'Thus says the Lord,' and recalling the people to the law. So the prophets were regarded as next in authority. But the law and the prophets needed to be interpreted. There was the problem of language: when the Jews returned from exile in Babylon many of them could no longer understand Hebrew and had to have the law translated into Aramaic. But there was also the need to know how to practise the demands of the law in the complex situations of everyday life. Various teachers and schools set themselves to providing this interpretation. But what authority could be claimed for this? The Pharisees believed that a God-given tradition of interpretation of the law had been passed from Moses to Joshua, and on down to Ezra and 'the men of the great synagogue' at the time of the return from Babylon. They called it the 'tradition of the elders'. From then each new generation of teachers passed on the traditions to their disciples with their own additions.[26] The authority of the scribe was, therefore, a derived authority. He might cite Moses, then perhaps the prophets, then the interpretation of the great synagogue, then would come the teaching of earlier famous rabbis like Hillel or Shammai, and finally the opinion of the present teacher on whatever the question may have been. The whole system was an appeal to authority, resting on an unbroken chain of tradition allegedly going back to Moses and, ultimately, to God.[27] No wonder the people were astounded when Jesus ignored all this and spoke God's words as though he possessed a knowledge of divine things within himself. He did not even use the prophet's introductory formula, but spoke simply and directly as one who knew. His characteristic introduction to words that he wished to impress upon his hearers was 'Truly, truly, *I* say to you …'[28] Mark uses a very strong word when he describes the people's response: they were *astounded*. This was something quite new.

Someone who assumes authority always begs questions, of course. What is its source? Is it legitimate authority, or is it usurped? Jesus' manner provoked such questions: Who is this man, that he speaks in this way? Followed perhaps by a demand that do something to demonstrate his credentials. That was the reaction he got in Nazareth, but on this particular day in Capernaum it was different.

An Exorcism

I can report from my own experience that when someone jumps up and shouts out in the middle of a church service, the effect on the congregation is electrifying. It is usually no less so for the preacher, who must suddenly respond to the totally unexpected. Politicians may be accustomed to and even revel in it, but the orderly context of worship is different. Mark describes the person who shouted at Jesus as 'a man in an unclean spirit'; Luke says he had 'a spirit of an unclean demon'. He cried, 'What do you want with us, Jesus of Nazareth? Have you come to destroy us? I know who you are. You are God's Holy One!'

The man is psychic and afraid: he senses and reacts to what is not yet apparent to the others. The presence of Jesus disturbs and angers him. The phenomenon of possession was not uncommon in the first century, amongst Jews and Gentiles, nor is it today in some communities; we will have more to say about it in chapter 10. Whether this man was previously known as a demoniac, or as a disturbed person, we do not know, nor do we know how his condition manifested itself on other occasions.

Jesus spoke directly and roughly to the spirit within him; rebuking it and telling it to 'shut up and come out of him'. The effect was dramatic. The man was seized with convulsions and screamed out as the evil spirit left him. Luke says the demon tore him so that he fell to the floor in the middle of the people, though he was unharmed by the experience.

Once more the congregation were astonished at Jesus' authority. Not that they were altogether unfamiliar with the exorcism of demoniacs. It was practised widely in the first century, as it is in many societies today. But the procedures they knew involved elaborate preparation, rituals and incantations – very different to what they had just witnessed Jesus do. Some psalms used in exorcism have been found among the Dead Sea Scrolls, and some of David's psalms were thought to have been composed for use in casting out demons.[29] Josephus describes an exorcism performed by a Jew in the presence of the Emperor Vespasian, at which he was also present:

> He [the exorcist] put to the nose of the possessed man a ring which had under its seal one of the roots prescribed by Solomon, and then, as the man smelled it, drew out the demon through his nostrils, and when the man at once fell down, adjured the demon never to come back into him, speaking Solomon's name and reciting the incantations which he had composed.[30]

All the modern exorcism procedures that I have personally heard of or seen have been similarly involved and lengthy. But Jesus, without any ritual performance, simply commanded the evil spirit to be silent and depart, and it obeyed him. It was this which amazed them. He not only *taught* with authority; he could command evil spirits. Perhaps this was one factor which later led an official enquiry to conclude that he had some alliance with the demonic powers (Mark 3:22).

Anyone can *teach* with apparent authority (though it is not as easy as it might seem), but Jesus had now *demonstrated* an authority which went beyond anything they had ever seen or thought possible. The latter reflected back on the former, so that there was no challenge at that point in Capernaum to the reality of his authority. Instead the news went out through the length and breadth of Galilee. In Nazareth they heard of what Jesus was doing in Capernaum!

A Healing in Peter's House (Mark 1:29–31)

Leaving the synagogue it was only a short walk to the house of Peter and Andrew. It is unusual to be able to make a statement like that in relation to anything in the gospel story, but in this case the house of Peter has been identified with a good degree of certainty among the remains of the first-century houses of Capernaum. Across the street in front of the synagogue were a group of houses and courtyards about twenty-five metres deep and then another street. Across that street are the ruins of an octagonal Byzantine basilica. Archaeological investigations of the foundations have shown that it rests on the remains of a Christian church which was constructed in the middle of a residential block belonging to the Capernaum of the first century. Egeria who visited Capernaum about AD 383 wrote that a church had been made out of the house of Peter, and that the walls of the house still stood as they were. Under the centre of the remains of the basilica archaeologists found the foundation of a 7 by 6.5 metre room which appears to be the house–church of the second-century Jewish Christian community in Capernaum, and before that the house of Peter and Andrew.[31]

Peter's mother-in-law was sick with a fever; Luke calls it a *great fever* and says Jesus *rebuked* it: another manifestation of his authority. The area was malarial until the draining of the swamps by the Jewish settlers of the twentieth century, so it may have been an attack of malaria.

Many are Healed

The strict Sabbath regulations prevented anything much else happening that day. A short walk was allowable, but to carry a sick person, or to come requesting healing was not. The Sabbath ended at sunset (having begun at the same time on Friday), and the townspeople lost no time in bringing their sick. Mark says the whole town gathered at the door; possibly an echo of Peter's somewhat exaggerated impression of having many descend on his house. On the other hand, it is unlikely that anyone who had witnessed what went on at the synagogue, or had heard about it, would not be there with the crowd. They brought their sick and those who were *demonized* (Mark's word).

This scene gives us an insight into another dimension of town life in the time of Jesus. The sick could not be conveniently removed to a hospital, nor paraplegics to a place of special care. Nor could those with psychic disturbances be gathered together out of the public eye. Sickness, deformity and insanity were familiar sights – at home and in the streets. If we ask ourselves how Jesus intended to carry out his programme of restoring Israel – 're-leasing the captives and setting free the oppressed' – we have the beginning of an answer here. Political subjugation was familiar enough to these people, though, in reality, not such a burden in Capernaum as they might have liked to think. But sickness, the care of the sick, and the fear of being sick, these were ever present forms of bondage. Jesus healed the sick and cast out many demons.

The healing must have lasted well into the evening. There was not time to deal with everyone and some went home, determined to return the next day when they would have a better chance. But Jesus was up well before dawn and had gone to find a lonely place to pray. When his absence became apparent, his friends went out to look for him. Finding him they informed him that the crowds wanted him, and begged him to come back. The way Mark reports this incident is peculiar. He says that *Simon* and the others *pursued* him. Peter may be differentiated from the others because it was his idea to go after Jesus, and he led the search party; it was also his story which Mark relates. The intensity of the word 'pursued', which is normally used in a hostile sense of tracking an enemy, may suggest something of his state of mind at the time; his eagerness to find Jesus and bring him back to the action.[32] But Jesus did not wish to come back. At least he would not return to stay and heal. He would move on to other towns and announce the gospel. For that, he said, is why he had come.

Such was that first memorable day in Capernaum. All of it is typical of what the gospels show us of Jesus' activity in the early days in Galilee: healing, exorcising and preaching in synagogues. Jesus' priority at this time was preaching; Luke and Mark are explicit that it was *kingdom* preaching (Mark 1:15; Luke 4:43). His task was to herald the arrival of the kingdom of God. The healing and the freeing of the spirit-oppressed was important – we will explore its meaning in chapter 10 – but strictly subservient to the announcement. Although he made Capernaum his home and would return there many times, Jesus resisted the temptation to become a 'local hero', the property of the town. We may not be far from the truth in seeing further resistance here to what he experienced as temptation to turn from his course. He was not at anyone's disposal but God's: not the town's, nor his disciples'. That surely is the significance of his escape to solitude and prayer, and of his words, 'This is the reason I have come.'

Authority

Capernaum was the location of much of Jesus' teaching and miracle working. A number of incidents in the gospels are connected with the town, and others that are not given any specific location may well have taken place there. Despite Jesus' determination not to let the town possess him, there can be no doubt that it was very privileged in what it witnessed. Jesus himself said as much when he finally turned to condemn it for its failure to respond to all that it had seen (Luke 10:15). Mark places the healing of the paralytic and the call of Levi in Capernaum (Mark 2:1ff.); Matthew and Luke add Q's account of the healing of the centurion's servant (Matthew 8:5–13). John mentions that the great discourse which Jesus delivered following the feeding of the five thousand took place in the Capernaum synagogue (John 6:59). Later, Mark tells how in the house in Capernaum Jesus used a child to teach his disciples about true greatness (Mark 9:33). Matthew, finally relates an incident concerning the payment of the temple tax (Matthew 17:24). As these events show, Capernaum's first impression – of a man endued with a remarkable authority – was reinforced again and again.

A Paraplegic Forgiven
(Matthew 9:1–8; Mark 2:1–12; Luke 5:17–26)

In one we find Jesus 'at home' after a trip away. As is often the case, Mark's telling of the story is by far the most vivid and circumstantial; he tells most of his stories in the present tense giving the impression he is relaying the verbal account of an enthusiastic story-teller. It is probably Peter's house and it is no doubt Peter's story. Matthew has pruned all features of the setting of the story. Luke has simplified it, but adds the interesting information that Jesus was seated with Pharisees and teachers of the law who had come from Galilee, Judaea and Jerusalem. This suggests that the occasion may have been a little different from the usual, and explains why they were indoors with people outside straining to hear.

Four men arrive carrying a paralysed man on a stretcher, but, because of the crowds, are unable to get him into Jesus' presence. The man would be described today as paraplegic or perhaps quadriplegic. At least his legs were useless. Of the cause of his condition we have no knowledge. Frustrated in their attempt to get their friend to Jesus through the door, the men carry him up to the flat roof.[33] (The roofs of the houses were used to escape from the heat, especially of stifling summer nights.[34]) They succeed in removing a portion of the roof and lower their friend, tied to the stretcher, into the middle of the room where Jesus is teaching.

One of the characteristics of the Jesus we meet in the gospels is that he is never nonplussed. He is able to sum up a disconcerting situation and respond in a positive and human manner. He notes the men's faith (they must have been looking down expectantly from the hole in the roof), and says to the man on the stretcher, 'Son, your sins are forgiven.' If Mark's Greek tense conveys accurately the force of Jesus' words, he was saying that *at that very moment* the man's sins were being forgiven.[35] His words sent an immediate shock through the audience, understandable if a number of them were professional theologians. It amounted to blasphemy; for who can forgive sins but God alone? Jesus was usurping the prerogative of God.

The theologians on this occasion were undoubtedly right. Only God can forgive. Admittedly if a person sins against another, it is the right of the latter to forgive if they wish to, since they are the offended party. But that is not the end of the matter. According to the thought world of the Bible, every sin is an offence against God, even when it is not deliberately aimed at him. I may be forgiven by the person I have injured, but I still need to reckon with the offence I have committed against God. Only God can forgive this. In the minds of the scholars, Jesus was either acting as though he himself were God, or he was pretending an authority given by God to forgive in his name. Either way it was dangerously close to an implied blasphemy.

So Jesus turns from the problem of the paraplegic to the questionings of his audience. He poses a question: Which is easier to say to the paraplegic, 'Your sins are forgiven,' or 'Stand up, pick up your stretcher and walk'? It is an interesting query. On the surface Jesus appeals to his ability to work miracles as validating his authority to forgive sins. Anyone could *pretend* to forgive sins. The transaction and its results are invisible, so it is impossible to know whether any real forgiveness has occurred or not. Clearly, it is easier to say someone's sins are forgiven, than it is to tell a paraplegic to walk. However, on a deeper level, we may suspect that there is some irony in Jesus' question. For this 'blasphemy' and others like it will in the end cost him his life at the hands of apparently God-honouring men. It is not so easy to say something which you think may endanger your life. Furthermore, if we accept Jesus' words that his death would be a 'ransom for many' (Mark 10:45), the purchase price of the forgiveness he is now declaring to the paraplegic will be his own life. If this was clear to him at the beginning of his ministry, healing may have seemed a good deal easier than forgiving![36]

At this point the men on the roof above must have been feeling somewhat dismayed. They came seeking healing, and their friend on the floor is now becoming the object lesson in a heated theological debate. However, Jesus does not wait for an answer to his question. It was obvious anyway. He simply declares the fact of his authority to forgive sins, and offers proof of it by telling the paraplegic to get up and go home.

It has been a question of debate amongst New Testament scholars for the past hundred years whether Jesus himself claimed to be the Messiah.[37] In recent times an increasing number of scholars have come to see that whatever he may or may not have *said* about his identity, the authoritative way he taught, forgave and did many other things implied that he understood himself to stand in a unique relationship to God.[38] To the people who heard him, Jesus' words and actions implied an authority that was either derived from God, or else was a blasphemous arrogance. They raised in an acute form the question, who is this man? The story shows that Jesus too was conscious of the question. He does not explain his authority at this point, but, in no uncertain terms, asserts and defends it. It is of a piece with the messianic understanding of himself we have seen at several points.

The Man who Amazed Jesus
(Luke 7:1–10; Matthew 8:5–13)

The healing of the Capernaum centurion's servant is remarkable for the way it too pinpoints the issue of authority as fundamental in Jesus' self-understanding. The story comes from Q, where it stood at the end of the Sermon on the Mount. Some think it is the same healing as that described in John 4:46–54, but this is unlikely, for although both involve an important person in Capernaum and a healing at which Jesus was not present, they are otherwise dissimilar. It is not impossible that reports of the other healing helped lead the centurion to his conclusion about the source of Jesus' power.

The centurion must either have been the commander of the garrison in Capernaum or a retired officer. A centurion would normally command one hundred men, which seems about the right size for the job that was required at Capernaum. He must have been very wealthy and have been established in Capernaum for a long time to have built the Jews their synagogue. The Roman army kept its officers moving, but the army of Herod Antipas may have been different.

It is important to understand that there was no direct Roman rule in Galilee at this time. In 4 BC the client kingdom of Herod the Great was split amongst his three sons, Archelaus (Judaea and Samaria), Herod Antipas (Galilee and Peraea) and

Philip (Gaulanitis [the Golan], Trachonitis and Auranitis). Archelaus' ethnarchy in Judaea and Samaria reverted to direct Roman rule in AD 6; Herod Antipas continued to rule as Tetrarch of Galilee and Peraea until AD 39. If the centurion was a Roman, it was because he was employed by Antipas' government, perhaps as an advisor in military matters. We do not know his nationality, only that he was not Jewish.

The respect in which this man was obviously held by the Jews gives an interesting balance to the usual picture of Jew–Gentile relations in the first century. The sheer unexpectedness of finding a Gentile in such relation to the Jews and the synagogue vouches for the authenticity of the story. A 'Gentile benefactor-centurion' is not a characterization anyone would have thought to invent for a military officer in Jewish–Galilean territory, though the story of Cornelius (Acts 10:1ff.) suggests that God-fearing soldiers were not unknown in the first century.[39] It was not uncommon in the ancient world for rich people to undertake great public works at their own expense, such benefactions being known as *leitourgia*.[40]

Hearing of Jesus, the centurion sent a delegation of Jewish elders to request he come and heal a much loved servant who was at the point of death. Jesus agreed to go, but while on his way was met by a second delegation of the centurion's friends conveying a message that he should not bother going to the house, but simply 'speak a word' and the servant would be healed. To us this appears rather impolite, but we need to remember the extreme difficulty and sensitivity of Jew–Gentile relationships at this time. A Gentile home was regarded by Jews as defiled and defiling. An observant Jew could not think to eat in the house of a Gentile.[41] How any self-respecting Gentile managed to love this nation in the face of such an attitude is a miracle, but the centurion's sensitivity to Jewish feelings testifies to the fact that some understood and accepted it. As he saw it there was no need to place Jesus in this awkward position. The centurion understood authority, and perceived Jesus to be a man of authority. Those with real authority do not need to do the thing themselves, it is their word of command which is all important. If Jesus really is possessed of the authority he seems to have in the realm of sickness and healing, he does not need to be present or to touch; all he needs to do is command.

When Jesus heard this he turned in amazement to the crowd. He had not found faith like this in any Israelite. It is the only place we ever hear of him being amazed at anyone's faith, and his response reveals that to his mind the centurion had properly understood the nature of his power. It is significant that it took a military man to see it. So Jesus did exactly as he had asked, he did not visit his home, but when the friends returned, they found the servant alive and well.

A Second Key to Understanding Jesus

Thus, if the kingdom of God is a first key for unlocking the meaning of Jesus' ministry, his authority is a second. And of course the two are linked, for a kingdom implies a king. Jesus behaved as one endued with enormous authority, in part at least because he believed himself commissioned by God and empowered to carry out his mission. His spectacular success in healing and exorcism makes it risky lightly to dismiss him. It is this authority which makes Jesus different from other healers and exorcists in the past and in the present. Though there may be and have been many healers and exorcists, their art is complex and their results uncertain; I know of none other who succeeded by a mere word of command.

The appropriate response to genuine authority is belief and obedience. If someone makes a pronouncement within their sphere of authority then it should be believed. Not to believe it is to dispute either their authority or their competence. If they give an order, the appropriate response is obedience. To disobey is to challenge their authority. The centurion saw that in the area of sickness and health Jesus was endued with full authority and could therefore be called on for help. Once Jesus had agreed to his request, the centurion could be sure that his servant would be made well. And precisely because Jesus healed by an authority that was vested in him, and not by magic or ritual or psychic contact, in the centurion's eyes it was quite unnecessary that he should endanger Jesus' reputation with the Jews by bringing him to his home. He was willing to rely on Jesus' word.

Here we see the nature of faith as Jesus understood it and commended it. It is not a religious inclination, but a simple willingness to accept his authority and rely on his word. Its best example was a man of the military, and he understood it because he practised it every day of his working life. Jesus was to say to many people, 'Your faith has made you well.' These were not people of religious inclination, but those whose desperate need and confidence in his competence drove them to come and ask for help.

Notes

[1] Josephus, *War*, 3.516ff. Josephus elsewhere mentions being thrown from his horse in the region at the north end of the sea of Galilee and being taken to a village named Cepharnocus. Some take this to be a variant spelling of Capernaum.

[2] C. Kopp, *The Holy Places of the Gospels*, 174–6.

[3] Josephus, *War*, 2.635; 3.531.

[4] S. Wachsman, *The Sea of Galilee Boat: An Extraordinary 2000 Year Old Discovery*.

[5] V. Tzaferis, *Excavations at Capernaum*.

[6] This road is shown on many recent maps as the Via Maris (Way of the Sea). According to B.J. Beitzel ('The Via Maris in Literary and Cartographic Sources', 65–75) this is a mistake. The Via Maris shown on mediaeval maps is the crusader road from Capernaum to Ptolemaus.

[7] Josephus, *War*, 1.204–207; *History*, 14.158–162.

[8] Josephus, *War*, 1.303–313; *History*, 14.413–433.

[9] Josephus, *War*, 2.55–59; *History*, 17.271–298.

[10] Theissen, *Shadow*, uses such notions to paint the social background of the gospels.

[11] Note the comments of F. Millar, *The Roman Near East 31 BC–AD 337*, 342: 'They [the gospels] remain authoritative testimony to the concerns, and the historical consciousness, of Jewish society, in Galilee and Jerusalem above all, before the fall of the temple'.

[12] R.A. Horsley (*Galilee: History, Politics, People*, 219) gives the impression of a triple tax.

[13] Josephus, *War*, 1.425.

[14] Josephus, *History*, 20.219–223.

[15] Josephus, *History*, 15.365; 16.64.

[16] Josephus, *History*, 15.305–316.

[17] Josephus, *War*, 3.43. Josephus claimed to have raised an army of 100,000 in Galilee in preparation for the Roman invasion (*War*, 2.576; 2.583). Millar comments 'It is not necessary to take these figures literally; but the impression of a dense population, in large villages and small towns, is not misleading' (*Roman Near East*, 347).

[18] It is hotly debated how much trade and intercourse occurred between these big centres and the villages of Galilee. It is hard to credit Horsley's picture of a peasantry so heavily taxed that trade was the sole preserve of the government. He is correct in saying that Tyrian coins found in Galilean towns do not necessarily mean they were trading directly with Tyre, but they do indicate trade links, albeit indirect. R.A. Horsley, *Galilee*, 202–221; *Archeology, History and Society in Galilee*, 66–87. S. Freyne argues that the Galileans of Jesus' time enjoyed peace and a reasonable standard of living (*Galilee*, 155–207).

[19] *Gospel of the Nazaraeans*. See E. Hennecke, *New Testament Apocrypha* I, 152; Wenham, *Enigma*, 41–42.

[20] Freyne, *Galilee*, 15. Cf, Josephus, *War*, 3.41ff.

[21] Eusebius, *Ecclesiastical History*, 3.39.15.

[22] Taylor, *Mark*, 91.

[23] For the various points of view see L.I. Levine, *Ancient Synagogues Revealed*.

[24] M. Avi-Yonah, 'Some Comments on the Capernaum Excavations', 60; G.L. Kroll, *Auf den Spuren Jesu*, 288ff.

[25] The scribe (*grammateus*) was trained in writing skills as well as the interpretation and application of Scripture.

[26] In Jesus' time there was some conflict and diversity amongst teachers of different traditions, but the people leaned toward the teaching of Pharisaic scribes

to the extent that the Sadducees had to acquiesce with their procedures, at least in public services at the temple. Even among the Pharisees there were differences, as the schools of Hillel and Shammai, roughly contemporary with Jesus, demonstrate. See Riesner, *Lehrer*, 173–6.

[27] *Mishnah Aboth* 1:1ff.

[28] Matthew 5:18; 6:2, 5 etc.; Mark 3:28; 8:12, etc.; Luke 4:24; 11:51, etc.; John 1:51; 5:19, etc.

[29] 11QPs (*DJD*, IV, 92) says David composed four psalms for singing over 'the stricken', probably meaning 'the possessed'. According to rabbinic tradition Psalm 91 was one such psalm. A number of psalm fragments from Qumran also look like they were composed for the purpose of exorcism (11QPsAp[a]; J.P. van der Ploeg, 'Un petit rouleau de Psaumes Apocryphes'). The 'Song of the Wise Man' from Cave 4 speaks of the wise man declaring God's splendour to terrify the various evil spirits, especially those that strike suddenly to drive people insane (4Q510; *DJD*, VII, 216; cf. *DJD*, VIII, 226, 228).

[30] Josephus, *History*, 8.45–48.

[31] V. Corbo, 'The Church of the House of St. Peter at Capernaum', 71–76; Kroll, *Spuren*, 294f.

[32] Luke suppresses any mention of Peter at this point (Luke 4:42). It is the crowds who seek and find Jesus and want him to come back. One motive for this rearrangement is that Luke deliberately does not introduce the disciples until chapter 5. However, he also had no reason to single Peter out in the negative way that Mark did.

[33] Evidence of external staircases have been found in the ruins of the first century buildings in the immediate vicinity of Peter's house. They generally lead up from an enclosed courtyard. The stretcher bearers apparently managed to get into the courtyard, but as Jesus was in the house and the courtyard was crowded, they could get no further.

[34] During an early morning swim in the Sea of Galilee after a sleepless summer night, I swam out and pulled myself up onto the side of a small boat that was moored about fifty metres from the shore. The owner was fast asleep in the bottom of the boat and did not stir as I slid back into the water and returned to the shore.

[35] See B.M. Metzger, *A Textual Commentary on the Greek New Testament*, 77; C.E.B. Cranfield, *The Gospel according to St Mark*, 97.

[36] I received this insight from a lecture of Bruce Smith at Moore Theological College.

[37] The original study was W. Wrede's *The Messianic Secret*. Wrede held that while Jesus did not see himself as the Messiah, the church did and dealt with the anomaly by inventing the notion that Jesus did, but kept it a secret.

[38] Jeremias, *New Testament Theology*, 250.

[39] Two such unlikely stories in a defence of Christianity to cultured and connected Gentiles (Theophilus may have been a military man) would tempt a critic to see them as the author's creation, were it not for the fact that the Capernaum centurion is part of Q.

[40] For an account of the ancient benefaction system see M.I. Finley, *The Ancient Economy*, 150–154.

[41] The story of Peter and Cornelius in Acts 10–11 revolves around the unlawful and unprecedented action of visiting and eating in a Gentile home. See also John 18:28.

Chapter 9

All The King's Men

Kingdom and People

When Jesus was finally arrested he was questioned first about 'his disciples and his teaching' (John 18:19). Evidently the extent and nature of his following was of some concern to the authorities. The proclamation of a new kingdom raises weighty questions: who is to rule being the obvious first. 'Kingdom of God' suggests God is the ultimate ruler, but who would rule for him in the world? The Jews expected someone in the line of David to fill that role. We have already seen evidence that Jesus saw himself that way, though for his contemporaries his relationship to the kingdom still hung as an unanswered question. But a kingdom is more than a king; it is a king and his people and the land within which they live. A king without a people is a joke. According to the vision of Daniel, which so influenced Jesus' thought and language, the king of God's kingdom would rule with and over a rescued Israel and over every nation, tribe and language group (Daniel 7). One presumes that all this is to happen on earth. It is important then that we pay some attention now to the question of Jesus' following and how he saw it.

The First Followers

We have seen the startling sense of authority which made such an impression on Jesus' first hearers, and have observed how this authority manifested itself in different ways. We are now struck with the authority inherent in the way he began to lay claim to the lives of human beings. It must have been very exciting for those around Jesus, hearing him teach with authority, watching him expel evil spirits, heal sick people, forgive a man his sins. But there was a world of difference between these external things, and having him turn personally to you and claim your service.

> And passing along by the Sea of Galilee he saw Simon and Andrew the brother of Simon casting their nets into the sea, for they were fishermen. And Jesus said to them, 'Come after me, and I will make you fishermen of men.' And immediately they left the nets and followed him.
> (Mark 1:16–17; cf. Matthew 4:18–20)

The same pattern was repeated with others. James and John were also fishermen, in a partnership with Simon and Andrew (Mark 1:19–20; Matthew 4:21–22). Levi (or Matthew) was one of the officials in the customs office in Capernaum. He was actually at work there when Jesus approached him. 'Follow me,' Jesus said, and he got up and went after him there and then (Mark 2:14; Matthew 9:9; Luke 5:27f.).

The earnest authority of Jesus' claim on people's lives may be illustrated from two other encounters in the gospels. In the first, when Jesus called a man to follow him, the man asked permission to first go and bury his father. There was no higher duty for a Jew than the burial of the dead![1] When it was the man's own father, it was monstrous that Jesus should not immediately send him off to perform his duty. Yet Jesus refused, with the shocking words, 'You follow me, and leave the dead to bury their own dead' (Matthew 8:21f.; Luke 9:59f.). So saying, he trampled upon one of the most sacred traditions of his people, but underlined with startling clarity his own authority and the supreme urgency of the task to which he was calling people.[2] On another occasion, when a young nobleman asked Jesus how he might be sure of entering the kingdom of God, Jesus told him to sell all his possessions for the poor, and then come and be his disciple. Stricken with grief, the man departed; he was rich and could not bring himself to part with his possessions. After he went Jesus made it clear to his disciples that the man had not simply exercised an allowable option, but had refused the kingdom of God.[3] Not surprisingly his other followers were amazed and dismayed (Mark 10:17–31; Matthew 19:16–30; Luke 18:18–30).

What is the meaning of the sovereign manner in which Jesus laid claim to these people's lives? Martin Hengel, in an important inquiry into the possible background against which these 'calls' could be understood, examined the way rabbis and revolutionaries in the New Testament period, and Old Testament prophets earlier, recruited their disciples. He came to the startling conclusion that Jesus' practice can be likened to none of these, but only to the way in which, in the Old Testament, God himself called his prophets.[4] In other words, we are dealing with a man who, at the level of authority, dealt with others in a kingly, almost God-like manner.

It is not necessary to imagine, as some have, that Jesus called these men on the first occasion that he met them, and that they responded in blind faith to some sort of irresistible personal magnetism. Mark and Matthew easily give that impression, but this is a function of the brevity of their accounts. What they are really emphasizing is Jesus' authority to command, and the immediate following which is the proper response to his call. It is clear from John's Gospel that Jesus had had considerable previous contact with some of these men, and Luke tells a story which suggests that the call of the four partners may have had more to it than is told by Mark and John.

A Remarkable Catch of Fish (Luke 5:1–11)

Some have dismissed Luke's story of the miraculous catch of fish
as a legend which grew up in the early church, but this just does
not square with the fact that Peter and John were well-known
teachers at the time Luke was writing his gospel. They had both
been in Jerusalem and throughout Israel, and had travelled widely
in Asia Minor. They must have been asked to tell their stories
repeatedly and in many places; it is difficult to see how a legend
could gain currency at this time. Whether Luke had met either of
them personally or not, he would certainly have known of them
through Paul. He would have been interested in knowing how
they had become disciples, especially given the brevity of Mark's
account. The way in which the story highlights Peter's confession
of sinfulness is an indication that it originated with him.[5]

The incident took place after Jesus had been teaching the
crowds by the lakeside. To deal with so many people he got
Peter to moor his boat a little from the shore and used it as a
pulpit. A better arrangement for open air preaching would be
hard to find. It was a method he evidently used more than once
(Mark 4:1), and shows him to have been a practical man. When
he had finished his teaching he told Peter to take the boat out
into deep water and set the nets. It was a good way of dispersing
the crowds. Peter protested that they had fished the whole
night previous and caught nothing. When it came to boats and
fishing he was the expert. Whether he wanted to warn the
carpenter-cum-teacher not to expect too much, or whether he
was unaccustomed to receiving orders in his own boat, it is
clear that as far as he was concerned, out on the water he was
not to be thought of as a disciple. Nevertheless he did what
Jesus asked. The result was a catch of fish, so large that they had
to call their companions to save their nets from tearing. Being a
keen fisherman myself, I cannot help imagining that moment –
there is nothing so enthralling as pulling in a heavy net. I am
sure that with the shouting and swearing that must have gone

on, no one gave Jesus another thought until the last fish was thrown into the boat. Only as the excitement subsided, brows were wiped and the catch surveyed, did it hit them. Peter was overwhelmed with guilt and fear: he fell to his knees in front of Jesus and said, 'Go away from me Lord for I am a sinful man.' Jesus told him not to be afraid, that from then on he would be catching people.

There follows immediately in Luke the story of the leper, which Matthew, Mark and Luke all utilize in different contexts. In Luke it answers Peter's confession of sinfulness, which receives no response in the story of the catch of fish. Luke may see a similarity between Peter's call and that of Isaiah (Isaiah 6:1–8). Isaiah has a vision of God's glory at which he becomes stricken with guilt and fear and exclaims, 'Woe is me! For I am as good as dead. I am a man of unclean lips and I live in the midst of a people of unclean lips, for my eyes have seen the King, the Lord of Hosts.' An angel then brings a hot coal from the altar, touches Isaiah's mouth with it, and says, 'This has touched your lips; your iniquity is taken away and your sin purged.' The Lord then gives Isaiah his call to be his mouthpiece to the nation. Just as Isaiah's guilt was dealt with before he was appointed to his prophetic mission, so Luke suggests through the story of the leper that Jesus is willing and able to cleanse Peter for his service. If I have not misread Luke's purpose at this point, Peter is depicted as overwhelmed by the realization of the holy in Jesus' presence, strongly underlining Hengel's point that Jesus' call of his disciples is best understood against the background of God's call of his prophets.

Sinners

Matthew's response to his call was to invite all his friends to a banquet to meet Jesus and some of his disciples (Mark 2:13–17; Matthew 9:9–13; Luke 5:27–32). It says a great deal about the effect that Jesus had on people. Andrew's first reaction to meeting

Jesus was to introduce him to Simon; Philip's was to go and find
Nathaniel. Matthew too wants to show Jesus off to his friends,
and he is not deterred by the fact that they are not religious.
There must have been something about him which disarmed the
common fear of exposing irreligious friends to one who is publicly aligned with God.

Matthew was a man of some wealth to be able to hold the size
of banquet that Mark suggests. Given his profession, this is not
surprising. Duty collection was a lucrative business. Direct taxes
were collected by officials of the government (in this case Herod
Antipas' government), but the right to collect customs duties
from a particular region were sold by tender to tax farmers. Only
wealthy individuals or business consortiums could enter the
bidding. The successful applicant contracted to return a certain
fixed amount to the government, but kept whatever could be
earned beyond that. The task could then be subcontracted to
smaller tax farmers or put in the hands of employees. Money was
to be made at every level, and it was expected that a customs
collector would be dishonest.[6] We meet these customs men
frequently in the gospels.

The many tax collectors and 'sinners' who came to Matthew's
home on that particular day explode the popular notion that tax
collectors were lonely individuals ostracized by their society, and
that Jesus was drawn to this class of people because of their social
wretchedness.[7] It is certainly true that the Pharisees regarded them
as reprobate, and that anyone accepting their hospitality would
have been seen as contaminating themselves, but they evidently
had their own considerable circle, and the benefits of money to
ease their plight. The 'sinners' were people whose existence in the
covenant community was compromised because of their neglect
of the law. They included those whose business interests conflicted
with strict observance of the law. Tax collectors were included, but
so were people who associated too much with Gentiles, dealt in
unclean commodities (e.g. pigs), indulged in immoral occupations
and the like. Many of them probably did well on it. It was

inevitable that Jesus would attract criticism, particularly from the purity-conscious Pharisees,[8] for accepting their hospitality.

Purity

The principles of purity and the practices which assured it are difficult for non-Jews to understand, though analogous ideas are still to be found in other societies.[9] The law of Moses defines two realms, the clean and the unclean, which correspond in an outward, symbolic way to the spiritual realms of the holy and the unholy (that which belongs with God and that which does not). At the outset Israel was chosen by God and declared holy and clean; the Gentile nations were seen as unclean. This division was symbolized and emphasized by the declaration of some foods as clean and others as unclean. Israelites were forbidden to eat unclean meats like pork; if they did, they became unclean like Gentiles and could not consider themselves part of the holy people until their uncleanness was removed. Many other things were defiling: menstruation, contact with a corpse, and so on. Such defilement did not actually remove one from the people of God, but to a degree which is not fully agreed upon by scholars today, created distance from God and needed to be removed. Furthermore, the uncleanness could be communicated to others directly by deliberate or accidental touch, and indirectly, for example by someone sitting on a chair in which an unclean person had previously sat. Indirect defilement was known as *midras* uncleanness. How seriously all this was taken can be seen from the fact that devout Jews would not live in the new city of Tiberias which Herod Antipas built on the Sea of Galilee, a few kilometres south of Capernaum. An ancient cemetery was uncovered during the construction which threatened to defile anyone who lived close to it.

Social intercourse in Jesus' day was largely determined by these laws of purity and the elaboration of them in 'the tradition of the elders'. There was a state of purity in which one could commune with God and his people, and most wanted to be in it as much as they could. The more pious you were the more careful you were. No one could be clean all the time – attendance at a funeral was defiling, even though it was regarded as a necessary act of piety – but if you were serious you took steps to minimize defilement and to remove impurity as soon as possible. In particular, it was risky to eat in the home of a neighbour, because you could never be sure that the food you were eating had been properly tithed, nor that the one who had prepared the food was not in her menstrual period. There were also gradations of purity related to various ritual requirements. The priests were obliged to eat the food offerings that were their due in a certain state of purity. Other ritual tasks required an even higher degree of purity. Some people sought to maintain a higher degree of purity than the law demanded of them.[10] The Pharisees are a case in point; because of their strict adherence to the law, they could safely eat in each other's homes without the risk of unconscious defilement. They also had ritual washings to protect them against becoming unclean from inadvertently touching impure things and persons in the market place (Mark 7:3–4). Strange as their practices seem to us, the Pharisees were far from extreme judged by the standards of their day. Members of the Dead Sea community lived in the state of purity demanded of priests at the temple. Full ritual immersion was required before a meal could be eaten.[11] There is evidence in the New Testament that ordinary Jews by and large observed at least the more important traditions of purity, and would have been anxious about knowingly remaining long in a state of impurity. Peter, for example, on one occasion protested that he had never in his life eaten anything unclean (Acts 10:14).

Midwife of the New Age

It was inevitable then that Jesus would create a scandal by accepting Matthew's invitation. Mark tells us that the Pharisees questioned Jesus' disciples on why he had shared the food of such people. But it was probably not only the Pharisees who were surprised. The most insightful, though not the most historical, scene in Zefferelli's *Jesus of Nazareth* is where Peter protests against Jesus' intention to go to the house of Matthew and tries to explain to him that his mission and reputation will be put in jeopardy if he does.

Jesus' answer to the Pharisees' complaint was to liken himself to a doctor who must go to where the sick are whatever the risk of 'infection'; his mission was to sinners. Despite the constant criticism and hostility it drew upon him, he continued to associate with such people throughout his ministry, so that he came to be lampooned as 'a friend of tax collectors and sinners' (Matthew 11:19; Luke 7:34). In truth there was no person or group with which Jesus refused to associate. He ate with tax collectors when invited (sometimes he invited himself), and with Pharisees. The question was not whom *he* would accept but who would accept *him*, and who would accept those whom he accepted. It was 'the acceptable year of the Lord' and Jesus made that acceptance felt.

Jesus is revealed in this incident as more than the herald of the new age. To change his metaphor a little, he also saw himself as a midwife helping people into that age. To do this he was prepared to come into close, sometimes defiling contact with those he sought to help. However, he did not leave people where he found them. Jesus showed them God in a way that made them want to know more. Judging from the gospels his strategy was successful, for many from these unexpected quarters turned to God. The parable of the two men in the temple (Luke 18:9–14) shows that Jesus may even have seen their response as something of a model of what it should have

been like for everyone. The 'sinners' were under no illusions
about where they stood in relation to the law of God, and
about where they would stand in any judgement. They
identified Jesus as coming from God, and were able to
recognize God's forgiveness when it was held out to them in
the concrete form of Jesus' accepting fellowship. The religious,
however, were able to justify themselves in their own eyes, and
failed to see their need. The Pharisee in the parable thought his
moral achievement gave him standing with God and was
unable to see beyond this to the real state of his heart, and to
the reality of his alienation from God.[12] The tax collector, who
acknowledged the truth about himself and begged God for
mercy, was accepted by God and went home his friend.

Sinners and the Kingdom

What did Jesus think sinners gained by their 'conversion'? His
was no preparatory mission to get people into a fit state to meet
their God. In meeting Jesus and turning to God they were actually entering the kingdom, and beginning to experience its
fellowship. 'Truly I say to you [Pharisees], the tax collectors and
prostitutes are entering the kingdom of God ahead of you'
(Matthew 21:31).

This notion of entering the kingdom is characteristic of Jesus;
it is found on his lips in all the gospels, and only once in the rest of
the New Testament.[13] It is one of the indications that he saw the
kingdom, not as later rabbis did as the rule of heaven to which
one submitted obediently in hope of a place in the new age, but as
the new age itself. Jesus' gospel declared God's acceptance of his
afflicted people (the poor); the only thing which kept them out
was their own refusal to enter. He rebuked his disciples for
keeping children away and declared their inclusion in the
kingdom, adding the dictum 'Whoever does not *receive* the
kingdom of God like a child shall not *enter* it' (Mark 10:13–16).

The kingdom of God is like the promised land, which Israel received as its inheritance and entered.

The Kingdom and Israel

What, then, did Jesus understand was happening when a person entered the kingdom of God? Clearly they were restored to God's favour, but what did this mean in terms of their communal identity? Were they now removed from Israel and constituted as the church? There are clear indications that far from removing people from the ancient community, Jesus saw himself restoring them to true membership of Israel as the people of God. He said he had been sent only 'to the lost sheep of the house of Israel' (Matthew 15:24). Of the restored tax collector Zacchaeus, he said, 'Today salvation has come to this house, because he too is a son of Abraham – for the Son of man came to seek and to save the lost' (Luke 19:9–10).

Did Jesus see himself appointed to restore fallen sinners to the main body of the people, or did he see the whole nation as lost? His three parables of the lost sheep, the lost coin and the lost son could suggest the former: the main flock is intact, the shepherd seeks the one lost sheep. But this was hardly his meaning. The parables were not intended to confirm the position of those who saw themselves as righteous, but to help them understand his mission to sinners. He desired that everyone should perceive their lostness and come home. Like John the Baptist before him Jesus viewed the whole people as spiritually apostate on the one hand, and in a state of abandonment on the other; lost and needing to be found, scattered and needing to be gathered. These are images of Israel's exile; behind them stands Ezekiel's oracle of doom on Israel's leaders, who far from shepherding God's flock, exploited it for their own purposes, leaving the sheep harassed and helpless (Ezekiel 34:11–16). The lost sheep are Israel's elect; alienated from their God and cut off from their rightful blessing, but whom

God has promised to gather, restore, feed and shepherd himself. In a collection of sheep and shepherd sayings in John 10 Jesus characterizes himself as the shepherd Messiah who comes and is recognized by his sheep. Unlike the hireling who scatters, the good shepherd comes to gather the flock and give them eternal life. When he calls the sheep they hear and follow him. Jesus addressed his disciples as 'little flock' (Luke 12:32), which means little Israel. It was little, because so few gave heed to his call. Jesus, then, sees himself doing nothing less than gathering and restoring scattered Israel.

Celebration

Once we see that Jesus construed his eating with sinners – his offer of friendship and their acceptance of it – as tantamount to entrance into the kingdom of God, we see how appropriate was the conviviality and celebration which got him his reputation as 'a wine drinker and a glutton' as well as 'a friend of tax collectors and sinners'. Their meals together were an expression of their new relationship with Jesus, which was celebrated as though it was a new relationship with God. According to Luke, Jesus told the parable of the lost son (Luke 15:11–32) in response to those who criticized him for eating with tax collectors and sinners. On the surface it is a magnificent picture of a father's love for a rebellious and runaway son, and his willingness to welcome and reinstate him when he finally comes home. But there are brush strokes in the artistry of the parable which carry us to a deeper understanding. While the returning son is still a long way off the father runs to meet him; hardly a God whose acceptance awaits full repentance and reparation. Jesus' apparently reckless giving of himself to table fellowship with sinners is an expression of the Father's overwhelming desire for the return of his lost sons. The extravagance of the father's welcome, which so arouses the jealousy of the 'righteous' brother, mirrors Jesus' enjoyment of fellowship with sinners. Far from being a sober persuading of them to change their lives, this was an overflow of celebration of the wonder that 'my son was dead and is alive again, he was lost and is found.'

In the short episode which in Mark follows the story of Jesus' meal with Matthew and his friends, Jesus is asked why he and his disciples did not observe any tradition of fasting (Mark 2:18–22; Matthew 9:14–17; Luke 5:33–9). Fasting was a mark of spiritual earnestness and penitent entreaty for the forgiveness of God and the coming of his kingdom. Pharisees fasted twice weekly, and fasting was also common amongst the disciples of the Baptist – logical, since they were earnestly and pointedly waiting for the coming of the Messiah and his kingdom. But Jesus replied that for his disciples fasting was inappropriate, for the bridegroom was with them.

This was a weighty answer, since, according to Matthew's Gospel, those who put the question were disciples of John the Baptist.[14] We have already seen that John likened Jesus to a bridegroom, and himself to the groom's friend.[15] Not only does Jesus see himself as the bridegroom, but he speaks as though the wedding is already in progress. His disciples – and they now included tax collectors and sinners – were the guests, and the celebration which was taking place could only be the wedding feast of the messianic kingdom. An ancient Jewish commentary on Exodus explains

> This world is like the betrothal, for it says: *And I will betroth you to me in faithfulness* (Hosea 2:20) ... The actual marriage ceremony will take place in the messianic days, as it says: *For your Maker is your husband* (Isaiah 54:5).[16]

The ideas behind this quotation stem from the Old Testament image of God as the husband of his people, divorced from them because of their unfaithfulness, but to be reunited in a new marriage at the beginning of the new age.[17] Jesus' use of the parable of the bridegroom shows that he saw himself already in the days of the kingdom. As Jesus understood his position, celebration was not an option but a duty. His will was that all should share it, even tax collectors and sinners. Those like the Pharisees – perhaps even some of the disciples of John – who would not enter into this joy were overlooking the presence of the kingdom; refusing to enter when it stood wide open before them.

Jesus' refusal to fast, or to let his disciples fast, was thus not a quirk, but a consequence of a new state of affairs which had broken into Israel's life with the commencement of his kingdom-heralding mission in Galilee. God had returned to accept and marry his people. Everyone knew that a wedding was a time for great rejoicing. Even rabbis would stop their study to join in the celebrations. There is a story told of Rabbi Tarphon (about AD 100) who was sitting teaching his disciples when a bride passed by. He ordered his disciples to accompany her and had his mother and wife bathe, bedeck themselves and dance in front of her until she reached the house of the bridegroom.[18]

On one occasion Jesus was discoursing on the subject of table fellowship, when a man interrupted with the exclamation 'Blessed is the one who eats bread in the kingdom of God.' Jesus responded with the parable of the banquet (Luke 14:15–24), showing how naturally he associated the kingdom of God with feasting and celebration. In the parable of the ten maidens the kingdom is likened again to a wedding feast (Matthew 25:1–13). Jesus also spoke of the many who will come from east and west to sit at table 'with Abraham, Isaac and Jacob in the kingdom of heaven' (Matthew 8:11). Each of these examples looks to a future beyond Israel's refusal of the opportunity which was before her at the present time. We shall examine this more closely later on. What is clear for the moment is the direct relationship between the celebration which will characterize the consummated kingdom, and the happy occasions Jesus was enjoying with sinners.

Many Disciples

It is in Mark's description of the dinner party at Matthew's house that he makes the first explicit mention of disciples. He says that some of Jesus' disciples attended the feast, and then, almost as though realizing that he had not mentioned disciples up to this point, adds a comment that Jesus had 'many disciples' who 'followed him' (Mark 2:15). We have already seen how Jesus called Peter, Andrew, James, John and Matthew to follow him, and are accustomed to thinking of these men and of the twelve as 'the disciples'. It is a little confusing, therefore, suddenly to encounter many more. How many disciples did Jesus have, how did he acquire them, and what was their status and significance?

To begin with we should note that nowhere in the gospels is the call of Peter, Andrew, James, John and Matthew equated simply with the call to discipleship. Since each of these was destined for membership of the twelve designated 'apostles', and called to actually accompany Jesus, it is possible that the manner of their call was not typical of many who were nonetheless counted disciples. This is a little confusing because the gospel writers appear to tell their stories to exemplify the right response to Jesus' lordship. They model what they hope will be true of ordinary disciples in their own day who, through the preaching of the gospel, would hear themselves called to 'come follow' Jesus, and would meta-phorically or literally leave everything to do so.

Nevertheless, during the time of Jesus' ministry there is little to suggest that this was the only way into discipleship, and much which implies that Jesus was happy to regard as disciples all who came to him and believed his message. In each of the gospels there is evidence of a group of disciples wider than the twelve.[19] Luke notes the presence of 'multitudes' of disciples (6:17; 19:37). John knows of secret disciples (12:42). Joseph of Arimathea named a disciple (John 19:38), but could scarcely have been a companion of Jesus. It is unlikely that the gospels are using the terminology of a later time to describe Jesus' pre-Easter followers as they are not called disciples (*mathetai*) outside the gospels, except in Acts. It is more probable that the large group who considered themselves Jesus' disciples during his ministry, continued to think of themselves in the same way for a while after his departure.

What was a Disciple?

All this raises the question of how well the form of discipleship which Jesus allowed to develop around him can be understood from contemporary parallels. There is some evidence from the time of schools where anyone able to pay the entrance fee could attend and might then be called a 'disciple' of the teacher.[20] More commonly, however, teachers of the law of Moses[21] had disciples, who in modern terms are best thought of as apprentices. They studied, worked and often lived with their master. Their goal was to memorize as much as they could of his teachings and learn from his way of life. At the same time they were expected to serve him – as slaves, except that a teacher could not expect disciples to take off his shoes or wash his feet –reducing them to the level of slaves, which they were not.[22] The aim was to carry on one's master's teaching after him. Although it was a worthy aim to 'raise up many disciples',[23] it is hard to think that one rabbi would have had more than a few this close to him. Rabbi Johanan ben Zakkai, a survivor of the holocaust in AD 70, had five.[24] There is some parallel here to the group of twelve whom Jesus singled out, but not to the multitude of disciples. How are we to think of these?

From time to time in the New Testament we encounter disciples of John the Baptist. John had a group of workers who helped him with his baptizing; these were certainly known as disciples. Andrew was one of them before he transferred to Jesus. But it is likely that all whom John baptized were seen as his disciples in a wider sense; this would explain how groups of them were encountered in later years. The word 'disciple' was used in a loose way of anyone who followed someone's teachings, much as the Pharisees on one occasion chided a man for being Jesus' disciple and declared themselves to be disciples of Moses (John 9:28).

How were Jesus' Disciples Distinguished?

In this respect, then, John and Jesus may have operated in a similar fashion, preaching to great crowds, appealing to the whole nation, and desiring a positive response from all. E. Fascher thinks Jesus' (and John's) open air teaching of crowds distinguished them from the rabbinic teachers.[25] However, unlike Jesus' disciples, John's were sacramentally differentiated from the rest of the people by baptism, even if they were not among his group of workers. In this respect Jesus' movement also contrasted with that of the Teacher of Righteousness of the Dead Sea community. Like John and Jesus, the Teacher also believed that the restoration of Israel was near, and like them he identified his followers with the true Israel. However, he separated them from the common herd and created an exclusive community which was difficult to join without an elaborate noviate. Only after a year of testing did one get anywhere near the communal meals enjoyed by the brotherhood. Jesus made it much easier, in effect, opening his table indiscriminately to every Israelite and letting their response determine who was 'a son of Abraham' (Luke 19:9).

The gospels are silent about any line of demarcation between those who were and were not disciples. It appears that Jesus allowed people to attach and detach themselves from him at will. This is one of the reasons we hesitate to speak of him founding a 'church' during his lifetime. His word alone was the instrument which drew people closer or drove them away. He considered all who did his Father's will as his true family (Mark 3:35), but they were Israel renewed, not some new grouping. For as long as Jesus was calling upon Israel to believe in his kingdom and inherit Israel's blessings, it was counterproductive to draw a hard line between his disciples and the rest of the nation.

However, it would be a mistake to think that Jesus had a casual attitude to discipleship. Outsiders may well have identified people as his disciples just by their enthusiasm for his teaching, but we note that Jesus encouraged his hearers to see themselves as his disciples in a deeper sense. Luke tells us that on one occasion Jesus addressed great crowds on the cost of discipleship (Luke 14:25–35). He wanted them to be his disciples, but not without due consideration that following meant going all the way, to death if necessary. The Sermon on the Mount is a discourse on discipleship, which again Jesus addressed to the crowds. At the beginning he speaks of being hated 'on account of the Son of man' (Luke 6:22); at the end is a challenge for genuine allegiance: 'Why do you call me Lord, Lord (Rabbi, Rabbi?), and not do what I tell you?' (Luke 6:46). Allegiance to himself was, therefore, one of his ministry objectives. If he saw himself as Israel's king this is understandable. It was not to separate them from Israel that Jesus drew people to himself, but to gather them as true, restored Israel. Nowhere is this intention more poignantly expressed than in his cry as he contemplated his last journey to the capital: 'O Jerusalem, Jerusalem, you who kill the prophets and stone those who are sent to you! How often would I have gathered your children together as a hen gathers her brood under her wings, but you would not!' (Luke 13:34). John the Baptist did nothing like this. He pointed people away from himself, to God and to the 'coming one'. Jesus sought to gather Israel, by gathering them to himself.

Jesus' method was to address all comers with his gospel teaching, and to heal their sick. His teaching on discipleship, demanding as it was, was not restricted to the inner group. People could make up their own minds about whether they were with him or not. Most of them, when they had heard, went home, either as his disciples, to act and hope as he had taught, or to forget him and get on with their lives. He instituted nothing to hold people in this relationship; they remained free to come and go at will. There was one occasion when many of his disciples withdrew (John 6:66). Jesus had no desire for numbers if they were not firmly committed to his teaching.

The Twelve

Against the background of mounting pressure from the large crowds, Jesus spent a full night in the hills in prayer, and the next day selected from among his many disciples twelve to be permanently in his presence and to be sent out to preach (Mark 3:13–19; Luke 6:12–16). Luke says he named them apostles (6:13).

Apostle (*apostolos*) is a curious term. In normal Greek it meant a ship, fleet of ships, or a naval expedition. It is seldom found outside of Christian writings with the sense of a messenger. Behind this usage probably lies the Jewish *shaliah*, an agent and legal representative of a sending person.[26] In designating the twelve this way Jesus was commissioning them as mouthpieces in his absence.

They were also his disciples according to the rabbinic pattern. A number, if not all of them, probably had an elementary education, and would have been quite capable of memorizing his sayings and parables in the manner of the rabbis' disciples.[27] We should keep in mind when we read the gospels that Jesus chose and trained these men to transmit his teachings, both on missions during his lifetime, and beyond. Disciples were not accustomed to writing things down; their education trained them to learn by heart. In the opinion of the rabbis 'a good disciple was like a well plastered cistern which did not lose a drop' (of his master's teaching).[28] It was the practice of teachers of his day to repeat their sayings on many occasions, and also to make short, memorable summaries of their major teachings so that their disciples could learn them by heart.[29] There is no reason to think that Jesus did not make use of the same techniques. Many of the sayings we meet in the gospels could be summaries of mini-sermons, which is why it is sometimes difficult to follow a clear sequence of thought between them.[30]

Twelve is a large number of disciples of the personal attendant type. The task Jesus had for them required more than four or five. But the number twelve has more significance than this. Even if Jesus had said nothing, we would suspect it was dictated in some way by the twelve-fold tribal division of Israel. But he left us in no doubt: 'Truly I say to you, in the new creation (*palingenesia*), when the Son of Man sits on the throne of his glory, you who have followed me will also sit on twelve thrones judging the twelve tribes of Israel' (Matthew 19:28; cf. Luke 22:28–30).[31]

An increasing number of scholars over the past thirty years have seen Jesus' appointment of the twelve as an indication that he was intent on Israel's restoration. He appears to have had a quite detailed view about how Israel would finally be restored. The term *palingenesia*, which I have rendered 'new creation' literally means 'regeneration' and refers to the resurrection of the dead and the renewal of the environment which the prophets had foretold.[32] Israel would then be in its definitive, complete form, and Jesus promised the twelve that they would rule as judges. There is no reason to take this in the negative sense of condemning judges. They are to be rulers or princes according to the ancient Israelite pattern of the judges. He must have seen his mission in terms of bringing together the community which would bring Israel to its completion and fulfilment. Its ultimate leaders are drawn interestingly not from its founding fathers, but from the twelve workers of the decisive generation.

Attention has rightly been drawn to the odd fact that Jesus did not choose eleven disciples and himself as Israel's judges. E.P. Sanders hesitates to admit that Jesus thought himself the Messiah, but thinks he must have seen himself as some sort of ruler: 'I think that even "king" is not precisely correct, since Jesus

regarded God as king. My own favourite term for this concep-
tion of himself is "viceroy". God was king, but Jesus represented
him and would represent him in the coming kingdom.'[33]

How one can come as close as this to admitting what all
Jesus' first followers finally believed and every New Testament
writer affirms, and pull up short is bewildering. A viceroy is
precisely the Old Testament notion of Messiah. God is the ultimate King, but his anointed son rules as his human king on
earth. Just as the tribal rulers of the perfected Israel are drawn
from the end of its history, so its king is not David, but David's
eschatological archetype.

The Sermon on the Mount
(Matthew 5–7; Luke 6:12–49)

As Jesus descended the mountain, having spent the night in
prayer and having chosen his twelve apostles, he met up with a
great crowd and proceeded to instruct them. That is how Luke
tells the story. We will examine his sermon, for its content appears
to have been heavily influenced by the task which lay before the
new apostles. It should tell us more about how Jesus saw his disciples and their role.

The fact that the Sermon comes to us in two different forms
and in different contexts presents us with a preliminary problem.
Were there two different sermons? Or are what we have today
artificial compositions, never uttered by Jesus as a single discourse?
When we discern what the two versions have in common, both in
setting and content, we can affirm three things with reasonable
confidence. First, that Q contained something like Luke's version.
Secondly, that it represents a real discourse of Jesus, in a mountain
setting, beginning with blessings, and ending with a parable
appealing for people to build their lives on his teaching. Thirdly,
the Sermon was related to the theme of discipleship and contained
teaching about love and non-retaliation.

Although Matthew and Luke place the Sermon in different contexts, the points of similarity – the mountain, the crowds, the just appointed apostles – suggest that they both knew its historical circumstances. The artificiality of Matthew's setting is apparent. Both he and Luke felt the lack in Mark of an adequate account of Jesus' teaching. Luke dealt with this by bringing forward the Nazareth sermon and placing it where Mark has Jesus teaching in the Capernaum synagogue (though without telling us what he taught). Matthew filled the same hole with the Sermon on the Mount,[34] and supplemented it with teaching on discipleship from other sources. This corresponds to what we observe of his compositional technique elsewhere; Matthew collects Jesus' teaching into five large thematic blocks.[35] Jesus' teaching on mission, for example, is brought together from various contexts and presented on the occasion of the sending out of the twelve (Matthew 10). Luke is also familiar with the art of collecting, but does it in a different way; he collected most of Jesus' teaching that did not belong in the context of his narrative into a large block later in his gospel (10:25–19:27).[36]

We may take it, then, that Luke's Sermon represents what was said by Jesus on the occasion of the appointment of the twelve. Such a setting would explain why it was remembered as a whole, and not broken into its modular components, as happened with some of Jesus' other teaching. Matthew underlines the importance of the Sermon by bringing it to the prime location in his gospel; using it to introduce Jesus' message. Although he is forced in doing this to loose it from its exact historical setting at the appointment of the twelve, he places it at an analogous point, the call of the first four. There is nothing improper in him supplementing the Sermon with further dominical teaching on the subject of discipleship. Some of this other material is to be found in Luke in other locations.

I have anticipated myself somewhat in repeatedly speaking of the Sermon as a discourse on discipleship. To justify this it is necessary that we first take note of a long history of interpretation of the Sermon and a number of other views.

What is the Sermon on the Mount?

How we appraise Jesus' intention in the Sermon on the Mount will have a large bearing on how we interpret it. Is it an impossible ideal intended chiefly to arouse an awareness of how deeply we have failed, and send us running to God for forgiveness?[37] Is it the new Law of Christ, intended to supersede the old Law of Moses?[38] Is it a revolutionary manifesto for a new kind of non-violent society?[39] Is it an 'interim ethic' meant for the time of emergency immediately preceding the end of the age, and inapplicable to the world in which that age has failed to appear?[40] Is it the law of the millennial kingdom which has not yet come?[41] Or is it a 'rule' for disciples, perhaps an early Christian catechism?[42]

All these are widely held views. It is clear that we need to look closely at the Sermon and its setting to determine what it is. It obviously makes a great difference to how we understand 'turn the other cheek', if the Sermon is viewed as a political manifesto rather than an instruction of ordinary disciples about interpersonal relationships. Some of the above views even question whether it is appropriate to apply the Sermon to life today at all.

The first clue to the nature of the Sermon is its setting. If it belongs to the occasion of the appointment of the twelve, the question of discipleship can be expected to feature strongly. Luke hints that one of the reasons why Jesus took the step of selecting the twelve was because of mounting official opposition to his mission (Luke 6:11ff.). John the Baptist, we recall, was in prison at the time and was shortly to lose his life. This situation may be presumed to be the immediate background of the suffering and persecution material in the Sermon. We may hazard, then, that whatever else the Sermon may be, it contains an address to those who are joining Jesus in a mission which is already beginning to generate dangerous opposition.

There is a further factor in the setting, which complicates our assessment of the Sermon somewhat. Luke tells us that although Jesus spoke with an eye on his disciples, the Sermon was given in the presence of great crowds. After making his choice of the twelve, he came down with them to a level place (still on the mountain) where the crowds had already gathered. Present were a great crowd of his disciples and a multitude of Jews from all over the holy land and from as far away as Tyre and Sidon. Luke's use of the word *laos* (people) to describe the audience marks them as the chosen people. 'Judaea and Jerusalem' denotes those from within the holy land; 'Tyre and Sidon' exiles from the diaspora.[43] Such a representative gathering of Israel should warn us against too narrow an interpretation of discipleship in the Sermon; it is about the discipleship of the twelve 'professionals', but also of all the others whom Jesus is calling to himself. Matthew also mentions a larger group (Matthew 7:28).

The people have come to be healed and to hear Jesus' teaching. The crowds wanted to touch him, 'for power came out of him and he healed them all'. The extravagant language betrays Luke's interpretation of the setting: here is the anointed Messiah standing before the people of Israel, healing their diseases and giving them his teaching. But it is vital to observe that they are a people in process of division: some already believe in him , some are still making up their minds. Jesus appeals to those who are *really* hearing him, interrogates those who call him Lord, and warns of the desperate consequences of rejecting his message.

We may tentatively conclude that the Sermon on the Mount is both a discourse on the disciples' mission in a situation in which persecution is likely, as well as an appeal for people to become disciples. We will refine and develop this conclusion in the next two sections.

Herald on the Mountain

The scene of the Sermon may be reminiscent of Moses receiving
the law on Mt Sinai and descending to deliver it to the people,
but much more powerful are the points of contact with the
Herald and Servant whose work is depicted in Isaiah 40–66.[44] We
have already seen how at his baptism Jesus was given the Servant's
commission, and how at Nazareth he took up the mantle of the
Herald. The primary role of the Herald, as it is depicted in Isaiah,
is to stand on the mountains and proclaim the arrival of God's
salvation (kingdom).[45] The task of the Servant was to actually
establish salvation, chiefly by means of his teaching and
suffering.[46] There are many themes and motifs common to both
the Sermon on the Mount and the Servant Songs: the Messiah as
teacher, the declaration of the gospel from the mountain, the
gathering of Israel, the salvation of the poor, the kingdom of God,
satisfying the hungry, giving gladness and laughter to those who
weep and mourn, the reproach of people, being cast out for the
sake of the Servant's name, reward, consolation, the importance
of hearing, the blind and those who see, turning the other cheek,
the mercy of God, the coming of the light, obedience to the
Servant. It is essential, therefore, that we consider these Songs as
background to a proper understanding of what Jesus was saying.

The beginning of the Sermon is gospel; Jesus appears as the
Herald on the mountains, proclaiming the kingdom of God. His
blessings are evangelistic, for they add up to a declaration to God's
suffering people that the kingdom is about to be theirs:[47]

> He lifted up his eyes upon his disciples and said,
> Blessed are the poor, for yours is the kingdom of God.
> Blessed are those who are hungry now, because you will be satis-
> fied.
> Blessed are those who weep now, because you will laugh.
> Blessed are you when men hate you and ostracize you and
> reproach you and cast out your name as an evil thing on account

of the Son of Man. Be glad in that day and leap for joy, for behold, your reward is great in heaven; for this is the way their fathers treated the prophets.

(Luke 6:20–23; cf. Matthew 5:1–12)

It is a common mistake to interpret the blessings either in moral or in socio-economic terms, as though Jesus were spelling out the spiritual or economic qualifications of those who would find admittance to the kingdom. However, Jesus announces the kingdom, not as the reward of the virtuous, but as God's gracious answer to human need (Israel's need actually). The poor are blessed by the removal of their poverty. Matthew's first beatitude ('Blessed are the poor in spirit, for theirs is the kingdom of heaven') only generalizes the need, for the same expression in the Dead Sea Scrolls shows that 'poor in spirit' is not a moral quality, but means 'crushed and downtrodden', in a context which identifies these poor with the suffering remnant of Israel.[48] The words and categories Jesus used here to declare salvation to his people are the same ones spread most thickly in the Old Testament in Isaiah 40–66. Against this background the meaning of the blessings for Jesus and for his Jewish audience can readily be seen. At one point in Isaiah the Servant is addressed in words which concentrate most of the ideas we meet in the blessings (underlined) with some we have already met in Jesus' Nazareth sermon (italicized):

Thus says the Lord, at *an acceptable time* I have answered you, and in a day of salvation I have helped you. I will preserve you and give you as a covenant to the people, to raise up the land, to make them inherit the desolate heritages, *saying to those that are bound, Go forth, to those that are in darkness, Come to the light!* They shall feed in the ways and on all the bare hills they shall find pasture. They shall not hunger nor thirst, nor shall heat or sun afflict them. For he that has mercy on them will lead them ... Sing O heavens, and be joyful O earth, and break forth into singing O mountains, for the Lord has comforted his people and will have compassion upon his *poor.* (Isaiah 49:8–13)

We have already noted how, against the background of Isaiah and its later development in Jewish tradition, the Jews understood themselves as 'the poor', 'the captive people', 'the mourners', 'the blind' and 'the hungry'.[49] Although there were sectarian groups like those at Qumran who laid claim to some of these titles for themselves,[50] Jesus' audience would have had no difficulty in recognizing in 'the poor, the hungry and the weeping' a characterization of their own oppressed nation, and in the blessing announced to them possession of the restored realm of Israel, or even a restored world (Matthew 5:5). With this would come the end of captivity and oppression, of poverty and hunger, of sighing and mourning, sickness and sin. What would have startled them was *Jesus* announcing the kingdom to them at the same time as he lifted people out of their downtroddenness by healing the sick and spirit-oppressed.

The other thing which would have appeared strange was the fourth blessing and the four woes which followed. The first three blessings are recognizable poetic summaries of their national hope, but the fourth falls into prose and promises a joyful future to those who suffer because of the Son of Man. The fourth blessing acts as a key to show how Jesus means the first three to be interpreted and applied:[51] true Israel will not avoid painful identification with the suffering Servant of God, which brings its destiny as the 'poor–hungry–mourning' people of God to a real climax. With the woes Jesus goes on to warn his hearers that it is possible for them to miss out on the promised kingdom if they refuse to stand with the Son of Man in his suffering, and opt instead for the good things and the good reputation which the world offers to its children.

In his announcement at Nazareth Jesus offered the kingdom to all who were present, but they were unwilling to receive it from him and forfeited it. In the blessings and woes of the

Sermon on the Mount he makes it explicit that although the kingdom is announced freely and without distinction to all Israel, it cannot come apart from the Son of Man. Unless they are prepared to side with him in his cause, they will miss out. Identifying with him now will run them into danger of persecution, but the outcome will be eternal joy. Siding with the present world-order, although it may bring happiness now, will ultimately mean eternal loss.[52]

It is now apparent why there were no clear boundaries to Jesus' disciple band. Jesus preached salvation to the whole nation and therefore allowed no sectarian breaking away. But because the kingdom was so closely bound up with his own person and mission, and because he was already meeting with opposition and rejection, it was impossible for a group of disciples not to emerge. This is probably why Luke begins the Sermon with the curious note that Jesus spoke to the whole people, but with his eyes upon his disciples.[53] It is upon those who stand with him, even in suffering, that the blessings of Israel finally rest.

Mission and Suffering

It is in the Sermon on the Mount that we first learn that Jesus' mission will entail suffering. His audience would not have seen anything in his speaking of himself as the Son of Man other than an odd avoidance of referring to himself directly. However, taken in the light of everything he was later to attach to this name, Jesus evidently saw himself as 'the one like a son of man', who in Daniel 7 represents the downtrodden people of God, and is ultimately awarded an everlasting kingdom on their behalf. Thus, mention of the Son of Man at this point hangs very much together with the characterization of God's people as poor, hungry and weeping. Jesus suggests that the nation's suffering is not quite complete, despite his announcement of the time of fulfilment.

It is significant that when we leave the blessings and woes and move to the more ethical section of the Sermon we meet immediately with the theme of suffering, though it is the suffering not of Jesus but of his disciples.

> But I say to you that hear, love your enemies, do good to those that hate you, bless those who curse you, pray for those who mistreat you. To the person who strikes you on one cheek, give him the other, and from the person who takes your cloak, do not withhold your coat as well. (Luke 6:27–29)

Love of enemies and non-resistance in the face of assault and robbery are a revolutionary philosophy of life. I am not aware that anyone has ever taught such an ethic independent of Jesus' teaching. Nothing like it occurs in the law of Moses, to which Jesus ascribed full authority as the definitive expression of God's will. The Psalms, with which Jesus was intimately and fondly familiar, are full of the suffering and persecution of the innocent, but they know little of love of enemies and non-resistance. They speak rather of vengeance and retribution. This strange new teaching demands some explanation, and it is no surprise to find the only precedent for such behaviour, apart from a saying in the book of Proverbs,[54] precisely in the songs of the Suffering Servant.

> The Lord God has given me the tongue of a disciple, that I should know how to sustain with a word the one who is weary. Morning by morning he awakens my ear to hear like disciples do. The Lord God has opened my ear, and I was not rebellious, nor did I turn back. I gave my back to those who beat me, and my cheeks to those who tore out my beard. I did not hide my face from shame and spitting. (Isaiah 50:4–6)

To find this striking image of offering one's cheek to the aggressor both in the Servant Songs and in the Sermon on the Mount makes it almost certain that this is the background of Jesus' thinking. The Servant's mission is to restore the tribes of Israel to their glory before God, and then to extend salvation and justice to the ends of the earth. He is distinctive in the Old Testament in that in the exercise of this task he is exposed to rejection and persecution, which will bring him to the end of his life, but from which he cannot turn away. His sufferings, however, lead to great good for others, and finally bring vindication from God and the success of his world-winning mission. The important things to note are that his suffering is necessary to his task of establishing the kingdom and that he willingly embraces it.

The Servant's Strategy

There has been a good deal of discussion amongst scholars over whether Jesus saw himself in the Servant role.[55] The Sermon on the Mount is evidence that he at least saw his disciples this way. They, of course, never made much sense of voluntary suffering during Jesus' lifetime. Love of enemies and non-resistance to evil were the pattern of *his* life, and the Servant Songs tell us that they were part of a strategy for winning the world.[56]

Jesus' task was to win the hearts of a broken and disobedient people back to God. He set out to do this by teaching, by acts of compassion and by his willingness to suffer. A man employed as a government social worker in a mixed community of aborigines and whites in Western Australia told me that he despaired of ever being able to do anything much for the black community. They had been so badly treated, by whites and by one another, that a cycle of hurt, counter-hurt and suspicion ruled in the community. 'The only way I could see myself doing any good,' he said, 'is if I were to go and live with them and do what good I could, and, when they hurt me, not retaliate, and maybe break the cycle of revenge.' He went on to explain that he could not expose his wife and family to such a life, and doubted that he himself could cope with what would be involved if he were alone. 'Perhaps a community could do it,' he concluded, 'or someone like Jesus.' With that I think he came close to understanding part of the strategy of the Servant's mission. God is in search of a runaway world. Jesus comes representing him and meets suspicion and hostility. Those who share Jesus' mission can expect the same. Retaliation puts an end to any attempt at reconciliation.

At the time of the Sermon on the Mount Jesus evidently did not see himself carrying out the Servant's mission as an isolated individual. We observe how, having declared the gospel, he appeals to all who have ears to hear. This is a plea for response, and the nature of that response is to become his disciple and join him in his mission of suffering; he warns them that if they will not, they will never see the kingdom. This is because, first, the role of the Suffering Servant was Israel's role;[57] secondly, only in default did the task pass to disciples, and finally with their defection, to one individual. Thus Jesus called upon all who heard to join him in an active programme of outgoing love and generosity that would engage with others and demonstrate God's goodness. It would meet opposition with generosity, prayer, and a willingness to suffer. God was seeking to be reconciled to his enemies, and his sons were called to participate in the peacemaking initiative (Luke 6:27–38).[58]

If I have rightly discerned the direction of Jesus' Sermon it has little to do with questions of law and order or war and peace as these are usually understood. It is indeed a discourse on discipleship, but more precisely, instruction for Jesus' followers as they join him in the Servant mission. Its applicability today hangs on whether the promise of the kingdom is still a viable reality, and whether God still wants to welcome home his enemies. Christian mission still entails suffering. If Christians retaliate against those who abuse them, other than with forgiveness, prayer and love, their mission to those people is finished. In this respect the Sermon has full relevance to those who still see themselves engaged in Jesus' kingdom-bringing mission of reconciliation.

A Matter of Destiny

The Sermon goes on to deal with the need for a good heart (the attitude to self and others which thy Sermon teaches demands it!), and another preoccupation of thy Servant: seeing and helping others to see.[59] It ends with an appeal for obedience (another concern of the Servant), and a parable.

> Everyone who comes to me and hears my words and does them – I will show you what he is like: he is like a man building a house who dug deep and laid his foundation on the rock. When it flooded, the river burst upon that house and was not able to shake it, because it had been well built. But the person who hears and does nothing is like a person who builds a house on the ground without a foundation. The river burst, and it collapsed in a moment, and the ruin of that house was terrible.
> (Luke 6:47–49; cf. Matthew 7:24–27)

Jesus here exploded any notion that his hearers (or their descendants) might have had that his teaching was not for immediate application. Hearing and obeying were all important. He called every Jew into a disciple-like relationship of hearing and doing his words, and warned that their response to his teaching would determine their destiny. It is an enormous claim which goes beyond anything he could have made by appropriating for himself this or that Old Testament title. He does not point forward like the Baptist to another who would come later, nor even point them to God and their need to obey him. Instead he places himself at the point to which all obedience is to be directed, and where the question of destiny is determined. He not only promised survival to those who obeyed him, but added the more troubling negative, that to ignore his teaching was to decide for ultimate calamity. The calamity to which he alluded can only be the catastrophe against which John the Baptist warned. It is the first indication from Jesus that he foresaw an alternative to the speedy arrival of the kingdom in its fullest form. Israel's destiny and the destiny of each individual hung on their response to his word. The Sermon on the Mount was a call to conversion: to believe in the kingdom and the one who had appeared to make it a reality. It meant joining Jesus in active and loving witness, teaching, and suffering. But this meant no more than becoming a true Israelite, a true servant of God. The alternative was to recoil from Jesus to the enjoyment of what the present age could offer, and that meant turning one's back on Israel's present and future. In the Sermon on the Mount we see people at the moment of decision. Some decided to be his disciples. The nation as a whole ignored him, and in less than forty years was swept away in a flood of destruction.

Kingdom Living

Before bringing this examination of Jesus' disciples to a close we should consider other aspects of the lifestyle he taught them. From time to time Jesus has been characterized as essentially an ethical teacher. He was not. The Sermon on the Mount may give that impression, but as we have seen, for all the ethical material it contains, it was originally an instruction for those who were joining Jesus in his mission. There are a few ethical parables, but most deal with issues specifically related to the kingdom of God. Nowhere in the gospels is there any sign of Jesus teaching a moral system. A cursory examination of one of the other major collections of his teachings, the central section of Luke (Luke 10–18), reveals what would normally be classified as ethical subjects (love of neighbour, perception, almsgiving, hypocrisy, greed, repentance, the Sabbath, humility, use of possessions, causing others to stumble, thankfulness, obedience), interspersed with a variety of other issues, like the priority of attention to Jesus, what to pray, boldness in prayer, Satan, the wrongness of asking for signs, judgements on leaders, judgements on Jerusalem, avoidance of anxiety, watchfulness for the coming of the Son of Man, divisions in families, recognition of the signs of the times, the manner of the coming of the kingdom of God, the number of those who will be saved, the replacement of those who refuse to enter the kingdom, the cost of discipleship, seeking the lost, the 'days of the Son of Man,' and prayer for the kingdom. Evidently we are not going to understand Jesus if we pursue him along the ethical teacher path.

One reason for the lack of a comprehensive catalogue of ethical issues, or of a particular ethical system, is that Jesus subscribed wholeheartedly to the Mosaic law and refused to be drawn by those who sought something different. When a lawyer, and later a young ruler, questioned him about the way to eternal life, he responded by reminding them of the law (Luke 10:25–37; 18:18–20). When he was urged to provide a miracle to persuade people to repent he insisted that the law was a sufficient guide (Luke 16:27–31). He had no moral requirements different from the laws (Matthew 5:17–20; Luke 16:17). Rather, he exposed people's evasions of the law.

The key to Jesus' teaching is once again the kingdom of God. He came to announce the kingdom, and most of his teaching – some of it ethical, some of it not – is kingdom-related. When his disciples asked him to teach them to pray, for example, he did not respond with instruction on methods or principles of prayer, but with what to pray. And everything he told them to pray was related to the coming of God's kingdom. 'Hallowed be your name, your kingdom come, your will be done on earth …' is a petition for three aspects of the coming of God's kingdom. Even the request 'Give us daily our daily bread' is probably kingdom-related. It contains a word unknown elsewhere in Greek, and is probably better translated 'Give us daily our *future* bread.' The reference is not to food alone, but to the good things that belong to God's kingdom.[60] Jesus was in the process of dispensing forgiveness and reconciliation, and celebrating the new age with his disciples.

Nevertheless, there was a distinctive way of life which was lived and commended by Jesus. His kingdom announcement was

followed by a call to absolute allegiance. The demand for loyalty
to him as God's king permeated his preaching and carried with it
an obligation to pay close attention to his lifestyle and teaching.
As we have seen, part of this lifestyle was mission – not an option
or special calling, but a life call on all who would join in his
conviction about the reconciling of people to God as the way to
the kingdom.

The ultimate kingdom was to be about more than just
spiritual healing. It promised the total end of evil and a world of
peace, harmony, righteousness and plenty. Much of Jesus' ethical
teaching goes in the direction of actualizing this new state of
affairs to the extent to which this is possible in the continuing evil
age. Love of neighbour, for example, makes real now the attitude
which will exist in the consummated kingdom. Insofar as the
kingdom is present, love will be the rule between its sons and
daughters. But since the kingdom is also coming, love means
work. Thus the person who inquired how he might find eternal
life was told to go and find people to whom he could become
a neighbour (Luke 10:25–37). A static acceptance of the
status quo is replaced by an outgoing, relationship-building
neighbourliness. Similarly, in the Lord's Prayer, the request that
God forgive us is followed by the assurance that we will forgive
those indebted to us. The reconciliation which will be the chief
feature of the perfect kingdom thus begins now. Jesus' emphasis
on helping the unfortunate, be it through giving to the poor,
lending without interest, forgiving the defaulter, clothing the
naked, feeding the hungry, visiting prisoners, or inviting the
needy to feasts, points in the same direction. What the kingdom is
to be in its ultimate perfection should become the disciple's
aspiration and ideal now. If the kingdom means mutual forgiveness they will seek to actualize that now. If the kingdom is a great
banquet where God's hungry people will all be fed, the disciple
will try to make that a reality now. Thus it is appropriate to speak
of 'a kingdom ethic'.

Jesus' 'Ethical System'

Naturalistic ethical systems identify the goal of individual human life either as personal happiness or some form of self-actualisation. There are also social versions of these systems, which see the greatest happiness of the greatest number, or world-actualisation as the ultimate good. Having identified an ultimate good as the proper goal of life, an ethical system is then deduced as the logical way to achieve it. Three realities drive such systems. First is the dominating role played by pain and pleasure, happiness and sorrow in people's lives. Second is the elusive nature of happiness, which is not attained simply by the pursuit of pleasure. Third is the pressure of other people, who limit the individual's happiness but are also indispensable to it. This suggests that ultimate good must be communal as well as personal. Once the ultimate good is identified, then the ethical system emerges as the way to achieve that good.

Considered from this angle, the kingdom of God may be viewed as Jesus' version of the ultimate good: meaning ultimate happiness both for individual and community; total self-actualisation (and more) for persons, for society and for the universe. It does not emerge, however, as a theoretical construct: something that Jesus has worked out. It is what he understands God to have revealed through the prophets and now to have inaugurated in his mission. It is something being brought about by the action of God and is not of human making.

Thus we do not see Jesus *reasoning* in the way Plato or Aristotle do, but *announcing*. And what he proclaims is not an ideal which must be actualized by ethical actions, but a coming reality to be believed or disbelieved. Belief, however, ushers one into a realm of kingdom living where ultimate kingdom realities *are* actualized in individual and communal behaviour.

A Social Ethic?

All Jesus' ethical teaching is directed to individuals. He does not appear to call for social reorganization or political action. However, that does not mean his teaching is individualistic, devoid of a social conscience. Disciples taking his lifestyle and teaching seriously will inevitably create communities. This is evidenced by Jesus' common meals and the people who flocked around him. The early Christians' imitation of him in the days following his resurrection naturally created community, and always has. And although he did not seek to impose his way on non-believers or authorize any form of coercion, such relationship-building activity and the communities that resulted from it inevitably had a wider social impact. One may add that the ideals and values of kingdom-minded people in positions of social and political influence will also effect these wider spheres. But that is to look to a future beyond the gospels' story.

The Kingdom and Possessions

There is not space here to survey all of the teaching of Jesus; many ethical and lifestyle issues are dealt with elsewhere. A review of his teaching on possessions will suffice as a further example of the way his unusual ethical stance naturally comports with his kingdom ministry.[61] Almost twenty per cent of Jesus' recorded teaching deals in some manner with the themes of rich and poor, wealth, poverty, and possessions. Admittedly this is concentrated in Luke, for whom it held a particular fascination, but its presence in all layers of the gospel tradition shows it was characteristic of Jesus himself. We will not go too far wrong if we see it once again in relation to his kingdom proclamation.

To begin with, possessions constituted a pull on people's allegiance, which competed with Jesus' rightful demands as king. He pointedly responds to a young nobleman's inquiry about the way to the kingdom with the demand that he get rid of his possessions: 'Sell whatever you have and give to the poor, and you will have treasure in heaven, and come follow me' (Mark 10:21). The disciples were horrified, though Mark says Jesus did it in love. It was not a demand he usually made of would-be followers. Something in this case required it, and the young man's refusal revealed that he valued his wealth above the eternal life he had come asking after. When Jesus discussed his case with the disciples he made it clear that nothing must come between a person and himself. Conversely, 'no-one who has left house, or brothers, or sisters, or mother, or father, or children, or lands, for my sake, and for the gospel's sake shall fail to receive one hundred-fold now in this time, houses and brothers, and sisters and mothers and children and lands, with persecutions, and in the age to come eternal life' (Mark 10:29–30). This makes it quite clear that Jesus was not advocating poverty for its own sake, but establishing the absolute priority of his own call. No one can serve God and mammon, he says in another place. And when he was setting out to face persecution and death in Jerusalem he challenged his would-be followers with the words, 'Whoever of you does not bid farewell to everything that is his cannot be my disciple' (Luke 14:33).

Jesus saw money and possessions competing for people's attention and allegiance with the call to the kingdom. In sayings and parables he warned of the power of wealth over people's minds, and thus its ability to blind and ultimately deprive them of the kingdom. He declined an appeal to arbitrate in the distribution of an inheritance with the strongest words of warning recorded in the gospels: 'Watch out and be on your guard against greed in all its forms. For even when a person has more than enough, yet life (*zoe*) is not from his possessions' (Luke 12:15). *Zoe* means quality of life. Greek employs another word (*psyche*) to express life as opposed to death. Jesus uses 'life' (*zoe*) and 'eternal life' (*zoe aionios*) interchangeably, and both are virtual synonyms for the kingdom of God. The latter emphasized the political dimensions of the age to come, the former its character as a new quality of life, be it in its future perfection or its present partial manifestation. To seek life in more and more possessions, as the greedy person does, is to seek a counterfeit which will disappoint and doom. Life does not come from possessions, but from God who wishes to bestow it in all its fullness through the gift of the kingdom.

To his warning on greed Jesus added the story of a rich farmer, who faced with the blessing of a bumper harvest thought only of how to increase the size of his barns and ensure a comfortable retirement (Luke 12:1–21). Not only does the man lose out on the life that could have been his, but God judges him for his greed. This parable is full of commercial innuendos. Responding to the richness of his harvest (fruit = interest) he seeks better storage for his goods (goods = capital). But at the moment of self-congratulation on his successful retirement God announces foreclosure on his life, which all the while, unknown to the farmer, was a loan he was failing to service.

Anxiety

Possessions remained a problem even for people who had decided for the kingdom. Jesus' disciples did not cease to worry about livelihood and the welfare of their families when they left home to follow Jesus on the road. He addressed their natural anxiety with the assurance that this God whom they had discovered as Father would care for them:

> Consider the ravens. They neither sow nor reap ... and God feeds them. Of how much more value are you than the birds ... Consider how the field flowers grow, how they neither toil nor weave, yet I tell you, not Solomon in all his glory was arrayed as one of them. If God so clothes them, though they are grass in the field today and tomorrow are thrown into the oven, how much more

will he clothe you, you of little faith. And you, do not be seeking
what you shall eat and what you shall drink and do not be
anxious and unsettled. For the nations of the world seek all these
things. And your Father knows that you need these things. But
seek his kingdom and these things will be added to you'
(Luke 12:24, 27–31).

It is mistaken to think Jesus is simply forbidding anxiety, or
demanding that they counter it by reordering their priorities,
or that he is advocating a careless lifestyle. He addresses people
who are threatened with persecution (see Luke 12:4–12) and
deprivation as a result of their commitment. His call of the twelve
to join him on the road and the danger into which that thrust
them was an obvious threat to their families' livelihood. Thus the
anxiety he combats is a consequence of their commitment. Its
solution is to consider the power and love of their Father–God.
Jesus makes a studied contrast between *God* who cares for the
birds and the flowers, and the *Father* who can be even more relied
on to care for his disciples. God is mindful of their needs and is
able to attend to them in his own way should their commitment
to his kingdom make it impossible for them to do so themselves.
There is no call here for a deliberately thoughtless lifestyle, but
rather an assurance that God can be trusted to do for his children
what they cannot do for themselves when they are engaged in his
service. Nor does Jesus think the Father will be frugal in his
provision; Solomon was arrayed in less glory than the field
flowers and how much more will the child of the Father-God be
cared for!

Right Use of Possessions

Jesus advocated a non–acquisitive, non–ascetic, generous lifestyle.
In the parable of the unjust steward (Luke 16:1–9) he indicates
that his desire for radically generous followers was also motivated
by a well-considered kingdom philosophy. An estate manager is

accused of mismanagement and given notice to quit. Faced with this crisis (a picture of coming kingdom judgement) he acts decisively and makes a plan. Using his managerial powers in the short time he still has them he calls in various debtors and drastically reduces their accounts. He expects that they will later treat him as a friend and welcome him into their homes. The master praises the unrighteous manager because he has acted prudently, 'For the sons of this age are more prudent in their own generation than the sons of light. And I (Jesus) say to you, "Make friends with the mammon (wealth) of unrighteousness so that when it fails they may receive you into the eternal tents." ' Jesus contrasts the resolute shrewdness of the man of the world with his disciples, who though claiming to believe in the coming kingdom are not taking the appropriate action. In the new aeon worldly wealth will suffer a complete devaluation. What action is appropriate for people who believe this? Jesus here reveals something of how he conceives the new age. He pictures it as a community of friends, whose welcome or otherwise will determine one's destiny. It is possible to use worldly wealth while it still has value to make friendships which have eternal value. At this point we see a profoundly positive, though qualified, assessment of the value of money and possessions.

This comes out even more clearly in the sayings which follow the parable. 'If therefore you have not become faithful with unrighteous mammon, who will give you the real wealth?' (Luke 16:11). The real wealth is what belongs to the kingdom of God, contrasted with the illusory and transient wealth of the age which is passing away. 'And if you have not been faithful with that which is alien who will give to you that which is you own?' (Luke 16:12). Jesus regarded money as essentially alien to his disciples because it belonged to the evil age. There is a wealth that pertains to the coming kingdom but it will never be entrusted to those who do not learn to act faithfully – that is, generously – with money. In the parable of the rich man and Lazarus, which follows in Luke, Jesus illustrates the converse: the man who could have made a friend of the brother who lay begging each day at his gate (they are both sons of Abraham), squandered his opportunity and ended in hell (Luke 16:19–31).

Perplexing Questions

Attention to the subject of possessions has shown us how the life-style Jesus lived and advocated arose naturally from his announcement of the kingdom of God. We have also seen how closely the disciple group itself was bound to Jesus' messianic purpose. They were the people of the kingdom, called to begin living its life now. Jesus' desire was that all God's historic people should grasp hold of their destiny and inherit the regenerated world, so he addressed Israelites indiscriminately with the message that their long-promised and passionately awaited future had arrived. Just because he associated the coming kingdom with his own presence he celebrated the new age with all who believed. Most, however, remained obtuse, and so it fell to those who followed him to be the people of the kingdom and actualize it by a generous lifestyle that treated others with the same friend-ship and forgiveness that God had shown them.

There remained a future dimension to Jesus' expectations of the kingdom. The day of resurrection and world restoration was not quite yet. Lost Israelites were yet to be gathered. This meant work, not only for Jesus, but also his disciples. 'He who is not with me scatters,' he said (Luke 11:23). Conversely, 'he who is with me gathers'! Disciples are missionaries.

Just because the kingdom-bringer was held in suspicion by many, persecution threatened, and disciples were likely to get hurt. In this they shared in the ministry of the Servant of Yahweh and fulfilled Israel's vocation. They could be sure that if they so actualized the suffering destiny of God's true people as the poor of Yahweh, they would also experience the full joy of the day of salvation when God's kingdom brought an eternal feast of good things and the end of all need. On the other hand, if people backed away from identification with the kingdom bearer, opting for the present age and its good things, they would meet destruction when the present evil age arrived at its appointed end.

At this point questions clamour to be answered. If Jesus envisaged a continuation of suffering, what real content can we give to his announcement that the kingdom was present? If Israel as a nation refuses the kingdom in the way it is offered to them, will it come willy-nilly for the remnant? Or will there be a replacement Israel of some kind – a largely Gentile church, for example? Will Israel's hope of national restoration die forever in the catastrophe of Jerusalem's fall? Will the prophetic promise of salvation and a renewed environment be transformed into something purely spiritual in the time beyond AD 70? Or did Jesus still envisage a 'material' future for his people? These questions must remain on our agenda as we proceed. In the next chapter we will see that the kingdom carried a very material payload, even in the ambiguity of the ongoing evil and suffering that accompanied the ministry of Jesus.

Notes

[1] See Tobit 1:17ff.; 2:3ff.; 4:3f.; 12:12f.; 14:10ff.

[2] Compare Jeremiah 16:1–9, where Jeremiah is commanded neither to marry nor to involve himself in any of the burial and mourning rituals of his people in view of the 'final solution' which God was about to bring on the nation. Also compare Leviticus 10:6f., where Aaron and his sons were forbidden to mourn the death of Nadab and Abihu while they were holy and carrying out the duties of the sanctuary.

[3] For a more detailed analysis of this story see Seccombe, *Possessions*, 118–125.

[4] M. Hengel, *The Charismatic Leader and His Followers*. For a prophet calling a disciple see 1 Kings 19:19–21. For God's call of a prophet see Jeremiah 1:4–10.

[5] One factor that has cast suspicion on the story is its similarity to John 21:1ff. But it may be the similarity of the two occasions which gives the latter its full significance. After their betrayal, Peter and the others encounter Jesus and his call in the same way as they did at the beginning, though this time it is sheep to be fed rather than fish to be caught. For further discussion of Luke's story see I.H. Marshall, *The Gospel of Luke*, 199–201.

[6] See Freyne, *Galilee*, 190–192; J.R. Donahue, 'Tax Collectors and Sinners: An Attempt at Identification', 39–61.

[7] Gnilka (*Jesus*, 176) includes tax gatherers with the sick, demoniacs, epileptics, debtors, etc. as the poor and dispossessed who received preferential treatment from Jesus. This is strange to say the least.

[8] On the Pharisees see Josephus, *War*, 2.162f.; *History*, 13.288ff.; 408ff.; 17.41ff.; 18.12ff.; *Life*, 10ff.; 191; Schürer, *History* II, 2, 381–403; J. Neusner, *Early Rabbinic Judaism*, 45ff.; E.P. Sanders, *Judaism: Practice and Belief 63 BC–66 CE*, 380–451.

[9] In some parts of England a woman will not appear in society after childbirth until she had been 'churched' to remove the contamination of the birth.

[10] See H. Maccoby, *Early Rabbinic Writings*, 94–100.

[11] Philo, *Every Good Man is Free*, 75–9; Josephus, *War*, 2.119–161; *History*, 18.18–22; Schürer *History* II, 555–574.

[12] In various writings E.P. Sanders has sought to overthrow what he sees as a Protestant misrepresentation of Pharisees as legalists who saw their relationship with God in terms of works rather than grace. From the writings of the period and of the later rabbis he establishes that the predominant Jewish understanding was what he calls 'covenantal nomism': Israelites stand in relation to God by virtue of being Israelites under a gracious covenant and remain in that state of grace by keeping the law. The so-called Protestant misrepresentation goes back, of course, to gospel stories like the Pharisee and the Tax Collector. Covenantal nomism may well be correct as a statement of official Jewish theology, but how it was practised in the first century is a question on which the New Testament is our closest witness. The weakness of Sanders' case is his neglect of this evidence (see *Judaism*, 380–451). When he does consider it, he frequently moves it from Jesus to the later church (e.g., *Jesus and Judaism*, 270–293). Why Jesus was immune from misunderstanding the Pharisees, when in his view the early Christians were not, he does not explain. It is possible for people to have formularies which express a doctrine of grace and a spirituality which is Pelagian or semi-Pelagian, witness Anglicanism (so J.R.W. Stott, *The Message of Romans*, 28–29). Paul is an obvious example of a first century

Pharisee who before his conversion saw his standing with God to be heavily bound up with performance of the law, whatever he may elsewhere have said about God's election of Israel (e.g., Philippians 3:3–9).

[13] E.g., Mark 9:47; 10:15, 23–25; Matthew 5:20; 7:21; 23:13; Luke 18:17, 24–25; John 3:5. Outside the gospels only in Acts 14:22.

[14] It is difficult to see why Matthew would have invented this unusual detail.

[15] John 3:28ff.

[16] Exodus Rabba 15:31; cf. Leviticus Rabba 11:2; *SB* 1, 517. It is unlikely that a tradition like this would have grown up in Judaism after the birth of Christianity.

[17] E.g., Isaiah 50:1; 54:5ff.; 62:4f.; Ezekiel 16; Hosea.

[18] *Aboth Rabbi Nathan* 41; *SB* 1, 511.

[19] E.g., Matthew 8:19–22 (Q?) and 12:49f.; (Mark 3:33–5; Luke 8:21); Luke 6:17; 19:37; John 6:66; 7:3. Further, see Seccombe, *Possessions*, 101–5.

[20] Josephus, *War*, 1.648ff. mentions the school of Judas and Matthias which was attended by a large, youthful audience.

[21] Later they were known as rabbis; in the NT they are called scribes (*grammateis*), lawyers (*nomikoi*) and law teachers (*nomodidaskaloi*). See Schürer, *History* II, 322f.

[22] *Babylonian Talmud Ketuboth* 96a. For an insight into the life of a disciple see *Mishnah Aboth* 6:6; D. Daube, *The New Testament and Rabbinic Judaism*, 266–267.

[23] *Mishnah Aboth* 1:1.

[24] *Mishnah Aboth* 2:8.

[25] E. Fascher, 'Jesus als Lehrer', 331ff.

[26] *TDNT*, 1, 407–420.

[27] Riesner, *Lehrer*, 411–414, 422ff.

[28] *Mishnah Aboth* 2:8.

[29] Riesner, *Lehrer*, 422ff.

[30] Notice the way in which the letter of James picks up many themes from the Sermon on the Mount and re-inflates them into sermonettes. The links between different sections even in James are difficult to see, if they exist at all.

[31] Only Matthew has this saying in the story of the rich ruler. Either he knew it independently in relation to this story or brought it from another context to explicate the disciples' reward. Whether it is the same Q saying which Luke reproduces in relation to the last supper is impossible to say. Such a momentous idea is unlikely to have been spoken only once.

[32] Isaiah 25:6–8; 11:6–10; 65:17, 25; 66:22 etc.

[33] Sanders, *Historical Figure*, 248.

[34] This can readily be seen from its position in Matthew and from the way he has omitted Mark 1:21–28 but retained 1:22 for the conclusion to the Sermon on the Mount (Matthew 7:29).

[35] Matthew 5–7 on discipleship; 10 on mission; 13 on parables of the kingdom; 17:24–18:35 on community relationships; 24–25 on the coming of the Son of Man.

[36] Luke was still concerned with the true setting of Jesus' teaching, however, is quite clear. If he had not been he could have placed the Nazareth Sermon into Mark's Capernaum synagogue story. He evidently preferred to give it in its original context.

[37] This is the view of Carl Stange (1924) and Gerhard Kittel (1925). For a summary of their views see W.S. Kissinger, *The Sermon on the Mount: A History of Interpretation and Bibliography*, 66–70.

[38] The view of B.W. Bacon, *Studies in Matthew*; see also E.J. Goodspeed, *A Life of Jesus*, 76ff.

[39] Tolstoy is the most famous exponent of this view. See Kissinger, *Sermon on the Mount*, 52–56.

[40] Albert Schweitzer is the best known exponent of this view: Jesus thought the arrival of the new world was so close that he summoned people to a radical obedience that had no regard for any continuation of the world order. Because Jesus was wrong in his expectation the ethic is quite impossible in the modern world. See Kissinger, *Sermon on the Mount*, 56–60.

[41] The view of the Scofield Reference Bible. See Kissinger, *Sermon on the Mount*, 61–66.

[42] The view of J. Jeremias, *The Sermon on the Mount*. See Kissinger, *Sermon on the Mount*, 108–110.

[43] Tyre and Sidon are also suggestive of *the coastlands* who wait for the Servant's law. See Isaiah 42:4.

[44] It is possible, of course, to read these as two separate figures, but the evidence of the gospels suggests that Jesus saw himself fulfilling both roles.

[45] Isaiah 40:9; 52:7.

[46] Isaiah 50:4–11; 51:4, 16; 52:13–53:12. The Targum to these passages, suggests that the Servant could have been interpreted as the Messiah in the synagogues of Jesus' time. See W. Zimmerli & J. Jeremias, *The Servant of God*, 67–72.

[47] The evangelistic character of the blessings is argued at length by E. Percy, *Die Botschaft Jesu*, 40ff.; J. Dupont, *Les Béatitudes*; and H. Schürmann, *Das*

Lukasevangelium, 325–336. For a review of this and my own treatment of the question see Seccombe, *Possessions*, 34f, 85ff.

[48] 1QM 14.7.

[49] For 'the Poor' see Isaiah 41:8–20; 49:13; 61:1; Psalms 9:12, 18; 68:10; 74:19, 21; 76:9; 149:4; Zechariah 11:7, 11 (Damascus Document 19:7–9); Isaiah 18:7 (LXX); 25:1–5; Psalms of Solomon 10:6; Midrash Psalms 9:12; 60:3; 68:11; *Genesis Rabbah* 71:1; *Numbers Rabbah* 11:1; *Pesikta Rabbati* 36 (162a); *Protevangelium of James* 20:2. Also Seccombe, *Possessions*, 35–43. For 'the captives' see Isaiah 52:2; Psalms 79:11; 102:20; 126; Testament of Dan 5:10–13. Also Seccombe, *Possessions*, 51–58. For 'those who mourn', see Isaiah 61:2f., 7; 66:10; 30:19; 35:10; Psalms 126; 137:1; Jeremiah 31:10–13; IQM 12:13–15; 17:7f.; 18:14f.; *Derek Erez Rabbah* 2:20 (56a). Also Seccombe, *Possessions*, 88. For 'The blind' see Seccombe, *Possessions*, 59–61. For 'The hungry' see Seccombe, *Possessions*, 79–81.

[50] For the use of 'the Poor' as a self-designation of the Qumran community see Seccombe, *Possessions*, 41–43.

[51] Daube, *Judaism*, 198f.; Seccombe, *Possessions*, 98ff.

[52] Seccombe, *Possessions*, 94–96.

[53] There may also be an echo here of Isaiah 49:18.

[54] The exception may be the isolated proverb 'If your enemy is hungry feed him; and if he is thirsty, give him water to drink; for you will heap burning coals on his head, and the Lord will reward you' (Proverbs 25:21f.). This could be practical advice on how to shame an enemy out of being an enemy, and as such is not far removed from the strategy that is apparent in the Sermon on the Mount and in Jesus' life. Cf. Romans 12:19–21.

[55] M.D. Hooker (*Jesus and the Servant*) argues that Jesus did not see himself in the light of the Servant's mission; J. Jeremias (in Zimmerli & Jeremias, *Servant*, 99–106) argues that he did.

[56] Neither Jeremias nor Hooker give any attention to the possible influence of the Servant passages on the Sermon on the Mount.

[57] Isaiah 41:8ff.; 42:1ff.; 42:18ff.; 43:10; 44:1; 49:1ff.; 50:4–10; 52:13–53:12.

[58] Matthew's seventh beatitude, 'Blessed are the peacemakers,' fits the context, not by delineating a certain virtue, but by characterizing those who share in the Servant mission.

[59] Israel prided herself on being a teacher and light-bearer because of her possession of Torah (Romans 2:19), but she failed. Jesus appears in the Sermon as a teacher of God's law and demands its wholehearted fulfilment. At the same time he indicates a share in this teaching role for all who will purify themselves,

removing the logs from their own eyes (Luke 6:39–42; Matthew 5:14–19; 6:22f.; 7:3–6, 15–23).

[60] See the discussion in E. Lohmeyer, *Our Father*, 134–159. Insofar as Jesus' meals were anticipations of the kingdom, the request for food is included.

[61] The approach in this section is broadly what I have argued in Seccombe, *Possessions*. See also Yoder, *Politics*; H.J. Degenhardt, *Lukas – Der Armen Evangelist*; L.T. Johnson, *The Literary Functions of Possessions in Luke–Acts*; D.L. Mealand, *Poverty and Expectations in the Gospels*.

Chapter 10

Miracle Worker

A Contradiction

The observant reader is probably aware by now of a glaring contradiction in my presentation of Jesus. On the one hand, I have argued that the newness of his ministry consisted in the fact that he announced the kingdom of God not as something for the future, but as something immediate, either actually present, beginning to be present, or so close that it could be reckoned with as an urgent reality. The age of promises and waiting was over, the day of God's release had dawned. On the other hand, nothing of what the Jews justifiably expected to be characteristic of the kingdom had arrived. Things remained much as they had been, and even Jesus implied that suffering would continue; that the joy and laughter of the kingdom's manifestation was not *now* but *in that day* (Luke 6:20–26). This is the same question mark that Schweitzer and many others in the twentieth century raised over the ministry of Jesus: he said that the kingdom of God would come, but nothing happened. What possible justification could Jesus have for speaking as though the messianic age had arrived when conditions of oppression and injustice continued and while he prepared his listeners for suffering?

The first thing to realize is that Jews in Jesus' day distinguished between the period of time in which the Messiah would actually do what was necessary to establish his kingdom and 'the world (age) to come'; the kingdom itself. The Dead Sea community, for example, expected the coming 'Prince' to establish God's kingdom by means of a long and intense conflict.[1] It would not have surprised Jesus' listeners, then, to learn that suffering was in the offing and that difficult things were expected of them, even as they were told that the time of fulfilment had arrived. But was *anything* happening? Anything, that is, but talk?

John the Baptist's Dilemma

One person who at the time felt this contradiction very deeply was John the Baptist. He had warned the nation to prepare for 'the coming one' who would gather the righteous into God's granary and burn the chaff with unquenchable fire. Following what he thought was God's leading he had even identified Jesus as the 'coming one'. So where now was the promised liberation and light? John was wasting away in a lightless cell, captive of the half-Gentile Herod, his most likely and immediate prospect being that *he* would be treated as chaff and burnt up in the conflict of political and emotional passions of Herod and Herodias. Every day he must have strained for news of something big beginning to happen outside, but Jesus appeared to be doing little more than talking. It is understandable that he began to doubt.

So he sent two of his disciples to Jesus with the question, 'You are the Coming One aren't you? – or are we to wait for another?' (Luke 7:18ff.; Matthew 11:2ff.). The form of his question shows that John has not altogether given up hope on Jesus, but wants to see some action. Perhaps the question was intended to give him a nudge to get on with the job. In any case that was precisely what Jesus did; he continued his work with the crowds, and then sent the messengers back to report to John what they had seen and heard: 'Blind people see again, crippled people walk, lepers are made clean and the deaf hear, dead people are brought back to life, the poor are hearing the gospel, and blessed is the person who does not take offence at me.' Manifestly, something more than talk was taking place. Captives of a kind were being released, and restoration was a reality at least in Jesus immediate environment (for those who did not take offence at him).[2] Jesus pointed to his miracles as proof of the presence of the kingdom.[3]

Miracles

Assessment of Jesus' miracles is complicated by the dominance of materialist philosophy over the past two centuries. In the name of science, though not on scientific grounds, the universe has been treated as a closed mechanical system in which everything proceeds according to fixed laws, every event is logically and theoretically predictable, and miracles are impossible. Many writers have been prepared to grant that Jesus had a natural aptitude for healing the physically and emotionally distressed, which was perhaps the origin of his reputation as a healer, but they do not allow that this could have moved beyond the limits of what is in accord with 'nature'. The various nineteenth-century lives of Jesus took either a rationalist or a mythological approach to 'anti-nature' miracles. The rationalist approach sought to explain the miracles in purely natural terms. For example, the five thousand whom Jesus fed exercised 'an extreme frugality' and therefore survived in the desert, 'and in this there was naturally seen a miracle'.[4] Again, Jesus did not really die on the cross and so was able to appear afterwards to his disciples.[5] The mythological approach treats the miracles as non-historical means of conveying a believed truth. For example, the healing of the leper is a story invented by disciples who wanted to give expression to their belief that Jesus was greater than the prophets of the Old Testament.[6] Rationalistic explanations of the miracles have now mostly been recognized as desperate expedients to save the essential historicity of the gospel narratives without doing damage to materialist assumptions. Treatments of the miracles as legendary or mythological, however, are still very much to the fore. Bultmann's dictum ('Modern science does not believe that the course of nature can be interrupted ... by supernatural powers')[7] remains axiomatic for many treatments of the life of Jesus. As otherwise sympathetic an author as Michael Grant feels forced to relegate the gospel miracles to Jewish story-telling traditions which could not distinguish the natural from the supernatural, nor metaphor from reality.[8]

Miracles and Science

It is a modern-day myth that the world prior to the birth of modern science was so poor in its understanding of nature that miracles were perceived as almost everyday occurrences. Any reading of literature from the centuries around the time of Jesus will quickly show that a miracle, then as now, was regarded as normally impossible; only made otherwise by the intervention of God or gods.[9] Some of the ancients were more alive to the possibility of such intervention than some moderns, but any amount of modern literature, produced within the milieu of the scientific world, could be cited to show a greater expectation of the miraculous than in some ancient literature. The difference is not that between scientific and non-scientific worldviews, but whether the material universe is seen as either closed or open to intrusion from a higher power. Has science proved the non-existence of God, or discovered some reason why divine intervention is impossible? Certainly not! It is not science as such which rules out the miraculous, but a philosophy which arose because of the success of scientific endeavour.

There is a paradox in this, for the beginnings of modern science are to be found in the work of those with deep, often Christian convictions about God. Believing that the universe was the handiwork of an intelligent God they looked for rationality in its structure, in the form of orderly relationships in its workings and parts, and they found them. Johann Kepler, for example, believed that there had to be some simple, understandable pattern in the movements of the planets around the sun. He spent much of his life working with a set of astronomical measurements, looking for that relationship. After thirty years of trying and discarding various theories and hypotheses he eventually succeeded: the planetary orbits are elliptical.[10] There was and is no scientific law which says that nature has a pattern and order comprehensible to the human mind. It was something which Kepler and others expected because of their belief in a rational God who had made humanity in his own image. That it turned out as they expected is something of a miracle itself: it is inexplicable in a materialist framework, even though it is the fundamental axiom of all scientific endeavour.[11]

So successful was the scientific method in unlocking the rationality of the universe that it was not long before philosophers – I will not call them scientists – felt they could safely ignore God because his presence did not feature in the nexus of cause and effect. The philosopher–mathematician Laplace is alleged to have said, when asked by Napolean where God fitted into his system, 'Sir, I have no need of that hypothesis'. All he was really saying was what the biblical notion of creation had always implied: that God is not a part of his creation; that in any analysis, measurement or observation of the physical universe, God will not appear. He is the originator of it and the ground of its being, not one of its contingent parts.

The twentieth century saw a gradual wane in the influence of the kind of 'scientism' typified by Laplace's comment.[12] Science as the benevolent deity who would solve all problems and grant us a glorious new age is dead. It is now generally seen to create as many problems as it solves. Scientists (and philosophers) have also become more humble about the limits of scientific method. I have noticed in many universities that the number of science students professing Christianity significantly outnumbers those studying in the humanities. Powerful as science is in helping us to understand the workings of the physical universe and develop a technology to control it, it is not competent to pontificate on what may or may not lie beyond its observation, nor to judge whether outside intervention is possible or not. The only thing which can decide this last question is the proper scientific method of observation and study of the evidence. Bultmann's dictum is an unsupported meta-physical postulate which hopelessly prejudices any enquiry into the life of Jesus, because it disallows, without consideration of the evidence, the miracle working, which on any reckoning is one of his chief character-istics in the gospel portraits.

Seeking Evidence for Miracles

When we turn to the evidence for miracles, and in particular to Jesus' miracles, we immediately confront a problem. Normal scientific method depends on being able to make repeated observations of the same phenomenon. A miracle, by its nature, happens once only; if it is repeatable it becomes part of the natural process and ceases to be a miracle. Alleged miracles can only be investigated by historical means. As such the evidence for them is chiefly the testimony of witnesses, though sometimes circum-stantial evidence may weigh for or against a positive judgement. Contrary to what is often claimed, miracles do not radically disturb nature. If Jesus did create bread to feed five thousand, most effects of the miracle could be expected to have been absorbed into the natural environment within a few days. The bellies which received the food would be empty and crying for more; the scraps would have turned mouldy and even if taken and examined in a laboratory would not have yielded any evidence of their true origin. The ongoing ramifications of the miracle, if such it was, would be found not in the natural environment, but in the thoughts of those who witnessed it – perhaps in the argument that was going on in the synagogue at Capernaum (John 6:25ff.).

The next thing that confronts us in examining the evidence for Jesus' miracles is a problem of overkill. The significance of miracles lies in their being 'impossible' and unexpected. But we find no shortage of alleged miracles, in history and in the modern world, threatening to cast doubts either on the reality of Jesus' miracles or on the uniqueness of his miraculous power. In relation to the former, it is certainly illogical to conclude that all miracles have logical explanations, however much one may be drawn in that direction. Many alleged miracles can neither be proved nor disproved, and even if all others were disallowed, it would not be an argument for or against Jesus' miracles. As for the latter doubt, it is important to note that little of importance usually hangs on the truth or otherwise of this or that alleged miracle. Once in a prayer group in Sydney I heard someone relate a tale of a person in New Zealand who had a glass eye. He prayed for sight and was able to see – through the glass eye. So the story went. I confess I was unable to suppress a giggle. But is God incapable of such a thing? Surely not, if he created the world. Nevertheless the thing seemed inappropriate and grotesque. And it did not matter much one way or another. If investigation proved it had happened, it would only support what can be known on other grounds, that God is merciful and powerful. On another occasion I was involved in prayer and laying on of hands for a young woman who had suffered from severe epilepsy from the age of two. She ceased her daily fits and until I lost contact with her had never suffered another attack except on one occasion when she was thrown from a horse. But what was the significance of it? At the time it certainly confirmed to those who were involved that God was real and listening; I well remember being in a state of fear for weeks afterwards. It led to no Christian faith on the part of the woman. Nor did it have any long term faith effect for me. It was just one of those things. The significance of a miracle really depends on the framework of meaning in which it takes place. Does it signify anything? Does it signify anything of significance? If it does not, it is hardly worth the bother of investigation.

The miracles of Jesus are of great significance, for they are part (not all) of the reason people believe his claim to have come from God. They invite investigation, therefore, by those who wish to check whether belief in him is justified – by those who want to know whether to believe in him and by those who wish to dispute his claims. However, the moment one begins any such investigation two other first-century miracle workers also demand attention. Jesus was one of a whole line of wonder-workers, it is sometimes said, and therefore not so unique as Christians have tried to pretend.[13]

Other First-Century Wonder-Workers

First we should rid ourselves of the notion that the ancient world was full of miracle workers. No single miracle was attributed to John the Baptist, great as his fame was (John 10:41). According to the gospel writers the intense excitement of the crowds who flocked to accompany Jesus was generated in part by his miracles. People were excited because 'Never since the world was created has it ever been heard that someone opened the eyes of a man born blind' (John 9:32). This hardly describes the reaction of people for whom 'miracles' were commonplace.

Miracle workers are not commonplace even in the Bible. They occur at only three points in the two thousand year span of its story: with Moses and his disciple Joshua at the time of the Exodus and entry into Canaan, with Elijah and his disciple Elisha at the time of the great conflict between the followers of Yahweh and Baal, and with Jesus and his disciples. There are occasional other happenings of a miraculous kind, but these are sporadic and isolated; often answers to prayer such as occur in all ages.

Vermes' theory that Jesus was part of a 'charismatic stream' of miracle workers in early Judaism is built on an impossibly slender foundation. He cites only one figure from before the time of

Jesus, Onias the Circle-maker, who is accredited with one startling answer to a prayer for rain.[14] As far as the Jews of Jesus' time went, they had only Moses, Joshua, Elijah and Elisha with whom to compare him. There are no other significant miracle workers from pre-Christian times. Jesus must have been startlingly new, if even half the miracles recorded of him took place. It is an oddity that itself begs some explanation, that later in the same century we hear of two other miracle workers, one from the Greco–Roman world and one from the Jews.

Apollonius of Tyana

The first of these was Apollonius of Tyana. He was born around the beginning of the Christian era in the Cappodocian town of Tyana. He was sent to Tarsus for his education where he embraced the philosophy and lifestyle of the disciples of Pythagorus. He spent his life as a wandering philosopher, living in temples and seeking to reform their worship. His wanderings took him to Babylon to study the wisdom of the Magi, to India to learn from the Brahmins and to Egypt to the Gymnosophists ('naked philosophers'). Apollonius' story is told by a Greek, Philostratus, at the request of the wife of the Emperor, Septimius Severus. His sources were the stories he found in the temples Apollonius had visited, hitherto unknown memoirs of a disciple of Apollonius, which had been given to the Empress, some letters and treatises of Apollonius himself, and a history of Apollonius' career in Agae. Philostratus consciously ignored four books about Apollonius by a certain Moeragines.

Prior to his time with the Brahmins, Apollonius is not attributed with anything worthy of the name miracle. He is only credited with the healing of a man suffering from dropsy, through wise advice to simplify his diet,[15] and with chasing off a hob-goblin by the abuse he heaped upon it.[16] Amongst the Brahmins he is said to have witnessed the sages provide a mother with a letter which they claimed would drive out a demon if it was read before her possessed daughter. They also restored a young man's withered leg by massage, gave sight to an eyeless man, cured a paralysed man, and prescribed a ritual involving a live rabbit for a woman suffering difficulties in childbirth![17] This bracket of incidents is imbedded in a travel narrative that gives detailed descriptions of the various kinds of dragons that are plentiful in India, including one that eats elephants and is only caught by charming it to sleep by magic letters (when killed its head is found to be full of precious gems).[18] This, with stories of griffins and phoenixes,[19] does not inspire confidence in the memoirs of Apollonius' Indian adventure.

After his return from India his miracles become more plentiful, though not so frequent if one considers them spread over the rest of his one hundred year lifetime. He stilled a plague at Ephesus by recognizing its instigator as an old beggar and urging the Ephesians to stone him to death. On doing so they realize the beggar is a demon in disguise, and on removing the heap of stones find a huge foam-vomiting dog.[20] In Athens, realizing that a young man in his audience was possessed, he conversed with the demon and ordered it to leave and give visible evidence of doing so. It obeyed and pushed over a statue on its way.[21] In Corinth Apollonius saved a young man from the fangs of a lamiat (vampire).[22] In Rome he is credited with raising a dead girl through touching her and whispering a secret spell, though Philostratus is careful to point out evidence to the effect that she was not really dead.[23] In Tarsus he cured a boy who took on the behaviour of the dog who had bitten him; Apollonius divined the identity of the dog, made it lick the boy's wounds so curing him, and finally cured the dog.[24] When he was in prison in Rome his disciple realized that he was no man at all, but a divine superman – he was at will able to put his feet in and out of the fetters which bound him, without sacrifice, prayer or any word.[25] He disappeared mysteriously from the courtroom, after giving his defence before the Emperor

Domitian also translating himself to another town where he had previously sent his disciple.[26] Various conflicting accounts are given of his death,[27] and a tale is told of his revealing himself in a dream after his death to a doubter who had prayed to him for nine months for a revelation.[28] Apollonius is also said to have often displayed a gift of prescient vision.

Such are the miracles of the 'divine man' with whom Jesus is most often compared. Though, as Eusebius in his critique of Apollonius points out, until the attempt to bolster paganism against the inroads of Christianity at the beginning of the fourth century, no one had ever made the comparison.[29]

Even if we take a charitable attitude towards the stories themselves, we must still ask about their significance. There is no indication that for Apollonius himself they had any significance at all, except perhaps as a demonstration of his wisdom and prescient skills.[30] For Philostratus they sometimes serve to show his greatness, at the same time as being something of an embarrassment, for, apart from the sheer interest of the story, one of his main purposes in writing was to defend Apollonius against the charge of being a magician. He hardly succeeds; the man who emerges from his story is attractive as a philosopher, but the magical colouring of the situations he confronts and the means he employs to solve them are bizarre.

Rabbi Hanina ben Dosa

Rabbi Hanina ben Dosa is the miracle worker par excellence of rabbinic literature. Apart from the fact that he came from 'Arab in Galilee' and was a disciple of Rabbi Johanan ben Zakkai (and therefore belongs to the second half of the first century), nothing is known of him except a string of stories and an occasional saying. He comes from a very different milieu than does Apollonius of Tyana. There is nothing of magic about Hanina; he is a man of prayer to whom God paid special attention. This is attractively illustrated in the story of his healing of Rabbi Johanan's son:

> He put his head between his knees and prayed for him and he lived. Said R. Johanan ben Zakkai: if Ben Zakkai had stuck his head between his knees the whole day, no notice would have been taken of him. Said his wife to him: Is Hanina greater than you are? He replied to her, No; but he is like a servant before the king [he is constantly in the kings presence], and I am like a nobleman before the king [who is granted access only at fixed times].[31]

Hanina also healed the son of Rabbi Gamaliel, on this occasion from a distance. Servants come asking him to pray, he goes upstairs and then returns and tells them they can leave, because the boy is healed. They ask him whether he is a prophet, but he replies that he has learnt from experience that if his prayer is fluent his request has been granted. The servants make a note of the exact time, and when they arrive home find that the son indeed asked for food at that precise moment.[32] These are the only healings attributed to Hanina, though the Mishnah makes it clear that he was known as one who healed through prayer.[33] He is also said to have had prescient knowledge in relation to the condition of a girl who had fallen into a well.[34] On another occasion he was so engrossed in his prayers that he did not feel a snake wrap around his leg and bite him. The snake was subsequently found dead at the entrance to its hole.[35] On one occasion he is said to have prayed for rain, to come and it came, to go and it went.[36] Another time he was entreated by a woman who was building a house and found that the roof beams were not long enough. He prayed and the beams became long enough to project half a metre on either side of the house.[37] Stories are also told of an encounter he had with the she devil,[38] about his goats, and about his ass (so saintly that it refused to eat the untithed food of the robbers who had stolen it).[39]

What are we to make of Rabbi Hanina ben Dosa? The first thing to ask is what did those of his own time make of him? The answer would seem to be, a saintly man whose prayers were particularly efficacious. Beyond this we could hardly go, unless suspicions were aroused that he represented an attempt on the part of Judaism to compete with Christianity and claim its own miracle worker. There is little indication of this, although the similarity between Hanina's healing of Gamaliel's son and Jesus' healing of the centurion's servant is hardly to be put down to 'a recognized charismatic pattern'.[40] Some influence from the gospel story seems more probable. With two healings, a number of bizarre haggadic tales involving himself, his wife and his animals, and few recorded teachings to his name,[41] Hanina is little more than a curiosity in the total structure of Judaism. It cannot be said that it gains anything essential from him, nor would it lose much if a sceptic were to dismiss his miracles from the scene. Very different for Christianity is the case of Jesus ben Joseph!

Jesus the Miracle Worker

In assessing the miracles of Jesus we need first to note the closeness of the sources to his life. Even taking the latest datings of the documents given by mainstream scholars (Q: AD 50–60; Mark: AD 64–70; Luke: AD 70–80; Matthew: AD 80–90; John AD 90–100), we are still within the lifespan of those who witnessed Jesus' ministry.[42] Secondly, we should note their variety. We are dealing in the gospels with four compilers employing at least five different sources. And, as we shall see, we can also add the testimony of some of Jesus' opponents.

In the miracle stories themselves we must examine the base upon which the miracles are erected. Are the situations to which Jesus responds believable, or do they strain credulity to the point at which we must conclude the author to be romanticizing or operating with a distorted perception of the real world? For example, when Apollonius displays his prescient powers by perceiving that the beautiful young woman with whom his disciple has fallen in love is really a vampire-spirit, or when he sees in the old beggar a plague-carrying spirit and orders him stoned, or when Hanina confronts the she-devil and restricts the patrols of her 180,000 destroying angels to Wednesday and Saturday nights, are we not justified in being suspicious? In comparison, the problems to which Jesus responds with miraculous answers are remarkably ordinary. None of them transgresses the bounds of the natural, except perhaps the cases of demon-possession. I will discuss these in due course, but for the moment let us simply regard them as cases of mental disturbance, epilepsy, deaf-muteness, or whatever they are presented as in their respective stories. Possession, after all, was not a visible condition, but a diagnosis of the cause of certain conditions which are all too common even in our own time. So remarkably human are the situations to which Jesus responds that even to read a list of the miracles recorded in the gospels is to gain a vivid impression of ordinary life in the first century: the wedding feast, men at their work, the common ailments of rich and poor, the fringe-dwelling lepers, the embarrassment of the unclean woman, the near demented harlot (if that is what she was), the funeral, the crowds, the 'odd' person in the synagogue, the incurably insane. If we were to judge the character of the gospel writers (or those who first framed these stories) from these base situations, we could hardly accuse them of an over-imaginative or sensational turn of mind.

Perhaps the oddest base situation is that of the man waiting to be healed at the Pool of Bethesda (John 5:2–7). In John's account he is waiting for the pool to be stirred so he can throw himself into the water and be healed. Yet the credibility of this is confirmed by recent archaeological discoveries. The pool of Bethesda has now been identified and excavations have uncovered healing grottos, indicating that a tradition of healing must have been associated with the place. The additional line in some later manuscripts to the effect that an angel would periodically stir the water, and that the first into the pool after such a disturbance would be healed, may inform us accurately of the legend associated with the pool.[43]

Characteristics of Jesus' Miracles

What are the chief characteristics of Jesus' miracles? The first is the sheer number of them. On a rough count there are thirty-five separate miracle stories prior to the resurrection, belonging to a period of something like two years. In addition to the separate stories are summary descriptions of Jesus healing among the crowds, indicating that healing and exorcism were a constant accompaniment of his mission. 'The news of him spread into all of Syria. And they brought to him all who were sick with various diseases and suffering from severe pain, demoniacs and lunatics and paraplegics, and he healed them' (Matthew 4:24; cf. Mark 1:33–34). Healing activity on this scale was unique in the ancient world, however recent or distant the memory. John records that many Jews in Jerusalem believed in Jesus because they could not imagine that the Messiah could possibly do more miracles than he had done (John 7:31). Has there been anything like it since?

The crowd healings obviously belonged to large meetings where Jesus would also instruct the people. Characteristic of the miracles that are related individually, however, is their natural setting. They took place not in contrived meetings, but 'on the way' or wherever Jesus encountered the situation. They thus distinguish themselves sharply from the healings that took place in cultic shrines, such as those attributed to Asclepius at Epidaurus.[44] Consonant with the absence of any contrived or favourite setting is the lack of any ritual or magical technique. Nor is there ever any indication that he is performing something which is difficult for him. All the miracle stories give the impression that such activity was natural, and made no more demands on him than anything else. The impression of a miracle comes only from the reaction of the witnesses, rarely from Jesus himself.

Sometimes Jesus performs his miracles by a word of command, as when he orders the storm to cease (Mark 4:35–41). Often, however, he makes no reference to the problem itself, but simply moves to treat the situation as though the problem no longer exists, as when he tells the paralytic to take his bed and go home (Mark 2:1–12), and when he sends the ten lepers to show themselves to the authorities (Luke 17:12–19). Sometimes he touches the person he is healing. Indeed, this may have been his common practice, for we often hear of people bringing their sick 'that he might touch them'. But, as the case of the centurion shows, it was by no means necessary (Luke 7:1–10). On a few occasions Jesus employed some intermediate means, as when he spat and touched the tongue of the man who had a speech impediment (Mark 7:33), when he spat on the eyes of the blind man at Bethsaida (Mark 8:22ff.), and when he sent another blind man to wash in the pool of Siloam (John 9:7). The most surprising 'technical' feature of the gospel miracles is Jesus' almost complete lack of observable prayer. All the gospels portray him in other respects as a man who loved to pray, but he does so in only one of the miracle stories (John 11:41–42), and then almost apologizes to God for it! This is not to say that he did not pray in relation to miracle working, but it does indicate that he usually felt under no compulsion to make this obvious.

For the most part Jesus' miracles were done out of compassion. This is in glaring contrast to the malicious miracles that are attributed to him in his childhood by later apocryphal writings,[45] and to the miracles his disciples would have liked to perform (Luke 9:54f.). He consistently refused to accede to demands for a sign,[46] but seems never to have refused the genuine cry for help. The great majority of the miracles, therefore, are healings. On two occasions Jesus is portrayed as experiencing unusual emotions in the context of working a miracle. At the healing of the leper (Mark 1:43) and at the raising of Lazarus (John 11:33, 35, 38) he shows deep anger, the cause of which is not at all clear, though its preservation in the narratives is a positive sign of genuine reminiscence.

Although he refused requests to do signs proving his divine authorization, Jesus nevertheless performed a number of miracles whose chief purpose seems to have been to give a sign. The healing of the paralytic, we have already seen, was to show the scribes that he had authority to forgive sin. It is hard to explain the feeding of the multitude or his walking to his disciples on the water on the grounds of pure compassion (Mark 6:31–51), especially if the feeding miracle was repeated in another setting (Mark 8:1–10). Certainly an element of compassion is present, but the chief reason for the miracle was to signify to the people and his disciples something about himself and his mission. The cursing of the fig-tree is best understood as a highly dramatic parable, whose sole significance was as a sign of what was coming (Mark 11:13–14, 20–21).[47] A number of sayings in the Gospel of John, in which Jesus appeals to the evidence of his miracles, are therefore entirely credible.[48] Some of the miracles appear to have been designed chiefly for the instruction of the disciples. Jesus could have avoided the storm altogether, as Apollonius did on one occasion – changing ships before the one in which he was travelling was wrecked, but he chooses instead (or God chooses for him) to go into the eye of the storm and command it to cease. The same is true of his walking to his disciples on the water. It was hardly necessary. Its purpose seems to have been to reveal himself to his disciples, as was also the case with the transfiguration (Mark 9:2ff.).

With perhaps one exception, none of the gospel miracles are performed for Jesus' own benefit. The exception is the story of the tax collectors coming to Peter to collect the half shekel tax. Jesus sends Peter to catch a fish in whose mouth he will find a coin to pay both his own and Jesus' tax (Matthew 17:24–27). The story seems so out of character with the rest of the miracles that it has been explained as a metaphor – Peter was meant to sell the fish for the required sum. However, no fish could possibly have been worth a shekel (four denarii),[49] and the story does suggest a miracle of sorts. We would do better to see it as part of Jesus' instruction of his disciples and admit that we do not have the full context to explain it more clearly.[50] It also stands as a warning against being too categorical in our classification of the miracle stories. They display a remarkable variety of motives.

Much of Jesus' healing is done as a response to faith. We have seen, however, that he did not seem to have interpreted this in a religious manner. He helped those who trusted his ability and good will enough to come and request his help. Faith was tantamount to simple reliance on him. 'Come to me!' appears to have been characteristic of his stance: 'Come to me all who are weary,' 'Let the children come to me,' 'Whoever comes to me I will not cast out' (Matthew 11:28; Mark 10:14; John 6:37). Jesus esponded to people's faith in him, and also sought to strengthen it. On the occasion when the woman with the chronic haemorrhage touched his garment in the crowd and felt herself healed, Jesus was aware that 'power had gone out from him', and demanded to know who had touched him (Mark 5:25–34). Of the many who were touching at the time, one person knew she had *really* touched him, and Jesus insisted she identify herself. This she did, 'in fear and trembling', and Jesus sends her away with 'Daughter, your faith has saved you. Go in peace and know that your sickness is cured.' From these words we may infer that Jesus took her further along the road of faith than the healing she perceived within herself had taken her. She is brought into personal relationship to Jesus (now she has really *come* to him) and receives her healing as a conscious gift. Along with it she receives the promise of eternal life. 'Your faith has saved you' is frequently rendered as 'Your faith has healed you.' This is justified to the extent that the Greek *sozo* can mean either to heal or to save. However, on Jesus' lips it often contains its larger meaning of 'save'. For example, he told the 'sinner' who anointed his feet with her tears that her faith had saved her when there was no question of physical healing. This means that for Jesus there was more involved in the healing transaction than a bodily cure; as well as healing people he indicated the inclusion in the kingdom of those who came to him in true faith. This points unmistakably to a greater significance for the miracles in Jesus' understanding than just acts of temporal compassion. We will look more at this after we have dealt with the question of exorcism.

One last characteristic of Jesus' miracle working activity, which rounds off the picture, is its transferability to his disciples. When the time came he invested them with an authority of their own to heal and to cast out evil spirits.

Demon Possession

Chief among Jesus' mighty works, according to the first three gospels, was his releasing people from the power of evil spirits. Mark introduces Jesus' Galilean ministry with his healing of the demoniac in the synagogue at Capernaum. In his first ministering 'tour' he describes him as 'preaching and casting out demons', overlooking the ordinary healing which also took place. The centrality of this activity in the synoptics has posed a problem to modern scholarly understanding of Jesus. For although the existence of demonic spirits was hardly questioned until quite recently, and is still a fact of life in many parts of the world, western medicine has dismissed them from its purview, and modern theology and philosophy for the most part have followed suit. While the scientific worldview commanded great popular prestige and authority, this attitude extended to the general populace in most developed countries, but with its decline over the last twenty years, with the resurgence of the occult, and with growing interest in eastern religions and spirituality in general, belief in spirits is on the rise once more. It is not uncommon nowadays to meet people who profess no faith in God, but who, because of personal experiences, have no doubts about the existence of evil spirits.

Spirits and the Modernist Worldview

The most telling reason for denying the existence of spirits is that to assume otherwise seems to endanger the very foundations of the scientific approach to the universe. In an animistic culture which is ruled by the fear of spirits there can be no thought of any consistency or order in nature; everything is influenced by a multitude of spirits, each with its own arbitrary wishes. The only way to find any order or safety in such a world is to placate the local demons as best one can so that they do not disrupt life too much. The idol-worshipper, for example, is driven by fear to make offerings to various gods in whose hands the different powers of life are thought to reside. But there is always the danger that paying too much attention to one may arouse the jealousy of another and cause trouble. At best life is a gamble. According to scientific presuppositions, however, nature is mechanical and orderly; it will behave tomorrow as I observe it to behave today. If the scientist, the engineer, the maintenance staff and the pilots (and these days the security personnel) do their tasks properly the aeroplane will fly; you can count on it. In reality there are no 'gremlins' in the system. If there is a problem, investigation will discover the fault, and it will not be the work of a demon.

If the animistic understanding of the universe is compared with the scientific, and the two are judged by which works best there can be no question that the scientific wins a thousand times over. It would seem to follow from this that spirits are either non-existent or powerless to effect the physical world, and therefore irrelevant. With the latter conclusion the Bible agrees, with a couple of qualifications.

Spirits and the Bible

The worldview of the Bible gives no grounds for thinking that spirits have any power to effect physical things. A spirit cannot bump your hand when you are driving, nor can it drive a kangaroo or kudu into the path of your car (otherwise I would be dead!). The Bible teaches that one God made and maintains the universe and that, for humanity's benefit he made it function in an orderly manner; he did not make chaos (Isaiah 45:18; cf. Genesis 1). There is no conflict with science when the Bible attributes every happening in the physical world ultimately to God, since scientific laws may be viewed simply as the orderly patterns which he has established. But there would be chaos if we were once to suppose that spiritual agencies outside of God's will had independent power over the physical realm. Whenever the Bible appears to attribute something physical to the agency of Satan, as for example the afflictions of Job, it is usually made clear that what actually happens is done with God's permission, and is therefore still ultimately attributable to the providence of God.[51]

On this understanding of the universe there is no objection in principle to a miracle. If the underlying order of our world is but the creative expression of a rational God who desires that we should live in an orderly environment, then a miracle is not an 'impossibility' or a contradiction, but an extraordinary (out-of-the-ordinary) working whose 'order' or rationality is not to be found in scientific laws but in the revelational or saving purposes of God. We may learn from the God-fearing pioneers of modern science, who sought for the order and rationality they were sure would be present in God's creation, by insisting just as firmly that miracles, if they occur, will not be arbitrary 'freaks' of nature, but *signs* which take place in a profound context of meaning.

Temptation

What then of the activity of Satan and evil spirits? The one possibility which is not exhausted by what we have already said is their effect upon the human mind. Christian tradition has always affirmed the possibility of people being *tempted* by the Devil. It is never suggested that *all* temptation derives from the Devil. The *world* (societal ideas, pressures, fashions) and the *flesh* (a person's own desires and ambitions) are also potent sources of temptation. But in addition to these the Devil is able to introduce suggestions to the mind. If this be granted, it implies at least some form of psycho-spiritual contact. Not necessarily control: people are not compelled to obey these suggestions, but if they do they allow the Devil's will to find expression in the physical world. It is always human beings who pull the triggers and push the buttons and issue the orders, but the evil and chaos they unleash may be of demonic inspiration.

Possession

Temptation, however, is not the same as possession. Possession indicates that satanic influence of an individual has gone a stage further; a separate, self-conscious spiritual entity has come to reside in the human organism and is competing for control of mind and body. Is such a thing conceivable? It is common in psychology and psychiatry to encounter cases where one person's mind is so heavily under the influence of a more dominant individual that a pathological situation develops. An Indian student once asked my advice with a problem: 'I always have my mother in my head,' was how he described it. It is in my opinion conceivable that demonic suggestion could become oppressive in an analogous manner. It is significant that in the modern resurgence of interest in spirits, and the corresponding revival of exorcism as a therapeutic method, the category of 'spiritual oppression' has come to describe those who appear to be under some kind of spiritual bondage, but show no evidence of an actual indwelling foreign intelligence. Again, however, this is not possession.

It must be said that the actual condition of possession is today relatively rare in western societies. It is not an illness that ordinary people contract, no matter how 'wicked' their lifestyle may be. I say this because there is a reactionary tendency in some circles to want to attribute many illnesses and psychiatric conditions – even bad habits – to possession, and to make exorcism a panacea for all ills. This can only have disastrous consequences. Nevertheless, the possibility that under particular circumstances the mind could be invaded by a demonic intelligence must at least be opened up for investigation. Some psychiatrists would rule it out of consideration from the beginning, but their reductionism is no more reasonable than that of those who want to attribute *all* mental ills to demonic activity.

Resurgent occultism seeks to make contact with spirits of one kind or another, and in some occult techniques people actually invite spirits to enter their minds and control them. In a case familiar to me, a sixteen year old student at a Sydney girls' school watched a television programme in which a woman demonstrated 'spirit writing'. In the following weeks when lessons were boring she would take a pen in her hand and invite a spirit to write with it. She began to receive messages. At the beginning it was a game which she could play when she wanted. In time, however, the messages began to come not only with the pen, but directly into her mind as she was trying to go to sleep. Eventually she lost all control of when they would come, and began to be afraid of what was happening to her. In conversation with another schoolgirl she heard (for the first time!) of the Holy Spirit and the two girls prayed together that the attacks on her mind would cease. They did, and she became a follower of Christ as a result.

I hesitate to bring forward a case like this, because I have no psychiatric qualifications and am unsure what a psychiatrist would have made of it. But it seems to me to illustrate the emergence of a pathological spiritual condition, which, had it continued its course, would probably have ended in a psychiatrist's clinic. What the psychiatrist's cure would have been I do not know, but the case is interesting in that a 'cure' was effected, not by an elaborate exorcism ritual but by the believing prayer of a schoolgirl. I know of other similar cases which are sufficient to convince me that possession is indeed a possibility where the mind's 'psychic door' is voluntarily opened. However, we are dealing with an uncharted area where quackery and deception are endemic. What is needed is for scientifically minded, well qualified and experienced psychiatrists (sceptics and believers) to keep good clinical notes on cases where there is occult involvement.[52]

Jesus encountered many sufferers in his day whom he diagnosed as 'demonized', or 'in an unclean spirit', and whom he restored by commanding the spirit (or spirits) to depart. Rationalistic theology has handled this by claiming that Jesus understandably shared the limited medical knowledge of his own generation, which saw all mental disturbance (some writers say all illness) as the work of evil spirits. However, this goes well beyond our evidence of medical knowledge in the Jewish world of the first century. It is certainly true that Jesus and his contemporaries regarded all evil and suffering as ultimately due to the Devil, but not in the sense of immediate cause. There is no evidence in or out of the New Testament that spirits were held to be the direct cause of all sicknesses. There is evidence of the penetration of Greek medical procedure into the first century Jewish world.[53] It is certainly true that some forms of mental disturbance were seen as the work of spirits – some of the Qumran hymns speak of 'the possessing spirits which attack without warning to take away sanity'.[54] But it runs ahead of the evidence to claim that all mental illness was seen in this way.[55] Two further things which should make us hesitate to dismiss Jesus as a child of his age are his undoubted success in healing these people (attributed by rationistic theology to the effect of his powerful personality), and the integral connection of his exorcistic work to his whole understanding of his mission. If he was mistaken in believing that he was contending with Satan and evil spirits, we will have to conclude that he was completely mistaken in his whole understanding of his mission.[56] On the other hand, we should at least hold out the possibility that a man so deeply attuned to things of the spirit may have had a better grasp of them than does our own still primitive science of psychiatry.

Jesus and Evil Spirits

Jesus achieved instant fame in Galilee on his first appearance in the Capernaum synagogue by commanding an evil spirit to leave its victim. We know nothing of the previous condition of the man, only that he interrupted the synagogue service shouting that he knew who Jesus was. When Jesus ordered the spirit to leave him he was convulsed and thrown to the floor. The awareness he had of who Jesus was and the fear he manifested in his presence is echoed in a number of other cases in the gospels. It seems to have been psychic in origin. In his summary description of Jesus' healing activity at the end of that Sabbath, Mark says that Jesus healed many possessed people and that 'he would not allow the demons to speak because they knew him' (Mark 1:34).

It is odd, to say the least, that the only people who seem to be recognizing Jesus for who he is at this point in the gospel story are the demon-possessed; odd too that Jesus should want to silence them. Various theories have been brought forward for this, the best known being Wilhelm Wrede's idea that it was an invention of the early church.[57] According to Wrede, Jesus never personally claimed to be the Messiah. The early church believed that he was, and solved the problem of him not having made the claim, by saying that he had kept it a deliberate secret. Why they should have involved the demons in this is unclear. One would have thought that if they were making it up it would have made a more edifying story to have *believers* confessing him and being sworn to secrecy.

Another explanation, which is no doubt correct as far as it goes, is that Jesus was unwilling to receive publicity from evil sources. But this leaves unanswered the question of why demons would want to give him publicity in the first place. The most obvious explanation for this is related to the very sensitive political situation within which Jesus worked. For someone to say they were the Messiah was to claim the legitimate kingship of Israel while Palestine was under the total control of the Emperor Tiberius. This was treason, and the penalty for treason was death. Every Jew in Jesus' day knew how earnestly that was to be taken. In the last great outburst of messianic fervour shortly after the death of Herod the Great, the Roman legate Varus had two thousand people crucified for treasonable activities.[58] According to Matthew, Jesus' family was in Egypt when this was taking place (Matthew 2:13–14, 20–23), but tales of it must have filled his childhood. The city of Sepphoris, six kilometres north of Nazareth had been burned to the ground and all its population sold as slaves.[59] The continuing sensitivity to possible revolutionary activity can be seen in Herod Antipas' reaction to John the Baptist. There was no dichotomy between spiritual and political in Jesus' day; the concept of a purely spiritual Messiah would have been a contradiction in terms.

This situation makes Jesus' silence about his identity fully understandable. It is probably the reason why John the Baptist usually spoke of 'the coming one' and not of the Messiah. The loud public exclamations of the demon-possessed, parading their knowledge of Jesus' identity and naming him as 'the Holy One of God' were malicious attempts to attract the kind of attention which would quickly have led to serious trouble. That Jesus wished to silence them is understandable. That he was able to command their obedience is further testimony to the authority he wielded and the weakness of demonic spirits before him.

Legion (Mark 5:1–20; Luke 8:26–39; Matthew 8:28–34)

The best known exorcism in history must be the story of Jesus' healing of the man called Legion. They meet on the opposite side of the Sea of Galilee in a region belonging to the ten Greek cities called the Decapolis. From a psychiatric point of view the man is suffering from a serious personality disorder. From a Jewish point of view (there is no suggestion that he is not a Jew) he is in a situation of total defilement – alienated from God and man – living in a cemetery, in a Gentile area where pigs are being farmed (what did he eat?). When he sees Jesus he is terrified and cries out to him not to torment him. He knows who Jesus is, but this time, no doubt because there were no crowds to worry about, Jesus does not silence him. Instead he engages the man, or rather, the spirit in the man, and learns that there are many of them. The spirits beg him not to send them 'out of the country' and at their request Jesus gives them permission to depart to the herd of pigs grazing nearby. The effect on the pigs is madness and a stampede which ends with the herd destroying itself in the lake. When the townspeople arrive on the scene they find the man clothed and in his right mind. In their fear of Jesus, and perhaps their anger over the loss of their herd they ask him to leave their territory. The healed man begs to accompany Jesus but is sent home to tell what God has done with him. He goes off and spreads Jesus' fame in the Decapolis.

Comparison of this story with others in the gospels allows us to make some general observations about Jesus' ministry of exorcism. First, with regard to outward symptoms: the man suffered from a disintegration of personality involving violence, self-destructiveness and loss of self-care consistent with the warring demands of different centres of consciousness on the one mind and body. Except that he is possessed of the same fearful awareness of Jesus' spiritual qualifications, his condition is not typical of other cases mentioned in the gospels. In fact none of the cases can be said to be typical. The man in the Capernaum synagogue is given no profile; that he suffered a convulsion in the process of being freed does not necessarily mean he was an epileptic. His external condition cannot have been too severe for him to have had a place in the synagogue. The source Q records the healing of a mute who begins to talk when a demon leaves him (Matthew 9:32–34; Luke 11:14–15). In another case the victim is blind and mute and receives both speech and sight (Matthew 12:22–24). A boy is described as deaf and mute and subject to periodic attacks in which he 'is torn, foams at the mouth, grinds his teeth and becomes rigid' (Mark 9:14ff.; Matthew 17:14ff.; Luke 9:37ff.). This could describe a severe case of epilepsy, but not necessarily so; there is no mention of unconsciousness following the attack. Finally, there is the case of the woman who has 'a spirit of weakness' and is unable to stand upright (Luke 13:10–16), it is not at all certain that Luke means this to denote a form of possession. Jesus simply declares her free of her weakness and she stands up, praising God; there is no ordering out of any evil spirit as in the other cases. Thus there is no basis in the gospels for associating possession with any specific set of symptoms, except perhaps the frequent presence of psychic knowledge. Deafness and muteness occur more than once, but there are other cases of deafness and speech impediment in the gospels where there is no suggestion of possession (e.g. Mark 7:32).

Secondly, the case of Legion attests the possibility of possession by a number of spirits. There is no need to take the name Legion to mean that he was literally possessed of six thousand, nor to suppose that there must have been at least one spirit for each of the two thousand pigs, but he is clearly represented as subject to attack by an unusually large number of demonic spirits. The only other case in the gospels of possession by more than one spirit is Mary Magdalene, who is said to have been freed of seven (Luke 8:2). There is insufficient information in the New Testament to do any more than note these two cases.

Thirdly, it appears to be a mark of Jesus' exorcisms, once he has established that he is dealing with a case of possession, to bypass the victims and address the demons directly.[60] The story of Legion, however, is the only case where he seeks the demon's name or enters into any dialogue other than to command their departure.[61]

Fourthly, the case of Legion is the one instance where clear evidence is given of the objective nature of the possession, though this coheres with a number of descriptions of exorcisms outside the gospels.[62] The stampede of the pigs would have proved to anyone who was doubtful the reality of the man's possession and the finality of his cure. Perhaps this was Jesus' reason for letting the demons go to the pigs, though there is no need to think that he foresaw their suicidal rush; the demons certainly did not.

Lastly, like many of the miracle stories this one is told with overtones which suggest that we are meant to perceive more than just an act of power. In this particular section of his gospel (4:35–6:6), Mark portrays various aspects of Jesus' miracle working authority. The first incident, in which he commands a storm to cease, evokes the image of God bringing the chaotic 'deep' to order by the command of his world-creating word.[63] There are similar overtones in the healing of Legion. The denizens of the great 'abyss' (Luke actually uses this word in 8:31) have broken free from their appointed place, and have turned this man's life into chaos. Jesus issues his word: the demons are returned to the deep and the life of a child of God is restored to order and peace.

Did Jesus Really Do These Things?

Some modern theologians place history and theology (meaning) at loggerheads, and assume that if a story has theological significance it is non-historical. This is an unfounded assumption, which prejudices itself from the outset against the gospels, for they tell the *story* of Jesus precisely because they are convinced that its history is profoundly significant and meaningful. Miracles and exorcisms play an important part in this. There is an odd idea that it is possible to capture and keep the meaning (theology) of a story, and at the same time discard as packaging the appearance of history.[64] But of course the meaning of the miracles has to do with the authority and power of Jesus, and if he did not do them they signify nothing at all about him. If anything they would cast doubt on the very thing the gospel writers set out to proclaim. For they are written to display a part of the basis on which people came to believe in his power, and if that part of the basis is fictitious we are inevitably led to question whether any real and adequate basis exists.

What evidence is there, then, that Jesus really did miracles? As I have indicated elsewhere, the main evidence for the whole of the Jesus story is the testimony of witnesses and those who wrote on the basis of their testimony. Our judgement of the miracles will be largely determined by our wider assessment of their whole enterprise. What we will look at here is whether there is any other evidence to support or undermine their testimony.

To begin with, two curious episodes could be mentioned. Both are hard to explain by any other means than that miracle working was an accepted part of Jesus' ministry. In one his disciples rebuke a man whom they discover is using his name to cast out evil spirits (Mark 9:38–39). Jesus corrects the disciples' possessiveness. The story shows the disciples in a bad light and is therefore unlikely to have been invented. It shows that Jesus' power as an exorcist was so well known that people were using his name for their own exorcism procedures. In the other episode

James and John ask Jesus whether they should call down fire from heaven on a Samaritan town which has refused to show him hospitality (Luke 9:51–56). Again Jesus rebukes his disciples and they are shown in a bad light. The story reveals how highly the disciples estimated Jesus' miracle working power, and even their own if acting with his permission.[65]

The claim that Jesus worked miracles goes back to the very first Christian preaching: 'Men of Israel, hear these words. Jesus of Nazareth, a man attested to you by God with mighty works and wonders and signs which God did through him in your midst, as you yourselves know' (Acts 2:22; cf. 10:38). It is difficult to see how the early preachers could have made much headway unless the people they addressed really did know that this was so. But Jesus was not only perceived as a miracle worker by those who preached him; there is evidence that even his opponents saw him that way.

The View of Jesus' Opponents

Mark describes the visit of a group of scribes from Jerusalem, who look suspiciously like a delegation sent to check out Jesus's activities (Mark 3:22–30). Their opinion of Jesus – and it looks like the gist of an official report – was 'He has Beelzebub (Satan).[66] He casts out demons with the help of the ruler of the demons.' This appears to have been the official explanation of Jesus in his own time, for it reappears on a number of other occasions.[67] It indicates that it was impossible for his opponents to deny the reality of his exorcisms (and probably his miracles). The only thing they could do was to dispute their origin.

It is telling that Judaism never disputed the reality of Jesus' miracles. Josephus says that Jesus was 'a doer of incredible deeds'.[68] In the Talmud it is given as the reason for his execution: 'He is going forth to be stoned because he practised sorcery and enticed Israel to apostasy'.[69] This assessment is repeated in various early anti-Christian sources which explain Jesus as a sorcerer who learned his art in Egypt.[70] It is also the view of one modern historian.[71] Arguing that Jesus was rightly interpreted as a magician, Morton Smith mounts a strong case for the reality of Jesus' miracle-working activity. Mark's story of Jesus' visit to Nazareth and his admission that Jesus was unable to do any mighty works there is inexplicable as a Christian invention, says Smith, it can only be historical. And if it was remembered that he did very few miracles in Nazareth, it must be true that he did more in other places.[72] The taunt of his enemies as he hung on the cross, 'He saved others, he cannot save himself,' also presumes that Jesus was well known as a healer.[73] Indeed, it would be difficult to see how Jesus ever got the following he did if it were not for the fact of his miraculous activity.[74] Strangely, at the end of his book Smith runs for the safety of the rationalist denial of miracles, and, on the basis of a preconceived worldview, seems to cut the ground from under his own conclusions.[75]

The Ongoing Effects of Miracles

It is obviously impossible in most cases to say anything in evidence of individual miracles. Their physical effects are quickly absorbed by the environment, those who experienced them are gone and only the written testimony of friends and enemies remains. However, each miracle related in the gospels, if it really happened, would clearly have had ongoing ramifications in someone's life, for each of them represented the invasion of God into an area of acute human need. The obvious example, which we have already discussed, is the resurrection, for which the very birth of Christianity stands as witness.

> If the coming into existence of the Nazarenes, a phenomenon undeniably attested by the New Testament, rips a great hole in history, a hole the size and shape of Resurrection, what does the secular historian propose to stop it up with?[76]

Mary Magdalene

Are there any other cases? Mary Magdalene we know to have been the most prominent of the women who gathered around Jesus and moved on into the early church. We have seen that her prominence came from her being the first to see the resurrected Jesus, though obviously she had some importance before this. The significant thing in relation to the miracle question is that Luke, in introducing her in his gospel, says that she was one of those whom Jesus had freed of evil spirits; prior to her coming to him she had been possessed by seven demons (Luke 8:2). It is unlikely that any early Christian writer would make such a negative statement about the origin of the best known woman in Christian memory, unless it was a known fact. Thus we have indirect evidence both of the extremity of Mary's original condition and of the fact that Jesus healed her in a way that was permanent.

Feeding the Five Thousand

The feeding of the five thousand has always been the most difficult miracle to believe. Yet, with the exception of the resurrection, it is the one that may have left the clearest mark on later history. Josephus describes the appearance less than thirty years after the time of Jesus of a number of extraordinary 'false prophets' who gathered great crowds of Jews together and promised to show them 'miracles':

> There arose another body of villains, with purer hands but more impious intentions, who no less than the assassins ruined the peace of the city. Deceivers and imposters, under the pretence of divine inspiration fostering revolutionary changes, they persuaded the multitude to act like madmen, and led them out into the desert under the belief that God would there give them tokens of deliverance.[77]

One of them, called the Egyptian, led his followers into the desert and then to the Mount of Olives, where he promised that at his word the walls of Jerusalem would fall and they would be able to enter the city and make him king. His 'miracle' was forestalled by the procurator Felix who met him with the Roman army.[78] Another, named Theudas, promised that at his command the Jordan river would part to allow his followers through. He too fell foul of the Roman army and was beheaded. Josephus gives the impression that others made similar attempts.[79]

Such an extraordinary behaviour pattern demands some explanation. P.W. Barnett has suggested that the first example of this pattern: a messianic pretender taking his disciples into the desert and showing them signs of deliverance, was the feeding of the five thousand. This being the case, it is not unlikely that Jesus' miracle provided the pattern and inspiration for later desperate attempts to force God's hand to intervene and establish his kingdom.[80]

We have looked at some of the philosophical, scientific and historical problems relating to Jesus' miracles and exorcisms and have seen both that there is no cogent reason for disallowing them without consideration of the evidence, and that there is good evidence for accepting the gospel witness to Jesus as a miracle worker and exorcist. It remains, finally, to look at the question of what Jesus' miracles meant.

Signs of the Kingdom

I began this chapter by drawing attention to John the Baptist's uncertainty about whether Jesus really was the coming Messiah. Jesus' answer was his works. The things he was doing belonged to the days of fulfilment, to the time of the King–Messiah. That Jesus was doing them was sufficient to show that he was the one and that the promised future was now present. Admittedly, it was not yet present in its completeness; that is why there was a danger that people (even John) might take exception to Jesus. Nevertheless enough was happening to signify that the kingdom of God was really and substantially breaking into the world. The powers of that kingdom were there where Jesus was and in the crowds that gathered around him. In his presence sickness gave way to health, deformity to wholeness, blindness to sight, deafness to hearing, madness to sanity. Even the unruly and destructive power of the storm was tamed. The poor of Israel were being invited to enter, there and then, into a fellowship with God which belonged to the time of restoration.

It was to these things that Jesus referred in response to the Pharisees' questions about the kingdom's coming, 'The kingdom of God is not coming with observation; nor will they say, "Behold here, or there!" For behold, the kingdom of God is among you' (Luke 17:20–21).

In similar vein he said to a group of Pharisees and Sadducees who challenged him to perform a sign from heaven, that they were experts in forecasting the weather, but were quite unable to discern the signs of the inbreaking kingdom which were all around them (Matthew 16:1–3).

The whole of Jesus' kingdom preaching, miracle working and exorcistic activity can be seen as a sign and an activity of God's kingdom, even when the majority of his healings may have been done out of pure compassion, without any thought on Jesus' part of performing a sign. For nothing is more expressive of the character and presence of the kingdom than that unaffected and effectual compassion which was so unique a mark of his ministry. The scribes accused him of performing his exorcisms by the power of Satan. The parables with which Jesus gave answer to that slander are the clearest indication of how he understood his own miraculous activity:

> Every kingdom divided against itself is laid waste, and if a house is divided against a house it falls. And if Satan has become divided against himself how will his kingdom stand? ... and if it is because

> I am possessed by Beelzebul that I drive out the demons, how do
> your sons drive them out? They then will be your judges. But if it
> is with the finger of God that I drive out the demons then the
> kingdom of God has come upon you.
>
> Whenever the strong man, fully armed, guards his own palace his
> possessions are in peace, but if a stronger than he comes upon him
> and conquers him, he seizes the armaments he was relying on and
> divides his spoils. Whoever is not with me is against me,
> and whoever does not gather with me scatters. (Luke 11:17–23;
> cf. Matthew 12:25–30; Mark 3:23–27)

We see first from this answer, that Jesus regarded Satan as the
holder of a kingdom, to which the kingdom of God was opposed.
His miracles, and in particular his exorcisms, are powerful evidence that the kingdom of God is in some way, or in some measure, present. He suggested that other Jewish exorcists be brought
in to testify to that.[81] Secondly, we see that Jesus imagined himself
as breaking into the castle of an armed strongman. The fact that
he was presently engaged in liberating captives was sure proof
that he was stronger than the strongman and had overpowered
him. Thirdly, we see that Jesus regarded those around him as part
of his mission. They were either helping him gather spoils from
Satan's kingdom – they were with him gathering together the
lost and captive people of God – or they were scattering. The
source of this last parable is Isaiah 49:24–25:

> Shall the spoils be taken from the strong man or his rightful
> captives be delivered? But thus says the Lord, Even the captives of
> the strong man shall be taken away, and the spoils of the tyrant
> shall be delivered. And I will contend with him who contends
> with you, and I will save your children.

In Isaiah the natural reference of the strong man is to the king of
Babylon who has taken the people of Israel captive from their
land to work as slaves enhancing the glory of his kingdom. It is
reasonable to suppose that Jews in the first century would have

updated the reference, making it refer to their captor, the Emperor of Rome. It is very important, therefore, to see that Jesus uses this image to describe his own kingdom-winning ministry, not in contrast to the empire of Rome, but to the kingdom of darkness, whose captives he was restoring to their place with God as he broke their bonds of satanic oppression. It begins to be apparent why, against all expectation, Jesus did not move in the direction of armed revolution, and why he refused to treat any human being as an enemy. As he saw it his real enemy was not flesh and blood, but the dark power behind all human beings and all human institutions. He was directing his attack against the very stronghold of evil, within whose power all humans were to be found, from the Emperor of Rome to the High Priest of Israel down to his own disciples.

Summary

Jesus appeared in Galilee proclaiming that the time of God's great jubilee had arrived. He announced salvation to Israelites, good or bad, inviting them to join him in inheriting the kingdom of God. With those who accepted his message he celebrated as though the kingdom had already come and likened them to the guests at the messianic banquet. However, from the outset he also met with suspicion and rejection, especially from officialdom. He then made it explicit that the kingdom was the inheritance of the poor of Israel, those who would actualize their suffering-servant destiny in the company of the suffering Son of Man. But the prospect of continued suffering raised in acute form the question of whether his announcement of the kingdom was not an obvious mistake and even a contradiction in terms, since the kingdom was to mean the end of all tears. Jesus answered that question by pointing to his miracles and preaching as the sign of the presence of the kingdom. Conflict was inevitable, for God's kingdom was breaking into a realm which had its tyrant. But the one commissioned to lead the invasion was already proving his superior strength, and people were being snatched from the old power to the new. Wherever Jesus was it could truly be said that God's kingdom was there, though battles were yet to be fought to decide the destiny of individuals and of the world.

Notes

[1] The best place to see this is in the War Scroll (1QM), especially 1QM11ff. See also *Psalms of Solomon* 17.

[2] Jesus' catalogue of his works calls to mind the promise of healing in the new age in Isaiah 35:5–6. Along with this is the promise of a new highway, 'the way of holiness'. Isaiah 35 was probably well known to the Baptist.

[3] This is disputed. Some hold the story of the messengers as a creation of the later church, but it is most unlikely that Christians would have invented John's doubts, especially when we consider John's positive testimony, which they evidently treasured. If at any time John did have doubts about Jesus, Jesus' disciples would have had a keen interest in their master's response. Jeremias (*Theology*, 87, 103–105) thinks Jesus' words originally had a metaphorical meaning, and described the enlightening and strengthening effect of his teaching. But this would not have answered the Baptist's doubts as he could certainly have claimed the same for his own teaching.

[4] E. Renan, *The Life of Jesus*, 103.

[5] This view is falsely attributed to Schleiermacher by Schweitzer, (*Quest*, 64f.) It is actually the view of H.E.G. Paulus.

[6] Strauss, *Life*, 437–441. It was Strauss who first propounded in detail the mythological approach to the gospels.

[7] Bultmann, *Mythology*, 15.

[8] Grant, *Jesus*, 33–44.

[9] See, e.g., *The Treatise of Eusebius against the Life of Apollonius of Tyana*, Philostratus, *The Life of Apollonius of Tyana* 2, 497–503.

[10] See R. Hooykaas, *Christian Faith and the Freedom of Science*, 17. *Encyclopaedia Britannica* article: Kepler, Johannes.

[11] If the human mind is ultimately a product of random forces, how does it come about that there is a congruence between its rational processes and the physical universe, which follows orderly mathematical patterns?

[12] For recent studies on miracles see C. Brown, *Miracles and the Modern Mind*; R.D. Geivett & G.M. Habermas, *In Defence of Miracles*.

[13] See H.D. Betz, 'Jesus as Divine Man' for the thesis that Jesus was originally understood as one of a hellenistic 'species' of 'divine man'.

[14] G. Vermes, *Jesus the Jew*, 58–82.

[15] Apollonius I, 9.

[16] Apollonius II, 4.

[17] Apollonius III, 38–40.

[18] Apollonius III, 6–8.

[19] Apollonius III, 48–49.

[20] Apollonius IV, 10; VIII, 7.

[21] Apollonius IV, 20.

[22] Apollonius IV, 25.

[23] Apollonius IV, 45.

[24] Apollonius VI, 43.

[25] Apollonius VII, 38.

[26] Apollonius VIII, 8.

[27] Apollonius VIII, 30.

[28] Apollonius VIII, 31.

[29] Eusebius, *Treatise against the Life of Apollonius*, 1.

[30] In his defence before Domitian he denies being either a god or a magician (Apollonius VIII, 7).

[31] *Bab. Talmud Berakoth* 34b.

[32] *Bab. Talmud Berakoth* 34b; *Mishnah Berakhot* 5:5.

[33] *Mishnah Berakoth* 5:5.

[34] *Bab. Talmud Baba Kamma* 50a.

[35] *Tosefta Berakoth* 3:20; *Jer. Talmud Berakoth* 5:1. cf. *Bab. Talmud Berakoth* 33a.

[36] *Bab. Talmud Taanith* 24b.

[37] *Bab. Talmud Taanith* 25a.

[38] *Bab. Talmud Pesahim* 112b.

[39] The Ass: *Aboth Rabbi Nathan* 8; the goats: *Bab. Talmud Taanith* 25a.

[40] Vermes, *Jesus*, 75.

[41] For his most important sayings see *Mishnah Aboth* 3:10, 11.

[42] See chapter 3 for my much earlier datings of the gospels.

[43] John 5:4 is not part of the oldest manuscripts, but is old and widespread, occurring in many of the versions and in the Diatessaron.

[44] Many cures are attributed to the god Asclepius in inscriptions at the shrine at Epidaurus. See H.C. Kee, *Miracle in the Early Christian World*, 78ff. It is not

clear over what period of time these cures took place and how many went away without a cure. Modern counterparts exist. See, e.g., the inscriptions celebrating help given by the Black Madonna of Einsiedeln in Switzerland.

[45] In the Gospel of Thomas Jesus terrorizes his playmates and their families by his destructive antics. See Hennecke, *New Testament Apocrypha*, 392ff.

[46] Mark 8:11f.; Matthew 12:38f.; 16:1–4; Luke 11:16; 12:54–56; John 6:30.

[47] C.L. Blomberg, 'The Miracles as Parables', 330–333.

[48] John 5:36; 10:25, 32, 38; 14:11.

[49] R.J. Bauckham, 'The Coin in the Fish's Mouth', 200.

[50] However, see Bauckham's treatment which elucidates the miracle as an integral part of Jesus' teaching that God does not tax his children ('Coin', 224f.).

[51] Job 1:38–42; 2 Samuel 24:1; 1 Chronicles 21:1.

[52] The only work I am aware of is K. Koch's *Christian Counselling and Occultism*. A doctor in an Australian psychiatric hospital told me that in one and a half years in which she saw hundreds of patients she felt that one or possibly two could have involved demonic interference. E.g., a married man dabbled in occult practices (tarot cards, seances, ouija boards, etc.) and also kept a diary. In his diary he recorded that a dark power was enticing him to give in to it. His last entry was the statement 'I have given in and surrendered myself.' He was subsequently found by the police, wandering around the city in a dressing gown, dazed and withdrawn. He was taken to a psychiatric hospital where his behaviour was found to fit none of the psychiatric classifications outlined in the then major psychiatric text *DSM III*. The doctor suggested to her consultant that perhaps they should take into account the spiritual factors which his wife (who had participated with him in occult practices) believed had lead him to his present state. The consultant asked the doctor whether such factors were mentioned in *DSM III*. She replied not, and he replied, 'then don't mention it'.

[53] 4QTherapeia. See H.C. Kee, *Medicine, Miracle and Magic in New Testament Times*, 128ff.

[54] 4Q510:6; cf. 4Q511:2f. See Kee, *Medicine*, 116, n. 13.

[55] Matthew 4:24 gives a list of conditions which Jesus healed, including *daimonizomenoi* but also *seleniazomenoi*. This may indicate a category of mental disturbance that he does not subsume under the title of demonization.

[56] This is argued persuasively by E. Fascher, *Jesus und der Satan*.

[57] Wrede, *Messianic Secret*, 24ff.

[58] Josephus, *History*, 17.295. Further, see Schürer, *History*, I, 330–335.

[59] Josephus, *History*, 17.289.

[60] Mark 1:25; 3:12; 9:25.

[61] Compare 11QPsApᵃ col. iv (Ploeg, 'Psaumes Apocryphes', 135ff.)

[62] E.g., in the Jewish exorcism performed in the presence of Vespasian the exorcist placed a pot of water nearby and ordered the demon to overturn it as it left (Josephus, *History*, 8.45–49). In Apollonius' exorcism at Athens the demon itself offered to knock down a statue on its departure.

[63] Genesis 1:2ff.; cf. *Pseudo Philo* 60:3.

[64] For a clear presentation of this position see E.& M.-L. Keller, *Miracles in Dispute*.

[65] See G.B. Caird, *The Gospel of Luke*, 140; E.E. Ellis, *The Gospel of Luke*, 152.

[66] The Jews had many names for the Devil. Beelzebub was one of the old Canaanite idol-gods (2 Kings 1:2ff.). Jesus usually referred to the Devil as Satan.

[67] Matthew 10:25; John 7:20; 8:48, 52; 10:20; 11:47.

[68] *paradoxon ergon poietes: History*, 18.63. The so-called *Testimonium Flavianum* is suspected of having been interfered with by Christians, but Vermes (*Jesus*, 79) thinks this description of Jesus as a miracle worker is genuine. He points out that Josephus describes Elishah in the same way (*Jesus*, 242f., n. 106). According to H.G. Liddell & R. Scott (*A Greek–English Lexicon*, 1309) *paradoxopoios* means 'miracle worker'.

[69] *Bab. Talmud Sanhedrin* 43a.

[70] See Origen, *Against Celsus*, 1.28, 68, 71; 6.42 (*ANF* 4); *Bab. Talmud Shabbath* 104b; Jerome, *Letter to Asella*, 6 (*NPNF* 2ⁿᵈ series, VI, 60).

[71] M. Smith, *Jesus the Magician*. For a critique see Kee, *Medicine*, 112–114.

[72] Smith, *Magician*, 15f.; 140–142.

[73] Smith, *Magician*, 42, 142.

[74] Smith, *Magician*, 8ff.

[75] Smith, *Magician*, 149.

[76] C.F.D. Moule, *The Phenomenon of the New Testament*, 3.

[77] Josephus, *War*, 2.258f.; cf. *History*, 20.168.

[78] Josephus, *History*, 20.168ff.; *War*, 2.261ff. The Egyptian escaped. (Paul was mistaken for him in Acts 21:38).

[79] Josephus, *War*, 2.258ff.; 6.285f.; *History*, 20.97ff, 167.

[80] P.W. Barnett, 'The Jewish Sign Prophets – AD 40–70: Their Intention and Origin'.

[81] At the time of the exodus Moses did various miracles but Pharaoh would not accept their divine origin and brought forward his own magicians to match him. They succeeded in a few cases but finally capitulated and witnessed to

Pharaoh that what Moses was doing was 'the finger of God' (Exodus 8:19). Jesus suggests that the best judges of his exorcisms should be other recognized exorcists.

Chapter 11

Parables Of Divine Strategy

Parable Maker

At the end of chapter 4 I commented how fascinating it would be to know what went through Jesus' mind when he realized that his task was to take up the mantle of the Servant–Messiah and win the world for God. How ever was he expected to do such a thing?

During his forty day fast in the wilderness we saw him do battle with the present ruler of the world, and in the process put behind himself three possible strategies which might have given him some chance of achieving at least the outward goal of world dominion. In an early protest against abuses at the temple, and in his later conversation with a Samaritan woman, we saw evidence of Jesus' interest in purifying the worship of his people, or rather, of creating a community whose true and spiritual worship would supersede the shrine-based cult of the Jews and Samaritans. On reaching Galilee his mission began in earnest. Centre stage was his proclamation of the arrival of the kingdom of God, supported by teaching, disciple gathering, exorcism and miracle working. In his proclaiming we saw Jesus taking up the role of Isaiah's end-time herald, and in his teaching the role of the Servant-law-giver. In his disciple-gathering he called the whole nation to share his Suffering Servant task prior to the final manifestation of the kingdom. In his exorcisms and miracles he broke into the domain of Satan; began to undo his works and liberate his captives.

Summarized in this fashion, Jesus' activity begins to appear purposeful and deliberate. When we come to his parables, and especially the parables of the kingdom, we get a much clearer insight into his conscious strategy. For although the kingdom parables are often seen to be about what the kingdom *is*, closer examination shows that they say much more about *how it comes*.

Jesus was a master parable maker; without doubt the greatest ever. For all their hesitation about many aspects of the Jesus story, and given that they may debate the authenticity of this or that parable or fragment of parable, there are few scholars who do not readily grant that in the parables we are in touch with Jesus of Galilee. The parables show such a profound and original genius that we just cannot see anyone else in the early church who could have created them.[1]

People often ask whether Jesus wrote anything, and when they learn that the answer is probably no,[2] become doubtful about his teachings, in some cases even questioning his existence. In searching for something with his own signature on it, so to speak, we need look no further than the parables. For although he was not a writer, Jesus has produced something quite distinctive and just as enduring.

Mark characterizes Jesus as a parable maker: 'He did not say anything to them without using a parable' (4:34). Every good teacher will illustrate points with stories, anecdotes and illustrations, but for most of us they don't come easily; I have sat all day trying to work out a good sermon illustration. Others may find it easier. But the point is this: a good parable is a work of art, and Jesus used them constantly. One wonders whether he did not think in parables, for beyond the list found in books and commentaries (Jeremias lists forty-one), parabolic images are found everywhere throughout his teaching. He is walking along the beach and comes upon some fishermen cleaning their nets, 'Follow me,' he says, 'and I will make you people-fishermen'

(Mark 1:17). People challenged him about eating with unscrupulous business people: 'Those who are well do not need a doctor, but those who are sick do' he replied. The gospels give the sense of a man who was familiar with God, and also had a wonderful understanding of ordinary life. Effortlessly he speaks of the one in terms of the other.

In their quality and in their sheer number, Jesus' parables are unique. There never has been a parable maker like him. If you did nothing else with him, you would have to give him a place in the 'literary' history of the world. You may invent a legendary figure and call him the Son of God and even say he was a great teacher. But to give him a unique teaching method and then make up his teachings – well, who could do it? It is like suggesting someone wanted to start a legend of a great English playwright. So you give him the name Shakespeare. But of course he would need some plays, so you just pen Macbeth, King Lear, The Merchant of Venice and The Winter's Tale. No one in the early church taught in parables; not Paul, nor Peter, nor John, nor James, nor Jude. The man Jesus is no legend, he is as self-evidently real from the parables as William Shakespeare or Charles Dickens are from their works.

Expert Communicator

We have already encountered a number of Jesus' parables. In one he likened those who heard his teachings to house builders. Whether they believed him or not, who could ever have forgotten his warning that if they ignored him their house one day would crash in ruins? Jesus did not explain abstract concepts like a philosopher; he promised and warned, commanded and encouraged, forgave and condemned, informed and explained, argued and proclaimed, about the coming of the kingdom and how to live in the light of it, always with vivid images, examples and stories.

Jesus had no difficulties holding a crowd, even when he was not healing them. 'Give and it will be given to you: good measure – pressed, shaken, overflowing – will be given into your bosom' (Luke 6:38). He could have spoken of God's generous gift, but instead created an unforgettable image of someone holding up their shirt tails to receive wheat and staggering away unable to stop the overflow from spilling around their feet. 'Can a blind man lead a blind man? They'll both finish up in the pit, won't they?' (Luke 6:39). The Jews of Jesus' time saw themselves as light-bearers and teachers of the world. Paul unpacks the concept in his own way in his letter to the Romans:

> But if you bear the name of a Jew, and rest on the law, and glory in God, and know his will, and approve the things that are excellent, being instructed in the law, and are confident that you are a guide of the blind, a light for those who are in darkness, a corrector of the foolish, a teacher of babes, having in the law the form of knowledge and of the truth – you therefore who teach others, will you not teach yourself? (Romans 2:17–21)

How long would Jesus have held his open-air crowd if he had preached like that? Actually, I cannot imagine him teaching in those parables without also throwing his body into their telling. Many of his picture parables lend themselves wonderfully to mime, just because they are so concrete and expressive. It is not hard to imagine an audience being convulsed with laughter at the half acted story of two blind men leading each other around, or of the man with the log in his eye, solicitously concerned for the poor chap with the speck of sawdust (Luke 6:39–42).

There is nothing mysterious or dark about these parables; they are crystal clear illustrations which would have been difficult to forget, even for those who consciously resisted their meaning. However, when we come to the so-called parables of the kingdom, and especially the group that are clustered together in Mark 4 and Matthew 13, we meet with something designed as much to obscure the truth as to reveal it.

Seeds of the Kingdom

It was one of those occasions when the crowd pressed so hard that Jesus had to teach from a boat moored close to the shore. He taught them many things, among them the parable of the sower and others about the kingdom of God. After recounting the parable of the sower, Mark interrupts the story to indicate its meaning. Not even Jesus' followers had understood it, and when they were alone they asked him for an explanation. His reply is surprising. I remember reading a gospel for the first time, coming to this passage in Matthew and thinking that if this was what Christianity was about, I wanted nothing to do with it.

> To you has been given the mystery of the kingdom of God, but to those outside everything comes in parables, 'so that seeing, they may see and yet not see, and hearing they may hear and not understand, lest they should turn and should be forgiven'. (Mark 4:12; the quotation is from Isaiah 6:9–10; cf. Matthew 13:10–17; Luke 8:9–10)

Jesus' Teaching or the Church's?

Wilhelm Wrede's solution to the offensiveness of this passage was to see it as the creation of Mark's community. As we have seen, Wrede thought that Jesus never claimed to be the Messiah, and that the early church invented sayings like this and the idea of a messianic secret to fit its later beliefs about him.[3] The most obvious refutation of Wrede's idea lies in Jesus' 'triumphal' entry into Jerusalem and subsequent crucifixion as 'King of the Jews'. Yet this aside, Wrede's thesis hardly accounts for the creation of this passage, which makes no obvious reference to the question of Jesus' identity; it simply does not do what Wrede suggests Mark meant it to. It is the mystery of the *kingdom*, which Jesus says needs to be concealed, and although, as we shall see, this ultimately does involve the question of his identity, it does not do so here. The fact that Matthew and Luke both include what can only be said to be a very difficult concept, that John is also aware of it,[4] and that it is in harmony with certain other difficult teachings of Jesus,[5] cautions us against taking the easy way out and removing it from him.[6]

The Mystery of the Kingdom

In speaking of the *mystery* of the kingdom of God, Jesus indicates that there are things about the kingdom which can only be known through revelation from God.[7] They are not accessible to the normal researches and guesswork that afford information in other spheres of human life. In the Old Testament Daniel was the great revealer of mysteries.[8] God revealed through him the meaning of a number of dreams relating to the political fortunes of his people until the time when he would set up his eternal kingdom. At the end of the book of Daniel certain secrets are revealed, but when Daniel enquires further he is told that 'the words are shut up and sealed until the time of the end' (12:9). A further revealing of mysteries was therefore to be expected at the time of fulfilment. In speaking of 'the mystery of the kingdom of God' (Matthew and Luke say 'mysteries'), Jesus claimed to know how God would bring about the final consummation of his purposes; something not fully revealed before, even to the prophets. He implied that some of this revelation was locked up in his parables. He was happy to unlock it for those who came to him and asked, but for 'those outside' some things had to remain for the moment as riddles. In quoting Isaiah 6 Jesus revealed that part at least of the reason for this lay in the fact that Israel was under judgement.

A Decree of Judgement?

The notion that Jesus may have preached to hide truth that might otherwise have saved people seems impossibly harsh. It is understandable that some would hasten to soften it. That in itself is an indication of its originality; who would have invented such an idea, if Jesus had not said it? That he relates it to Isaiah's experience suggests that it was part of a deeply held theological understanding that derived, in part at least, from Jesus' reflection on the Scriptures. At the conclusion of his ministry in Galilee he touched again on the theme, attributing to God's predestinating will the fact that most of the Galileans had refused his message: 'I bow to your understanding, Father, Lord of heaven and earth, that you have hidden these things from the wise and understanding and revealed them to babes. Yes, Father, for this was your sovereign decree' (Luke 10:21).[9] Such a statement only makes sense if we recognize: first, the general rebellion against God which Jesus encountered; second, his understanding that God was perfectly capable of removing that hardness and bringing about the immediate repentance and salvation of his people; third, his acceptance that God declined to do that, for whatever reason. The joy that Luke tells us Jesus experienced in the midst of what appeared to be the failure of his mission in Galilee relates to his recognition that some have heeded, but also to his accepting that some greater plan of God is in process, which can only result in an even more glorious salvation in the end (Luke 10:21). John the Baptist's mission, 'to make ready for the Lord a people prepared', had failed. Nor did Jesus have any illusions that there would be a great turning resulting from his own work. That this was so implied that God's decree of judgement still stood against his people, despite the fact that Jesus was in the process of declaring salvation. His own ministry, then, necessarily had a paradoxical character.

Reasons for Preaching

But why would Jesus have bothered to preach at all if judgement had already been passed? His reference to Isaiah suggests three possibilities. Isaiah was sent as a prophet to his people with no illusions that his prophesying would move them to repentance. On the very day he was called he was told that the people would seem to listen well enough, but would not really heed him. Nevertheless, he had to go on preaching until the land was a burnt-out wilderness. The first reason for this was to be a *witness against them*. God would not judge without first telling them why, nor without giving them every opportunity to repent. And of course some did repent, which must be counted as a second reason for his preaching. Isaiah attracted disciples and a remnant survived the judgement of the nation (Isaiah 8:16–22). But the third and greatest significance of Isaiah's preaching was for the future. Hope lay not in Israel heeding the message then, but in what would happen beyond the cataclysm which would fall on their disobedience. Thus, it was not judgement alone which was operative in the case of Isaiah, there was also a sifting out of the responsive and a preparation for the future.

Interpreting Parables

Before looking at the parable of the sower to see whether any of this is present there, we shall briefly consider some general principles of parable interpretation. The new 'science' of parable interpretation originated in 1888 with Adolf Jülicher's great critique of the time-worn allegorical method. The way in which the images, stories and situations of Jesus' parables appealed to the imagination was nigh on being destroyed by wooden allegorical interpretations (those which made, for example, the good Samaritan Jesus, the man who fell among thieves a symbol of humankind, the thieves the Devil and his angels, Jerusalem paradise, Jericho mortality, the donkey the flesh of

Christ, and the inn the church).[10] This tradition of interpretation invited the ingenious to inject into the parables as much of their own understanding of Christian doctrine as they could. It neglected the obvious consideration of what Jesus could have expected his listeners to grasp. Following the rules of Aristotle, Jülicher insisted that parables differed from allegories in having but one point of comparison. By applying this principle he began a new era of responsible historical interpretation, in which sensitivity to how Jesus' listeners would have heard the parables became key. However, in rejecting in principle the possibility of allegory in Jesus' parables, implying that it was something fundamentally inferior and post-Jesus, and in insisting that Jesus' parables could only have had one point, Jülicher went beyond the evidence and put an artificial straitjacket on interpretation.[11] 'There is a difference between making an allegory and giving an allegorical interpretation of a story which is not in itself allegorical. A story which is itself allegorical should be so interpreted. But to treat a story which is not as if it were – to allegorize it – can only frustrate the intention of the story.'[12] Jewish parables are extremely diverse in their type, and allegory was a popular art form. Jesus' parables have many allegorical elements which can only be eliminated by as unnatural a form of surgical excision as some allegorizing is an unnatural grafting-in of foreign ideas.[13] If some of the 'classical' interpretations made the parables into contrived dogmatic formulations, Jülicher's interpretations often reduce them to commonplace moral lessons.

The interpretation of any form of symbolic speech (or writing) must recognize first that the speaker is wishing to advance the understanding of hearers, by telling them something new or by helping them to see something in a new way. For this to take place there needs to be an amount of familiar ground between them, as well as something which carries the hearers beyond where they were before. We must try to listen to parables as the Jewish crowds would have.[14] This means paying attention to any information the evangelists give us about the contexts in which Jesus spoke. If they have invented or misrepresented these, then they have misled us. It is foolish to think that a twentieth-century scholar can recover a lost context, beyond the most tentative surmise. Similarly, modern interpretations which transpose the parables into a worldview unknown to Jesus' Jewish hearers, though they may be ingenious and have validity as *reinterpretations*, are of little help in discovering *Jesus'* meaning.[15] Jülicher's biggest mistake was to overlook the excitement of Jesus' kingdom preaching, which drew him and his audiences together; he reads the parables as simple wisdom-for-living lessons.

To interpret the parables we need to seek an understanding of what was common to Jesus and his hearers, and then to wrestle with the new. Allegorical elements may come from a shared stock of images – a king is likely to stand for God; a vineyard may signify Israel – or they may come from Jesus' own worldview. The better we understand Jesus, therefore, the better we will judge what is meaningful in a parable and what is stage dressing. Of course, that throws us into a certain circularity. Our whole study seeks an understanding of how Jesus saw things. The parables will help us achieve that. But seeing how he saw things will help us interpret the parables. The process is not entirely circular, however; it is more akin to a spiral, the so-called 'hermeneutical spiral'. Each increment in understanding, be it gleaned from a parable or something else in the story, brings us closer to Jesus' mind, and closer to an understanding of all that he meant in a particular parable. Of course, we can never be sure we have seen it just right. We should remember that Jesus withheld some of the clues vital to reading him correctly until late in his ministry. A degree of misinterpretation, or failure of interpretation, was part of his strategy of concealment with a view to greater revelation.

Thus the art of parable interpretation is to try to put oneself in the shoes of the first hearers. What did they hear? What sounded obvious to them? What sounded odd? What images already had meaning for them? What broke with their previous understanding? What did the parable challenge them to do or think?

Parable of the Sower
(Mark 4:3–9; Matthew 13:1–9; Luke 8:5–8)

The first thing to notice about the parable of the sower is that there is no internal indication of what it is explaining. The parable of the housebuilders begins with an explanation ('Whoever hears my words and does them, I will show you what he is like'); the audience knows that the difference between those who heed and those who ignore is being explained in a picture. But the parable of the sower is simply told as a story, with no clue to what it was about, except perhaps the concluding 'Whoever has ears let him hear!' It is not even clear that Jesus indicated he was talking about the kingdom of God, as he did later to his disciples. So it must have been a puzzle, and it is quite natural that some should have come later and asked for an explanation. It is probably an exaggeration to say they were given no clue, for I cannot imagine that this parable could ever have stood alone. If, as Mark indicates, it was in the context of other teaching about the kingdom, it is not unlikely that someone should have guessed that Jesus was referring to his own teaching and its relationship to the coming of the kingdom – especially considering the way he drew their attention at both beginning ('Listen!'), and end ('Whoever has ears to hear, hear!'). After all, is not *broadcast* sowing such a fitting image of spreading the word that the pioneers of wireless took it over to describe their new method of disseminating (!) words? Yet most people seem not to have got Jesus' point. His followers didn't; it was he who had to tell them that the parable was a revelation of the kingdom, and specifically about the role of the word of God in its coming. The majority thus probably left the shore with a story in their minds whose reference and meaning they did not know. Probably most of them did not have the interest to worry about it any further. Some, however, might have been puzzled: 'Did I miss something? I don't remember what he was getting at by that story about the sower. Maybe he got sidetracked? But he seemed very anxious that we should pay careful attention.' And every time one of them saw a field of wheat or barley, or a farmer broadcasting his seed it would have come back. Like the seed, the parable was well and truly planted in many minds.

Mark goes on to provide a clue as to why Jesus wanted to plant such seeds.

> He was saying to them, The lamp is surely not brought in to be placed under the corn measure or under the bed? Isn't it placed on the lamp stand? Nothing is secret except that it may become manifest; nothing has been hidden but that it should be clearly revealed. If anyone has ears let him hear! (Mark 4:21–23; cf. Luke 8:16–17)

Jesus admitted that a certain part of the light (truth) was being hidden, but insisted that this was with the intention that it should ultimately be clearly revealed. He urged his hearers to dig out the secret themselves (Mark 4:24). His purpose was to reveal, but to do that effectively there were certain things which had to be hidden for a while. Thus the parable will certainly have been effective as a way of sifting out those with real interest from those with only a casual curiosity. To those who have, more will be given, but the rest will lose even what they think they have (Mark 4:25). Thus the mystery parables seem to have been designed in part to attract the right kind of disciples.

Dangerous Truth

But why did Jesus make it so difficult for them? Would he not have made more disciples had he preached his message without a veil of obscurity? Part of the reason for his strange strategy must lie in the politics of his time. As I have already pointed out in relation to the malicious outbursts of demoniacs, the political climate was such that if Jesus said too much too soon about the kingdom, and especially about his own connection with it, his enemies would very quickly have used it against him, long before he had the chance to say all that he knew he must. This would not have been the problem it was, had the people been open to God. But their hardness of heart, to which Jesus alluded in the Isaiah quotation, made it an issue. The meaning of the parable of the sower, subsequently disclosed to his disciples, was that the kingdom is to come through the preaching of the word. And we must not overlook that it was *his* word and preaching which were the most obvious referents. To us this appears harmless, but for his hearers there was a double offence. First, any obvious claim on Jesus' part that he would bring the kingdom by his own action would have made him the immediate target of a political reaction; the kingdom of God, however it came, meant the overthrow of the existing order. It was one thing to announce that *God* was bringing the kingdom into being; no one would dispute that, but to suggest that *Jesus* by his own action would do it was quite a different matter. The second offence would have been to those who wanted God to establish his kingdom quickly and violently. To learn that a process of growth and development was required *in them* before the kingdom could come would have turned many away from Jesus before they had heard him out. If the people were under judgement it was because they were in rebellion against God, though most of them were quite unaware of it. They wanted the kingdom of God desperately. That is why they flocked around Jesus with such excitement. But their understanding of the kingdom was removed from themselves. They wanted the renewal of the environment which the kingdom promised, and the end of oppression, the glorification of Israel, the healing of the sick and the resurrection of the dead. But they overlooked the claim of God upon their own persons. They did not realize and would not face the fact that there could not be a kingdom, at least not the kind Jesus wished to establish, without obedient and faithful subjects – true worshippers – and that required a complete inward revolution. Jesus seems to have been keenly sensitive to the shock this personal demand would have. It is this which suddenly brings to the surface all the vested interests and proud independence that is characteristic of human beings. In time they would realize that they were so opposed to the rule of God in their hearts and lives that they would kill the man who came to lay God's claim before them rather than accede to his demands. We see this clearly in the rulers with their very visible vested interests, but it was also true of many others. The parables allowed Jesus to give them truths, which for the moment were unacceptable; would even turn them in bitter hostility against him. So for friends and enemies, and for the confused and undecided, the parables lay ticking away like timebombs. When the right time came they would explode into light.

In summary we might say that the mystery parables are a piece of strategy in themselves. They were necessitated by the hostility of the ruling establishment to any change, and people's rebelliousness to the inward rule of God. To some extent they were a judgement on that double rebellion. On the other hand, they were designed to excite inquiry on the part of those willing to learn, and to be retained for the future by those who for the moment were closed or hostile. They allowed Jesus to teach publicly without fear of his enemies taking his words and using them against him.

Individual Response

The parable of the sower points to the centrality of message in the mission of Jesus, and the vital importance of its proper reception in the heart of each individual. To discover, as those who asked did, that 'the seed is the word' was not the end of it of course. An intelligent guess could have yielded the same answer. It was the personal realization that *their* heart needed to be open to Jesus' word, that *they* must hang on to it at all costs, which was the real secret of this parable. Unlike most of the other kingdom parables, this one is about individual response; it is not about the final harvest, but about the course of things before that harvest. God had promised to sow his kingdom–land with the seed of humankind (Jeremiah 31:27–28), but each plant had to be good and true (Isaiah 61:3), and for that to be so each individual had to be sown with the good seed of Jesus' word, to hold it fast and bear fruit. Jesus saw his word as the seed which would create the new kingdom community, yet, because of Israel's continuing hardness, it would be rejected by many and prove unfruitful in many more. The separation of the righteous and the wicked, which John the Baptist had declared to be the task of the 'coming one', would take place initially through people's individual responses to Jesus' message.

Harvest

> And he said, This is what the kingdom of God is like: it is as if a man should throw the seed onto the earth, and he goes to bed and gets up, night and day. And the seed sprouts and grows long – he doesn't know how; the earth bears fruit of itself, first the stalk, then the ear, then the full grain in the ear. And when the grain is there, at once he puts in the sickle, because the harvest is ready. (Mark 4:26–9)

A time of sowing, a time of growing and a time of mowing – that is what the kingdom of God is like. But where did Jesus and his hearers find themselves in this process, and what implication did he mean those who understood to draw? Were they sowers, or in the process of growing, or did they stand at the end when harvest was the business in hand?

Where did the Original Hearers Stand?

The gospels have their own interpretation of the time frame of
the parables of growth and harvest. The interpretation given to
the parable of the sower by the synoptics, and to the weeds and
the catch of fish by Matthew, assume that the sowing was going
on at the time the parable was being heard, the time of growth lay
immediately ahead, and the harvest would come at the end of the
age. However, C.H. Dodd argued that this could not have been
the meaning *Jesus* gave to these parables, because he saw himself
living at the *end* of the age, in the time of harvest.[16] He told his
disciples as they were passing through Samaria that the fields were
white to harvest and it was time for them to reap what others had
sown (John 4:35–38). On another occasion, perceiving that the
harvest was so great, he urged them to pray to the Lord of the
harvest to send out more workers to do the reaping (Luke 10:2;
Matthew 9:37–38). Dodd concluded that Jesus' focus in the parables of growth must have been on the harvest which had arrived
and required gathering in. The time of sowing and growing – the
work of former prophets, of John the Baptist, of God's providen-
tial work in people's hearts – was past, and therefore only a
prelude to the real action. The parables challenged people to
throw themselves into the work of harvesting. The early church,
however, reset the parables in a different time frame, applying
them to their own concern of preaching the word.

Dodd's approach is very persuasive and has been followed by
many later interpreters.[17] It certainly seems unnatural in the light
of two clear statements on Jesus' part that the time of harvest had
come, to turn around and make him a sower. And yet I am uneasy
with it, for it seems to dismiss as 'dramatic machinery' too much
of what appears central to the parables. Dodd's view of what Jesus
intended in the sower is, who would refrain from harvesting
because there were bare patches in the field?.[18] Yet, as we have
seen, the parable makes no mention of harvest and concerns itself
predominantly with the varying fortunes of different parts of the

crop. If it means to say what Dodd infers, it is not a good parable, whereas if the gospels' interpretation is correct, it is a master-piece.[19]

It is characteristic of a lot of modern parable research to reject the settings and interpretations which the gospels provide, and then seek to discover (or invent) better ones. But one must seriously ask whether such efforts can be anything more than guesswork. If the gospel writers have led us astray, it is doubtful that the modern researcher has any reliable technique for bringing us back. But have they in fact led us astray? Philip Payne makes the important observation that the parable of the sower is typical of a number of Jesus' parables in depicting varied responses, and inviting hearers either to make their own response, or to identify with the responses depicted.[20] Such a pattern strongly suggests that the varying fate of the seed is the real point of the parable. This does justice to its content; it also assumes that the hearer stands at the time of seeding, not at harvest. It is necessary, therefore, that we ask whether Jesus could have seen himself both as a harvester and a sower.

Was Jesus Sower or Harvester?

There is no argument that Jesus saw himself as involved in the harvest of the end of the age. He proclaimed the presence of the kingdom and gathered people into its fellowship. The little parable of the wedding guests declares the bridegroom present and the festivities of the new age begun. But this is not the whole story. We have seen that from the outset Jesus and his message were discounted and opposed. The kingdom was present in the midst of opposition. Israel's suffering vocation had not yet run its course. Disciples had to prepare themselves to suffer for the Son of Man and his kingdom. A division of the people was in progress. The final abolition of poverty, hunger and tears still lay in the future.

It was John the Baptist who first identified Jesus as the one who would effect the great harvest. With winnowing fork in hand he would garner the grain and incinerate the chaff. It soon became apparent that, for the moment at least, Jesus was taking up only one side of this mission. The grain he was gathering, but the chaff disposal seemed to have been postponed to a later time. Nevertheless, it has not dropped out of Jesus' thoughts altogether, as though he totally repudiated the concept of judgement. The parable of the two house builders makes this frighteningly clear (Matthew 7:24ff.; Luke 6:47ff.): a cataclysmic deluge could be expected which would ruin every person whose life was not solidly grounded on his teaching. Jesus urged people to take his teaching to heart and build their lives on a foundation which would survive the coming judgement. There is no way here of sliding the time scale backwards, bringing this 'consummation' into the present, because the end of the story is a still future judgement.

It is not a long step from the idea of building a solid house to cultivating a fruitful crop. The parable of the house builders and the parable of the sower urge the same action; the former making a simple contrast between the destinies of those who take Jesus' teaching seriously, the latter paying more attention to the variety of responses, focusing on the maturing fruitfulness of those who hold onto Jesus' word.

It appears, then, that Jesus saw his mission not only in terms of bringing in an existing harvest, but also of preparing for a future crisis involving an ultimate harvest and separation which would finally and absolutely determine the destiny of human beings. His understanding of the relationship of these two may be found in his parable of the fruitless fig tree (Luke 13:6–9).

According to Luke, Jesus told this parable in explanation of a most solemn warning of judgement. People had drawn his attention to a recent outrage in Jerusalem when Pilate had killed some Galilean pilgrims at the temple. We know nothing more of the incident than Luke tells us, but it is not untypical of some of the clashes that took place during Pilate's administration. Jesus' reaction is extraordinary; he shows no concern for the injustice of Pilate's action, but uses the tragedy, and another in which a tower collapsed, to warn his hearers of the terrible catastrophe that lay before all of them if they would not repent. 'I tell you,' he says (twice), 'if you do not repent, you will all likewise perish' (Luke 13:3, 5). His insistence that those who died were no worse sinners than anyone else, and that *all* ('you all'), in contrast to the few, faced a similar prospect if they refused to repent, shows that he saw a terrible judgement of a this-worldly (probably military) kind looming before the nation. Then comes the parable of the fig tree; threatened with the axe, but given a short reprieve, in which, if it would, it might bear fruit.

Jeremias draws attention to a similar, quite ancient parable which probably provided a prototype to Jesus' fig tree.[21] It comes from the story of Ahikar, various versions of which circulated among the Jews and other peoples for centuries before Jesus. Ahikar was treacherously betrayed by a nephew to whom he had done great good.

> And Ahikar said to him, 'O my boy! You are like the tree, which was fruitless beside the water, and its master wanted to cut it down, and it said to him, "Remove me to another place, and if I do not bear fruit, cut me down." And its master said to it, "When you were beside the water you did not bear fruit, how will you bear fruit when you are in another place" '.[22]

Jesus' parable is something of a reversal of this, and the contrasting deviation doubtless marks something significant in what he wanted to teach.

But who in Jesus' parable is this gardener who begs a stay of execution? Jeremias is undoubtedly correct in seeing behind the gardener the figure of Jesus himself.[23] I suggested earlier that the forty day fast at the beginning of Jesus' ministry makes most sense when seen against the background of John the Baptist's warning of impending destruction; a penitential supplication of God to restrain judgement. This may explain why the 'day of vengeance' disappears from Jesus' Nazareth sermon, and why his ministry differed so markedly from what John expected. It indicates that Jesus saw his role not only as the harvester wielding the winnowing fork, but also as the farmer doing everything to make sure that when harvest time comes there will be something to gather. He is even ready to push back the time of harvest if it will mean an ultimately greater crop.

Thus we may proceed, at least provisionally, with the thought that Jesus reckoned himself a sower as well as a harvester, and see the tension between these two as yet another manifestation of the strange way in which Jesus brought the future kingdom into the present, yet continued to orient himself towards its final unveiling. The wedding guests are already celebrating with the groom, the fishermen are already hauling their nets in, the harvest is already being reaped, indeed the wind of his word is already separating the wheat from the chaff. Yet the groom is to be taken away and his wedding still lies in the future, the final net is still to be cast, the harvest still awaits the end of the age; the final separation is not yet.[24]

A Period of Growth

What, then, is the meaning of the parable of the seed which grows by itself? First, it says that the kingdom begins with the preaching of the word. Then it will grow, and finally the end of the age will witness its completion. After the previous long and complex argument this seems almost too trivial and obvious. But think for a moment of the background against which Jesus spoke this and other similar parables.

If the community at Qumran had coined a parable to describe the manner in which the kingdom would come it might have sounded something like this:

The kingdom of God is as if a king should send a favoured prince to reconquer a province that has been overrun by his enemies. But when he came to rouse the people of the land to overthrow the enemy, he found most of them happy with the way things stood. In the desert, however, was a community of the faithful who had not forgotten their true king. They were few in number but pure and faithful and prepared for the battle which would surely come. Led by the prince and reinforced by armies from beyond, they attacked the citadel of the enemy and with great slaughter cleansed the land of all the sons of darkness. From there the battle continued until the whole empire of wickedness fell and all the ends of the earth acknowledged the true king.

Most of Jesus' audience, while not members of the Qumran community, would have held a similar view. What greater contrast could be imagined to a conquering prince than a farmer sowing seed? Jesus' parable sounds a completely alien strategy, and yet it is full of confidence that the strategy will succeed. The focus of interest is the mysterious growth of the seed. As surely as it is sown it will grow; there is a divine process at work which guarantees it. The farmer need have no fear; a harvest will surely follow.[25]

God's Empire

What else do the parables teach us about the coming of the kingdom? In the parable of the mustard seed the insignificance of its beginning is contrasted with its ultimate size (Mark 4:30–32; Matthew 13:31–32; Luke 13:18–19). The mustard plant is no tree, but an annual with an average height of about four feet.[26] Jesus' odd description of it as 'greater than all the vegetables' (*lacanon*) suggests it was the largest plant commonly found in a domestic garden, and that he was well aware of its character.[27] However, uncharacteristically (miraculously?) it begins to produce great branches and by the end of the parable is more like the proverbial cedar of Lebanon than a mustard plant. Commentators have had a hard time with this, seeking to save Jesus' credibility by stretching the mustard plant, or by toning down the description of the tree. One writer refers to 'goldfinches and linnets coming in flocks to perch in this tree-like herb and to eat its seeds'[28] – hardly what Jesus had in mind by the birds of heaven making their nests in its shade. This kind of jarring incongruity is not uncommon in Jesus' parables; its effect would have been to rivet the attention of hearers to that particular point and incite questioning: Is Jesus ignorant or is he hinting at something?[29] In this case the something was not difficult to discern. In the book of Daniel the great tree which is host to the birds of heaven is a picture of Nebuchadnezzar standing for the vast Babylonian empire (Daniel 4:21). Ezekiel pictured the Assyrian empire in a similar way (Ezekiel 31:3–18), and predicted that God would one day plant such a tree of his own in Israel (17:22–24). In each case the tell-tale motif of the birds nesting in the branches points both to the size of the tree and to the many peoples and nations who find their place under the umbrella of the great empire. Jesus' use of this standard picture reveals his own understanding of the final state of God's kingdom: a universal empire in whose compass the nations of the world would have a place. The parable says that God's empire will rise from the tiniest of seeds – himself and what he is doing, we may surmise. I don't think we are straining the parable to see in his choice of a mustard seed, destined in the normal course of things to become a large garden plant, a hint that you would not expect a kingdom to result from the sort of beginning he has made – at least, not until something quite strange begins to happen to this Jack-and-the-Beanstalk-like plant. This parable too would have implanted itself, and would not have been easily forgotten.

A Hidden Kingdom

The parable of the hidden yeast is frequently treated as a poor relation to the mustard seed, but it has a great deal more of its own to add to our understanding of how Jesus thought of the coming of the kingdom. 'The kingdom of heaven is like yeast which a woman took and hid in three measures of flour, until it was all leavened' (Matthew 13:33; cf. Luke 13:20–21). Short as it is, a number of oddities must have arrested the attention of Jesus' hearers. In Jewish thinking yeast was a common symbol for evil and corruption. To hear Jesus using it as an image of the kingdom would have excited immediate attention.[30] Second, the woman took the yeast and *hid* it in some flour. What on earth was she doing? Was she making bread? Why does he say she *hid* it? This detail is obliterated by some translators, who, unaware of its importance, simply have the woman *mixing* it with the flour (NIV). Third, she hid it in *three measures* of flour. We are familiar today, from cartoons and comic books, with the cook who over-does it with the bread mix and returns to the kitchen to find the dough has risen out of the bowl and is running off the table onto the kitchen floor. This woman has hidden her yeast in *twenty-five kilograms* of flour – sufficient to feed a hundred people if she had enough ovens to cook it in.[31] In truth, what she appears foolishly to have done is hide her yeast in the flour barrel. The result is predictable. Thus in this tiniest of the parables we meet three attention-catching incongruities. What does it mean? Perhaps that the kingdom is brought into being by something more powerful and more pervasive than evil. Though at the beginning it must needs be hidden (the mystery of the kingdom), it will finally transform the whole world.

A Compromised Kingdom

The parable of the weeds (Matthew 13:24–30) rivals the sower in the level of its detail, and, if its interpretation in Matthew (13:37–43) is accepted as dominical, it is by far the most revealing of how Jesus saw his own ministry in relation to the kingdom of God. The gospel interpretation is commonly dismissed on the grounds that it takes the parable as an allegory and gives it a point for point meaning, but we have seen that such an a priori judgement is unjustified. What the critic should ask is whether there is anything in the interpretation which is out of keeping with the thought world of Jesus and his hearers. I do not think there is.

Indeed, this patently symbolic story is too complex to be exhausted by a one point comparison. Jeremias rejects Matthew's interpretation,[32] but gives a meaning no less allegorical, simply stressing different features of the story.[33] According to Matthew, Jesus explained the parable to his disciples in the following terms: the sower is the Son of Man, the field is the world, the good seed is the sons of the kingdom, the darnel is the sons of the evil one, the enemy is the Devil, the harvest is the end of the world and the harvesters are angels.

What might the original parable have conveyed to the first hearers, and how does that accord with the interpretation given to the disciples? Notice first that Jesus began by saying that the kingdom *has been* likened to a sower who sowed good seed. He had *already* in other parables spoken of the growth of the kingdom resulting from the efforts of the sower; the subject of this parable is the work of the enemy who followed him. Talk of an enemy of God's kingdom would naturally have aroused in many people's minds thoughts of Romans and their Jewish collaborators. Those who were favourable to Jesus' cause might have seen in the enemy a reference to all and anything which was hostile to his message, in particular opposing Pharisees, Herodians, Sadducees, Essenes, violent revolutionaries and others

– seen as hindering the kingdom's progress by their opposing teachings. We have already seen enough of Jesus' outlook to know that he would not view any of these persons or groups as enemies in themselves; he saw their opposition, rather, as an out-working of the activity of Satan, the real enemy. It would have been important for Jesus to clarify this to his disciples, so 'the enemy is the Devil' was needed and appropriate.

The primary thrust of the parable is to warn that Satan's work will go on for some time yet, and to insist that compromise and uncertainty, the presence together of the sons of light and the sons of darkness – Jesus employs Qumran terminology – are necessary to the kingdom builder's strategy: a strategy of care for the preservation of the individual plants of the crop. Jeremias is right to see the parable as a call for patience in the face of the seeming confusion that attends the coming of the kingdom. Matthew's interpretation assumes this, and goes on to strengthen the disciples' patience by explaining in precise terms the final outcome of things at the close of the age.

Much of this might well have been evident to the first listeners, for the Baptist had warned people that a great one was coming to separate wheat from chaff, to gather one and burn the other. Here, at last, Jesus was talking about what everyone was waiting for. It was probably the lack of chaff-burning which caused the Baptist's disquiet. Jesus' hearers would not have missed the fact that he had relocated this judgement to the separation which would take place at the end of a period of confused growth. They were not to expect the kingdom in its consummate form to appear immediately; nor could they expect the presence of the kingdom in its unconsummated form to be unambiguously clear. They may even have registered that he shifted the commission of this judgement from the 'coming one' himself to the harvesters, though they might well have assumed themselves to be counted among these. The revelation that the agents of the great separation were to be angels, was not something that could have been inferred from the parable, but it is consistent with first-century Palestinian thinking; in the Qumran War Scroll angels are involved in the final judgement.[34] There is no substantial reason for refusing to allow that Jesus could have coined this aspect of the parable and its explanation.[35]

The next thing we notice is the scope of the parable: 'The field is the world (*kosmos*).' Since Jesus limited his ministry to the Jews, we might have thought his field would be Israel. Or, if the interpretation was one provided by later believers, the church. That is the way Christian interpreters – troubled by the presence of unbelievers in the church – have usually read it. But Jesus conceives the final form of the kingdom on the widest possible scale. Did he foresee a time when the world beyond Israel would be sown with the seed of the kingdom? Many have denied it, but they do so in the face of much in his teaching. The birds who make their nests in the branches of the great tree-empire are pictures of foreign peoples finding their home in Israel's kingdom. In N.T. Wright's words, 'from the historian's point of view, one would strongly expect that anyone announcing the kingdom ... would envisage that part of the result of his work would be the ingathering of the nations of which the prophets had spoken. When YHWH finally acted for Israel, the Gentiles would be blessed as well.'[36] How did Jesus visualize this taking place? 'You are the light of the world. A city set on a hill cannot be hidden,' he said to his disciples (Matthew 5:14), urging them to take to heart Israel's historic vocation to the nations.[37] It ought not to be ruled out that he was preparing them, ultimately, for a world mission. If Jesus saw himself as Yahweh's Servant, the words with which God addressed the Servant in Isaiah 49:6 – 'I will give you as a light to the nations, that my salvation may reach to the ends of the earth' – must have entered in some way into his vision of the future. It is not surprising, then, to find him speaking in the week of his death, of the drawing of Gentiles into his kingdom, and the gospel being preached in the world.[38] Thus, 'the field is the world' fits.

Perhaps the most surprising feature of the parable to the modern reader is the way Jesus describes the final resolution.

'The Son of Man will send his angels, and they will gather out of his kingdom everything that causes sin and all doers of lawlessness.' It is as though the world and the kingdom have coalesced. All that is required is the removal of evil in order that the children of the kingdom might shine in their true light. Jesus' original hearers would hardly have noticed this, since they thought of the coming age as something to be enjoyed in a renewed earth. But for moderns accustomed to thinking of the kingdom of God as heaven, or as a spiritual presence of God in the heart of the believer, or as his actual but abstract rule, it is sharply discordant. Should it not be the righteous who are gathered and removed? Jesus' way of speaking is nonsensical on any of these interpretations. Only as we see the kingdom as the king with his people, in the world about to be cleansed of all contamination, does talk of removing the wicked, and the righteous shining like the sun in their Father's kingdom make sense. Of course, this is not to be thought of as part of the meaning of the parable, as though Jesus set out to teach it. Nevertheless, the way he has crafted the story is indicative of the shape of his thinking. It is worth noting, too, that his picture of the righteous shining like the sun, is drawn from a description in Daniel of the post-resurrection glory of God's people (Daniel 12:2–3).

Jesus' Strategy

What do the parables we have examined add up to in the way of an understanding of, and a strategy for the coming kingdom? First, the final form of the kingdom is to comprise the whole world, embracing all nations in its scope. In using images of the tree and the birds of heaven, Jesus showed his understanding of the kingdom to be profoundly political. In his mind the kingdom of God was a universal empire. This accords well with much that we have already seen of Old Testament and contemporary Jewish expectations. Where he did part company with such expectations was on the question of *how* the kingdom would come. It would result from the growth of a message, which must be received, take root and bear fruit in every individual who is to find a place in the ultimate kingdom. The beginning of the process is therefore small and hidden, but it will grow inexorably until it is of such size that the whole world belongs to it.

How is this growth to be understood? At the beginning of the twentieth century exponents of the 'social gospel' rightly seized on the theme of growth as central to the parables of the kingdom, but interpreted it to mean that the kingdom would evolve on earth as the result of human social improvement.[39] This accorded well with the nineteenth century idealization of progress. However, such an understanding hardly flows naturally from the parables, which envisage the kingdom's growth in terms of the gathering of more and more of its ultimate subjects and of their growth to a fruitful maturity. Whether this would lead to an improvement of the world – if one allows that the process may stretch beyond a generation – is beyond the view of the parables, which imply that confusion and ambiguity will continue until the final weeding out of all evil.

On the other hand, there is little in these parables to support the traditional spiritual approach which abandons the world to the Devil, looking for salvation only in the escape of the sons of the kingdom to a heavenly realm. Jesus' thought structure is the reverse of this: it is evil and all its causes which will finally be rooted out of the world, so that the righteous can appear in their true light as sons of the Father and citizens of the kingdom. In this there can be no justification for passiveness in the face of evil, but only earnest engagement. Not because the kingdom will be created through human striving, but because it is the character of the sons of the kingdom to resist evil in the midst of a world which belongs to God, despite the many things which for the moment cause stumbling.

In light of Jewish understanding which saw the kingdom's coming very much in terms of a final judgement on the state of human beings at the moment of its arrival, the place of the individual's response to the message of the kingdom is a remarkable feature of Jesus' strategy. We must remember that he was not teaching about how it would be *when* the kingdom came, nor what people should do to find a place *then*. For him the kingdom was already present. The word he proclaimed was a call to enter *now* and become a child of the kingdom. This is nowhere better illustrated than in the parable of the treasure, and the pearl merchant (Matthew 13:44–46). The kingdom was present, waiting to be discovered (though note that it is hidden), and it is so precious that when someone finds it (note the individuality) they gladly give everything they have to possess it.

Thus for Jesus the kingdom was more than the final reward of those who received his message and carried it until it bore fruit. It was something to be discovered and entered into now. Any growth on the part of the individual takes place on the inside, as it were. Jesus' word was the invitation which drew people into the kingdom. Community was one essential dimension of this. The presence of the Messiah and a transformed environment would be purposeless were there not also a community of people to enjoy them. Jesus' word was the active power, which was creating this community. This is why he numbered 'preaching the gospel to the poor' amongst the miracles which should have convinced the Baptist that the kingdom was present (Luke 7:22; Matthew 11:5).

Jesus' strategy was to proclaim the word and through it create the community of fruit-bearing (righteous) people. His refusal to commence judgement, and therefore to make a separation of his own people from the Devil's, consciously doomed his message and his kingdom to be misunderstood, compromised, denied, vilified and persecuted. All this seems to be embraced in his strategy. It accords well with his commitment of himself and his people to the Servant mission. It also fits with his unwillingness to delineate sharply between those who were and were not his disciples. He expected his word to be the instrument which would draw

people closer or repel them. Yet for all the inevitable confusion
this strategy entailed, Jesus was convinced that his word would
not be lost. Against all odds it would grow steadily and effect a
hidden revolution for the time of the kingdom's final unveiling.

The Mysteries of the Kingdom

'To you is given to know the mystery of the kingdom of God',
Jesus said to his disciples when they inquired about the meaning
of the parables (Mark 4:11). We noted earlier Matthew and
Luke's substitution of 'mysteries' for Mark's 'mystery'. There is
little to be gained by a detailed investigation of whether Jesus
spoke in the singular or the plural; he might well have used both
expressions at different times. Our examination of the parables
would thus far suggest that we are dealing not with a single idea,
but with a broad set of understandings of how the kingdom will
come. The way things were unfolding was very different to how
John the Baptist had envisaged them. Jesus was conscious of this –
conscious of having new 'mysteries' to unfold. Tentatively, he
began to do this in his parables.

So far we have said nothing about Jesus' own place in the
parables of growth. Was he simply the teacher of truths, or did he
see himself as an indispensable player in the growing kingdom?
'The sower sows the word.' But it is easy to overlook that it is
uniquely *his* word that is in view. At the point in the story to
which these parables belong Jesus is the sole preacher. Soon
others will take up the task, but even when they do it is his
message they will carry.

The smallness and hiddenness of the beginnings of the kingdom applied as much to him as to the word he proclaimed.
'The one who sows the good seed is the Son of Man' (Matthew
13:37), and whether one thinks here of the creation of the
kingdom by a *mere man*, or in terms of Daniel's prophecy – a
frail human being in contrast to the beastly empires of the

world – the thought is similar. God brings his kingdom into the world through an agent who appears insignificant, but at the finish conquers all. Jesus as the humble kingdom-bringer is thus one of the mysteries of the kingdom.

The Son of Man

This is the best place to say something about the way Jesus repeatedly referred to himself as the Son of Man. For that too, in my opinion, is a 'parable' or riddle of the kingdom. I have already drawn attention to the physical danger that in Jesus' time dogged any attempt to proclaim the kingdom of God. By the use of parables Jesus was able to teach publicly without making unambiguous statements which might prematurely seal his fate. It was the work of a brilliant strategist to present his teaching in a form that anyone who had ears to hear could 'find the treasure', while the rest nonetheless swallowed a time-release capsule which might at any moment claim them for the kingdom too. At the same time, his enemies would have nothing which they could hold against him in a court of law. The confusion of the witnesses at his trial over what Jesus had said, and what he meant, is testimony to this. The greatest danger, of course, was anything that could be construed as a claim to be the Messiah. This was surely part of the reason that he called himself 'the Son of Man', a term which only he uses and which is therefore certainly original.[40]

'Son of man' in Hebrew or Aramaic need mean no more than *a man*, or one of the human species. It is a common expression in the Old Testament. For example, God continually addresses the prophet Ezekiel as *son of man*, probably to emphasize his human frailty. Thus Jesus could have been heard to be calling himself 'the human being'. On the other hand, there is the particular 'son of man' mentioned in Daniel, who, after the judgement of the beastly empires, is awarded total sovereignty over all nations of the world. Did Jesus mean he was that person? It is debated whether Son of Man would have been recognized by Jesus' contemporaries as the title of a messianic figure. The Similitudes of Enoch (1 Enoch 37–71) apply the term to a supernatural figure they also refer to as the Righteous One, Elect One and Messiah. As long as it was thought that the Similitudes were part of the pre-Christian book of Enoch, it seemed Jesus was openly claiming an exalted status. However, the absence of any part of the Similitudes from the Dead Sea Scroll fragments, when the rest of 1 Enoch is well represented, led J.T. Milik to the conclusion that they were post-Christian, perhaps even Christian.[41] Other scholars disagree, and hold them to be Jewish writings from before AD 70.[42] However, even if they were in existence in Jesus' time, it by no means follows that they were widely known, nor that Son of Man would always be recognized as a messianic title. Jesus' opponents suspected him of messianic ambitions, but clearly did not read his Son of Man talk as a claim to be Daniel's exalted ruler. In marked contrast is people's emotional reaction to the terms 'Son of David' (Mark 10:47–48) and 'king' (Luke 19:38–40). The obvious inference is either that the Similitudes did not exist, or that they were not well enough known for 'Son of Man' to be heard as an automatic reference to the future king.[43] People needed some clue if they were to make the connection with Daniel 7 (or with the Similitudes). Jesus' calling himself the Son of Man caused no offence to his hearers until he made the connection explicit at his trial.

Thus, unless he gave them the connection (which he mostly did not) Jesus' hearers could hardly understand him to be doing anything more than using an odd turn of phrase to refer to himself as a human being. Certainly no one could assert that he was making a messianic claim simply by calling himself the Son of Man. It would have been raised against him at his trial if they did. Yet it was an odd way to speak, and like the oddities of some of the parables, must have drawn attention and produced puzzlement. It was always possible that an individual might tumble to the tentative conclusion that Jesus saw himself as *Daniel's* Son of

Man. On some occasions and in some company the way Jesus spoke seems calculated to draw this forth.[44] Yet for his enemies it would remain a riddle until the day of his trial. Then all would burst into light, but only at the moment that Jesus himself chose to be finished with secrecy; making clear that he believed himself to be the Son of Man destined to come on the clouds of heaven as the world's eternal ruler: a revelation which shocked the High Priest (Mark 14:61–64).

A Ministry of the Word

How did Jesus' ministry actually measure up against his farmer imagery? It explains at once what we have already observed, that he saw preaching as central to his task and resisted any pressure which might deflect him from it (Mark 1:38). This is illustrated in a most dramatic way in the undoubtedly historical incident when he was teaching in a house, and his mother and brothers came to restrain him (Mark 3:20f., 31–35; Matthew 12:46–50; Luke 8:19–21). All three gospels place the incident in relation to the parables of the kingdom, probably because of the thematic similarity. We not only have testimony in this event to the commitment of Jesus to his teaching and preaching, but also to the fact that he saw response to his word creating a community which transcended even the ties of blood. In another incident a woman called to Jesus out of the crowd, 'Blessed is the womb which bore you and the breasts you sucked.' Jesus replied, 'Blessed rather are those who hear the word of God and keep it' (Luke 11:27–28). He counted those who through his word stood in a new relationship of obedience to God, as his closest kin, blessed in an ultimate way by their membership of the kingdom.

Towards the end of his ministry, when Jesus sent out the seventy-two into towns he intended to visit, he briefed them in a way that is very revealing of the power he saw residing in his message, even when it was delegated to agents. He told them that when they entered a house they were to say, 'Peace be to this house.' If there was a 'son of peace' there the blessing would rest on them; if not, the blessing would return to the missionary (Luke 10:5–6; cf. Matthew 10:12–13). In Jesus' mind the blessing of peace carried a real payload, presumably acceptance into the kingdom they were announcing. He went on to emphasize to his disciples that they were invested with full authority as his agents, just as he had full authority as his Father's plenipotentiary.

> The person who hears you hears me, and the person who rejects you rejects me, and the person who rejects me rejects the one who sent me.
>
> Everything has been delivered to me by my Father and no one knows who the Son is except the Father, and who the Father is except the Son, and whoever he wills to reveal him to. (Luke 10:16, 22; cf. Matthew 10:40; 11:27)

He saw himself commissioned to deliver a message which would reveal God, create relationship with him, and bring people into a divine fellowship which was constitutive of the kingdom of God. From this there is a clear line into the Gospel of John, where we find most of the themes relating to the word of Jesus which we have already encountered, though in a somewhat different and more concentrated form. John's focus is more on Jesus' impact on the individual than on the coming of the kingdom in its totality. He usually speaks of eternal life rather than the kingdom, though the two are closely related. Jews referred to the coming kingdom as 'the age to come', and to its life as 'the life of the age to come'. This is rendered in Greek as 'eternal life', literally 'the life of the age (aeon)'. Whereas in the first three gospels Jesus announces the arrival of the kingdom of God, and speaks only occasionally of eternal life, in John he most often invites people to enter into eternal life, understood as a relationship with God brought about through knowing God and the One he has sent (John 17:3). The instrument by which they are invited and brought in is his word. Whoever hears his words and does them is delivered from judgement, passing there and then from death to life (John 5:24). Jesus speaks of his word as a life-giving power which wakens the spiritually dead (among whom he walks), and will one day call back to life even those who are dead in their tombs (John 5:25–29). It is remaining in his word which is the hallmark of a true disciple (John 8:31); his voice gathers the flock of God (John 10:27), and his word prunes the branches of the vine so that they bear much fruit (John 15:3). In one place Jesus says he only speaks what God has told him to say, and that all his words add up to one thing, namely eternal life. Nevertheless if anyone rejects him, the very words he has spoken will turn around and condemn them on the day of judgement (John 12:47–50).

John's final assessment of Jesus is well known. He came from God, and he spoke the words of God because he was endowed with the Spirit of God in a manner which was total and measureless (John 3:31–36). His mission was to speak life by his word to all who would hear him. He was more than just a *messenger* of God's word, he was the Word of God in human flesh (John 1:14, 18). Such was the final form of John's faith, born of his intimate experience of Jesus and his message. In the gospel he conveys the substance of what led him to that point. It does not appear to me that he has moved far from the picture conveyed by the first three gospels, particularly in the parables of the kingdom.

Notes

[1] See Dodd, *Founder*, 37–41, for a superb description of Jesus' parable-making art. Dodd sees it as one of Jesus' clearest personal traits. Also P.B. Payne, 'The Authenticity of the Parables of Jesus', 329–344.

[2] There used to be a letter in the library at Edessa, purportedly from Jesus to the ruler of Edessa, answering a written request that he come and heal him. A translation of the correspondence is preserved in Eusebius, *History*, 1.13.10.

[3] Wrede, *Messianic Secret*. For a critique see Schweitzer, *Quest*, 334–350; also chapter 10.

[4] John 10:24; 12:39f.; 16:25.

[5] Matthew 7:6; Luke 10:21–23.

[6] On the theme of the messianic secret see C.F.D. Moule, 'On Defining the Messianic Secret in Mark'; M. Boucher, *The Mysterious Parable*, 80–83.

[7] This is the regular meaning of the Greek term *musterion* in the New Testament: Romans 11:25; 1 Corinthians 2:1; 15:51; Ephesians 1:9; 3:3; 6:19; Colossians 1:26; 4:3; 2 Thessalonians 2:7; 1 Timothy 3:9, 16; Revelation 1:20; 10:7.

[8] See especially Daniel 2; 4:9.

[9] In this highly predestinational context I have tried to bring out what I think is the force of the terms *exomologoumai* and *eudokia* with 'bow to your understanding' and 'sovereign decree'.

[10] Luke 10:29–37. Augustine identified these and many more parts of the story. See W.S. Kissinger (*The Parables of Jesus: A History of Interpretation and Bibliography*, 18ff.; 26–27) for allegorical interpretations of other parables.

[11] For a comprehensive common-sense treatment which establishes the presence of allegory in many of Jesus' parables see C.L. Blomberg, *Interpreting the Parables*.

[12] D.O. Via, *The Parables*, 4.

[13] See P.B. Payne, 'The Authenticity of the Parable of the Sower and its Interpretation', 169–71; 'Parables', 334–337.

[14] Linnemann, *Parables*, 22–23.

[15] In this category I would place some of the existentializing interpretations of Via (e.g., *Parables*, 113–122 on the talents), and J.D. Crossan's philosophically ingenious interpretation of the hidden treasure in *Finding is the First Act*.

[16] Dodd, *Parables*, 179f.

[17] E.g., Linnemann (*Parables*, 114ff.) follows Dodd's general approach. However, she places the parable in the context of an argument (hypothetical) over whether the kingdom had really arrived or not, arising out of Jesus' belief (hypothetical) that the huge response to the Baptist's preaching was evidence that it had. Others allegedly disputed Jesus' understanding, pointing out that many had not believed John's message. Jesus sought to bridge the gulf between himself and his hearers by telling a parable which drew them into making the judgement that the harvest could be real enough even when some of the sown seed has been lost along the way. She gives the parable more stomach than Dodd. However, she can only do this with the aid of two very doubtful hypotheses. Even then her interpretation leaves the impression that the parable really

missed the point, if such it was, for it neither mentions nor implies a harvest. Indeed, the attention it directs to the varying yields of different plants is irrelevant if not confusing to the meaning she puts forward.

[18] Dodd, *Parables*, 183.

[19] Some have objected to this interpretation on the grounds that it does not fit the parable. But see Payne, 'Sower', 168ff.; B. Gerhardsson, 'The Parable of the Sower and its Interpretation', 165–193; R.E. Brown, 'Parable and Allegory Reconsidered', 36–45; C.F.D. Moule, 'Mark 4:1–20 yet Once More', 95–113; *The Birth of the New Testament*, 149–52.

[20] Payne, 'Sower', 163–165. He lists ten such parables: the sower, the wicked husbandmen, the good employer, the marriage feast, the great supper, the talents, the pounds, the good Samaritan, the barren fig tree, the shrewd manager.

[21] Jeremias, *Parables*, 170.

[22] See Charles, *Pseudepigrapha*, 775.

[23] Jeremias, *Parables*, 169–171. Note that he feels forced to concede a deliberate allegorical element stemming from Jesus.

[24] Jeremias (*Parables*, 115ff.) appears to follow Dodd's realized eschatology in principle, but when it comes to the actual business of interpreting individual parables he is still forced to concede a future harvest in the thinking of Jesus (150f.).

[25] Jeremias' attempt to avoid paying heed to the process of growth by dismissing it as a western preoccupation seems a little desperate (*Parables*, 148f.).

[26] Some varieties of mustard, when allowed to grow wild, can reach heights of up to ten feet, but the connection of the parable with Daniel and Ezekiel's great tree makes it clear that this is not what Jesus has in mind.

[27] The existence of a Mishnaic law forbidding the planting of mustard in a vegetable garden (Jeremias, *Parables*, 27, n. 11; *Mishnah Kilaim* 3:2) does not mean it was not grown in Galilee in the first century.

[28] D. Wenham, *The Parables of Jesus*, 54.

[29] Examples of incongruity: the comparison of the kingdom with leaven (Luke 13:21); the intercession of the orchardist in the parable of the fig tree (Luke 13:6–9); the likening of Jesus to Archelaus in the parable of the three entrepreneurs – also his giving the one mina to the man who already had ten (Luke 19:11–27); the size of the debt in the parable of the unmerciful servant (Matthew 18:23–35); the Samaritan in the parable of the good Samaritan (Luke 10:30–37); the commendation of the unjust steward (Luke 16:8).

[30] E.g., Matthew 16:6, 11f.; Mark 8:15; Luke 12:1; 1 Corinthians 5:6–8; Jeremias, *Parables*, 149.

[31] Jeremias (*Parables*, 147) sees the large quantity of flour as 'eschatological colour' added by Matthew and Luke. It is surely part of the genius of the original parable.

[32] Jeremias, *Parables*, 81–85.

[33] Jeremias, *Parables*, 226.

[34] 1QM12.

[35] See Riesner (*Lehrer*, 435f.) who argues that Jesus could have been expected to give such interpretations to his disciples. Also D. Hill (*The Gospel of Matthew*, 235) who contends for at least an original core to the interpretation, and Blomberg (*Parables*, 197–200), who defends the dominical character of both parable and interpretation. Boucher, (*Parable*, 39–40) thinks the interpretation is Matthew's, but feels that some such interpretation was necessary and could have been given by Jesus.

[36] N.T. Wright, *Victory*, 309. Similarly Meyer, *Aims*, 167–168, 171.

[37] In Isaiah 60:1–3 Israel's light will be seen by the nations and prove to be irresistibly attractive.

[38] John 12:20–32; Mark 13:10; 14:9.

[39] See Kissinger, *Parables*, 97–102.

[40] There is no case in the gospels of 'Son of Man' on anyone's lips but Jesus'. It is not used as a title anywhere else in the New Testament, except once when Stephen says he sees the Son of Man standing at God's right hand (Acts 7:55–56).

[41] J.T. Milik, *Ten Years of Discovery in the Judaean Wilderness*, 33–34.

[42] So J.H. Charlesworth (*Jesus Within Judaism*, 40) who thinks Jesus was influenced by the Similitudes.

[43] It is noteworthy that 'Son of Man' as a messianic title occurs in no other fragment from the Dead Sea Scrolls, nor in any other pre-Christian Jewish writing.

[44] E.g., John 12:23, 34.

Chapter 12

Opposition

Many Enemies

For a man who advocated love of enemies Jesus had any number of them to test himself on. At various points in our journey thus far we have touched on opposition. John the Baptist's activities were under hostile scrutiny from Jerusalem and Herod. Jesus' action at the temple drew the attention of the authorities and made them wary. Initially they may have seen him as less of a problem than John, but when he began to outstrip John with his preaching and the number of his disciples multiplied, attention soon shifted in his direction (John 4:1–2). It was this unwelcome notice which, according to the Gospel of John, motivated his decision to go back to Galilee. Mark says it coincided with the Baptist's arrest (Mark 1:14). It must have been a tense time.

Herod struck at the Baptist as ruler of the Trans-Jordanian territory of Peraea, where much of John's preaching and baptizing took place. But Herod was also the ruler of Galilee, so flight there hardly removed Jesus from his reach. However, we have seen that Herod was probably preoccupied with his sensitive southern province at this time,[1] and Jesus may have judged Galilee a safe haven. We do not hear much of Herod regarding Jesus as a threat until later in his ministry, though Mark informs us that members of the Herodian party made their appearance early, in company with other hostile parties (Mark 3:6).[2]

The move to Galilee, however, did not remove Jesus from opposition. He generated it wherever he went. He soon offended his own townspeople and alienated his family. The scribes considered his unilateral declaration of forgiveness to the paraplegic blasphemous. The Pharisees were offended by his free socializing with notorious law-breakers. A delegation of scribes was sent from Jerusalem to investigate his activities. Thus despite the crowds which flocked to hear him – indeed because of the crowds – Jesus was a marked man from the outset, and it cannot be said that all the opposition came from one quarter, nor even that it came only from the various ruling groups. John, more than the other gospel writers, indicates that Jesus was resented not just by special interest parties, but also by a wider circle of ordinary Judaeans and Galileans.[3]

Foremost amongst Jesus' critics were the Pharisees. This was particularly so in the Galilean phase of his ministry, though they were also prominent when he transferred his activities to Judaea and Jerusalem. We do not hear much of opposition from the Sadducees in Galilee, but since they were an aristocratic party composed mostly of priests, whose activities were chiefly concentrated in Jerusalem, this is not surprising. They became more important once the scene shifted to Jerusalem. At the time of Jesus' arrest the ball fell into the court of the Jerusalem officials, the High Priest, other influential priests, elders and members of the Council. Most of these were Sadducees, though there were also Pharisees involved. Once they are acting in an official capacity their party affiliations become less evident. Finally, Jesus was handed over to the Roman administration for execution.

Thus there is an unusually varied complex of opposition, including at least three national parties, three different government administrations, and members of the public who may or may not have had special affiliations. In this chapter we will focus on the build up of opposition to Jesus in the first year of his Galilean ministry. The story of the last year is so much dominated by the succession of events which led to Jesus' death that it requires separate attention.

Two Great Issues

Opposition to Jesus gathered at two distinct storm-centres. These were the question of his own personal claims and aspirations, and the issue of his teaching. Memories were still fresh of witnessed massacres and civil war brought about by prophet-like figures who excited the populace with promises of help from God if only they would be courageous and strike against Rome. Thus, popular preachers like John and Jesus were inevitably of concern. For most of the story the concerned authorities were Jewish. In Galilee and Peraea the government was Jewish, and we should not think that even in Judaea there were Roman soldiers everywhere. The Romans used a native administration headed by the High Priest to control most of the country. The small Roman garrison in Jerusalem was a military presence in case of trouble, and the procurator and his legion most of the time were out of the way in Caesarea on the Mediterranean coast.

This resulted in a complex situation. The majority of Jews never gave up hope that God would fulfil his promise to liberate them from foreign powers, and expected that this would come through a human deliverer. Thus, despite a necessary wariness of false prophets, who could wreak untold damage, Jewish leaders could not be too heavy-fisted in crushing every sign of messianic fervour without danger of opposing the real thing. Even if some of the Sadducean rulers had abandoned all hope of future divine intervention – and we don't know that they had – and looked only to the maintenance of their own temporal power under the Romans, they would not have had the cooperation they needed to suppress all possibly messianic activity. There is a telling incident which John locates in Jerusalem at the Feast of Tabernacles in AD 29. The chief priests and Pharisees gave orders for Jesus' arrest, only to have the arresting party return empty handed with the words, 'No one ever spoke like this man' (John 7:32–49). Such ineffectual delegation is only credible in a situation where ordinary people exercised independent judgement about who was truly representing God.

Testing Jesus' Authority

Jesus' declaration of the nearness (presence) of the kingdom of God, and his large following assured him of close, but initially respectful, scrutiny by the Jewish authorities. We have seen that he did not proclaim himself publicly as the Messiah. His message focused on the new order that was breaking in. For the authorities the crucial questions must have been how Jesus imagined the kingdom would come, and what role he envisaged for himself in bringing it about. There was also the question of whether he had a God-given authority for acting as he did, or was in fact a false prophet. John the Baptist was asked directly who he claimed to be; there is only one clear instance in the gospels prior to his trial where we see Jesus faced with such an inquiry, though it is unlikely to have been the only occasion. In that instance he is evasive, unwilling simply to surrender himself to his enemies by means of a direct answer (John 10:22–29; cf. 8:53–59). On the other hand, many of Jesus' actions and words implied an authority little less than God's, and he does not seem unwilling that sympathetic people should draw messianic conclusions. Accordingly, the most frequent line of challenge we encounter from his opponents is the request for a sign.

> The Pharisees came and began to test him, seeking from him a sign from heaven. Groaning in his spirit he says, 'Why does this generation seek for a sign? Truly I say to you, It is out of the question that any sign should be given to this generation.' (Mark 8:11–12)

This saying bristles with difficulties, the most obvious being that Jesus is frequently seen doing miracles which should have been signs to anyone with eyes to see. He never does them on demand though, or with the intention of authenticating himself to sceptics. Yet his miracles were an integral part of his kingdom-bringing mission, most often motivated by compassion. He appears to have desired that people draw messianic conclusions, but would not actually stage miracles to overwhelm his critics. It is unclear whether the words 'test (tempt) him' refer to the motives of the Pharisees, or to the real temptation such challenges presented Jesus, but given his experience in the wilderness it is likely to include the latter. It is not easy to see why Jesus regarded it as wrong to comply with the Pharisees' request – it could not have been difficult for him. Evidently he desired something more in the way of a believing response than the grudging assent that might be wrung from the unenthusiastic by an overawing display of power. Or perhaps there was something fundamentally perverse about the request. Besides announcing the kingdom, Jesus, and John before him, were calling on people to do only what was self-evidently good, and in complete accord with the law and the prophets. In his parable of the rich man and Lazarus (Luke 16:19–31), Jesus criticized his opponents for disregarding the law and the prophets, despite their apparent zeal. If they are unwilling to listen to the prophets, says Jesus, they would not believe even if someone were to rise from the dead. We see here a profound connection in Jesus' thinking between a person's moral stance and their ability to believe, which made sign – miracles pointless and wrong. Nevertheless, Jesus was doing the works his Father had appointed to manifest the presence of the kingdom, which should have been sufficient to convince anyone that he had a God-given commission.[4] To require that he further prove himself by dancing to their tune would have placed them in the position of lordship – just the kind of inappropriate testing that Israel indulged in during its wilderness days. Besides, the power to work miracles was not decisive on its own. Moses warned of the possibility of a false prophet performing signs in order to draw Israel away from God (Deuteronomy 13:1–5). Thus it was possible for a critic to witness a miracle and still judge Jesus an evildoer. That is precisely what happened in the case of the delegation from Jerusalem. They did not dispute that he cast out demons, but charged that it was with demonic power (Mark 3:22). According to the Talmud Jesus was condemned for practising sorcery and leading Israel astray, an acknowledgement of his signs and a judgement of their evil inspiration.[5]

We are now in a position to see how questions about Jesus' identity and the source of his authority lead naturally to anxiety about his teaching. It was crucial to know of any new teacher, regardless of miracles, whether they were leading Israel towards or away from God. Four years before the outbreak of war with Rome a man named Jesus ben Ananias began wandering about Jerusalem crying woes against the city. He was arrested and chastised by the Jewish rulers, and when he refused to cease, handed over to the Romans. Though severely flogged he refused to give any reply to his questioners, and was finally released when the procurator concluded he was mad. What saved him, to continue his cries of warning for another seven years, was his lack of a following. He was a loner who spoke to neither friend nor foe. He was in no danger of becoming influential. Such was not the case with Jesus of Nazareth.[6] His seemingly revolutionary announcement coupled with the size of his following made an investigation of his teaching unavoidable. And it was the Pharisees, the watchdogs of the nation's faithfulness to the law, who were the ones most sensitive to the question of his leading Israel astray.

The Pharisees

Josephus describes four schools of thought among the Jews of Jesus' time.[7] The Pharisees, Sadducees and Essenes were long-standing 'parties', each with a defined membership and distinctive philosophy (theology). The 'Fourth Philosophy,' as he calls it, had originated in relatively recent times in the revolutionary fervour aroused by the introduction of direct Roman rule and taxation to Judaea in AD 6. It was a philosophy of no compromise with the Roman occupiers. The revolt it occasioned was crushed. It is not known whether an organized movement existed in the time of Jesus or whether the philosophy was present only as an influence. Later it was to crystallize into a number of revolutionary organizations, among them the 'Zealots' and 'Sicarii' (Dagger-men), which were active in the revolt against Rome. It is scarcely to be doubted that Jews with revolutionary tendencies were interested in Jesus, though they are never mentioned as a distinct group. Neither are the Essenes, though they too could not have failed to be interested in his message. It is the Pharisees who overwhelmingly dominate the opposition in the gospel records. We meet them repeatedly: disapproving, passing judgement, setting up trick questions, asking for signs, involving themselves in debate with him and his disciples. Who were these people, and what were the causes of their disquiet?

Their origins probably lie in another movement known as the Hasidim (the Pious). From 167 to 164 BC the Jews fought a war of liberation against the Greek kingdom of Syria. Prior to that they had been an uneasy province, sometimes of the Egyptian, sometimes of the Syrian section of the Greek empire. Hellenistic thought and customs were making serious inroads and many Jews were in favour of adopting Greek ways in place of their own outdated culture. Things came to the boil when the Syrian king Antiochus Epiphanes determined to standardize the culture of his empire and imposed forced hellenization on the Jews. Circumcision was made illegal, a pig was sacrificed in the temple at Jerusalem, and commissioners were sent throughout the villages to ensure conformity. Jews were required to sacrifice to the Greek gods and eat pork to demonstrate their abandonment of the old religion and loyalty to the

new. In the village of Modin a rebellion took place, leading to a
passionate guerilla war in defence of historic Judaism. The
Syrians were ousted and a Jewish regime was established that
lasted until the coming of the Romans in 63 BC. Judas
Maccabaeus, the leader of the initial struggle, was supported by
the religiously orthodox Hasidim.[8]

As a distinct party the Pharisees appear first in the reign of
the Hasmonean (Maccabaean) prince, John Hyrcanus (135–105
BC).[9] Whereas their chief concern was loyalty to the law, his
was power, so that although in earlier days the Pharisees and
their predecessors were closely allied to the Hasmonean rulers,
a struggle now commenced. When a certain Pharisee declared
that Hyrcanus was disqualified from holding the high priesthood a bitter feud broke out and the Sadducees, who are also
first met at this time, took their place as advisors and interpreters of the law.[10] The conflict reached its climax when Alexander
Jannaeus (103–76 BC) had eight hundred Pharisees crucified in
his presence in Jerusalem.[11] However, his widow, who succeeded him to the throne, made peace with the Pharisees (on
the advice of her dying husband), reintroduced Pharisaic law,
and made them the rulers of the country in all but name.[12] This
was the high point of Pharisaic ascendancy. With the coming of
Roman power, the disintegration of the Hasmonean dynasty
and its replacement by Herod the Great, they lost their official
position. However, in the minds of the people they remained
identified with loyalty to the law and probably also with the
national struggle for an independent theocratic constitution.
More than six thousand Pharisees refused to swear an oath of
obedience to Caesar and Herod the Great.[13] It was a Pharisee
who along with Judas the Galilean, introduced the 'Fourth Philosophy' of resistance to Roman rule.[14] An early second century
descendant of the Pharisees declared Simon ben Kosiba to be
the Messiah and supported another war against Rome.[15] This is
not to suggest that the Pharisees were violent revolutionaries;
most of them for most of their history lived peaceably under

whatever administration prevailed, but they were not uncon-
cerned with Israel's traditional hopes.[16]

Recent Debate about the Pharisees

It is necessary to prefix what else I have to say with the warning
that the nature of the Pharisaic movement in the time of Jesus has
been the subject of intense study and debate since the Second
World War. There was a tendency in former Christian writing
and preaching to portray the Pharisees as villains: paradigms of
hypocrisy and shallow, external religion. Sometimes this went a
step further, and, in the service of anti-Semitism, a simplistic
identification was made of Pharisees and Jews. Recent Christian
and Jewish writing has raised a legitimate and helpful protest.[17]
Recognizing that the gospel picture of Pharisaism is inevitably
one-sided, some scholars have legitimately attempted to understand the Pharisees on their own terms, to see to what extent they
really were guilty of the accusations Jesus made against
them. Neusner, Sanders and Maccoby have all given attractive
portrayals of first century Pharisees.[18] Some writers have then
gone to the extreme of denying Jesus had any quarrel with them.
Accounts of conflict are attributed to later Christian writers
projecting onto Jesus the struggles of church and synagogue in
their own day.[19]

This is quite improbable. First, for all that is said about gospel
writers fabricating sayings and incidents and attributing them to
Jesus, there is no evidence that they did and many indicators that
they did not.[20] Secondly, the issues over which Jesus and the
Pharisees disagree in the gospels are different to the contentions of
the early church. Thirdly, the evidence points to a more friendly
and open relationship between Pharisees and Christians after the
resurrection (at least until the sixties) than had existed before.
Fourthly, Luke shows no hostility to Pharisees as such.[21] Many
became Christians and may have maintained their membership of

the Pharisaic party.[22] Indeed, Luke goes out of his way to show as much of the positive side of Pharisaism as possible.[23] His, for example, is the only gospel which records a number of incidents in which Jesus shared meals with Pharisees.[24] No doubt he had a motive for this: he wrote to convince people sympathetic to Judaism (perhaps Jews) that Jesus was the Messiah and Christianity was not contrary to true Old Testament Judaism. Anything positive in Jesus' relationship with these recognized exponents of Judaism was thus helpful. If there had been more accord between them Luke for one would have had every reason to highlight it. That he also includes the controversy demonstrates both that it was part of history, and that he did not jettison material that made his own thesis difficult to maintain. Luke's two volumes are the only New Testament books written by a non-Jew, and they are by far the most sympathetic and conciliatory towards Pharisaism.[25] The other gospels appear harsher, but are by no means uniformly so. John follows with sympathy and interest the development of faith in the Pharisee Nicodemus.[26] Matthew, who has the appearance of being the most anti-Pharisaic (a tendency some-times attributed to conflicts with Pharisees in his own time) records Jesus' surprising acknowledgement that the scribes and Pharisees are to be obeyed because they 'sit on Moses' seat' (Matthew 23:2–3). It is absurd to think that later Christians would have invented such a saying. It must go back to Jesus, and acknowledges, despite his trenchant criticisms, that the Pharisees' interpretations were the de facto law of the land.[27]

National self-criticism has a long history among the Jews, going back to the Old Testament prophets. It has nothing to do with anti-Semitism. The harsh words of John the Baptist, Jesus, and other New Testament writers should all be understood within this context. To attribute to them anti-Semitic sentiments is as silly as accusing Moses and Isaiah of anti-Semitism. They all longed passionately for Israel's salvation. To use the gospels for anti-Semitic purposes is therefore flagrant abuse.

The Pharisees According to Various Sources

Recognizing that the gospels are highly critical of the Pharisees, and that reconstructions based on them alone are likely to be one-sided, the attempt has been made to understand Pharisees from other sources. This has been complicated by debates about the reliability of Josephus' information: was he ever a Pharisee as he claims, and are his writings for or against them? Then there is the difficulty of identifying Pharisaic writings and traditions that go back to the first century: necessary if we are to understand their teachings in their own terms. Nevertheless, despite some uncertainties, a reasonably clear and consistent picture has emerged.

The Pharisees were, for the most part, a party of lay people who wanted to be faithful to God's law, and lead the nation to obedience. It was disobedience which had brought Israel into bondage and disgrace, and only a renewal of faithfulness would get them out. A second century (AD) disciple of Rabbi Akiba said that if every Israelite would keep two Sabbaths according to its laws the kingdom would come.[28] They studied and interpreted the law, worked out the details of how it should be applied in everyday life, lived it, taught it, and lobbied for its observance at a national level. This inevitably brought them into conflict with parties holding different views, particularly the Sadducees who predominated amongst the ruling priestly aristocracy. The people regarded the Pharisees as the true interpreters of the law and leaned towards them in preference to the more remote Sadducean aristocracy.[29] Such was the authority of Pharisaic opinion that the Sadducean priests themselves were sometimes forced to carry out some of their temple rituals in accordance with Pharisaic rules.[30]

Neusner and Sanders have both queried the extent of the Pharisees' influence. Seeing them as a small group, pursuing life according to their own rules without wishing to impose their viewpoint on others,[31] they depict them having little impact on national life. This goes against the explicit testimony of Josephus, as well as the picture painted by the gospels,[32] and makes it difficult to understand how Pharisaism quickly established itself as official Judaism in the reconstruction period following the first Jewish–Roman war. Maccoby thinks the Pharisees were widespread and influential.[33] If we accept the evidence of the gospels, and it is the nearest to being contemporary with the Pharisees, we can see that they were represented throughout the towns and villages of Judaea and Galilee, and active at the highest level in Jerusalem. They were a scholarly movement, dedicated to accurate interpretation of the law, not purely for their own benefit and practice, but also for observance by the people. Some think they were even responsible for the proliferation of synagogues as places of instruction in the law.[34] They were not all scholars or teachers. Nevertheless, study, teaching and practice was what the movement was all about. It is an anachronistic retrojection of modern pluralism to think of Pharisees pursuing a particular interpretation of the law for themselves alone, happy that others should live in other ways. The law was for everyone, and if their rules interpreted it correctly, then they were right for every Jew. Only this makes sense of their attacks on Jesus and his disciples for not observing the traditions of the elders.

One of the debates surrounding the Pharisees relates to the rationale behind their rules of purity. These went beyond what the Torah required of ordinary Jews. The preponderance of Pharisaic laws dealing with dietary matters, which Neusner identifies in the Mishnah and Tosefta, leads him to the view that the Pharisees of Jesus' time were a pure food club; no longer concerned with politics, only with the internal affairs of their own group. Their basic aspiration was to live ordinary life in a purity akin to what was normally required of priests.[35] That they were concerned to live as much as possible in some degree of ceremonial holiness seems clear.[36] But it goes against the evidence to suggest that they regarded this as purely a rule for their own community, even allowing that some of their practices were regarded as voluntary works of supererogation.[37] All Israel was called to be holy, and it stood to reason that what they had come to believe was the right way to be holy, was for all who were serious about godly living.[38] Their dietary rules made them cautious about receiving hospitality from non-Pharisees whose food might not be clean, making it likely that the movement enjoyed a high degree of communality over the meal table. Inviting non-Pharisees to eat with them may not have presented an equal risk, so it is not a contradiction to find that Jesus at times was the guest of Pharisees.

Let this thumbnail sketch suffice for the moment. It brings us to the Pharisees encountered by Jesus: men who saw themselves as expert interpreters of Moses, models of true obedience, particularly sensitive to matters of ceremonial purity, and watch-dogs of the nation's faithfulness to the law. It is impossible that one like Jesus should not have aroused their interest and suspicion to the highest degree.

Three Early Clashes

In my telling of the story thus far, we have met the Pharisees in relation to three issues. They were understandably incensed by Jesus granting forgiveness to the paraplegic (Mark 2:1–12). There is no reason for doubting the detail supplied by Luke, that on this occasion Jesus' audience was composed of Pharisees and teachers of the law from all over the country (Luke 5:17); their presence evidences a desire to check on his activities. The disquiet at Jesus' sovereign grant of forgiveness is no negative reflection on the Pharisees. Anyone of spiritual sensitivity would have questioned it. Jesus answered them with a 'sign' of his authority, and it should not go unnoticed that they responded to this positively in their subsequent praise of God (Luke 5:26). Some also took exception to his eating meals with 'tax collectors and sinners' (Mark 2:16), and this was a continuing source of aggravation. It was more than the understandable affront, which must have been felt by many more than the Pharisees, that Jesus seemed to give such favoured attention to 'bad elements' of the population.[39] The 'purity' of the people, one of the Pharisees paramount concerns, necessitated a clear line of demarcation between Jews and Gentiles, and between righteous and sinners. For a person who claimed a close relationship with God to fellowship with sinners was tantamount to saying that *God* fraternized with sinners. Unthinkable! No doubt the Pharisees found it difficult to counter Jesus' likening himself to a doctor, and the argument that he had come to bring sinners to repentance, but it could not have gone unnoticed that he began his fellowship with these people *before* they had given any sign of repentance or made any public act of restitution. The third issue concerned exorcisms (Mark 3:22–30). Had Jesus merely taught and acted in an unconventional manner he would have been very much easier to deal with. It was his miracle working and exorcisms which established him, as far as the general public was concerned, as 'a man come from God'. We know of one Pharisee at least who shared this judgement (John 3:1–2); doubtless there were others of the same opinion. To dismiss Jesus' work as being of satanic inspiration was about the only theological way out, though it does not seem to have carried much weight: attempts to trip him up on other grounds continued, and a good number of Pharisees continued to be sympathetic to his cause.

Lord of the Sabbath

The most common complaint about Jesus in the gospels is that he broke the Sabbath. It was probably the one clear and repeated instance of what seemed like undeniable law breaking, that gave real substance to the Pharisees' complaints against him. His most frequent misdemeanour was healing on the Sabbath. The first case of Sabbath irregularity related by Mark is the only instance where healing is not in view, and in this case it was not Jesus who broke the law, but his disciples (Mark 2:23–28; cf. Matthew 12:1–8; Luke 6:1–5). This is significant, for there is no occasion recorded where Jesus did break the law except where higher principles were involved. As the question of his paying the temple tax illustrates, he seems to have been sensitive to not giving unnecessary offence to the scruples of others unless something important was at issue (Matthew 17:24–27). Nevertheless, his disciples were under his tutelage and were expected to be imitating his pattern of life, so their behaviour understandably reflected back on him and he was questioned on it.

The law of Moses said 'Remember to keep the Sabbath day holy ... you shall not do any work in it' (Exodus 20:8–11). Keeping the law was the obligation of every Jew, but to observe it correctly it was first of all necessary to know what was work and what was not. The Pharisees took upon themselves the task of making this definition, and expanded the law of Moses with myriads of detailed ordinances about what was and was not permitted on the Sabbath. The process of definition had been going on for some time before Jesus, and it continued after him. The first detailed written record of it was the Mishnah of Rabbi Judah the Patriarch, written at the end of the second century AD. Thus the Mishnah tractate *Shabbath* gives us the law of the Sabbath at the end of the second century, but its development was already well advanced by the time of Jesus. Though it is difficult to say exactly how many of the Mishnaic provisions were in force in Jesus' day, the general character of the law is clear.

Sabbath According to the Mishnah

Thirty nine major categories of work are named, among them reaping and threshing. In addition, there are hundreds of detailed ordinances which bespeak an even larger body of tradition:

seemingly endless definitions of what could and could not be done on the Sabbath. Many of them were difficult cases which were discussed by the scholars or brought before them for judgement. There were rules, for example, about what could be placed on a stove which was still hot from Friday[40] (Sabbath began at sunset on Friday), and what could or could not be carried out of a house (including an argument about whether a cripple is permitted to take his wooden leg outside with him on the Sabbath).[41]

There is no question that what the disciples were doing was classified as work, but Jesus was quick to spring to their defence, even though the transgression was not his own. He reminded his accusers of the occasion in the Old Testament when David, in his flight from Saul, took the sacred bread from the tabernacle in Nob and gave it to his men, although according to the law only the priests were permitted to eat it (1 Samuel 21:1ff.). It was a case of human need overriding an ordinance of the law. Jesus inferred that his disciples' hunger also overrode the Sabbath. This was a dramatic relaxation. The scribes debated what was permissible in the case of emergencies; when there was a real threat to life the Sabbath could be overridden.[42] But normally even the putting out of a burning house was forbidden, and only certain things, like copies of the Scriptures could be rescued from it.[43] Johanan ben Zakkai, who lived near Nazareth not long after the time of Jesus, seriously doubted whether a person who placed a dish over a scorpion so it would not bite anyone was not guilty and liable to a sin-offering.[44] Thus overriding the Sabbath on the grounds of ordinary hunger would have been unthinkable.

Jesus' Attitude to the Law

Yet Jesus supported his position by appeal to a precedent of holy Scripture. In this he was very much within the tradition of scribal debate and practice. He understood their method and used it. If his opinion hung only on his interpretation of this passage his argument was answerable; if the people who questioned him failed to come up with an answer there and then, they could have referred it to their scribes who would not have had difficulty finding a counter-argument. But his interpretation indicated something much deeper than could have been ultimately grounded on one Old Testament story. A position which allowed mere hunger to override the Sabbath, would, if it were accepted, turn Sabbath keeping into such a relaxed and subjective business that legislation except against the most obvious abuses (Sabbath trading for example) would have become impossible. Thus there is something here in Jesus' attitude to the Sabbath, and perhaps to more of the law, which is fundamentally different to the Pharisaic tradition. It emerges very clearly in two of his sayings.

> Woe to you lawyers too, for you load people with burdens which are heavy to bear, but you yourselves do not touch these burdens with one of your fingers. (Luke 11:46; Matthew 23:4)

> Come to me all you who are tired from carrying a heavy load, and I will let you rest. Pick up my yoke and learn from me, because I am gentle and humble-minded, and you will find refreshment for your souls, for my yoke is easy to wear and my burden is light. (Matthew 11:28–30)

Jesus accused the Pharisaic law-makers of turning the law into a heavy burden for ordinary people, which they themselves, possibly because of their cleverness or their wealth, were able to evade. On the other hand, he invited people to learn the law from him and discover that it was not a burden, but something which gave refreshment. This need not mean Jesus was creating a new law. His commitment to Moses comes through on numerous occasions.[45] But he had a different approach to it than the Pharisees. To use a term from the computing world, he viewed it as 'user friendly'. This inevitably meant radically different interpretations to those of the Pharisees, as the incident in the grain fields makes clear.[46]

The Law as Pillar of the Cosmos

It was no accident that the law had become so burdensome. The Pharisees believed that the law of Moses was older than humanity, older than the world. Many years prior to Jesus, under the influence of the Platonic and Stoic concept of a universal *logos* ('word', 'idea'), some Jews began to identify the Mosaic law with divine wisdom, which had been with God as he laid the foundations of the world (Proverbs 8). According to the Stoic notion, behind the universe of visible things stood a divine idea, a kind of heavenly blueprint. It is not difficult to see how this concept was connected with the idea of God's wisdom, but it was a bold and dramatic step, which claimed that this 'blueprint' had been revealed to Israel in the law of Moses.[47]

Three consequences flowed from this new concept. First, the answer to every conceivable question must lie hidden somewhere in the law. Secondly, humanity is made for the law, not the law for humanity. And thirdly, any breach of the law strikes a blow at the God-ordained structure of the cosmos. This latter point meant that the law needed to be carefully protected. To do this it was necessary to 'build a fence around the law'. This fence consisted of the mass of detailed laws seen as necessary to protect the six hundred and thirteen primary scriptural laws from being transgressed.[48] We have already seen some of the laws which fenced the Sabbath.

This view also implied the subversiveness of incorrect attitudes to the law. It was not merely a question of different interpretations, which could coexist harmoniously. The Torah was one of the pillars that sustained the world;[49] to break it was to threaten the order of the cosmos. A reflection of this is seen in the earnestness with which the Qumran community regarded some of its variant interpretations, particularly those related to the calendar and the dates of festivals.[50]

For Jesus to declare that the law was made for people and not people for the law was in fundamental conflict with Jewish beliefs of the day (not just Pharisaism), and totally subversive of the Pharisaic system which was then in process of construction. He evidently saw the law as something given to protect human life, more than something which people are charged to protect for its own sake.[51] It explains his user-friendly approach to the law and also his final statement that the Son of Man is lord of the Sabbath. Jesus may have meant that he as King was master of what could be done on the Sabbath, but more likely he spoke generically of human beings. God had not decreed the details of how the Sabbath was to be kept; therefore human beings, even private individuals, might take the responsibility for deciding for themselves. They were not to enjoin their rules on others as divine decrees.

Healing on the Sabbath

On a number of occasions Jesus is said to have healed people on the Sabbath, and this appears to have caused particular offence to the Pharisees. Indeed this particular transgression looms so large in the gospels that one wonders whether it was not the one clear case where Jesus himself observably broke the law.

In the case of the man in the synagogue with the withered hand (Mark 3:1–6; Luke 6:6–11; Matthew 12:9–14), Mark says the Pharisees were observing to see if Jesus would heal on a Sabbath. Luke says the scribes and Pharisees were trying to find basis for a charge against Jesus. Healing was regarded as work and was therefore illegal; only when there was a manifest danger to life could the Sabbath be overridden.[52] The particular case before Jesus suited the purposes of the scribes perfectly. There could be no question of a danger to life in a crippled hand; it was forbidden even to set a broken limb on the Sabbath.[53] Would Jesus heal in such a case or not?

He did – with emphasis. For, knowing that he was under observation, Jesus first called the man into the middle of the

group, and then addressed those who were watching him. 'Is it
lawful on the Sabbath to do good or to do evil, to save life or to
kill?' This is very different to his approach to the incident in the
grain fields. Jesus does not bother with the question of the
scriptural grounds on which one might override the Sabbath, nor
does he approach the question of whether what he is doing is
work. Indeed, he sidesteps the whole issue of work and what one
should *not do*, basic to Pharisaic understanding of the Sabbath, and
poses a question about what one *will* do. It is impossible to do
nothing, even on the day of rest, so what should one do? As Jesus
understands the situation before him, he cannot do nothing.
Nor indeed are his critics doing nothing; they are conducting an
examination whose intended aim is to find grounds to accuse
him. The ultimate goal of their efforts as Jesus perceived it was his
death. He too must do *something*, and the question he places
before his critics is whether he should do something good or
something evil, something life-giving or something murderous.
Their business at that moment was murder, his was life. The
question of work was irrelevant.

Jesus could, of course, have done what a certain synagogue
ruler demanded on another occasion: told the man to return the
next day to be healed (Luke 13:14) – in surgery hours, as it were.
That would seem the reasonable thing in the circumstances. It
would have removed all grounds for offence, and the man could
still have been healed. Yet it appears that for Jesus to appease the
hostility and hardness of heart which confronted him in the
synagogue and walk away from a man he was able to heal there
and then, was to walk in the direction of evil and death, surely the
ultimate desecration of the day God had set apart to be kept holy.
He ordered the man to stretch out his hand and it was immediately restored to soundness.

The disproportionate number of stories of this kind gives the
impression that for Jesus there was something especially
appropriate about healing on the Sabbath. This is understandable
if he saw the Sabbath as Paul and the author of Hebrews did, as a

prophetic foreshadowing of the ultimate rest of the new age (Colossians 2:16–17; Hebrews 3:7–4:11). To be condemned for restoring the diseased and damaged creation to wholeness on the day that was to be a symbol and a foretaste of the new creation, was to be condemned for doing the thing which was the very essence of his mission. Jesus' words about a crippled woman point in this direction: 'this daughter of Abraham as she is, whom Satan bound for eighteen years, ought she not to be released from her bond on the Sabbath day?' (Luke 13:16). We can understand his grief over hard hearts that would allow legalities to blind people to the manifest fulfilment of the Sabbath – to the healing presence of the kingdom of God.

Jesus defended his Sabbath day healing of the man at the Pool of Bethesda by arguing that God was still at work, and that he who only did what he saw his Father doing, had also to be at work. His work and his Father's work were ultimately to give life to the dead: to establish the kingdom and to fulfil the Sabbath. Since the time had now arrived for all this to take place, it was unthinkable that the manifestation of the life-giving powers of the new age should be suspended on the Sabbath (John 5:16–30). The offence of this particular healing was still an issue a year later when Jesus returned to Jerusalem for the Feast of Tabernacles (John 7:19–24).

Mark tells us that after the healing of the man with the withered hand, the Pharisees began to discuss with the Herodians how they might destroy Jesus. It is not necessary to imagine that this one situation alone sparked off organized opposition to Jesus. Mark reports the plot as the climax of a series of opposition stories involving Jesus forgiving sins, consorting with sinners, ignoring fasting, and allowing his disciples to treat the Sabbath with laxity. We may surmise there was much more. What is clear is that the Pharisees did see Jesus as a threat to the continuance of the people in the law, and that they were willing to go to the ruling power to have the threat removed.

God's Commandments and Human Traditions

Thus far we have seen very little to indicate that in his own eyes Jesus was a law-breaker, though in the eyes of the Pharisees he not only broke it himself, but encouraged others in a laxity which was highly subversive to their whole concept of law-keeping. In Mark 7 we see him once more in conflict with them, this time over the matter of purity. Mark explains to his non-Jewish readers that the Pharisees and all the Jews follow the 'traditions of the elders' and do not eat unless they first wash their hands; he also mentions some of their other baptismal customs. Jesus' answer, which is recorded in greater detail than the controversies we have looked at so far, gives us a good insight into his attitude to the law as a whole, and to its Pharisaic interpretation.

Again it was the disciples' behaviour which caused offence. The Pharisees and the 'scribes who came from Jerusalem' observed that some of them ate with their hands unclean ('common'). This had nothing to do with hygiene. It was a ritual matter to ensure that meals were eaten in a state of holiness (the opposite of 'common'). According to the Mishnah tractate *Yadaim* (Hands), half a litre of water was deemed sufficient to cleanse the hands of one hundred people, and they could dry their hands by rubbing them on their head or wiping them on the wall without undoing the purification.[54] It was probably some sort of official or unofficial party sent to check on Jesus' orthodoxy that came to dispute with him; they asked why his disciples did not walk according to the tradition of the elders, but ate their bread with 'common' hands. It cannot be correct that Pharisaic teaching saw extra-biblical purity rituals as purely voluntary. Whether this conflict was with Jesus or the church, it indicates disapproval of those who did not observe 'the traditions of the elders'. Again, instead of excusing his followers Jesus rose to their defence and attacked the very basis of Pharisaism. 'Isaiah prophesied the truth about you hypocrites, for it is written, "This people honours me with its lips, but its heart is far away from me.

They worship me in vain, their teachings are rules of men." You abandon the commandment of God and hold the traditions of men' (Mark 7:6–8, quoting Isaiah 29:13). Jesus made a sharp distinction between the traditions and the commandments of God. The traditions are of human origin, the commandments of God come from God. The Pharisees made no such distinction. Although they believed that the Mosaic Torah was primary, they also believed that it could not stand without an accompanying body of rules which told people how to 'walk' in accordance with Moses' law. They believed that as well as giving the written law Moses had passed down a body of subsidiary oral tradition which formed the basis of the tradition of the elders.[55] People were no less obligated to this tradition than they were to the written law; in some ways more so, for this was exact and specific, whereas the written was general and vague.[56]

Yet what for them was intended to secure a proper obedience to the Torah had according to Jesus resulted in their abandoning and making it of no effect. The honour they paid God's law was only an appearance. In reality their hearts were somewhere else. That is what he meant by calling them hypocrites. He did not mean that they were insincere or necessarily aware of the gulf he saw between their system and God. His reply must have been a shock, and they would not have countenanced it for a moment, but Jesus reinforced his contention with an illustration of how their tradition overrode the law (Mark 7:9–13).

Vows

The Mishnah tractate *Nedarim* (vows) is devoted to the question of vows. A quick perusal reveals how common they were, how seriously they were taken, and how strictly they were enforced. It was common for a person to vow that they would take no benefit from someone they were angry with. A man once vowed that he would take no further benefit from his wife.

She then sued him for the return of her dowry. He pleaded for release from his vow, but Rabbi Akiba declared that he must pay back her dowry even if he had to sell the hair of his head. Only when he declared that he would never have made the vow if he had known it included the dowry did Akiba release him.[57] It was also common to vow that the benefits someone might expect from you were *konam* or *korban* ('dedicated'). This had the same effect as if the other party had vowed not to take any benefit.

The case which Jesus mentioned (Mark 7:9ff.) was probably not uncommon. A man became angry with his parents and declared any benefits they might receive from him *korban*. He was then conveniently and religiously released from further financial obligations to his parents. According to Jesus, even if he later repented of such rash action, the scribes would not permit him to help his parents, and thus God's commandment to honour father and mother was overthrown. It seems incredible that such practice was possible, but the Mishnah confirms that it was so. Later on the rabbis debated whether 'a way of repentance' could be opened by 'the honour due to father and mother',[58] but the very existence of such a debate confirms the currency of the problem Jesus pinpointed, and may even have been partially stimulated by his acid critique.[59]

Jesus brought this issue forward not as an isolated instance but as typical of many Pharisaic practices, which had the effect of 'making void' the word of God. Their treatment of divorce and remarriage was another case in point. For Jesus the written commandments of Moses were 'the word of God', and he defended them in the most rigorous manner. The traditions of the elders, on the other hand, were mere human rules which, although intended to help people keep the law of God, sometimes circumvented it while maintaining an appearance of law-abidingness, and sometimes made it unnecessarily burdensome.

Jesus and the Ten Commandments

One positive thing which emerges is the great regard in which Jesus held the commandments of Scripture, and in particular the ten commandments. This comes to the surface at a number of other points in the gospels. When the young ruler came to Jesus and asked him what he needed to do to inherit eternal life (Mark 10:17ff.; Matthew 19:16ff.; Luke 18:18ff.),[60] Jesus told him to keep the commandments, reciting a number to make it clear that he meant the ten commandments. The young man was surprised and disappointed and replied that he had been keeping the commandments since he was young. Everyone knew that keeping the commandments was the way to life; what was expected of a rabbi was some special line on *how* to keep them, or directions as to which were the most important ones to concentrate on.[61] But Jesus would have none of it. Embellishment of the law only led to its destruction; he would place people before it in its starkness and simplicity and allow no slipping sideways.

On another occasion, when a lawyer tested him with the same question as the rich ruler, Jesus answered as before: 'In the law, what is written, how does it read to you?' (Luke 10:25ff.). The lawyer replied with a summary of the law: you should love God with all your heart and your neighbour as yourself. Jesus approved his answer (he had summarized the law in identical fashion himself); 'You have answered correctly,' he said, 'do this and you will live'. The lawyer immediately moved in the direction of the scribal tradition and asked Jesus to define who was meant by 'neighbour'. Jesus' response was the parable of the good Samaritan. A traveller was attacked by bandits and left wounded on the roadside. Two pious passers-by were unwilling to interrupt their journeys to help, but at last a Samaritan came along, took pity, and did all that he could to help. At the end of the story Jesus invited the lawyer to answer his own question: 'Which of the three, in your opinion, *became* neighbour to the man who fell among bandits?' He then sent him off to do likewise.

At this point the difference in the two approaches to the law becomes dazzlingly clear. Paradoxically, for all its massive size and attention to detail, the Pharisaic approach can be viewed as an attempt to limit and control the law. The law limited one's freedom, and it became urgent to precisely define the extent of the limitation. Jesus, on the other hand, saw the law as a revelation of the will of God, to which people should respond, not as a negative restriction but as a positive challenge to greater humanity. The former approach would seek to put a limitation on who might be regarded as a neighbour, the latter would seek to be a neighbour to whomever needed a friend.

A few reflections on this might be in order. The Pharisaic system placed people in a relationship to God which easily engendered deep hostility. This is not to say that they believed God was hostile, nor that many of them did not love God. But the system tended toward one of three things. For the conscientious it made the service of God a crushing burden. For some this led to despair and their giving up altogether the attempt to be law-abiding. For the clever it tended towards their manipulating the law to remain within its letter, at the same time as they transgressed its spirit. Each of these responses was fatal to the positive loving relationship with God that Jesus held forth.

Marriage and Divorce

Their very different approaches to the law also came to the fore over the issue of divorce. Jesus taught on this matter on more than one occasion. Matthew records his teaching in summary form in the Sermon on the Mount (Matthew 5:32), and later gives Mark's account of an occasion when some Pharisees asked Jesus to give his judgement on the question (Matthew 19:1–9). Luke passes over the account of this inquiry and records an accusation of hypocrisy which Jesus brought against the Pharisees on account of their frequent practice of divorce (Luke 16:18).

Luke's account is of particular interest because it highlights the nature of the wider controversy between Jesus and the Pharisees. It occurs in a sequence, which, although severely abbreviated, may well preserve the gist of an original debate (Luke 16:1–31). It begins with the parable of the unjust manager, to which the Pharisees responded with mockery. Jesus retorted that they made themselves appear righteous in the public eye, while to God, who knew their hearts, they were an abomination. He then added, 'The law and the prophets were until John. From that time the kingdom of God is being announced, and everyone is forcing their way into it' (Luke 16:16).

This constituted a warning to the Pharisees that their dominance over Israel was at an end; the age of law was over, and the kingdom was open to whomever wished to enter. The law could no longer stand as a barrier to someone who wanted to come to God. This could have led to the immediate accusation that Jesus was destroying the law, but he anticipated this by adding that it is easier for heaven and earth to pass away than for a single punctuation mark in the law to fall. Whatever he meant by the age of the law and the prophets coming to an end, Jesus evidently did not intend that the law had no further relevance. It was to emphasize this point, and illustrate his original criticism of the Pharisees' hypocrisy that he raised the question of divorce and remarriage.

'Everyone who divorces his wife and marries another commits adultery and the person who marries a woman divorced from her husband commits adultery' (Luke 16:18). To understand what is happening here we need to know something of the scribal debate which was going on over this issue, and also something of Jesus' more detailed response to it in Mark 10. The Mishnah tractate *Gittin* (Bills of Divorce) deals mostly with the formalities of preparing and serving bills of divorce. It ends, however, with a description of the different opinions of the Pharisaic scholars on what constituted adequate grounds for divorce.

> The School of Shammai say: 'A man may not divorce his wife
> unless he has found unchastity in her, for it is written, "Because
> he has found in her *indecency* in anything".' And the School of
> Hillel say: '[He may divorce her] even if she spoiled a dish for him,
> for it is written, "Because he has found in her indecency in *any-*
> *thing*".' Rabbi Akiba says: 'Even if he found another fairer than
> she, for it is written, "And it shall be if she find no favour in his
> eyes".'[62]

The schools of Hillel and Shammai were active in Jesus' time,
though their masters were of his parents' generation. Akiba
belongs to the early second century; his view is related to that of
Hillel. The passage quoted is Deuteronomy 24:1; the same
passage which the Pharisees referred to in discussion with Jesus in
Mark 10. They had asked him whether it was lawful for a man to
divorce his wife for any and every cause (exactly the issue
between the schools). He asked them what the law said, and they
replied from Deuteronomy 24 that Moses allowed divorce, so
long as a bill of divorce was given by the man to his wife. Jesus,
however, replied that God's original and positive will concerning
marriage was not expressed in Deuteronomy 24, but in the
second chapter of Genesis where God declares man and woman
joined together in marriage as 'one flesh'. 'What God has joined
together', said Jesus, 'let not man separate'. The law about divorce
and bills of divorce was given because of 'hardness of heart', that
is, because of the necessities arising from the sin-spoilt human
situation, and should not be used to determine the question of
whether divorce was right or not. That could only be decided in
relation to God's positive desire for the permanent union of those
who marry.

To return to Jesus' words to the Pharisees: he told them that for
someone to divorce his wife and marry another (i.e. *in order to*
marry another woman), was to commit an act of adultery against
his original wife, regardless of whether the correct formalities
involving bills of divorce had been observed.[63] Divorce for the

purpose of remarriage was a relatively frequent practice, understandably so given the ease of divorce under Pharisaic law. All a
man had to do was write his wife a bill of divorce (anyone could
do this – it did not require a lawyer)[64] and have it delivered into
her hand. It could be so sudden that legislation existed for the
case where a husband changed his mind: if he could catch up
with the messenger who was carrying the bill to his wife, or reach
his wife before the messenger did and tell her that the bill was
void, it was void. If the bill reached her first, it was binding. People
were even divorced on the basis of a vow. A man once said to his
wife, '*Konam* if I do not divorce you.' He divorced her and later
when he wanted to take her back was only granted permission by
the scribes as an act of exceptional leniency.[65]

Under these circumstances it is understandable that a very
frequent reason for divorce (probably the most frequent) was the
desire to marry again. But according to Jesus the character of such
an action was exactly the same as adultery. Under such conditions
a woman who wanted to could very easily aggravate, persuade, or
even sue her husband to write her a bill of divorce so that she
would be free to marry someone else.[66] Jesus declared that for a
man to be waiting to snap up a woman as soon as she was
divorced was also an act of adultery.[67] Once again we see how
Pharisaic casuistry was able to use the law against itself, and how
Jesus exposed such behaviour as hypocrisy. A man could persuade
the public and even himself of his righteousness, but his act might
differ from that of the person who slept with his neighbour's wife,
in nothing but the bill of divorce. Before God, it would pass as
nothing less than 'abomination'.

Real Defilement

'Abomination' described something which God loathed. It also
brought about the highest degree of defilement in the biblical or
Pharisaic system. A heathen idol was an abomination; the action

of Antiochus Epiphanes sacrificing a pig on the altar of the temple in Jerusalem was known as 'the abomination which desolates'. For Jesus to have used this word of the Pharisees' inward condition was a most horrible and cutting rebuke, which could not have helped but arouse indignation against him. Yet it is consistent with much else he said.

After his dispute with the Pharisees over the washing of hands Jesus addressed the crowds with this parable: 'Hear me all of you and understand, nothing outside a person can defile him by going into him. But the things which come out of a person are the things that defile him' (Mark 7:15). Self-evident as it may seem to us, this was another of those parables which does not appear to have been immediately understood in its time. Jesus had to explain privately to his disciples that food passes through the body without reaching the heart (mind); it is the evil thoughts, acts of fornication, theft, murder, adultery, greed, spite, deceitfulness, licentiousness, envy, blasphemy, arrogance and foolishness which really defile.

The Pharisees would certainly not have disputed that these things corrupt and defile. However, because their system laid such emphasis on purity rituals as the way to holiness, it had an in-built danger of overlooking them. There is a tendency in most religious movements to be preoccupied with whatever differentiates you from others. I have argued that the Pharisees saw their rules of purity as what all Israelites should do; why else would they have criticized Jesus' disciples for not washing in the prescribed manner? But the fact is, *they* did them, and many others did not. To have defined their movement in terms of a ritual purity which separated them from the rank and file ('Pharisees' probably meant 'the separate ones'[68]) was to run an extreme risk that real holiness would be seen by many in terms of group membership and performance of the required rituals. The tragedy which Jesus brought to light was that in their zeal for the symbolic and ritual aspects of the law they had blinded themselves to the presence of real moral evils, even allowing the law to cloak their presence. 'You are like whitewashed tombs,' he taunted them, 'which appear beautiful on the outside, but inside they are full of dead people's bones' (Matthew 23:27). Contact with the remains of a corpse brought about first degree defilement. Jesus implies that others were unwittingly defiled by contact with these people. It is hard to imagine a crueler rebuke of those for whom purity rated so high. It is tempting to wish to remove from Jesus anything so harsh. Yet it would not serve the cause of history to do so. Better to face up to the fact that this was the way things were between them, and seek an understanding of their differences. These criticisms were not made behind their backs.

Once, in the home of a Pharisee, Jesus responded to criticism of his failure to perform the correct washing ritual with the observation: 'Now you Pharisees cleanse the outside of the cup and the dish, but your inside is full of grasping and wickedness. Fools, didn't he who made the outside also make the inside? Rather give alms of that which is within, and behold, everything will be clean for you' (Luke 11:39–41). The dish has become a picture of the person. One can be scrupulous about the surface of the dish and overlook its disgusting contents. Jesus counsels them to bring acts of kindness and mercy from their inmost being in order that they may be truly holy.

The Commandments and the Kingdom

It is time we asked what Jesus' peculiar approach to the law has to do with the kingdom of God. We know he saw a new age dawning, which succeeded the age of the law and the prophets. People regarded as disqualified by the law from membership of the future community were deemed acceptable to the kingdom and welcomed. The law seems to have been eclipsed and superseded. And yet, we have also heard him defending the law of Moses as God's law, and demanding that people obey it. The beginning of an answer is to be found in a saying of Jesus preserved in Matthew's Sermon on the Mount.

> Do not think that I have come to destroy the law or the prophets. I have come not to destroy, but to fulfil. For truly I say to you, until heaven and earth pass away not one tiniest detail of the law shall pass away. Whoever therefore breaks one of the least of these commandments and teaches others to do so will be called least in the kingdom of heaven; but whoever shall do them and teach them shall be called great in the kingdom of heaven. For I tell you that unless your righteousness exceeds that of the scribes and Pharisees you will certainly not enter the kingdom of heaven. (Matthew 5:17–20)

Could the same Jesus who welcomed tax-collectors and sinners have said such a thing? Some think not, and put it down to Matthew's sensitivity to the rabbinic opposition allegedly faced by his community.[69] But we have already seen that Luke records similar ideas. We have also noted that Jesus had no disregard for the law of the Scriptures. His complaint was that it was being evaded. The key to appreciating what Jesus is saying is the idea of fulfilment. The kingdom brings the fulfilment of all God's promises; it also means the perfection of Israel as God's servant people. This must mean, along with everything else, their perfection in obedience. E.P. Sanders has summed up Palestinian Judaism's understanding of the law as 'covenantal nomism'.[70] 'Covenantal nomism' means first that God has graciously brought Israel into covenant relationship with himself; secondly that they remain within his covenant by obedience to his law; and thirdly that if they broke the law they could be restored by repentance and the system of atonement. Controversial as this has become, it seems to me essentially correct. It is certainly a correct description of Old Testament religion, and there is no reason for doubting that it was the official theology of people like the Pharisees. However, when Sanders goes on from this to infer that there could have been little quarrel between the Pharisees and

Jesus, he overlooks what should be plain to us now, that Jesus (and John before him) understood his countrymen to be so far removed from God and his covenant that only a complete conversion and a miracle of mercy were of any avail. The 'covenantal nomist' system (to use Sanders' terminology) had been rendered totally inoperative by the people's rebellion. 'Their hearts are far from me (God),' Jesus said of the paragons of law keeping. 'Do not begin to say to yourselves, "We have Abraham as our father",' said John. For most people the covenant was cancelled. But, Jesus' kingdom announcement of the acceptable year of the Lord was an invitation to all to enter again into the sphere of God's mercy. That is why it transcended the law, and why Jesus could say 'Everyone forces their way into it' (Luke 16:16). If the kingdom is to bring about the real fulfilment of Israel's vocation to be God's people, however, it must also include a dynamic to bring about that true goodness which the law (covenantal nomism) could not achieve. Jesus said he had come to fulfil the law, and part at least of that is bringing together a people whose real righteousness would exceed that of the scribes and Pharisees. He can hardly mean just a more scrupulous observance of more laws. What he wants is an honest, loving and heartfelt obedience to the ordinary requirements of the law, and to their spirit. He summed this up in terms of love for God and neighbour. When Jesus said he came to call sinners to repentance, it was to this that he was calling them.

Such obedience is described in the so-called antitheses, which follow in the Sermon on the Mount (Matthew 5:21–48). A person should not just refrain from murder, but from the inner attitudes which add up to murder by intention. More than that, all should be peacemakers, ever seeking reconciliation with offended sisters or brothers. A person should not just refrain from adultery, but from all attitudes and mental acts which amount to the same thing. Oaths and vows are unnecessary; good people will speak the truth and be true to their word. All else is an accommodation to evil (like the bill of divorce).[71] Forgiveness, mercy, generosity – even towards enemies – these will be marks of the children of the heavenly Father. Their almsgiving, their prayers and their fasting will be matters between them and God, not matters for commending them in the eyes of other people.

Conclusion

The Pharisees' opposition to Jesus originated in their suspicions about his faithfulness to the law. One who drew the crowds as he did threatened to do irreparable damage to the national life if he promulgated different interpretations of or laxity towards the law. For although Jesus publicly counselled the people to obey their laws (Matthew 23:1–3), it cannot be doubted that he undermined their authority. Their examinations of his teaching and way of life revealed a couple of cases of questionable behaviour on the disciples' part, but on Jesus' part only the question of Sabbath keeping. That it was only with miracles of healing that he broke the Sabbath made it difficult to tie down a serious charge of law breaking even there. They also uncovered a deep-seated antagonism to the fundamental basis of their system of interpretation, which must have appeared threatening to say the least.

At every point of their attempt to investigate him, however, Jesus revealed more and more of a fundamental illness which their own system engendered. It tended to externality and show and led to blindness to their own spiritual condition – to hypocrisy: 'the yeast of the Pharisees'. Gentle as he could be with others, Jesus was harsh to the point of cruelty in exposing this hypocrisy. For the Pharisees there could only be two possible outcomes of such criticism: either they would have to own it and repent, or they would destroy him to silence it. The Pharisees were not unaccustomed to petitioning the ruling power to remove a troublemaker. That, in the end, is the course they took.

Postscript

I said at the beginning that Jesus had many enemies. It was the Pharisees who became his chief enemies, first because of their self-appointed role as guardians of the nation's purity and orthodoxy, but also for the simple reason that there were many of them spread throughout the land. Wherever Jesus went he encountered Pharisees. Whenever he ministered in their domain there was conflict, and to pretend they would not have used the government to deal with him permanently is unhistorical and anachronistic. They were accustomed to using all possible means to protect what they saw as the interests of God and the nation.

Yet to 'blame' the death of Jesus on the Pharisees would be equally unhistorical. It is significant that once Jesus passed into the jurisdiction of the priestly establishment, dominated as it was by the Sadducean party, he met opposition quite as fierce if not fiercer than that of the Pharisees. When at the end he threatened to touch the vested interests of the Roman procurator he fared no better there. But this is to jump ahead. It is not easy to write dispassionately about the Pharisees, for there are still many who own something like the Pharisaic system as their faith and would certainly want to defend it against the charges which Jesus brought. But those who would use Jesus' teaching as a stick to beat Jews, or anyone else, need first to apply the teaching to their own hearts. The hypocrisy Jesus exposed is endemic to every religion, Christianity included. Religious people and secular people alike seek ultimate security in their beliefs and observances, particularly those which make them different from others. But where greed, lust, hatred and indifference to the needy lurk in the heart there can be no security. The evils upon which Jesus put his finger are to be found in every human being. It is close to the truth that only Jesus could ever with integrity have brought such a charge against any *particular* group of people. Anyone else would have been found to have a larger log in their own eye.

The Pharisees created a system to enable them to live in a way that was pleasing to God. Yet for all its rigours, according to Jesus, it did not succeed. Like every other system which has set out to achieve similar ends it was unable to deal with the deep problems of the heart – pride, lust, greed and the like – nor produce true goodness – love, mercy and self-denying justice. To achieve these ends an altogether more powerful medicine would be required. Only the person who knew that they were sick would take that medicine. The Pharisees had already performed the task of exposing the unrighteousness of the tax collectors and sinners; it fell to Jesus to administer the healing of the gospel. It seems they were well prepared ground. For the Pharisees themselves, however, a sharp scalpel was first necessary to reveal the cancer that lay hidden beneath the surface. The presence of Pharisees in the early church is testimony to the effectiveness of the treatment. It was a Pharisee who was later to declare, 'Faithful is the saying, and worthy of full acceptance, that Jesus Christ came into the world to save sinners, of whom I am the chief' (1 Timothy 1:15).

Notes

[1] It is paradoxical that John, a Judaean, was dealt with by Herod, whereas Jesus, a Galilean, finished up in Roman hands in Judaea. It is not clear whether an extradition was involved in John's case, or whether he was arrested in Peraea.

[2] Apart from what their name suggests, nothing is known about the Herodians, though in the complex political situation of Palestine it is obvious that a support base would have existed for the rule of the Herods and of Antipas.

[3] John frequently uses 'the Jews' to describe Jesus' opponents. This is due in part to his writing for non-Jews who tended to look on the Jews as an homogeneous mass. However, it also indicates a more diverse opposition than just Pharisees or other party members. See John 2:18; 5:10ff.; 6:41, 52; 7:11f.; 8:51ff. For an imaginative insight into how Jesus might have alienated ordinary people, see Theissen, *Shadow*, ch. 8.

[4] Matthew 11:2–6; Luke 7:18–23; 11:20; John 10:25, 38. The final two references refer to more than Jesus' miracles, but they include them.

⁵ *Bab. Talmud Sanhedrin* 43a.

⁶ Josephus, *History*, 6.300–309. Attention is drawn to the peculiar similarities between the case of Jesus ben Ananias and that of Jesus by Sanders, *Jesus and Judaism*, 302–303. The point of their followings as the reason for their different fates is made by M. Hengel & R. Deines, 'E.P. Sanders, "Common Judaism", Jesus and the Pharisees', 13–14.

⁷ Josephus, *History*, 18.11–25; *War*, 2.119–166.

⁸ Schürer, *History*, I, 157.

⁹ Josephus, *History*, 13.288ff.

¹⁰ For an account of the reign of John Hyrcanus I, see Schürer, *History*, I, 200–215.

¹¹ For an account of the reign of Alexander Jannaeus, see Schürer, *History*, I, 219–228.

¹² For an account of the reign of Alexandra, see Schürer, *History*, I, 229–232.

¹³ Josephus, *History*, 17.41–45.

¹⁴ Josephus, *History*, 18.3ff.; 18.23–25; *War*, 2.117–118.

¹⁵ Schürer, *History*, I, 534–552.

¹⁶ Rivkin, *What Crucified Jesus?* 20–32, says the Pharisees had developed a doctrine of 'two realms' and had a pact with the secular administration to remain out of politics. I fail to see the evidence for this. It is one thing to be forced into compliance and compromise; quite another to develop a theology which makes it a virtue.

¹⁷ J. Neusner, *From Politics to Piety; Judaism in the Beginning of Christianity*, esp. ch. 3. Sanders, *Jesus and Judaism; Judaism*, 380–451.

¹⁸ Neusner, *Politics*; Sanders, *Jesus and Judaism*; H. Maccoby, *Rabbinic Writings*, 11–16.

¹⁹ Sanders, *Jesus and Judaism*; Maccoby, *Judaism*, 260–267, 274–281.

²⁰ See L. Morris, *Studies in the Fourth Gospel*, 81–86.

²¹ See J.A. Ziesler, 'Luke and the Pharisees'.

²² Acts 15:5. Also notice the way Paul boasts his membership of the Pharisees in Acts 23:6; 26:5.

²³ It was the sect of the Sadducees who, according to Luke, were primarily responsible for the persecution of Christians in Jerusalem (Acts 4:1; 5:17). On more than one occasion Christians are defended by Pharisees (Acts 5:34ff.; 23:9).

²⁴ Luke 7:36ff.; 11:37ff.; 14:1ff.

²⁵ J.T. Sanders (*The Jews in Luke–Acts*) accuses Luke of being anti-Semitic, on the basis of some of Jesus' harsh sayings. He greatly underplays many evidences

in the Gospel and Acts of a great sympathy towards Jews, Jewish history and traditions, and the salvation of Jews. Against Sanders see J. Jervell, *Luke and the People of God*; D. Seccombe, 'Luke's Vision for the Church'; 'New People of God', 366–370.

[26] John 3:1–15; 7:47–52; 19:39.

[27] It is a mistake to project our own highly organized national systems of law, law enforcement and jurisprudence into the first century. Israel's law was the Torah of Moses. It needed interpretation and application, and the Pharisees and their scribes were those most commonly looked to for this. Law enforcement for the most part would have been the business of local leaders. This saying probably reflects a setting outside Jerusalem; the Pharisees would not have had such undisputed status there. M.A. Powell ('Do and Keep what Moses Says', 419–435) surveys different interpretations of this difficult saying. His own view is far-fetched. He thinks the Pharisees were the official *readers* of Scripture (most others allegedly being illiterate), and that Jesus was telling his followers to listen to their scripture reading, but not their interpretations.

[28] Rabbi Simeon ben Yohai, *Bab. Talmud Shabbath* 118b. See J. Bright, *The Kingdom of God*, 175.

[29] Josephus, *Life*, 191.

[30] *Mishnah Sukkah* 4:9.

[31] Sanders, *Judaism*, 380–451; Neusner, *Politics to Piety*; *Beginning of Christianity*, 45–61.

[32] The weakness of Sanders' position lies in his almost total disregard of the evidence of the gospels. On my dating they provide testimony, albeit of a tendentious nature, from the time when the Pharisees were active. On Sanders' dating they are still the earliest evidence we have. Sanders thinks that most of the controversies between Jesus and the Pharisees in the gospels were actually later ones, written back into the Jesus story. But to attribute such a dubious procedure to all the gospel writers and Q is unwise, though Sanders is not the first to do it. Besides, as Hengel & Deines ('E.P. Sanders' 7) point out, the disputes in the gospels (tithes, gifts to temple, handwashing, purity) are not those that were uppermost in the early church. Circumcision, table fellowship with Gentiles, idol meat, etc. were of more concern.

[33] Maccoby, *Rabbinic Writings*, 11–16.

[34] Hengel & Deines, 'E.P. Sanders', 32–33.

[35] Neusner, *Beginning of Christianity*, 57.

[36] J. Neusner ('Mr Sanders and Mine', 84) clarifies his position: the Pharisees ate food in purity, not as priests, but as one rung down from them. D.R. de Lacey ('In Search of a Pharisee', 353–371) defends this. There was a hierarchy of holiness from priest to Pharisee to the *'am ha-aretz*.

[37] Maccoby (*Rabbinic Writings*, 94–100) thinks they did not enjoin non-biblical purity practices on the general population.

[38] Hengel & Deines, 'E.P. Sanders', 47: 'Since the *basic obligation to be holy* applied to the *entire people*, the Pharisees wanted to deduce what was involved from Scripture and tradition, and then live this out as an example to the rest' (emphasis original). Although Neusner (*Beginning of Christianity*, 56–60) thinks the special purity laws were not generally observed, and that Jesus' disciples were reproached for not being Pharisees (!), he appears to contradict this when he says, 'Since the Pharisees claimed that the laws they kept were not "sectarian", but derived from the Torah of Moses at Sinai, they would have said they kept the rules and regulations of the Creator of the World, and their laws constituted perpetual observance of his will' (*Politics to Piety*, 90).

[39] See the reaction of the onlookers at Jericho to Jesus going to the house of a 'sinner' (Luke 19:1–10).

[40] *Mishnah Shabbath* 3.

[41] *Mishnah Shabbath* 6:8.

[42] *Tosefta Shabbath* 15:11–17; *Mekilta Exodus* 31:12–17.

[43] *Mishnah Shabbath* 16:1–6.

[44] *Mishnah Shabbath* 16:7.

[45] Hill (*Matthew*, 207f.) points out the connection between Matthew 11:28–30 and Jeremiah 6:16. It is noteworthy that 'rest' is to be found in a return to 'the old paths', i.e. the law of Moses.

[46] It is significant that in Matthew's arrangement of the gospel material the incident in the grain fields and an account of Jesus' healing on the Sabbath are placed directly after the invitation to 'learn from me' (Matthew 11:28–12:14).

[47] I take this point from Moore, *Judaism*, I, 263–270; M. Hengel, *Judaism and Hellenism*, 169ff. See Ecclesiasticus 24; Baruch 3:24–4:4; *Genesis Rabbah* 1:1.

[48] *Mishnah Aboth* 1:1: 'They said three things: Be deliberate in judgement, raise up many disciples, and make a fence around the Law'. Further on the fence see Moore, *Judaism*, I, 259–262.

[49] *Mishnah Aboth* 1:2: 'Simeon the Just … used to say: By three things is the world sustained: by the Law, by the [Temple] service and by deeds of loving-kindness'.

[50] E.g., *Damascus Document* 4, 5, 6. On the calendar in use at Qumran and their attitude to it, see Vermes, *Scrolls in English*, 42f.

[51] Rabbi Simeon ben Menasiah (2nd century AD) interpreted Exodus 31:14 to mean 'The Sabbath is given to you, but you are not surrendered to the Sabbath' (*Mekita Exodus* 31:12–17). This interpretation may reflect the influence of Jesus, but in any case it is spoken in reference to a clear danger to life.

[52] *Mekilta de Rabbi Ishmael* on Exodus 31:12–17.

[53] *Mishnah Shabbath* 22:6.

[54] *Mishnah Yadaim* 1:1; 2:3.

[55] *Mishnah Aboth* 1:1: 'Moses received the Law from Sinai and committed it to Joshua, and Joshua to the elders, and the elders to the Prophets; and the Prophets committed it to the men of the Great Synagogue. The law referred to here included the oral law or 'traditions of the elders'.

[56] *Mishnah Sanhedrin* 11:3: 'Greater stringency applies to the words of the scribes than to the words of the [written] Law'. This was probably so because the words of Scripture were held to be self-evident, whereas rejection of the rulings of the scribes was more subversive of the system. This rule probably dates from later than Jesus but it shows the tendency of the system.

[57] *Mishnah Nedarim* 9:5.

[58] *Mishnah Nedarim* 9:1.

[59] It is not unlikely, in my opinion, that later scribal debates could have had their origin in some of the trenchant criticism levelled by Jesus.

[60] Mark 10:17ff.; Matthew 19:16ff.; Luke 18:18ff.

[61] See *Babylonian Talmud Berakoth* 28b; Seccombe, *Possessions*, 122f.

[62] *Mishnah Gittin* 9:10.

[63] This understanding of the passage is argued at length by B.W. Powers, *Marriage and Divorce: The New Testament Teaching*, 155–178.

[64] *Mishnah Gittin* 2:5.

[65] *Mishnah Gittin* 4:7.

[66] On a wife's powers to sue for divorce see *Mishnah Ketuboth* 7:10; Maccoby, *Rabbinic Writings*, 101–102.

[67] As far as I can see there was no barrier to a divorced couple having second thoughts and mutually agreeing to invalidate the bill of divorce and/or remarrying. This means that in real terms the marriage was not finally severed by divorce. Only when one or the other party remarried did reconciliation become impossible (Deuteronomy 24:1–4, Jeremiah 3:1). This means that it was those who remarried who severed the first marriage irrevocably. This could be the spouse who initiated the divorce in order to

marry another, or the third party who took advantage of, or even provoked the divorce.

[68] See Schürer, *History*, II, 396–398.

[69] Sanders, *Jesus and Judaism*, 260–264. For a defence of the originality of part of the saying see Meyer, *Aims*, 167, 297, n. 124.

[70] For a succinct summary of the concept see E.P. Sanders, *Paul and Palestinian Judaism*, 422.

[71] Personally, I would not understand Jesus to have completely ruled out oaths and bills of divorce. There are situations of brokenness ('hardness of heart') where they may still be necessary. Jesus' point is that provisions for dealing with the results of evil should not become moral justification for initiating those evils.

Chapter 13

Who Is This Man?

Expanding the Mission

About a year after Jesus began to work in Galilee the ministry entered a critical phase which brought to a head the question of his identity and the role he would play in the kingdom. Events at this time led to speculation, confusion and, finally, for his disciples, clarity about who he was. But to speak of a sequence of events requires some justification. In the preceding three chapters we have looked at the miracles and exorcisms, the parables of the kingdom, and at Jesus' differences with the Pharisees. It was unnecessary in these chapters to inquire into the actual order of events. What I said about the story of the leper applies to most of the material we looked at: some sayings and stories are not given anything more than a very general location in time, others are located differently in different gospels because their importance was topical rather than chronological. Even the story of Jesus' visit to Nazareth, which as moderns we would expect to find in a consistent time frame, occurs at three different places in the first three gospels. It is because the gospels treat the material in this way that it was necessary to follow a thematic approach in these chapters. In Mark 6–8, however, we find a series of events, clustered around the feeding of the five thousand, which shows every appearance of being chronologically connected. The twelve are sent out.

Herod hears of it and begins to ask about Jesus. The twelve return, and Jesus takes them across the lake to where the feeding of the five thousand takes place. Recrossing the lake, Jesus walks to the disciples on the water. After a further period of teaching Jesus moves into Gentile territory. On his return he miraculously feeds another crowd. Sometime later he questions his followers about public opinion relating to his identity. Peter says he is the Messiah and Jesus tells them that to fulfil his mission, he must die. A few days later, on a mountaintop Jesus is gloriously transformed in the sight of three of his disciples.

Matthew and Luke do not reproduce every part of the sequence, but each of them preserves the impression that at this stage of Jesus' ministry momentous things were happening which had enormous consequences for Jesus and the disciples, and also for Galilee.

Jesus' Road Team

Quite early in his Galilean ministry Jesus selected twelve of his disciples 'to be with him, and that he might send them out to preach' (Mark 3:14). Their first task was simply to be there: to help manage the crowds, and to learn as much as possible in the process. The object was that in time they would be able to represent him. When he went around the various towns and cities proclaiming the coming of the kingdom of God Jesus took the twelve with him as well as a largish group of women who supported and fed them (Luke 8:1–3). It must have been quite a spectacle: this rabbi with his twelve disciples and retinue of women supporters – even more surprising when it was discovered that one of the women was the wife of someone highly placed in the government.[1] Jesus' touring party was something of a sign in itself. The twelve were chosen to signify the twelve tribes of Israel (Luke 22:30; Matthew 19:28). A community composed of such disparate men and women, assisting one another in the work and sharing fellowship at meal times, must have been a powerful sign of the new community which Jesus' preaching was bringing into being. Ordinary (though not impious) workmen like Peter, Andrew, James and John, the wealthy, once ostracized tax collector, Matthew, Simon the 'zealot', and Nathaniel the scholar(?),[2] constitute an odd combination to be sharing a common mission and a common table. When we add women, in particular the socialite, Joanna, and the healed demoniac, Mary Magdalene, we have a picture which by any standards verges on the bizarre. And yet what a persuasive demonstration of the tendency of Jesus' ministry and message. Most surprising, although people were scandalized by his fellowship with tax collectors and sinners, there is no trace that any suggestion of sexual impropriety was ever levelled. There must have been something about Jesus, which made any such suggestion appear patently false.

Jesus wanted to take the kingdom message to every Jewish community (Mark 1:38), something he could not do unassisted. Initially that meant getting the word out to the communities in Galilee that he had been unable to visit himself. When did he judge it time to send out the twelve? The gospels do not say, but less than a year after his mission began they had gone and returned.

The Mission of the Twelve
(Mark 6:7–13; Luke 9:1–6; Matthew 10:5–15)

This was no ordinary mission. The disciples were to go out with none of the things one would expect someone away from home to carry. They took nothing but the clothes they wore – even a welcome extra tunic (it was late winter) was forbidden. It seems odd that Jesus would give them a specific command to wear sandals and take a staff; presumably they would have taken these anyway unless it was explicitly forbidden. The reason for Mark's emphasizing this probably derives from the fact that when Jesus later sent out the seventy two, they were to go barefoot – but we shall come to that in due course.[3]

A Mission Strategy

Why were they to go in such a precarious manner? Were they to travel light because of the urgency of their mission? This was certainly the case in the later mission of the seventy two, but there is less indication of it here. The effect of journeying without food or money would have been to make them totally dependent on God's providing, presumably chiefly by means of hospitality. From a purely practical point of view this would have bound them closely to those to whom they preached. Jesus may have anticipated blessing from this for their hosts, and this is probably why he included instructions on how they were to treat invitations to hospitality. One can readily imagine that once they began to perform miracles everyone in the village would want to have them as guests. Jesus also intended that they should be cared for on their journey in a way that would seem miraculous (Luke 22:35). Thus we should see these strange instructions partly as a practical strategy for the success of their mission, and partly as a sign of God's presence in their mission. They were not only to preach the kingdom of God, but also to be proof of its presence. That was also the significance of their healing and exorcisms.

Messianic Ambassadors

Jesus particularly designated the twelve disciples as his 'apostles' (Luke 6:13). We have seen that this probably renders the Hebrew *saliach*, an 'agent' in the legal sense.[4] The distinctiveness of the *saliach* was their authorization by the person who sent them to act on his behalf. They were plenipotentiaries with the full authority of their master. According to the rabbis, 'the one sent by a man is as the man himself'.[5] Thus Jesus said to his disciples 'Someone who receives you receives me, and anyone who receives me, receives the one who sent me' (Matthew 10:40). Jesus saw himself as God's apostle!

I mentioned in chapter 10 that one of the unusual characteristics of Jesus' miracle working was his ability to delegate it to others. For the time of their mission, and in view of their acting as his ambassadors Jesus gave his disciples authority over evil spirits, a sign of the in-breaking messianic age. Twice in the pre-Christian *Testaments of the Twelve Patriarchs* it is said that the coming saviour would bind Satan (cf. Mark 3:27) 'and give power to his children to tread upon evil spirits'.[6] The disciples also healed the sick, and here Jesus gave them a sacramental sign which he does not appear to have used himself: they anointed the sick with oil, probably to indicate that the power was coming not from themselves but from the Holy Spirit, whose presence was also to characterize the new age (Isaiah 32:15).

It would be interesting to know exactly what the twelve said. Mark tells us no more than that they preached that people should repent. Luke and Matthew add that they announced the kingdom. Presumably Jesus sent them to proclaim the same gospel he himself preached. Did they also preach about him? It is hard to imagine that they did not talk a great deal about him, they were his apostles after all, and only repeating his message. But although they spoke and healed in his name, it does not appear that they had any official message about *him*. Jesus' connection with the kingdom was still a question mark.

The disciples were given one further sign to perform. If they were not received in a place they were to shake the dirt from their feet as they left, a witness to that town that its status was now that of Gentile territory.[7] Its rejection of the message of the kingdom would signify its citizens' rejection from Israel and the forfeiture of their place in the kingdom of God. This procedure seems such a radical and summary judgement that it raises the question of what significance Jesus saw in this mission.

Did Jesus Miscalculate?

The lynchpin of Albert Schweitzer's interpretation of Jesus' missionary aim was the significance he believed Jesus gave to the mission of the twelve. In the course of Matthew's mission discourse Jesus tells his disciples: 'When they persecute you in one city flee to another; for truly I say to you, you will not have completed your round of all the cities of Israel before the son of man comes' (Matthew 10:23). According to Schweitzer this all important clue shows that Jesus expected the arrival of the kingdom in the immediate future. Before the twelve returned from their mission he would be revealed by God as the majestic Son of Man coming on the clouds of heaven. But Jesus was mistaken. When the twelve arrived back without anything so dramatic having taken place, he was forced to rethink his position and eventually came to the conclusion that he must die to set in motion the final denouement.[8]

Schweitzer's particular reconstruction has not commended itself to many scholars. It is built too completely on the single leg of this intriguing but unparalleled saying. I have already mentioned that Matthew 10 is a compilation of Jesus' mission teaching on various occasions. It could even include teaching from between his resurrection and ascension. This particular saying envisages a mission throughout Israel in which the preachers are to expect severe persecution. There is no indication that the mission of the twelve was intended to take them much further afield than Galilee, and the most that is anticipated in the way of persecution is that they may be rejected and have to 'dust their feet' on their departure. The saying does not belong to the mission of the twelve.[9]

An Evangelistic Crusade?

To dismiss Schweitzer's radical notion of a coming of the Son of Man in the course of the disciples' mission is not to deny that something very big was happening. Vincent Taylor saw it as the turning point in the Galilean ministry. It generated great excitement, but failed to meet with repentance. As such it was all of a piece with Jesus' preaching activity. At that point, faced with the failure of his own and his disciples' ministry to produce a real turning to God amongst the people, Jesus began to withdraw from the enthusiastic mobs, reassessed his direction, and finally came to the conclusion that his future course was to fulfil the mission of the Suffering Servant.[10]

On the surface of it there is a glaring problem with the mission of the twelve. Anyone who has had anything to do with preaching knows that you do not persuade a town of the truth of your message in a day or two. To declare an unresponsive village damned because of its failure to respond to a short visit from two scantily clad missionaries seems impossibly naive. Or so it appeared to me once when I was wrestling with the disappointing lack of an account of what the disciples were to teach. I had been personally involved in various missions, including attempts to evangelize country towns, and the account of the mission of the twelve seemed singularly unhelpful in the brevity of its description. I was overlooking something which made this particular mission quite unlike any other before or since. The twelve were not engaged in the kind of teaching and persuading which has been common Christian practice ever since, but were making *a public announcement* – that the kingdom of God was at hand – and warning people to do something about it. The gospels do not tell us any more because there was no more. Realizing this, after many years of misunderstanding, made me so excited that I must have made a lot of noise, for the door of the upstairs room where I was working in the Theological Faculty in Tübingen flew open and some anxious people burst in to see if I was all right. Mine was not a small misunderstanding. The kingdom of God meant something very particular and decisive for the people of Jesus' time. It meant the coming to an end of the present evil age and the arrival of the government of God in the world. On this point Schweitzer was certainly correct. All the other teaching and wonder working was ancillary to this simple promise (or warning) of an impending crisis. In modern terms, Jesus' gospel is better likened to a newsflash of an approaching invasion fleet (with the drone of aircraft overhead to further confirm it) than to an evangelistic crusade.

What could one do in the face of such a proclamation? Either believe it and turn to God in readiness for the end, or disbelieve it and continue your present course of life. Most of the Galileans apparently did the latter; for all their excitement about the outward aspects of Jesus' and the disciples' mission, they did not repent. Jesus' instruction to the disciples to dust their feet indicates that he viewed this as their last chance.

What if Israel will not Repent?

If I have correctly understood the character of the mission of the twelve, the question arises as to what the effect of a wide-scale failure to repent would have been on the promise of the kingdom bound up in Jesus' gospel? When he was rejected in Nazareth Jesus simply moved on. He had declared to all of them, irrespective of moral standing, the time of God's acceptance and the arrival of the age of jubilee, but they found him and his message unacceptable. So he went on to the next town and took his blessings with him. It is this procedure that Jesus instructs his disciples to imitate if they have to. Such a town forfeits its place in the Israel of promise and will fare like Sodom and Gomorrah on the day of judgement (Luke 10:12). But what if all the towns reject him? I am not suggesting that the disciples were run out of every town they visited, any more than Jesus was; the evidence suggests that their mission had spectacular results. But what if they failed to elicit the required response of a deep turning to God? What if Jesus also failed to find it? What would become of the promised kingdom if its intended sons and daughters thrust it from them? Perhaps Jesus was not mistaken in declaring the kingdom at hand. But it was not, as Schweitzer suggested, that he expected the end of the age to break in regardless. Perhaps it did break in – in himself and his mission – and in its fully consummated form came within the grasp of those favoured Galileans. But they refused it and sent it away.

I have run ahead of the evidence at this point, but it is well that the main thesis I wish to propound concerning the aim and outcome of Jesus' mission be clear. As we continue to unpack the gospel story we will be able to fill this thesis out and see whether it holds water. For the moment let what I am suggesting be clear. Jesus, having proclaimed the arrival of the kingdom in a small area of Galilee, sent his disciples out to complete the task (or at least to significantly further it). They were to be the final heralds performing the final signs of the promised kingdom. Indeed, they were signs themselves. People's response was deemed by Jesus to be their final answer to the invitation to enter the kingdom of God.

Herod Hears
(Mark 6:14–29; Matthew 14:1–12; Luke 9:7–9)

The disciples' mission did not go unnoticed. For Herod Antipas makes his appearance in the story at this time. One of the peculiarities of the Gospel of Mark is the way it sandwiches between the going out of the twelve and the feeding of the five thousand which took place at their return, a note about Herod hearing of Jesus' fame, and the story of John the Baptist's death. The latter is lengthy, considering its seemingly small relevance to Mark's overall purpose, and it creates the confusing impression, heightened in Matthew, that Jesus' withdrawal across the lake was a reaction to hearing the news of John's death. Many accounts of the life of Jesus accordingly make the death of John a turning point in Jesus' career.[11] This can hardly have been the case, since in both Mark and Matthew John's death is a flashback explaining Herod's reaction to news about Jesus' miracle working. What was it that Herod heard? The context in Mark implies that it was the mission of the twelve, as a result of which Jesus became even more widely known. The disciples' miracles were apparently attributed by the public to Jesus, hardly surprising, since they healed and spoke in his name.

At first glance it is surprising that the Tetrarch had not been aware of Jesus before this. Capernaum was only twenty kilometres from his capital (Tiberias). However, we need to keep in mind that Herod was the ruler of two geographically separated territories (Galilee and Peraea). There is some evidence that at that time he was dealing with an unstable situation on his southern frontier in Peraea, which may have kept him preoccupied and away from Galilee. Herod had secretly determined to divorce the daughter of Aretas, king of Petra and marry Herodias. His rejected wife learned of the plot against her, went for a holiday to the Machaerus fortress in the south, and made her escape to her father's kingdom. This became the cause of trouble between Herod and Aretas, which was later to lead to war. It was in this tangle that John the Baptist became embroiled, and to this that we owe Josephus' description of him.[12] At the time John was beheaded Herod was at the Machaerus, and the fact that his Galilean dignitaries had to come there to celebrate his birthday may indicate that his residence was of some duration.

The execution of John is generally taken to have happened somewhat late in the period of Jesus' Galilean ministry, but this could not have been so. For Herod to think that Jesus was John come back from the dead, it must have been some time after John's execution that he first took note of Jesus. It is a startling opinion, even if Herod latched onto it half in jest,[13] testifying both to Jesus' sudden rise to fame, and to his reputation as a miracle worker. One can sympathize with his perplexity: he has no sooner beheaded John, than he receives word of someone else preaching a similar message, but this time doing miracles! The opinion did not originate with Herod, it was suggested to him by others, and it is quite unintelligible unless there were many people whose first hearing of Jesus' miracle working took place only *after* the death of John had become public. If John was beheaded shortly before the mission of the twelve (a confusion that really goes back to a misreading of Matthew[14]), there would have been too many people who knew that Jesus had been active well before John had departed the scene. It seems more probable that the incident in which John sent messengers to Jesus occurred early in the Galilean ministry and that his execution was not very much later.[15] Jesus' ministry, then, was not visibly effected by it. Certainly it caused no dramatic change of direction, though it would have added strength to his conviction, met in the Sermon on the Mount, that the path of a disciple leads through persecution.

It is a significant moment when a movement of the kind that Jesus initiated comes to the notice of the ruling power. Most ancient historians concerned themselves more with the activities of kings and governors than with religious movements and the goings on of ordinary people. It is often only when these intersect the concerns of rulers that they come to our attention. Josephus, for example, tells us about John the Baptist only because many people thought Herod's treatment of him was the reason why Herod's army was later destroyed. If there had been anyone to write the court history of Herod Antipas we would probably have learned a great deal more about Jesus at this point in the story. It is one of the 'tragedies' of history that Josephus, who was so wonderfully informed about the reign of Herod the Great, and had his own memories of the Jewish War, had such a paucity of material for the period that most interests us.[16] I suspect that the undue space that Mark gives to the story of John's execution is because at this point (and at Jesus' crucifixion) he was conscious of telling history in the style he would have known it from other history writers.

The Time Frame

It is some confirmation of the historical seriousness of the gospels that all the indications and clues to dating the period of Jesus' ministry converge on the same period. Within the extremes provided by the procuratorship of Pontius Pilate (AD 26–37), the High Priesthood of Caiaphas (AD 18–36), and the conversion of Paul (AD 33 at the latest) fit the fifteenth year of Tiberius (AD 26–29)[17] (Luke 3:1), Jesus' approximate age of thirty (Luke 3:23),[18] the 'forty six year saying' at the first temple incident (AD 27), and the Friday death of Jesus at Passover (AD 30 or 33). Thus the general period of Jesus' activity between AD 26 and AD 33 can hardly be disputed. Precise dates are different. I have already given reasons for thinking that the appearance of John the Baptist took place about AD 27–28 and that the first Passover at which Jesus appeared in Jerusalem was in April AD 28. Some scholars place the beginning of John's and Jesus' ministry some two years later. As for the end of his ministry, it has been established by astronomical and calendrical means that in the relevant period Passover fell on a Thursday or Friday only in AD 30 and AD 33.[19] If Jesus made his appearance in AD 28 and was crucified at the Passover of AD 30, everything recorded in the gospels containing any hint of a time reference, with one possible exception, can be fitted in.[20] However, there are a number of uncertainties which make dogmatism about exact dates unwise. Hoehner argues cogently that the ministry took place between AD 29 and 33.[21] The overall picture of Jesus' ministry is little changed, whichever set of dates one opts for.

There is little in the first three gospels to give us any indication of how events were chronologically distributed throughout Jesus' ministry. We can fix the beginning and the end, but little in between. The arrangement of John, however, is different; most of its action occurs in connection with Jewish feasts. These enable us to give the period of Jesus' ministry a rough skeletal framework. Significant for our purposes in this chapter, John supplies the information that the feeding of the five thousand took place when 'the Passover of the Jews was at hand'. This places it, according to our reckoning, in the spring of AD 29 (Passover was 18 April), midway through Jesus' ministry.[22] The twelve had completed their mission a short time before.

The Feeding of the Five Thousand
(Mark 6:30–44; Matthew 14:13–21; Luke 9:10–17; John 6:1–15)

The return of the twelve was a heady and confusing time. We may imagine something of their excitement if they had been instrumental in healing the sick and possessed. But we need also to imagine the excitement that was generated amongst the population of Galilee by these miracle working emissaries and their kingdom message. In A.C. Headlam's words, 'It looked like real revolution.'[23] Anyone who came in touch with Jesus' message for the first time during the mission must have been eager to see the master himself. This may be the situation reflected in Mark's comments that 'many were coming and going and there was no time at all even to eat', and that those who took part in the wilderness feeding were 'from all the cities' (Mark 6:30f., 33).[24]

So Jesus took his disciples away from the crowds to the other side of the lake, where they might have expected to find some rest and quiet to assess their mission. The beaches at the north-east end of the lake are ideal for swimming and relaxing; today they are a haven for holidaymakers. We do not need to doubt that the news which Jesus received of Herod's interest in him also had something to do with this withdrawal, particularly his selection of an area outside Herod's territory. But there is nothing at this stage to indicate that Jesus was in any danger from Herod. Herod's interest, according to Luke, was curiosity, like those who were 'coming and going'. Nevertheless, a ruler's curiosity is never purely idle. Hugh Montefiore has argued that the crowds which gathered to Jesus were 'engaged in preparations for a messianic uprising'.[25] This goes beyond the evidence, but that they were in a state of high excitement generated by Jesus' and his disciples' kingdom preaching is probable. If this were to increase and come to Herod's attention his desire to see Jesus might become dangerous. So Jesus took his disciples away.

However, they underestimated the enthusiasm and persistence of the crowds. It is about six kilometres by boat from Capernaum to the country south of Bethsaida, but because they were so close to the top of the lake it was not much further by land, and the people could keep them in sight most of the way. There was a sizable crowd waiting for them when they touched ashore. Jesus' reaction is significant. Although exhausted, he was moved with compassion at the sight of so many lost and leaderless people. He saw them as 'sheep without a shepherd, and he began to teach them many things' (Mark 6:34).

We have no way of knowing whether or not Jesus actually said anything to this effect on the occasion, for ostensibly the comment is Mark's. If he did, or if Mark has interpreted him correctly, it was a deeply messianic reaction. It is easy to miss this, because today the image of sheep and shepherd is soft and sentimental. In the Old Testament it is a political image of king and people, or sometimes of God and his people. On the occasion of Joshua's accession to leadership over Israel Moses prayed that God would appoint a man, 'that the Lord's congregation may not be as sheep without a shepherd' (Numbers 27:17). The prophets foretold the coming of the Messiah as a shepherd who would rescue the sheep from their oppressors and rule them in peace and plenty.[26] Whatever may have been said to stimulate Mark's comment, Jesus certainly told parables at other times which indicate that he saw himself as the one shepherd who was capable of leading the people of God into their promised inheritance.[27]

Jesus' reaction to the leaderlessness of his people was to teach them – fitting his servant–teacher concept of how he would establish the kingdom. According to one of his shepherd parables it was the sound of his voice (his teaching) which would draw together the flock of God and repel those who were not his sheep. 'My sheep hear my voice, and I know them, and they follow me, and I give them eternal life, and no one shall snatch them from my hand' (John 10:27–28). At the end of the day his disciples urged him to disperse the crowds, as they were in a deserted place and the people had been most of the day without food. His care for the flock then took an unexpected turn, and he fed the multitude from five small loaves and two fish. Mark tells us there were five thousand men (males) present; everyone had as much as they could eat, and twelve baskets full of scraps were collected afterwards.

There have been basketfuls of attempts at a rationalistic explanation of this story, designed to remove it from the realm of miracle. It has been seen as a carefully staged hoax with Essene henchmen handing Jesus loaves from the entrance of a concealed cave,[28] or as a miracle of contagious generosity in which the crowds were impressed by the boy who volunteered his lunch and finally shared their own previously concealed food.[29] Renan saw it as a case of survival through extreme frugality. Another writer explained that rich ladies from Tiberias used to inquire where Jesus was teaching and deliver baskets of food for the hungry crowds.[30] Schweitzer reckoned it as a sacramental meal in which everyone was given a fragment as a pledge that they would later share the messianic banquet.[31] Thiering makes it an ordination ceremony in which Gentile laymen were transformed into 'loaves' (ministers who could serve at communion).[32] Such attempts fail to convince. All four gospel writers present it as an outstanding miracle. If it were not, it is hard to view their accounts as anything but clumsy and fraudulent.

Mark concludes his account of the feeding by saying that Jesus *forced* his disciples to get into the boat and leave without him. He does not say why, and we would be left to guess, were it not for the Fourth Gospel. John adds that, astounded by his miracle, the crowds identified Jesus as the coming Prophet and determined to make him king (John 6:14–15). It is an interesting example of the manner in which the gospels sometimes unwittingly complement one another, bearing testimony to the history behind their accounts. We can well imagine that the twelve would have been very much in favour of any move to declare Jesus king, and that they would have been loath to depart on such an exciting occasion. Jesus had to impel them into the boat and remove them from the scene before the situation became unmanageable. He escaped into the hills.

Mountains rise steeply about a kilometre from that side of the lake. From his vantage point on the hill Jesus could well have seen the progress of the boat if there was sufficient light. He had told them to go up the lake to Bethsaida, but the wind blew them off course and they were struggling to make it to Capernaum.[33] At about three o'clock in the morning he came to them walking on the water. It is another of Mark's stories which, when transposed into the first person, reads like the account of Peter (Mark 6:48–52; cf. Matthew 14:22–34; John 6:16–21).[34]

Departure from Galilee
(Mark 6:53–8:10; Matthew 14:34–15:39)

Escape from the dangerous enthusiasm of the wilderness crowd did not lessen Jesus' popularity. Wherever he went he was recognized and crowds gathered with their sick. When he entered a town the market place quickly became choked with people and stretchers. Such was his reputation that people were eager to touch his clothes as he passed, and Mark tells us that even this way they were healed. But popularity also brought opposition. Pharisees and scribes from Jerusalem seized upon irregularities in his disciples' behaviour and a heated clash took place (Mark 7:1–23).

It is not surprising, then, that shortly after the miracle of the feeding Jesus left Galilee for the Gentile lands to the north. It is a period of his ministry that we know little about. Mark's inclusion of it is best accounted for by its being one of the few occasions that Jesus' ministry touched Gentiles. Mark was involved in a later mission to Gentiles north of Israel, and from there had travelled with Paul to Cyprus and Asia Minor. He would have a natural interest in this movement of Jesus, and anything which impinged on the later Gentile mission. There is a theory that Jesus was engaged in a Gentile mission at this time, but this is contradicted by the one incident Mark relates. A Gentile woman (a Syrian–Phoenician) came asking him to heal her demon-possessed daughter (Mark 7:25–30). Jesus refused on the grounds that it was unfitting to give the children's food (the blessings that he had brought for Israel) to the dogs (Gentiles). In her famous rejoinder she accepted the limitations of his mission, but pleaded that even dogs eat what falls from the children's table. For the faith that her reply expressed she received all that she requested. It is an extraordinary story, if, as some contend, the early Christians invented material to lend justification to their later activities. Who, seeking legitimacy for a mission which treated Christian Jews and Gentiles as equals, would create an event in which Jesus grudgingly acceded to the request of a Gentile 'dog'? The incident must go back to a Jesus who saw his commission in terms of Israel, but who occasionally went outside of his brief in a way that augured possible future blessings for Gentiles.

Some have suggested that his journey north was an extension of Jesus' frustrated attempt to be alone with his disciples and give them private instruction. Vincent Taylor believed that during this period Jesus was on his own, absent even from his disciples (though this contradicts Matthew's account), and that it was a time of reassessing his ministry in the light of the disappointing response to the mission of the twelve.[35] Others think he was running from Herod. The gospels suggest that it was popularity threatening to become political that Jesus was escaping.[36] It may have been part of his intention to give the crowds a cooling-off period.

In the Decapolis

On his return to Galilee through the Decapolis Jesus engaged in further public ministry. The Decapolis was a territory in which Jews and Gentiles lived in close proximity. To be consistent with his own statements, Jesus must have worked primarily amongst the Jews, though some Gentiles may have been involved, for their reaction to Jesus was to praise 'the God of Israel'.

According to Mark, at this time Jesus healed a man who was deaf and had a speech impediment, and also fed another crowd of four thousand (plus women and children) who had been with him for three days (Mark 7:31–8:10; Matthew 15:29–39). Many commentators dismiss this account as a duplicate of the feeding of the five thousand.[37] According to the theory of doublets a story undergoes development as it passes from person to person and may develop in different directions to the point where what was originally one incident is now thought to be two. This is a possibility that needs to be reckoned with in dealing with material with a long history of oral transmission, but it is not a satisfactory explanation for the stories of these two feedings. Even if some doubt Papias' information that Peter stood behind the writing of Mark, we still have to reckon with it as a gospel written well within the lifetime of people who remembered the ministry of Jesus. Such an obvious error would not have escaped correction, especially to be repeated by Matthew.[38] The doublet theory overlooks the special significance to Jesus of these actions as signs. This is indicated by Jesus' later reference back to the

two feedings (Mark 8:19–20; Matthew 16:9–10). The existence
of a saying in which Jesus draws his disciples' attention to the
significance of both feedings must tip the scale in the direction of
the independence of the second miracle.[39]

A Story of Human Struggle

The Gospel of Mark is an evangelistic tract whose main
purpose is to convince its readers that Jesus is the Messiah. One
way it does this is to present the bare bones of Jesus' ministry
between his baptism and his disappearance from the tomb,
allowing its readers to see how the disciples muddled through to
their ultimate conviction. It is in part a story of the disciples'
struggle. Some, following the theory of Wrede, view this as the
artistic creation of the gospel writer. If it were, Mark would
have to be rated as an outstanding work of creative fiction from
the ancient world. However, Wrede's thesis has been closely
scrutinized by many scholars and its deficiencies noted. Jesus'
triumphant entry into Jerusalem at the last Passover, his bold
action at the temple, and his crucifixion on the charge of
claiming to be 'King of the Jews' make it certain that the idea
of him being the Messiah did not originate after Easter. The
resurrection confirmed what Jesus believed and the authorities
denied. Besides, it is implicit in the authoritative way Jesus
spoke, called disciples, and related to people throughout his
ministry, that he knew himself to be God's agent.[40] That he did
not openly proclaim his messiahship earlier is understandable,
given the political temperature of the time and his desire to
complete his teaching and disciple training.

When did the disciples come to share his view? Not from
the start, according to Mark, but as the climax of a lengthy
process. Mark tells the story in the hope that it will lead others
to the same faith. The most effective instrument for bringing
others to faith ought to be the *true* story of how the disciples

reached their's. If their whole faith were built on experiences after the resurrection, these would surely be the things an evangelist would wish to highlight. The fact that Mark presents a long struggle involving many misunderstandings, most of which took place within the historical ministry of Jesus, is a firm indication that it was here, before the resurrection, that the ground work of their christological understanding was laid. The strong probability that Peter stands behind Mark suggests we are primarily hearing Peter's story, though others of the disciples were no doubt moving with him, or even in front of him. When we see how the history is told, especially in the sections before us, we will see that it is indeed Peter's story, told with a frankness and honesty that could only have originated with the apostle himself. Matthew and Luke each tone down Mark's ruthlessly frank portrayal of Peter.

The Meaning of the Loaves

About the time of the two feedings the confusion of the disciples reached its climax. The first note of this comes at the end of the story of Jesus walking to them on the water (Mark 6:49, 51–52). According to Mark, their fear and bewilderment was due to the fact that their hearts were hardened and they had failed to understand about the loaves. The feeding of the five thousand contained an obvious clue to Jesus' identity and the meaning of his ministry. It is hard to put this down to Mark's particular story-telling interests. Matthew's account shows much more the tendency of later Christian story telling (Matthew 14:26–33): when Jesus comes into the boat they worship him as the Son of God. It is much more probable that Mark's account puts us in touch with Peter's recollections of the effect of the situation on himself and the other disciples. At the time they honestly could not take it in. The miracle of the loaves had not effected any breakthrough in their understanding. From the standpoint of their later knowledge it seemed as though their hearts had been hardened to the point that they were unable to see the obvious.

On the next occasion they were together in a boat, crossing once more from Galilee to the far side of the lake, and had forgotten to take bread with them (Mark 8:13–21; Matthew 16:5–12). Jesus warned them solemnly to watch out for the yeast of the Pharisees and Herod, sparking an argument amongst them about the forgotten bread. Perhaps they were apportioning blame, or disputing whether to go back.[41] In any case Jesus perceived that they were absorbed with something quite trivial in comparison with the matters of destiny unfolding around them and chided them in a manner that is notably agitated.

> Why are you arguing about not having bread? Don't you yet perceive or understand? Are your hearts hardened? You have eyes, don't you see? You have ears, don't you hear? Don't you remember how many baskets full you picked up when I broke the five loaves for the five thousand? And when I broke the seven loaves for the four thousand how many baskets full of pieces did you pick up? Don't you understand yet?

We can sympathize with the disciples. It is easy enough to put all the pieces together as we study them in a book, and think that the meaning should have been clear, but to have encountered these situations one at a time, in the flesh, would have been very different. Especially when, in spite of Jesus' message of the kingdom, their world continued much the same as it ever had been. For although every miracle and much more in the ministry of Jesus was a sign of the presence of the kingdom, there were many more signs to the effect that all was as it had ever been. The miracles were still *exceptional* events, pointers to something that was not yet clear. But the little story of the forgotten bread is eloquent testimony to the dominant reality that the disciples' world continued to be an ordinary place. They were still capable of becoming totally engrossed in the question of where their next meal was going to come from.

What Jesus seems most to have wanted for his disciples at this point was that they should come to an understanding of *him*, and a trust that was commensurate with who he was. That, oddly, is what most seems to be lacking in them at this point. I say oddly, because at the beginning of our story it seemed they followed him in the belief that he was the Messiah. A year later all that confidence has evaporated. Surely if Jesus did the miracles recorded in the gospels it would have been confirmed over and over.

We need to remind ourselves here that Jesus was not in any way carrying out the essentials of the messianic programme as his contemporaries pictured it. It was of the very definition of Messiah that he should be the king of Israel. If he were not, whatever else he might be, he was not the Messiah. And Jesus certainly did not behave like a king, nor like someone who had his sights set on being one. When kingship was within his grasp he took urgent measures to avoid it. Also, Jesus does not appear to have overtly claimed to be the Messiah in this first half of his ministry, not even to his disciples. It was John the Baptist who had done this for him, and even he had subsequent doubts when Jesus failed to carry out the messianic programme. Jesus had to appeal to him on the basis of certain signs, against many other contrary appearances, not to lose faith in him (Luke 7:22–23). Jesus proclaimed the presence and coming of the kingdom of God, but his own relationship to it was always a mystery. If he expressed it at all it was in the form of parables, and these were capable of various interpretations. The only people who openly acknowledged him as Messiah were the demon-possessed.

The miracles too were capable of different interpretations. Apart from the scribes' dismissal of them as demonically inspired, we have encountered opinions that saw them as the work of the resurrected Baptist and of an old time miracle-working prophet.

There was much to commend this latter interpretation. Jesus was primarily a teacher like the prophets, and not at all the messianic conqueror like David. We may guess that the disciples, after a certain period of hoping that Jesus might be the Messiah, quietly settled back to this more modest view. Or perhaps they vacillated between this and renewed ideas that he might be the king. For the overall ordinariness of their life and their world continued to be punctuated with signs, every one of which brought the question, 'Who is this man that he does such things?' Miracles like the feeding of the five thousand challenged the view that Jesus was a mere prophet.

Whatever it was that Jesus wanted them to understand as they quarrelled over who had forgotten the bread, it was evidently bound up with the significance of the two feeding miracles. This means that in Jesus' mind they were more than compassionate responses to a hungry crowd; they were deliberate pointers to his identity and significance. It is important, then, that we too try to see them as Jesus hoped the disciples would.

The obvious thing to note initially is John's comment that the first feeding took place when the Passover was near, though that Mark does not think it necessary to supply this information indicates that in his mind the miracle spoke for itself. The connection with the manna in the wilderness was obvious whatever season the miracle took place in. Passover, and the Feast of Unleavened Bread which accompanied it, was the season when the events of the exodus were specially recalled: the escape from Egypt, the crossing of the Red Sea, and God's supernatural provision of food in the desert. There is ample evidence of a belief among the Jews that this was more than mere history: in the messianic age the manna would again come down from heaven. 'And it will happen at that time that the treasury of manna shall come down again from on high, and they will eat of it in those years, because these are they who will have arrived at the consummation of time'.[42] The people who in John declared Jesus 'the prophet who is to come into the world' evidently saw the connection, and it is hard to think it could have been completely lost on the disciples. Why did they not draw the conclusion? Probably they did, but Jesus upset that understanding by withdrawing from their attempt to make him king. He could not be the Messiah because he was not going about the messianic mission in the only way they could conceive.

Sight For The Blind (Mark 8:22–26)

The miracle Mark relates after Jesus' appeal to the disciples in the boat is told principally to illustrate the progression of their understanding. It is unique in all the gospels in being the only healing in which Jesus appears to have experienced some difficulty in effecting a cure. A blind man was brought to him and he was asked to touch him. They were near Bethsaida, a new city just beyond the border of Galilee, at the top end of the lake. As the next location in Mark's itinerary is Caesarea Philippi further to the north, it probably took place on the way. Jesus took the man by the hand and led him out of the village. There he spat on his eyes, touched him with his hands and asked if he could see. The blind man saw, but only very indistinctly; the people looked to him like walking trees. Then Jesus laid his hands once more on the man's eyes and he saw everything clearly.

The time had now come for the disciples to 'receive their sight'. After Jesus' impassioned plea in the boat they must have begun seriously to ponder the meaning of the feeding miracles. As they journeyed north to the villages of Caesarea Philippi Jesus asked them who they thought he was. Is it possible that he put that question to them then because at last they were again asking it of themselves, and that, with the nudge he had given them, were reaching a better conclusion?

Who is He?

> In the way he questioned his disciples, and he said to them, Who
> are people saying that I am? And they said to him, John the
> Baptist, and others Elijah, and others one of the prophets. And he
> questioned them, What about you? Who do you say I am? Peter
> replied and said, 'You are the Messiah.' (Mark 8:27–29; cf.
> Matthew 16:13–20; Luke 9:18–21)

It is an extraordinary question. Of whom do we ever ask, 'Who is
he or she?' We may ask it to establish a person's name, or an
occupation, but beyond that we would scarcely go. Not even of
the most famous people would it seem an appropriate question,
unless perhaps we were trying our hand at psychoanalysis; finding
the real person beneath the exterior. It is no different with
historic personages. I am not aware of anyone other than Jesus of
whom it was ever seriously asked, 'Who is he?' The only
circumstance in which the question might be appropriate is if we
suspected there was more to a person than met the eye. If they
were using a false identity, for example, or were pretending an
authority we were unsure about. If a stranger walked into a
theatre and ordered everyone to move outside, form up into a
group and wait for further instructions, you might say, 'Who is
he/she?' or 'Who does he/she think he/she is?'. In such a case
you would not be seeking to learn their name but the basis of
their authority.

It is in this last sense that the question was asked of Jesus, and
it is important to see that it was the natural question generated
by the interaction in people's minds of everything he did and
said with their own understanding of the prophetically revealed
scheme of God's purposes. At his first appearance in the
synagogue at Capernaum the people exclaimed, 'What is this?
A new teaching? With authority he commands even the
unclean spirits and they obey him' (Mark 1:27). His words to
the paralytic brought forth an immediate protest from the

learned onlookers, 'Who can forgive sins but God alone?' (Mark 2:7). The disciples in the boat cried out in fear, 'Who is this that even the wind and the sea obey him?' (Mark 4:41). His townsmen in Nazareth asked, 'Where does he get these things, isn't he the carpenter?' (Mark 6:2–3).

Jesus' question makes it clear that the issue of his identity was the subject of wide discussion. It is significant that even the Tetrarch had an opinion and wanted to see Jesus for himself. That people were seriously entertaining the possibility that he might be John the Baptist returned from the dead witnesses to the felt need to connect John's prophetic ministry and its abrupt termination with Jesus' appearance, comparable message, and altogether greater endowment of supernatural power. The suggestion that he might be Elijah is another consequence of Jesus' miracle working, and also indicates the eschatological fervour that his ministry generated. To see him as an old style prophet was a little less bold, but still a witness to people's observation of an authority that might originate in God. It was imperative for the Pharisees to come up with some alternative explanation if they wished to maintain their own authority in the face of Jesus' very different manner of teaching. Their explanation, that he wielded the power of the prince of the demons, is no less tribute to him than the opinions of his supporters. From a question put to Jesus after the transfiguration it is plain that the possibility of his being the Messiah had been canvassed. 'How is it that the scribes say that Elijah must come first?' his disciples asked (Mark 9:11). The scribes must have asserted that Jesus could not be the Messiah, because Elijah had not yet come. Their opinion carried weight, even with Jesus' disciples. It troubled them until the time God afforded them definite proof.

Thus the disciples no less than the people were caught up in this ferment of questioning. They heard it all and saw it all. There was no doubt in their minds that Jesus' authority derived from God. The question was what role Jesus was playing in the plan of

God and where he fitted in terms of the various identities that could be found in the prophetic scriptures. It is this question that Jesus finally put to them roughly a year after the commencement of his Galilean ministry, and it was the two feeding miracles which were pivotal in bringing Peter to his declaration that Jesus was the Messiah.

This is what Mark surely means us to understand with his sequence of: feeding miracle; observation of the disciples' lack of understanding; second feeding miracle; Jesus' passionate appeal that they understand these signs; his parabolic miracle of the blind man gradually receiving sight; and finally Jesus' question and Peter's answer. Luke's gospel also testifies to the important connection between the feeding miracle and Peter's confession, for he places Jesus' question to Peter immediately after the feeding of the five thousand, and omits everything between.

It is a reasonable historical inference, then, that the disciples (or at least Peter) attributed their conviction that Jesus could be no less than the Messiah to the influence of these feeding miracles. Every miracle attested Jesus' divine authority, but when they finally allowed themselves to ponder the feeding of the five thousand they were pushed beyond seeing him as a prophet or even as *the* Prophet, to what for them was the ultimate ascription to a man. Against all the evidences to the contrary they named him Messiah.

Why Messiah?

But why Messiah? The obvious comparison suggested by the feedings was to Moses – the one who had provided the manna – and thence to the expected Moses-like great prophet. But reflection might have raised queries about the adequacy of even this comparison. For it was not really Moses who had given the manna. It was God who said 'I will rain bread from heaven for you' (Exodus 16:4). Moses was simply the prophet who mediated God's word to them to go and pick it up. Jesus' actions of taking the bread in his own hands and multiplying it suggested a better comparison was with God than with Moses (John 6:31–32). This is also true of his walking on the water. In later biblical reflection on the crossing of the Red Sea it was not Moses who walked before Israel, but God: 'Your way was in the sea, and your paths in the great waters, yet no one saw your footprints. You led your people like a flock, by the hand of Moses and Aaron' (Psalm 77:19–20).

I am not suggesting that the disciples began to think of Jesus as God at this time; only that his actions pushed him closer to the sovereign autonomy of God than anything that could be said of a prophet, even a prophet as great as Moses. I think the only final recourse to them was to believe that he must be the Messiah; a Messiah in many ways less than they would have expected, yet in other ways perhaps immeasurably greater. It is doubtful that they would have expected even the Messiah to act with the autonomy which Jesus displayed.[43]

Bread From Heaven (John 6:24–71)

A further factor which may have been influential in the growing conviction of the disciples is the dialogue which, according to the Gospel of John, took place in the synagogue at Capernaum some time after the feeding of the five thousand. The long discourses in the Fourth Gospel are reckoned by some to be compositions of the author. Their lack of conformity to the style of the other gospels, their similarity to the overall style of John, and their concentration on the identity of Jesus is thought to support this conclusion. On the other side, allowing for the fact that in this discourse John may be reporting the gist of Jesus' teaching in his own words, there appears to be a remarkable conformity to what we have seen were Jesus' concerns at this time, in particular, the relationship between the miracle of the feeding and his own identity. Jesus not infrequently taught in synagogues, so he must at times have delivered lengthy discourses.[44]

Paradoxically, Jesus accuses the Jews of following him not because they saw signs but because they had filled their bellies with food. On the surface this is manifestly absurd; their excitement was due to the remarkable miracle he had done. But it makes sense if we consider what we have observed was the problem Jesus encountered at this time: an excited curiosity which enjoyed the miracles but refused to penetrate to their real significance. Such an interest in his miracles was not an attention to them as *signs*, but a carnal fascination on a par with an appetite for food. Even if it be said in the Jews' favour that they understood the miracle enough to want to make him king, it was king on their terms, to continue to provide food and whatever else they craved. To Jesus it still boiled down to a preoccupation with the bread of this age. He urges them to seek the food which endures to eternal life which, he says, he has been appointed by God to give them.

They then ask him for a sign (exactly what Mark 8:11 indicates some were requesting at this time), and remind him that Moses gave their forefathers bread from heaven. Are they discounting the once-only character of the feeding and challenging him to give them something more continuous, like the manna? Or are they asking him, if he is the one sealed by God to give them eternal life, for some greater sign than Moses gave? Whatever the implications of their question, Jesus replies by denying that Moses gave bread from heaven: 'it is my Father who gives you the real bread from heaven.' The manna, in other words, was symbolic, like the bread Jesus had given them. It was intended to point to something real and ultimately life-giving which God was wishing now to give his people. 'The bread of God is that which comes down from heaven and gives life to the world.' They then ask him to give it to them, and he responds '*I* am the bread of life, whoever comes to me will not hunger and whoever believes in me will never thirst.'

Could Jesus have made such an affirmation at this point in his ministry? Some doubt it. Yet it is exactly where, according to Mark, he was driving his disciples' understanding at this time. In any case the whole discourse never ceases to be parabolic in its nature. Jesus does not say he is the Messiah, but that God has appointed him to 'give life to the world', a way of speaking of the resurrection and the new age. In parabolic fashion, and parallel to his words to the disciples at Caesarea Philippi, Jesus then goes further to indicate that he intends to do this by the surrender of his life for the life of the world. However, he is not understood, and his offensive reference to eating his flesh and blood causes confusion and disaffection. According to John many ceased to follow him at this point. Even the twelve are embarrassed. They remain with him, they say, because he has 'the words of eternal life' and they have nowhere else to go. Peter acknowledges Jesus as 'the Holy One of God'. They are unhappily 'hooked'. In the scheme of John this discourse and its results fulfil a similar role to the story of Peter's confession at Caesarea Philippi. If John's purpose was to complement Mark, this episode may have been a stage along the road to Peter's confession.

Conviction

The disciples have now replied to the question about Jesus' identity with the highest answer they were capable then of giving. They began their association with him believing him to be the Messiah on the basis of John the Baptist's testimony, but with Jesus' failure to do anything to substantiate this, soon slid back to a more modest assessment. Either that, or they fluctuated confusedly between thinking him a prophet, and hoping anew that he might be the Messiah. Jesus did not tell them who he was, but let them experience and share his kingdom-heralding ministry until they were driven by the sheer majesty of his actions to acknowledge with conviction that he had to be the Messiah. Yet this latter conviction was of a different quality to the first. The first was hearsay, based on nothing more than someone else's word, carrying with it the full programme of what *they* and John expected him to do. The latter embraced the reality – even the disappointment – of what he was, but was grounded on what their own eyes and ears had witnessed. This is the turning point of the Gospel of Mark and there is every reason to think it was a decisive moment in the life of Jesus.

A Suffering Messiah

In Mark's story it was when Peter acknowledged him as the Messiah that Jesus began to speak openly about his impending death. Matthew and Luke say the same, and we have seen that John preserves a similar progression. How are we to account for this? The nineteenth century's Lives of Jesus were especially interested in Jesus' psychological development and seized eagerly on this evidence of a change of outlook. Jesus began his ministry thinking that the kingdom would develop naturally from his teaching, but in the face of rejection became subject to a death-wish; such was one reading of the story. Schweitzer saw the mission of the twelve as the turning point: when the disciples returned without God having revealed him as the heavenly Son of Man, Jesus went through a time of reassessment, concluding that he must bring on the end of the world by giving himself as a sacrifice. Vincent Taylor attributed the change to Jesus' realization of the growing hostility towards his non-political approach. Many scholars reject the whole attempt to monitor any change in Jesus' outlook because of their scepticism about the order of the gospel narratives. We have seen that this scepticism is exaggerated: while not everything can be placed in sequence, much of the story can. And whether Jesus' thinking changed radically at this point, or whether he began to reveal to his disciples what was clear to him all along is a question of some importance for our understanding of his mission.

Did Jesus Anticipate Violent Death?

The first matter we need to settle is whether, in the early part of his ministry, Jesus anticipated a violent death. There are indications that he did. First, Mark tells of Pharisees and Herodians in early agreement to kill Jesus (Mark 3:6). Herodians are strange people to find allied with Pharisees, and this indicates the historical nature of the plot, since they play no significant role elsewhere in the gospels.[45] It also places the incident in the Galilean (early) phase of Jesus' career. Secondly, when Jesus explained his non-fasting as the appropriate lifestyle of the bridegroom with his guests, he foretold a time when he would be taken away, and fasting (Matthew says 'mourning') would become appropriate (Mark 2:19–20; Matthew 9:14–15). Thirdly, the Sermon on the Mount obviously expects persecution, to the degree that Jesus must instruct his disciples in the right way to respond. If he expected his disciples to suffer, and willed that they refrain from retaliation or self-defence, did he not see himself in the same peril? Fourthly, his unfortunate visit to Nazareth must also have made clear what reaction he could expect from an unveiled messianic claim. Fifthly, at a feast in Jerusalem in the first year Jesus came under attack for healing someone on the Sabbath, and John says there were threats on his life when he spoke in a way that implied a unique relationship with God (John 5:1–18; 7:19–25). There is, therefore, no reason to doubt that death loomed large in Jesus' reckoning well before the mission of the twelve or Caesarea Philippi.

Death and the Kingdom

Is there anything to indicate how Jesus viewed his death in relation to the coming of the kingdom? Again we are not without clues. Although the presence of the kingdom might logically have implied the cessation of suffering, for Jesus it did not. Though present in part, its full consummation remained in the future, and depended on his mission. Thus he saw solidarity with Israel's identity as the poor as vital for himself and his disciples. Such poverty was to be actualized in the disciples' commitment to suffer for righteousness, which in the present context meant maintaining loyalty to the Son of Man. That he would be rejected and persecuted is implied. Jesus likened such suffering to that of the prophets; he regarded persecution as inevitable to the prophetic vocation. This goes some way to explaining a commitment to suffering throughout his kingdom-bringing career: the one who stands for God (the true Israelite) will always suffer persecution. Those who pursue any God-given commission must needs suffer. This does not imply that suffering has any instrumental role in achieving the kingdom, only that the mission would not succeed without it. This is not all, however.

The heavenly voice at his baptism pointed Jesus to the Servant of Yahweh as his messianic prototype. Isaiah's Servant profile includes difficult labours, discouragement, apparent failure, rejection, and death.[46] Some of these troubles are the opposition hindering the Servant's mission; others are instrumental in achieving it. Jesus applied the Suffering Servant pattern to his disciples when in the Sermon on the Mount he told them to turn the other cheek. This was part of a strategy of reconciliation and peacemaking. He was certainly not unaware of its possible future application to him. Did he also see himself fulfilling the sacrificial aspects of the Servant mission? He certainly did in the last year, as we shall see. The only indications of it in the first half of his ministry are in the Fourth Gospel. Jesus tells Nicodemus that just as Moses raised a bronze snake for the snake-bitten people to look at and be healed, so the Son of Man would be lifted up, 'that whoever believes in him may have eternal life' (John 3:14–15). Then, in his bread of life discourse in the Capernaum synagogue, Jesus refers in an unmistakably sacrificial image to his flesh and blood as the instrumental cause of eternal life (John 6:51–59). The kingdom of God and eternal life were near synonymous correlates in the language of Jesus' time. John's preference for the more individualistic term should not confuse us that it is still the coming of the kingdom which is in view.

There is no cause for surprise, then, when Jesus begins to speak of the inevitability of his death. That he began to communicate this to his disciples only at Caesarea Philippi need not mean that he had undergone a turnabout in understanding his mission. It could have been just as the gospels portray it, that his first objective was to bring the twelve to a firm conviction about his messiahship, and only then to broach the difficult task of preparing them for his death.

The Son of Man Must Suffer

> He began to teach them that the Son of man must suffer many things and be rejected by the elders and chief priests and scribes, and be killed and on the third day be raised. And Peter took him aside and began to rebuke him, but he turned and saw his disciples and rebuked Peter and said, 'Get behind me Satan, you are not thinking in God's way but in the manner of men.' (Mark 8:31–33; cf. Matthew 16:21–23; Luke 9:22)

If ever a story had the ring of truth it is this one: Peter rebukes Jesus! Jesus rebukes the prince of the apostles and as much as calls him the Devil! It reminds one of the game of Snakes and Ladders. Peter has climbed almost to the top of the board and now he has slid to the bottom again. Jesus' preoccupation with his death will characterize the latter part of the gospel story. It now becomes the occasion for a fresh wave of confusion on the part of the disciples. Perhaps the two-stage healing of the blind man prefigured the very partial gain in insight that came with Peter's climactic confession of Jesus' messiahship; the faith journey is not yet complete. And yet, although they must now accommodate the ultimate setback to their hopes and expectations for the man they have named king, they do not really go backwards. Something happened to make sure that they would not retreat from their newly found conviction.

Jesus' Kingship Confirmed
(Mark 9:2–13; Luke 9:28–36; Matthew 17:1–13)

Six days after their Caesarea Philippi experience Jesus took Peter, James and John to a mountaintop and was transfigured before them so that he shone with a whiteness they had never before seen. Elijah and Moses appeared and spoke with him, according to Luke, 'about his *exodus* which he was about to fulfil in Jerusalem'. The story descends from the sublime to the ridiculous as Peter suggests to Jesus that he put up three shelters for him and his two guests. A cloud comes over them and they hear the voice of God saying 'This is my Son, the Chosen One, listen to him.' When the cloud moves everything is normal again.

What can one say about such a story? It is possible to point to elements that look authentic, like Peter's clumsy suggestion and Mark's (Peter's?) comment, 'For he did not know what to say because they were terrified.' One can point out its significance for the developing faith of the disciples: against all the learning of the scribes and Pharisees and their apparent loyalty to the traditions of Moses and the prophets, Peter, James and John have now seen Moses and Elijah in personal, intimate association with Jesus. More than that, they have been on the mountain of God and have heard the voice of God. They have it now as a word of God himself that Jesus is his Messiah. Many years later Peter referred back to this in one of his letters (2 Peter 1:16–18).[47] In the final analysis some things are established only on the testimony of those who have seen them. One accepts their word or refuses it according to how one judges them on other grounds. The experience of the transfiguration explains why Peter, James and John never retreated from their conviction that Jesus was God's man despite all the disappointment, perplexity and disillusionment of the eventful year to follow.

As they came down from the mountain after the trans-figuration Jesus solemnly charged his three disciples not to tell anyone what they had seen 'until the Son of Man should rise from the dead.' A week previously, when Peter declared Jesus as Messiah, Jesus had in like manner forbidden the disciples to tell anyone. It is curious that he should be so anxious for them to believe in him, yet command them to hold it as a secret. One wonders, if he saw himself as Messiah, why at the feeding of the five thousand he did not allow his disciples and the crowds to make him king as they wanted to. What was it that caused him to turn away from the kingship he believed was his, when it was freely offered him, and command his disciples to keep his identity a secret?

Once previously Jesus had been offered the kingship and had refused it. In the wilderness Satan offered him all the kingdoms of the world if he would only bow down and worship him. Jesus declined then because his worship belonged to God alone. In that case, although he may have succeeded in gaining kingship, it would not have been an independent lordship, but a dominion under Satan. In reserving his worship to God alone Jesus made it clear that he would have the kingdoms only in ultimate submission to God, and therefore as the kingdom of God. He evidently considered an absolute exercise of rule either undesirable or impossible. This suggests a possible explanation of his reaction to the crowd's offer of kingship. If he were to receive kingship from them he would hold it in submission to them and on their terms. He would be in the position of a democratically elected leader, ruling the people by the will of the people. To our ears that sounds good, but we should notice that a subtle inversion has taken place. The real rulers are the people, not the king. He is put in position by them, to serve their purposes, for as long as they see fit to keep him there. As democratically sounding as this appears, Jesus may have seen it as only one step removed from submission to the rule of the Devil.[48] He would become king in God's way at God's time, exercising his kingship under God, executing God's programmes.

When Peter took Jesus aside and disputed the necessity of his suffering we observe this same process of inversion at work in his disciples. They wanted Jesus to be a king according to their conceptions of kingship, and they wanted to direct the manner in which he would get there. No doubt their programme had its attraction to Jesus. For one thing it would allow him, like many of history's rulers, to sit back in safety while his servants did the fighting and dying. God's programme (the Servant mission) meant suffering and death for *him*. His savage repudiation of Peter's well-meaning opposition shows how threatening he felt it to his mission.

On the mountain God placed beyond all doubt that Jesus was his Messiah. He also charged the disciples to listen to him. While they were trying to run things themselves, according to their own understanding, they were in the deepest sense denying his kingship; so were the crowds who wanted to make him king by force. If he was the Messiah, the logical response was to follow him, no matter how strange the path along which he led.

From this point forward Jesus' way moved steadily in the direction of rejection and death in Jerusalem. For the disciples it would bring much confusion and sorrow. Yet, except for those few dark hours at the end, most of them would not cease to believe that however paradoxical things appeared, Jesus *was* God's anointed King, and that somehow or other, one day, he would rule.

Notes

[1] Joanna is described as the wife of Chuza, Herod's *epitropos*. An *epitropos* could be a guardian of children (Galatians 4:2 – unlikely in this context), a governor (also unlikely), an estate manager, or even a treasurer. The name Chuza may be Idumaean; it occurs in a Nabataean inscription and may derive from the name of an Idumaean god, Kos. The Herods were of Idumaean descent. F. Godet (*Commentary on the Gospel of St John*, II, 135) speculates that Chuza may be the royal official whose son Jesus healed (John 4:46–54). This would explain such a prominent official allowing his wife to accompany Jesus' party.

[2] It has been suggested that the shade of fig trees was a favoured place for scholars to sit with their disciples. Nathaniel's question to Philip (John 2:46) indicates a critical knowledge of Scripture.

[3] Chapter 14. There are some significant discrepancies between Mark's account of the mission charge and that of Luke and Matthew, that show that Q's account of the mission was a little different to Mark's. The variations may have originated in confusion with the sending of the seventy two. Matthew fused details from these two missions together and added further material to form an extended teaching block on the subject of mission. Q may also have displayed some influence of cross fertilization between the two mission charges.

[4] See p. 247 above.

[5] *Mishnah Berakhot* 5:5. See *TDNT* 1, 407–445.

[6] *Testament of Levi* 18:12; *Testament of Simeon* 6:6; cf. *Testament of Zebulon* 9:8.

[7] *Mishnah Tohoroth* 4:5; *Mishnah Oholoth* 2:3; *SB*, I, 571.

[8] Schweitzer, *Quest*, 357f.

[9] It is an encouragement to missionaries that there will always be a place for them to run to, always a city remaining to be evangelized until the time of Christ's parousia.

[10] Taylor, *Life*, 112–138. For a critical appraisal of Taylor's view see Cranfield, *Mark*, 202f.

[11] See Goguel, *Life*, 346ff.

[12] See above pp. 72ff.; Josephus, *History*, 18.116–119.

[13] Luke, who had an inside source on the Herods and perhaps a reason for sensitivity in his portrayal of them, amends Mark's rather unflattering portrayal of Herod's superstitious reaction, by framing it in the form of a question: 'John I beheaded, but who is this, about whom I hear such things' (Luke 9:7). His is the only gospel to mention Joanna the wife of Herod's steward (Luke 8:3; 24:10). Wenham (*Enigma*, 85) thinks she may have supplied some

of Luke's information. In Acts 13:1 he mentions a Manaan who had been brought up with Herod the Tetrarch. In Acts 25:13–26:32 he gives a sympathetic account of Herod Agrippa II's hearing of Paul's case.

[14] Matthew 14:12f. gives the initial impression that it was Jesus' hearing of John's death that caused him to withdraw with his disciples. But this would then imply that Herod's hearing of Jesus took place after the feeding of the five thousand, which Matthew obviously does not intend. The contradiction is removed if we see that 14:3–12 is an extended digression explaining Herod's reaction to Jesus, and that it was this reaction that Jesus heard about, and on account of which he withdrew. Hoehner (*Herod Antipas*, 169–171) recognizes that the story of John's execution is a flashback, but continues with the opinion that it took place later in the Galilean ministry, a year after his imprisonment. Robinson (*Priority*, 139f.) takes a similar view. Headlam (*Life*, 271) thinks the news of John's death cut short the mission of the twelve.

[15] In Matthew 11:2ff. John's execution appears after the mission of the twelve, but this is a topical, not a chronological arrangement. The aorist participles allow us to translate 'When John had heard in prison, the works of the Christ and had sent to him through his disciples'. Jesus' words about the Baptist's light, in which the Jews were content to walk for a while (John 5:33–35), do not demand, but are consistent with his being dead at the time.

[16] The period AD 6–37 is covered in *History*, 18.26–89, 116–119; *War*, 2.117–180. Much of this is international affairs, touching only lightly on the Jews in Palestine. It is significant that two things he does find space for are accounts of Jesus and of John the Baptist.

[17] The uncertainty is due to our ignorance of which calendar Luke employed, what point was reckoned as the beginning of Tiberius' reign (his rule of the provinces, or his accession to sole emperorship at the death of Augustus), and whether his first year included the few months of the year of his accession. Finegan (*Biblical Chronology*, 262–269) gives sixteen different computations ranging from AD 26–29.

[18] Jesus was born late in the reign of Herod the Great who died in 4 BC. If he was born in 6 or 5 BC, suggested by the fact that Herod, when he heard of a possible messianic pretender in Bethlehem, tried to eliminate all boys two years and under, he would have turned 30 in AD 25 or 26.

[19] All the gospels agree that Jesus died on Friday. According to the synoptics this was the day after Passover (Nisan 15), whereas in John it is Passover itself (Nisan 14). Finegan (*Biblical Chronology*, 295) gives a table of days for Nisan 14 & 15 in the years AD 27–34. Actually, the only year in

which Passover fell on a Thursday was AD 27, pointing to a crucifixion on Passover itself. See Robinson, *Priority*, 153ff.

[20] Between the first Passover and his arrival in Galilee, Jesus said to his disciples, 'Don't you say, "There are yet four months, and the harvest comes"? I tell you, raise your eyes and behold the fields; they are white for harvest' (John 4:35). If Jesus was referring to the actual situation in the fields he must have been in Samaria in the winter (December–January) and a Passover not mentioned in the gospels must have occurred before the summer that preceded the feeding of the five thousand. So Finegan, *Biblical Chronology*, 283; Hoehner, *Chronological Aspects*, 56–57. However, Jesus may have been quoting a common saying about the time between seeding and harvest, indicating the immediacy of the harvest of ready-to-believe Samaritans before them. It may then have been the sight of ripening grain fields that suggested this image to him. So Robinson, *Priority*, 132–135.

[21] Hoehner, *Chronological Aspects*, 45–63.

[22] By Hoehner's reckoning it would have occurred in Spring AD 32.

[23] Headlam, *Life*, 270.

[24] Luke condenses Mark's account but preserves the relationship between the return of the twelve and the occasion of the feeding (Luke 9:10). Matthew loses it through his thematically motivated relocation of the mission to an earlier point in the gospel (Matthew 10).

[25] H. Montefiore, 'Revolt in the Desert?', 135.

[26] Isaiah 40:10f.; Ezekiel 34; Zechariah 11, 13:7ff.

[27] John 10. Note that in 10:14 'the good shepherd' means the *expert* or *capable* shepherd (*kalos*).

[28] K.F. Bahrdt's view. See Schweitzer, *Quest*, 41.

[29] Goodspeed, *Jesus*, 105.

[30] P. Nahor. See Schweitzer, *Quest*, 326.

[31] Schweitzer, *Quest*, 374f.

[32] B. Thiering, *Jesus the Man*, 121–125. She appears to make up meanings. Her footnotes do not substantiate her assertions. In this chapter one footnote refers to the biblical text; all the rest are references back into her own book.

[33] A harmonization of Mark's comment that Jesus sent them to Bethsaida, and John's that they headed for Capernaum.

[34] So Cranfield, *Mark*, 224.

[35] Taylor, *Life*, 134–138.

[36] So Schweitzer, *Quest*, 362.

[37] E.g., Hooker, *The Gospel According to St Mark*, 187; Taylor, *Life*, 129f.

[38] The absence of the second feeding story from Luke is readily explained by his omission of all Mark has between the feeding of the five thousand and Peter's confession. It implies no judgement on Mark's historical worth. The theory that Mark repeated the story to indicate that Gentiles as well as Jews are to have a share in the messianic banquet requires some definite indication on Mark's part that it had anything to do with Gentiles. While this could conceivably be argued in the case of Matthew, there is no indication of it in Mark.

[39] The mention of both feedings could be a Markan amendment, but if Mark had the saying before him with reference only to the first feeding would he not, in the interests of economy, rather have dropped the second feeding. His gospel would have lost nothing in the process. Hooker (*Mark*, 187–189) notes that the two feedings were of obvious importance to Mark but can suggest no reason. I submit that the reason was historical. Further to the independence of the second feeding, see Cranfield, *Mark*, 204–205.

[40] Several scholars have tackled the problem of Jesus' self-understanding, not by way of his titles, but by inquiring into the implications of how he carried out his ministry. Hengel (*Charismatic Leader*) focused on the enormous authority implicit in the way Jesus called disciples. B. Witherington (*The Christology of Jesus*) leaves the Caesarea Philippi incident to one side and attends to what is implicit in the way Jesus related to people, his words and his works. The result is positive for the view that Jesus understood himself to be the Messiah, even if he did not share all the messianic views of his contemporaries.

[41] The suggestion of T. Zahn, *Das Evangelium des Matthäus*, 536.

[42] *2 Baruch* 29:8, a Jewish writing of the early second century AD (translation in Charlesworth, *Pseudepigrapha*, 631). Also *Mekilta Exodus* 16:25; *Ecclesiastes Rabbah* 1:9. Cf. Micah 7:14ff.; Isaiah 49:9f.; and see Brown, *John*, I, 265f.; Dodd, *Interpretation*, 335f.

[43] For an insightful development of the paradoxical manner in which Jesus failed to live up to the expectations of his contemporaries at the same time as he transcended them, see O. Borchert, *The Original Jesus*, 23–37.

[44] P. Borgen (*Bread From Heaven*) establishes the unity of the discourse on the basis of its elaboration of certain Old Testament texts and Jewish haggadic ideas.

[45] This is well argued by H.G. Wood, 'Interpreting This Time', 262–263.

[46] Isaiah 42:4; 49:4, 7; 50:6–9; 52:13–53:12.

[47] Many scholars think 2 Peter is a pseudonymous writing (falsely purporting to be written by Peter). See Kelly, *Peter and of Jude*, 223–237; R.J. Bauckham, *Jude, 2 Peter*, 138–163. For defences of its authenticity see Robinson, *Redating*,

169–199; M. Green, *2 Peter and Jude*, 13–39. Whichever way one takes it, directly or indirectly, the letter preserves Peter's solemn testimony to his strange mountaintop experience.

[48] Early in his ministry many people in Jerusalem believed in him because of the signs he did, but, according to John, Jesus would not allow himself to fall into their hands because he knew the human heart (John 2:23ff.).

Chapter 14

Last Chance

Final Months in Galilee

Six months were still to run after the momentous events of the last chapter, before Jesus brought his time in Galilee to a close. The gospels tell us little about them. Having already given a vivid account of the shape and character of the Galilean period there was probably little need. Mark makes the curious comment that as they passed through Galilee Jesus wanted no one to know his whereabouts because he was teaching his disciples (Mark 9:30–31). Were they forced to keep on the move by the crowds which soon massed whenever he stopped very long in one place? John says of the same period that Jesus deliberately stayed in Galilee because the Judaeans were seeking to kill him (John 7:1). There could be a relationship between these two. Jesus was wary of the political aspirations of the Galilean crowds; some people in Judaea may have been equally anxious about *his* political aspirations. He was announcing the kingdom of God, after all, and no one was aware that he had ever denied outright being the Messiah himself. Yet Jesus did not envisage God's kingdom being established by a popular uprising; any realist knew that such a thing was just what it would take to bring the legions marching from Syria, soaking the countryside in blood. His reticence was as much to protect Galilee as for his own security. It is significant that this caution never took the form of a public denial of messianic aspirations which could have settled the problem once and for all.

Little is said of this time, so ministry of the kind the gospels have previously described may have continued. However, the few incidents which are recorded confirm that Jesus was concentrating his attention on the twelve, and reveal the divergent directions in which their thoughts began to move.

A Suffering Son of Man?

Not long after the transfiguration Jesus made a second solemn utterance about his impending death. To appreciate its force one must imagine the disciples' state of mind. First, they had come to the point of confessing his messiahship and Jesus had not denied it. His kingship was acknowledged. Secondly, three of them had seen him mysteriously transformed and talking with Moses and Elijah. His kingship was confirmed. Then, as they descended the mountain, they encountered utter confusion. The other disciples had attempted to heal a demon-possessed boy and failed. A crowd was there to witness and share their distress; the power of evil was too strong for them, but Jesus rebuked the evil spirit and gave the boy back to his father healed. The power of his kingdom was displayed.

At this point, Luke tells us, the crowd was thunderstruck at the majesty of God. We can well imagine it, and it is impossible to think that Peter, James and John were not whispering something of what they had seen on the mountain to the other disciples. Thus, it was in the midst of the disciples' euphoria over his kingship that Jesus turned to them and said, 'Put these words in your ears, for the Son of Man is about to be delivered into human hands' (Luke 9:44).

We saw previously that Jesus spoke of himself as the Son of Man because for hostile or disinterested listeners it might be no more than a quaint way to speak of his own humanity. For himself and those who believed him to be the Messiah, however, it referred to the glorious Son of Man of Daniel 7. The large number of Jesus' Son of Man sayings which also envisage suffering has led many scholars to the conclusion that Jesus saw suffering as integral to the Son of Man concept. They point out that Daniel's Son of Man stands for the saints of the Most High who have been battered down by oppressive heathen empires. He is therefore a suffering figure. This appears to me to be mistaken. It is true that the tyrannical beasts of Daniel 7 have persecuted and oppressed the saints. However, there is nothing in Daniel's description which connects this suffering with the Son of Man. Quite the reverse: though he shares humanity with those he comes to save, he is depicted as a glorious figure whose destiny is power and dominion. It is difficult to see how any Jewish reader, Jesus included, could have made a sufferer of him on the basis of Daniel alone. He is the future king described in the most exalted terms found anywhere in the ancient Scriptures. Jesus' solemn words to the disciples should be seen, therefore, as deliberately paradoxical: the one who is destined to rule all peoples is about to be delivered into the hands of people. Small surprise that the disciples were unable to make any sense of it.

Who Will Be Greatest?
(Mark 9:33–37; Matthew 18:1–5; Luke 9:46–48)

The thrust of their thinking at that time is apparent in an incident recorded by all three synoptic writers. They had been arguing about who would be the greatest – naturally, if they imagined Jesus would soon set up a messianic regime. Back in the house in Capernaum Jesus took a small child in his arms to teach them that greatness in his kingdom had nothing to do with status. 'Whoever receives one such child in my name receives me, and whoever receives me, does not receive me, but the one who sent me'.

In human affairs the higher up you are the greater are the people with whom you associate. An army of public servants is in place to see that leaders are not bothered by people of lesser importance. People gauge their importance by the status of those whom they receive. To receive a president into your home is to be great yourself. But Jesus says that if, as a representative of his kingdom (in his name) you receive a child, you receive him, the King. The child in the first century was a person of very low status, but Jesus associates himself with the lowly to the extent that he reckons the way the child is treated as the way he is treated. How seriously he meant them to take him is seen in what he adds: to receive him is to receive God. He saw himself as the earthly representative of the heavenly Lord.

Who May Belong? (Mark 9:38–41; Luke 9:49–50)

It may have been on the same occasion that John drew to Jesus' attention that they had come across a stranger using Jesus' name to cast out demons. They had forbidden him to do so any longer, since he was not one of Jesus' travelling band. The twelve did not wish to lose control; if there was going to be a kingdom and they were the top men, they did not want people acting in Jesus' name without approval. But Jesus had no concern for that sort of exclusiveness. As he saw it a person acting in his name like that could hardly be against him. 'And whoever is not against us is for us!' – a remarkable statement implying that Jesus did not think it was possible for people, in the end, to be indifferent towards him.

Reacting To Opposition (Luke 9:51–56)

A third incident belongs a little later but Luke brackets it with these two episodes because of the way it reveals the disciples' state of mind at the time. Jesus sent his disciples into a Samaritan town to get food, but they were refused because they were Jews on the way to Jerusalem. There was strong antipathy between Jews and Samaritans, particularly when it came to pilgrimage. A few years later some Jewish pilgrims would be murdered on their way to Jerusalem. The animosity is understandable; the Samaritans' rival temple had been destroyed in 128 BC by the Jewish king, John Hyrcanus.[1] The feelings of the disciples at their treatment is also understandable. It was an insult to their Messiah and his kingdom. They urged him to let them call down fire from heaven upon the town. Elijah had once done something similar (2 Kings 1:9–15). But Jesus rebuked them and went elsewhere. Whatever he may previously have said about judgement on those who rejected the kingdom, it had nothing to do with a temperamental desire for revenge. Jesus wanted to see people saved from the judgement, even if ultimately their obstinacy might land them there anyway.

Feelings in Jerusalem (John 7:2–52; 8:12–10:21)

On one occasion during this last phase Jesus went to Jerusalem. The Feast of Tabernacles, the celebration of the ingathering of the harvest, took place in Autumn. In AD 29 it was October 12–19.[2] The most popular of the annual festivals, Tabernacles was celebrated by camping for the week in makeshift shelters, remembering the years of nomadic existence in the wilderness at the time of the exodus. At the Temple an elaborate water ritual took place commemorating God's provision of water from the rock, and anticipating the life-giving river that was expected to flow from Jerusalem in the messianic age. There was also a ceremony of lights and a wonderful torch dance.[3]

Although his brothers urged him to make a dramatic appearance at the feast, Jesus at first appeared unwilling to go. Only later when everyone else had left did he go up privately. People were on the look out for him and there was a great deal of speculation and debate. Some claimed he was a good man, others, probably with reports of the wilderness feeding in mind, thought he was leading the masses astray (John 7:12). The authorities were known to be against him, so people were careful about speaking openly. We can appreciate Jesus' caution. Towards the middle of the feast, when most would have concluded he was not coming, and the authorities were probably less wary, he suddenly appeared in the Temple and began teaching. People were amazed at his learning. Jesus claimed his teaching came from God. According to John, the city seethed with disagreement. Controversy focused on the question of Jesus' righteousness. If he were not righteous he could hardly speak for God; and had he not broken the Sabbath on his previous visit to Jerusalem, when he healed the man at the pool? Jesus retorted that they circumcised their children on the Sabbath, why should they be angry with him for making a whole man well? If circumcision, which could be viewed as a symbol of wholeness, took precedence over the Sabbath, how could restoring a crippled man be judged a sin? He urged them to exercise a true judgement.

John describes in some detail Jesus' teaching and the arguments it provoked, even relating an aborted attempt to have him arrested, and a spontaneous attempt to stone him. Most at issue was the question of who he claimed to be. The authorities were adamant that no one from Galilee could be a prophet – nor any Sabbath-breaker. Jesus then exacerbated the situation by healing a blind man on the Sabbath, even employing what could have appeared to be a medical cure. What he had done throughout the villages and countryside of Galilee he was now doing in the capital before the eyes of the theological elite. About his own identity Jesus remained enigmatic. He called to himself those who wished to experience the life-giving waters of the age-to-come and the light of the eternal kingdom, and he spoke of God as his Father in a way which to some sounded blasphemous, but it was difficult to be certain. He continued to refrain from any explicit messianic claim; it was for them to draw their own conclusions. Jesus went back to Galilee, presumably with the returning pilgrims, leaving Jerusalem acutely divided.[4]

Decision to Die

It could not have been long after his return from the Feast of Tabernacles that Jesus made the momentous decision to quit Galilee and head for where he knew death awaited him. There is no suggestion that he ever returned to Galilee during his natural lifetime.

'It happened when the days were fulfilled for him to be received up that he steeled his face to go to Jerusalem, and he sent messengers to go before him' (Luke 9:51–52). The gospel writer's statement is pregnant with his assessment of the meaning of Jesus' decision. The predestined time had now arrived for Jesus' 'assumption' (*analempsis*, a being taken up), in which term Luke probably includes his going up to Jerusalem, death, resurrection, and reception to the place of highest honour in the universe.[5] The way to this ascent to glory is rejection and death, and for these he must 'set his face like flint' as it was prophesied of the Suffering Servant (Isaiah 50:7).[6] At this point Luke is at his most theological. Whether his interpretation reflects Jesus' own thinking we will need to judge for ourselves as we continue to unpack the story. We have seen Jesus' preoccupation with impending suffering and also the mood of Jerusalem. We know Jesus envisaged his mission in terms of establishing God's kingdom. We have had some indication that he saw his death as instrumental in this, and that he looked forward to a future resurrection. Luke's statement, therefore, seems close to the mark. In any case it is clear from all the gospels that, for whatever reason, Jesus did at this time shift the focus of his operation from Galilee to the south.[7] Luke and Matthew go further, telling us his feelings about the outcome of the year-long mission in Galilee.

Result of the Mission in Galilee

How then did the Galilean mission end up? We traced Jesus' ministry of kingdom preaching, disciple gathering, healing, exorcism and teaching through Capernaum and around the lake. We saw how he widened the field of his kingdom-announcing by sending out the twelve into the many towns of Galilee, how this brought him to the notice of a much greater public, including the Tetrarch himself, and culminated in the unscheduled feeding of the five thousand. At that point, when his popularity was at an all time high and dangerous political feelings were being whipped up, Jesus withdrew to the north. Some time later he set out towards Caesarea Philippi and Peter made his crucial acknowledgement of Jesus' messiahship. The place of the transfiguration is unknown, though visitors to Israel are often taken to Mount Tabor. The scribes arguing with Jesus' disciples at the foot of the mountain show they were back in Jewish territory. Between the transfiguration and their departure to Judaea, Mark records only a visit to Capernaum and the teaching we have just reviewed. From this tiny amount of information it would be foolish to draw any conclusions about the latter end of the period in Galilee. It gives the impression that most of the public ministry was over by the feeding of the five thousand, but this may be only an impression, since at least six months were to elapse before Jesus' final departure.

What we do have are a series of sayings uttered as Jesus set out for Judaea, in which he expressed his feelings about the results of the Galilean mission. The first of these gives the impression of a failed campaign.

> Woe to you Chorazin, woe to you Bethsaida; because if the miracles that have happened among you had happened in Tyre and Sidon they would have repented by now, sitting in sackcloth and ashes. It will be more bearable in the judgement for Tyre and Sidon than for you. And you Capernaum, will you be exalted to

heaven? You will descend to the pit. (Luke 10:13–15; cf. Matthew 11:20–24)

Chorazin was three kilometres north of Capernaum. Bethsaida was the original home of Peter and Andrew. These places must have been especially favoured with disproportionate amounts of Jesus' teaching and miracle working. And yet they failed to turn to God. Capernaum's boast that she would ascend to heaven may have some basis in the previous history of the town, but more likely it describes the euphoria and pride that Jesus' presence and activity occasioned there. Yet the host town failed to bear the one kind of fruit that Jesus counted as worth anything. The people did not repent. The striking condemnation of Capernaum, echoing Isaiah's prediction of Babylon's fall (Isaiah 14:14–15), could only have come from Jesus; the tendency of later times was always to venerate the scene of a holy man's activities. The gospels do not indicate any conscious rejection of Jesus' person on the part of the inhabitants of Capernaum. It was more a question of a growing resistance to his central message of the kingdom and its concomitant demand for repentance. Jesus also hated the arrogance his ministry had brought to the surface. That he could declare his family not his family unless they heard and obeyed the word of God (Mark 3:33ff.; Luke 8:21), and could now resign to judgement his home of choice because it had not turned to God, shows how severe Jesus' judgements could be.

What Kind of Judgement?

What was this judgement to which Jesus consigned these towns of Galilee? Christians are accustomed, when they hear of judgement, always to think of the last day, when God is to raise the dead and call the whole world to account. John the Baptist and Jesus both speak of such a judgement. John saw it coming almost immediately, with the manifestation of the 'coming one'; Jesus, we have seen, focused on the present as a time of salvation. The idea of a great separation does not disappear, however; it is rather pushed forward to the end of the age.[8] Yet it does not appear that this judgement of every individual at the end of the age is what Jesus had in mind when he spoke of the fall of towns and cities. The clue to his meaning is given by his comparison with Sodom. He hardly imagined that Sodom as a city was to suffer a further collective judgement at the end of the age. It had perished in sulphurous fire two thousand years earlier.[9] Had it witnessed the signs that Capernaum witnessed, Jesus said, it might well have still been around. It will have been better for Sodom in its judgement than Capernaum.[10] This saying pictures a holocaust analogous to Israel's previous destruction by the armies of Babylon. Jesus' later prediction that the temple in Jerusalem would be overthrown makes it clear that this was his meaning.[11] Does this imply that with the offer of the kingdom of God rejected, and the possibility of its full revelation in the immediate future withdrawn, the Galilean cities would now be handed over to judgement in a historical form, to be executed by human agents of destruction? When we come to the mission of the seventy-two we shall see that this was so.

Was Jesus Bitter?

A number of nineteenth-century lives of Jesus concluded on the basis of Jesus' woes against these cities that he suffered disillusionment at the end of the Galilean ministry. Theodor Keim coined the expression 'Galilean springtime' to describe the first part of the ministry;[12] later Jesus was rejected and became angry and disillusioned. His denunciations were felt to be a regrettable though understandable regression from the joy and love of his early ministry. According to Renan, Jesus' 'wandering life, at first so full of charm, now began to weigh upon him ... Bitterness and reproach took more and more hold upon him ... He was not able to receive opposition with the coolness of the philosopher'. Renan excuses Jesus for what he calls a characteristic Semitic lack of polish and moderation.[13] Putting Renan's racial aspersions to one side, is this a fair assessment of Jesus' final reaction to his ministry in Galilee?

From very early in the ministry we have noted the background possibility of judgement if the offer of the kingdom was spurned. We have also seen that Jesus employed a strategy which took seriously the fickleness and unreliability of the response he was likely to get. John's comment, that he would not entrust himself to the people in Jerusalem who believed in him, 'because he knew all men ... and he knew what was in a man' (John 2:23–25), accords well with the character of Jesus' mission in Galilee, especially his withdrawal when they wanted to make a king of him. Jesus may well have been disappointed at the failure of his mission, but it is doubtful that he was taken by surprise. There is also a fundamental difference between an angry threat and a solemn judgement, though to the critic they may sound identical. Those who threaten wish to inflict an injury which need not be; those who warn speak of something which is inevitable unless urgent action is forthcoming. They speak in the hope that their warning will avert the crisis.

But did Jesus see his Galilean ministry as a failure? Other words he spoke not long afterwards are quite unlike what might be expected of a man suffering disillusionment.

> In the same hour he rejoiced in the Holy Spirit and said, 'I praise you Father, Lord of heaven and earth, because you have hidden these things from the wise and understanding and revealed them to babes. Yes Father, for such was your good pleasure. All things have been committed to me by my father, and no one knows who the son is except the father, and who the father is except the son, and whomever the son wills to reveal him.' (Luke 10:21–22; cf. Matthew 11:25–27)

According to Luke Jesus said this at the return of the seventy-two, but they look back on the whole of his ministry up to that time. The outcome of the later mission would have been little different to that of the former, as his warning to the missionaries not to rejoice in their outward success makes clear. The deeply predestinarian language in which Jesus' outburst of praise is couched expresses deep satisfaction at the achievement of God's sovereign purpose in the way things were turning out.[14] Though, judged at the human level his mission might be regarded a failure, seen from the point of view of the divine plan everything was proceeding according to God's predestined purpose. Many ordinary people had embraced the kingdom and its herald. The refusal of the 'wise and understanding' had not led the plan of God to miscarry, but was in reality part of that plan. Jesus implies that things could have been otherwise if God had so chosen; he could have overcome their resistance to his will, but withheld that grace (hardened their hearts),[15] so that they ran according to their own sinful instincts. Jesus' paradoxical joy is due first to his perception that what is happening is the will of the Lord of heaven and earth, but also no doubt because he trusts that his Father's plan is the expression of a wisdom which, though denying what would have seemed the obvious and immediate good, would finally achieve something immeasurably greater. Years later Paul agonized over this very question of Israel's refusal of Jesus, and concluded that God had hardened a part so that the full manifestation of the kingdom might be delayed, and a door of opportunity opened to Gentiles. Eventually the blindness would be removed and the Messiah would return to his people (Romans 9–11).

Jesus' words give an impression of finality and satisfaction. Though the mission marked the end of one stage of his work and the beginning of another, it was no transition from failure to a fresh try elsewhere. The plan of God was treading its appointed path. The 'babes' destined to see the light had seen it. Necessary truth had been imparted. For the moment it seemed to have been to no avail; its positive results would lie in the future. For now the work in Galilee was complete.

Proclaiming the Kingdom to Judaea (Luke 10:1–24)

The decision to head for Jerusalem entailed the recruitment and briefing of a team of seventy-two disciples to precede him into all the towns he was planning to visit. I do not suppose this means that Jesus himself visited all the villages; he probably travelled from area to area, with the thirty-six teams fanning out to cover the surrounding countryside; and the whole operation concluding in Jerusalem. If this corresponds to the historical facts, the mission of the seventy, as it is usually known, cannot but be of vital significance to our understanding of Jesus' mission.

Was There A Second Disciple Mission?

But is it history? The fact that it is related only by Luke has caused some to suggest that it arose from a confused telling of the mission of the twelve.[16] When gospel scholarship was dominated by the quest for the literary sources underlying every sentence of the gospels it was common to doubt anything that was not to be found in Mark or Q, and to treat similar stories and sayings as variant forms of one underlying original ('doublets'). But why should Mark and Q be the only reliable sources? Luke says that he received information from many sources, written and oral (Luke 1:1–2). Two of these (Mark and Q) we can identify. There is no reason to think his other sources were any less reliable. As for the so-called doublet theory: it is possible that two variant oral accounts of the same event might, with the passage of generations, diverge from each other enough to look like two different events. But that Luke should make a blunder of this magnitude, writing only thirty years after the events (or even fifty) stretches the imagination. No matter what written sources he may have employed, he was still within the memory range of living witnesses.

Indications within the story itself also vouch for its authenticity. First, there is good reason for thinking Q contained an account of both missions. That Matthew's composite mission discourse contains most of Jesus' charge to the seventy-two suggests that there was a version of the mission of the seventy-two in Q. But there are also indications that it contained an account of the mission of the twelve.[17] Although the likelihood of two separate missions in Q does not absolutely settle the question, it does move the two accounts closer to Jesus' ministry and greatly strengthens the presumption in favour of historicity.

The second indication of the second mission's historicity is Jesus' saying about the harvest being plentiful, but the labourers few (Luke 10:2). The disciples are urged to pray to the Lord of the harvest to send out labourers. This does not fit the first mission, limited to the twelve.[18] It implies an occasion in Jesus' ministry when he was experiencing difficulty finding the numbers of suitable missionaries to cover the ground. Indeed, we even have the account of someone offering for service, if only he may first go and say farewell to his family.[19]

A third indication is the dramatic difference in the instructions that were given to the two groups of missionaries. Mark is quite insistent that the twelve were to wear sandals, almost as though he knew there was some confusion on the point. This on its own would raise the suspicion that there had been a mission in which footwear was forbidden; the confusion is readily explained by the curious instruction to the seventy-two not to wear shoes. The demand is so strange that it would hardly have been invented, nor would it have been easily forgotten.

What about the suggestion that Luke has invented the number seventy for symbolic reasons?[20] It would be a stronger argument against historicity if it were clear that this was the number. The manuscripts are so evenly divided between seventy and seventy-two that the Bible Society text of the Greek New Testament leaves which number was original an open question. However, the oldest existing manuscript of Luke (p[75] – second or third century) has the reading seventy-two, and it is hard to imagine a scribe altering seventy to 'seventy-two'; copyists tend to simplify what is complex, not the reverse. The symbolism of the number seventy is so rich that if it were original it would surely have been preserved.[21] On the other hand, it is readily understandable that a copyist might change seventy-two to seventy in the interests of both symbolism and simplicity.[22]

If Luke (and Q) originally recorded that Jesus chose seventy-two extra missionary preachers it is doubtful that his interests were primarily symbolic. Seventy-two sounds like a number related to the original choice of twelve. Perhaps each of the twelve was to take charge of three pairs, or maybe each of the initial six pairs was given a group of twelve to lead. We cannot be sure, but certainly seventy-two is more in line with the practical logistics of a further mission, than with theological symbolism of uncertain reference. We may safely conclude that such a mission did take place. Jesus selected seventy-two additional disciples and sent them ahead of him into the various places he was intending to go.

Barefoot Missionaries (Luke 10:4–12)

Ancient readers of the gospels were troubled by the apparent contradictions in Jesus' instructions in the various mission accounts. Different attempts have been made to account for his command to wear shoes, and not to wear shoes. Perhaps he forbade heavy shoes but allowed sandals. There is also a problem with staffs. Part of the answer lies in the fact of two missions, elements of both of which are found intertwined in Matthew. But why the difference and why in particular the strange prohibition of shoes in the latter mission?

It was forbidden to wear shoes in the temple, so the suggestion has been made that Jesus was indicating that the land they trod was holy ground – until it proved hostile to the message of the kingdom?[23] But then why were the twelve not similarly attired on their mission? So was it a symbol of impending judgement, as when Isaiah prophesied naked to warn of coming captivity (Isaiah 20)? This seems out of character with the positive message of the nearness of the kingdom Jesus' missionaries carried.

There are several clues which point to a simpler explanation: Could Jesus have intended these barefoot messengers to remind people of those beautiful feet which, according to Isaiah (Isaiah 52:7) were to appear on the mountains and proclaim to the cities of Judah the arrival of God's kingdom of peace?

> How beautiful on the mountains are the feet of the *gospeller*, who announces peace, who *gospels* good, who announces salvation, who says to Zion, 'Your God reigns'.

The couriers of ancient Israel were marathon runners. When they reached their destination after a twenty or thirty kilometre race over rough ground their feet were not likely to have been a pretty sight. Yet scratched and bloodied though they may have been, they were beautiful feet if their owner carried good news. In this case they carried the best: God has arrived to rescue his people.

Jesus sent the seventy-two out barefoot and carrying nothing, though few were likely to have been toughened runners. They were to greet no one because they were couriers of urgent news. The coming of the kingdom and the declaration of peace, the content of Isaiah's herald's message, is precisely the news that was born by Jesus' couriers. When they reached their destinations they must have been a footsore and bloodied spectacle, and it would not have taken a great leap of the imagination for some to see in them a possible fulfilment of prophecy. It must have created a stir, and that surely was Jesus' intention. What a brilliant communicator he was! Isaiah's prophecy hardly calls for such a literalistic fulfilment, but Jesus sent his messengers attired so that people hearing the kingdom announced and witnessed its power in the healing of their sick, could not help but see a visible fulfilment of Isaiah's promised herald, appearing on the mountains of Judah, proclaiming the coming of God's salvation. There for those who had eyes to see was another sign of the kingdom.

As with the previous mission, the response to their call was to determine the destiny of whole towns. They were Jesus' agents and he was God's. The response to them was deemed to be the response to him, and the response to him, the response to God (Luke 10:16). The town that rejected them would suffer a fate worse than Sodom's. The offer was wonderful, but as in Galilee, it was a final offer.

Final Offer

How final the offer presented by the seventy-two was may be judged from two of Jesus' later sayings. He tells the crowds who follow him that they are very good at interpreting weather patterns. From the formation of the clouds and from the direction of the wind they know what sort of weather is coming: rain or scorching heat. How can it be then, he asks, that they do not seem able to interpret the happenings of the present time (Luke 12:54–56)? Then he appeals to them through a parable which shows how much his message was shifting from the positive offer of the kingdom to its negative counterpart, and how urgent the situation had become.

> Why are you not judging for yourselves what is right? For as you are going with your opponent before the authorities, work hard to reach a settlement with him in the way, lest he drag you before the judge, and the judge deliver you to the officer, and the officer throw you in prison. I tell you, you will not get out from there until you have paid the last cent (*lepton*). (Luke 12:57–59)

Taken on its own this could be a practical lesson on avoidance of court cases and the need to work hard at reaching settlement with an offended neighbour. In the context of Jesus' message of the kingdom and here in Luke it carries a greater meaning.[24] The last opportunity for a favourable settlement has arrived. It is as though they are debtors being hustled to court by their creditor. They are already on the way, yet there is still time to reach a settlement if they will seize it. The time is near when that opportunity will be lost. The forces of justice once unleashed will leave no stone upon another. Before Jesus' mind loomed an approaching catastrophe, which need not happen should the salvation which God was offering be accepted, but was inevitable if it were not. The shape of that cataclysm was a destruction of the nation in the near future. Once, when his attention was drawn to a massacre of Galileans, Jesus asked whether they thought the victims were worse sinners than everyone else. In fact, he warned, if they did not repent they would all perish in a similar way (Luke 13:1–5). In the parable of the fig tree that follows the gardener begs for time to do all in his power to make the tree fruitful. If he fails, he allows that there would then be no alternative to felling the tree (Luke 13:6–9). The fig tree was an obvious image of Israel.

Thus the sending out of the seventy-two and Jesus' departure for Jerusalem brought the whole eschatological timetable to a new state of urgency. The people along the way were to receive their last invitation to embrace the kingdom of God while it was present and open to them. Jerusalem too would then have its last opportunity, though it had already had many.[25]

Jesus' Vision

The missionaries did as they were told and returned to Jesus in a state of high excitement. What elated them most was that even the demons had obeyed the commands they had given in his name. He saw their victory as the coming true of a dream, that one day human beings would trample the Devil. 'God the Lord, the Great One in Israel, will be manifest upon the earth [as a man].[26] By himself he will save Adam. Then all the spirits of error shall be given over to being trampled underfoot. And men will have mastery over the evil spirits' (Testament of Simeon 6:5–6). This and other statements from the second century BC document the *Testaments of the Twelve Patriarchs* reflect a pre-Christian expectation, grounded on the promise of Genesis 3:15, of a future reversal of the satanic defeat of the human race.[27] The promise that the seed of the woman would one day bruise the serpent's head indicated an eventual victory of Adam's descendants. At Jesus' temptation we observed Satan still flaunting his authority over the earth, but Jesus greets the missionaries' return with the assertion of a dream: 'I saw Satan fallen like lightning from heaven' (Luke 10:18). We cannot say when Jesus had this vision, nor what its nature was, nor from his statement when the vision would be fulfilled. The aorist 'fallen' indicates simply that he foresaw it as an accomplished fact; the success of the seventy-two brought it back to his mind. A week before his death Jesus was still calling Satan 'the ruler of this world,' but declaring that this would cease as a result of his death.[28] Thus Jesus did not view his disciples' exorcisms as constitutive of Satan's defeat. They were proleptic signs of something greater lying ahead. That is why his thoughts ran beyond the excitement of that moment to what he saw as the ultimate fruits of Satan's fall: 'do not rejoice that the demons submit to you, but that your names have been written in heaven' (Luke 10:20).

The jubilant disciples were not to rejoice in their authority over the forces of darkness, which was partial, and of doubtful ultimate value. Satan was far from being a spent force, and worse tribulation than they could imagine still lay ahead. Their ultimate security and the ground of their deepest joy should be that God in his mercy had inscribed their names in the book of life.[29] If that were so, come what may they would stand at the end amongst the truly living. Jesus' ultimate goal in storming the satanic stronghold was nothing less than the rescue of human beings and their transfer to the kingdom of God.[30] Thus Jesus went on in words we have already discussed to praise God for revealing the truth to the chosen 'babes'. And so, in words of deep significance for our inquiry, Jesus blessed his disciples privately. With this Luke closes his account of the mission of the seventy-two: 'Happy are the eyes that are seeing what you see. For I tell you that many prophets and kings wished to see what you are seeing and did not see it, and to hear what you are hearing, and did not hear it' (Luke 10:23). The disciples are the babes to whom Jesus has revealed the mysteries of the kingdom of God. They know him for who he is, and knowing him they know his Father. They are the remnant chosen from eternity in the good pleasure of the Lord of Heaven and Earth, who, in the midst of Israel's blindness, have been chosen to see. To see what? Nothing less than what prophets foretold and kings prefigured, 'the desire of all nations', God visiting his people in the person of his anointed King. This saying leaves no doubt that Jesus saw the kingdom of God present in their midst, though in a form that only those who were born again from above could see.

The Journey to Jerusalem

For most of the history in this chapter we have depended heavily on Luke. Where Matthew and Mark simply record that Jesus went south to Judaea and Peraea, Luke relates Jesus' momentous decision to go to death in Jerusalem, and tells of the recruitment and instruction of disciples, their sending forth, an unpleasant episode in Samaria, and their eventual return.[31] The journey, however, continues from Luke 9 to Luke 19, giving the impression of a solemn march culminating in Jerusalem amidst crowds of pilgrims a week before Passover. This 'journey' is one of the distinctive characteristics of the Gospel of Luke.

The Gospel of John, on the other hand, has Jesus in Jerusalem at the Feast of Dedication three months previous to the final Passover, and in Peraea in the period between (John 10:22, 40). How are we to deal with this conflict? It has chiefly been handled by treating John as non-historical, dismissing Luke's mission of the seventy-two as a doublet, yet agreeing with his picture of a single journey from Galilee to Jerusalem.[32] Following this procedure, Jesus is seen completing his Galilean ministry and making a final, perhaps meandering journey to Jerusalem for a showdown with the authorities. But to discount John's information for this period is perilous, especially when it is partially corroborated by Mark.[33] Luke uses the 'journey' as a literary vehicle to carry the majority of Jesus' teaching, so his stylized account of Jesus' journey to death and exaltation may deliberately ignore much coming and going. We are dealing with a period of some five months here, between the sending out of the seventy-two and the final Passover.

If for the moment we accept that between his departure from Galilee and his arrival in Jerusalem at Passover, Jesus was at least once in Jerusalem, and spent some time in Peraea, does anything remain of Luke's 'journey'? To be fair, he says that Jesus 'set his face to go to Jerusalem', not that he made a neatly describable single trip. This would not preclude a preliminary appearance in Jerusalem, nor an amount of ministry in Peraea between the time of his decision and his final arrival in Jerusalem. What it means is that from the time of that decision Jesus' mind was made up that he must bring his ministry to its God-intended climax in Jerusalem. From then everything was taking him closer to that goal.

When Did the Mission of the Seventy-Two Take Place?

Jesus and the seventy-two must have completed their journey in Jerusalem (Luke 9:53). Between the Passover at which he fed the five thousand and the final Passover, John records his presence in Jerusalem at two other feasts. The first was Tabernacles, which in AD 29 took place in mid-October, six months after the first miracle of the loaves (John 7:1ff.). The second was Dedication, two months later (John 10:22ff.). Of the period between Tabernacles and Dedication John says nothing; for some of the time between Dedication and the last Passover Jesus was in Peraea (John 10:40ff.).

One of the distinctive features of Maurice Goguel's reconstruction of Jesus' ministry is his identification of the journey to Jerusalem with John's visit of Jesus to Jerusalem for the Feast of Tabernacles.[34] According to Goguel, Jesus came to Jerusalem in October and remained there until the feast of Dedication in December. Towards the end of the period he spoke of destroying the temple and raising it again in three days, and was forced to leave Jerusalem for Peraea. On his return at Passover Jesus made his 'triumphal entry'. But it is hard to see how the secret and unprepared trip to the Feast of Tabernacles which John describes could possible correspond to one which was preceded by the recruitment and sending ahead of scores of disciples. According to John, Jesus was goaded by his brothers to go up to Jerusalem for the feast of Tabernacles and go 'national' (international?) with his mission. He withstood their efforts with the assertion that *his time had not yet come*. One can only be struck with the contrast between this and Luke's statement that the mission of the seventy-two was triggered by Jesus' realization that *the time for his going up was fulfilled*. One expresses a feeling of *not yet*, the other of *now*. There is no improbability in supposing that after Tabernacles Jesus returned to Galilee as after every other feast, until he judged the time was ripe for a decisive revelation of himself in Judaea and Jerusalem.

From Tabernacles to Dedication was only two months. It must have been in this period, therefore, that the mission of the seventy-two took place, since Jesus was in Peraea after Dedication. Given the shortness of the period the mission would have ended not long before or during the Feast of Dedication. John says that Jesus was met at Dedication with the demand that he state clearly if he was the Messiah (John 10:22–24). He still refused to give a decisive answer, but the close relationship with God implied by his manner of speech seemed blasphemous to the Jerusalem Jews and he escaped another attempt on his life by fleeing to the other side of the Jordan (John 10:25–42).

Why Did Jesus Flee?

Why Jesus did not bring his mission to a climax at the feast of Dedication we are not told. Apparently the time or the circumstances were not quite right. Although the opposition was real enough, perhaps it had not crystallized to the point of an outright rejection of him by the city. There were murderous feelings, which periodically threatened to erupt in a spontaneous lynching, as had happened once before in Nazareth. But that would not have constituted a decision of the city or the nation. People in Jerusalem, the authorities themselves, were still making up their minds about Jesus. Something would need to happen to bring that process to a head. According to John that something was occasioned by the unexpected death of one of Jesus' closest friends.

Thus the real end of the journey which Luke intimates did not come at the end of AD 29 with the conclusion of the mission of the seventy-two, but three months later, after a short exile in Peraea, and a time of lying low in Ephraim. Whether this fits the definition of a journey is for the reader to decide. It began with a decision in Galilee to bring things to a head in Jerusalem and it ended on a Roman gallows. The gospel writers give us the beginning and the end; they are somewhat hazy about what happened in the middle. Two features of the inside of this 'journey' stand out: the disciples' absorption with questions of power, and Jesus' preoccupation with his approaching suffering and death. We will consider each in turn.

The Power And The Glory

Following Peter's momentous recognition of the Messiah at Caesarea Philippi, the mind of Jesus and the minds of his disciples divided along two very different tracks. The Messiah was to be Israel's king. He was to set up a government more glorious than that of David and Solomon, to bring peace to Israel and blessing to the world. Against many contraindications the twelve were now convinced that Jesus was this king, and strange as it must have seemed to them, he had chosen them as his closest confidants and indicated to them a role in judging (i.e. ruling) the twelve tribes. It is understandable, therefore, that, unwilling or unable to make sense of Jesus' premonition of death, their thoughts should have turned to questions of government and their own future privilege. This preoccupation continued right up to Jesus' arrest and execution. Jesus did nothing to divest them of a political understanding of his messiahship and kingdom – if he did, there is no record of it. Whatever he had been doing previously in the north, he had not been teaching his disciples 'a higher view of messiahship', or, if he had, he had completely failed to get through.

Somewhere in the 'journey' period an incident occurred which clarifies for us the very different thinking of Jesus and his followers at that time, but underlines their common conviction about a real kingdom in this world. 'James and John, the sons of Zebedee approach him saying, "Teacher, we want you to do for us what we ask of you." He said to them, "What do you want me to do for you?" They said to him, "Grant that one of us may sit on your right and one on your left in your glory" (Mark 10:35–37). In Matthew's version it is the mother of the two men who petitions Jesus. She was Jesus' aunt so this is not unlikely.[35] Jesus himself may well have been the cause of this jockeying for position among the disciples – at Caesarea Philippi he told Peter of the special role he was assigning to him in the kingdom. Peter had just declared Jesus to be the Christ and Jesus responded with the words:

> Blessed are you Simon bar Jona, for flesh and blood has not revealed this to you, but my Father in heaven. And I say to you that you are Peter, and on this rock I will build my church (*ekklesia*), and the gates of Hades will not be victorious against it. I will give you the keys of the kingdom of heaven; whatever you bind on the earth will be bound in heaven and whatever you loose on the earth will be loosed in heaven. (Matthew 16:16–19)

The historical accuracy of this report (found only in Matthew) has frequently been assailed, because of its absence from Mark and its seemingly anachronistic talk of church.[36] However it is the translation 'church' which is anachronistic, not Jesus' statement. *Ekklesia* (Hebrew *qahal*) is one of two common words used in the Greek Old Testament to describe the people of Israel when they gathered as a community, or when they were thought of in communal terms. When Moses brought the Israelites out of Egypt he assembled them as God's *qahal* at Mt Sinai and God constituted them as his kingdom. Kingdom and 'church' are correlate terms, the one describing Israel politically, the other communally. From their coming into Canaan they would gather year by year at the national festivals as 'the great - assembly'. Talk of such a community would not have been strange to the disciples. It fitted perfectly with Jesus' intention to gather the community of God's restored people. What must have sounded odd was his reference to it as *his* assembly. Surely only God could say that – or perhaps the promised King, destined to represent God on earth.

Jesus declares here his intention to build an eternal community. The gates of Hades (Sheol) have nothing to do with hell (Gehenna). The reference is to death, visualized as an invincible kingdom through whose gates all living creatures must pass and never return. Jesus asserts that the grave will never swallow up his community. In saying he will build the community *at* or *on this rock* Jesus may be alluding to Mt Sinai (the rock Horeb) where the original Israelite *qahal* was formed. Just as at the rock Horeb God constituted the rabble of Israel as the congregation of his people, so now Jesus intends to raise a new community of those who acknowledge him as God's King.[37] Peter, as first to make this confession of faith, is the first stone in the building (*petros* means stone, as does the Aramaic equivalent *kephas*). It follows from this way of looking at Jesus' words that Peter's uniqueness lies in his being first to make the confession of faith; as others follow him they too will be incorporated as stones into the building, an idea clearly expressed in 1 Peter 2:5.

Jesus then promised to give Peter the keys of the kingdom. Again we must beware of anachronistic interpretations that would have been meaningless to the disciples. In the old kingdom of Judah the keeper of the keys was a state official of great authority and importance, akin to a minister of home affairs in a modern government. He was probably second to the king. Isaiah declared that God would hurl just such an official out of his office and replace him with another (Isaiah 22:15–25). Peter was to have the keys of the kingdom of heaven, so the decisions of the opener and closer, the binder and looser, would affect not only earthly things but the very relationship between heaven and earth.[38] We can see what kind of office Jesus might have been seen to be offering Peter, and how easily an avalanche of speculation could have been set off among the other disciples. Peter had been indicated his place. What about the others? It is interesting that the next ones we hear about are James and John, the two disciples who with Peter formed the inner circle of the disciple group.

In reply Jesus described to them the style of government they were familiar with, but as an object lesson in how it was not to be amongst them. Those who seem to rule the Gentiles lord it over their people. Positions of status are seen in terms of how many people someone has at their disposal, to be commanded and to do their bidding. Government is like a pyramid with the person at the top commanding all, and being served by all. Those at their left and right hands are next in line; they must obey the top man, but can in turn expect to have everyone else at their service. Jesus did not want it to be so among his followers. Whoever wishes to be great must be a servant, and the person who wishes to be number one must be the slave of everyone. The pyramid of government is effectively inverted. The person at the top (bottom) is serving everyone; the higher up (or lower down) you go the more people you have to serve. He, the King, has come to make himself the servant of all. In this manner Jesus began to show his disciples the radical difference between the kingdom of God and the kingdoms of the present world.

To What Degree did Jesus Change his Disciples' Idea of the Kingdom?

How radically did Jesus alter the disciples' ideas of the kingdom? We have seen that he challenged their exclusiveness; he taught them that greatness in the kingdom comes through serving rather than wielding power, and that status is obtained through associating with the little people and not with the greats. Does any of this amount to a complete overthrow of the Old Testament idea of a real, material and political messianic kingdom? Jesus has not challenged this notion at all. In reply to James' and John's request he freely admitted that there were places of honour at his right hand and at his left. They were just not his to award.

Thus there is little justification for the notion, common amongst Christians, that Jesus struggled valiantly to divest his thick-headed disciples of their earthly Jewish ideas of kingdom and messiahship in favour of a 'spiritual' view.[39] There is nothing unspiritual about the prophets' hope of a world renewed under the government of a God-loving, people-loving, peace-loving king, unless by spiritual we mean non-material. The Jews did not equate spiritual with non-material. To the very end Jesus presented the kingdom to them in 'political' terms, albeit ultimate political terms. We must use the term 'political' with caution, since a regime that entails resurrection, universal judgement, the abolition of death, and a transformation of the environment involves radically different political structures to those we are familiar with. Nevertheless, in 'kingdom of God' Jesus chose a deliberately political term, which signified for the Jews the consummation of their political life, as well as the final solution to the world's political strife, in an ultimate, glorious messianic government. Jesus insisted this could not come without him suffering, but this hardly transforms his understanding into something out of this world. Even after the resurrection we find his disciples asking, 'Lord will you *now* restore the kingdom to Israel?' And him answering, not that they have totally misunderstood, but only that the time is not yet (Acts 1:6–8). What awaited Jesus in Jerusalem at the end of the journey was not government and glory but rejection and death. However, he never thought these would be the end of his story. Rather, death was to be instrumental in establishing the kingdom.

Why Must Jesus Die?

Immediately after Peter's confession Jesus began to speak seriously to his disciples about the necessity of suffering if he was to fulfil his mission (Mark 8:31). In this first so-called passion prediction he told his disciples that he would be rejected by the elders, chief priests and scribes (i.e. ruling Jewish officialdom), be killed and after three days rise again. The same thing is repeated in Mark on two further occasions (Mark 9:31; 10:32–34). In the last of these Jesus added that the Jews would deliver him to the Gentiles.

Rationalistic theology has generally rejected these predictions because they express supernatural knowledge and must therefore be the work of later Christians putting sayings into Jesus' mouth. Other scholars, without such presuppositions, have been happy to accept that Jesus could well have predicted his death. A third approach has pursued the idea that Jesus was an astute enough observer of events to know which way the political tide was running, a fourth that he had determined to act in such a way as to make execution inevitable. Albert Schweitzer thought that Jesus was forced to the desperate expedient of engineering his own rejection and death by the failure of the kingdom to appear during the mission of the twelve. By giving himself up as a sacrifice for the people's sins he would forcibly roll the wheel of history and bring in the new age.[40] Vincent Taylor thought that Jesus spent a long period in the north reflecting on his failure to move Galilee to repentance, reaching the conclusion that he must suffer.[41]

We have already seen that as early as the Sermon on the Mount Jesus saw himself engaged in the mission of the teaching, suffering Servant of Yahweh. In the period of the 'journey' we find, in addition to the three 'passion predictions', a number of other outbursts in which he expresses iron determination to confront an unpleasant ordeal that was in some manner necessary to the accomplishment of his mission (Mark 10:38; Luke 11:47–51; 12:49f.; 13:32–34; 14:25–27; John 10:11, 17–18). The sense of inevitability which characterizes some of these sayings could be viewed as a fatalistic realization that death would surely soon catch up with him. John the Baptist had been killed for less, and Jesus now had as many enemies as he. Already in Nazareth he had experienced an attempt on his life. Yet Jesus could have avoided death had he so wished. Several times he extracted himself from dangerous situations.[42] For the most part the trouble was provoked by his own presence and activity, particularly in Jerusalem. He could have stayed in Galilee, or if that became risky, gone north as on a previous occasion. The reality is that Jesus set off south to the very place where he knew the greatest danger lay. Even in Jerusalem the crisis could have been defused. He could have ceased to provoke the scribes on sensitive matters like the Sabbath, and softened his attacks on their integrity. On the super-sensitive issue of whether he was the Messiah he could easily have put their minds at rest.

We have already noted Jesus' awareness that a premature messianic claim would bring about his swift demise. If he really believed himself to be the Messiah – and it seems to me a desperate expedient to deny it – he could have expected only one of two things once he made his claim open. Either it would be accepted and the nation would stand to do his bidding, or rejected, and the form of that rejection did not require too great a political imagination. An overt claim to be the King–Messiah was exactly the kind of move which could be predicted to bring an immediate death sentence – even a sentence of crucifixion, depending on the circumstances in which it was made.[43] The alternatives were the uprising of his followers to support him militarily, which it was clearly his intention to avoid, or the agreement of the nation to his claim, which Jesus knew in the circumstances was unlikely. We can well appreciate the sombre resolution with which he set his face to go to Jerusalem. It was a question of taking his cause to the one place where it could be ratified or rejected, or abandoning it altogether. Jesus went, knowing that the only way to his ultimate goal was first to allow a decisive rejection.

Martyr or Redeemer?

The question that troubles us as we contemplate the life of Jesus is *why* he viewed death as a necessity. It cannot be said that the gospels are full of information on this point. For all that is said today about their being theological documents, they submitted themselves to a severe limitation in presenting the deeds and words of Jesus himself. To get a comprehensive theological explanation of his death we need to go to the other New Testament writings. Nevertheless, it is important for us to know how much of what Christians were later to believe was anticipated by

Jesus himself. To learn his interpretation of his death we are confined to his own words. Prior to the last supper the most telling are those he spoke to the disciples when James and John made their request for precedence in the new kingdom. 'Whoever wishes to be first among you must be the servant of all. For the Son of Man himself came not to be served, but to serve and to give his life as a ransom for many' (Mark 10:44–45).

Jesus evidently saw his death as central to the purpose of his coming, providing a positive service in the rescuing of people's lives. Thus far there has been little to suggest that Jesus' death might have a positive effect. We have seen that death was a very likely prospect, if he continued his provocative kingdom preaching, and almost a certainty if he openly claimed to be the Messiah. Yet the only positive effect one can imagine in a death like this is the example of a brave martyr's witness, and this needs to be balanced with the negative effect of bringing judgement on those who sought his death. This is a far cry from a *service* of many or indeed of any, and one struggles to see how even a hero's death could be instrumental in establishing the kingdom of God, unless it were to force God's hand as Schweitzer suggested. But that would go directly against Jesus' earlier determination not to test God.

'A ransom for many' indicates that Jesus saw his death paying a price that would set people free. The ransoming of slaves and captives was common practice in Roman times, familiar to Gentiles and Jews. The Jews regarded the ransoming of prisoners and Jewish slaves as a valuable act of piety.[44] Redemption had a rich background in Israel's history. The whole nation had been 'redeemed' from slavery in Egypt. Because it is not immediately clear that a ransom price was involved in this transaction – it was effected by divine force – it has been conjectured that redemption in the Old Testament lost its reference to a price paid and became simply a metaphor of rescue from slavery. Everywhere else though, redemption terminology maintains the idea of payment or sacrificial substitution,[45] and closer reflection on the exodus reveals its presence there also. For Israel only escaped the death that fell on every firstborn by the substitution of a Passover lamb in every family, and from that time on every firstborn male was redeemed with a half shekel. Behind these rituals stands the idea that the lives of the first-born sons – heirs and representatives of the whole people – were forfeit unless ransomed.[46] Jesus' avoidance of attempts on his life, until he appeared deliberately in Jerusalem at Passover, must surely be seen in the light of this. In using ransom termi-nology, then, Jesus attempted to inform his disciples that his death would result in the liberation of 'many' from some form of bondage comparable to Israel's Egyptian enslavement. The Roman yoke would have sprung immediately to their minds, though how his death could effect release from that must have baffled them. They should have recalled that Jesus had always targeted Satan as the real tyrant, and indicated his intention to rescue captives from that quarter.[47] 'A ransom for (instead of) many' (*lutron anti pollon*) indicates that Jesus saw his death providing the payment necessary to effect release. For an answer to how that might be we must wait until the night before his death.

Jesus' Death And the Restoration Community

The Gospel of John contains another significant saying that rein-forces what we have just seen. It comes at the end of a discourse occasioned by the request to see Jesus of some Greeks visiting Jerusalem at Passover (John 12:20–33). Jesus begins by speaking of the need for a seed to die if it is to bear much fruit, and con-cludes with the words: 'Now is the judgement of this world. Now the ruler of this world will be cast out. And I, if I am lifted up from the earth, will draw all people to myself.' It is one of the vagaries of book writing that one begins a theme and never concludes it. Mark's great unfinished theme is Jesus' conflict with Satan; the first half of his gospel is full of it, and then it fades away and is never brought to any obvious resolution. Luke takes it one stage further when he records Jesus' words on the return of the seventy-two that he had seen Satan fallen like lightning from heaven. But it is left to John to give some final sense and resolution to this conflict. It is also another of those accidental tie-ups between the different gospels which assure us that we are dealing with a man of history, whose story was bigger than any one writer could tell.

Jesus saw his death as the historic turning point, at which the authority of Satan over the human race would be broken and he, Jesus, would be raised up as the new Lord, to gather people of all nations to himself, Greeks included.[48] Could this have been in his mind since the days of his desert ordeal? There we saw Jesus emerge from a period of battle with the one who, because of his hold on human beings, could rightly claim to be called the ruler of this world. Flinging every temptation afforded by the circumstances, the Devil sought to turn Jesus from his Father and bring him under the influence of his own will. He did not succeed; Jesus maintained unbroken trust in God and remained his own man. But that was only a preliminary skirmish.

We saw Satan seek to abort Jesus' mission through the hostile revelations of the demon possessed; we saw the suggestion of his manipulative malice behind the attempts of Jesus' family to use their influence to remove him from his field of work; we even saw his own chief disciple become a front for Satan's efforts to dissuade him from his commitment to suffer. We will see something similar at his betrayal, and finally in the temptations which fell upon him in the garden on the night of his arrest. There was no relenting: even as Jesus suffered physical torture he was urged to do a miracle and come down from the cross.

The cross would be the last battle. For at the end, in the effort to tempt Jesus to retreat, Satan would push him so close to the precipice of death that he would fall, and then at last one of Adam's sons would have run the gauntlet to the end. One man would have fulfilled his destiny without surrendering to the enemy the lordship that was meant to belong to human beings. Jesus looked beyond death to his glorification as the Son of Man destined to rule the nations, when he would draw to himself the multinational community of the new age (John 12:23). Did he see this purely in terms of his own lordship, or also in the power of a redemptive death which could generate a kingdom of forgiven people by cancelling out the guilt which gave Satan his authority?[49] Jesus spoke of a seed, which if it fell into the earth and died would produce much fruit. Such focus on the effect of death could suggest the latter was also in his mind. His death would bring the new community into being, both by establishing him as King, and by releasing his future subjects from the guilt that held them under the sway of the kingdom of darkness.

Jesus viewed his death, therefore, as something essentially positive: necessary to bring into being the community of the kingdom. This does not mean he did not die a martyr's death; in holding to his course, faithful to the will of God even in the face of death, Jesus bore testimony to God's lordship as his ultimate concern. But that was incidental to the purpose which drew him step by step to a death which would redeem and liberate the many into the freedom of God's kingdom.

The Disciples and the Cross

At several stages in the course of the last journey we are given glimpses of the excitement of the crowds who expected Jesus to make a move on the government when he got to Jerusalem. At the same time we are reminded of Jesus' solemn commitment to a confrontation which he knew would end in his humiliation and death. These conflicting sentiments interacted at one point to produce passionate words[50] – words which reveal a wish that he should not go to death alone.

> If anyone comes to me and does not hate his father and mother
> and wife and children and brothers and sisters, yes and even his
> own life, he cannot be my disciple. Whoever does not carry his
> own cross and follow after me cannot be my disciple ... Whoever
> of you who does not bid farewell to all that is his cannot be my
> disciple. (Luke 14:25–33)

It is an extraordinary statement on the part of one who counted
love as the greatest commandment, and castigated the Pharisees
for providing loopholes for people to dodge their obligations to
their parents. The clue to what Jesus meant is to be found in a
consideration of his own behaviour. At the beginning of his
ministry he had to turn his back on the normal obligations and
expectations of an eldest son when the father was no longer alive.
Later, when the family tried to reclaim Jesus, he repulsed them in
a way that could only have been extremely hurtful. 'Who are my
mother and my brothers?' he said, and it must have been gossiped
around Capernaum that *he seemed to hate his own family*. That at
least was what his behaviour *looked like*, even though we know
from the aftermath that the course of action he was forced to take
towards his family was motivated by something very different to
hate.[51] In fact, many members of Jesus' family finished up as
disciples. His decision to go to Jerusalem and die might be seen as
his last action of 'hate' towards his family, for it meant his final
renunciation of all obligation towards them. It was also an act of
'hate' against his own life. However, in this saying Jesus tells *all*
would-be disciples that they too must imitate him. He was going
to die in Jerusalem. If they were true disciples they would follow
him to the end. They could only do this by abandoning every
other human obligation, even the most basic love of all, the love
of their own life.

   In Jesus' own mind he was already on the way to crucifixion. It
would not have been an uncommon sight to see a condemned
man bearing the top section of his cross to the place of execution
where the upright was already in place in the ground. Around his

neck he would carry the placard which detailed his crime, and the crowds on the way were free to heap on him all the physical and verbal abuse they wished. Jesus imagined himself already walking on that way, and he demanded that those who would be his disciples be with him also, bearing their own crosses.[52]

All this indicates Jesus' desire that he should not be alone in death. He believed that his disciples should accompany him in it, and this is consistent with others of his sayings. At Caesarea Philippi Jesus had warned that if they sought to save their lives they would lose them, but if they were willing to surrender them for him they would gain them in an ultimate way.[53] On another occasion he encouraged his disciples not to fear those who could kill their bodies and do no more; to confess him was the one thing that mattered, to disown him would mean being finally disowned themselves (Luke 12:4–9). In the Sermon on the Mount he warned all who would hear him that the way to the kingdom was to identify with the Son of Man in his suffering and share with him the Servant mission. This appears to be at the bottom of the terrible demand he made of those who followed him to Jerusalem. The Servant of Yahweh was a figure of the faithful people of God, and the Son of Man was the representative of God's suffering saints. Ideally the Servant's sufferings were theirs, and it was to be at the end of their suffering that the Son of Man would be awarded universal dominion on their behalf. What might have happened had his disciples listened and steeled themselves to remain by his side we will consider later.

And After Three Days Rise

On several occasions Jesus added to his warning of violent death a prediction that he would rise again in three days.[54] The Servant of Yahweh, though he was to give his life as a ransom for many, was not to be left in the grave; the prophet foresaw his days prolonged as he shared out the spoils of his victory (Isaiah 53:10–12). Resurrection was therefore a proper inference to draw from this passage, and there was much else in the Old Testament scriptures that might have convinced Jesus that God would raise him up.[55] However, there was no indication of how long might elapse between the shameful death and the consequent exaltation, so this expectation of resurrection in three days requires some explanation. The Pharisees believed that the resurrection would take place in the messianic age, but as we have seen, Jesus believed himself already to be in the messianic age.

There is only one prophecy – in Hosea – that could have given Jesus the conviction that God would not leave him *long* in the grave, and it is this which probably shaped his words about being raised in three days. 'Come and let us return to the Lord, for he has torn and he will heal us; he has smitten and he will bind us up. After two days he will revive us; on the third day he will raise us up and we shall live before him' (Hosea 6:1–2). This is hardly a direct prophecy of the Messiah's raising. It is an appeal to Israel to repent in the knowledge that God's mercy would pick them up and restore them if they did. The third day is no more than an expression of the confidence that they will not need to wait long for God to begin and complete his work of healing amongst them. Yet could not Jesus have understood it precisely in this sense and seized the words to express his own confidence that, as he surrendered himself voluntarily to be torn and smitten, God would not delay in raising him again to life? The words with which he answered those who warned him of Herod's intention to kill him show how he could use this three day motif without any intention of meaning a literal three day period. 'Behold I cast out demons and perform cures today and tomorrow, and on the third day I am perfected. Nevertheless I must go on my way today and tomorrow and the day following' (Luke 13:32f.). Herod needed to be told that Jesus had a God-determined course to run which would not be effected by any threats. It looks as though Jesus has adopted Hosea's prophecy to describe his whole ministry as three days culminating in resurrection. He corrected a possible literalistic misunderstanding of his words by adding that for the next three literal days he must be on his way to Jerusalem – it would be a miscarriage of God's plan as he saw it if he were to die in Herod's territory and not in the holy city. Thus we are not bound to think that Jesus necessarily saw his resurrection taking place in precisely three days. God would determine how long those days would be. This explains why Jesus could tell his disciples that some of them would not taste death until they saw his kingdom established (Mark 9:1). Jesus did not know whether his resurrection would be soon enough to precede the deaths of all his disciples, but he was certain not all of them would have died.

Another influence on Jesus' expectation of resurrection was Jonah. Jonah is the only prophet to whose experience he directly compared his own. Jonah's tomb stood in the village of Gath Hepher only a few kilometres from Nazareth.[56] Jesus may well have visited it. To those who asked him for a sign he replied that no sign would be given except the sign of Jonah. In fact there was no sign associated with Jonah; he simply preached and the Ninevites repented (Luke 11:29–30, 32; Matthew 16:4). That is why Jesus said they would rise up in judgement against the generation which had seen so much. Something greater than Jonah was here! On another occasion, however, he pointed to the experience of Jonah in the belly of the fish as the one sign that would be accorded his generation: 'As Jonah was three days and three nights in the belly of the sea monster, so shall the Son of Man be three days and three nights in the heart of the earth' (Matthew 12:40). This cannot be jettisoned as a creation of the early church; they would not have emphasized a 'three days and nights' motif, because Jesus was in fact only two nights and one full day – a mere thirty six hours – in the tomb.[57] Jonah's prayer from the belly of the fish is the prayer for salvation of one who is descending into the grave (Jonah 2). One can readily imagine Jesus reflecting on it in relation to his own death and the prophecy of Hosea 6. His conviction that God would raise him up in 'three days and three nights' or 'the third day', was expressed without at all meaning to specify precisely how long it would be between his dying and rising.

This makes more understandable the disciples' uncertainty about what he meant by the resurrection of the dead (Mark 9:10), and the lack of any expectation on their part that anything dramatic would happen on the third day. They no doubt had a faith like Martha's that he would rise again in the resurrection at the last day (John 11:24). Jesus' was convinced that for him that day was close, but perhaps not even he knew how close.

Notes

[1] Schürer, *History*, II, 18–19.

[2] Robinson, *Priority*, 157.

[3] For details see D.A. Carson, *The Gospel according to John*, 321–322, 337–338.

[4] What happened at Tabernacles possibly goes on to John 10:21. The next verses relate the following festival in December.

[5] *analempsis* literally means 'taking up', 'receiving'; it also can mean 'death' or 'assumption' (into heaven). There was a book known as *The Assumption of Moses* extant in New Testament times. Some think Luke deliberately uses *exodus* in Luke 9:31 and *analempsis* here to allude to the experiences of Moses and Elijah (Elijah was 'assumed' into Heaven).

[6] The Hebrew of Isaiah 50:7 contains an interesting word play. The Servant knows he will not be ultimately humiliated (*nicelamiti*) because God is with him; therefore he has set his face like flinty rock (*halamish*). The LXX has 'but I have set my face as strong stone' (*hos sterean petran*) to which Luke's 'steeled' (my translation of *esterisen*) probably alludes.

[7] Mark 10:1; Matthew 19:1; John 10:22ff.

[8] Luke 12:2f.; Matthew 25:31ff.

[9] Genesis 19:24ff.

[10] Greek has no future perfect tense. To translate the future as here is allowable if the context requires it. That Jesus envisages a historical judgement of Israel was argued in various places by G.B. Caird. See his *Luke*, 143; 'Les eschatologies

du Nouveau Testament', 217–227; *Jesus and the Jewish Nation*. Caird's ideas have been followed and developed by Wright, *Victory*, xviii–xix; 320–368.

[11] Mark 13:2; cf. Luke 19:41–44.

[12] See Schweitzer, *Quest*, 211; Cadoux, *Mission*, 189–193.

[13] Renan, *Life*, 181–182.

[14] *eudokia* (Luke 10:21) commonly expresses the predestinating pleasure of God. See Luke 2:14; Ephesians 1:5, 9; cf. Mark 1:11 (Luke 12:32); 1 Corinthians 1:21; Galatians 1:15; Colossians 1:19. The Hebrew equivalent *ratson* is frequently used in this predestinarian sense in the Dead Sea Scrolls.

[15] Cf. Mark 6:52; 8:17; Matthew 13:15.

[16] One theory is that Luke found an account of the mission of the twelve in Mark and a slightly different account in his other source Q, which he took to be a different mission. As there were indications in the second account that more than the twelve were involved he created a second mission (another doublet!), this time of seventy (two) to correspond to the traditional number of nations of the world. The mission thus prefigures the later Gentile mission and gives expression to Luke's universalist leanings, but, according to this theory, it did not actually happen.

[17] If Mark contained the mission of the twelve and Q contained a different version of it which Luke mistook for a separate mission, we would expect him to follow Mark closely in his telling of the mission of the twelve, and Q in the mission of the seventy-two. However, Luke has some striking deviations from Mark's account of the twelve which indicate that he was also influenced by another source. The most obvious inference to be drawn is that Q contained an account of both missions. Manson (*Sayings*, 73ff.) does not consider this possibility. He divides Luke's material in the mission of the seventy between Q (vv. 2, 3, 8–12, 13–16) and L (Luke's special source) (vv. 1, 4–7, 17–20). If he is right about L we have two sources for the mission of the seventy-two, which must strengthen the case for its historicity.

[18] Matthew uses the saying to introduce his composite chapter on mission. Although Matthew 10 is built around the mission of the twelve it is intended to gather all of Jesus' instructions for missionaries for the benefit of the later church's mission. As such the saying fits well.

[19] It is something of a problem to know where to place the three stories in Luke 9:57–62, because Matthew who records the first two gives them an entirely different setting close to the beginning of Jesus' ministry (Matthew 8:18–22). They may have been similar incidents which took place at different times, which Matthew and Luke each placed at the point he knew one of them

belonged. Luke's third story seems to envisage a definite journey in which disciples were being called upon to proclaim the kingdom. It is difficult to think
of any other time in the ministry of Jesus where such a saying, if it were not
uttered by one of the twelve, would fit. It may well be that the saying about the
man who wanted to bury his father belongs here too.

[20] See M. Miyoshi, *Der Anfang des Reiseberichts*; W. Manson, *The Gospel of Luke*,
123; Marshall, *Luke*, 412–413.

[21] Jacob's seventy children went down to Egypt (Exodus 1:5); seventy elders
ascended Mt Sinai with Moses (Exodus 24:1, 9); seventy elders were
appointed to share with Moses the burden of the people (Numbers 11:16,
24f); the Sanhedrin had seventy members in addition to the High Priest; the
traditional number of nations in the world was seventy according to the
Hebrew text. Three symbolic possibilities are commonly given for the
number seventy-two: Whereas the Hebrew text of Genesis 10 lists seventy
Gentile nations, the Greek text lists seventy-two. (However, the *traditional*
number is seventy not seventy-two. See 1 Enoch 89:59ff.; *Tanchuma Toledoth*
32b); seventy-two elders prepared the Septuagint translation of the Old
Testament (though it is called the LXX = seventy); The seventy elders of
Numbers 11 are corrected to seventy-two by the inclusion of the two men
who prophesied in the camp. It is noteworthy that in each of these cases the
traditional number is seventy not seventy-two.

[22] Kurt Aland is astonished that the reading seventy-two should occur at all if it
were not original. See Metzger, *Textual Commentary*, 150.

[23] T.W. Manson, *Sayings*, 181; based on *Mishnah Berakoth* 9:5: 'A man may not
enter the Temple Mount with his staff or his sandal or his wallet, or with the
dust upon his feet.'

[24] The same parable is found in Matthew's Sermon on the Mount where the
reference is not so clear. Its association with the threat of judgement in 5:22 and
especially the denial of leniency in 5:26 makes apparent it is not to be understood as general wisdom on seeking reconciliation, but, as in Luke, a plea to
make peace with God before it is too late.

[25] This may be inferred from John's record of Jesus' visits to Jerusalem and
Luke 13:34.

[26] The words in parentheses are thought to be a Christian interpolation.

[27] *Testament of Simeon* 6:6; *Zebulon* 9:8.

[28] John 12:31–32.

[29] Jesus' reference to the names of his disciples being written in heaven recalls Daniel 12:1, where, out of a time of trouble such as never had been experienced, those whose names were written in the book would be delivered.

[30] Mark 3:27; Luke 11:21–23; Colossians 1:13.

[31] The order of Luke 9:51 is somewhat jumbled. The Samaritan episode clearly belongs to the mission, but has been attracted into the series of episodes illustrating the disciples' lack of understanding (9:44–62).

[32] Mark 10:32ff.; Matthew 20:17ff. supports the notion of some kind of journey to Jerusalem.

[33] According to Mark 10:1, when Jesus left Galilee he went to Peraea (cf. Matthew 19:1). While not impossible on a journey through Samaria to Jerusalem, this is odd. John places Jesus in Peraea after an attempt on his life in Jerusalem (John 10:40–42).

[34] Goguel, *Life*, 238ff., 400ff. This theory is adopted and developed by T.W. Manson ('Cleansing', 271–282) who argues that Jesus' triumphal entry to Jerusalem and the cleansing of the temple actually took place at the Feast of Tabernacles, and not, as the gospels say, at Passover. Taylor (*Life*, 164) also leans toward this theory.

[35] Wenham, *Enigma*, 34–35.

[36] For a defence of its originality see Meyer, *Aims*, 185–197.

[37] To the vexed question of what was meant by the office of the keys, we need first to distinguish between the kingdom in its consummated existence, of which we know little and hardly need to know much, and the period of its partial manifestation in apostolic times and in the present. For the apostolic period the best approach to the question is to ask whether we see any activity on the part of Peter which might be thought to bind or loose in an eternal fashion. In fact we do. The preaching of the gospel was regarded by the apostles as determining people's eternal destiny. I would infer from this that the ministry of the keys was exercised in the apostolic age by the preaching of the gospel. It is in accord with this that Peter left the leadership of the Jerusalem church in the hands of James and devoted himself to missionary preaching.

[38] This has been argued in various, as yet unpublished, papers by D.B. Knox.

[39] See, e.g., Headlam, *Life*, 265, 275; Manson, 'Life of Jesus', 218f. For the contrary view see Wrede, *Secret*, 45f.

[40] Schweitzer, *Quest*, 357–395.

[41] Taylor, *Life*, 134–138.

[42] E.g., Luke 4:28–30; John 6:15; 8:59; 10:31–40; 11:53–54.

[43] D. Seccombe, 'Take up your Cross', 142–145; *Possessions*, 109–113.

[44] See *Mishnah Shekalim* 2:5.

[45] L. Morris, *The Apostolic Preaching of the Cross*, 11–27.

[46] L. Morris (*Apostolic Preaching*, 18–22) locates payment in the effort which God expended in rescuing Israel 'with an outstretched arm'. This certainly denotes great power, but not price.

[47] Mark 3:22–27.

[48] The coherence of John 12:20–36 is argued in D. Seccombe, 'Jesus and the Gentiles', 32–41.

[49] Revelation 12:7–11 is a description of Jesus' victory on the cross in apocalyptic style. Note that the casting down of the Accuser from his place in heaven is coincident with the coming of the kingdom of God.

[50] J. Denny, 'The Word "Hate" in Luke 14:26', 41–42.

[51] Proverbs 13:24 ('He who spares his rod hates his son') uses concrete and emotive language to express the thought that to withhold discipline from a child is to act *as though* you hate it, even though your actions may stem from anything but hate. Compare Malachi 1:3.

[52] See Seccombe, 'Cross'.

[53] Mark 8:34ff.; Luke 9:23ff.; Matthew 16:24ff.

[54] Mark 8:31; 9:31; 10:34; Matthew 12:40.

[55] E.g. Job 19:25–27; Psalm 16:9–11; Psalm 116; Psalm 139:18; Isaiah 25:6–8; 26:19; 53:10–12; Ezekiel 37. More profound than these, however, is the direct apprehension Jesus had of the intrinsic fitness of resurrection. This allowed him to see words like 'I am the God of Abraham, Isaac and Jacob' as proof of the resurrection (see Mark 12:26f.) I think he would have seen Psalm 91, which he was tempted to misuse, rightly as a challenge to faith in God who could be relied on to raise up those who had died in obedience to his will.

[56] G. Dalman, *Sacred Sites and Ways*, 111f.

[57] For the theory that this motif was a later Christian invention see Perkins, *Resurrection*, 73.

Chapter 15

The Coming Of The King

The Raising of Lazarus (John 11:1–44)

About November AD 29 Jesus came to Jerusalem in the wake of a large band of kingdom heralds. He taught there – we do not know for how long – gained many supporters and aroused much opposition. The opposition was ragged, however, having not yet solidified into a united determination to do away with him. Nevertheless, it reached the point that if he stayed in the city his life was in serious danger of coming to a premature end; the result of an outburst of anger from one or other disaffected group. Jesus had no desire for this kind of conclusion to his ministry; he wanted the final decision of the nation, so withdrew across the Jordan to Peraea (only thirty five kilometres away) and ministered there until his 'time' should come.[1] Such is our reconstruction of the latter part of Jesus' ministry. Something needed to happen to bring the process of decision to a head. And that something was provided, according to John, by the death of Lazarus.

News reached Jesus from his friends Martha and Mary in Bethany that their brother Lazarus was seriously ill. Would he come? Jesus delayed his departure two days before announcing to his disciples that Lazarus was dead and that he was going to awaken him. The disciples were fearful of returning to Judaea, where only a short time before people had wanted to stone Jesus to death. The situation in Jerusalem was perilous and Bethany was only three kilometres away. Nevertheless they reluctantly agreed to accompany him. 'Let us go with him ourselves so we can die with him,' were Thomas' words of resignation, which decided the other swaying disciples. Perhaps he was beginning to understand about hating his life and taking up his cross.

From where they were to Bethany would have been a day's journey or perhaps two.[2] When they arrived Lazarus had been dead four days, the burial was over, and the customary mourning in progress. That meant he died before the messengers even got to Jesus. We are not told whether Jesus guessed this from their description of Lazarus' condition or intuited it supernaturally. Either way, with his eye ever on his Father's clock, he greeted it as the striking of the eleventh hour (John 11:9–10).

The account of Jesus' conversations with Martha and Mary and his calling Lazarus from the tomb is by far the most detailed and personal description of the lead-up to any miracle in the gospels. On one occasion when I was travelling to speak to a man whose young wife had just died, I was lamenting the lack of anything in the Bible to show me how to deal with the situation. In fact, this story shows Jesus in just such a situation and describes his interchange with the two women in some detail. My most urgent fear as an inexperienced minister was to know what to say. I noticed that Jesus at first said nothing; it was Martha who did all the talking. I was also struck by the way these women brought forward their standard life-after-death beliefs, which apparently were not helping them very much, and how Jesus parried these and made them face the question of resurrection as an immediate issue. I saw too how freely Jesus gave reign to his own emotions in the situation. I had cause that day to be very grateful to John for recording the story of Lazarus, I only regretted that unlike Jesus I could not raise the dead.

Did It Really Happen?

It would be fair to say that this is the most doubted of all Jesus'
miracles. It is passed over in embarrassed silence in many treatments of his life, even by those who are otherwise disposed to
accept that he worked miracles, and who accord some historical
value to John.[3] It is also only fair to admit that the reasons for
holding it in suspicion are weighty, the main problem being its
lack of mention in the other three gospels. If, as John indicates,
it was the means of bringing many undecided people to faith in
Jesus, and also the immediate cause of the plot which led to his
death, how could Mark or the other gospels have failed to
record it? It is also seen as inconsistent with Mark's account of
the shape and chronology of Jesus' ministry. It is viewed, therefore, as yet another indication of the non-historical character of
the Fourth Gospel. John supposedly wove the story together
from fragmentary suggestions in the other gospels: a number of
stories of Jesus raising people from the dead, a parable in which
the request is made that a dead 'Lazarus' be allowed to return
from the dead, and a cameo of the home-life of a certain Mary
and Martha.[4] The story's value thus becomes purely symbolic.
Though if part of its symbolism is to do with Jesus' power to
raise the dead, which in point of fact he did not do, one
wonders about its value.

Of all the miracle stories, this one, taken at face value, is the
least symbolic. It is told with a wealth of circumstantial and
personal detail, and as an essential component in the nexus of
events which quickly led Jesus to a very unsymbolic end. Thus it
does not lack in scholars who have come to its side, both to
defend it for its own sake, and to defend the integrity of John.[5]
What one makes of John has a great deal to do with how one
approaches the raising of Lazarus. If he is seen as a late first
century or early second century writer with little original
tradition at his disposal then it is not difficult to imagine him
creating such a story from, say, the parable of the rich man and

Lazarus (Luke 16:19–31). If, on the other hand, he was an original participant in the events, or even in close touch with the tradition, such inventiveness is difficult to credit, no matter when he actually wrote.

Actually, the similarity between Jesus' statement in the parable that the Jews would not be convinced even if Lazarus were to return from the dead, and the story we are considering does not weigh one way or the other as evidence of the historicity of the miracle. Certainly the parable might have inspired the story of the miracle, but dependence might easily run in the other direction.[6] It could be argued that the raising of Lazarus, had it really occurred, would have provided a powerful stimulus in later years to add his name to one of the parables. After all, Jesus' prediction that the Pharisees would not believe even if someone were to come back from the dead had come true twice over. What could be more natural than to draw attention to it? If there were reason to think Lazarus was a real person, the likelihood of his being constructed out of a parable recedes.

Was Lazarus Real?

One thing that weighs heavily in favour of the historicity of the Lazarus story is its connection with names and places that were familiar to the early church. Names and places do not feature heavily in the miracle stories.[7] It is unlikely that someone inventing a symbolic story would tie it to historical people and a real place, especially the most easily visited town in the holy land apart from Jerusalem itself. John goes out of his way to identify Lazarus, and does it in a decidedly odd manner: 'Lazarus of Bethany' the brother of 'that Mary who anointed the Lord with ointment and wiped his feet with her hair' (John 11:1–2). Why would he identify Lazarus with reference to a story he will not tell until later in his gospel, when it will be perfectly obvious that Mary and Lazarus are sister and brother (John 12:1–8)? The answer must be that 'the Mary who anointed the Lord with ointment and wiped his feet with her hair' was well known in the early church. The reason for this is found in Mark, who never mentions her by name, but tells the story of the meal at Bethany and of the woman who anointed him. 'Truly I say to you,' Jesus proclaims, 'wherever in the whole world the gospel is proclaimed, what she has done will also be spoken in memory of her' (Mark 14:9). So Lazarus was the brother of a Christian celebrity from a village three kilometres from Jerusalem, hardly what one would expect in a tale of symbolic fiction.

The other part of the story which is equally hard to dismiss is the effect which John says the miracle had on the authorities in Jerusalem, but we will look at that after we have considered why the other gospels might have omitted the story from their accounts.

Why Omit the Story?

We are obviously fishing in murky water when trying to divine why a story is *not* in a particular gospel. An obvious possibility is that it was unknown to that gospel writer. If that were so in this case it would mean the miracle did not happen. Another possibility might be that the details of the story were not as well known as others; Leon Morris points out that Peter is nowhere mentioned during the latter, pre-Jerusalem ministry period, and might not have witnessed this particular incident.[8] This solution would have more force if there were some other reason for thinking Peter was not with the group at the time, but in the absence of this it seems to be clutching at straws. A more probable explanation is that the story would have spoiled the literary form – what might be called the 'kerygmatic shape' – of the gospel. Mark deliberately employed the outline of the apostolic gospel as the shape of his written gospel (see Acts 10:36–43).[9] This outline represented a simplification of the actual ministry, but made it comprehensible in terms of a preachable pattern of movement from Galilee to Jerusalem. To have had Jesus coming and going from Jerusalem in between times would have destroyed the stylization that was familiar to those who had heard the gospel preached, and would have called for explanations which were not possible in the compass of Mark's short work.[10] It will have been for the same reason that Mark omitted any record of Jesus' regular visits to the feasts in Jerusalem. That he was followed by Luke and Matthew is evidence of the authority accorded Mark in the early days (understandable if an apostle was known to lie behind it), but perhaps also of the influence of this outline of the kerygma.

What then of the charge that Mark could not have failed to mention the story if it influenced the events leading to Jesus' death as John insists? There is evidence that the raising of Lazarus must have taken place about six weeks prior to Jesus' final Passover.[11] Thus it was not an *immediate* cause of Jesus' death; another gospel writer could well know of it, but treat it as one of a complex of events which led to his downfall. John's Gospel has a Jerusalem focus, whereas the other gospels view the Jesus event from a Galilean perspective. The story of Lazarus is of particular importance to John because it was the major factor which brought about the final polarization of public opinion in Jerusalem; it brought many Jerusalemites over to Jesus and convinced the authorities to strike. It was not fundamentally different, however, to things that took place earlier in Galilee, and the other gospel writers could legitimately represent Jesus' death as the result of tensions which built up there.

Jesus Becomes an Outlaw

Bethany was 'near Jerusalem, about fifteen furlongs away' (John 11:18). Because of this proximity many came from Jerusalem to comfort Mary and Martha when they heard of Lazarus' death. The family in Bethany must have been well known, and the situation was unusually tragic, since Martha's husband was a leper.[12] Many Jerusalem Jews saw Jesus call Lazarus from the tomb and began to believe in him. John speaks of a 'crowd' witnessing the miracle and many others being influenced by their report (John 11:19, 45; 12:9, 17–18). Some of these reported to the Pharisees. Whether in malice or with the intention of winning them to Jesus' side we are not told, but the effect was to galvanize them to action. Pressure was put on the chief priests, who were worried enough anyway, and a council was called to discuss the issue.

> The chief priests and Pharisees met in council and said, 'What are we to do, for this man does many signs? If we leave him alone like this everyone will believe in him, and the Romans will come and take away our place and our nation.' A certain one of them, Caiaphas, who was High Priest that year, said to them, 'You know nothing. Don't you reckon that it is better that one man should die for the people, than the whole nation perish?' … From that day on they moved a resolution that they should kill him. (John 11:47–50, 53)

Thus in John's perception, the raising of Lazarus brought Jesus' support in Jerusalem to such a dangerous level that the leaders were forced to move against him. The danger they foresaw was nothing less than national destruction! This is the only mention of such a thing in the gospels, and at first glance it seems somewhat extreme. However, it is not inconsistent with what is known of the balance of political forces at the time. John's statement that Caiaphas was High Priest that year is a subtle reminder that high priests were in office solely at the pleasure of the Roman government. Their value to the Romans lay in their ability to keep the population quiet. There had been a time when they were changed with such regularity that it looked like becoming an annual office, and the only reason Joseph Caiaphas stayed in his position from AD 18–36 was that he managed to do what his masters wanted.[13] His three predecessors and his successor lasted one year each.[14]

The last time the people had rallied to the cry of home-grown leaders the result had been catastrophic: parts of the temple razed, the temple treasure seized, Sepphoris and other towns put to the torch, their inhabitants sold as slaves, and two thousand rebels crucified. Most of the council would have been old enough to remember this.[15] What would happen if the people began to obey this Galilean? The Romans would hardly concern themselves with whether his message was violent or non-violent; was he a danger to their authority would be all that counted. There was no doubt in the minds of the chief priests, or of the scribes and Pharisees, that Jesus threatened to usurp their influence and authority. If the people followed him everything they stood for would become obsolete. As they saw it, it was him and his plans for the nation, or them and theirs; the peaceful coexistence with Rome they had struggled to achieve was in jeopardy. Caiaphas summed up the situation without any explicit condemnation of Jesus himself. It was a question of pure political pragmatics: someone must die, if not Jesus, then the nation.[16] John uses legal terms which indicate that the result of the Council's meeting was an order of proscription which effectively made Jesus an outlaw (John 11:53, 57). A resolution was passed condemning him to death, a warrant issued for his arrest, official search proceedings instituted, and orders given that he be denounced by anyone who knew his whereabouts. Jesus was now a wanted man. John's account of Jesus' proscription receives interesting confirmation from the Talmud.

> On the eve of the Passover Yeshu was hanged. For forty days before the execution took place, a herald went forth and cried, 'He is going forth to be stoned because he has practised sorcery and enticed Israel to apostasy. Anyone who can say anything in his favour, let him come forward and plead on his behalf.' But since nothing was brought forward in his favour he was hanged on the eve of Passover.[17]

Stoning was the presumed method of punishment in such a case. The Talmud does not say why this was changed to hanging, though the gospels make it clear. For the time being Jesus withdrew, though not to the place in Peraea where he had previously been ministering. He could quickly have been extradited from there. He went to a town called Ephraim on the edge of the wilderness, traditionally identified as the present day 'Et Taiyebah, but according to W.F. Albright more probably 'Ein Samiya, an isolated and inaccessible oasis, about twenty kilometres north-east of Jerusalem, surrounded by steep hills pockmarked with cave entrances.[18] There he laid low until the road down the valley began to thicken with the pilgrim traffic going up to Jerusalem for Passover.

Return to Jerusalem

We have been following John's account of things since Jesus' visit to Jerusalem at the Feast of Dedication. It is now time to rejoin the first three gospels, though there are well known difficulties involved in bringing them together with John at this point. John has Jesus in hiding in Judaea, in the others he appears on the road to Jerusalem at the head of a great throng of pilgrims coming from Galilee. The contradiction is solved when we realize that a few kilometres walk east of 'Ein Samiya is the Jordan Valley road. Jesus could simply have fallen in with the pilgrims who happened to be coming down that way. Alternatively, there may have been some forward planning and liaison involved and someone could have organized for a good number of his Galilean disciples to be at the right place at the right time. Jesus was a hunted man, so it was vital to his security that he be in the midst of a friendly crowd when he reached Jerusalem.[19] It is hard to account for Mark's observation of the disciples' amazement as Jesus set out for Jerusalem from his own story (Mark 10:32). It makes perfect sense if it relates to his leaving his hiding place in Ephraim. Three incidents along the way show us that for Jesus it was business as usual even at this late stage: at or near Jericho he dined with a tax collector, healed a blind man and told an important parable.

Zacchaeus (Luke 19:1–10)

Jesus' fame preceded him to Jericho. The crowds were such that one short man could only get to see him by running ahead and climbing a tree. Jesus spied him, and to the disgust of many invited himself to be the guest of yet another 'sinner'. It is common in telling the story of Zacchaeus to paint him as a friendless man, ostracized by the Jewish population for his professional collaboration with Rome. This is only partially true. He was not a government collector of personal or land taxes, but part of a private company dealing with tolls and customs. The right to these was tendered for by large consortiums or very rich individuals. As 'chief tax collector' in the important and prosperous border city of Jericho he must have been a very wealthy businessman, unpopular with those who transported goods and paid tolls, disapproved of by the religious, but hardly without friends. The next day was probably Saturday, and as travel on the Sabbath was forbidden, Jesus needed somewhere to stay.[20] He may have spent thirty-six hours in the tax-collector's home. Zacchaeus was staggered at the unexpected generosity of Jesus' desire for hospitality. A famous person, even one held in some suspicion, should be the guest of someone prominent. A holy man should entrust his reputation only to those beyond reproach. Zacchaeus put the grumblers to shame by pledging half his money to the poor, and fourfold restitution for anyone he had overcharged. Another lost son of Abraham found, was Jesus' satisfied response; salvation had reached another house in Israel. The gathering of the restored community of Israel was proceeding.

An End of Secrecy
(Mark 10:46–52; Matthew 20:29–34; Luke 18:35–43.)

We may assume that the party set out early on Sunday morning to make the steep ascent to Jerusalem. On the roadside leaving Jericho was a blind beggar named Bartimaeus.[21] Hearing the crowd and learning that it was Jesus approaching he began to shout in a very loud voice, 'Jesus, Son of David, have mercy on me.' 'Son of David' meant Messiah. It was a dangerous thing to cry in public; Jesus had previously restrained such outbursts. Understandably on this occasion the crowd tried to do it for him and ordered the man to hush up. But Bartimaeus cried even louder, and Jesus allowed it; the time for secrecy had evidently passed. He summoned the man, inquired what he wanted, and gave him his sight. An ecstatic Bartimaeus followed him up to Jerusalem, towards an even greater breaking of the silence.

The Kingdom is Delayed (Luke 19:11–27)

The title of this section is deliberately provocative. The so-called 'delay of the parousia' is much discussed by New Testament scholars. The first Christians, it is thought, believed Jesus would reappear gloriously within a few years of his resurrection. As the time lengthened there was forced upon them the notion of a delay in the second coming (parousia).[22] We are interested in Jesus' view of his future, especially now that rejection and death loomed large before him. According to Schweitzer, Jesus initially expected the kingdom to appear while the twelve were engaged in their first mission. God's delay in revealing him then as the heavenly Son of Man forced him to conclude that he must first suffer. Reasons have already been given for rejecting Schweitzer's theory. But in the parable of the postponed kingdom, just before his arrival in Jerusalem, Jesus himself broaches the matter of a delay in the kingdom's appearance.

Intriguingly, the dramatic entry Jesus was about to make into Jerusalem is itself described in terms of an ancient parousia. The Greek word *parousia* means 'a coming in order to be present'. A king coming to visit an ancient city would be met by its citizens some kilometres before his arrival and given a royal welcome. Jesus was about to be accorded just such an entrance. Those who provided it, many of whom were with him as he left Jericho – Bartimaeus probably included – thought that Jesus' arrival (*parousia*) in the capital would mean the establishment of the messianic kingdom. Jesus knew otherwise and told the parable to forewarn them. His Jerusalem parousia was to result not in the appearance of the kingdom, as it should have were his messianic claim accepted, but in rejection and death, which would effectively push it back to an unspecified point in the future.

All this is controversial. Some scholars even deny that Jesus had any notion of a parousia-like return. N.T. Wright thinks it is a mistake to refer the parable of the pounds (Luke 19:11–27) to Jesus' second coming: it speaks, rather, of the return of God to his people after the long delay of Israel's exile. According to Wright Jesus' journey to Jerusalem was an enactment of the return of the Lord to Zion, so the parable referred to the judgement that was to take place after God's long absence, not to a parousia postponed.[23] A true interpretation of the parable of the pounds is evidently vital to our understanding of Jesus' quest.

Are the Parable and its Setting Genuine?

Scepticism about Jesus' authorship of the present form of the gospel parables has been widespread for most of the twentieth century. The form critical movement saw the early Christians pressing their own ideas and concerns onto original teaching to such an extent that one could rarely be sure whether a parable's context or application stemmed from the Master. Jeremias' highly influential analysis of the parables purported to identify their stages of evolution in the hands of the church and recover the original masterpieces. In our case, Jeremias asserts that the three similar parables found in Matthew, Luke and the Gospel of the Nazareans all evolved from one primitive dominical parable. Boiled back to a lowest common denominator, and with every possible addition stripped off, the original turns out to be an exhortation to the scribes not to neglect what God had entrusted to them, namely the word of God. The application to Jesus' second coming, found in both Matthew and Luke, is attributed to the later church.[24] But this is pure supposition. Why could Jesus not have framed a number of similar parables? Wright sensibly protests 'It is highly likely that Jesus used such stories like this on numerous occasions, not just "twice", as cautious conservative exegetes used to suggest. There is no reason whatever to insist that either Matthew's or Luke's version was "derived" from the other, or both from a single original.'[25] And why should Jesus not have spoken of the period beyond his death, if he saw his death as the way to the kingdom? And why could Luke not have preserved the parable in its original context? In fact, there are positive indications that he did.

Jesus' authorship of this parable is vouched for by the clear comparison of himself to Archelaus, the original man of noble birth who went into a far country to receive a kingdom and return. At the death of Herod the Great in 4 BC Archelaus was named in his will as the successor to his throne. Before taking over the kingdom, however, he had to travel to Rome and hear the will read and ratified by Augustus. His brothers also hurried to Rome to plead their respective cases, and a Jewish delegation set out to ask for relief from the rule of the Herods and self-government under Rome.[26] Augustus effectively ratified Herod's will, though he reduced Archelaus' territory, giving Galilee and Peraea to Herod Antipas, and the territory north-east of Galilee to Philip. Archelaus received his 'kingdom', though his title was reduced from 'King' to 'Ethnarch' ('Nation Ruler') until he should prove himself worthy. He hurried home to Judaea to settle scores with his enemies. Thus the face of Archelaus is unmistakable in the parable. However, his reign was marked by such brutality and incompetence, that after ten years he was deposed by the Romans and sent into exile. Who in the early church would ever have thought to compare Jesus with this Idi Amin of the first century? Surely no one other than himself![27] Even modern authors have attempted to evade the comparison.[28] They overlook that this is yet another parable with an attention grabbing twist; the comparison was meant to surprise – even shock – and not be forgotten. It is typical of Jesus' story telling.[29]

A little way to the south of Jericho, where the road that comes along the Jordan Valley from Galilee turns right to ascend the mountains to Jerusalem, stood the winter palace of King Herod which Archelaus repaired after it had been gutted by fire.[30] Jesus would have passed it as he began his last journey to Jerusalem. With all Jericho's reminders of this recent ruler who had once to travel to a far country to receive his kingdom, it is not so strange that Jesus should have employed his memory to address his followers' mistaken belief that the kingdom of God was to appear in a matter of days. We may be confident that both parable and its context were as Luke tells it.

The Kingdom Will Not Appear Immediately

Wright's insightful suggestion that Jesus' journey to Jerusalem was a conscious enactment of the much prophesied return of God to Zion is not to be put aside.[31] Nevertheless, it is only by the severest contortion that our parable can be pushed into this mould. The three foci of the parable are the unusual going away and returning of the nobleman, by which the coming of the kingdom is delayed, the challenge to the servants to entrepreneurial vision in the interim, and the judgement of the rebels at the end. The parable is not a clumsy fusing of two smaller parables; the reminder of Archelaus is there throughout: in the departing and returning nobleman, in the austere master at the reckoning, and the avenging king at the end. The action of the servants and the returning king arise naturally from the uncertain conditions of the would-be king's absence, making the whole an artistic piece. Luke makes it clear that the time of uncertainty lies in the future, for the parable answers the disciples' eagerness for an immediate manifestation of the kingdom in Jerusalem.[32]

Did Jesus see it differently? Was he referring to an imminent appearance of the kingdom after God's long absence? 'A certain man of noble birth' is a very strange way to introduce a comparison with God, if he did. The obvious connection is with 'the Son of David' to whom Bartimaeus has just appealed. Equally inappropriate is the notion of God receiving the kingdom; it is Jesus' (the Messiah's) kingship which is the subject of uncertainty. And the rewarding of servants and punishing of enemies is precisely what is not going to eventuate in the immediate future,[33] despite the disciples' ardent longings. Jesus' view of the parable and Luke's are therefore one.

Jesus has spent the past two years announcing the kingdom of God and warning of the dire consequences for Israel if it were refused. At an official level it has already been rejected. Jesus, a man with a death sentence against him, is about to reappear in the capital. He does not intend to seize power by force and there has been no hint that he expected God to act for him miraculously at this point. So he is going to die. It is, therefore, of the greatest moment to hear Jesus addressing his disciples' hopes, not with an admission of failure, but an assertion that the kingdom will yet appear, though not at once. He must first depart, but will most surely return.

In speaking of the kingdom's *appearance* Jesus addressed his followers' reasonable expectation that sooner or later the secrecy surrounding his identity must be lifted and the kingdom seen in its full, unambiguous glory. What the prophets predicted and the Baptist proclaimed – a new order under the rule of a God-anointed human king, in which evil, suffering

and death have vanished forever – must have its fulfilment if
Jesus is not to be judged a fraud. The excited crowd thinks it
will happen in Jerusalem, no doubt by means of a miracle-
assisted coup. We have seen various indications that this was the
disciples' mentality; they had even discussed who would be who
in the new cabinet.

Jesus evidently foresaw an ambiguous period beyond his
death, when his messiahship would be real but hidden. He
would be acknowledged by his followers, but not by all. It
would be a time when different players would be backing
different scenarios of the future. Those who knew the truth
would be about their master's business, utilizing all the resources
he had left at their disposal to the full extent of their power,
doing things which would be of profit to him on his return.[34]
Judgement would wait until the king's return and it would be
severe: Jesus paints himself as a demanding master, though
exceedingly generous in his rewards. The rule of cities in return
for faithful service in the time of uncertainty is what would be
expected of an Archelaus, but could not have been far removed
from what the disciples expected of their involvement with the
Messiah. It is surprising to us how little interest Jesus' shows
in disabusing them of such this-worldly aspirations again
evidencing his belief in a real, historical, space–time
consummation of his kingdom promise, beyond his imminent
rejection. The disciples' mistake was not one of concept but of
programme and timing. To the very end Jesus presented the
kingdom to them in 'geopolitical' terms, though he also never
stopped insisting that he (and they) must first suffer.

The postponed kingdom parable of the pounds thus forces
upon us the notion of a second coming of Christ, though some
kind of glorious appearance of the kingdom is already inherent
in Jesus' commitment to a strategy of non-resistance and death.
How this relates to his anticipated resurrection, and his
warnings of Israel's destruction, is not yet clear. The final
chilling words of the parable ('As for these enemies of mine

who did not want me to rule over them, bring them here and slay them before me') recall Archelaus' gloating return, but also point to some future judgement. Whether in Jesus' mind this was the national catastrophe he had already foreshadowed, or the final judgement of individuals at the end of the age, or whether these were in some way united in his thinking cannot here be discerned.

The Disillusioned Disciple
(Mark 14:3–11; Matthew 26:6–16; John 12:1–8)

It was a hot and weary twenty five kilometre climb from Jericho to the top of the range. Jesus' destination was Bethany, a small village nestled in the hills just out of sight of Jerusalem. It was the home of Mary, Martha and Lazarus, and a meal was waiting for the travellers.[35] During the meal Mary took a flask of oil of nard, broke it open and anointed Jesus' head and feet. Her action caused some disquiet. Had it been sold, it could have fed a poor family for a year. She was roundly criticized for what seemed a terrible waste. Jesus defended her. To his way of thinking she had anointed his body for burial. The poor they would always have with them, but not him. It is unlikely that *Mary* thought of herself as preparing him for burial, but she may have been more sensitive than the others to Jesus' commitment to face the inevitable in Jerusalem, and to the fact that the days were rapidly closing in on him. It must have been an act of high emotion; love, perhaps with a presentiment of tragedy. She may have been the one member of the party on Jesus' wavelength, and his defence of her against the hurtful insensitivity of the disciples is understandable. The incident was something of a revelation to Judas Iscariot, who pointed out to the other disciples the cash value of her gesture.

Speculation over why Judas betrayed Jesus is never-ending. It was this particular evening which appears to have actually decided him against his master. Mark tells the story as a flash-back to explain the betrayal. Did Judas' sharp interchange with Jesus not only put his nose out of joint, but also jolt him to the realization that Jesus intended to do nothing to prevent his own death? He may have been the political realist among the disciples. If Jesus intended no political action to establish the kingdom then the cause was lost, and he was not about to be caught on a sinking ship. Some have suggested that Judas thought to force Jesus' hand by betraying him, but it is unlikely he would have negotiated a sizable reward for himself had that been his intention. John's statement that he had been stealing from the common purse may not be mere slander. Judas may have determined that night that he would abandon the group with whatever he could take to help him in his new life; he did not intend to be one of those poor, who, according to Jesus, would always be around.

Jesus' words here about the poor should not be overlooked. It is a clue to how he saw the future his disciples faced. He envisages conditions in the world continuing much as ever. When the Israelites were about to enter the 'promised land' Moses assured them that there would be no poor among them if they obeyed God's laws, but, almost in the same breath, he predicted that the poor would never cease out of the land (Deuteronomy 15:4, 11). The poor were thus a sign of Israel's disobedience and the lost possibility of a land blessed through its unbroken relationship with God. Against this background Jesus' words may mean that the promised kingdom, in which poverty, hunger and tears were to be a thing of the past, would not materialize immediately. His rejection meant the thrusting away of the glories of the new age, which his message had promised and his presence given a foretaste of.

Royal Procession
(Matthew 21:1–11; Mark 11:1–11; Luke 19:29–44; John 12:9–19)

If it was Friday when Jesus joined the pilgrim crowd and entered Jericho, he would have spent the remainder of Friday and Saturday with Zacchaeus, and on Sunday made the journey with the crowds from Jericho as far as Bethany. Sunday night was then spent with the family in Bethany, where he may have made some necessary arrangements for the activities of the next day. On Monday he entered Jerusalem.

Mark tells how Jesus sent two of his disciples into a nearby village with instructions to fetch a previously unridden donkey and bring it to him. The story is told with a touch of intrigue, suggesting to those who love a conspiracy evidence of an intricate plot. They may be close to the truth here. Jesus was in danger of arrest and had to be exceedingly careful about his arrangements. If the word had spread prematurely in Jerusalem that he was planning to stage an impressive entrance, he would certainly have been forestalled. Josephus relates how some years later an Egyptian false prophet led a party of his followers from the wilderness to the Mount of Olives where he promised that the walls of Jerusalem would fall at his command. His party was met by the Roman heavy infantry who made short work of them.[36] Evidently Jesus has not told his plans even to his disciples, which accounts for the surprise that Mark's record reflects. The arrangement evidently made an impression on them.

Then began a strange procession into the city. As the top of the Mount of Olives is reached the walls of Jerusalem on the opposite side of the Kidron Valley come suddenly into view. Dominating the scene before them was the temple which, according to Josephus, 'appeared to approaching strangers like a snow-clad mountain – for all that was not overlaid with gold was of the purest white'.[37] The enthusiastic crowds, some who travelled with Jesus from Bethany, others who heard of his approach and ran from the city, spread garments on the donkey and laid cothing and branches on the way before him. The waving palm fronds recalled the Great Hallel that was sung to the waving of palm 'hosannas' at the Feast of Tabernacles,[38] and the crowd began to chant the familiar words.

> Hosanna! (Save us now!)
> Blessed is he who comes in the name of the Lord.
> The king of Israel (add Luke and John)
> Blessed is the coming kingdom of our father David
> Hosanna in the Highest.

The traditional interpretation of Jesus' action on that day is not to be evaded, though many have tried. Everything indicates that he was at last raising the veil of mystery which had necessarily surrounded his mission, and allowing himself to be acclaimed as the King–Messiah. The Jewish scholar, Joseph Klausner, had no doubt that Jesus was announcing his messiahship.[39] The special donkey, the 'red carpet' and the acclaim are found in each of the gospels. They are not the invention of later Christians. The only thing which might be laid at the door of the church is their inter-pretation. Admittedly neither Mark nor Luke say what Matthew and John make explicit, that Jesus' riding the donkey was the fulfilment of a prophecy of Zechariah (9:9–10). The important question is whether Jesus intended it to be so.

The donkey was a common form of transport, so the connection with Zechariah's prophecy would not have been immediately apparent to those who witnessed the procession; even the disciples did not see it at the time. To that extent the action still had something of the parable about it (John 12:16). Yet Jesus obviously saw this colt as more than a normal mount. He took great care to obtain a donkey that had never been ridden. This would seem to indicate that he saw both occasion and rider as holy. The ark of God had once been transported in a similar way![40] The garments and the branches are consistent with the reception accorded to a king. Jehu was proclaimed king in this manner (2 Kings 9:13). In a few days time Jesus would have another prophecy of Zechariah on his lips (Mark 14:27), so it is probable that he knew exactly what he was doing with the donkey, and exactly what he wanted to say. He was coming to his people in the paradox of their victorious yet humble king, bringing them dominion and peace. Yet on the way down the mount Jesus would pause to weep over the city which refused to recognize its visitation and know the things which made for peace. If any doubt remains about the symbolism of Jesus' actions, the cries of the crowd remove all uncertainty. The words they chanted are from the psalm of praise which would be sung in a week's time at the conclusion of the Passover meal; an anticipatory song of welcome to the coming King–Messiah.[41] To have sung it before Jesus in this way could only have been to acclaim him as the coming king of the house of David, and Jesus accepted the acclaim.

The situation was now exceedingly dangerous and it is not surprising that some of the better educated of those present urged Jesus to silence his disciples. Jesus declined their well-meant advice, 'I tell you, if they were to be silent, the stones will cry out!' (Luke 19:40).

Some view these words as a cry of sarcastic despair over the incurably political messianic hopes of the crowd. They were so irrepressible that if Jesus tried to shut them up the stones would probably have tried to make him a king! After all he had taught them they were still expecting an ordinary king.[42] But what *had* he taught them that would make what they were doing that day inappropriate? They hardly expected one who raised the dead, healed the blind and chose such ordinary men for his companions to be an *ordinary* king. But expect him to be a *king* they clearly did. Does not all of Jesus' teaching and action converge on this point, and is not the natural meaning of his answer to the Pharisees that what his disciples were doing that day was appropriate to the point that silence would have been nothing short of monstrous? Matthew tells us that the children continued to chant acclaim even when Jesus was in the temple, and that even there he refused to silence it (Matthew 21:15–16).

Unrecognized Visitation

Somewhere on the way down the hill Jesus stopped and wept over Jerusalem. This was the city which killed the prophets and stoned God's messengers, whose people he nonetheless wished to gather together as a hen gathers its chicks under its wings (Luke 13:34). For all the exhilaration of the day it is little wonder that he wept. Entry into that city meant death, yet his tears were not for himself.

> If you knew this day, even you, the things that make for peace –
> but now they have been hidden from your eyes. Because days will
> come upon you when your enemies will throw up a barricade
> against you and encircle you and close you in on every side, and
> they will raze you to the ground, you and your children within
> you, and they will not leave in you one stone upon another
> because you did not know the time of your visitation.
> (Luke 19:42–44)

Such irony! The leaders of Jerusalem have decided to do away with Jesus to save the city from the peril of the Romans, yet in Jesus' eyes they are signing the nation's death warrant. It is a paradox he expressed to his disciples once before: 'He who seeks his life will lose it, but he who loses it for my sake and the gospel's will save it' (Mark 8:35). There can be no mistaking what form Jesus thought that 'loss of life' would take. Israel had been given a gracious visitation that could have yielded the promised kingdom of peace, but she was about to thrust it from her. She was about to choose the rule of Rome in preference to the kingdom of the Messiah; Rome it would be, then, who would determine her fate.

We may believe Matthew's report that when Jesus entered Jerusalem the whole city was stirred. 'Who is this?' asked those who did not know, and the crowds who did gave answer, 'The prophet Jesus from Nazareth in Galilee' (Matthew 21:10–11). The entrance had been well planned and executed. Jesus and his party had come from the Mount of Olives into Jerusalem and up to the temple, peacefully, and without any interference from the temple police or Roman garrison. Jesus surveyed the situation in the temple, probably decided on the next morning's activities, and, as the sun was setting and a new day (Tuesday) was beginning,[43] returned to Bethany with the twelve disciples.

The Fig Tree's Fate
(Mark 11:12–14, 20; Matthew 21:18–20)

According to Mark, Jesus returned to the temple the next morning. On the way he saw a fig tree resplendent with its leafy foliage, and being hungry went to see if he could find something to eat. It was early April and figs do not ripen in Jerusalem until late in May, but small figs can be found at this time which sometimes fall to the ground and ripen enough to be edible.[44] The tree was without any fruit at all and Jesus cursed it. The disciples must have wondered whether the strain of the days was beginning to show on him. A day or two later when they passed by they were amazed to see that the tree had withered. In the light of Jeremiah's picture of Israel-about-to-be-judged as a fruitless and withered fig tree (Jeremiah 8:13), and Jesus' own parable of the fig tree it was an ominous sign. The tree for which he had begged a season of respite was still without fruit. As insipid salt was good for nothing but to be trampled in the street, so a fruitless tree was good for nothing but cutting down and burning.[45]

The Temple

'By three things is the world sustained: by the Law, by the temple-service, and by deeds of loving-kindness.' So said Simeon the Just.[46] The temple was the heart of Israel's cultic worship of God. There God had given them a place where they could regard his presence as residing, and to which they could direct their devotion to him. In theocratic terms the temple was God's palace where he was resident as king in their midst. Mark says Jesus drove out the traders, upended the tables of the moneylenders and prevented the caryying of goods through the temple (Mark 11:15–17; Matthew 21:12f.; Luke 19:45f.).

In chapter 6 we discussed John's account of the cleansing of the temple at the beginning of Jesus' ministry. I disagreed with the view that John placed it there for 'theological' reasons, and argued that if we had to choose between John's and Mark's location of this incident the evidence favours John's. We must now ask whether Mark (and Matthew and Luke) have placed it in the last week for theological or literary reasons, or whether it is conceivable that Jesus cleansed the temple on two different occasions.

Were there Two Cleansings?

This last suggestion is often scorned, chiefly because it is difficult to imagine an essentially symbolic action happening more than once. If more than once, then how many times? Did Jesus cleanse it every time he visited Jerusalem? This objection would fall away, however, if the temple trading to which Jesus objected so strongly was not normal.

According to the Mishnah the money-changers' tables were set up in the temple three weeks prior to Passover to receive the annual half-shekel tax due from every Israelite.[47] The tax was only acceptable in Tyrian currency, so money changing was necessary.[48] If the tax was not paid voluntarily it was exacted by force – from Levites, Israelites, proselytes and freed slaves (not from priests). This practice must have aroused much heart-searching.[49] How long the collecting in the temple went on is not known, but it is unlikely that it could all have been carried out in two weeks.[50] It probably went on at least until Passover to catch up with the many Jews and proselytes who came to Jerusalem only at that time. That is probably the reason it was collected so close to Passover. This would mean that the money changing Jesus encountered in the last week of his life was not something that went on all year round. Since he had not attended the previous Passover,[51] the last time he had seen this business was the occasion John indicates two years earlier.

As for the selling of sacrificial animals in the temple precinct, we do not know whether it was a normal practice or not. E.P. Sanders helpfully counters the prejudice that there was something inherently evil in the sale of sacrificial animals. Some-one had to provide the many animals required for the God-appointed sacrificial system. It was impractical for country folk to bring their offerings with them. They bought them in Jerusalem along with the city people. Thus there needed to be a substantial economy in sheep, goats, cattle and doves.[52] But with the exception of sacrificial doves, most of this probably normally took place outside of the temple.[53] The sale of large animals in the temple area may well have been a special provision to deal with the approximately thirty thousand sacrifices required at Passover. If it was controlled by the high priestly family it would have been a source of considerable revenue.[54] It may also have been the subject of controversy quite apart from Jesus' action.

What might Jesus' attitude to the business in the temple have been on a second occasion? One gets the impression that he almost commandeered the temple for his own purposes during this last week. He would not even allow people to carry anything through.[55] It became his teaching seat and perhaps also a place of sanctuary.[56] The authorities regarded it foolhardy to arrest him there in the presence of so many enthusiasts. The unpopularity of the temple trading probably made it difficult for them to protest too loudly and rallied more of the common people to his side. The authorities seem to have been paralysed to know what to do until they received unexpected help from Judas. Thus it is most unlikely that Jesus would not have 'cleansed' the temple, if he had done it on the former occasion. It is not the desire to harmonize the gospels at all costs which draws me to this conclusion, but the believable picture which emerges.

A New Jeremiah?

There are also important differences between the cleansing described by John and that of the other gospels, which discount the possibility of literary dependence between them, but which may also indicate the very different situations in which each took place. Jesus' final words of protest on each occasion betoken different circumstances. The first time he simply issues a command, 'Do not make my Father's house a house of trade.' The last time he uses more ominous words, echoing Jeremiah, 'My house shall be called a house of prayer, but you have made it a bandits' cave'.

These words alert us to the fact that Jesus saw his actions in this last week as in some way hearkening back to the prophet who six hundred years earlier had been called to declare the doom of the temple and the destruction of the nation. The very imagery which Jesus used to describe the fall of Jerusalem as he wept over it is borrowed from Jeremiah, and although one can hardly speak of his tears being borrowed, the likeness to Jeremiah is notable.[57] Jeremiah was told by God to go and stand in the gate of the temple and call the people to repentance. If they refused he would eject them from the land and not even the temple would save them. 'Is this house which is called by my name become a *den of robbers* in your eyes?' God asked, that they should continue in their evil deeds and then come running to the temple to rejoice in the security of its shadow. Jeremiah was to point them to Shiloh where God had previously had his sanctuary, to see what he would do if his people continued in their evil ways (Jeremiah 7:1–15). For Jesus to have called the temple a bandits' cave was tantamount to announcing its imminent destruction if there was not an immediate and radical turning to God amongst leaders and people.

An Oracle of Destruction?

Some argue that Jesus' overthrow of the tables was an enacted prophetic oracle announcing the temple's destruction.[58] There is little evidence for this, despite what has been said above. Jesus' attitude to the temple is still positive. It is called by God's name and he acts in zeal to restore its holiness. It was still within the reach of Israel's leaders to agree with his action and repent. Had his action been perceived as an attack on the temple it would certainly have been the central charge against him at his trial. All that was brought against him was hearsay to the effect that he had said he would destroy the temple and build it again in three days (Mark 14:56–59). It is understandable his judges could make nothing of this if it was a riddle of uncertain meaning uttered two years earlier, but quite inexplicable if he was known to have made a transparent attack on the temple that very week. Each of the gospel writers saw Jesus' action as fundamentally pro-temple, and so it seems did his opponents.

Jesus in the Temple

The scene is remarkable. Here was a man, proscribed by law, an outlaw who was guilty unless proved otherwise, entering the capital city of the Jewish world, moving into its holiest place in a peaceful manner and making it his teaching seat. From another angle, we have the promised King entering Jerusalem, 'the City of the Great King', taking his seat in the very house of God. The authorities are paralysed. The High Priest held his office because of his proven capacity for preventing rebellion and rioting. He was not about to provoke a riot himself; a popular uprising at the beginning of the feast of liberation was to be avoided at all costs. He must have been more than a little relieved that Jesus had thus far made no aggressive move to subvert the government, though this was surely what the disciples and the crowds wanted him to do; what else did they mean by calling him the Son of David? The authorities probably expected that sooner or later Jesus would act, especially when he began denouncing the scribes (though not the priests) in the temple.[59] Yet for the moment there was some comfort in that all he was doing was teaching. So the leaders joined the crowds in the temple and took what opportunities they could to probe him. They set traps to discredit him in the eyes of the people, or embarrass him before the Roman administration.[60]

The Question of Authority
(Mark 11:27–33; Matthew 21:23–27; Luke 20:1–8)

Jesus' opponents began probing for weaknesses. The first attempt involved the old question of authority, which had been raised again in acute form by his temple action. Jesus proposed a counter-question: was the baptism of John from heaven or human beings? In other words, did John's movement carry the authority of God, or was it sanctioned merely by John's charismatic power? It was a clever manoeuvre on Jesus' part: challenge them to answer their own question – for John had borne witness to one who would come after him – or declare publicly that John was a fraud. They were unable to give the answer they wanted for fear of being stoned by the people, who revered John as a prophet, so they equivocated and said they did not know. Jesus, accordingly, refused to answer their question; he was not about to 'come clean' with people who would not deal straight with him. Even at this late stage, despite his royal entry into Jerusalem and his allowing the people to say of him what they would, Jesus was not playing into the hands of his enemies by speaking of himself unequivocally as Messiah. They were not seeking to know the truth, but only to find grounds to accuse him. Thus the time for riddles was not quite over, though they were becoming more and more transparent.

The Parable of the Tenants in the Vineyard
(Mark 12:1–12; Matthew 21:33–46; Luke 20:9–19)

At this point Jesus told a story about a man who sent his servant to collect his share of a vineyard he had let out to tenants. Successive servants were beaten up – if they were not killed – and sent away empty-handed. Finally he sent his only son. The parable fits its context so well and includes such an obvious allusion to the temple that here is where it surely belongs. Significantly, it is based on an idea from Jeremiah's temple discourse (Jeremiah 7:25–26), adding to the impression that Jesus saw himself in a Jeremiah-like situation.

The vineyard was a transparent figure for Israel (Isaiah 5:1–7); the servants who were wounded and killed were obviously the prophets (Jesus emphasized their number). The attention catcher in the parable is the last desperate act of the vineyard owner: 'Still one he had, a beloved son. He sent him last to them saying, "They will respect my son." ' But no, the tenants saw this as their chance to take possession of the vineyard for themselves once and for all. So they killed the son and heir and cast him out of the vineyard. No father in his right mind would ever think of sending his son into such a situation. Jesus again introduces an incongruity to rivet attention to a crucial point. And the point here is that the Messiah coming at the end of a long line of prophets will fare no better than they; he will be murdered by Israel's own caretakers.

Jesus is frequently understood to have spoken in this parable against Israel as a whole, and intimated its rejection in favour of the Gentiles – for he went on to say that the owner would come and destroy the present tenants and give the vineyard to others. But if it was addressed to the leaders in the way that is indicated, it speaks not of the rejection of the nation, but of the authorities in their role as leaders and guardians of the people. Jesus as much as charges them with high treason against God. They have not tended his vineyard for him but for themselves, and now they are about to lay hands on his beloved son and make themselves absolute lords. God will have no recourse but to destroy them and place the vineyard in the care of others. At this point in the parable Luke notes the horrified reaction of the listeners at the enormity of the suggestion that the tenants might kill the beloved son. This could be outrage at the idea that *they* would do such a thing, but more probably they were giving vent to the unthinkable idea that the true Messiah should be so treated by his people. It is another example of how Jesus' parables carried his audience along. They were unwittingly passing judgement on themselves. He reminded them then of a stanza from the Great Hallel, which a short time before had been on the lips of his followers. 'A stone which the builders rejected: this has become the cornerstone; This is from the Lord and it is marvellous in our eyes' (Mark 12:10–11 from Psalm 118:22–23). They were the nation's builders, entrusted with shaping and preserving the national life, theirs was the responsibility of deciding whether a person was a threat to Israel's wellbeing, and therefore to be 'cast out'. They had examined Jesus and found him the wrong shape for the edifice they were constructing and maintaining; they must therefore reject him. Yet God would recover him and make him the cornerstone, the stone whose perfection of shape qualified it to determine the lines of the whole building.[61] There is a possible play on words in the Hebrew between son (*ben*) and stone (*eben*).[62] Jesus' hearers must have caught in this building imagery a glimpse of the temple of the new age, to be built without human hands.[63] Once before Jesus had said he would in three days raise up just such a temple. He had now gone further in implying even to the authorities that he understood himself as the Son of God (Messiah) who would be determinative for the shape of the new age. However, the kingdom would not come without his first being rejected and killed; it would be a miraculous work of God, recovering the rejected one and employing him to reconstruct the temple and community of the age-to-come. The stone saying hints at resurrection, but also implies a future appearance of the kingdom, as in the parable of the pounds.

Perhaps the way Jesus described his sonship also suggested there was something more to his identity than anointed kingship. In explaining the words of God at his baptism, and to the three disciples at the transfiguration, I hesitated going beyond seeing 'Son of God' as Messiah by virtue of his office as God's earthly representative. It was difficult to think Jesus' disciples and the gospels' first Jewish readers could have had any other view. But Jesus' own public reference to himself as 'the beloved son of God' calls for deeper reflection. The 'beloved son' of the Old Testament is Isaac. God tells Abraham to sacrifice 'your son, your only son, whom you love' (Genesis 22:1), and refers to him twice more in the chapter as 'your only son'. However, the Septuagint, possibly following a Jewish interpretative tradition, describes Isaac three times as the 'beloved son'. A beloved son of Abraham is one thing, but what could be intended by a beloved son of God? The parable suggests a more fundamental and intimate filial relationship between God and the final messenger than can be accounted for from normal messianic categories. That Jesus intended to provoke such inquiry about his person becomes even clearer in another question he put to his hearers at the same time.

Who Is the Messiah?
(Mark 12:35–37; Matthew 22:41–45; Luke 20:41–44)

How can the Messiah be David's son if David calls him Lord? According to Jesus there must be more to messiahship than sitting on Israel's throne as David's successor. There would be nothing in that to establish the Messiah in anything more than an inferior relationship to David, his 'father' and the head of the dynasty. Yet according to Psalm 110 David acknowledged the lordship of his promised son. It is the clearest indication we have yet encountered that Jesus claimed something more for himself than the title to Israel's kingship. It carries us back to that occasion in his childhood, years before his messianic commission, when his parents missed him in the group of pilgrims returning from Jerusalem and found him in the temple sitting amongst the teachers discussing the things of God. 'Did you not know that I had to be in my Father's house?' was his surprised answer to the news that his parents had thought him lost (Luke 2:41–51). Now, twenty years later, God's Son was once again in his Father's house, the place where he truly belonged.

There were now only three courses open to the 'authorities'. They must dismiss him as a madman, but how could they do that to one who taught daily in the temple and had the crowds hanging on his every word? Or they could join him and sit at his feet. Or they must destroy him. Who was the ultimate authority? Who spoke for God? Who had the right to determine Israel's path? These were the issues at stake.

Notes

[1] Carson (*John*, 400) thinks it was Batanea. Mark 10:1 has Jesus ministering in Peraea in the latter part of his career.

[2] It has been argued that Jesus must have been much farther away than Peraea for Lazarus to have been dead four days. However, it is not unlikely that the

messengers could have taken two days to travel across the Jordan and locate Jesus. Jesus purposely delayed his departure for two days. He would have taken at least one day to travel to Bethany. This makes five days. If Lazarus died one day after the messengers left the four days in the tomb are accounted for.

³   Taylor (*Life*, 103) footnotes it as a didactic story whose historical basis is not known. It is not mentioned by Dodd, *Founder*, or Grant, *Jesus*.

⁴   Mark 5:22ff.; Luke 7:11ff., 22; 16:19ff.; 10:38ff. See A. Richardson, *The Gospel According to Saint John*, 139.

⁵   E.g., Brown, *John*, I, 428–430; Morris, *John*, 532–536; A.M. Hunter, *According to John*, 76f.; Westcott, *John*, 163f.; Carson, *John*, 403–404.

⁶   R. Dunkerley ('Lazarus [Jn. 11; Lk. 16:19–31]') argued that Jesus might have told the parable when his disciples urged him that raising Lazarus would be a powerful way of convincing the Jews in Jerusalem. Jesus replied that they would not be convinced even if someone were to come back from the dead. Although in the parable the request for Lazarus' return is refused, faced with the grief of Mary and Martha, Jesus later decided to raise him anyway. This is unconvincing. It contradicts too much of what John depicts as the occasion of the miracle and ignores the thrust of the major part of the parable, directed as it is towards the rich.

⁷   In the Gospel of John there are none but Lazarus and Malchus (John 18:10–11; Luke 22:50–51). Elsewhere Simon's mother-in-law (Mark 1:30–31), Jairus' daughter (Mark 5:22–43), Mary Magdalene (Luke 8:2), Bartimaeus (Mark 10:46–52).

⁸   Morris, *John*, 534–535.

⁹   See C.H. Dodd, 'The Framework of the Gospel Narrative', 1–11.

¹⁰   The apocryphal Secret Gospel of Mark actually does include an account of Jesus raising a young man between Mark 10:34 and 35. 'And they come into Bethany. And a certain woman whose brother had died was there. And, coming, she prostrated herself before Jesus and says to him, "Son of David, have mercy on me". But the disciples rebuked her. And Jesus, being angered, went off with her into the garden where the tomb was, and straightaway a great cry was heard from the tomb. And going near Jesus rolled away the stone from the door of the tomb. And straightaway, going in where the youth was, he stretched forth his hand and raised him, seizing his hand. But the youth, looking upon him, loved him and began to beseech that he might be with him' (M. Smith, *The Secret Gospel: The Discovery and Interpretation of the Secret Gospel According to Mark*, 447).

¹¹   According to Bab. Talmud Sanhedrin 43a the formal decision to put Jesus to death was forty days before Passover. See p. 488–491 below.

[12] Mark 14:3 identifies the house where the later anointing took place as the 'house of Simon the Leper'. There is no other mention of him so he could not have lived at home, even if he were still alive.

[13] P.W. Barnett, 'Under Tiberius all was Quiet', 589–590.

[14] Schürer, *History*, II, 230.

[15] Josephus, *War*, 2.39–79; *History*, 17.250–298.

[16] Further see O. Betz ('Probleme des Prozesses Jesu [Mk. 14.15]', 598–609) who recounts other instances of the same policy and argues that the sacrifice of one man for the preservation of temple and people was a part of Sadducaean politics, born in the sacrificial cult.

[17] *Babylonian Talmud Sanhedrin* 43a. J. Jeremias, (*Eucharistic Words*, 19, n. 7) follows Dalman in denying that this Yeshu is our Jesus, but rather the disciple of R. Joshua b. Parahiah (100 BC). However this disciple was probably originally unnamed and later falsely identified with Jesus, leading to the association with *Sanhedrin* 43a. See *Bab. Talmud Sotah* 47a; *Sanhedrin* 107b. Further J. Klausner, *Jesus*, 24–28.

[18] See Robinson, *Priority*, 145; Brown, *John*, I, 441. W.F. Albright ('Ophrah and Ephraim', 124–133) points out that 'Et Taiyebah is not on the edge of the wilderness as John describes, and is one of the coldest places in Israel at that time of the year. It is quite exposed and does not appear to commend itself as a hiding place. His archaeological soundings indicated a first century town at the present 'Ein Samiyah.

[19] From Jericho to Jerusalem Jesus was with a large crowd (Mark 10:46; Matthew 20:29; Luke 18:36; 19:3, 37).

[20] John 12:1 has Jesus coming to Bethany six days before Passover. If Passover began on the eve of the following Friday this would be Sunday (they would not have travelled on Saturday). If Passover was Thursday the day would be Saturday or Friday. The entry to Jerusalem is also unlikely to have been on a Saturday, so a Friday arrival does not square with John 12:12.

[21] Only Mark names him: Bartimaeus the son of Timaeus. He was evidently known to Mark or his community. Matthew says there were two blind men involved. Mark's focus on the more prominent person is not untypical: compare Mark 5:2 with Matthew 8:28 and Mark 16:5 with Luke 24:4. Luke relates this story at Jesus' entry into Jericho. He probably wanted to climax the central section of his gospel (the 'journey') with the salvation of Zacchaeus, and to preface the entry into Jerusalem with the parable of the pounds. There is no obvious reason for Mark to have made a rearrangement, so I accept his placing of the event.

[22] H. Conzelmann (*The Theology of Saint Luke*) thinks Luke responded to the non-appearance of Jesus by developing a new sense of time. Instead of viewing Jesus' coming as the end of the age, soon to be consummated with his reappearance, it becomes the middle of time (the original German title of his book was *Die Mitte der Zeit*), an age for the expansion of the church, and Jesus' return is pushed into the indefinite future. However, the presence of the delay motif in Q, Matthew, and perhaps even Mark makes this no creation of Luke.

[23] Wright, *Victory*, 632–639.

[24] Jeremias, *Parables*, 58–63.

[25] Wright, *Victory*, 632–633.

[26] Josephus, *War*, 1.664; 2.1–39, 80–95, 111; *History*, 17.188–249, 299–320, 339–354.

[27] M. Zerwick ('Die Parabel vom Thronanwärter', 654–674) points out that the clear allusion to Archelaus which runs from the beginning to end of the parable (including the 'austere' man in the central part) undermines the case of those who see it as a Lukan elaboration of Matthew's parable of the talents. Whatever the relationship between the two parables, Luke's must be authentic.

[28] R. Winterbotham ('Christ or Archelaus?', 338–347) sees the figure of Archelaus behind the 'austere' businessman of the parable but recoils from any application to Jesus. Cf. J. Ellul, 'Du texte au sermon 18: Les talents Matthieu 25:13–30', 134–136.

[29] See above.

[30] Josephus, *History*, 17.340; Kroll, *Spuren*, 392–395.

[31] Wright, *Victory*, 612–653. See especially his setting out of the Old Testament and extra-biblical evidence for this idea (616–624).

[32] L.T. Johnson ('The Lukan Kingship Parable [Luke 19:11–27]', 139–159) thinks the parable *confirms* the disciples' expectation of an immediate appearance of the kingdom. He sees no idea of a delay in the parable. How he can say this when Luke juxtaposes the disciples' belief in the immediate appearance of the kingdom with the nobleman going away to receive his kingdom and leaving them with work to do is beyond me.

[33] Johnson ('Kingship Parable', 155–159) thinks the leaders were rejected and the disciples given authority when Jesus came to Jerusalem and declared his kingdom. It certainly did not appear so! In an earlier work (*Literary Function*) Johnson developed the concept that apostolic authority was symbolized in their control of possessions. While I do not wish to dispute that the kingdom was, in a manner, declared and established in the events which were about to

take place in Jerusalem, it cannot be said that the kingdom *appeared*. In Acts 1:6 the disciples are still asking 'when?'

[34] Compare the parable of the servants waiting for the return of the bride-groom (Luke 12:35–48). The one thing the master requires to be done in his absence is for his (lesser) servants to be fed and cared for.

[35] Mark gives the impression that Jesus reached a level with Bethany, made arrangements to procure a mount, and then made a dramatic entry into the city that same day (Mark 11:1ff.). John makes it clear that they actually spent a night in Bethany (John 12:1ff.). Mark is streamlining his story in the way we have seen all the gospels do on occasions. There is a further problem reconciling John and Mark's placing of the meal. When it is seen that Mark relates the story of the meal at the point of Judas' going to the authorities as a flashback explaining his defection, it is clear we must follow John's order.

[36] Josephus, *War*, 2.261ff.; *History*, 20.167ff.

[37] Josephus, *War*, 5.223.

[38] Suggested by Cranfield, *Mark*, 351.

[39] J. Klausner, *Jesus of Nazareth*, 309f.

[40] 1 Samuel 6:7f.; cf. 2 Samuel 6:3.

[41] See Jeremias, *Eucharistic Words*, 255.

[42] V. Taylor, *Life and History of Jesus*, 186f.

[43] It is important in understanding the chronology of the last week to know that the Jewish day began at sunset.

[44] T.W. Manson, 'Cleansing', 277. Goodspeed (*Jesus*, 166) says they are even offered for sale.

[45] Luke 3:9; 13:6–9; 14:34f.; Matthew 5:13.

[46] *Mishnah Aboth* 1:2, Simeon the Just was High Priest either in 280 BC or 200 BC.

[47] *Mishnah Shekalim* 1:3. See Robinson, *Priority*, 128.

[48] The half shekel coin from Tyre had a reliable silver content.

[49] Bauckham ('Coin') thinks Jesus had strong objections to the very principle of the temple tax: God does not tax his own children (Matthew 17:24–27).

[50] B.H. Branscom (*Mark*, 204) says the money changers operated for only one week since the tax was due by 1 Nisan, a fortnight before Passover. He overlooks, however, that exactions were then made of unpaid taxes, and also that the majority of visitors who were to pay the tax in Jerusalem would not arrive until the week prior to Passover.

[51] Jesus was questioned about his non-payment of the temple tax that year by the collectors in Capernaum. His journey to the north apparently caused him to miss the usual collection time (Matthew 17:24–27).

[52] Sanders, *Jesus and Judaism*, 61ff.

[53] SB, 1, 851 describes the markets for sacrifices on the Mount of Olives. J. Jeremias (*Jerusalem in the Time of Jesus*, 48–49) reviews the evidence for trade in the temple. There is evidence for the regular sale of doves. *Mishnah Shekalim* 6:5 describes thirteen money chests in the temple, two of them for bird offerings, one for wood and one for frankincense. The lack of any mention of money for larger animals suggests these were not regularly provided for worshippers in the temple precincts.

[54] M. Bockmuehl (*This Jesus*, 69–71) gives evidence for the questionable commercial reputation of the priestly hierarchy.

[55] Mark 11:16. Cf. *Mishnah Berakhot* 9:5.

[56] Luke 19:47; Mark 11:17–19, 27; 12:41; Matthew 21:14–17, 23; 24:1.

[57] Jeremiah 6:6–15; 9:1; 13:17.

[58] Sanders, *Jesus and Judaism*, 61–90.

[59] Mark 12:38–40; Matthew 23:1–39; Luke 20:45–47. The triple testimony to Jesus' severe criticism of the scribes renders improbable the idea that it arose from conflict between Christians and Jews later in the century.

[60] Luke 20:20; Mark 11:27ff.; Matthew 21:23ff.; Luke 20:1ff.

[61] Cf. Ephesians 2:20–21; 1 Peter 2:7. According to Jeremias, *TDNT*, I, 792, the reference is not to the 'cornerstone' but to the key stone that completes the building and holds it together.

[62] So Wright, *Victory*, 501.

[63] The 'precious corner stone' of Isaiah 28:16 was known at Qumran as a prophetic image of the new temple/community. See 1QS 8:5ff.; Ellis, *Luke*, 231.

Chapter 16

Day Of Judgement

Official Reaction

There is a certain platinum–iridium bar kept in the International Bureau of Weights and Measures in Paris which is exactly one metre long. You may take your own metre rule and measure this bar. If it turns out to be a little more or less than a metre, however, it is not the bar which is at fault but your own rule. Those who judge others, in their act of judgement often pass judgement on themselves. Never was this more true than in the events of the last days of Jesus' life. God's cornerstone was about to be measured and found wanting.

We learn from Matthew of a meeting of the authorities which took place in the palace of Caiaphas two days before Passover, probably on Wednesday (Matthew 26:2–4).[1] The business of the day was to find a way to seize Jesus and do away with him without provoking an uprising. The only positive result of the meeting that we learn about is that it ruled out the possibility of arresting him during the feast; the danger of sparking off a reaction which might unseat their government was too great. Did they hope they might be able to dispose of Jesus before the feast? They must dearly have wished they could, for with Jesus surrounded by crowds of disciples in the temple, and hundreds of thousands of worshippers streaming into the city, the authorities must have been dreadfully apprehensive about his real intentions. It may have been that very day that word came to them that someone was offering to lead them to Jesus at a time when he was away from the crowds.[2]

The Last Meal
(Mark 14:12ff.; Luke 22:7ff.; Matthew 26:17ff.; John 13:1ff.; 1 Corinthians 11:23ff.)

On Thursday Jesus sent Peter and John to prepare for their Passover celebration. There is evidence of careful planning on Jesus' part; not even the twelve knew where the meal was to be held. Secrecy was essential for a man who was liable to instant arrest. Knowing that one of his men was not to be counted on meant keeping his plans even from them. Two disciples were sent into the city where they would be met by a man carrying a stone water jar. He would take them to a house where they could arrange the meal in a large upstairs room that had been reserved for them. In the evening Jesus and the others came; Judas was among them. We have several sources of information for what happened at this meal. In addition to Mark there is Luke's separate source, John's extended treatment and an account in 1 Corinthians.

Jesus' Love

What a person does on their last day says a great deal about them. It was the conclusion of Jesus' ordinary ministry among his disciples and his last evening of freedom and normal life. We cannot be sure that he knew he would see them again in a mere three days. Nowhere in the gospel records is his love for his disciples so transparent as on this evening. Soon after their arrival, he expressed his affection in a physical way by washing their feet.

In days when roads were dusty and sandalled feet were always dirty, the washing of feet before a meal was more than a luxury. Normally it was a slave's job to remove the guests' shoes and perform this task. Peter and John had been sent to make ready the meal, but their preparations evidently did not reach to this. A disciple was expected to serve his master in everything except removing footware.[3] To have gone to that length would remove the last distinction between disciple and slave. John's heavily interpreted account of what took place shows the deep impression made on him by Jesus' unexpected action (John 13:1–5).

Moving from one to another, Jesus placed himself in the position of the slave, and in a most intimate way expressed something of his feeling towards each individual disciple. We may guess that silent messages came back. By the time he had been around the twelve he could probably have identified his betrayer had he not already known. Peter's body language also betrayed him: he withdrew his feet, unable to endure Jesus acting the slave to him. In the intense interchange that followed, Jesus made it clear that his action was more than a spontaneous token of love; it was a parable of what he was about to do for them through his death.

> Lord, are you going to wash my feet?
> What I am doing you do not know now, but you will know later.
> Never will you wash my feet.
> If I do not wash you, you have no part with me.
> Lord, not my feet only, but my hands and my head.
> (John 13:8)

What Jesus was about to declare in giving them his 'body' and 'blood', he made clear here through washing their feet. The one who said 'Whoever of you wishes to be first, let him become the slave of all,' showed the way. The Servant of the Lord serves his friends by removing the defilement which barred their way to fellowship with God. Membership of his kingdom, first of all means being loved and served in this way by its king; only then can there be any thought of reciprocal service.

The incident shows how deeply the Servant role permeated Jesus' mentality. He followed it with a plea that they love and serve one another. Though he was about to be removed from them, he clearly envisaged them going on together as a community (John 13:12–17). The last meal was a natural climax to their many times of fellowship on the road, but it also pointed forward to the fellowship of forgiven men and women which he expected to go on beyond his death. His most fervently expressed desire for them was that they should go on loving one another as he had loved them (John 13:34–35).

Was This Passover?

The four gospels agree that the last supper took place on Thursday evening and Jesus' crucifixion on Friday. However, while Mark, Matthew and Luke say that Jesus ate *the Passover* with his disciples, implying that the sacrifice of the lambs took place that very Thursday afternoon, John says the supper was the day before Passover.[4] The Talmud says 'On the eve of Passover Jeshu was hanged,' agreeing with John.[5] Astronomical evidence also indicates the probability that Passover in AD 30 (and 33) fell on Friday.[6] The crux of the problem is that in the synoptic gospels Jesus and his disciples clearly understand themselves to be eating the Passover on Thursday night, whereas in John the priestly authorities are anxious on Friday to keep themselves undefiled so they might eat it later that day.

A great deal of scholarly labour has gone into the elucidation of this problem and various solutions been proposed. Some think the supper took place on Passover eve, but John has placed it earlier so he could represent Jesus dying at the time the Passover lambs were killed. Others suggest Jesus celebrated an early Passover as he knew he was about to be arrested. Some suggest different groups celebrated Passover at different times, others that the authorities had to eat their Passover late because of the trial the previous evening. None of these suggestions is proven.

The most promising direction is the probability that there was some latitude over the day on which people ate the Passover. This is declared impossible by some, and it must be admitted that the days of great festivals are generally fixtures. It is difficult to think of people celebrating Christmas on different days.[7] Passover, however, presented some special problems. First, its date had to be determined by a sighting of the 'new light' indicating a new moon.[8] This meant the exact date of Passover could not be known far in advance. There was an official announcement of the month's beginning, but there could have been disagreement. The situation was further complicated by groups who favoured different calendars.[9] There was also a logistical problem: more than ten thousand lambs needed to be sacrificed in the temple for everyone to eat Passover, and enough space found for all to cook and eat.[10] There is evidence that some ate Passover at an irregular time by the expedient of presenting their sacrifice as some other offering (they could do this on any day) and then utilizing it for a Passover celebration.[11] Thus the date on which people ate the Passover may not have been as rigidly determined as our Christmas – there was even a second Passover for those who missed the first.[12] It is not unthinkable, therefore, that Jesus and his disciples shared what may have been seen as a legitimate celebration the day previous to the official festivities.[13]

I offer this as a very tentative solution, knowing it is not the only possibility.[14] But common sense rebels against thinking that the chief priests would have involved themselves with the scribes and elders in an arrest and all night trial on the evening of the most solemn feast of the year, even if it were a legal possibility.[15] It would mean them spending the busiest day of their official year organizing an arrest and trial, involving a good part of Jerusalem's Jewish leadership on a night when it was obligatory for the poorest person to drink four cups of wine.[16] It stretches the imagination to think that the chief priests would have planned such a thing, especially if there was an alternative, which even Mark's chronology suggests there was.

According to Mark the meeting of the Council which decided *not* to arrest Jesus during the feast, and Judas' disclosure to the authorities took place two days before the Passover and feast of Unleavened Bread.[17] If the official slaughter of the lambs took place two days later as this indicates, the possibility lay before them to strike the next day and have the execution over before the festivities began in earnest at noon on Friday. Surely their only other alternative was to wait until the feast was over, with the obvious risk that Jesus might make his move earlier.

Passover and Kingdom

Jesus' first words in Luke's account of the supper confirm that in his and the disciples' eyes they were celebrating Passover, and may also indicate that there was something premature or irregular about their celebration.

> How I have longed to eat this Passover with you before I die. For I tell you I shall never eat it again until it is fulfilled in the kingdom of God. Taking a cup he gave thanks and said, Take this and divide it among yourselves, for I tell you, from now on I will not drink from the fruit of the vine until the kingdom of God comes. (Luke 22:15–18)

Jeremias thinks Jesus is giving expression here to an unfulfilled desire. Though it was a Passover meal and he dearly wanted to share it with his disciples he refrained because he had taken a vow to fast on behalf of his disobedient countrymen until the establishment of the kingdom. Jesus himself, therefore, did not eat.[18] His words over the cup certainly indicate that he did not drink, but the first part of the statement hardly amounts to an intention to fast. Surely if Jesus had longed to eat the Passover with his disciples he would not then have refrained from doing so. However, the ordeal which lay ahead of him precluded wine. He would not drink again until the kingdom of God had come. The kingdom would follow his death and was related to it in his mind.

Passover was the Jews' celebration of liberty. They rehearsed together how God had rescued them from slavery in Egypt and anticipated how he would in some future passover save them finally from all the powers of evil.[19] When Jesus spoke of the Passover's fulfilment in the kingdom of God he was talking about something very familiar, for on the first Passover they were redeemed, and on the 'last', when the kingdom came, they would be redeemed.[20] The focus of the celebration was the lamb itself, representative of the lambs whose blood had marked the Israelite dwellings, ensuring that the destroying angel would pass over and spare them in the hour of Egypt's judgement. That redemption was now enjoyed by the whole nation. Rabbi Akiba used to pray 'Let us praise you for our redemption and for the ransoming of our soul. Blessed are you, O Lord, who has redeemed Israel.'[21] We recall Jesus' words, 'The Son of Man came not to be served, but to serve and to give his life a ransom for many' (Mark 10:45).

Jesus' Intention

Consideration of a person's life-quest seldom includes their death. Though this may be entailed, it is usually forced upon them, or accidental. We would generally say they would have achieved more if they had not died. With Jesus it is different. We have seen several hints of deeply considered purpose in his thinking about his death, signs that he saw it achieving something which could be done no other way. From the outset his over-riding purpose and mission was to inaugurate the kingdom of God – to establish himself as king over a world reconciled to God. Various elements of his strategy have emerged: announcing the kingdom gospel, planting the seeds of life transformation through teaching, manifesting the powers of the age-to-come, training disciples, coming to Jerusalem, taking his rightful messianic place in the temple. All this is comprehensible in terms of a pattern which might conceivably lead to Israel saying 'Yes' and its acknowledging him as king. Yet Jesus did not believe that they would. He knew they would kill him. This raises the question of whether he viewed this as defeat or as part of his kingdom-inaugurating plan. And if the latter, what did he think it would achieve? Jesus' words in the course of the last supper allow us to penetrate his thinking.

My Body, My Blood (Mark 14:22–24)

There is no mention of the actual lamb at the last supper, but when Jesus took bread and called it his body, and wine and called it his blood, he alluded to it.[22] In inviting his disciples to eat and drink Jesus made them participants in the forgiveness and life which he saw would flow from his sacrifice, just as he had intimated in his discourse on the 'bread from heaven' in the Capernaum synagogue.[23] His blood would 'be poured out for many' to cancel guilt and seal a new covenant of forgiveness between God and his people.

There can be little doubt that we should connect all this with the mission of the Suffering Servant, which we have seen from the beginning of our study was never far from Jesus' mind. Isaiah's Servant is the one place in the Old Testament where sacrificial ideas are applied to a human victim.

> Yet it pleased the Lord to bruise him; he has caused him to suffer. When he makes himself a guilt offering he shall see his seed, he shall prolong his days; the will of the Lord will prosper in his hand. He shall see the fruit of the suffering of his soul and be satisfied; by his knowledge shall my righteous servant justify many and he shall bear their sins. (Isaiah 53:10–11)

According to the fourth Servant Song God's Servant would be exalted before the kings of the earth, but only as he is first despised and rejected and led to slaughter like a helpless lamb. His life given in this way, in accord with the will and plan of God, would function as a sacrificial guilt offering. The 'chastisement' owing to the many would be borne by the one. He would die without issue, but live again to see the fruit of his suffering in the many who would be forgiven, washed and acquitted on his account. Jesus' saying that he would give his life as a ransom for many, the resolute path he trod towards his own destruction, and his words at the last supper make it plain that he saw his death in these terms.[24]

Sacrifice

The idea that forgiveness might come through blood shed in sacrifice is foreign and repugnant to many twentieth-century people, and it is understandable that some would wish to shy away from it in relation to the meaning of Jesus' death. However, if we are to understand him in his own terms we must be careful not to saddle him in advance with the predilections and dislikes of our own thinking. He was a Jew amongst Jews of the first century, when the temple with its sacrificial cult stood at the centre of the national life. He deliberately entered Jerusalem at a time which would place his death in a Passover context, when it would readily be understood in sacrificial terms. At the very time of the last meal more than a hundred thousand Israelites were gathering to participate in a solemn sacrificial ceremony at the temple. Two men from each eating party came to the temple with their lamb, lined up opposite the priests, cut their animal's throat, drained its blood into a bowl and handed it to a priest to throw on the altar. They skinned and gutted their lamb and took it home to roast on a spit. Then the party would consume the sacrifice, thankfully conscious of their participation in Israel's redemption. Joachim Jeremias, an expert on Jewish antiquities, was adamant that Jesus' death must be seen against this background.

> The oft repeated assertion that it is inconceivable that Jesus should have ascribed atoning power to his death, that such statements belong rather to the 'dogmatic' of the Early Church or to the apostle Paul, is astonishing to anyone who knows the Palestinian sources ... The sources compel the conclusion that *it is inconceivable that Jesus should not have thought of the atoning power of his death*.[25]

Schweitzer, and more recently Wright, are firm on this point: a sacrificial doctrine of Jesus' death was not something which made its appearance later; Jesus himself pursued his ministry and moved towards his death under 'doctrinal' influences: he believed that God wanted him to bear the guilt of the nation by means of his own death, so moved his life in that direction.[26]

The psychological, spiritual and instinctual roots of sacrifice run deep. Most ancient societies practised it in one form or another; some present-day cultures still do. Guilt that is deep and real requires something dramatic and supernatural to expunge it. Sacrifice could be understood as crudely as the irretrievable giving up to God (or to a god) of something precious to make amends and turn away divine anger (or secure divine favour). For the Hebrews it had a more refined meaning, for the sacrifice of an animal in the prescribed manner was a *God-given* mechanism for dealing with guilt and restoring an individual or community to right standing with him. The animal's death gave graphic expression to the seriousness of sin, which severed relationship with God, and ultimately led to death. At the same time it declared the possibility of restoration for the guilty person or community through the payment of a ransom. The focus of attention was not on the value of the animal. Most sacrifices were eaten by the people who offered them. Rather, it was the death of an unblemished victim which was essential, and God had designated certain animals for this purpose. To share in eating a sacrifice was to participate in the benefits which flowed from it: remission of guilt, reconciliation with God, and restoration to the covenant community.

It is paradoxical that we have Jesus to thank for freeing us from the necessity of offering blood sacrifice. If it had not been for him it is likely that sacrifice would be as common today as it was in the ancient world. It is still common in Hindu, Buddhist, Islamic, animistic and ancestor-venerating societies. Yet we should never forget that he brought the system to an end not by condemning it, declaring it redundant or repugnant to God, but by affirming and fulfilling it. Jesus offered himself as the sacrifice to end all sacrifices, and wherever Christianity has gone sacrifice has ceased. People look at him and see that something real and substantial has happened to deal with their guilt. They also see what their forgiveness cost. The concepts of ransom and sacrifice coalesce. We are able to contemplate a world without blood sacrifice because Jesus saw himself as the sacrifice towards which all others pointed as symbols and prophecies.

Restoration Still in View (Luke 22:28–34)

According to Luke, at the last meal Jesus renewed a promise to the disciples:

> You are the ones who have remained with me in my trials. I covenant with you, just as my Father has covenanted with me to give you a kingdom (*basileian*), that you may eat and drink at my table in my kingdom (*basileia*), and sit upon thrones judging the twelve tribes of Israel.

In translating this extraordinary statement to convey what I think is its meaning, I am conscious that I have given it an unusual interpretation. The first instance of the Greek word *basileia* could be rendered 'royal authority', to give this passage a more dynamic sense. However, when Jesus speaks of sitting at table in his kingdom he clearly has in mind the coming state of affairs in which he will rule as king over the restored people of God in a restored world. To speak of his followers exercising 'royal authority' in this context implies the existence of kingdoms within an overarching kingdom, and Jesus identifies these with the tribes of Israel. In language that implies a solemn and binding deposition, Jesus promises that the twelve will reign as judge–kings over these communities. This notion reappears in the book of Revelation (4:4, 9–10).

The hope that Israel would be restored obviously still shone as bright as ever, but it would be a very different Israel whose new leaders governed in the manner of service and love to which Jesus was training them. The memory of their Messiah crouched at their feet like a slave would be difficult to escape. Nevertheless they still had a way to go before they would be ready for their new task. Satan was demanding to 'sift them like wheat', and none would pass the test. But Jesus was praying that they might not fall forever. Peter in particular would turn again and become the ministering servant of the others (cf. John 21:15–19). It was unthinkable to Peter, whose loyalty to Jesus seems almost passionate, that he should desert. He vowed and declared, as did the others, that he would go to prison and death before he would deny his master. Jesus knew his followers well; none of them would stand in the ordeal that was approaching. Before the break of day Peter would deny even knowing him.

Jesus A Criminal (Luke 22:35–38)

In his last words to them before they left the room Jesus warned them that, in accordance with the prophecies about the Servant of Yahweh, he was now to be 'reckoned with transgressors' (Isaiah 53:12). His being deemed a criminal and executed would have grave consequences for his followers. He reminded them of when he had sent them out without purse or bag or sandals; in

the exercise of their kingdom–bringing mission they had wanted
for nothing. But in the future things would be different. The
ejection of their master would mean the signs of his kingdom
would also disappear. They could not henceforth rely on God
always to provide and protect in the miraculous way that befitted
the kingdom-like conditions of their former missions. From now
on normal preparations and equipment would be needed, even at
times a sword. The disciples were able immediately to lay hands
on two. It was hardly what Jesus intended. One of them left the
meal strapped to the side of Simon Peter. Perhaps he thought that
Jesus was at last beginning to talk sense.

Gethsemane (Mark 14:32ff.; Luke 22:39ff.; Matthew 26:30ff.; John 18:1ff.)

Judas took his leave before the end of the meal and went to meet
the priests to lead them to the place on the Mount of Olives where
Jesus would spend the night. The way John speaks suggests a walled
garden owned by one of Jesus' Jerusalem followers. Gethsemane is
a Hebrew name meaning 'oil press'. It was not uncommon for
teachers to make use of such gardens for the private instruction
of their disciples.[27] Jesus had been there often (John 18:1–2).
On Passover night people slept within the extended bounds of
Jerusalem. Bethany lay outside these limits; perhaps there was also
danger to their friends if they slept there. Judas knew where they
would be and the best time to catch them unawares.

Despite the difficulty of Jesus' private prayers, many otherwise
sceptical scholars give credence to the Gethsemane story. Its
attestation in different forms in the gospels and a further possible
reference in Hebrews 5:7, along with its depiction of a frightened
Jesus and witless disciples, speaks for essential historicity.[28]

The disciples settled down. Jesus took Peter, James and John a
little way from the others and asked them to pray with him. He
was in a state of some mental anguish. There is something about

the story of Jesus' agony in the garden which eludes normal critical study. It is possible to explain the words and yet to remain totally outside what happened. He seems to have gone through an experience of horror such as most of us only ever approach in nightmares, yet he was the most awake person in the garden. Many have reflected on the fact that his demeanour before death was in sharp contrast to certain other heroes of history, Socrates most notably. Even the later Christian martyrs seem to have gone to their deaths with a good deal more equanimity than Jesus. To be fair, we should observe that at the time of his actual death Jesus seemed to have moved beyond the horror of the garden. Do we know anything about the moment when these others faced head on the reality of their impending doom? When a human being stands before a life and death decision, the mental battle leading to the determination to go forward can be more difficult than the death itself. Yet to say this is only to touch the edge of Jesus' experience that night.

Mark uses two words to describe Jesus' emotional state, one meaning distress and one whose meaning is not altogether clear (*ekthambeisthai*). It indicates intense emotion, but was it amazement, or fear, or distress? Matthew replaces it with a word meaning grief. Jesus' own words certainly betray deep sorrow. 'I am so sorrowful I could die' (Mark 14:34). This is a strange utterance from one who is bracing himself to die, expressive surely of something more than the natural sorrow of impending death. One of his handpicked men, whom he had lived with, nurtured and trained for the past two years, had turned against him. For all his protestations of loyalty, Jesus knew that Peter would not stand. Indeed, all his followers would turn tail when trouble struck. Even in the garden his three closest friends were unable to stay awake a mere hour with him in his agony. Was his sorrow compounded with the knowledge that his own sufferings entailed the ultimate closure of opportunity and favour toward Israel? The forgiveness for which he had once fasted forty days – the stay of execution and season for renewal for which the gardener had petitioned – had elapsed, and what lay ahead for Israel was too terrible to contemplate. 'Do not weep for me, but weep for yourselves and your own children,' he would say as they led him out to execution the next day (Luke 23:28). On one level what Jesus faced in the garden was the failure of two years of pleading with his countrymen to return to their God. For one who loved as Jesus did deep, depressing grief is understandable.

Temptation

Jesus told three of his disciples to 'keep watch' while he prayed. Some think he posted them to watch for intruders; that he intended to run if he got sufficient warning. But his actions and words point in another direction. The rest of the disciples had been left on their own with no instructions. The three were only a few yards from Jesus, who was preoccupied, not with escape but with facing the coming trial. The word used (*gregoreite*) means to stay awake or to be alert; Jesus had often spoken of the watch-fulness required in the face of temptations and trials.[29] Passover was traditionally a night of vigil (Exodus 12:42). Thus the enemy against whom they were to be watchful was not Judas and his party, but Jesus' old antagonist from wilderness days. In the upper room Jesus had implied that he saw the whole period of his ministry as a battle against the Devil (Luke 22:28); now 'the ruler of this world' was coming armed with greater power than ever (John 14:30). As Jesus saw it, such a struggle could only be fought by watchful prayer. The object of the attack, after all, was to make him (and the disciples) break faith with his Father; it was crucial that he stayed awake and maintained an unbroken and clear-minded contact with his Father's will.

The powerful weapon which the Devil threw against Jesus on this occasion was the prospect of his own death. In some sense this had also been the case in the wilderness, and when Peter pleaded with him on the road to Caesarea Philippi, and when he set his face to go to Jerusalem. But there was a great difference between action that put him on the road to the cross and actually peering into the darkness of the 'cup'. What Jesus saw that night was so horrible that he begged his Father to remove it from him if at all possible. Yet even then he repeated his preparedness to 'drink' if that was what his Father wanted.[30]

What did Jesus see in this cup of suffering? We can never fully know. Who in this world sees and understands the content of their own death? How then can we hope to penetrate the full reality of 'that most cruel and disgusting of all punishments' as Cicero described crucifixion.[31] But we are surely correct to insist that Jesus saw more in his cup than the agonies of crucifixion. 'The cup' is a frequent Old Testament image for the full measure of punishment which God meted out to nations or individuals.[32] Jesus saw his death as 'a ransom *instead of* many', and an atoning sacrifice. Who can say what that may have added to the content of his cup?

Karl Heim was surely right to take issue with those who minimize the seriousness of what Jesus faced in the garden, and speak as though the outcome could never have been any different than it was.[33] If the Garden of Gethsemane was not 'a piece of theatre', then Jesus on that night was as close as ever to giving up. Without the real and enticing possibility of turning aside from his Father's will, the obedience, which according to the New Testament achieved 'our salvation', would have been an empty show. Jesus stood in that garden, as Adam stood in a garden once before, the decision before him not over a piece of fruit, but over his own life. More than anything else in the gospels his agony in the choice proves the reality of his humanity. If he had chosen away from the will of God he would have gone the way of Adam and all talk of a restored Israel and a renewed humanity would be an empty mockery. He saw the worst, and felt the pull of life as strongly as anyone ever felt it, and yet chose to go with God.

Arrest

When the arresting party arrived with Judas, Jesus alone was prepared. The others, still rubbing the sleep from their eyes, panicked. The soldiers themselves were not without anxiety. They no doubt expected resistance, whatever Judas may have said, but perhaps there was more to their fear. John records the curious fact that when Jesus stepped forward and identified himself they shrank back and fell to the ground. We need to remember that Jesus had a reputation as a miracle worker; what might a person with such powers do to his enemies on a dark night? Only when he as much as put himself in their hands did they bind him and lead him away. Peter alone made any attempt at defence, drawing his sword and swiping at one of the High Priest's servants. But Jesus commanded him to put his sword away. He had determined to drink the cup. Jesus was led away, Peter and John followed him at a safe distance, and the others fled.

Whereas the first three gospels speak only of an armed 'crowd' coming with Judas to effect Jesus' arrest, John explains that the group was composed of police belonging to the chief priests and Pharisees, and part of the Roman cohort under the command of the tribune.[34] There was a Roman garrison stationed permanently in Jerusalem, which was strengthened with troops from Caesarea Maritima for the great festivals, when disturbances were more likely to break out. The involvement of the Romans at this point is surprising, and has been dismissed by some as historically unlikely. Given the situation, it seems to me anything but improbable, and a confirmation of the anxiety of the authorities. Judas had no doubt assured them that Jesus was not likely to offer resistance, and that he was taking them to him at a time when followers would be few. Whether the priests were willing to trust him altogether is doubtful. A move on someone with as much popular support as Jesus was fraught with risk; it is unlikely they would have left anything to chance. They were planning to involve the Romans

the following day anyway, so it could only have aided their
cause to request help in apprehending him. In fact the participation of the Romans appears to have been crucial to the chief
priests' strategy. The prospect of rioting – even of a coup –
when the populace learned that Jesus had been arrested, must
have loomed large in their planning. In laying hands on Jesus
with so many Galileans and others of his followers in the city,
they were taking a calculated political risk, which is only
explained by them regarding it an even bigger risk to leave him
at large during the feast. If we may infer their plan from the way
things turned out, it was to have Jesus in the hands of the
Governor, being executed under his authority, with security
guaranteed by his troops, so early the next morning that the
risk to themselves was minimal. Had everything gone according
to plan they might have expected Jesus to be on a cross before
most people in Jerusalem knew that he had been arrested.

The Judgement of the Jews

The arresting party took Jesus first to the house of Annas
(John 18:12–14, 19–24). Ananus, as Josephus calls him, was
Caiaphas' father-in-law and the real power behind the high
priesthood. He had been High Priest himself from AD 6–15
and, except for three or four years, his sons and close relatives
held the office until the forties.[35] Josephus says he was known as
'the most fortunate' of men,[36] and he appears to have been
regarded by many in the time of Jesus as the High Priest, even
though technically it was Caiaphas who held the office
(Luke 3:2; John 18:19). Our sole source of information for
Annas' preliminary examination is the Gospel of John.

Strange as it seems, John had some kind of relationship with
the High Priest, whether Annas or Caiaphas is not clear. He was
able to enter the palace courtyard and bring Peter in as well. His
contacts within the palace were good enough that he knew the

name of the servant whom Peter wounded in the garden, and
recognized one of the servants who later challenged Peter as the
wounded man's relative. Thus he could easily have discovered the
gist of what transpired between Annas and Jesus. Of the hearing
before Caiaphas John tells us nothing, though his comment that
Annas delivered Jesus bound to Caiaphas shows he knew of it.
Probably he thought there was no need since Mark had made it
common knowledge.

Annas questioned Jesus 'about his disciples, and about his
teaching', just what we would expect if the priests felt their own
position was threatened. Jesus answered only that he had never
taught in secret; everything he had said was public knowledge
and could be learned from those who had heard him. In spite of
his unwillingness to answer most of the questions put to him that
night, he retorted strongly when one of the officers struck him
for insubordination, challenging him to state clearly the wrong
he had done or desist hitting him. Having got nothing from this
questioning, Annas sent him to Caiaphas.

Night Trial (Mark 14:53–65; Matthew 26:57–68)

There is uncertainty as to the exact status of the 'trial' before
Caiaphas and the Sanhedrin, and also about when it took place.
Some have doubted whether it happened at all. Mark describes
a night trial at which Jesus was condemned to death. According
to the Mishnah capital trials could be held neither at night nor
on a feast day.[37] It was also prescribed that judgement should not
be given until the day following the trial, ruling out a trial on
the eve of a feast day unless the judgement was held over. A
judgement on the morning of Passover for a trial which took
place on the previous day would have been in order, for
Passover did not begin until the afternoon and in Judaea normal
work continued until midday.[38] The real problem is the night
trial. However there has been a great deal of debate over

whether the Mishnaic provisions for trials were in force early in the first century; it is possible that some of its laws represent the ideal, not what actually took place. We saw evidence earlier that Jesus was placed under a proscription edict six weeks before his actual arrest. This might have drastically altered the required procedure since a trial of sorts had already taken place. Whatever the normal custom may have been, however, when a matter of national security was at stake, as in the eyes of the authorities it surely was, ways and means must have existed. That some manner of process took place at night before Caiaphas is plain. John says that Jesus was led bound to Caiaphas, though he does not describe the trial, and Luke has Jesus all night in the palace, though he only describes the meeting which took place in the morning. Mark and Matthew describe the night proceedings, but Mark also specifies that something of an official nature happened first thing in the morning (Mark 15:1). Luke says that in the morning Jesus was actually led into the Sanhedrin, which met in a separate building (Luke 22:66). If most of the Sanhedrin had been present at a night hearing, a formal pronouncement and recording of the judgement could have been carried out quickly in the morning in the appropriate chamber. Jesus could have been delivered to Pilate by dawn, even perhaps when it was still dark.

The historian A.N. Sherwin-White draws attention to various indications of the authenticity of the night trial. Even Lietzmann, who made the original case against the Jewish trial, argued that Peter's denial of Jesus in the High Priest's courtyard was unquestionably genuine: too damaging to Peter to have been fabricated. Sherwin-White asks what reason there could have been for lighting a fire at that hour of the night and for so many people to be hanging around. If there were a process of some kind going on it would be understandable. The night proceedings were necessary if Jesus was to be brought to Pilate the next morning, for as Sherwin-White points out, the Roman administrator was at his day's work before dawn and would have completed it by eleven in the morning. For this reason he doubts the possibility of a meeting of the Sanhedrin in the morning, but we have already suggested this may have been no more than a pre-dawn formalization of what had been done during the night.[39]

Trial Before Caiaphas

Mark tells us that many gave false but contradictory witness against Jesus. Jewish courts laid great importance on consistent testimony. Witnesses would be called one at a time to give their account of things; if there were any discrepancies their evidence was disallowed. The difficulty of finding consistent witness against Jesus went back, no doubt, to his parabolic method of teaching. Different people will have interpreted his words differently and have come to different conclusions. In a court of law this could cause chaos. One charge brought against Jesus was that he claimed he would destroy the temple and in three days build another by supernatural means. Two Passovers earlier, according to John, he challenged his critics to destroy the temple and let him build it again – he never threatened to do the destroying himself. It is not surprising that the witnesses gave conflicting accounts of the incident, and easy to imagine how frustrating the trial might have become.

Finally Caiaphas stood and addressed Jesus. There was clearly something substantial amongst all the confusion of witnesses, so he challenged Jesus to elucidate what it was that was being testified against him. This is an extraordinary request from a judge, and understandably Jesus declined to respond. What lay at the heart of most of what was testified against him was the question of who he imagined himself to be. The High Priest therefore made a frontal assault on this central issue, placing him on oath and asking him outright, 'I adjure you by the Living God to tell us if you are the Christ, the Son of God?' to which

Jesus at last broke his silence. 'You have said it, but I tell you
from now on you will see the Son of Man seated at the right
hand of the [divine] Power and coming on the clouds of
heaven' (Matthew 26:64).[40]

I have given Matthew's version of Jesus' response because it
probably corresponds most closely to his exact words. According
to Mark, Jesus replied outright, 'I am!' but both Matthew and
Luke indicate that his words were a little less direct than that.
Some see this indirectness as an indication of some reservation on
Jesus' part about the messianic title, as though he were saying he
was the Messiah, but not in the political way people imagined.
This is possible, but it may simply be an extension of a characteristic of his ministry, which we have seen again and again: Jesus did
not overtly claim to be the Messiah; he carried out the messianic
mission and allowed people to draw their own conclusions.
Caiaphas drew the messianic conclusion and Jesus did not deny it.
Far from it! In the words of two well-known scriptures, he finally
and irrevocably lifted the veil of secrecy and declared in the most
elevated terms possible his future office as the king of God's
kingdom.

> The Lord said to my lord, 'Sit *at my right hand* until I make your
> enemies your footstool.' (Psalm 110:1)

> Behold, there *came with the clouds of heaven* one like a son of man,
> and he came to the Ancient of Days ... and there was given him
> dominion and glory and a kingdom, that all the peoples, nations
> and languages should serve him; his dominion is an everlasting
> dominion which shall not pass away, and his kingdom one which
> shall not be destroyed. (Daniel 7:13–14)

The first of these Jesus had already used at the temple to suggest
that the Messiah must be more than just a descendant of King
David. He is to sit in the position of executive power next to the
very throne of God.[41] A brief glance at Psalm 110 shows that
Jesus is far from having surrendered the 'political' aspects of

messiahship, for, like the psalm alluded to at his baptism, it describes the victorious campaign by means of which God would establish the government of his Messiah. By combining this with the second scripture, Jesus declared his conviction that God would award him not only the government of Israel, but an eternal kingdom which would embrace all the nations of the world. This was just what God had declared to him at his baptism, and this would be what he would die for!

One might think that the High Priest should then have considered the evidence for or against Jesus' incredible claim. Presumably many members of the Council believed that sooner or later there would be a man for whom some of these things were true. But to hear them from the lips of one who had already alienated himself from the ruling and religious establishment, and who now stood bound before them, dishevelled from the effects of a long day, his agony in the garden, arrest, and the beatings he had already been subjected to, was too monstrous for rational analysis. The claim to the place at God's right hand may even have been heard as claim to penultimate authority in the universe. The High Priest tore his clothes and declared it blasphemy. What need was there for witnesses when the whole Council had heard it with their own ears. They declared him worthy of death. Between the end of these proceedings and his brief appearance in the court of the Sanhedrin proper, Jesus was mocked by those who at last had the chance to express their feelings towards the one who had held them up for ridicule before the people.[42]

The Judgement Of Rome
(Matthew 27:1ff.; Mark 15:1ff.; Luke 23:1ff.; John 18:28ff.)

By daybreak Jesus' judgement before the Jews was complete and his chief disciple had repeatedly denied all knowledge of him. One wonders what John was doing all this time. Probably staying quiet and feeling thankful that no one had challenged him! Jesus was bound and taken to the Praetorium to Pilate.

Pontius Pilate had been Prefect of Judaea about five years when Jesus appeared before him. He is described by Philo as 'naturally inflexible, a blend of self-will and relentlessness'.[43] Most of his recorded acts bear out this description, though in two notable confrontations with the Jews he finally backed down,[44] as in the case which was now before him. 'Opposition and eventual capitulation are remarkably consistent with the Pilate we know from Philo and Josephus,' writes Brian McGing.[45] All of the gospels give us accounts of Jesus before Pilate, John's being the most detailed. None of them are anxious to portray Pilate in a bad light. He is depicted as an unwilling pawn in someone else's game, who made every effort to have Jesus released, but failed through the cleverness of his opponents and his own weakness.

It is an unexpected feature of all the gospel accounts that Pilate went out of his way to have Jesus released. The only explanation is given by Matthew: he had received a message from his wife telling him to have nothing to do with 'that righteous man'; she had dreamt of Jesus and 'suffered much on his account' (Matthew 27:19). This ought not to be dismissed. There is no discernible reason for its insertion in the narrative other than that Matthew knew of it. Jesus made an impact on women in his time, some of them, we have seen, from the ruling elite. A Roman with susceptibilities to portents and omens might well have heeded his wife's warning, especially when he knew that a great deal of personal animosity on the part of the chief priests was involved in the complaint against Jesus (Mark 15:10; Matthew 27:18). The message from his wife explains what appears to have been a volte-face on Pilate's part.

As it was the day the Passover celebrations began, the chief priests were unwilling to defile themselves by entering the Gentile Praetorium and Pilate considerately met them outside. He began by asking them what accusation they brought against Jesus. The priests replied that they would not have brought him were he not a criminal. This rather odd reply suggests that the priests were not expecting Pilate to hear accusations and retry the case; only that he would take delivery of the prisoner and have him executed on the basis of the Jewish court's decision. They could only have expected this if there had been prior consultation, and that would only occur in a case that they thought involved national security.[46]

Pilate then tried to get rid of the case by suggesting that the priests take Jesus and deal with him according to their own law. They could have done this were they not pressing to have Jesus executed, a punishment beyond their powers (John 18:31). There has been much scholarly discussion about this. Was it true that the Jews had no authority to carry out executions?[47] There was an inscription in the temple which threatened even Romans with the death penalty if they trespassed beyond the Court of the Gentiles (though it does not say who would ratify and carry out the execution).[48] Stephen was executed by the Sanhedrin – though his looks more like a lynching than a judicial execution (Acts 7:57ff.). James the brother of Jesus was stoned to death on the orders of a later High Priest (though in this case he was deposed for exceeding his authority).[49] John's statement should be decisive as the witness of a contemporary, but the debate goes on. The weight of evidence clearly favours John. According to Sherwin-White, 'the capital power was the most jealously guarded of all the attributes of [Roman] government'.[50] He considers it most unlikely that conditions would have been different in Judaea than in the rest of the empire. The Romans were opposed to giving the power of the sword to any but their own governors for fear of their opponents eliminating Roman supporters among the populace. Indeed, according to Rosadi, Pilate himself could only have held the power to execute if he was vice-president of Syria as well as procurator in Judaea.[51] Nevertheless, Sherwin-White admits that governors might at times turn a blind eye to the activities of the local authorities, provided these were not subversive to their own interests. Was Pilate telling the Jews to inflict on Jesus some penalty that was within their mandate, or was he quietly suggesting that they deal with him as they pleased, in the knowledge that he would raise no objection? John indicates that the latter may have been the case when he adds that Jesus' prediction that he would die by crucifixion was now as good as fulfilled (John 18:32; cf. 19:6). Had the Jews dealt with him 'according to their own law', he would have been stoned.[52]

There are two reasons why the priests may have wished to have Jesus dealt with by crucifixion and not stoning. The first we have already touched upon: Jesus had too many supporters in the city. Stoning was essentially a means of communal execution.[53] It needed a crowd and could easily backfire. The High Priest would also have to carry too much of the responsibility. The law made the chief witnesses responsible for throwing the first stones, but who were the chief witnesses in this case? All the original witnesses had been discharged; the whole Sanhedrin was witness to Jesus' blasphemy. A stoning, therefore, would have been both complicated and dangerous. A second reason I put forward only as a suggestion. The priests were dealing with a man with a reputation for sanctity and miracle-working power, whom many believed to be the Messiah. There were possible dangers for those who touched such a one, even after he was dead. What better way to deal with him then, than to have him executed in a way that carried with it the stigma of rejection by God? The Old Testament associates the curse of God with 'everyone who is hanged on the tree' (Deuteronomy 21:23). Paul was later to quote this principle in support of his understanding that 'Christ became a curse for us' (Galatians 3:13). It is not unlikely that in his pre-Christian days of hostility against the church, this argument took the form, 'Jesus *could not have been* Messiah, for Scripture says that all who are hanged are under the curse of God.' It could have been the priests' intention to provide just such a proof that Jesus was not the Messiah. Clearly, the Jewish authorities had nothing to lose and everything to gain from a crucifixion ordered by the Roman governor. They declined, therefore, to deal with Jesus themselves, and reminded Pilate of the Roman law by which they were not entitled to inflict the death penalty.

The Charge Against Jesus

The priests then began to bring political accusations against Jesus. He had subverted the nation, forbidding people to pay taxes to Caesar and saying that he himself was a king. Pilate asked Jesus if he was the 'king of the Jews'; Jesus neither affirmed nor denied it. According to John, Jesus then spoke of his kingdom and admitted to being a king, though not according to the world's pattern. If it were otherwise, would not his servants have fought to save him from being arrested. His mission in the world was to teach the truth (John 18:33–38). Pilate had full knowledge from the tribune of the circumstances of Jesus' capture. He had given himself up without resistance, and only one of his disciples had attempted any defence. He knew that he was not dealing with a brigand. The conduct of Jesus' trial before Pilate is clear evidence that the Romans never perceived Jesus as a threat to public order. His 'triumphal' entry and 'cleansing' of the temple would have been known to the governor, but were evidently not seen as politically dangerous. To the other accusations Jesus would give no answer.

Before Herod (Luke 23:6–12)

Luke supplies the information that Pilate learned incidentally that Jesus was a Galilean, and seeking once more to rid himself of the case, sent him to Herod Antipas who was in the city for the festival. Their encounter was inconsequential. Herod had long wanted to see one of Jesus' miracles, but although he barraged him with questions and the priests joined in with their accusations, they could not penetrate his silence. After being subjected to ridicule and buffoonery Jesus was mocked up to look like a king and returned to Pilate. Luke, who had an informant within Herod's court,[54] intimates that a long-standing grievance between Herod and Pilate was patched up that day. Pilate cannot have disapproved of the treatment Jesus received from Herod; perhaps it reassured the unease his wife's message had aroused in him. Nevertheless, Herod and Pilate were agreed that there were no grounds for a death sentence.

Pilate Tries To Release Jesus (John 19:1–16; Mark 15:6–15; Matthew 27:15–26; Luke 22:13–25)

Pilate then suggested that, since neither he nor Herod had found anything to warrant execution, Jesus be punished and released. It was normal procedure to have a prisoner flogged as a warning against future troublemaking, if their crime fell short of a death sentence. Some years later another Jesus, the son of Ananias, who was unsettling Jerusalem with prophecies of doom was handed over to the Procurator Albinus and dealt with in precisely this manner.[55] Pilate also appealed to the crowd which had now gathered that he exercise his normal prerogative at Passover and release the prisoner. The crowd would have none of it. Were they a select group gathered for the occasion? They demanded the release of Barabbas who had been arrested some time earlier in relation to an 'insurrection' in the city. As for Jesus, they demanded he be taken away and crucified. Pilate must have decided to have Jesus flogged anyway in the hope that this sight might change their minds. It gave his soldiers some opportunity to have their fun; they were probably Samaritans and would have enjoyed some sport with a Jewish messianic pretender.[56] They gave him a crown of thorns and a purple robe and hailed him as King of the Jews. Pilate must have thought it a good joke; it suggested to him a way of telling the priests what he thought of them. Mark cuts what was becoming a long and complex story short at this point, but according to John Pilate came out again and declared that he had found no crime in Jesus. Jesus was led out in his bloody finery and presented to the people with the words 'Behold the man.' It should have been enough, but the crowd persisted with its chant, 'Crucify him,' and the priests insisted that since Jesus had made himself out to be the Son of God, he had to die.

Talk of a 'Son of God' aroused Pilate's superstitious fears again. He spoke once more to Jesus and renewed his efforts to release him, but this time the priests turned their attack on Pilate, threatening to denounce him to Caesar for sheltering a royal pretender. Pilate was a 'friend of Caesar', and this struck at his weak point. Amongst the Romans 'friendship' was a quasi-official term of patronage, having nothing to do with personal intimacy. Pilate stood in a position of privilege under the Emperor, which involved him in a host of reciprocal responsi-bilities.[57] He was a man of equestrian rank, easily removed from his privileges and office. In a few years time he would be.[58] Pilate knew the accusation the priests were suggesting could be made to look bad. Once before the Jews had embarrassed him before the Emperor.[59] Reluctantly, he gave in, and ordered that Jesus be crucified. He also gave orders that the title 'King of the Jews' be pinned above his head in Aramaic, Greek and Latin. It was a way of getting back at those who had manipulated him.

The Time

Places, dates and times serve to mark important events. Mark notes the moment of Jesus' crucifixion with the comment, 'it was the third hour'. For John, Pilate's solemn delivery of Jesus to the will of his accusers was the critical event, and he drew attention to it by marking the place and time (John 19:13–14). After all his attempts to spare Jesus have failed, and with the Jews threatening to accuse him to Caesar of shielding a king, Pilate brings Jesus forth with the words, 'Behold your king!' After the treatment he had already received Jesus must have looked a sorry sight. Pilate probably wanted them to see how ridiculous their suggestion was. But far from restoring perspective and awakening pity, the sight of this unregal figure, who imagined himself as Israel's Messiah, further antagonized the onlookers and they bayed for his crucifixion. 'Shall I crucify your king?' asked Pilate, to which they fatefully retorted 'We have no king but Caesar.' For John, the master of the double meaning, this whole interchange was historic and fateful. On Passover Friday at the sixth hour at the official place of judgement in Jerusalem the Jews refused King Jesus and declared their allegiance to Rome.

According to Mark, Jesus was crucified at the third hour, about nine o' clock in the morning (Mark 15:25). John, however, says that Pilate gave his final judgement at about the sixth hour: noon by the same reckoning (John 19:14).[60] B.F. Westcott solved the discrepancy by suggesting John was using a different system of reckoning to Mark, numbering the hours as we do from midnight and midday.[61] On that reckoning Pilate gave his judgement around 6am. Many modern commentators reject Westcott's solution, contending that the numbering of the hours from sun-up was the universal method of reckoning amongst ordinary people in the ancient world. Some then resolve the difficulty by pointing out that the reckoning of time was necessarily very approximate since the sun was the only thing to go by,[62] but this will hardly do.

Witnesses at law were allowed a discrepancy of two hours in their estimations of when an event took place, but no more.[63] If we supposed Mark an hour early in his reckoning and John an hour late we are still an hour out, without taking into consideration the time between Pilate's judgement and the actual crucifixion. We must also consider that John almost certainly knew Mark's Gospel. But in fact the reckoning of hours was not standard. Pliny wrote 'The Babylonians count the period between two sunrises, the Athenians that between the two sunsets, the Umbrians from midday to midday, the common people everywhere from dawn to dark, the Roman priests and the authorities who fixed the official day, and also the Egyptians and Hipparchus, the period from midnight to midnight.'[64] All John's references accord with a midnight to midnight system (the modern method), some of them better than with a sunrise to sunset reckoning, so a few modern scholars are returning to Westcott's solution.[65]

But is it possible that Jesus could have been formally condemned in the Sanhedrin, taken before Pilate, referred on to Herod, returned, and for Pilate to have given his judgement before 7am? It was probably Caiaphas' intention to have Jesus on the cross before Jerusalem had awoken to what had happened, so a very early first appointment with Pilate is what we would expect. A Roman governor's official day began before dawn,[66] so Jesus could have been before him as early as 5am. If his first examination, cut short when Pilate discovered he was a Galilean took half an hour, Jesus could have been before Herod at 5.45am. It was less than five hundred metres from Pilate's Praetorium (now believed to have been in the palace of Herod the Great on the western side of the city[67]) to the Hasmonean palace where Herod Antipas may have resided when he was in Jerusalem.[68] The referral of Jesus to Herod for what appears to have been an opinion was a conciliatory act on Pilate's part, so it is unlikely Herod would have delayed or prolonged his examination. Jesus could have been back by 6.30am and Pilate on the judgement seat before 7am. It may have been even quicker.

The Judgement of the World

Looking back over the various persons involved in bringing Jesus to his end it is tempting to make comparisons and apportion guilt. The Jews have been blamed – as though the crowd before the Praetorium were representative of the whole nation, even of all Jews at all times. In recent days great scholarly efforts have been made to clear them and pin the blame on the Romans. The historical reality, as Otto Betz points out, is that the Jews never hesitated to own Jesus' condemnation to death. The Talmud has forgotten that the Romans were ever involved. Yet Betz goes on to note that if blame is being apportioned, the boot, since Auschwitz, is surely on the other foot. What can a Gentile say to a Jew after the attempted annihilation of the whole Jewish nation?[69] Can Germans say, because they were not personally involved, that they are not to blame? Can Gentiles say they carry no responsibility because they are not Germans? And if Germans or Gentiles can disclaim responsibility for the holocaust, then Jews can say they were not involved in the death of Jesus. But the reality which stares at us from the story of Jesus' death is that each person involved at the point that their own self-interest conflicted with the mission of Jesus, acted to secure those interests, and left Jesus to die. It was just this fear and self-interested unwillingness to take a stand against evil which made the holocaust possible. Whether we look at Judas or Peter, at Caiaphas or Herod or Pilate, at the Pharisees or the crowds, all were out to secure their own interests, and their actions in the end conspired to destroy the only man who seemed to have everybody's interest but his own at heart. History decreed – God decreed – that the Jews of the first century should play host to Jesus as one of their own sons. The Pharisees and the Sadducean aristocracy of that time suffered the most obvious threat to their interests and spearheaded the attack. They carry the stigma of his death. But many others were involved: Jews, Samaritans, Romans, an Idumaean, and even his own disciples leaving him at the last, an outcast from the human family, 'the rejected stone', 'reckoned amongst the transgressors', and crucified between two criminals.

The human condition is deep and complex. We can ask who was to blame for something of the magnitude of Auschwitz and look perhaps at Hitler, National Socialism or the German nation. Or we can ask ourselves what we would have done if our career, family, economic position, or life itself were threatened if we did not cooperate with the prevailing policy. There is a mysterious solidarity about the human race which makes efforts to dissociate ourselves too far from the sins of others sound hollow. When the early Christians began to preach they would say that 'Herod and Pilate with the Gentiles and the people of Israel' had conspired together against God's holy servant Jesus (Acts 4:27–28). It was a crime of the human race, and not of any one group or nation. A few days before his arrest Jesus declared that 'the judgement of *this world*' was about to take place (John 12:31). No one was more sensitive to the paradox that this involved than the apostle John who recorded these words. Jesus had come not to judge the world but to save it. However, the world, in its reaction to him, judged itself: 'This is the judgement, that the light has come into the world, and human beings loved the darkness rather than the light, because their deeds were evil' (John 3:19).

The result of Jesus' trial was very dark – human beings exposed as rebels against their Creator – murderers of the one God sent to represent him. Yet correct diagnosis can be the beginning of cure. As Jesus explained to his disciples at their last meal together, although his death would expose for the world the horrible corruption of its own moral and spiritual condition, it would also reveal the possibility of a new basis for standing before God and signal the final end of all evil in the world (John 16:8–11).

Israel's Fateful Decision

Without denying anything just said, it would be anachronistic and unhistorical to ignore the clear way in which the gospel writers portray the rejection of Jesus as a Jewish action with peculiar consequences for themselves. In John the Jews angrily repudiate Jesus and declare Caesar their only king. In Matthew Pilate ceremoniously washes his hands of 'this man's blood' and the Jews declare, 'His blood be upon us and our children' (Matthew 27:24–25). It is not surprising that some modern writers have charged the evangelists with being anti-Semitic. Yet Matthew, Mark and John were all Jews and the only non-Jewish gospel writer refrains from any such declaration. In fact, Matthew and John are establishing something deeply theological which has nothing to do with anti-Semitism. Each tells a Jewish story, of a king sent to Israel by God to establish his kingdom, who is rejected, with catastrophic consequences for that people (Luke 13:34f.). The glorious new age that Jesus announced will not appear – at least not now – instead there will be national destruction. The involvement of Gentiles in this phase of the story is almost incidental.

The Last Battle (Mark 15:20–41; Matthew 27:31–56; Luke 23:26–49; John 19:16–37)

It was normal that someone sentenced to crucifixion be flogged, and then led out to the place of execution carrying the horizontal beam of their cross. The upright was a permanent fixture at the execution site. Having been scourged already in the course of his examination, it is unlikely Jesus endured this a second time. It may have killed him if he had. He was stripped of the finery in which the soldiers had decked him, given back his own clothes, and led off carrying the wooden beam and a placard which announced his crime to all. It was part of the punishment that he would suffer the abuse of the crowds on the way to the place of execution. In Jesus' case some women raised a wailing lamentation over him. He told them not to weep for him, but for themselves and their children; what was being done to him was only a foretaste of the horrors that would fall on the city when its corruption reached maturity (Luke 23:27–31). Somewhere along the way Jesus collapsed under the weight of the timber and a passer-by, Simon of Cyrene, was pressed into service to carry it for him (Mark 15:21). Simon's two sons were known later to Mark and probably the church in Rome; Simon may have led his family into Christianity as a result of this unexpected association with Jesus.

Crucifixion

In 1968 the bones of a crucified man were found near Jerusalem.[70] It was the first such archaeological find. A single nail was still imbedded in his right heel bone, indicating that he had been crucified in a contorted position (as sometimes happened),[71] or that his feet were nailed separately to the sides of the upright beam.[72] Most likely his arms were attached by rope as there was no clear indication that his hands or arms had been nailed. With only one specimen in existence it is impossible to know how typical this was. There was considerable variation in the manner of crucifixion. Interestingly, the man's ankles had been smashed by a heavy blow from a club or axe. This may be what happened to the two men crucified with Jesus and almost happened to him, or it may have been damage inflicted when the corpse was removed from the cross.

At the site of the cross Jesus was stripped of his clothes, which became the property of the four executioners.[73] Once his hands or wrists were nailed,[74] the horizontal beam would have been hoisted to the upright and his feet fixed in place. In Jesus' case a *titulus*, placarding his crime, was fixed above his head, though it is not known whether this was normal practice. A strong person might then last two or three days before pain and exhaustion claimed them. Crucifixion was designed to inflict as much pain as possible for as long as possible, in a manner that brought about the complete public humiliation of the victim. Naked, incontinent, bloody, unable to ward off the swarms of flies – the sufferer became an object of horror and revulsion. This was Rome's way of exposing the foolishness of anyone with political pretensions. There was no honour or heroism in such a death. Origen spoke of 'the utterly vile death of the cross'.[75] The will to live made the victim push down on his feet to relieve the weight on his chest, multiplying the agony. The end came when his knees finally gave way, and he sagged to allow the full weight of his body to hang from his arms. A person suspended in such a way can scarcely breathe, and death follows quickly.

Jesus' Demeanour

Did Jesus scream with pain when the nails were hammered in? I ask the question with a purpose. The gospels do not tell us, and therefore it is not a question that can properly be answered. Yet people will always bring their imagination to bear and provide answers to such questions for themselves. In the twentieth century in Northern Europe the tendency was to depict Jesus steeling himself against any show of emotion and pain; he would have suffered in silence, for that was people's image of the ideal man. Today the ideal is changing and the legitimacy of emotions is recognized anew.[76] The Jesus of today is not ashamed to display his natural feelings, and if there is no reason to hide his agony, will scream with pain. I only raise the question to point out how easily we project our own ideals onto Jesus.

What does stand in the gospel tradition is that he refused the drugged wine that was offered him (Mark 15:23; Matthew

27:34), and that he prayed for his persecutors. 'Father, forgive them for they don't know what they are doing' (Luke 23:34). This prayer, one of the best known and most loved of Jesus' utterances, does not stand in the earliest manuscripts.[77] The words are unlikely, therefore, to have been penned by Luke, unless he made an addition to a later manuscript of his gospel. They were probably added very early, perhaps inscribed in the margin by a copyist who knew that Jesus had so prayed and did not want to leave the prayer unrecorded. The crucifixion was a most public event, and all that was done and said would have been treasured and repeated. Such memories were far more than could be contained in any one gospel, or all four together, so it is not surprising if some of them turn up in the margins of early manuscripts. The prayer's historical value is no less than if it had stood in Luke's original.

The Two Rebels
(Luke 23:32–43; Mark 15:32; Matthew 27:44)

Jesus' execution was shared by two rebels. Crucifixion was practised only against non-Romans convicted of treasonable offences, and slaves. The three whom chance brought together on that particular day were all political offenders, though their ideologies could not have been more different. The one charged with claiming to be King of the Jews preached peace and prayed for his enemies. The other two were brigands who had committed murder in some sort of anti-Roman disturbance, possibly the same one in which Barabbas was arrested. Mark says they joined in the general abuse of Jesus, but Luke says that one of them rebuked his fellow insurrectionist and asked Jesus to remember him when he came into his kingdom. It is an amazing story, and standing alone in Luke perhaps invites scepticism. But there is nothing intrinsically improbable about it. Jesus' kingdom proclamation was common knowledge, and would have had special appeal to a man with revolutionary leanings. Jesus' refusal to take the path of political revolution was a disappointment to those who early in his ministry had set high hopes upon him as a national liberator. Now, however, when this rebel's revolutionary hopes were dashed, when the passion that had led to violence had spent itself and he had tasted the futility and guilt of murder to no purpose, when his own life was coming to a close, and when he had had opportunity to observe Jesus at close quarters, who is to say that his eyes were not opened to see Jesus' kingdom as his only remaining hope? Jesus assured him that they would be together in paradise that very day. The first to taste the joys of the paradise of the new age was to be a convicted murderer!

The Last Temptation of Christ
(Mark 15:29–32; Matthew 27:39–44; Luke 23:35–38)

As Jesus hung on the cross a last attempt was made to induce him to use messianic power to save himself before the eyes of an eager public. If he could raise a temple in three days, could he not come down from the cross? If he was really Israel's Messiah here was his big opportunity to prove it. He had saved others, could he not save himself?

Could he have? It appears he thought so. When Peter sought to protect him at the time of his arrest Jesus told him to sheath his sword with the words, 'Don't you think I cannot appeal to my Father, and he will at once send me more than twelve legions of angels?' (Matthew 26:53). That being so, this must be seen as his last temptation. In the wilderness it was the driving force of hunger coupled with the inevitable weakening of his forty day fast which empowered the suggestions that came to him. Resisting temptation is all the more difficult when energy levels are low. On the cross Jesus was driven by agony, humiliation and a life-sapping fatigue. He hung and remained silent.

God-forsaken? *(Mark 15:33–34; Matthew 27:45–46)*

According to the first three gospels, it became dark from noon till three o'clock. There is mention of this outside the New Testament. Thallus, perhaps a Samaritan in Rome, writing probably about the middle of the first century, explained the darkness as a natural eclipse of the sun. Julius Africanus disputes this view, noting the impossibility of a solar eclipse at Passover time. Luke's word, *eklipontos* (23:45), can mean either an eclipse or simply a failure of light from the sun from some other cause. Africanus also cites the third century writer Phlegon of Tralles, who mentions an eclipse at full moon from the sixth hour to the ninth in the time of Tiberius Caesar.[78] These writers could have taken their information from the gospels, but as neither was a Christian this cannot be assumed.

As the period of darkness neared its end Jesus cried out with a loud voice 'My God, my God, why have you forsaken me?' Such startling and troubling words must be genuine. Nor would they have been preserved had not Mark and Matthew seen them as deeply significant.[79] Schweitzer saw them as Jesus' moment of truth. For two years he had believed God would intervene to reveal him as the glorious Son of Man and establish his kingdom. Now he realizes there will be no miracle. His whole apocalyptic worldview is false. God does not break into human history. At this point Schweitzer's work is at its most persuasive. To modern ears Jesus' cry sounds like pure despair.

But modern ears have also grown unfamiliar with the lament, a form of prayer common in the Old Testament. The faithful sufferer verbalizes his agony in the form of a complaint against God. Jeremiah, for example, cries, 'O Lord you have deceived me, and I was deceived; you are stronger than me, and you have prevailed. I have become a laughingstock all the day; everyone mocks me' (Jeremiah 20:7). The modern reader recoils from the thought of blaming God, but for the ancient Israelite it was the natural expression of his view that God was in ultimate control.

Such laments almost always end with expressions of faith: 'But the Lord is with me as a dread warrior; therefore my persecutors will stumble, they will not overcome me' (Jeremiah 20:11).[80] Jesus' 'cry of dereliction' was the opening line of a familiar lament (Psalm 22), which pours out the pain of the suffering psalmist against the one he knows has ultimately allowed it, but who can also remove it. The lament moves from despair to prayer to exultation that God 'has not despised or abhorred the affliction of the afflicted ... but has heard when he cried to him'. It climaxes with a declaration of God's kingship over the whole world: 'All the ends of the earth shall remember and shall turn to Yahweh, and all the families of the nations shall worship before him. For to Yahweh belongs dominion and kingship over the nations' (vv. 27–28). It is significant that Jesus died with a kingdom psalm on his lips.

Jesus' words, then, are quite the reverse of an admission of failure. The sense of forsakenness is unmistakable, the agony unimaginable. The darkness that pervades the scene shows that even the gospel writers believed God had in some manner turned away.[81] Nevertheless, the man of faith continues to pray, and in a form which anticipates a glorious end.[82]

A little later Jesus called out that he was thirsty. A sponge soaked in vinegar was held up to him on a stick. He drank a little, called out 'It is finished,' and died with a loud cry.[83]

Burial (Mark 15:42–47; Matthew 27:57–61; Luke 23:50–56; John 19:38–42)

As soon as Jesus was dead Joseph of Arimathea, a member of the Sanhedrin and secret disciple of Jesus, requested Pilate's permission to take possession of the body. Pilate was surprised to hear that Jesus was already dead, but when he learned from the commander of the execution squad that it was so, granted the request. The Jews had also requested that the legs of the condemned be broken early enough for them to be dead and removed from their crosses before the second star appeared in the sky and the Sabbath commenced. Once their legs were broken it was impossible for them to push down and prevent the full weight of the body from constricting their chest, causing rapid suffocation. The Jewish law of hanging required that the body be buried before nightfall. That evening was also the night of Passover. Jesus' legs had already ceased to support him when the soldiers came to carry out their task; he was dead. A lance thrust made absolutely sure the job was complete. The three fellow-sufferers were removed from the wood, two taken to the common grave, the third to a newly hewn tomb belonging to Joseph.

Several rock tombs of the period have been discovered in the Jerusalem area. Typically, a low entrance leads to a small chamber with its floor lowered to allow two or three people to stand and work at the stone bench forming part of one wall. Body-length holes in the walls of the chamber held the corpses until they were decomposed and the bones could be collected into a stone ossuary (bone box). One very ornate ossuary, discovered in 1990 in the burial cave of what must have been a wealthy family, is inscribed with the name Yehosef Qayafa', possibly the Joseph Caiaphas of Jesus' trial.[84] Some tombs have several interconnected chambers, developed over many generations. Joseph of Arimathea's was a newly cut tomb, so it probably had a single chamber. Just outside the entrance a trough was cut in the rock into which the heavy circular stone door was rolled to seal and lock the cave.

Joseph and another councillor, Nicodemus, had Jesus carried to the tomb, and with the help of some of the women from Galilee did a temporary job of laying out his body, wrapping it in a linen shroud packed with spices they had brought for the purpose.[85] They rolled the circular stone door into its slot, and departed until the Sabbath was finished and they could return to complete the task.

Notes

[1] Although only Matthew is explicit about the meeting, some such conference must have taken place about this time; see Mark 14:1–2; Luke 22:1–2. If the entry took place on Monday, the cleansing and occupation of the temple on Tuesday, then Wednesday (two days before Passover) seems about right.

[2] Mark's narrative, with its flashback to Jesus' censure of Judas to explain his defection, places the collusion between Judas and the authorities 'two days before the Passover'. *Apostolic Constitutions* 5:15 says 'He has directed us to fast on Wednesday and Friday, the first day because of his betrayal, the second because of his passion'.

[3] See p. 273, n. 22 above.

[4] Mark 14:12; Luke 22:7; Matthew 26:17; John 13:1; 18:28.

[5] *Bab. Talmud Sanhedrin* 43a.

[6] Finegan, *Biblical Chronology*, 295. The only proximate years when Nisan 14 could have fallen on a Thursday were AD 27 and 34.

[7] Christmas customs also differ. Europeans have their main celebration on Christmas Eve, others on Christmas Day.

[8] Jeremias, *Eucharistic Words*, 36–37.

[9] A. Jaubert (*The Date of the Last Supper*) finds a solution in the solar calendar of the book of *Jubilees*, according to which Passover always fell on a Wednesday. Her attempt, however, to find in the gospels a basis for a Tuesday supper and arrest, hearings stretching over Wednesday and Thursday, and crucifixion on Friday is unconvincing. But the existence of groups favouring different calendars must have complicated things. It has been suggested there were differences between Galilee, Judaea and the Diaspora.

[10] Jeremias (*Eucharistic Words*, 42, 47; *Jerusalem*, 77–84) estimates the normal population of Jerusalem in Jesus' time as 25,000–30,000 and the number of Passover pilgrims at 85,000–125,000. The quorum and usual size of a Passover *haburah* was ten. Jeremias' figures are based on the number of people he estimates could fit into the temple in the three shifts when the Passover victims were sacrificed. Josephus (*War*, 6.420–425) says a count of lambs was made at a Passover in Nero's reign in order to estimate the number of people in Jerusalem. 255,600 victims indicated 2,700,000 people in the city. The logistical difficulties may have been far greater than Jeremias allows.

[11] M. Casey ('The Date of the Passover Sacrifices and Mark 14:12') presents evidence that many people celebrated on 13 Nisan in accordance with the

stipulation of Exodus 12:6 that it should be eaten 'between the evenings'. *Mishnah Zebahim* 1:1, 3; cf. *Pesahim* 6:5.

[12] Numbers 9:9–14; *Mishnah Hallah* 4:11; *Pesahim* 9:1–3; 2 Chronicles 30:1–27.

[13] Finegan (*Chronology*, 290–291) points out that Jesus and his disciples may have followed an old Israelite reckoning by which Nisan 14 began at sunrise on Thursday, while the authorities reckoned it from sunset Thursday to sunset Friday. If this were so there was bound to be argument over the correct afternoon for slaughter. Mark's comment that Jesus ate the Passover with his disciples 'on the first day of Unleavened Bread when they sacrificed the Passover,' clearly brings their celebration under the rubric of Passover. Those who celebrated a day early would also need to remove leaven from their houses a day in advance. 'When the Passover was sacrificed' may be a general reference to the character of the Feast of Unleavened Bread, though note France (*Man*, 136–137) who points out that technically Jesus would have eaten the last supper on the day that the Passover lambs were sacrificed, since that day actually began at the preceding sunset.

[14] Another possible way of putting together the data is to have Jesus arriving in Bethany on Friday, resting on Saturday, entering Jerusalem on Sunday, cursing the fig tree and cleansing the temple on Monday, passing the withered fig tree and spending the day in the temple on Tuesday, Judas' meeting with the authorities also taking place on Tuesday. Two days later (Thursday) Jesus ate the Passover at the regular time. The authorities ate their Passover a day late.

[15] *Mishnah Betzah* 5:2; *Sanhedrin* 4:1.

[16] *Mishnah Pesahim* 10:1.

[17] Mark's passion week consists of the triumphal entry on day 1, the cursing of the fig tree and cleansing of the temple on day 2, sighting of the withered fig tree and disputes in the temple on day 3, Judas' betrayal two days before the feast. If the entry was Monday, as I have argued, and the betrayal took place the day after the cleansing of the temple (the most likely time for the authorities to be meeting) then Mark himself indicates Friday ('after two days') as the official Passover. If the entry was Sunday, as some think, Jesus must have travelled to Bethany on the Friday (he would not have travelled on the Sabbath) and spent the Sabbath there.

[18] Jeremias, *Eucharistic Words*, 207–218.

[19] For the original institution see Exodus 12. For its later meaning see Jeremias, *Eucharistic Words*, 205–207.

[20] *Mekilta Exodus* 12:42; Jeremias, *Eucharistic Words*, 206.

[21] *Mishnah Pesahim* 10:6.

[22] Whether the idea of 'flesh' or 'body' lies behind the Greek *soma*, the two-fold identification of Jesus with the Passover sacrifice is hardly to be avoided, as is attempted, for example, by Cranfield, *Mark*, 426. See Jeremias, *Eucharistic Words*, 220ff.

[23] John 6:25–59. The dialogue arises from the feeding of the multitude and Jesus' concern that his hearers not 'live by bread alone'. The real bread which ultimately sustains human life is what he has come to give them. To the Jews' challenge that he prove himself, and their citation of Psalm 78:24, 'he gave them bread from heaven to eat', Jesus responds that he and his life-giving mission, not the manna are the bread from heaven. As the discourse develops he becomes more specific, asserting that the bread he will give for the life of the world is his flesh. A sacrificial interpretation of these words is hardly far fetched, especially when he adds that only those who eat his flesh will have eternal life. That they must also drink his blood is provocative beyond measure, but far from rupturing the sacrificial metaphor, it intensifies the sense of participation in the sacrifice which makes the recipient a sharer of its benefits. See 1 Chronicles 11:18–19.

[24] At the last supper Jesus cites Isaiah 53:12 in reference to his approaching rejection (Luke 22:37). There is influence from Isaiah 53:12 in Luke 11:22. Jesus' silence at his trial may have been motivated by Isaiah 53:7. Some think the phrase 'to give his life as a ransom for many' alludes to Isaiah 53:12. It is clear from the Targum to Isaiah 53 that the passage was seen as messianic by Jews in Jesus' time, though its Servant-as-victim theology does not seem to have influenced Jewish messianic concepts. See Zimmerli and Jeremias, *Servant*, 67ff.

[25] Jeremias, *Eucharistic Words*, 231.

[26] Schweitzer, *Quest*, 351ff.; Wright, *Victory*, 368ff., 553–611, especially 592–594. Wright has given a new interpretation of Jesus' sacrifice: Jesus saw himself enacting the story of Israel's exile and restoration. Having warned of the inevitability of destruction at the hands of Rome if Israel did not mend her ways, Jesus 'would go, as Israel's representative, and take it upon himself' (596). I fail to see the evidence or logic of this. Nowhere does Jesus suggest that his death will ransom Israel from its historical judgement. Rather, he saw their rejection of him as sealing Jerusalem's destruction (Luke 19:41–44; 23:28–31).

[27] Riesner, *Lehrer*, 439.

[28] See Hooker, *Mark*, 346–347. As to the prayers, three disciples were very close to Jesus, who may well have said something to them about what was concerning him and what he was praying. If not, they had ample

opportunity to question Jesus in the six weeks following his resurrection. It would be strange if they did not inquire about something so important.

[29] E.g., Matthew 24:42; 25:13; Mark 13:34, 35, 37; Luke 12:37; cf. Acts 20:31; 1 Corinthians 16:13; Colossians 4:2; 1 Thessalonians 5:6; 1 Peter 5:8; Revelation 3:2.

[30] Mark 10:38; 14:36; John 18:11.

[31] Cicero, 'Speech against Verres' 2.5.165; see M. Hengel, *Crucifixion*, 8.

[32] Psalm 11:6; 60:3; 75:8; Isaiah 51:17, 22; Jeremiah 25:15, 17, 28; Lamentations 4:21; Ezekiel 23:31ff.; Habukkuk 2:16; Zechariah 12:2.

[33] K. Heim, *Jesus the World's Perfecter*, 80ff.

[34] The chief priests controlled a force of 'constables of the court' in connection with their judicial responsibilities. John uses the regular words for a cohort and tribune to describe the Roman contingent. There was a cohort (600 men) regularly stationed in Jerusalem. The tribune was the commander-in-chief of the garrison. See Robinson, *Priority*, 238ff.; Schürer, *History*, I, 363–366.

[35] Schürer, *History*, II, 230f.

[36] Josephus, *History* 20.198.

[37] *Mishnah Betzah* 5:2; *Sanhedrin* 4:1.

[38] *Mishnah Pesahim* 4:5.

[39] A.N. Sherwin-White, *Roman Society and Roman Law in the New Testament*, 24–47. Mark 15:1 connects the morning meeting of the Sanhedrin with Peter's denial of Jesus at cock-crow. Cock-crow in Jerusalem in April is about 3am. See B. Corley, 'Trial of Jesus', 846.

[40] Cf. Mark 14:61–62; Luke 22:67–69. Mark's version looks like a simplification of the fuller vision of Matthew. Luke's version suggests an even more complex interchange, which the gospel writers have simplified in various ways.

[41] Wright (*Victory*, 642–644) thinks Jesus, in using Psalm 110, envisaged himself sharing the throne of God, and that it was this which drew the cry of blasphemy. However, the psalm pictures the Messiah as God's vice-regent in the position of ultimate executive authority.

[42] Mark 14:65; Luke 22:63–65; Matthew 26:67–68.

[43] Philo, *Embassy to Gaius*, 301.

[44] Josephus, *War*, 2.169–177; *History*, 18.55–62, 85–89; Philo, *Embassy to Gaius*, 299–305.

[45] B.C. McGing, 'Pontius Pilate and the Sources', 437.

[46] This is basically the argument of Morison, *Stone*, 52–56.

[47] The case for the Sanhedrin having capital powers was given originally by J. Juster, *Les Juifs dans l'Empire Romain: Leur condition juridique, économique et*

sociale, II, 133ff. The same case has been argued more recently and in great detail by P. Winter, *On the Trial of Jesus*, 75ff. The case against may be found in G. Rosadi, *The Trial of Jesus*, 139–145; Sherwin-White, *Society*, 35–43; Bruce, *History*, 190–191.

[48] See Josephus, *War*, 5.193f.; 6.124f. One of these inscriptions has been found.

[49] Josephus, *History*, 20.200–203.

[50] Sherwin-White, *Society*, 36. Compare Rosadi, *Trial*, 139: 'The right of life and death is the principal attribute of their [Rome's] sovereignty and was never relinquished …'

[51] Rosadi, *Trial*, 142. The Justinian Code did not give a procurator capital powers, only the governor (in this case of Syria) and his vice-president (at this time Pilate).

[52] According to John Chrysostom, *Homilies on St John*, 1, 83 (*NPNF*, 14, 310) they could have stoned him, but *wanted* him crucified 'that they might make a display of the manner of his death'. See the discussion in Morris, *John*, 787.

[53] See Blinzler, 'Stoning', 148–149.

[54] See p. 435f., n. 1, 13 above.

[55] Josephus, *War*, 6.300–309. Albinus eventually pronounced him mad and let him go.

[56] According to Schürer (*History*, I, 363) most of the soldiers who served the Roman procurators in Judaea were not Romans but auxiliaries recruited around Sebaste (Samaria).

[57] E.A. Judge, 'St Paul as a Radical Critic of Society', 195–197.

[58] Josephus, *History*, 18.85–89.

[59] Philo, *Embassy to Gaius*, 299–305. Robinson (*Priority*, 265–266) suggests that Pilate may have been particularly vulnerable as Sejanus, through whose influence he may have obtained office, was also falling from imperial favour and would be executed the following year.

[60] Epiphanius said that the sign for three had been altered to six in certain manuscripts of John.

[61] Westcott, *John*, 282.

[62] E.g., Morris, *John*, 800f.; T. Zahn, *Johannes*, 648, n.76.

[63] *Mishnah Sanhedrin* 5:3. If one witness said something happened at the third hour and another at the fifth their witness could be held valid (though this was disputed). However, if one said the fifth and the other the seventh hour their witness was certainly invalid since the sun was on opposite sides of the sky. A discrepancy between the third and the sixth hour seems too large to account for by the inaccuracy of time reckoning.

[64] Pliny, *Natural History*, 2.79.188.

[65] Finegan, *Biblical Chronology*, 12–13; Walker, 'The Reckoning of Hours in the Fourth Gospel', 69–73.

[66] See p. 539f. above and n. 39.

[67] According to B. Mazar (*The Mountain of the Lord*, 39, 78–80) archaeological investigations have established that Herod's palace served as the official residence of the Roman procurators.

[68] We do not know where Antipas resided. R.E. Brown (*The Death of the Messiah*, 1, 766) suggests the Hasmonean palace since Herod Agrippa II resided there in the 60s.

[69] Betz, 'Probleme des Prozesses', 566f., 570–580.

[70] See J.H. Charlesworth, 'Jesus and Jehohanan: An Archaeological Note on Crucifixion'.

[71] Josephus, *War*, 5.451 notes that the Roman soldiers crucified many of the captives from Jerusalem in different postures, though he gives the impression this was not the normal procedure.

[72] J. Zias & E. Sekeles, 'The Crucified Man from Giv'at ha-Mivtar: A Reappraisal', 22–27. Earlier it was thought the victim's feet may have been nailed into a small wooden frame which was lightly tacked to the upright. See Charlesworth, 'Jesus and Jehohanan', 147–150.

[73] To share the victim's clothes was an accepted right of the execution squad. See Sherwin-White, *Society*, 46.

[74] John 20:25 makes it certain Jesus' hands or wrists were nailed, since the Greek *cheir* could mean hand and wrist. It was more common to nail the wrists

[75] 'Mors turpissima crucis' from Origen's *Commentary on Matthew*, 27:22ff., was the original title of Martin Hengel's study of Jesus' crucifixion. See Hengel, *Crucifixion*, xi.

[76] E.g., H. Kung, *Eternal Life*, 172.

[77] The saying is absent from a variety of Greek, Latin, Syriac and Coptic manuscripts. It was included in Aland's Greek Text in brackets because it was felt to be dominical, though not Lucan. See Metzger, *Textual Commentary*, 180.

[78] Julius Africanus, *Fragment of Chronography*, 18 (*ANF* 6, 136–137).

[79] H.R. Weber (*The Cross*, 40) examines the question of whether the cry of dereliction could have been created by later Christians on the basis of Psalm 22. He thinks it must have been historical.

[80] For further examples of the lament see Lamentations, especially 3:1–39. Also 2 Samuel 1:17ff.; 2 Chronicles 35:25.

[81] Since the exodus, when darkness fell everywhere in Egypt except Goshen where the Hebrews lived, darkness was associated with the absence of God's presence. It is noteworthy that the Messiah's coming was expected to bring light (Isaiah 9:2; 60:1–3).

[82] It may be this cry that is in mind among others in Hebrews 5:7.

[83] Morris (*John*, 814f.) thinks that the loud cry with which Jesus died was 'It is finished' – 'the triumphant recognition that He has now fully accomplished the work that He came to do'.

[84] Z.V. Greenhut, 'Burial Cave of the Caiaphas Family', 29–36; R. Reich 'Caiaphas' Name Inscribed on Bone Boxes', 38–44; W.R. Domeris & S.M.S. Long 'The Recently Excavated Tomb of Joseph Bar Caiapha and the Biblical Caiaphas', 50–58. The identification with Caiaphas is questioned by W. Horbury & E. Puech, 'Caiaphas' Identification Questioned', 20.

[85] The fate of this shroud is a story in itself. The Turin Shroud, a 4m×1m linen cloth preserved since 1578 in the cathedral of Turin is believed by many to be Jesus' burial shroud. It was photographed at a public veneration in 1898 and the photographic plates showed a negative image of the front and back of a human body marked with the stigmata. In 1988, to settle the question of the shroud's authenticity, samples were given to three laboratories in Tuscon, Oxford and Zurich for radiocarbon dating. Each laboratory reported their sample to be mediaeval. Some hold that the samples were switched and continue to contend that the shroud is genuine. See Kersten & Gruber, *Conspiracy*, 2–100.

Chapter 17

The Future

Journey's End?

In the normal manner of things we might have thought that whether he was good or bad, whether what he struggled for was right or wrong, Jesus' journey would have been over when they laid him to rest in Joseph's tomb. The story began at the Jordan where John was calling the nation to turn to God and prepare for the coming of the mighty saviour-judge. Jesus went down into the river to be baptized with the rest, and heard the voice of God name him as the one who would baptize with the Holy Spirit and fire. Thus commissioned as God's Servant–Messiah, the Holy Spirit who now rested upon him drove Jesus into the wilderness, where for forty days he endured the efforts of the Devil to weaken his obedience to God and turn his mission down an evil path. Returning victorious from this skirmish Jesus plunged into activity alongside John, calling the nation to repentance. As John's ministry drew to a close Jesus saw that the time of preparation was over and the season of fulfilment had arrived. When John was arrested he moved to Galilee and began to proclaim that the promised time of salvation had come, that the kingdom of God was at hand. To Galileans, regardless of class, status, wealth or moral standing, Jesus announced the time of God's favour, that all could enter into the open kingdom. Wherever he went he healed and delivered, touched and restored, and wherever people received his message he bound them to himself in a joyful fellowship of eating, drinking and celebrating the arrival of the new age. Jesus' message and mission met with a varied response. Some were overwhelmed at the generosity of God meeting them in Jesus' outgoing love; they hastened to join him and experienced a new fellowship with God in his company. Others were delighted by his authoritative preaching, his challenging the religious elite, and by his acts of power, but when it came to changing their lives and living in new openness before God they remained untouched. Some reacted strongly against his message and lifestyle; they could not accept a world-changing programme from such an ordinary person, or saw in his message and way of life a threat to their own ascendancy or the well-being of the nation. Jesus made it clear that the kingdom could not be enjoyed without him, a son of man whose immediate destiny was to be rejected.

Jesus established his base in the lakeside town of Capernaum, gathered twelve disciples and a group of women to accompany him on the road, and set out on various preaching and healing missions into the villages of Galilee. As the movement expanded and it became impossible for one man to cover the ground, he sent out twelve disciples, familiar now with his message and method, into all the towns and villages of Galilee, proclaiming that God's kingdom was at hand, that all must immediately and urgently repent. Their success brought the movement to Herod's notice, and curious crowds flocked to see Jesus for themselves. In an unsuccessful attempt to get away from the crowds' coming and going, Jesus found himself to the east of the Lake of Galilee with a crowd of five thousand, whom he miraculously fed. This action sparked an attempt to make him king, but Jesus was quick to defuse it, sending his disciples away in a boat and escaping into the hills. Later that night he went to them, walking on the water. A trip to the north, again in part to escape enthusiastic crowds, culminated in another feeding somewhere in the Decapolis. Soon after, on their way to Caesarea Philippi, Jesus for the first time openly questioned his disciples as to who they thought he was. Peter concluded a long period of uncertainty and misunderstanding by unequivocally declaring him the Messiah. From that point Jesus spoke often of the necessity of his death, of the disciples' need to suffer with him, and his resurrection 'after three days'. At first this aroused strong opposition from his disciples, but after the transfiguration they settled back to a fearful acceptance of whatever he was doing.

Jesus had made various short trips to Jerusalem for the great feasts, so was well known there. Some came to be his disciples, a few maintaining their loyalty in secret. Most of the leaders saw him as subversive and wanted him done away with. Many were uncertain, swayed by the opinion of the learned on one side, and Jesus' teaching and miracles on the other. Sometime in the second year of his ministry, prior to the feast of Dedication, Jesus brought his Galilean work to a close and commissioned a band of seventy-two kingdom heralds to precede him with the kingdom message into all the towns on his way to Jerusalem. The preachers were enthusiastic about their success, but again Jesus judged the response not to be the repentance for which he had called. In Jerusalem things became very dangerous with people suspicious of his intentions and belief about himself. He fled from an attempt to stone him, carrying on his ministry in Peraea until the death of a friend called him back to Jerusalem. The raising of Lazarus on the outskirts of Jerusalem caused such a stir in the city, and brought so many people to his cause, that the authorities at last made up their minds and issued orders for his arrest. Jesus withdrew to a town on the edge of the wilderness and remained in hiding until Passover. Then he joined the pilgrims coming from Galilee and journeyed for the last time to Jerusalem. He entered the city amongst enthusiastic crowds, whom he allowed to hail him as the promised king. The following day Jesus cleansed the temple and made it his teaching seat. Each day he came to the temple with crowds of supporters, and in the evenings he would leave the city to spend the night in a secret place. Judas, however, had decided to quit the movement, and two days before Passover went to the priests, who were desperate for a way to get Jesus out of the temple before the feast began. With an informant from amongst his disciples they decided to arrest him. That evening Jesus gathered his disciples and ate a Passover meal at which he made explicit that he saw his death as a sacrifice which would deal with the sin of 'many', thus making possible a forgiven kingdom community. After their meal they spent the night in a garden on the Mount of Olives, and Jesus underwent his hardest time of testing, facing the full horror of the cup which his Father had given him to drink. He reaffirmed his willingness to do whatever God saw as necessary, and, when Judas arrived with the soldiers, gave himself up without a struggle. Jesus was tried and condemned by the Jews, examined and sentenced by Pilate, flogged, and taken out to be crucified by soldiers. After seven or eight hours of agony on the cross, he died, and was hurriedly buried at sunset, just before the beginning of the Sabbath. At dawn on Sunday women came to his tomb to complete the preparation of his corpse for burial and found it empty.

Beyond the Tomb

We have seen something of the shape of the story that emerges from the various resurrection accounts, and the circumstantial and personal evidence which undergirds them. The women coming to Jesus' tomb, hoping that the guards might open it and allow them in, discovered them gone and the tomb open. Mary Magdalene ran to tell Peter and John. The other women heard from a young man/angel that Jesus was alive and left the tomb, only to be met by him on their way. Peter, John and Mary arrived back to find things just as Mary had said. After they went away she remained at the tomb, crying because she assumed his body had been stolen, and Jesus revealed himself to her. The same day he appeared to Peter, to two men on the road to Emmaus, and in the evening to the twelve. In the six or seven weeks that followed he showed himself again and again to the twelve and to his brother James. He also appeared to his many disciples in Galilee; on one occasion five hundred saw him. He instructed the twelve in the full significance of what had taken place, and then took his departure from them with the promise that he would return at the end of the age.

Who Was He?

We are reaching the point where we can hardly put off any longer making our own personal judgement on who Jesus was or is, and on whether his message and mission is a curiosity of the past, or something which extends into our own time to challenge and claim us. In the end it is a personal question. Throughout the ministry of Jesus people answered it for themselves in various ways. Jesus once put it to Peter who gave the answer that seemed right to him from what he had seen to that point. Herod, Caiaphas, Pilate, the Pharisees – all had to consider the question, and the consequences of their decision affect the world to this day. Before we seek to give a final answer ourselves, it is worth seeing what some of the gospel writers said. Each recorded the story of Jesus' ministry in the conviction that God had been at work in a unique and continuingly relevant way. The first three in particular were remarkably restrained in the degree to which they intruded their own interpretations into the picture, but in their selection and arrangement of material and in the total shaping of their story, they let their convictions be known.

Christ, the Son of God

Mark entitled his work 'The beginning of the gospel of Jesus Christ.'[1] We recall that Peter stands behind this gospel, and how

vividly his hardness of heart and misunderstanding come to the
fore, until he is driven by the sheer weight of evidence to
declare Jesus as the Christ. Even that does not settle things for
him, and he nurses resistance to Jesus' commitment to suffer
until finally he has denied that he ever knew him. It is nature
itself which finally bears witness to the truth. The sun is blotted
out as Jesus hangs dying, and at the moment of his death the
great curtain – according to the Mishnah a handbreadth thick[2] –
which separated the holiest place of God's presence from the
place of the people, was torn in two (Mark 15:33, 37). These are
Mark's ways of telling us of the cosmic significance of Jesus'
death, and its achievement in opening a way for human beings
to become friends of God. But who is to say it was not also
God's way: that at this most critical moment in human history
nature did indeed raise its voice, as, according to Josephus, it was
also to do when the temple was finally desecrated thirty-six
years later?[3] To an ordinary observer the death of Jesus was just
another crucifixion; its significance could only be a matter of
revelation. That God would use events of nature to assist the
process is no surprise to those who are familiar with his former
dealings with Israel. In Mark the ultimate judgement on Jesus is
given not by any of the disciples, but by the Gentile centurion
who commanded the execution party: 'Truly this man was the
Son of God.' The force of these words is often diminished by
translating his exclamation as 'Truly this man was *a* son of God'
(Mark 15:39). It is felt that a Roman soldier would hardly have
used such an exalted Jewish title as 'the Son of God' even if he
were greatly impressed by the manner of Jesus' death. In Luke's
account the centurion says only that Jesus was a righteous man.
However, Luke's overriding purpose in the story of Jesus' trial
and death was to demonstrate Jesus' innocence in spite of his
suffering the supreme penalty of Roman law, so he may well
have re-formulated the centurion's words to highlight that
point. The centurion undoubtedly proclaimed Jesus' innocence,
but he may have done a great deal more. It is a mistake to think

that he was necessarily a pagan Roman; he might have been a Samaritan,[4] with some understanding of Jewish beliefs, who heard the charge that Jesus had made himself the Son of God. It is quite possible that Jesus' behaviour throughout the process of execution, and the portentous events which also took place, vindicated him in the centurion's eyes and brought forth the exclamation that he must indeed have been what the priests said he claimed. Peter and Mark's ultimate conclusion to the whole Jesus story is that he was and is the Messiah, the Son of God, whom even King David will address as Lord. Through his life and death he made it possible for human beings to be reconciled to God and find a place in the kingdom – which became concretely present with its king, is manifested in power through his resurrection and reign at God's right hand,[5] and is yet to come in its fullness.

Israel's Promised Redeemer

The story of the two men on the road to Emmaus gives us a clear window into what was important to Luke (Luke 24:13–35). They are joined on their journey by a stranger who asks what it is they are so intently discussing. They are surprised that anyone should not know what has been going on in Jerusalem, and tell him of Jesus of Nazareth, the prophet mighty in deed and word, whom they had hoped would redeem Israel. Their hopes were not to remain shattered. Jesus explains to them from the Old Testament scriptures how it was necessary for the Messiah to suffer, and thus to enter into his glory. He reveals himself to them and later declares that repentance and forgiveness of sins must now be proclaimed to all the nations. Then indeed the restoration of Israel will come and the Messiah will appear visibly in his kingdom (Acts 1:6–7, 11; 3:20–21). It is the Gentile writer Luke who shows himself most interested in Israel's future glory.

God Incarnate

John wrote to provide the evidence which would enable his readers to believe 'that Jesus is the Christ, the Son of God' and believing 'have life in his name' (John 20:31). More than the others, however, he makes clear that more is bound up in the title 'Son of God' than Jesus' messiahship. His gospel begins with the assertion that the 'Word' (God's eternal self-manifestation) has become flesh (John 1:14), and climaxes with the story of Thomas. Despite being one of the twelve, Thomas was not with them on the Sunday night when Jesus first appeared, and refused to believe their story until he received tangible proof that he was alive. A week later he got what he asked for, and was so overwhelmed by the sight of Jesus that he addressed him as 'My Lord and my God'. Far from reprimanding him for this extravagance, Jesus pronounced Thomas blessed, and along with him, all, who without such visible reassurance, should nevertheless believe (John 20:24–29). As 'the disciple whom Jesus loved' ultimately saw it, Jesus was no less than the eternal God become man to carry out the rescue of the human race.

Divine Ruler of Israel and the Nations

Matthew commences his story with the birth of a king, whom Herod feared and foreign dignitaries came to worship, and completes it with Jesus' appearance to his disciples on a mountain to commission them for their future ministry (Matthew 28:16–20). Some worshipped him, though others remained hesitant. In kingly words, appropriate to the Son of Man whose destiny was to receive dominion over the nations (Daniel 7:14), Jesus tells them that all authority in heaven and earth has been placed in his hands. They are mandated to declare his kingship to the nations, baptizing people into the name of the Father, Son and Holy Spirit, and instructing them in his teaching. Matthew, like John, makes it clear that Jesus' person is so closely bound to God that the single divine name comprehends Father, Son and the Spirit of God, and that it is appropriate to worship and obey Jesus as God. Jesus promises his disciples his invisible presence (the Holy Spirit) until the close of the (evil) age and his visible reappearance.[6]

We could go on looking at other New Testament writers to see how they answered the question, but our main concern in this study has been the four gospels so we will content ourselves with them. What is clear is that each was forced by sheer weight of evidence of Jesus' person, message, miracles, mission, demeanour, death and resurrection, to the conclusion that he was the promised king – though he had pursued his messianic mission in a way totally foreign to their expectations. Beyond this they realized that he was no ordinary person, graciously seized upon to fulfil a divine purpose, but one whose origin was deep in God – who came forth into the world as a human being to overcome the enemy before whom every other living person was powerless and defeated.

The Question of the Future

There is a further question which needs to be answered before we can give a final answer to the Jesus question. It is taken as fact by many that Jesus was mistaken about what would happen in the future: he claimed he would return within the lifetime of his disciples. Some admit that he made an error, but feel this is understandable given the limitations of his human condition, and insufficient cause to reject what can be believed about him on other grounds.[7] Others feel that what he said about the future was so complex, and perhaps so intertwined in the gospels with the beliefs of the early church, that it is best to suspend judgement on this particular issue. But it is understandable that many would feel that a mistake on something as fundamental as this would radically discredit him.[8]

The matter is of some importance. The Old Testament lays down criteria for recognition of a true prophet, and one of these is that what the prophet says about the future comes true. Otherwise they do not speak the words of God and can safely be dismissed (Deuteronomy 18:21–22). In the earliest days of the Christian movement Peter preached Jesus as the great prophet in succession to Moses, and called on the people to surrender him their obedience. If Jesus was wrong in what he said about the future, Peter's message is untenable. The question is especially important today. We live twenty centuries removed from the events of Jesus' life, and that is a long time. Even by the end of the New Testament period people were complaining that the Christian hope was false because everything was going on as it always had, and Christ had not returned (2 Peter 3:3–4). It is necessary to question Jesus' hope of the kingdom, and ask whether it is still realistic to expect the new age he promised, or whether we should look elsewhere, or perhaps resign ourselves to despair. We are the future; we cannot be indifferent to what Jesus said of it.

Is It Still Reasonable to Hope For A New Age?

Albert Schweitzer pioneered the last century's doubts about Christianity. Jesus' first mistake, he argued, was his belief that the kingdom of God would appear during the period of his actual ministry. His second was that it would come if he surrendered his life in sacrifice. Jesus' cry of defeat from the cross signalled disillusionment at the whole idea that God might intervene in history to put the world to rights. For those who thought Schweitzer was even roughly correct, Christian faith in its New Testament sense became an impossibility. All that remained of Jesus was a great hero and teacher of the past.

The majority of twentieth-century scholars were unconvinced that Jesus expected the kingdom's appearance in his own lifetime; the impression that he expected it within the lifetime of his followers, however, has been harder to avoid.

Schweitzer's case rests on his belief that Jesus made an absolute and unconditional proclamation that the Son of Man would come on the clouds of heaven and that the kingdom of God would dawn in the course of his ministry. He is adamant that the kingdom was not to be established *by Jesus*, nor was its coming in any way conditional on the repentance of Israel. It would come from the outside by a sovereign act of God; Jesus merely announced it, and people could only prepare for it by repentance. The announcement would soon be proved true or false. Schweitzer overlooked that Jesus' kingdom was not just a thing of the future, but came and was present in his ministry. Jesus demonstrated its presence in his mighty works and offered it to the Jewish nation as something they could enter into, take possession of, and see perfected in the manner the prophets had spoken of. The possibility lay before them even at the eleventh hour, as Jesus taught in the temple, that they might turn to God and inherit the glories of a renewed Israel and a world set free from sickness, disease, oppression and death. But there was also an alternative: national destruction if they refused.

What if Israel had Accepted Jesus?

There is a problem inherent in this view: what would have happened had the Jews actually repented and taken Jesus at his word? The gospels are so clear that he had to die to fulfil God's saving plan, and our minds are so attuned to what actually happened, that there seems to be no room for such a turnaround, even if the nation had desired it. Strong as this impression is, it cannot be a correct one, for it implies that Jesus' offer of the kingdom was never a real one. Yet to the end of his ministry he was passionate about the great possibility against which Israel was turning its back. Had they only recognized their 'visitation' things could have been so different, but they would not (Luke 19:14–44). How often he had tried to gather them as a hen gathers its chickens, but they would not (Luke 14:34). One can almost hear him crying to his people as God did in Ezekiel's day, 'Turn, turn from your wicked ways, for why will you die, O House of Israel?' (Ezekiel 33:11). Jesus did not call on his people to reject and kill him, and so fulfil the purpose of God, but to turn and inherit the promised kingdom. Nor did he engineer his own death, even if at the last he declined to fight or run away. Jesus' integrity demands that there be a possibility other than that which actually transpired. This being the case, the reader may forgive me a short flight of fancy. Consideration of what might have happened may help us to appreciate what did.

Let us return to the scene of the last week. Jesus, knowing himself to be the King–Messiah, the Servant of the Lord, and much more, has come to his Father's house and there he sits teaching the ways of God to all who will hear. The leaders have two possibilities before them. One is to assert their authority and have him removed, the other is to submit to his, to hear and obey. What if they had done the latter? Is it thinkable? What if the gentle Servant had remained in his place and been allowed to continue teaching the 'law of the Lord'? What if the nation flowed to the temple to hear his words and amended its life according to, say, the teaching of the Sermon on the Mount? Nothing less than national renewal would have resulted, brought about by Israel's de facto acceptance of Jesus as its God-given king.

What then might have been the Roman reaction? We know Caiaphas' view: 'the Romans will come and take away both our place (the temple?) and our nation' (John 11:48). Could there have been any other outcome? What if Jesus had taught the people to pay their taxes, even if they were unjust, and to love the Romans (their enemies). What if he taught them, when forced to carry a soldier's bag one kilometre, to carry it two? Might that have made a difference to the Roman reaction? Suppose after much investigation Rome decided to allow this strange situation to continue, since things were more peaceful than they had ever been, tax revenue had increased, and their own position did not seem to be threatened.

But what if, having finished with the restoration of his own people, Jesus sent forth emissaries – much as he had sent the twelve and the seventy two – to offer Gentiles a place in God's kingdom? What if he called the world to repentance, and what if, having completed his healing of Israel, he turned his acid criticism onto the Gentile power-lords? Would they too come and sit at his feet; let him be who he knew himself to be? Hardly! Somewhere along the line things would have erupted in violence. This would have happened much earlier than in the scenario I have sketched, but let us take the extreme possibility and suppose the reaction did not take place until the government of Rome itself was challenged by Jesus' call to repentance. When violence flared would Jesus and his people fight? If they were living by his teaching and seeking to win their enemies by love and truth, they would not. So sooner or later the world-rulers must come and take him from his place, and, them being Romans and him a rebellious Jew, crucify him with his supporters. Could a whole nation be crucified? Perhaps in a representative way it could.

What might have happened then? The logic of Jesus' message indicates that he and those who died with him should rise 'on the third day' and the kingdom of God be gloriously manifested. Those who lost their lives for his sake and the gospel's would find them again, the crucifying powers would be burned as chaff, and eternal dominion over the whole world would be awarded to the gentle Son of Man and his suffering people.

Why then did it not turn out like this? Why did the unthinkable happen and Israel reject her own Messiah? Was it not because the deep rebelliousness towards God, which would make a Pilate or a Caesar turn against anyone who imperilled their authority, was also operating in the High Priest, the elders, the Sadducees and Pharisees? And was not this same deep malaise, which Jesus called 'sin', just as much at work in the common people, and even in his own disciples, so that at the end he would hang alone in death with the whole world turned to its own interests? This seems to me to be the logic of Jesus' ministry: of what could have been and what actually was.[9] We must now come back to reality and look carefully at Jesus' actual predictions about the future.

Jesus' Predictions

In chronological order, the things which Jesus said about the future were, first that he would be rejected by the leaders of the nation and crucified. This was fulfilled to the letter, though as we have seen, he was to some degree active to ensure that things took place as intended. It is something quite unprecedented in prophetic history for someone to be consciously involved in working out the fulfilment of their own statements about the future, but it is only to be expected in Jesus' case, since he saw it as his mission to fulfil the prophets.

Resurrection

Jesus' second prediction was that he would be raised after three days. We saw earlier that Jesus did not interpret these three days in a literal way. He expected to see his disciples again, within their lifetime, but may have been as surprised as anyone to find himself alive again after only thirty-six hours. His expectation of resurrection was thus solidly fulfilled. One must say that in the annals of predictive prophecy this has to have been the boldest and least likely to be fulfilled of all prophecies. It is little wonder that the early Christians had such confidence in their Christ, and preached him to the end of their generation, whatever difficulties they may have encountered in interpreting some of his other words. If sceptics wonder why Christian faith is not abandoned on the basis of what they regard as a demonstrable falsehood in Jesus' promises, the answer is surely to be found here.

Jerusalem's Destruction

Jesus' third set of predictions relates to the Jewish nation and to the fortunes of his disciples up to the destruction of Jerusalem and its temple. He warned of a horrible judgement if his offer of the kingdom was rebuffed, and makes clear that he saw this being executed in war. Jerusalem would be invaded by armies, there would be suffering on a scale never before experienced, the city would be destroyed, and the temple levelled to the ground.[10]

The temple in Jerusalem was one of the wonders of the ancient world. It was rebuilt after the Babylonian holocaust, in the time of Haggai and Zechariah sometime after 537 BC. In 20–19 BC Herod the Great began a programme of extension and beautification, and although the main buildings were completed within ten years, the work went on for seventy-five years. On its completion in AD 64 eighteen thousand workmen were laid off.[11] To accommodate the massive complex, Herod constructed stone retaining walls to increase the size of the mountain platform. At places some of these went down to a depth of one hundred and fifty metres. Josephus speaks of stones more than twenty metres by two by three.[12] Visible in the foundations today are some weighing fifty tons – one in the western wall nearly four hundred tons.[13] Jesus' declaration that the whole edifice would soon be in ruins must have seemed like the wildest fantasy. Before this took place, however, he predicted a substantial period of history in which his followers would carry forward their witness to the gospel in the midst of trial and persecution, wars and rumours of wars, famines and natural disturbances, false prophets and false messiahs (Mark 13:5–13). These were not to be seen as signs of the end, but as 'labour pains', necessary to the birth of the new age (Matthew 24:8; Luke 21:9).

The sign for the destruction of Jerusalem and the temple would be the appearance of 'the abomination of desolation standing where it should not'. At this the disciples would know that the desolation of the land was at hand and flee into hiding in the mountains (Mark 13:14–20). An 'abomination of desolation' is something or someone which so desecrates the temple's holiness as to cause its abandonment by God. The idea is first met in Daniel 9:27. One fulfilment of this prophecy was seen in 167 BC when Antiochus Epiphanes sacrificed a pig on the temple's main altar. In 63 BC the Roman general Pompey entered the innermost sanctuary of the temple, but this caused no cessation of worship and therefore no desolation. Judaea was next convulsed on the temple's account when the emperor Gaius Caligula (AD 37–41) ordered a statue of himself to be erected in the sanctuary. Desolation was expected, but the crisis was avoided by his timely assassination. The events which more than any others brought about the visible desolation which lasts to this day, were the suspension of sacrifices for the Gentile world, and the Zealot occupation of the sanctuary.

A reading of Acts and Josephus' account of the years leading up to and including the Roman–Jewish war will confirm that everything did turn out as Jesus had indicated. By AD 70 Jerusalem was a ruin, and the just completed temple literally levelled. Only Masada held out and it too would fall with the suicide of its entire defending force.[14] Paradoxically, the abomination which finally rendered the temple unfit for worship was not the coming of Gentiles into the holy of holies or the sacrifice of unclean meat, but the suspension of sacrifices for Rome in AD 66, the accompanying prohibition of Gentiles offering sacrifice in the temple, and the seizure of the temple by Jewish revolutionary groups in AD 67 as a stronghold and a base for their operations.[15] Jesus, echoing Isaiah, had called the temple 'a house of prayer for all nations' (Mark 11:17; Isaiah 56:7). To Christians engaged in a mission to Gentiles sanctioned by the Old Testament, the suspension of sacrifice for Gentiles must have appeared a blasphemous affront to God. But even a non-Christian Jew like Josephus deemed these actions sacrilege and saw them leading directly to God's abandonment of the temple and its speedy destruction.[16] He even tells of a divine voice in the inner court of the temple announcing desolation in the words 'We are leaving this place.'[17] According to Eusebius, the Christians were warned by an oracle and made their escape to Pella in the Decapolis.[18] Jewish life as it had been ceased forever. Temple worship has never been re-established. The site is now occupied by the Muslim Haram esh Sharif (Dome of the Rock) and El Aqsa Mosque. Jesus' words were terrifyingly fulfilled.

A Mission to the Nations

'This gospel of the kingdom shall be preached in all the world as a witness to the nations and then the end will come' (Matthew 24:14). Jesus foresaw his followers engaging in a mission to the non-Jewish nations. Some doubt this, pointing to the fact that it was some years before the Christians moved in this direction – their reticence being hard to account for if Jesus had commanded it. In reality it was not many years. We do not know the date of the persecution which began with Stephen's death and led to Christian refugees preaching to Gentiles in Antioch, but it could hardly have been later than AD 35. The years prior were fully occupied with mission in Jerusalem, Judaea, Samaria, Galilee and to Jews further afield. The main reticence was not about preaching to Gentiles, but over sharing table fellowship with them and allowing them access to God's kingdom without the requirement of circumcision.[19] Many times, in deed and word, Jesus hinted at mercy for the

Gentiles,[20] and on several occasions spoke explicitly of a Gentile mission.[21] The gospels bear witness that the world mission of the later Christians was in accordance with Jesus' purpose and command. It was also fully in accord with Old Testament expectations.

Did Jesus Anticipate a Glorious Return?

The last set of predictions we meet in the teaching of Jesus regards his visible and glorious return to make the final separation of good from evil and to rule openly over a resurrected world. A few scholars, however, question whether he had any such expectation. T.F. Glasson thinks Jesus spoke of resurrection, and sometimes in a vague manner about 'coming', and that the early church, drawing on Old Testament images of God's coming, transformed this into a journey from heaven to earth.[22] Jesus' reply to the High Priest at his trial jumps immediately to mind as a rejoinder: 'I am (Messiah), and you will see the Son of Man seated at the right hand of power and coming with the clouds of heaven' (Mark 14:62). Unfortunately, this statement does not immediately settle the question. N.T. Wright accepts it as a genuine utterance of Jesus, but thinks it is a misunderstanding to read it of Jesus' return to earth. The original prophecy of Daniel 7:13 speaks of 'a son of man' coming with the clouds of heaven to 'the Ancient of Days' (God) to be made ruler of the world's kingdoms. According to Wright, the 'clouds of heaven' is a literary device to create a sense of awe and heighten the cosmic importance of the event. He mocks the traditional notion of a return 'downwards to earth, on a literal cloud' as a 'monstrosity' which we can safely leave behind. For Wright, Israel's promised restoration comes about through Jesus' ministry, death and resurrection, and is accomplished finally when the temple falls and the high-priestly regime is destroyed. Jesus is then seen to have been right and his disciples the true people of God. This is figured in apocalyptic language as the Son of Man's enthronement in heaven and his coming to God on the clouds of heaven.[23] 'Already present in Jesus' ministry, and climactically inaugurated in his death and resurrection, the divine kingdom will be manifest within a generation, when Jesus and his followers are vindicated in and through the destruction of Jerusalem.'[24]

Wright's view is not lightly brushed aside. It is not easy to be sure how literally or figuratively to interpret details of an Old Testament oracle ahead of its fulfilment, and Daniel's prophecy can be read in the way he says. Its main thrust is to declare God's eventual enthronement of a human representative of Israel as king of the world. It is not immediately clear where the coronation takes place – whether in heaven or on earth. Wright thinks it happens in heaven, and implies that Jesus saw his kingship as essentially an invisible rule from heaven. Is that how Jesus understood himself fulfilling Daniel's prophecy?

Jesus certainly spoke of his glorification through death, resurrection, ascension, and invisible rule at God's right hand, in terms drawn from Daniel's Son of Man prophecy. Two examples are sufficient to prove the point. A few days prior to his death he greeted the news that some Greeks wanted to see him with the words, 'The hour has come for the Son of Man to be glorified.' He then expanded on the necessity of his death and lifting up, by which he would draw all people to himself (John 12:20–32). Thus Jesus saw the establishment of the Son of Man's kingdom and his rule over the Gentile nations coming about, in part at least, through his death and glorification. Accordingly, in one of his resurrection appearances Jesus declares 'All authority in heaven and earth has been given to me,' and commissions his followers to disciple the nations (Matthew 28:18). Again Daniel's prophecy lies near to the surface. The award of dominion over the nations was an accomplished fact from the time of his resurrection. The evangelistic mission of the disciples was to make this known throughout the world. Wright and others think Jesus also referred to the judgement of Jerusalem as a coming of the Son of Man.[25]

This is not impossible;[26] it may be that Jesus also saw the Christian mission as a part fulfilment of the coming of the Son of Man.[27] But is the idea of Jesus' visible return so easily dismissed? Did he really mean us to see the fall of Jerusalem as the climactic moment in the fulfilment of his kingdom? Even if we allow that Jesus saw the cross-resurrection-ascension, fall of Jerusalem, and mission to the world as important aspects of the coming of his kingdom (they surely are), the question still remains whether there is not more, and whether he did not also look forward to an ultimate consummation – to a coming again to judge the living and the dead, as the Apostles' Creed puts it. Is the ultimate reference of Daniel's vision to a man ruling in heaven over a world still racked with suffering, or to his coming to earth to preside over a new age of peace, as Isaiah envisaged?[28]

If his contemporaries thought Jesus' language of coming with the clouds obviously referred to this worldly political upheavals like the fall of Jerusalem, it is a puzzle why the first Christians jumped so quickly to believing that he would return literally to earth. 'Maranatha' ('Our Lord come!'), the cry of Aramaic-speaking disciples, takes us into the earliest days of Christianity.[29] Jesus' return to be present with his people was at the heart of the faith and hope of the Christians addressed by the earliest of Paul's letters.[30] Wright thinks the idea of a second coming originated in the early days of the church, forced on them by Jesus' unexpected resurrection, which split what they expected of the kingdom's consummation into two parts. However, they did not mean a literal descent to the world; Jesus' 'coming' was a figurative way of speaking (a metanym) of 'the royal presence of Jesus, and the sovereign rule of God' in the new heavens and new earth that are the final destiny of God's presently blighted creation.[31] But to read the apostolic descriptions of the parousia as other than a dynamic *event* transposes them into something they are not. The insistent literalness of Acts 1:11, for example, is difficult to evade. Whether one takes it as Luke's creation, the view of earlier

Christians, or as an authentic angelic announcement it insists on a literal return to earth. In 1 Thessalonians 4:16 the resurrection of the dead and the eternal presence of Christ with his people is preceded by a dramatic arrival. A closer examination of Jesus' words at his trial indicates that such a view can be traced back to Jesus.

In the vision of Daniel the son of man comes to God to be enthroned. 'Coming' logically precedes 'enthronement'. It may seem a small point, but had Jesus only an invisible enthronement in heaven in mind, albeit manifest in historical upheavals on earth, would he not have said 'You will see the Son of Man coming (to God) with the clouds of heaven and seated at the right hand of power?' But coming follows enthronement in his saying. Is it not natural then to connect the coming with something beyond his exaltation as King? Daniel's prediction helps us see what this could be. For his vision of a son of man succeeding the beastly world empires declares the solution of the problem of power politics (who will rule?), with all the suffering it entailed for Israel, in a God-appointed human king ruling on earth for ever. 'On the clouds of heaven' is to be seen in contrast to 'the great sea', from which the monstrous beasts rise. The sea represents the turbulent human masses.[32] The son of man comes from God, by God's appointment. The rule of the heaven-given son of man thus displaces the rule of the beastly empires; it is a vision of God ruling on earth through his human representative, not of a synchronous rule of evil earthly kings with an invisible divine ruler. As such Daniel agrees with the other prophets' expectation of God's kingdom visibly manifested through a son of David ruling on earth.[33] One may wish to say that 'sitting at the right hand of power and coming on the clouds of heaven' envisages more than the two events of the Messiah's enthronement and parousia, that it comprehends his executive power and the manifestation of that power at various points in history. But one must not remove from it the ultimate manifestation: the visible appearance of the king – however much we may urge the unwisdom of trying to picture this.

Wright's focus on the fall of Jerusalem as the crucial act in the drama of the coming of the Son of Man (as Jesus understood it) seems to make the main object of his hope for the world a holocaust.[34] It translates the fulfilment of a hope of restoration for Israel into a sick joke; for it is actually its destruction. Consideration of Jesus' teaching shows this cannot be correct. Certainly he warned of an historic destruction of Jerusalem, but also of an ultimate judgement when every act and word would be assessed for punishment or reward,[35] and beyond this a glorious consummation. Usually he does not speak of this as coming at death, but on a day of judgement at the end of the age.

The Day of Judgement

'For the Son of Man is to come in the glory of his Father with his angels and he will repay everyone according to his work' (Matthew 16:27).[36] Here is Jesus' counter to the hopes raised by the mission of John the Baptist, that the 'coming one' would appear immediately to wield the winnowing fork and cut down the fruitless trees. The fall of a city is manifestly not a judgement of everyone according to their works. A coming for universal judgement also answers to the passionate desire of Jesus' disciples to see him overthrow the government in Jerusalem. Remember how he spoke then with a parable of a nobleman who went away leaving things much as they were, and later returned to manifest his kingdom and call his *servants* to judgement (Luke 19:11–27)!

The ultimate disaster was not to be Jerusalem's fall, terrible as that would be, but final rejection from the kingdom, which Jesus describes as being banished to outer darkness, where there is weeping and gnashing of teeth.[37] The final establishment of the kingdom would require the rejection of everything and everyone evil to a kind of cosmic rubbish heap, which Jesus called

Gehenna.[38] This was the name of the valley to the south of Jerusalem which may have served as the city's garbage dump. The Jews connected it with Isaiah 66:24 and used it as an image of being judged utterly worthless and consigned to destruction at the dawning of the new age.[39]

The Ultimate Vision

We would misrepresent Jesus if we saw destruction – of Jerusalem or of the wicked – as his ultimate vision. Beyond Israel's hostility and the world's wickedness he foresaw a future coming, visible and full of hope. 'Truly I say to you, In the re-creation (*palingenesia*), when the Son of Man sits on his glorious throne, you who have followed me will also sit on twelve thrones, judging the twelve tribes of Israel' (Matthew 19:28). There would be an 'end' when all God's promises of blessing and salvation would be accomplished and fulfilled. He called it the *palingenesia* (regeneration): a new beginning for God's creation brought about through the resurrection of the dead.[40] Jesus spoke of people of all nations sitting at banquet with Abraham, Isaac and Jacob;[41] of the righteous shining like the sun in the kingdom of their Father;[42] of the meek inheriting the earth;[43] of people being received with joy into eternal dwellings;[44] of the Messiah dividing his rule amongst his servants;[45] of life in all its fullness.[46]

There are also strong suggestions that this consummation would include Israel. 'Behold, your house is left to you desolate. For I say to you, you will certainly not see me again until you say, "Blessed is the One who comes in the name of the Lord" ' (Matthew 23:38f.). In this Q saying Jesus foretells the desolation of the temple, the departure of the 'coming one', and at least the possibility of a change of heart for Israel – followed by their seeing him again. He may imply more. It is possible Jesus thinks his return cannot take place until he has been recognized for who he is by his historic people.[47]

The 'end', when it comes, will be initiated by a spectacular coming or return (*parousia*). 'When the Son of Man comes in his glory, and all the angels with him, then he will sit on the throne of his glory and all the nations shall be gathered before him, and he shall separate them from each other, as the shepherd separates the sheep from the goats' (Matthew 25:31–32). The influence of Daniel's son of man prophecy is apparent; to Jesus' mind it clearly envisaged the coming of the king to rule on earth. He emphasizes the glorious public nature of this coming, which rules out its being merely intellectually perceived: believed by some, but not by others. It will be as the lightning which shines from one end of the sky to the other. If anyone tells you it has happened here or there, you need not even bother to look.[48] When it happens everyone will know, for 'it will come upon all who dwell upon the face of the whole earth' (Luke 21:35). By inference, if only one person is uncertain it has not happened. It was not an implied vindication through the fall of Jerusalem that Jesus had in mind, nor the coming of the Holy Spirit, nor a coming in the guise of a later prophet[49] – such constructions are purposefully ruled out. It was Jesus' own personal, public, powerful return to bring to completion the kingdom he had lived and died for.

Did Jesus Predict The Time Of His Coming?

Jesus' promise to return and manifest his kingdom is, on this reading, an unfulfilled prediction. May its fulfilment still reasonably be hoped for in our future, or has something happened to disqualify it from further consideration? Upon this question hinges the continuing validity and relevance of historic Christianity. Perhaps we could disqualify it if Jesus had placed a time limit on its fulfilment which has now elapsed. Many believe this to be the case; that Jesus predicted his final return would take place in the generation of his own contemporaries. But did he?

The first saying which seems to suggest it comes in the context of Jesus' warning and promise after Peter declared him to be the Messiah on the road to Caesarea Philippi.

> 'And he was saying to them, "I tell you truly, there are some standing here who will certainly not taste death until they see the kingdom of God having come in power"' (Mark 9:1; cf. Matthew 16:28; Luke 9:27).

Whether this is an unfulfilled prophecy depends on what Jesus meant by 'the kingdom of God having come in power'.[50] It is often taken to mean the arrival of the kingdom in its final, consummated form when the Son of Man returns on the clouds of heaven openly and unambiguously to claim the world as his own. But this is by no means the only possible meaning. It has also variously been seen as a reference to the transfiguration, cross, resurrection, ascension, coming of the Holy Spirit and fall of Jerusalem.[51] Jesus' mission alerts us to the fact that there is more to the coming of the kingdom of God than the final revelation of the heavenly king. He came announcing the presence of the kingdom as well as its future coming and offered immediate entrance to all who would heed his message. Israel as a nation thrust from itself the invitation to enter the kingdom there and then, and with it the possibility of seeing the fulfilment of the prophetic hope in their day. Yet even if they had not, it is clear that they would first have needed to suffer before entering into the glory of the fully consummated messianic kingdom. The kingdom was not to be established by an irresistible fiat of the supernatural and all powerful God, but had to be fought for and won against the opposing satanic kingdom by weak and mortal human beings. Throughout his ministry Jesus saw himself breaking into Satan's kingdom and liberating his captives; in the mission of his disciples he saw the promise of Satan's fall from heaven. The question arises as to whether Israel's refusal and Jesus' death somehow cancelled the kingdom for the present, and banished it to reappear only in the remote future.

This was certainly not the case. In the passage we are considering Jesus told his disciples that it was *necessary* for him to die. The necessity in Jesus' mind related to the establishment of his kingdom. Peter wanted him to establish it by political means, presumably by ousting those in power and taking their place, but Jesus consistently refused this path. His sights were set on the enemy he perceived to be the real ruler of humankind, and he proceeded steadfastly to meet him in battle. That battle climaxed, as we saw, in the night of his arrest and the events which followed. Jesus fought and won, and through his death established his own right to rule God's creation as a human being. Through his death he also made possible the redemption of other men and women to share the kingdom with him. Jesus said that in the approaching crisis of his death the ruler of this world would be cast out and he would draw all people to himself (John 12:31–32). The kingdom, in its aspect as people under his lordship, would thus be established by his death. This became evident to his disciples at his resurrection. His words to them, 'all authority in heaven and earth have been given to me' (Matthew 28:18), are the words of a king claiming a universal kingdom. They envisage the kingdom as a present powerful reality, even though the revelation of its final form lay in the future. Thus it is not at all certain that the saying we are considering refers to the ultimate unveiling of the kingdom. It may well refer to the victory Jesus most assuredly believed was coming through his death and resurrection. In fact it was the difficulty aroused in his disciples' minds by his determination to let himself be killed which appears to have given occasion to these words in the first place. If instead of seizing government he intended to surrender himself to death, what would become of the kingdom? Jesus assured them that it would indeed be established in power, within their very generation. We need to remind ourselves that he was not necessarily expecting to be raised from death in three literal days. He trusted that God would raise him at a definite time after his death, and obviously expected that to be well within the lifespan of his followers. He may not have been certain whether all of them would still be alive to witness his resurrection, but sure that some of them would be. As it turned out they were all there except Judas.

That the kingdom's coming in power referred to the result of his death and resurrection and not to his final return is in fact confirmed by his words. They indicate that his disciples would still need to taste death. If Jesus were thinking of the parousia, with its accompanying general resurrection, he would not have said his followers would not taste death '*until* ...' for there would be no more death. To say they would not die *until* the kingdom came, implies that the present age would still have some of its course to run, and that disciples would still need to reckon with dying.

This Generation Shall Not Pass Away Until ... (Mark 13:30; Matthew 24:34; Luke 21:32)

The saying which is held to establish beyond all dispute that Jesus thought his final coming would occur within the generation of his disciples occurs in his answer to their query about when the destruction of the temple would take place. It was once common amongst New Testament scholars to treat the discourse in which this saying occurs as a 'little apocalypse' which found its way into Mark from an early Christian source unrelated to Jesus. The problem of Jesus making a mistake was solved by denying he ever made the statement. But there is no justification for this procedure. G.R. Beasley-Murray's thorough study of the history of the little apocalypse theory shows it was motivated more by the desire to rescue Jesus from Strauss' contempt, than by anything in the gospels.[52] That we find the discourse in Mark, Matthew and Luke (in a form which suggests an additional source), and that many of its ideas are found elsewhere in the gospels, forbids us detaching it from Jesus.

Jesus' discourse about the future was designed to prepare his disciples for the extensive period of uncertainty which would precede the fall of Jerusalem, and to warn them that the temple's destruction would not itself be the end; beyond there would still be false messiahs and other problems. The coming of the Son of Man would be an unmistakable event of cosmic proportions, witnessed by all. In the saying about the fig tree he addressed the question of time.

> From the fig tree learn this parable: when its branch sprouts and puts forth leaves you know that the summer is near. So you, when you see these things happening, know that he is near, at the doors. Truly I say to you that this generation will in no way pass away until all these things have taken place. Heaven and earth will pass away, but my words will not pass away. But concerning that day or its hour no one knows, neither the angels in heaven nor the Son, but only the Father. Watch and be on your guard, for you do not know when the time will be. (Mark 13:28–33; cf. Matthew 24:32ff.; Luke 21:29ff.)

To modern ears this certainly sounds like Jesus saying he would return in his disciples' lifetime, but there are other ways of reading it. I have already mentioned the view of some that the 'coming' Jesus speaks of here is his coming to judge Jerusalem.[53] Others think the 'all these things' which are to take place within the generation are the signs which indicate the nearness of the Son of Man, and do not include his actual coming. The language and structure of the discourse in Mark and Matthew (though not in Luke) supports this view. The disciples ask when the temple will be destroyed, and perhaps also what the sign will be for Jesus' coming and the end of the age (Mark 13:4; Matthew 24:3). The things they can expect which will show that his coming was near cannot logically include the coming itself, and it is 'these things' (including the desolation of the temple) which he says they will experience in their generation.[54] In the Greek text 'these things' is forcefully contrasted with 'that day and hour' (of his coming), which no one knows (Mark 13:30–32). Jesus did not know that it would *not* happen in that generation, but nor does he affirm that it would. He affirms that he does not know when that day and hour will be. Throughout the discourse Jesus constantly speaks to his disciples of what they ('you') will see and experience, but when it comes to speaking of his ultimate return he switches to the vaguer 'they will see the Son of Man coming in the clouds with great power and glory' (Mark 13:26). Jesus was extremely positive about what he did know, but he was equally strict about what he did not know.

This Generation

There is also the very real possibility that by 'this generation' Jesus referred not to the life-span of his contemporaries, but to the sinful race of human beings or the timespan of the evil age. This suggestion is sometimes scorned as a desperate expedient to escape the inescapable. Generation (*genea*) admittedly usually mean a life-span, or the people alive at a particular time. But in one place at least Jesus uses it with another sense: 'The master praised the steward of unrighteousness, because the sons of this age are wiser in their own generation than the sons of light' (Luke 16:8). Two generations are contrasted here, and they are not those living at two different points of time. Rather, they are two races of human beings: the sons of this age, who are a distinct generation by virtue of the evil root, and the sons of light, whose generative principle lies in God. Jesus' temporal thinking is conditioned here by the Jewish division of history into 'this age' and 'the age-to-come'. Each age spawns a generation (race) with its special characteristics. Thus 'this generation' on the lips of Jesus could mean the inhabitants of the present evil age, or the age itself. It is part and parcel of his kingdom vocabulary. Peter appears to use the word with the meaning in his first sermon, where he calls on his hearers to save themselves from 'this crooked generation' (Acts 2:40). His words echo Moses' Song, where the 'perverse and crooked generation' is not a particular group living at one time, but all those Jews, present and future, whom Moses predicts will rebel against their God (Deuteronomy 32:5, 20). Such a way of speaking is also found in the Psalms (14:5; 24:6; 73:15; 112:2), and a related usage appears in the blessing of the High Priest in the Dead Sea Scrolls: 'May he fight at the head of your thousands until the generation of falsehood is ended.'[55]

Taking 'generation' in this sense does not empty Jesus' pronouncement. It signifies that everything he has prophesied will indeed take place before the inhabitants of the present age pass away. It stands well alongside his further assurance, 'Heaven and earth may pass away, but my words will not pass away' (Luke 21:33).

There is therefore no certainty that Jesus predicted his coming in glory within a generation of his death. He solemnly assured his disciples that most of them would live to see the kingdom established in power, and, according to the New Testament understanding of the kingdom, they did. He also told them they would see the fall of Jerusalem and many other things in their lifetime, and they did. But Jesus strongly disavowed any knowledge of the time of his ultimate return, which was entirely in the hands of his Father, and he spoke of it in language which, while not denying that his disciples might be alive to witness it, nevertheless left open that they might not, that their generation might indeed have passed away. In a number of parables he also prepared them for the possible eventuality of a long wait.[56]

Final Solution

A decision on Jesus must be a personal one. Each of the people involved in the drama of Jesus' ministry had to make up his or her mind, and their decisions determined their destinies. A Galilean fisherman who decided Jesus could be no less than the King–Messiah ended up crucified in the capital city of the empire.[57] His fishing partner's similar decision took him finally to Ephesus to author one of the most profound and influential books ever written, and die in peace at a ripe old age. A budding rabbinic scholar turned his back on his studies and ended up as the expert witness of Jesus' messianic integrity to the courts and governors of many of the great states of the first-century Roman world. A disciple who abandoned and betrayed Jesus committed suicide. A High Priest who saw him as a threat to the survival of the Jewish cause died in old age, 'the most fortunate of men', but the Judaism for which he fought and the dynasty which he controlled died, never to be revived. A Roman governor who sacrificed Jesus to his own political career scraped out another five years before he was disgraced and sacked. A wealthy nobleman who wanted to follow Jesus but could not bear the insecurity of abandoning his wealth lost it all within forty years, swept away in a storm of fire and blood. The Jewish nation, which despite its deeply held hope for an intervention of God and a new world, found, when offered these things, that the pull of the present and the familiar was too strong. Its national life fell into increasing chaos until it was torn to pieces from within and without. A rich tax-collector discovered that friendship with Jesus was of more value than all that he owned. His end, like that of countless others who decided in favour of Jesus is unrecorded and unknown. Yet, although for the most part they lived and worked without historians to record their stories for posterity, they spearheaded the most remarkable missionary movement ever seen, taking the name of Jesus within not much more than a century east and west and north and south, to almost every place in the known world.

In terms of the decision to be made, the information upon which it must be based, and the consequences which may flow from it, we are not in a much different situation. No one saw the whole of Jesus' ministry; most people witnessed only a little part, and on that basis had to make up their minds whether they would go further with him or depart. Things were never unambiguous; there were always those who had an alternative explanation to this or that. If we do not have the advantage of the first generation

– being able to witness one of his miracles or see him alive after his crucifixion – we are able to see the thing as a whole and consider it at our leisure. As to the consequences and risks, the position has not much changed in many parts of the world. To decide in favour of Jesus and his kingdom is to surrender one's allegiance to an invisible lord and to enlist as his disciple in the cause of a future world. No one can know where such a commitment may lead, in the short term or in the long. 'When Christ calls a man, he bids him come and die,' said one twentieth-century Christian whose own discipleship led him to the gallows.[58] Only the person who in addition to the challenge and danger of a call into the unknown, also sees enough of Jesus to awaken a solid trust that the direction of his call, though it lead through death, is ultimately to resurrection and a renewed world, will find the courage and motive to hazard everything for his kingdom.

Answers To Some Questions

In the first chapter I said that for a faith to hold water it must give a clear answer about the question of God, and also have something positive and hopeful to say about the mess in which we find ourselves in this world. Strictly, the question of God's existence can only be answered by God. There is no way that I as a creature within the bounds of time and space can know who or what may lie beyond these limitations, unless the one who is out there reveals himself. When I look around today, and scan the history of the world, asking whether there is evidence of a personal God making himself known, I am confronted pre-eminently with Jesus. He did not set out to convince his contemporaries that God was real; they knew that well enough already. What he did was bring them face to face with the reality of God in the concrete, demanding his rightful place in their lives and in their world. Nevertheless, for me and my generation, for whom the very existence of God is a burning question, Jesus is the clearest answer. Those who have tried to explain him apart from God have distorted him beyond recognition. To receive in Jesus the answer to the God-question is, however, to be confronted, like the people of his own day, by a person who calls us to take sides in the battle for a new age. For he does not only answer the God-question, but also the problem of evil and suffering. Jesus announced the kingdom of God, a renewed world without anything to spoil it. Around him the powers of evil retreated and people were released from their sufferings. But they would not have his kingdom, for it also demanded a renunciation of the wrong within, and active engagement to suffer for what was right. So the kingdom was rejected. Yet, paradoxically, in its moment of rejection Jesus declared it accomplished, through his faithful suffering and obedient death. He sent out his followers to declare his victory, to announce to all nations the forgiveness of sins, God's willingness to receive all who would come to him, and to offer a place in the perfected kingdom to all who would join themselves to its eternal ruler. We do not yet see that kingdom in its perfection, but there is no more important question for our generation (as for his) than whether it is real. If it is, then it is the all important reality of our time, growing inexorably amongst the weeds of ambiguity until the day of the great separation, when everything will be seen in its true light and 'the righteous will shine like the sun in the kingdom of their Father' (Matthew 13:43). And so Jesus also answers the hope question. The alternative is horrible to contemplate, whether we accept it as the judgement of God on a rebel planet or simply as the inevitable end of a meaningless and accidental world whose chaos spewed up a creature with a greed for life and fulfilment so strong that it brought itself and its world to an untimely end.

The Mission and Achievement of Jesus

The task that was given Jesus at his baptism was to establish the kingdom of God and extend its authority to the ends of the earth. Did he succeed? In the eyes of many of his contemporaries – as indeed of Reimarus, Schweitzer, Crossan, and many moderns – he died an abject failure. In his own eyes and in the new eyes of those who followed him he succeeded beyond measure and his cause lives. Jesus' entry into Galilee was like the entry of an anonymous prince into a rebel-controlled territory that had once been his own. A stranger, and yet moving with an ease and a grace beyond anything his countrymen had ever seen, he made the extra-ordinary announcement that the time of rebellion had come to its close and the true king had come to claim his people. It was ludicrous because all things were as they ever had been, the existing structures of power remained undisturbed. Yet wherever Jesus went remarkable things began to happen, things which belonged to the new order and contradicted the laws of the dark power of rebellion. There was a limited and localized sense in which one had to admit that the kingdom of God had come, and the power of Satan was no match for it.

There were many who were so impressed with Jesus that they were eager for him then and there to move against their oppressors, and willing to risk life and limb to help him. He refused to buy into political struggle, which would only set person against person and himself against the people he desired to rescue. He advanced to battle against the power of evil itself – like a general who will not waste his resources on unimportant skirmishes along the way, but hastens to do battle with his enemy's chief power. He knew that it was the outcome of that battle which would decide the war. His strategy was unconventional, but the outcome was victory. With his enemy defeated the war was as good as over. As surely as the backbone of Satan's power was destroyed, God's kingdom was established in the world and the way was clear for men and women of all nations to be drawn to the fellowship of the crucified but victorious King–Messiah.

The task of gathering the new age community Jesus gave to his followers. Having defeated the central rebellious power, he sent them out into lands which were still very much in the power of evil – much as a victorious general might divide his forces, sending them into the far reaches of a newly conquered land to declare his victory, offer amnesty and a place in the new order to all who would lay down their arms and surrender their allegiance to the king.[59] Their mission was fraught with danger, for everywhere they would meet the old authority, defeated but still holding vestiges of power. They would meet disbelief and ridicule about the victory of their king, and sometimes violence. As followers of the crucified one they could meet these challenges with nothing more than the love and willingness to suffer that had characterized their master. This kingdom would not grow through force of arms, but grow it would, until the king was satisfied that every place at the banquet table of the future was full. Then he will appear to make the final separation and remove from his kingdom all that spoils and corrupts and causes pain. All things will be revealed for what they are, and begin to be what they shall be. In the compass of this renewed universe, under the lordship of the King–Messiah, all God's promises to Israel and to the nations will come true. Then it will be said finally and truly that the kingdom of God has come, that it is all of Jesus' doing, and it is marvellous in our eyes.

Notes

[1] Many ancient manuscripts add the phrase 'Son of God', so there is some uncertainty about Mark's original wording.

[2] *Mishnah Shekalim* 8:5.

[3] Josephus, *War*, 6.288–309.

[4] Schürer (*History*, I, 363) says troops recruited around Samaria (Sebaste) probably composed the majority of the Judaean garrison.

[5] Mark 9:1; 14:62.

[6] Matthew 16:27; 25:10, 19, 31–46.

7 E.g., Beasley-Murray, *Jesus and the Future*, 183–191.

8 Reimarus, *Fragments*, 211–229, and Strauss, *Life*, 582–598, both attack Christianity on this point.

9 My thinking here has been influenced by Paul's argument in Romans 11. In Romans 11:15 he connects the final resurrection with the Jews' ultimate acceptance of Christ. His logic seems to imply that had Israel accepted Jesus when he came, the resurrection would have been then, and the Gentiles would have missed out. God allowed a hardening to come upon Israel so that the Gentiles might have the opportunity of faith. Only so will Israel finally receive mercy and be saved (11:26). Paul, of course, struggled deeply with the question of why Israel had rejected its Messiah. See D. Seccombe, *Dust to Destiny: Reading Romans Today*, 190–201.

10 Mark 13:1ff.; Luke 21:5ff.; Matthew 24:1ff.; Mark 12:9; Luke 13:1ff., 6ff., 35; 19:41ff.

11 Josephus, *History*, 20.219.

12 Josephus, *History* 15.380ff.; 20.219ff.; *War*, 5.184–189, 224; Schürer, *History*, I, 292, 308, 476.

13 H. Shanks & D.P. Cole, *Archaeology and the Bible*, II, 27.

14 Josephus, *War*, 7.252ff.

15 Josephus, *War*, 2.408–426; 4.151ff. It is intriguing to read Josephus' description of the portents which heralded the approaching desolation of the temple (*War*, 6.288ff.). Note Titus' protest at the Zealot's desecration of the sanctuary: *War*, 6.124–128.

16 Josephus, *War*, 4.386–388.

17 Josephus, *War*, 6.300.

18 Eusebius, *Ecclesiastical History*, 3:5.

19 Acts 10:28; 11:2–3; Galatians 2:11–14; Acts 15:1–35.

20 Luke 4:24–28; Mark 7:24–30; Luke 14:23; Matthew 8:5–13.

21 Mark 13:9–10; 14:9; John 12:20–32; Matthew 28:18–20.

22 T.F. Glasson, 'Theophany and Parousia', 259–270

23 Wright, *Victory*, 339–343, 517, 525, 642–643.

24 Wright, *Victory*, 365.

25 Also D.B. Knox, 'Five Comings of Jesus, Matthew 24 and 25', 44–54.

26 E.g., Luke 17:22–37.

27 Matthew 24:29–31 is seen by some scholars as an apocalyptic description of Jesus' sending forth of messengers (angels) to gather the elect.

28 Isaiah 9:1–7; 11:1–9; 25:6–9; 66:22–23.

29 1 Corinthians 16:22; Didache 10:6.

[30] 1 Thessalonians 1:9–10; 4:13–18.

[31] N.T. Wright & M. Borg, *The Meaning of Jesus*, 202.

[32] See chapter 7, n. 63.

[33] Jesus saw even the 'sitting at God's right hand' of Psalm 110 as a prelude to the victorious struggle which would result in all God's enemies being brought into submission to the king. Compare Mark 12:36 with 14:62.

[34] It is difficult to account for the absence outside the gospels of a looking forward to the fall of Jerusalem, if one supposes it formed such a focal position in Jesus' scheme.

[35] Matthew 5:21–22; 12:36–37, 41–42; 25:31–46; Luke 11:31–32; 13:23–30; John 5:28–29.

[36] See also Matthew 12:36; 13:39–43, 47–50.

[37] Matthew 8:12; 13:42, 50; 22:13; 24:51; 25:30; Luke 13:28.

[38] Matthew 5:22, 29–30; 10:28; 18:9; 23:15, 33; Mark 9:43–47; Luke 12:5.

[39] Gehenna was the Valley of Hinnom (*Ge Hinnom*) south of Jerusalem. King Ahaz had a place there for the worship of Molech, where human sacrifice was practised (2 Chronicles 28:3). Josiah defiled the place (2 Kings 23:10), and it is said later to have become a rubbish tip. See J. Wenham, *Facing Hell*, 238; Kung, *Eternal Life*, 133–135. The term occurs in Jewish literature before and after Jesus as the place of final punishment (e.g. *Sibylline Oracles* 1:103; 2:292; *Assumption of Moses* 10:10) and is common in rabbinic writings (e.g. *Mishnah Aboth* 1:5; 5:22, 24).

[40] Matthew 22:23–33; John 5:28–29; cf. Romans 8:18–24. 2 Peter 3:12–13.

[41] Matthew 8:11; Luke 13:28–30.

[42] Matthew 13:43.

[43] Matthew 5:5.

[44] Luke 16:9.

[45] Luke 22:29–30.

[46] John 10:10.

[47] Luke 21:24 probably implies something similar. Paul is explicit that Israel's acceptance will precede the resurrection (e.g., Romans 11:11–12, 15).

[48] Luke 17:22–24; Mark 13:21–22, 26; Matthew 24:23–27.

[49] Many Baha'is see their prophet Baha'u'llah answering Jesus' promise to return. Other twentieth-century prophets have made similar claims.

[50] Matthew 16:28 says 'until they see the Son of Man coming in his kingdom'.

[51] For a discussion of several interpretations see E. Nardoni ('A Redactional Interpretation of Mark 9:1', 365–384) who argues that the transfiguration is meant. K. Brower ('Mark 9:1: Seeing the Kingdom in Power', 17–41) thinks it is the cross.

[52] Beasley-Murray, *Jesus and the Future*, 1–80.

[53] See p. 585ff.

[54] So C.E.B. Cranfield, 'Thoughts on New Testament Eschatology', 512.

[55] 1QSb 3:7.

[56] E.g., Luke 12:35–40; 18:1–8; Mark 13:34–37; Matthew 25:1–13.

[57] G. Edmundson, *The Church in Rome in the First Century*, 143.

[58] D. Bonhoeffer, *The Cost of Discipleship*, 79.

[59] O. Cullmann (*Christ and Time*, 84) likens Jesus' programme for establishing the kingdom to the allied progress in World War II. VE Day meant the war was won, but many pockets of resistance still remained.

Bibliography

Aalen, S., ' "Reign" and "House" in the Kingdom of God in the Gospels', *New Testament Studies* 8 (1961-62), 215-240

Ackroyd, P.R., 'Reply', *Journal of Theological Studies* NS 10 (1959), 94

Albright, W.F., 'Ophrah and Ephraim', *Annual of the American Schools of Oriental Research* 4 (1922-3), 124-133

Anderson, J.N.D., *Evidence for the Resurrection* (London: IVF, 1950)

—, *The Witness of History* (London: Tyndale, 1969)

—, *A Lawyer among the Theologians* (London: Hodder & Stoughton, 1973)

Avi-Yonah, M., 'Some Comments on the Capernaum Excavations' in L.I. Levine (ed.), *Ancient Synagogues Revealed* (Jerusalem: Israel Exploration Society, 1981)

Bacon, B.W., *Studies in Matthew* (London: Constable, 1930)

Barnett, P.W., 'Under Tiberius all was Quiet', *New Testament Studies* 21 (1975), 564-571

—, 'The Jewish Sign Prophets – AD 40-70: Their Intention and Origin', *New Testament Studies* 27 (1981), 679-697

Bauckham, R.J., *Jude, 2 Peter* (Word Biblical Commentaries, Waco: Word, 1983)

—, 'The Coin in the Fish's Mouth' in D. Wenham & C. Blomberg (eds.), *Gospel Perspectives 6: The Miracles of Jesus* (Sheffield: JSOT Press, 1986), 219-252

Beare, F.W., *The Gospel according To Matthew* (Oxford: Basil Blackwell, 1981)

Beasley-Murray, G.R., *Jesus and the Future* (London: Macmillan, 1954)

Beitzel, B.J., 'The Via Maris in Literary and Cartographic Sources' in *Biblical Archaeologist* 54,2 (June 1991), 65-75

Bernard, J.H., *A Critical and Exegetical Commentary on The Gospel according to St John* (Edinburgh: T.&T. Clark, 1928)

Best, E., *1 Peter* (New Century Bible Commentary, London: Marshall, Morgan & Scott, 1971)

Betz, H.D., 'Jesus as Divine Man' in E.C. Colwell & F.C. Trotter (eds.), *Jesus and the Historian* (Philadelphia: Westminster, 1968), 114-133

Betz, O., 'Jesus' Gospel of the Kingdom' in P. Stühlmacher (ed.), *The Gospel and the Gospels* (Grand Rapids: Eerdmans, 1991), 53-74

—, 'Probleme des Prozesses Jesu (Mk 14:15)' in *Aufsteigund Niedergang der Römischen Welt*, 11/25.1 (1982), 565-647

Blinzler, J., 'The Jewish Punishment of Stoning in the New Testament Period' in E. Bammel (ed.), *The Trial of Jesus* (London: SCM, 1970), 147-161

Bloch, A.P., *The Biblical and Historical Background of Jewish Customs and Ceremonies* (New York: Ktav, 1980)

Blomberg, C.L., 'The Miracles as Parables' in D. Wenham & C.L. Blomberg (eds.), *Gospel Perspectives 6: The Miracles of Jesus* (Sheffield: JSOT Press, 1986), 327-359

—, *Interpreting the Parables* (Leicester: Apollos, 1990)

Bockmuehl, M., *This Jesus* (Edinburgh: T&T Clark, 1994)

Bode, E.L., *The First Easter Morning* (Rome: Biblical Institute Press, 1970)

Bonhoeffer, D., *The Cost of Discipleship* (London: SCM, 1959)

Borchert, O., *The Original Jesus* (London: Pickering & Inglis, 1933)

Borg, M.J., *Jesus: A New Vision* (London: SPCK, 1993)

Borgen, P., *Bread From Heaven* (Leiden: E.J. Brill, 1965)

Bornkamm, G., *Jesus of Nazareth* (London: Hodder & Stoughton, 1973)

Boucher, M., *The Mysterious Parable* (CBQ Monograph, Washington: Catholic Biblical Association of America, 1977)

Branscom, B.H., *Mark* (Moffat NT Commentaries, New York: Harper & Brothers, 1937)

Bright, J., *The Kingdom of God* (New York: Abingdon, 1953)

Brower, K., 'Mark 9:1: Seeing the Kingdom in Power', *Journal for the Study of the New Testament* 6 (1980), 17-41

Brown, C., *Miracles and the Modern Mind* (Grand Rapids: Eerdmans; Exeter: Paternoster, 1984)

Brown, R.E., 'Parable and Allegory Reconsidered', *Novum Testamentum* 5 (1962), 36-45

—, *The Gospel according to John* (London: Geoffrey Chapman, 1966)

—, *The Community of the Beloved Disciple* (London: Geoffrey Chapman, 1979)

—, *The Death of the Messiah* (New York: Doubleday, 1994)

Bruce, F.F., *New Testament History* (London: Nelson, 1969)

Bultmann, R., *Jesus Christ and Mythology* (London: SCM, 1960)

—, *The Gospel of John: A Commentary* (Oxford: Basil Blackwell, 1971)

—, 'New Testament and Mythology: The Problem of Demythologizing the New Testament Proclamation' (1941) in S.M. Ogden (ed.), *New Testament and Mythology and other basic writings* (London: SCM, 1984)

Cadoux, C.J., *The Historic Mission of Jesus* (London: Lutterworth, 1941)

Caird, G.B., *Jesus and the Jewish Nation* (London: Athlone, 1965)

—, *The Gospel of Luke* (London: Pelican, 1968)

—, 'Les eschatologies du Nouveau Testament', *Revue d'Histoire et de Philosophie Religieuses* 3 (1969), 217-227

Cardwell, K., 'The Fish on the Fire: John 21:9', *Expository Times* 102 (1990), 12-14

Carnley, P., *The Structure of Resurrection Belief* (Oxford: Clarendon, 1987)

Carson, D.A., *The Gospel according to John* (Leicester: IVP; Grand Rapids: Eerdmans, 1991)

Carson, D.A., D.J. Moo & L.L. Morris, *An Introduction to the New Testament* (Grand Rapids: Apollos, 1992)

Casey, M., *Is John's Gospel True?* (London: Routledge, 1996)

—, 'The Date of the Passover Sacrifices and Mark 14:12', *Tyndale Bulletin* 48 (1997), 245-247

Charles, R.H., *The Apocrypha and Pseudepigrapha of the Old Testament in English, II Pseudoepigrapha* (Oxford: Clarendon, 1913)

Charlesworth, J.H., 'Jesus and Jehohanan: An Archaeological Note on Crucifixion', *Expository Times* 84 (1972-73), 147-150

—, *Jesus Within Judaism* (New York: Doubleday, 1988)

Charlesworth, J.H. (ed.), *The Old Testament Pseudepigrapha* (Garden City: Doubleday, 1983)

Collins, J.J., 'The Kingdom of God in the Apocrypha and Pseudepigrapha' in W. Willis (ed.), *The Kingdom of God in Twentieth Century Interpretation* (Peabody: Hendrickson, 1987)

Cone, J.H., *God of the Oppressed* (London: SPCK, 1977)

Conzelmann, H., *The Theology of Saint Luke* (London: Faber & Faber, 1969)

Corbo, V., 'The Church of the House of St. Peter at Capernaum' in Y. Safrir (ed.), *Ancient Churches Revealed* (Jerusalem: Israel Exploration Society, 1993), 71-76

Corley, B., 'Trial of Jesus' in J.B. Green, S. McKnight & I.H. Marshall (eds.), *Dictionary of Jesus and the Gospels* (Downers Grove: IVP, 1992)

Craig, W.L., 'The Guard at the Tomb', *New Testament Studies* 30 (1984), 273–81

—, *Assessing the New Testament Evidence for the Historicity of the Resurrection of Jesus* (Lewiston: Edwin Mellen, 1989)

—, 'John Dominic Crossan on the Resurrection of Jesus' in S.T. Davis, D. Kendall & G. O'Collins (eds.), *The Resurrection* (Oxford: Oxford University Press, 1997)

Cranfield, C.E.B., *The Gospel according to Saint Mark* (Cambridge: Cambridge University Press, 1972)

—, 'Thoughts on New Testament Eschatology', *Scottish Journal of Theology* 35 (1982), 497-512

Crossan, J.D., *Finding is the First Act* (Philadelphia: Fortress; Missoula: Scholars, 1979)

—, *The Cross that Spoke: The Origins of the Passion Narrative* (San Francisco: Harper & Row, 1988)

—, *The Historical Jesus: The Life of a Mediterranean Jewish Peasant* (Edinburgh: T&T Clark, 1991)

—, *Jesus: A Revolutionary Biography* (New York: Harper Collins, 1994)

—, *Who Killed Jesus?* (SanFrancisco: HarperSanFrancisco, 1995)

Cullmann, O., *Christ and Time* (London: SCM, 1962)

Dalman, G., *The Words of Jesus* (Edinburgh: T&T Clark, 1902)

—, *Sacred Sites and Ways* (London: Levertoff, 1935)

Daube, D., *The New Testament and Rabbinic Judaism* (London: Athlone, 1956)

Davies, W.D., *The Setting of the Sermon on the Mount* (Cambridge: Cambridge University Press, 1964)

Davis, S.T., D.Kendall & G.O'Collins (eds.), *The Resurrection* (Oxford: OUP, 1997)

Degenhardt, H.J., *Lukas – Evangelist der Armen* (Stuttgart: Katholisches Bibelwerk, 1965)

Deissmann, G.A., *Light from the Ancient East* (London: Hodder & Stoughton, 1910)

Denny, J., 'The Word "Hate" in Luke 14.26', *Expository Times* 21 (1909), 41–42

Dodd, C.H., *The Parables of the Kingdom* (London: Nisbet & Co., 1936)

—, 'The Fall of Jerusalem and the "Abomination of Desolation"', *Journal of Roman Studies* 37 (1947), 47–54

—, 'The Framework of the Gospel Narrative' in idem *New Testament Studies* (Manchester: Manchester University Press, 1953), 1–11

—, *Historical Tradition in the Fourth Gospel* (Cambridge: Cambridge University Press, 1963)

—, 'The Appearances of the Risen Christ' in idem, *More New Testament Studies* (Manchester: Manchester University Press, 1968), 102–133

—, *The Interpretation of the Fourth Gospel* (Cambridge: Cambridge University Press, 1968)

—, *The Founder of Christianity* (London: Collins, 1971)

Domeris, W.R. & S.M.S. Long, 'The Recently Excavated Tomb of Joseph Bar Caiapha and the Biblical Caiaphas', *Journal for Theology for Southern Africa* 89 (1994), 50–58

Donahue, J.R., 'Tax Collectors and Sinners: An Attempt at Identification', *Catholic Biblical Quarterly* 33 (1971), 39–61

Dunkerley, R., 'Lazarus (Jn. 11; Lk. 16:19-31)', *New Testament Studies* 5 (1958-9), 321–327

Dupont, J., 'L'Origine de récit des Tentations de Jésus au désert', *Revue Biblique* 73 (1966), 30–76

—, *Les Béatitudes* (Paris: J. Gabalda, 1969-1973)

Edmundson, G., *The Church in Rome in the First Century* (London: Longmans, Green & Co., 1913)

Eisenman, R. & M. Wise, *The Dead Sea Scrolls Uncovered* (Longmead: Element, 1992)

Ellis, E.E., *The Gospel of Luke* (London: Nelson, 1966)

—, 'The Date and Provenance of Mark's Gospel' in F. Segbrock et al. (eds.), *The Four Gospels*, vol. 2 (Festschrift F. Neirynck; Leuven: Leuven University Press, 1992), 801–815

Ellul, J., 'Du texte au sermon 18: Les talents Matthieu 25.13-30', *Etudes Théologiques et Religieuses* 48 (1973), 134–136

Emerton, J.A., 'The 153 Fishes in John 21.11', *Journal of Theological Studies* ns 9 (1958), 86–89

Farmer, W.R., *The Synoptic Problem* (Macon: Mercer University Press, 1986)

Fascher, E., *Jesus und der Satan* (Tübingen: Max Niemeyer, 1949)

—, 'Jesus als Lehrer', *Theologische Literaturzeitung* 79 (1954), 324-342

Finegan, J., *Handbook of Biblical Chronology* (Princeton: Princeton University Press, 1964)

Finley, M.I., *The Ancient Economy* (London: Book Club Associates, 1979)

France, R.T., *Jesus and the Old Testament* (London: Tyndale, 1971)

—, *The Man they Crucified: A Portrait of Jesus* (London: IVP, 1975)

—, 'Chronological Aspects of Gospel Harmony', *Vox Evangelica* 16 (1986), 33-59

Freyne, S., *Galilee* (Edinburgh: T&T Clark, 1998)

Fuller, D.P., *Easter Faith and History* (London: Tyndale, 1965)

Funk, R.W., R.W. Hoover, et al., *The Five Gospels: The Search for the Authentic Words of Jesus* (New York: Macmillan, 1993)

Geivett, R.D. & G.M. Habermas (eds.), *In Defence of Miracles* (Leicester: Apollos, 1997)

Gerhardsson, B., *The Testing of God's Son* (Lund: C.W.K. Gleerup, 1966)

—, 'The Parable of the Sower and its Interpretation', *New Testament Studies* 14 (1968), 165-193

Gibson, J.B., *The Temptations of Jesus in Early Christianity* (Sheffield: Sheffield Academic Press, 1995)

Glasson, T.F., 'Schweitzer's Influence – Blessing or Bane?', *Journal of Theological Studies* 28 (1977), 289-302

—, 'Theophany and Parousia', *New Testament Studies*, 34 (1988), 259–270

Gnilka, J., *Jesus of Nazareth* (Peabody, Mass.: Hendrickson, 1997)

Godet, F., *Commentary on the Gospel of St John* (Edinburgh: T&T Clark, 1892)

Goguel, M., *The Life of Jesus* (New York: Macmillan, 1949)

Goodspeed, E.J., *A Life of Jesus* (New York: Harper & Brothers, 1956)

Grant, M., *Jesus* (New York: Simon & Shuster, 1995)

Green, M., *2 Peter and Jude* (Leicester: IVP, 1987)

Greenhut, Z.V., 'Burial Cave of the Caiaphas Family', *Biblical Archeology Review* 18,5 (1992), 29-36

Grigsby, B., 'Gematria and John 21:11 – Another Look at Ezekiel 47:10', *Expository Times* 95 (1984), 177-178

Gundry, R.H., *Matthew* (Grand Rapids: Eerdmans, 1982)

Habermas, G.R. & A.G.N. Flew, in T.L. Miethe (ed.), *Did Jesus Rise from the Dead?* (San Francisco: Harper & Row, 1987)

Harnack, A. von., *What is Christianity?* (London: Williams & Norgate, 1904)

—, *The Origin of the New Testament* (London: Williams and Norgate, 1925)

Harris, M., *Exodus and Exile: The Structure of Jewish Holidays* (Minneapolis: Fortress, 1992)

Harris, M., *Raised Immortal: Resurrection and Immortality in the New Testament* (London: Marshall, Morgan & Scott, 1983)

—, *Easter in Durham* (Exeter: Paternoster, 1985)

—, *From Grave to Glory* (Grand Rapids: Academie Books, 1990)

Headlam, A.C., *The Life and Teaching of Jesus the Christ* (London: John Murray, 1936)

Heim, K., *Jesus the World's Perfecter* (Edinburgh: Oliver & Boyd, 1959)

Hendin, D., *Guide to Biblical Coins* (New York: Amphora Books, 1987)

Hengel, M., 'Maria Magdalena und die Frauen als Zeugen' in O. Betz (ed.), *Abraham unser Vater* (Leiden: E.J. Brill, 1963), 243-256

—, *Judaism and Hellenism* (London: SCM, 1974)

—, *Crucifixion* (London: SCM, 1977)

—, *The Charismatic Leader and His Followers* (Edinburgh: T&T Clark, 1981)

—, *Studies in the Gospel of Mark* (London: SCM, 1985)

—, *The Johannine Question* (London: SCM; Valley Forge: Trinity Press International, 1989)

Hengel, M. & R. Deines, 'E.P. Sanders, "Common Judaism," Jesus and the Pharisees', *Journal of Theological Studies* NS 46 (1995), 13-14

Hennecke, E., *New Testament Apocrypha* (W. Schneelmelcher (ed.); London: Lutterworth, 1963, 1965)

Hill, D., *The Gospel of Matthew* (London: Oliphants, 1972)

Hoehner, H.W., *Chronological Aspects of the Life of Christ* (Grand Rapids: Zondervan, 1978)

—, *Herod Antipas* (Cambridge: Cambridge University Press, 1972)

Hooker, M.D., *Jesus and the Servant* (London: SPCK, 1959)

—, *The Gospel according to Saint Mark* (Peabody: Hendrickson, 1991)

Hooykaas, R., *Christian Faith and the Freedom of Science* (London: Tyndale, 1957)

Horbury, W. & E. Puech, 'Caiaphas' Identification Questioned', *Biblical Archeology Review* 20,6 (1994), 20

Horsley, R.A., *Jesus and the Spiral of Violence* (Minneapolis: Fortress, 1993)

—, *Galilee: History, Politics, People* (Valley Forge: Trinity Press International, 1995)

—, *Archeology, History and Society in Galilee* (Valley Forge: Trinity Press International, 1996)

Hunter, A.M., *According to John* (London: SCM, 1968)

Jaubert, A., *The Date of the Last Supper* (New York: Alba House, 1965)

Jeremias, J., *Jesus' Promise to the Nations* (London: SCM, 1958)

—, *The Sermon on the Mount* (Philadelphia: Fortress, 1963)

—, *The Eucharistic Words of Jesus* (London: SCM, 1966)

—, *Jerusalem in the Time of Jesus* (London: SCM, 1969)

—, *New Testament Theology*, vol.1 (London: SCM, 1971)

—, *The Parables of Jesus* (London: SCM, 1972)

Jervell, J., *Luke and the People of God* (Minneapolis: Augsburg, 1972)

Johnson, L.T., *The Literary Function of Possessions in Luke-Acts* (Missoula: Scholars, 1977)

—, 'The Lukan Kingship Parable (Luke 19.11-27)', *Novum Testamentum* 24 (1982), 139-159

Johnstone, P., *Operation World* (Carlisle: OM Publishing, 1993)

Jonge, M. de & A.S. van der Woude, '11QMelchizedek and the New Testament', *New Testament Studies* 12 (1965-66), 301–326

Judge, E.A., 'St Paul as a Radical Critic of Society', *Interchange* 16 (1974), 191-203

Juster, J., *Les Juifs dans l'Empire Romain: Leur condition juridique, économique et sociale* (Paris: Geuthner, 1914)

Justin Martyr, *Dialogue with Trypho the Jew* in A. Roberts and J. Donaldson (eds.), *The Anti-Nicene Fathers* I.194–270 (Grand Rapids: Eerdmans, 1979)

Kee, H.C., *Miracle in the Early Christian World* (New Haven, Yale University Press, 1983)

—, *Medicine, Miracle and Magic in New Testament Times* (Cambridge: Cambridge University Press, 1986)

Keller, E. & M.-L. Keller, *Miracles in Dispute* (London: SCM, 1969)

Kelly, J.N.D., *A Commentary on the Epistles of Peter and of Jude* (London: A.& C. Black, 1969)

Kersten, H. & E.R. Gruber, *The Jesus Conspiracy* (Brisbane: Element, 1995)

Kilpatrick, G.D., *The Origin of the Gospel according to St Matthew* (Oxford: Oxford University Press, 1946)

Kirk, A., 'Examining Priorities: Another Look at the Gospel of Peter's Relationship to the New Testament Gospels', *New Testament Studies* 40 (1994), 572-595

Kissinger, W.S., *The Sermon on the Mount: A History of Interpretation and Bibliography* (Metuchen NJ: Scarecrow & American Theological Library Association, 1975)

—, *The Parables of Jesus: A History of Interpretation and Bibliography* (Metuchen NJ: Scarecrow & American Theological Library Association, 1979)

Klausner, J., *Jesus of Nazareth* (London: Allen and Unwin, 1927)

Knox, D.B., 'Five Comings of Jesus, Matthew 24 and 25', *Reformed Theological Review* 34 (1975), 44–54

Koch, K., *Christian Counselling and Occultism* (Grand Rapids: Kregel, 1965)

Kopp, C., *The Holy Places of the Gospels* (Freiburg: Herder; London: Nelson, 1963)

Kroll, G., *Auf den Spuren Jesu* (Stuttgart: Katholisches Bibelwerk, 1979)

Kümmel, W.G., *Promise and Fulfilment* (London: SCM, 1961)

Kung, H., *Eternal Life* (London: SCM, 1984)

Lacey, D.R. de, 'In Search of a Pharisee', *Tyndale Bulletin* 43 (1992), 353–371

Ladd, G.E., *The Presence of the Future* (London: SPCK, 1974)

Lapide, P., *Auferstehung: Ein Judisches Glaubenserlebnis* (Stuttgart: Calwer; München: Kösel, 1977). ET: *The Resurrection of Jesus* (Minneapolis: Augsburg, 1983)

Lee, G.M., 'The Guard at the Tomb', *Theology* 72 (1969), 169–175

Levine, L.I. (ed.), *Ancient Synagogues Revealed* (Jerusalem: Israel Exploration Society, 1981)

Liddell, H.G. & R. Scott, *A Greek-English Lexicon* (Oxford: Clarendon, 1940)

Lightfoot, R.H., *St John's Gospel* (Oxford: Clarendon, 1956)

Linnemann, E., *Parables of Jesus*, (London: SPCK, 1966)

Lohmeyer, E., *Lord of the Temple* (Edinburgh: Oliver & Boyd, 1961)

—, *Our Father* (New York: Harper & Row, 1965)

Lüdemann, G., *The Resurrection of Jesus* (London: SCM, 1994)

—, *What Really Happened to Jesus* (London: SCM, 1995)

McEleney, N.J., '153 Great Fishes (John 21.11)', *Biblica* 58 (1977), 411–417

McGing, B.C., 'Pontius Pilate and the Sources', *Catholic Biblical Quarterly* 53 (1991), 416–438

Maccoby, H., *The Mythmaker: Paul and the Invention of Christianity* (London: Weidenfeld & Nicholson, 1986)

—, *Early Rabbinic Writings* (Cambridge: Cambridge University Press, 1988)

—, *Judaism in the First Century* (London: Sheldon, 1989)

Manson, T.W., *The Sayings of Jesus* (London: SCM, 1949)

—, 'The Cleansing of the Temple', *Bulletin of the John Rylands Library* 33 (1950–51), 271–282

—, *The Servant Messiah* (Cambridge University Press, 1953)

—, 'The Life of Jesus: A Study of the Available Materials' in idem, *Studies in the Gospels and Epistles* (M. Black (ed.); Manchester: Manchester University Press, 1962), 13ff.

Manson, W., *The Gospel of Luke* (London: Hodder & Stoughton, 1930)

Marksen, W., *The Resurrection of Jesus of Nazareth* (Philadelphia: Fortress, 1970)

Marsh, C., *Albrecht Ritschl and the Problem of the Historical Jesus* (San Francisco: Mellen Research University Press, 1992)

Marshall, I.H., *The Gospel of Luke* (Exeter: Paternoster, 1978)

Mazar, B., *The Mountain of the Lord* (Garden City: Doubleday, 1975)

Mealand, D.L., *Poverty and Expectation in the Gospels* (London: SPCK, 1980)

Meier, J.P., *A Marginal Jew* (New York: Doubleday, 1994)

Metzger, B.M., *A Textual Commentary on the Greek New Testament* (London: United Bible Societies, 1971)

Meyer, B.F., *The Aims of Jesus* (London: SCM, 1979)

Michaels, J.R., *1 Peter* (Waco: Word, 1988)

Milik, J.T., *Ten Years of Discovery in the Judaean Wilderness* (London: SCM, 1959)

Millar, F., *The Roman Near East 31 BC – AD 337* (Cambridge, MA: Harvard University Press, 1993)

Miyoshi, M., *Der Anfang des Reiseberichts* (Rome: Biblical Institute Press, 1974)

Montefiore, H., 'Revolt in the Desert?', *New Testament Studies* 8 (1961-62), 135-141

Moore, G.F., *Judaism* (Cambridge, MA: Harvard University Press, 1927)

Morison, F., *Who Moved the Stone?* (London: Faber & Faber, 1930)

Morris, L., *The Apostolic Preaching of the Cross* (London: Tyndale, 1965)

—, *Studies in the Fourth Gospel* (Exeter: Paternoster, 1969)

—, *The Gospel According to John* (London: Marshall, Morgan & Scott, 1972)

Moule, C.F.D., *The Phenomenon of the New Testament* (London: SCM, 1967)

—, 'Mark 4.1-20 yet Once More' in E.E. Ellis & M. Wilcox (eds.), *Neotestamentica et Semitica* (Edinburgh: T&T Clark, 1969), 95-113

—, 'On Defining the Messianic Secret in Mark' in E.E. Ellis & E. Grässer (eds.), *Jesus und Paulus* (Göttingen: Vandenhoek & Ruprecht, 1975), 239-252

—, *The Birth of the New Testament* (London: A. & C. Black, 1981)

Moule, C.F.D. (ed.), *The Significance of the Message of the Resurrection for Faith in Jesus Christ* (London: SCM, 1968)

Nardoni, E., 'A Redactional Interpretation of Mark 9.1', *Catholic Biblical Quarterly* 43 (1981), 365-384

Neill, S. & T. Wright, *The Interpretation of the New Testament 1861-1986* (Oxford: Oxford University Press, 1988)

Neugebauer, F., *Jesu Versuchung* (Tübingen: J.C.B. Mohr, 1986)

Neusner, J., *From Politics to Piety* (Englewood Cliffs: Prentice Hall, 1973)

—, *Early Rabbinic Judaism* (Leiden: E.J. Brill, 1975)

—, *Judaism in the Beginning of Christianity* (London: SPCK, 1984)

—, 'Mr Sanders' Pharisees and Mine: A Response to E.P. Sanders, *Jewish Law from Jesus to the Mishnah*', *Scottish Journal of Theology* 44 (1991), 73-95

Nolan, A., *Jesus Before Christianity* (London: Darton, Longman & Todd, 1977)

Owen, O.T., 'One hundred and fifty three Fish', *Expository Times* 100 (1988), 52-54

Pannenberg, W., *Jesus: God and Man* (London: SCM, 1968)

—, 'Did Jesus Really Rise from the Dead?' in R. Batey (ed.), *New Testament Issues* (London: SCM, 1970)

Paulus, H.E.G., *Das Leben als Grundlage einer reinen Geschochte Urchristentums* (Heidelberg: C.F. Winter, 1828)

Payne, P.B., 'The Authenticity of the Parables of Jesus' in R.T. France & D. Wenham (eds.), *Gospel Perspectives* 2 (Sheffield: JSOT Press, 1981), 329-344

—, 'The Authenticity of the Parable of the Sower and its Interpretation' in R.T. France & D. Wenham (eds.), *Gospel Perspectives 1* (Sheffield: JSOT Press, 1980), 169-71

Percy, E., *Die Botschaft Jesu* (Lund: Acta Universitatis Lundensis, 1953)

Perkins, P., *Resurrection* (London: Geoffrey Chapman, 1984)

Philostratus, *The Life of Apollonius of Tyana* (Loeb edition, tr. F.C. Conybeare; Cambridge, MA: Harvard University Press; London: Heinemann, 1950)

Ploeg, J.P. van der, 'Un petit rouleau de Psaumes Apocryphes (11QpsApa)' in G. Jeremias (ed.), *Tradition Und Glaube: das frëhe Christentum* (Göttingen: Vandenhoek und Ruprecht, 1971), 128-139

Pokorny, P., 'The Temptation Stories and their Intention', *New Testament Studies* 20 (1974), 115-127

Powell, M.A., 'Do and Keep what Moses Says (Matthew 23:2-7)', *Journal of Biblical Literature* 114 (1995), 419-435

Powers, B.W., *Marriage and Divorce: The New Testament Teaching* (Sydney: Family Life Movement & Jordan Books, 1987)

Reich, R., 'Caiaphas' Name Inscribed on Bone Boxes', *Biblical Archeology Review* 18,5 (1992), 38-44

Reicke, B., *The Epistles of James, Peter & Jude* (Garden City: Doubleday, 1964)

Reimarus, H.S., *Reimarus: Fragments* (C.H. Talbert (ed.); London: SCM, 1970)

Renan, E., *The Life of Jesus* (London: J.M. Dent & Sons; New York: E.P. Dutton & Co., 1927)

Richardson, A., *The Gospel according to Saint John* (London: SCM, 1959)

Riesner , R., *Jesus als Lehrer* (Tübingen: J.C.B. Mohr, 1981)

—, 'Bethany Beyond the Jordan (John 1:28)', *Tyndale Bulletin* 38 (1987), 29-63

Rissi, M., 'Voll grosse Fische, hundertdreiundfünfzig (John 21.1-14)', *Theologische Zeitschrift* 35 (1979), 73-89

Rivkin, E., *What Crucified Jesus?* (London: SCM, 1984)

Robinson, J.A.T., 'The Temptations' in idem, *Twelve New Testament Studies* (London: SCM, 1962), 53-60

—, 'The 'Others' of John 4:38' in idem, *Twelve New Testament Studies* (London: SCM, 1962), 61-66

—, 'A New Look at the Fourth Gospel' in idem, *Twelve New Testament Studies* (London: SCM, 1962), 94-106

—, *Redating the New Testament* (London: SCM, 1976)

—, ' "His Witness is True": A Test Case of the Johannine Claim' in E. Bammel & C.F.D. Moule (eds.), *Jesus and the Politics of His Day* (Cambridge: Cambridge University Press, 1984), 455-460

—, *The Priority of John* (London: SCM, 1985)

Romeo, J.A., 'Gematria and John 21.11: The Children of God', *Journal of Biblical Literature* 97 (1978), 263–264

Rosadi, G., *The Trial of Jesus* (London: Hutchison, 1905)

Ross, J.M., 'One hundred and fifty three Fish', *Expository Times* 100 (1990), 357

Sanday, W. *Outlines of the Life of Christ* (Edinburgh: T.&T. Clark, 1905)

Sanders, E.P., *Paul and Palestinian Judaism* (London: SCM, 1977)

—, *Jesus and Judaism* (London: SCM, 1985)

—, *Judaism: Practice and Belief 63BC – 66CE* (London: SCM; Valley Forge: Trinity Press International, 1992)

—, *The Historical Figure of Jesus* (London: Penguin, 1993)

Sanders, J.T., *The Jews in Luke-Acts* (London: SCM; Philadelphia: Fortress, 1987)

Schürer, E., *The History of the Jewish People in the Age of Jesus Christ* (G. Vermes et al. (eds.); Edinburgh: T&T Clark, 1973–1987)

Schürmann, H., *Das Lukasevangelium* (Freiburg: Herder, 1969)

Schweitzer, A., *The Quest of the Historical Jesus* (Baltimore: John Hopkins University Press, 1998)

Scobie, C.H.H., *John the Baptist* (London: SCM, 1964)

Seccombe, D., *Possessions and the Poor in Luke-Acts* (Linz: SNTU, 1982)

—, 'Take up your Cross' in P.T. O'Brien & D.G. Peterson (eds.), *God Who is Rich in Mercy* (Sydney: Lancer, 1986), 139–151

—, *Dust to Destiny: Reading Romans Today* (Sydney: Aquila, 1996)

—, 'Luke's Vision for the Church' in M. Bockmuehl & M.B. Thompson (eds.), *A Vision for the Church* (Edinburgh: T&T Clark, 1998), 45–63

—, 'The New People of God' in I.H. Marshall & D. Peterson (eds.), *Witness to the Gospel: The Theology of Acts* (Grand Rapids: Eerdmans, 1998), 349–372

—, 'Wanted – A New Approach to the Life of Jesus', *In Die Skriflig* 33 (1999), 32–41

—, 'The Story of Jesus and the Missionary Strategy of Paul' in P. Bolt and M. Thompson (eds.), *The Gospel to the Nations* (Leicester: IVP, 2000), 115–129

—, 'Jesus and the Gentiles (John 12:20–36)', *The South African Baptist Journal of Theology* 9 (2000), 32–41

Selwyn, E.G., *The First Epistle of Peter* (London: Macmillan, 1955)

Shanks, H. & D.P. Cole (eds.), *Archaeology and the Bible, vol. 2: Archaeology in the World of Herod, Jesus and Paul* (Washington: Biblical

Archaeology Society, 1990)

Sherwin-White, A.N., *Roman Society and Roman Law in the New Testament* (Oxford: Clarendon, 1963)

Smith, B.T.D., *The Parables of the Synoptic Gospels* (Cambridge: Cambridge University Press, 1937)

Smith, M., *Jesus the Magician* (New York: Harper & Row, 1978)

—, *The Secret Gospel: The Discovery and Interpretation of the Secret Gospel according to Mark* (Clearlake: Dawn Horse, 1982)

Stott, J.R.W., *Basic Christianity* (London: IVF, 1958)

—, *The Message of Romans* (Leicester: IVP, 1994)

Strauss, D.F., *The Life of Jesus Critically Examined* (London: SCM, 1973)

Taylor, V., *The Life and Ministry of Jesus* (London: Macmillan, 1954)

—, *The Gospel according to St Mark* (London: Macmillan, 1966)

Theissen, G., *The Shadow of the Galilean* (London: SCM, 1987)

Thiering, B., *Jesus and the Riddle of the Dead Sea Scrolls* (San Fransisco: HarperSanFrancisco, 1992)

—, *Jesus the Man* (London: Corgi, 1993)

Thompson, G.P., '"Called – Proved – Obedient": A Study in the Baptism and Temptation Narratives of Matthew and Luke', *Journal of Theological Studies* NS 11 (1960), 1-12

Trudinger, P., 'The 153 Fishes: A Further Response and Further Suggestion', *Expository Times* 102 (1990), 11-12

Tuckett, C.M., *The Revival of the Griesbach Hypothesis* (Cambridge: Cambridge University Press, 1983)

—, *Q and the History of Early Christianity* (Peabody: Hendrickson, 1996)

Tuckett, C.M. (ed.), *Synoptic Studies* (Sheffield: JSOT Press, 1984)

Tzaferis, V., *Excavations at Capernaum, vol. 1: 1978 – 1982* (Winona Lake: Eisenbrauns, 1989)

Vermes, G., *Jesus the Jew* (London: Collins, 1973)

—, *The Dead Sea Scrolls in English* (Sheffield: Sheffield Academic Press, 1995)

Via, D.O. Jr., *The Parables* (Philadelphia: Fortress, 1974)

Vine, V.E., 'The Purpose and Date of Acts', *Expository Times* 96 (1984), 45-48

Wachsman, S., *The Sea of Galilee Boat: An Extraordinary 2000 Year Old Discovery* (New York: Plewern, 1995)

Walker, N., 'The Reckoning of Hours in the Fourth Gospel', *Novum Testamentum* 4 (1960), 69-73

Weber, H.-R., *The Cross* (London: SPCK, 1979)

Weiss, J., *Jesus' Proclamation of the Kingdom of God* (London: SCM, 1971)

Wenham, D., *The Parables of Jesus* (London: Hodder & Stoughton, 1989)

Wenham, J., *Easter Enigma* (Exeter: Paternoster, 1984)

—, *Facing Hell* (Carlisle: Paternoster, 1998)

Westcott, B.F., *The Gospel according to St John* (London: John Murray, 1908)

Williams, C.S.C., *The Acts of the Apostles* (London: A. & C. Black, 1957)

Wilson, A.N., *Jesus* (London: Flamingo, 1993)

Windisch, H., 'Die Spruche vom Eingehen in das Reich Gottes', *Zeitschrift für Neutestamentliche Wissenschaft* 27 (1928), 163-192

Winter, P., *On the Trial of Jesus* (Berlin: W. de Gruyter, 1974)

Winterbotham, R., 'Christ or Archelaus?', *Expositor* 8 (1912), 338-347

Witherington, B. III, *The Christology of Jesus* (Minneapolis: Fortress, 1990)

—, *The Jesus Quest* (Downers Grove: IVP, 1997)

Wood, H.G., 'Interpreting This Time', *New Testament Studies* 2 (1956), 262-266

Wrede, W., *The Messianic Secret* (Cambridge: James Clarke & Co., 1971)

Wright, C.J.H., *God's People in God's Land* (Grand Rapids: Eerdman / Exeter: Paternoster, 1990)

Wright, N.T., *The New Testament and the People of God* (London: SPCK, 1993)

—, *Jesus and the Victory of God* (London: SPCK, 1996)

Wright, N.T. & M. Borg, *The Meaning of Jesus* (London: SPCK, 1999)

Yoder, J.H., *The Politics of Jesus* (Grand Rapids: Eerdmans, 1972)

Zahn, T., *Das Evangelium des Matthäus* (Leipzig: A. Deichert, 1910)

—, *Das Evanglium des Johannes* (Leipzig: A. Deichert, 1912)

Zerwick, M., 'Die Parabel vom Thronanwärter', *Biblica* 40 (1959), 654-674

Zias, J. & E. Sekeles, 'The Crucified Man from Giv'at ha-Mivtar: A Reappraisal', *Israel Exploration Journal* 35 (1985), 22-27

Ziesler, J.A., 'Luke and the Pharisees', *New Testament Studies* 25 (1979), 146-157

Zimmerli, W. & J. Jeremias, *The Servant of God* (London: SCM, 1957)

Scripture Index

Genesis
1:2ff   317
1:26-28   117
2   384
3:15   91,458
6:1-2   117
8:8-11   106
10   480
12:3   115
19:24ff   478
22:1   513
28:10-17   142
49:8-12   91

Exodus
1:5   480
4:22   101
8:19   318
12   562
12:6   562
12:42   534
16:4   424
17:1-7   129
19:6   180
20:8-11   371
24:1, 9   480
24:18   113
31:14   396
34:28   113

Leviticus
10:6f   271
25:8-55   195
25:9   199

Numbers
9:9-14   562
11:16, 24f   480
24:17   92
27:17   411

Deuteronomy
6:16   129
8:15f   112
13:1-5   362
15:4, 11   500
18:21f   577
21:23   545
24:1-4   396
24:1   384
32:5, 20   597
32:9f   112
32:43   102

1 Samuel
1:17ff   566
4:17   199
6:3   518
6:7f   513

10:1   98
16:1-13   92
16:13   98
21:1ff   372

2 Samuel
7   92, 101
7:12-16   181
18:19-33   192
24:1   316

1 Kings
4:20-34   181
5:4   118
11:14, 23, 25   118
19:8   113
19:15f   98
19:19-21   271

2 Kings
1:2ff   317
1:8   71
1:9-15   444
9:13   503
23:10   604

1 Chronicles
11:18f   563

17	92	91:11f	128	20	455
17:11-14	181	102:20	275	22:15-25	465
21:1	117	102:22	197	25:1-5	275
21:8	316	103:19	179, 197	25:6ff	153, 198,
		110	198, 514,		273, 482,
2 Chronicles			541, 564,		603
28:3	604		604	25:6	154
30:1-27	562	112:2	597	26:19	482
35:25	566	116	482	28:16	519
		118:22f	512	29:13	379
Job		126	275	30:19	275
1:6-12	117	137:1	275	30:21	31
1:38-42	316	139:18	482	32:15-19	81
2:1-8	117	145:13	179	32:15	402
7:17-19	121	149:4	196, 275	35:5f	314
				35:8	31
		Proverbs		35:10	275
Psalms		8	374	40-66	252, 254
2	198	13:24	482	40:1-11	77
2:2, 7f	97	25:21f	275	40:3	31, 112
2:8-11	131			40:9	274
9:12, 18	196, 275	**Isaiah**		40:10f	437
11:6	564	1:18	183	41:8ff	275
14:5	597	3:15	195	41:8-20	196, 275
16	31	5:1-7	511	42:1ff	97f, 106,
16:9-11	20, 482	6	324		275
22	559, 566	6:1-8	233	42:4	274, 438
24:6	597	6:9f	323	42:18ff	275
60:3	564	7-9	93	43:10	275
63:1	112	8:16-22	326	44:1	275
65:7	198	9:1-7	198, 603	45:7	179
68:10	196, 275	9:2	155f, 567	47:5	197
72	198	11	93, 198	49:1ff	198, 275
73:15	597	11:1-16	198	49:3	115
74:19, 21	275	11:1-9	603	49:4,7	438
75:8	564	11:4	196	49:6	344
76:9	275	11:6-10	273	49:8-13	254f
77:19f	425	13:19	197	49:9f	438
78:24		14:12ff	117	49:13,18	275
78:40ff	112	14:14f	448	49:13	196
79:11	275	14:30	196	49:18	275
89	198	17:12	198	49:24f	312
91	227, 482	18:7	275	50:1	153

50:4–11	274, 275	3:1	396	**Daniel**	
50:4–6	257	6:6–15	519	1:20	197
50:6–9	438	6:16	395	2	354
50:7	446, 478	7:1–15	509	2:31–44	184
51:4,16	274	7:25f	511	2:44	197
51:17,22	564	8:13	505	4:4–12	176
52:2	275	9:1	519	4:9	354
52:7f	192	13:17	519	4:17	197
52:7	274, 455	16:1–9	271	4:21	340
52:13–53:12		20:7	558	5:11	197
	274f, 438	20:11	559	5:16	197
53	31, 182	23:5	93	6:1	197
53:1	191	25:15, 17, 28		6:7	197
53:7	563		564	7	229, 350,
53:10–12	476, 482	31:10–13	275	442	
53:12	531, 563	31:27f	333	7:13f	93, 184,
54:4–8	153	31:31ff	183	541	
54:5	241	33:15ff	198	7:13	585
56:7	584			7:14	575
57:20	198	**Lamentations**		7:23f	198
58:4–8	87	3:1–39	566	7:27	198
58:6	158	3:3	180	9:24–27	160
58:12	106	4:21		9:24	102
60:1ff	198			9:26	198
60:1–3	356, 567	**Ezekiel**		9:27	583
60:1	128	16	273	10:13	197
61:1f	158	17:22–24	176, 340	11:2	197
61:1	192, 199,	21:27	91	12:1,10	75
275		23:31ff	564	12:1	480
61:2f,7	275	26:3	198	12:2f	345
61:3	333	28:12ff	117	12:2	31
63:19	183	29:14f	197	12:9	324
65:17–25	198, 273	31:3–18	340		
66:10	275	33:11	579	**Hosea**	
66:22f	603	34	198, 437	1ff	273
66:22	273	34:11–16	239	1–3	153
66:24	590	34:23f	93	2:14	112
		36:26f	183	2:20	241
Jeremiah		37	31, 198,	6:1f	476
1:4–10	271		482		
1:10,15	197	40:1ff	198	**Joel**	
2:2	112	47:1ff	198	2:28–32	81

3:18	198	3:13f	99	8:11	604
		3:13	104	8:12	604
Amos		3:14f	89	8:18-22	479
7:10-17	85	3:17	96	8:19-22	273
9:13ff	153, 198	3:22	362	8:21f	230
		4:1-11	109	8:28-34	303
Jonah		4:1	133	8:28	516
2	477	4:2-4	124	9:1-8	219
3:5	114	4:4	xi	9:1	201
		4:5	127	9:9	230
Micah		4:12-17	152	9:14-17	241
4:7f	187	4:12	152	9:14f	429
7:14ff	438	4:13	200	9:32-34	303
		4:16	155f	9:37f	334
Habakkuk		4:18-20	230	10	274, 403,
2:16	564	4:21f	230	437, 479	
		4:24	291, 316	10:5-15	400
Zechariah		5-7	249, 274	10:12f	352
3:1f	117, 121	5:1-12	252	10:23	403
4:7	197	5:5	255, 604	10:25	317
9:9f	502	5:13	518	10:28	604
11	437	5:14-19	276	10:29f	197
11:7,11	196, 275	5:14	344	10:40	352, 402
12:2	564	5:17-20	262, 388	11:2ff	278, 436
13:4	71	5:18	227	11:2-6	392
13:7ff	437	5:20	273	11:5	199, 347
		5:21-48	389	11:12f	155
Malachi		5:21f	604	11:14	105
1:3	482	5:22, 29f	604	11:19	237
3:1f	148	5:22, 26	480	11:20-24	448
4:5ff	75, 79	5:32	382	11:25-27	450
		6:2,5	227	11:27	352
Matthew		6:22f	276	11:28-12:14	
2:13f	302	7:3-6, 15-23			395
2:20-23	302		276	11:28-30	373, 395
3:2	81	7:6	354	11:28	294
3:5	79	7:21	273	12:1-8	371
3:7	82	7:24ff	336	12:9-14	375
3:10	114	7:24-27	260	12:22-24	304
3:11,14	105	7:28	252	12:25-30	312
3:11f	80	8:5-13	219, 222,	12:36f	604
3:11	85	603		12:36	604

12:38f	316	17:14f	304	24:8	583
12:40	477, 482	17:24–18:35		24:14	199, 584
12:41f	604		274	24:21	519
12:46–50	351	17:24–27	125, 293,	24:23–27	604
12:49f	273	371, 518		24:29–31	603
13	274	17:24	219	24:32ff	595
13:1–9	329	18:1–5	442	24:34	594
13:10–17	323	18:9	604	24:42	564
13:15	479	18:23–25	355	24:51	604
13:24–30	342	19:1–9	382	25:1–13	242, 605
13:31f	339	19:1	478, 481	25:10,19, 31ff	
13:33	341	19:16ff	381, 396		602
13:37–43	342	19:16–30	231	25:13	564
13:37	348	19:28	248, 399,	25:30	604
13:39ff, 47ff		590		25:31ff	478, 604
	604	20:17ff	481	25:31f	591
13:42, 50	604	20:29–34	493	26:2–4	520
13:43	600, 604	20:29	516	26:6–16	499
13:44–46	347	21:1–11	501	26:13	199
14:1f	406–409	21:10f	505	26:17ff	521
14:3–12	436	21:12f	506	26:17	561
14:12f	436	21:14–17	519	26:30ff	532
14:13–21	410–413	21:15f	504	26:53	130, 557
14:22–34	413	21:18–20	505	26:57–68	538
14:26–33	417	21:23ff	519	26:64	541
14:34–15:39		21:23–27	510	26:67f	564
	413–415	21:23	519	27:1ff	543
15:24	239	21:31	238	27:15–26	547
15:29–39	415	22:13	604	27:18	544
16:1–4	316	22:33–46	511	27:19	543
16:1–3	311	22:41–45	514	27:24f	553
16:1	130	23:1–39	519	27:31–56	553
16:4	477	23:1–3	390	27:34	555
16:5–12	418	23:2f	366	27:40, 42	131
16:6, 11f	356	23:4	373	27:44	556
16:9f	416	23:13	273	27:45f	558
16:13–20	422–424	23:15, 33	604	27:57–61	559
16:21–23	431f	23:27	387	28	54
16:24ff	482	23:38f	590	28:15	6
16:27	589, 602	24–25	274	28:16–20	575
16:28	592, 604	24:1ff	603	28:18–20	603
17:1–13	432–434	24:3	595	28:18	586, 593

Mark
1:1–14 100
1:3 31
1:6 71
1:9–11 89
1:9 104
1:11 96, 479
1:12f 109, 113
1:12 133
1:13 122
1:14f 152, 155
1:14 145, 152, 153, 357
1:15 151, 194, 218
1:16f 230
1:17 320f
1:19f 230
1:21–38 211
1:21–28 213ff, 274
1:25 317
1:27 422
1:29–31 216f
1:29 201
1:30f 515
1:33f 291
1:34 301
1:38 107, 351, 400
1:43 293
2:1ff 85, 219, 292, 369
2:1 201
2:7 423
2:14 230
2:15 243
2:16 369
2:17 321
2:18ff 134
2:18–22 241
2:18–20 86
2:19–22 154

2:19f 429
2:23–28 371
3:1–6 375
3:6 357, 429
3:12 317
3:13–19 247
3:14 399
3:20f, 31–35 351
3:22–30 307, 370
3:22–27 110, 482
3:22 216
3:23–27 312
3:27 133, 402, 481
3:28 227
3:33ff 448
3:33–35 273
3:35 245
4:1 232
4:3–9 329
4:11 xvii, 348
4:12 323
4:21–23 330
4:24 330
4:25 330
4:26–29 333
4:30–32 339
4:30f 176
4:34 320
4:35–6:6 305
4:35–41 292
4:41 423
5:1–20 303
5:2 516
5:22ff 515
5:22–43 515
5:25–34 293
6–8 398f
6:1–6 195
6:2f 423
6:3 196
6:5 165

6:7–13 400
6:14–29 406–409
6:16 72
6:17–29 72
6:23 175
6:30–44 410–413
6:31–51 293
6:34 411
6:48–52 413
6:49 53
6:49, 51f 417
6:52 479
6:53–8:10 413–415
7 378
7:1–23
7:3f 236
7:6–8 379
7:8 179
7:9ff 379, 380
7:15 386
7:24–30 603
7:25–30 414
7:31–10:10 415
7:32 304
7:33 292
8:1–10 293
8:11f 316, 360
8:11 130, 426
8:12 227
8:13–21 418
8:15 356
8:17 479
8:19f 416
8:22ff 292
8:22–26 421
8:27–29 422–424
8:31–33 431f
8:31 467, 482
8:34ff 482
8:35 199, 504
9:1 477, 592, 602

9:2ff	293	11:12-20	505	14:27	503
9:2-13	432-434	11:13f	293	14:32ff	532
9:10	478	11:15-17	506	14:34	533
9:11	3, 14, 77, 423	11:16	519	14:36	564
		11:17-19	519	14:38	121
9:14ff	304	11:17	148, 584	14:53-65	538
9:25	317	11:20f	293	14:61-64	351
9:30-31	440	11:27ff	519	14:61f	564
9:31	467, 482	11:27-33	510	14:62	585, 602, 604
9:33-37	441	11:27	519		
9:33	219	12:1-12	511	14:65	564
9:38-41	443	12:1-11	107	15:1ff	543
9:38f	306	12:9	603	15:1	539, 564
9:43-47	604	12:10f	512	15:6-15	547
9:47	273	12:18-25	190	15:10	544
10	383f	12:26f	482	15:20-41	553
10:1	478, 481, 514	12:35-37	514	15:21	554
		12:36	604	15:23	555
10:13-16	238	12:38-40	519	15:25	549
10:14f	177	12:41	519	15:32	556
10:14	294	13:1ff	603	15:33, 37	573
10:15, 23-25	273	13:2	479	15:33f	558
		13:4	595	15:39	573
10:17ff	231, 381, 396	13:5-13	583	15:42-47	559
		13:8	174	16:1	51
10:21	266	13:9f	603	16:5	516
10:29f	199, 266	13:10	199, 356	16:45	
10:31, 35-45	190	13:14-20	583		
		13:21f,26	604	**Luke**	
10:32-34	467	13:26	596	1:1f	452
10:32	491	13:28-33	595	1:2	41
10:34f	515	13:30-32	596	1:3	50
10:34	482	13:30	594	1:17	77
10:35-47	463	13:34-37	564, 605	1:28	194
10:38	468, 564	14:1f	561	1:36	99
10:44f	470	14:3-11	499	1:46-55	95, 189
10:45	221, 526	14:3	516	1:52	39
10:46-52	493, 515	14:9	199, 356, 487, 603	1:68-79	95, 189
10:46	516			1:74	39
10:47f	350	14:12ff	521	2:14	479
11:1ff	518	14:12	561	2:25, 38	189
11:1-11	501	14:22-24	527	2:40ff	96

2:41–51	514	5:17–26	219		515
2:46f	157	5:17	369	8:3	435
3:1f	71	5:26	369	8:5–8	329
3:1	409	5:27f	230	8:9f	323
3:2	537	5:33–39	241	8:16f	330
3:3–6	82	6:1–5	371	8:19–21	351
3:7	82	6:6–11	375	8:21	273, 448
3:8f	82	6:11ff	251	8:26–39	303
3:8	84	6:12–49	249	8:31	305
3:9, 17	78	6:12–16	247	9–19	459
3:9	518	6:13	401	9:1–6	400
3:10f	86	6:17	243, 273	9:7–9	406–409
3:12–14	87	6:20–26	277	9:7	435
3:16f	80	6:20–25	126	9:10–17	410–413
3:16	85	6:20–23	252f	9:18–21	422–424
3:22	96	6:22	246	9:22	431f
3:23–38	100	6:27–38	259	9:23ff	482
3:23	409	6:27–29	257	9:27	592
3:38	122	6:38	322	9:28–36	432–434
4:1–13	109	6:39–42	276, 322	9:31	478
4:1	133	6:39	322	9:37ff	304
4:2	134	6:46	246	9:37–43	441
4:5–8	131	6:47ff	336	9:44–62	481
4:6	116	6:47–49	260	9:44	441
4:12	107	7:1–10	222, 292	9:46–48	442
4:13	133	7:5	212	9:49f	443
4:14–23	200	7:11ff	515	9:51–56	307, 443f
4:14–21	152	7:18ff	278	9:51f	446
4:14f	156	7:18–23	392	9:51	481
4:14	101	7:19ff	107	9:53	460
4:16–30	156	7:22f	419	9:54f	292
4:18f	158	7:22	199, 347,	9:57–62	479
4:18	101		515	9:59f	230
4:20	41	7:24–26	72	10–18	261
4:24–28	603	7:26–28	75	10:1ff	30
4:24	227	7:31–35	86	10:1–24	452
4:28–30	481	7:33ff	133	10:1–20	479
4:42	227	7:34	237	10:2	334, 453
4:43	107, 199,	7:36ff	393	10:4–12	454
	218	7:36–50	126	10:5f	352
5:1ff	63, 227	8:1–3	399	10:12	405
5:1–11	232	8:2	305, 309,	10:13–15	448

10:15	219	12:37	564	16:17	262
10:16, 22	107, 352	12:49-51	108	16:18	382, 383
10:16	456	12:49f	468	16:19-31	270, 361,
10:18	133, 458	12:54-56	316, 456		486, 515
10:20	458	12:57-59	456	16:27-31	262
10:21-23	354, 481	13:1ff	603	17:12-19	292
10:21f	450	13:1-5	457	17:20ff	311
10:21	325, 479	13:3,5	337	17:22-37	603
10:22	126	13:6ff	603	17:22-24	604
10:23	459	13:6-9	114, 336,	18:1-8	605
10:25ff	381	13:10-16	355, 457, 518	18:9-14	237
10:25-37	262, 263	13:10-16	304	18:17, 24f	273
10:29-37	354	13:14	376	18:18ff	381, 396
10:30-37	355	13:16	377	18:18-30	231
10:32ff	481	13:18f	339	18:18-20	262
10:38ff	515	13:20f	331	18:35-43	493
11:4	121	13:21	355	18:36	516
11:14f	304	13:23-30	604	19:1-10	395, 492
11:16	130, 316	13:28-30	604	19:3	516
11:17-23	312	13:28	604	19:9f	239
11:20	133, 392	13:32-34	468	19:9	245
11:22	563	13:32f	476	19:11-27	355, 493-
11:23	270	13:34f	553		499, 589
11:27f	126, 351	13:34	246, 480,	19:14-44	579
11:29f, 32	477		504	19:29-44	501
11:31f	604	13:35	603	19:37	243, 273,
11:37ff	393	14:1ff	393		516
11:39-41	387	14:15-24	242	19:38-40	350
11:46	373	14:23	603	19:40	503
11:47-61	468	14:25-35	246	19:41ff	603
11:51	227	14:25-33	474	19:41-44	479, 563
12:1-21	266	14:25-27	468	19:42-44	504
12:1	356	14:33	266	19:45f	506
12:2f	478	14:34f	579, 518	19:47	519
12:4-12	268	15:11-32	240	20:1ff	519
12:4-9	475	16:1-31	383	20:1-8	510
12:5	604	16:1-9	268	20:9-19	511
12:15	266	16:8	355, 596	20:20	519
12:24-31	267f	16:9	604	20:41-44	514
12:32	240, 479	16:11f	269	20:45-47	519
12:35-48	518	16:16	155, 199,	21:5ff	603
12:35-40	605		383, 389	21:9	583

21:20–24	38	24:22	46f	3:31–36	144, 353
21:24	604	24:34	47	4:1–43	145
21:29ff	595			4:1–3	136, 152
21:32	594	**John**		4:1f	357
21:33	597	1:4f	104	4:20–24	149
21:35	591	1:6	105	4:21–23	151
22:1f	561	1:8	76	4:23f	148
22:7ff	521	1:14, 18	353	4:34f	151
22:7	561	1:14	146, 575	4:35–38	334
22:13–25	547	1:19–28	76	4:35	437
22:15–18	525	1:20–23	105	4:38	154
22:28–34	530	1:23	77	4:43–45	136
22:28–30	248	1:26	80	4:45–54	201
22:28	534	1:29–34	98f	4:46–54	222, 435
22:29f	604	1:29, 36	101	5:1–18	429
22:30	399	1:34	101	5:2–7	290
22:31	120	1:35–51	139, 141	5:4	315
22:35–38	531	1:35–40	76	5:10f	392
22:35	401	1:41, 45, 49	101	5:15–30	377
22:37	563	1:51	227	5:19	227
22:39ff	532	2:1–11	142f	5:24	135, 353
22:50f	515	2:12	201	5:25–29	353
22:63–65	564	2:16	148	5:28f	604
22:66	539	2:18	392	5:33–35	436
22:67–69	564	2:20	409	5:35	76
23:1ff	543	2:23–3:15	144	5:36	107, 316
23:6–12	547	2:23ff	439	6:1–15	410–413
23:26–49	553	2:23–25	450	6:14f	413
23:27–31	554	2:46	435	6:15	481
23:28–31	563	3:1–15	394	6:16–21	413
23:28	534	3:1f	370	6:24–71	425–427
23:32–43	556	3:5	273	6:25ff	282, 563
23:34	556	3:11	44	6:27	107
23:45	558	3:14f	430	6:30	316
23:50–56	559	3:16–21	144	6:31–32	424
23:56	51	3:19	552	6:37	294
24	49	3:22ff	139, 144	6:41	392
24:4	516	3:22–4:2	150	6:51–59	430
24:6f	50	3:23–30	150	6:52	392
24:10	51, 435	3:27–30	105	6:66	247, 273
24:13–35	574	3:28ff	273	7:1ff	460
24:13	52	3:29f	152, 154	7:1	440

7:2–10:21	444f	11:19, 45	489	17:3	352
7:3	273	11:24	478	18:1ff	532
7:5	29	11:33, 35, 38		18:10f	515
7:11f	392		293	18:11	564
7:12	445	11:41f	292	18:12–14	537
7:19–25	429	11:47–53	489	18:19–24	537
7:19–24	377	11:47	317	18:19	229
7:20	317	11:48	579	18:28ff	543
7:31	291	11:53, 57	490	18:28	228, 561
7:32–49	360	11:53–54	481	18:31	544
7:47–52	394	12:1ff	518	18:32	545
8:31	353	12:1–8	486, 499	18:33–38	546
8:48, 52	317	12:1	516	19:1–16	547
8:51ff	392	12:9–19	501	19:6	545
8:53–59	360	12:9,17f	489	19:13f	549
8:59	481	12:12	516	19:16–37	553
9:7	292	12:16	502	19:25–27	482
9:28	245	12:20–36	482	19:38–42	559
9:32	284	12:20–33	471, 586	19:38	243
10	240, 437	12:20–32	356, 603	19:39	394
10:10	604	12:23, 34	356	20:24–29	575
10:11, 17f	468	12:23	473	20:28	91
10:14	437	12:31f	133, 480,	20:31	91, 575
10:20	317	593		21	43f
10:21	478	12:31	116, 552	21:1ff	272
10:22ff	460, 478	12:35–48	518	21:15–19	531
10:22, 40	459	12:39f	354	21:24	44
10:22–29	360	12:42	243		
10:22–24	461	12:47–50	353	**Acts**	
10:24	354	13:1ff	521	1	53
10:25–42	462	13:1–5	522	1:1–11	49
10:25, 32, 38		13:1	561	1:1	50
	316, 392	13:8	522	1:6f, 11	574
10:27f	412	13:12–17	533	1:6–8	467
10:27	353	13:34f	533	1:6	518
10:31–40	481	14:11	316	1:11	587
10:40–42	481	14:30	116, 133,	1:14	29
10:41	72, 284	534		1:21f	153
11:1–44	483	15:3	353	2	1
11:1f	486	16:8–11	552	2:14–40	4, 20
11:9f	484	16:11	116	2:22	307
11:18	488	16:25	354	2:24–32	15

2:29-31	21	17:18	15	**1 Corinthians**	
2:40	596	17:22-32	4	1:21	479
2:41	22	17:30-32	15	1:22	128
3:14f	15	18:25f	31	2:1	354
3:20f	574	19:9	31	5:6-8	356
4:1	393	19:23	31	6:3	118
4:10	15	20:5ff	37	6:13f	19f
4:27f	552	20:31	564	11:23ff	521
5:1ff	121	21:38	317	15	6, 65
5:17	393	22	24	15:1-8	18
5:31f	15	22:4	31	15:3-8	24
5:34f	393	22:30ff	25	15:3-4	19
7:55f	356	23:6	15, 393	15:20, 23	19
7:57ff	544	23:9	393	15:44	19
9	24	24:1ff	25	15:51	354
9:2	31	24:10ff	31	16:13	564
9:20	31	24:14	31	16:22	603
10-11	32, 228	24:15	15		
10:1ff	223	24:22	31	**2 Corinthians**	
10:14	236	25:13-26:32		4:5f	xviii
10:28	603	436		12:1-9	26
10:36-43	487	25:13ff	25		
10:37-40	140	26	24	**Galatians**	
10:38	307	26:1ff	31	1:15	479
10:40f	15	26:5	393	1:18f	27
11:2f	603	26:19	26	2:1-10	32
12:2	30	26:23	15	2:11-14	603
12:12	41			4:2	435
12:15	53	**Romans**			
13:1	436	1:4	6	**Ephesians**	
13:5	41	2:17-21	322	1:5,9	479
13:13	42	2:19	275	1:9	354
13:16ff	31	4:13	118	1:10, 18-23	118
13:30-37	15	8:10f	19	2:20f	519
15	32	8:18-24		3:3	354
15:1-35	603	9-11	451	3:13	546
15:5	393	11	603	6:19	354
15:37-41	42	11:11f, 15	604		
16:11-18	37	11:15	603	**Colossians**	
16:40-20:5	37	11:25	354	1:13	481
17:3	6, 15	11:26	603	1:19	479
17:16ff	25	12:19-21	275	1:26	354

2:16f	377	3:9,16	354	5:13	42
4:2	564				
4:3	354	**2 Timothy**		**2 Peter**	
		4:11	42	1:16–18	433
Philippians				3:3f	577
3:3–9	273	**James**		3:12f	604
		1:1	29	3:15f	32
I Thessalonians					
1:9f	6, 14, 603	**Hebrews**		**1 John**	
4:13–18	604	3:7–4:11	377	5:19	119
4:16	588	5:7	532, 567		
5:6	564			**Revelation**	
		1 Peter		1:20	354
2 Thessalonians		1:1ff	32	3:2	564
2:7	354	1:3	28	4:4–10	531
		2:5	465	10:7	354
1 Timothy		2:7	519	12:7ff	117
1:15	392	5:8	564	12:7–11	4

Ancient Sources Index

Apocrypha
Tobit   53, 271
Sirach   106, 197, 395
Baruch   395
1 Maccabees   105, 197
2 Maccabees   197

Pseudepigrapha
Life of Adam & Eve   134, 135
Life of Adam & Eve (Slavonic)
   135
2 Baruch   420, 438
1 Enoch   350, 480
Assumption of Moses   105, 199,
   478, 604
Sibylline Oracles   604
Psalms of Solomon   94, 199,
   275, 314
Testaments of the Twelve
   Patriarchs   106, 196, 275, 402,
   435, 458, 480

Qumran Writings
Community Rule (1QS)   105,
   519
Damascus Document (CD)   275,
   396
War Scroll (1QM)   135, 199, 275,
   314, 356

Hymns (1QH)   106
Blessings (1QSb)   199, 597, 605
4QFlor   154
4QTherapeia   316
4Q174   154
4Q246   106
4Q252   106
4Q510   227, 316
4Q511   154, 316
4Q521   106
11QMelchizedek   106, 107, 135,
   196
11QPs   227
11QPsAp^a 227, 317

New Testament Apocrypha
Protevangelium of James   275
Gospel of the Nazareans   495
Gospel of Peter   8, 31, 52-53, 56
Gospel of Thomas   316

Other Post Apostolic Writings
Apostolic Constitutions   561
Didache   603

Rabbinic Writings
Mishnah
   Berakhoth   315, 435, 480, 519
   Kilaim   355

Hallah 562
Shabbath 395, 396
Pesahim 526, 562, 563, 564
Shekalim 482, 506, 518, 519, 602
Sukkah 394
Betzah 538, 562, 564
Ketuboth 396
Gittin 384, 396
Sanhedrin 396, 538, 562, 564, 565
Eduyoth 105
Aboth 31, 227, 247, 273, 315, 395, 396, 516, 518, 604
Zebahim 562
Oholoth 435
Tohoroth 435
Yadaim 396
Babylonian Talmud
Berakhoth 315, 396
Shabbath 394
Pesahim 315
Taanith 315
Ketuboth 273
Nedarim 396
Sotah 516
Baba Kamma 315

Sanhedrin 134, 307, 317, 393, 490, 515, 516, 523, 561
Jerusalem Talmud
Berakoth 315
Tosefta
Berakoth 315
Shabbath 395
Targum
Exodus 106
Isaiah 105, 199, 563
Amos 197
Micah 197
Zechariah 154, 197
Midrash Rabbah
Genesis 275, 395
Exodus 241, 273
Leviticus 273
Numbers 275
Ecclesiastes 438
Midrash Psalms 275
Mekilta Exodus 395, 396, 438, 562
Aboth Rabbi Nathan 242, 273, 315
Pesikta Rabbati 135, 195, 275
Derek Erez Rabbah 275
Tanhumah Toledoth 480

Author Index

Aalen, S. 197
Ackroyd, P.R. 69
Aland, K. 480
Albright, W.F. 491, 516
Anderson, J.N.D.
Augustine 6f, 15, 64
Avi-Yonah, M. 226

Bacon, B. W. 274
Bahrdt, K.F. 8, 15, 437
Barnett, P.W. 310, 317, 516
Barth, K. 10, 15
Bauckham, R.J. 316, 438, 518
Beare, F. W. 68
Beasley-Murray, G.R. xxiii, 594, 603, 605
Beitzel, B. J. 225
Bernard, J.H. 69
Best, E. 32
Betz, H. D. 315
Betz, O. 199, 516, 551, 566
Blinzler, J. 196, 565
Bloch, A. P. 134
Blomberg, C. L. 316, 354, 356
Bockmuehl, M. 519
Bode, E. L. 68
Bonhoeffer, D. 605
Borchert, O. 438
Borg, M.J. 171, 196, 604

Borgen, P. 438
Bornkamm, G. i, 133
Boucher, M. 354, 356
Branscom, B.H. 518
Bright, J. 394
Brower, K. 604
Brown, C. 315
Brown, R. E. 152, 355, 438, 515, 516, 566
Bruce, F.F. 31, 32, 565
Bultmann, R. 10, 15, 134, 152, 169, 280, 282, 314

Cadoux, C.J. 479
Caird, G. B. 173, 196, 317, 478f
Cardwell K. 69
Carnley, P. 30
Carson, D.A. 67, 478, 514, 515
Casey, M. 153, 561
Celsus 6, 46
Charles, R.H. 199, 355
Charlesworth, J.H. 134, 356, 438, 566
Chrysostom 565
Cicero 564
Collins, J. J. 199
Cone, J. H. 195
Conzelmann, H. 517
Corbo, V. 227, 435, 437, 438

Corley, B.   564
Craig, W.L.   12, 15, 56
Cranfield, C.E.B.   227, 518, 563, 605
Crossan, J. D.   12, 16, 31, 73, 105, 171, 196, 354, 601
Cullmann, O.   605

Dalman, G.   169, 174, 176f, 196f, 482, 516
Daube, D.   273, 275
Davies, W.D.   105
Davis, S.T. , D. Kendall & G. O'Collins   15
Degenhardt, H.J.   276
Deines, R.   393, 394, 395
Deissmann G. A.   199
Denny, J.   482
Dodd, C.H.   38, 62, 106, 109, 134, 140, 152f, 170, 196, 334f, 353, 355, 438, 515
Domeris, W. R.   567
Donahue, J. R.   272
Dunkerley, R.   515
Dupont, J.   110, 134, 274

Edmundson, G.   605
Eisenman, R.   106
Ellis, E.E.   67, 68, 317, 519
Ellul, J.   517
Emerton, J. A.   69
Epiphanius   565
Eusebius   68, 152, 226, 314, 315, 353, 584, 603

Farmer, W.R.   66
Fascher, E.   245, 273, 316
Finegan, J.   104, 153, 436, 437, 561, 562, 566
Finley, M.I.   228
Flew, A.G.N.   12, 15
France, R.T.   xxiii, 135, 153, 562

Freyne, S.   210, 226, 272
Fuller, D.P.   15
Funk, R. W.   196

Geivett , R. D.   315
Gerhardsson, B.   120, 124, 127, 134f, 355
Gibson, J. B.   120, 134f
Glasson, T. F.   585, 603
Gnilka, J.   272
Godet, F.   435
Goguel, M.   133, 435, 461, 481
Goodspeed, E. J.   274, 437, 518
Grant, M.   31, 280, 314, 515
Green, M.   439
Greenhut, Z.V.   567
Grigsby B.   69
Gundry, R. H.   67, 68

Habermas, G. R.   12, 15, 315
Harnack, A.   40, 168, 196
Harris, Monford.   134
Harris, Murray.   12, 15
Headlam, A.C.   153, 410, 436, 437, 481
Heim, K.   564
Hendin, D.   105
Hengel, M.   40, 43, 61, 68f, 231, 233, 271, 393, 394, 395, 438, 564
Hennecke, E.   226, 316
Hill, D.   356, 395
Hoehner, H. W.   105, 153f, 409, 436, 437
Hooker, M. D.   275, 437, 438, 563
Hooykaas, R.   314
Horbury, W.   567
Horsley, G.H.R.   199
Horsley, R. A.   195, 226
Hunter, A.M.   515

Jaubert, A.　561
Jenkins, D.　11
Jeremias, J.　170f, 196228, 274,
　　275, 314, 320, 337, 342f, 355,
　　356, 494f, 516, 517, 518, 519,
　　528f, 561, 562, 563
Jerome　64, 317
Jervell, J.　394
Johnson, L.T.　276, 517
Johnstone, P.　xii, 9, 15
Josephus　38, 72-4, 84, 105f, 129,
　　135, 153, 200, 202, 210, 215,
　　225, 227, 272f, 309, 316f, 362,
　　367, 393f, 408, 435f, 501, 516–
　　518, 537, 561, 564–566, 602f.
Judge, E.A.　565
Jülicher, A.　326–328
Juster, J.　564
Justin Martyr　6, 15

Kee, H. C.　315, 316
Keim, T.　449
Keller, E. & M.-L.　317
Kelly, J.N.D.　32, 438
Kendall, D.　15
Kepler, J.　314
Kersten, H. & E.R. Gruber　8f,
　　15, 567
Kilpatrick, G.D.　68
Kirk, A.　31
Kissinger, W. S.　274, 354, 356
Kittel, G.　274
Klausner, J.　502, 516, 518
Knox, D.B.　481, 603
Koch, K.　316
Kopp, C.　225
Kroll, G.　226, 227, 517
Kümmel, W. G.　170f, 196
Kung, H.　566, 604

Lacey, D.R. de.　395
Ladd, G. E.　170f, 196

Lapide, P.　11, 15, 30, 32
Laplace, P.S.　281
Lee, G.M.　68
Levine, L. I.　226
Liddell, H. G. & R. Scott　317
Lightfoot, R.H.　153
Linnemann, E.　194, 354
Lohmeyer, E.　174, 197, 276
Long, S.M.S.　567
Lüdemann, G.　10, 15

Maccoby, H.　272, 365, 368, 393,
　　394, 395, 396
Manson, T.W.　110, 134, 479, 480,
　　481, 518
Manson, W.　67, 480
Marsh, C.　196
Marshall, I.H.　272
Marxsen, W.　10
Mazar, B.　566
McEleney, N.J.　69
McGing, B. C　543, 564
Mealand, D. L.　276
Meier, J. P.　105, 106
Metzger, B. M.　227, 480, 566
Meyer, B. F.　105, 133, 173, 197,
　　356, 397, 480
Michaels, J. R.　32
Milik, J.T.　350, 356
Millar, F.　226
Miyoshi, M.　480
Montefiore, H.　411, 437
Moore, G. F.　105, 395
Morison, F.　22f, 31, 564
Morris, L. L.　393, 482, 487, 515,
　　565, 567
Moule, C.F.D.　11, 15, 31, 59, 309,
　　317, 354, 355

Nahor, P.　437
Nardoni, E.　604
Neugebauer, F.　134f

Neusner, J.   272, 365, 367, 368,
     393, 394, 395
Nolan, A.   78, 105

O'Collins G.   15
Origen   6, 15, 68, 317, 555, 566
Owen, O.T.   69

Pannenberg, W.   11, 15, 31
Papias   42, 68
Paulus, H.E.G.   7, 13, 314
Payne, P. B.   335, 353, 355
Percy, E.   274
Perkins, P.   482
Philo   272, 543, 564f
Philostratus   285-287, 314, 315
Phlegon   558
Pliny   550, 566
Ploeg, J. P. van der.   227, 317
Pokorny, P.   133, 134
Powell, M.A.   394
Powers, B.W.   396

Reich, R.   567
Reicke, B.   32
Reimarus, H.S.   xvii, 7, 9, 12, 23,
     51, 55, 167, 196, 601, 603
Renan, E.   314, 412, 449f, 479
Richardson, A.   515
Riesner, R.   64, 104, 195, 227,
     273, 356, 563
Rissi, M.   69
Ritschl, A.   167
Rivkin, E.   393
Robinson, J.A.T.   32, 69, 104,
     135, 138, 152-154, 436, 437,
     438, 478, 516, 564, 565
Romeo, J.A.   69
Rosadi, G.   565
Ross, J.M.   69

Sanday, W.   153

Sanders, E.P.   109, 147f, 154, 173,
     176, 197, 248, 272, 274, 365,
     367, 388, 393, 394, 397, 507,
     519
Sanders, J. T.   133, 394
Schleiermacher, F.D.E.   137, 314
Schürer, E.   195, 272, 273, 316,
     393, 397, 478, 516, 564, 565,
     602
Schürmann, H.   xiv, xxiii, 274
Schweitzer, A.   xiii, xxii, 10, 13,
     169, 274, 277, 314, 354, 403-
     406, 412, 428, 435, 437, 468,
     470, 479, 481, 493, 529, 558,
     563, 577, 601
Scobie, C.H.H.   106
Scofield. C.I.   274
Seccombe, D.   xxiii, 67f, 106, 135,
     195f, 199, 271, 273, 275, 394,
     396, 481, 603
Selwyn, E. G.   32
Shanks, H. & D. P. Cole   603
Sherwin-White, A.N.   539, 544,
     563, 565, 566
Smith, B.   227
Smith, M.   308, 317, 515
Stange, C.   274
Storr, G.C.   66
Stott, J.R.W.   11, 272
Strack, H.L. & P. Billerbeck.   176,
     273, 435, 519
Strauss, D.F.   xiii, 9, 15, 23, 31,
     137, 167, 196, 314, 594, 603

Tatian   xxiii
Taylor, V.   34, 134f, 226, 404, 414,
     428, 435, 437, 468, 481, 515, 518
Tertullian   68
Theissen, G.   105, 226, 392
Thiering, B.   8, 15, 412, 437
Thompson, G.P.   135
Tolstoy, L.N.   274

Trudinger, P.   69
Tuckett, C. M.   67
Tzaferis, V.   225

Vermes, G.   106, 199, 284f, 315,
   317, 396
Via, D. O.   354
Vine, V. E.   67

Wachsman, S.   225
Weber, H.-R.   566
Weiss, J.   168f, 196
Weisse, C.H.   66
Wenham, D.   340, 355
Wenham, J.   35, 51, 54, 67f, 226,
   435, 481, 604
Westcott, B. F.   10, 137, 152, 515,
   549, 565
Williams, C.S.C.   67
Wilson, A.N.   31

Windisch, H.   197
Winter, P.   39, 565
Winterbotham, R.   517
Witherington, B.   438
Wood, H.G.   438
Wrede, W.   228, 301, 316, 323,
   354, 416, 481
Wright, C.J.H.   195, 197
Wright, N.T.   14, 105, 106, 173,
   177, 185, 197, 199, 344, 356,
   479, 494, 495, 496, 517, 518,
   529, 563, 585, 603, 604

Yoder, J. H.   195, 276

Zahn, T.   438, 565
Zerwick, M.   517
Zias, J. & E. Sekeles.   566
Ziesler, J. A   393
Zimmerli, W.   274, 275, 563

Subject Index

Abomination of desolation   385f, 583

Abraham   121, 180-181

Adam (and Eve)   91, 114, 117-119, 121, 457f, 535

Adultery   384f

Agrippa II, Herod   25, 436

Akiba,Rabbi   367, 380

Alexander Jannaeus   364

Allegory   326, 328

Ananias: 26

Andrew   40, 202, 230, 233, 244

Angels   45, 51, 117-119, 127-131, 343f

Annas (Ananus, High Priest):   29, 537f, 598

Anti-Christ   132

Anti -Semitism   365f, 391f

Antiochus Epiphanes   363

Antipas   see Herod Antipas

Anxiety   267f

Apollonius of Tyana   285-7, 293

Apologetics   48

Apostles   30, 401-403, 530f, 243, 247

Apostleship: 26

Archelaus: 172, 495f

Aretas   407

Arrest, Jesus'   112, 536f

Ascension   49

Asclepius   291

Athens   4, 25

Atonement   101-102, 113-114, 159, 182, 529, 535

Augustus   436, 495

Authority   213

Authority, Jesus'   422-4, 214-225, 230

Authorship   40-44, 137

Babylon   126, 162, 182

Banquet, Messianic   412, 590, 602, 263

Baptism   xviii, 79, 80, 81-85, 88-90, 96-101, 108, 114, 122, 141, 145, 150-151

Barabbas   547f, 556, 210

Barnabas   41

Bartimaeus   493

Believing   61, 194 (see also, faith)

Bethany in Peraea   49

Bethany in Judaea   484, 499, 501, 505, 532,

Bethesda, Pool of   290f

Bethlehem   436

Bethsaida   411, 413, 421, 437, 448

Birth, Jesus'   xxiii, 42, 96

Blasphemy   220

Blindness (Blind)   163-164, 255, 421, 424, 432, 493

Blood   527

Bodily resurrection   53, 62

Bread   124-126

Bridegroom   144, 150, 152, 155, 242, 335
Buddhism   1-2
Burial, Jesus'   12

Caesar   548
Caesarea Maritima   205
Caesarea Philippi   421f, 427, 431
Caiaphas   409, 489, 520, 537-42, 560
Calendar   436, 524
Call of disciples   243
Capernaum   200-228, 295, 301, 304, 407, 413, 422, 425, 437, 448
Captives   255, 312
Celebration   240-2
Children   177-178, 219, 238, 443, 504
Chorazin   448
Chronology   211, 398-439, 409f, 428, 436, 523-5, 549f
Church   xix, 121, 239, 245, 464
Chuza   435
Circumstantial evidence   14-23
Clement of Alexandria   136-137
Cleopas   52
Commandments   *see* Law
Communism   125
Community   149, 177-178, 264f, 269, 347, 351
Compassion   292f, 511
Consummation   126, 185
Contradictions   51-52, 141
Corpse   387
Covenant   112, 129, 147, 162, 180-182, 389
Covenantal Nomism   388f
Creation   117-119, 180, 281, 297
Crucifixion (cross)   50, 167, 204, 302, 364, 469, 472f, 474f, 545, 553-9, 573

Daniel   324
Darkness   558, 573
Dating of Gospels   36-44, 71, 137, 146
David (King)   20, 92, 100, 112, 180-181, 514

Dead Sea Scrolls   *see* Qumran
Death   4
Death penalty   544f
Death, Jesus'   xxiii, 7 (also see Crucifixion)
Decapolis   303, 415f, 409, 427-436, 446, 467-78
Dedication, Feast of   401, 419, 459-462
Defilement   385f
Delay of Kingdom   493-499, 500, 577f
Demons   215, 295-305, 401, 419
Demon Possession   215, 290, 295-305, 419
Dereliction, Cry of   558f
Devil   *see* Satan
Disciples   59, 114, 139, 141-142, 150, 173-174, 229-276, 306f, 351f, 371, 378f, 399, 416-429, 522, 532
Divine man   287
Divinity   90-91, 101, 157
Divorce   382-5
Dominion   117-119, 131-132, 184-185
Doublets   415f, 452

Earthquake   54, 58
Economy of Israel   210-211
Education   247
Egeria   21, 216
Egypt   101-102
Ein Samiyah   491
Elijah   71-78, 113, 424, 432 (*see also* John the Baptist)
Emmaus Road   46, 49, 52
Ephraim   491
Essenes   8, 82
Et Taiyebah   491f
Eternal Life   266f, 352f, 412, 426, 431
Ethics   86-88, 261-271, 389
Evidence   37-66, 282-4, 305, 306, 310
Exile   114, 159, 173, 185
Existence of God   2

Exodus 102, 420, 432, 470f, 526
Exorcism 214-216, 299-305, 401 (*see also* Miracles)
Ezra 25

Face, Jesus' xviiif,
Faith 127ff, 137, 143, 224f, 268, 294,f416f
Fall 118-119
Family 230, 267f, 380
Family, Jesus' 302, 351, 448, 474
Fasting xviii, 86, 109-115, 124-126, 131, 150, 159, 241, 429, 533
Feeding of 4000 415-417, 420, 424, 433, 438
Feeding of 5000 279, 282, 309f, 410-413, 417, 420, 424, 433, 438
Felix 310
Figtree 336-8, 505
Fish, Fishing, Fishermen 202, 207, 232f
Food 368f, 386
Forgiveness 85-86, 89, 114, 159, 220-2, 251, 527-30
Fourth Philosophy 363f
Fulfilment of Scripture/Prophesy 77, 112-113, 160-161, 192-194, 387f, 574
Future 577f, 581-597

Gamaliel I 25
Gamaliel II 288
Galilean Ministry 140-141, 145, 151-152, 155, 178, 357f, 440, 446-452
Galileans 203, 405, 410, 537
Galilee 203-11, 405-7, 421, 429, 495
Gehenna *see* Hell
Genealogy 100, 122
Generation 596f
Gentiles 39, 93, 157, 183, 223, 235, 340, 344, 414, 451, 472f, 512, 544, 551f, 583-5, 586, 602
Gessius Florus 39

Gethsemane 121, 532-7
Ghost 53
Glory 463-6
Glory of God xviii
God, Jesus as 221, 231, 425, 575f
Gospel 155-156, 191-194, 404, 455, 487f
Gospel of Peter 18, 31, 52-53, 56
Great Commission 54
Greed 266f
Guards at tomb 54-58
Guilt 529f

Hanina ben Dosa 287-9
Hardness of Heart 325, 331, 384, 418, 451
Harmonization of Gospels 33-34, 58, 136ff, 139 -152
Hasidim 363f
Healing 283, 370-2
Healing,
   disciples 401
   Jesus 217f, 252, 277-318, 375-7, 415, 421, 445
Heaven 1, 89, 142, 144,
Hell 464, 589f
Herald 253-6
Herod the Great 95, 100, 146, 172, 203-206, 302, 364, 408, 436, 495, 582
Herod Agrippa II see Agrippa II
Herod Antipas 72-74, 152, 174, 204-6, 222f, 234f, 278, 302, 357, 406-409, 411, 415, 418, 423, 435, 476f, 547, 550
Herodians 428
Herodias 278, 407
High Priest 55, 29, 358
Hillel 25, 214, 384
Historical Jesus xix, 110
Historical reconstruction 33-35, 42, 64-66, 136, 145-147
History 306, 408f
Holocaust 551

Holy Spirit   *see* Spirit
Hospitality   401
Hour   151, 155
House, Peter's   216f
Hypocrisy   365, 379, 385, 390-2
Hyrcanus, John   444

Identity,
  Jesus   221f, 398-434, 572-6
Immorality of the soul   4
Incarnation   90
Intention, Jesus'   xvii, xxii, 526-31
Isaac   513
Isaiah   326, 590, 598, 602
Israel   114-115, 180ff, 239, 511f, 530f,
  551-3, 574, 578-581
Israel, destruction of   xxii, 114 (*see
  also* Jerusalem, fall)

James, brother of Jesus   27, 28, 29,
  157, 544
James, son of Zebedee   230, 400,
  432f, 465
Jeremiah   508
Jericho   492, 496
Jerusalem   59-60, 141, 143, 146, 150-
  152, 167, 187-189, 205, 462, 488,
  504f
Jerusalem, fall of   37-38 (*see also*
  Israel, destruction) 182, 582-4
Jesus Seminar   12, 171-172
Jesus, son of Ananias   362, 547
Jew-Gentile debate   55-57
Joanna   51
Job   119-120
Johanan ben Zakkai   244, 257f, 372
John the Apostle   43-44, 60ff, 76,
  202, 210, 230, 252, 400, 432f, 465,
  537f, 543, 598
John the Baptist   70-104, 112, 114,
  141-142, 144, 148, 150, 155, 164,
  171, 241, 244, 251, 278f, 284, 302,
  336, 343, 357, 406-9, 419, 423, 436,
  510f

John, Gospel of   136-151, 352f, 425,
  485, 491
John Hyrcanus   364
Jonah   114, 477
Joseph of Arimathea   243, 559f
Joshua   411
Journey to Jerusalem   459f
Jubilee   158-160, 162-164, 193, 405
Judaism   3, 24, 83-84, 147, 158, 169,
  189, 235f, 289, 307, 388
Judas Iscariot   8, 499f, 532, 598
Judas Maccabaeus   364
Judas son of Ezekias   203f
Judgement   4, 72, 78-79, 81, 85, 101,
  108, 114-115, 118, 162, 164, 170-
  171, 180, 325, 336-8, 343, 402f,
  444, 448f, 456f, 498f, 505, 551f,
  589

Kepler, Johann   281
King   *see* Messiah
Kingdom of God   xi, xviii, xxii, 3, 75,
  77, 85, 87f, 126, 130-133, 144, 149,
  150f, 155f, 164-194, 224f, 229, 279,
  310-13, 319-56, 238-42, 262-71,
  359-62, 387-90, 401, 405f, 418, 428,
  430f, 433, 440-82, 493-9, 525f,
  530f, 546, 556f, 559, 577-581, 591-
  4, 600-602
Kingship,
  Jesus   263, 302, 410-434, 463-7,
  502-4, 530f
Koran   2

Lamb of God   101-102
Lamb, Passover   526
Lament   558f
Last Supper   521-532
Law   76, 82, 86, 147, 155, 180, 262,
  361, 366-390
Lazarus   483-91
Leadership   411f
Liberation Theology   160-161
Life   126

Light   156, 163-164, 183
Lives, of Jesus   xiii,xvif,xxiii, 7, 8, 10, 279
Logos   374
Lord's Prayer   121
Love   257-9, 263, 381, 389
Love,
   Jesus   521-3
Luke (author)   37ff, 156, 249f, 265, 365f

Maccabees   39
Machaerus   407
Magdala   202
Magi   100
Magic, magician   287, 291, 307f, 362
Manna   420, 424-6
Mark, Gospel of   45, 416, 428
Mark, John   41-42
Markan Priority   36, 66-67, 42, 51, 137
Marriage   382-5
Martyrdom   469-71, 533
Mary Magdalene   45, 60-62, 305, 309, 400
Mary and Martha   483-9, 499-500
Mary, Mother of Jesus   45, 147, 142-143, 151
Mary, Song of   39
Materialism   279-82
Matthew (author)   219, 230, 233f
Matthew, Gospel of   249f, 366
Meals   235f, 240-2, 368f, 400, 418f, 523
Medicine   295, 300
Melchizedek   160
Messiah   3, 4, 21, 24, 25, 29, 50, 54, 75-77, 85, 90, 102, 108, 122-133, 142, 145, 151, 166-167, 181-183, 189, 221f, 240, 248f, 301f, 359-62, 410-434, 497, 502, 513f, 541f, 545f, 572, 575
Messianic expectation   38-39, 78, 80-82, 87, 91-96, 162-164
Messianic age   241f, 420, 444

Millennium   166
Miracles   xv, 65-66, 72, 111, 127-131, 143, 150, 165-166, 277-318, 360-2, 412, 418, 420, 426, 485-7, 536
Miracles,
disciples   407
Mishnah   83, 86, 288, 371f, 538f
Mission   256-9, 263
Mission of 12   400-409, 414
Mission of 72   401, 452-462
Mission to Gentiles   344, 414, 584f, 602
Modernism   116
Money   209, 266 (*see also* Possessions)
Mormonism   14
Moses   24, 25, 231f, 244f, 253, 262, 284f, 411, 424-6, 432 (*see also* Sinai)
Muhammed   1-2
Mystery, of Kingdom   xvii, 323f
Mythology   109, 115-116, 167, 280

Nathaniel   400, 435
Nature   279, 282, 296
Nazareth   142, 156ff, 308, 398f, 405, 423, 429, 477
Nebuchadnezzar   176, 184
Necessity of Jesus
death   50
Nero   25, 28, 36-37
New Age   xi,xxii, 248f, 376f, 402, 660 (*see also* Restoration of Israel)
Nicodemus   144-145, 147, 149, 362, 430f, 560

Occult   295
Old Testament imagery   38, 111-112, 149, 178-179, 183
Onias the Circlemaker   285

Papias   42-43, 211, 415
Parables   172, 175-176, 319-356, 412, 419, 427, 494-6, 502
Parousia   494 (*see also* Second Coming)

Passover 59, 64, 143–144, 146, 409f, 420, 437, 490ff, 520-532
Paul 12, 19f, 23–27, 37–39, 41, 65, 67, 232, 322, 376f, 409, 414, 451, 598
Peace 352
Peace making 259, 430
Pella 584
Pentecost, Day of 20–23, 58
Peraea 407, 459f, 495
Persecution 36, 251f, 403-8, 429, 582f
Peter 20–23, 27, 28f, 32, 37–38, 42, 47, 52–53, 63–64, 140, 202, 211f, 216–18, 230, 232f, 236f, 293f, 400, 413, 415, 417, 424, 431-3, 463–6, 487, 522, 531f, 536, 539, 597
Petra 407
Pharisees 11, 20, 76, 79, 82, 86, 114, 144f, 150, 190, 208, 213f, 219-22, 234-247, 311, 357-397, 414, 418, 423, 429, 432, 489
Philip 495
Philo 84
Philosophy 281
Pilate 55, 336, 409, 539f, 543-50, 598
Plan of God 50, 75, 89, 95, 122-123, 130-131, 133, 180ff
Political revolution xiii, 73-74, 78, 88, 110, 129-130
Polycarp 43
Poor 209, 238, 253–6, 430, 499f
Possessions 231, 265-271
Poverty 160-162, 266 (*see also* Possessions)
Power 442f, 463-7
Prayer 112, 120, 218, 262, 287-9, 292, 532-5, 556
Preaching xxii, 4, 13, 45–46, 64, 99-100, 140, 156, 191, 218, 329-32
Predestination 325, 451
Predictions 467-9, 581-97
Presuppositions 35

Priests 92, 180, 489f, 537-48
Prophet, Jesus as 419f, 423, 427, 576f
Prophets/prophecy 41, 49-50, 71, 75, 84, 92-93, 98, 130, 145, 185, 213f, 361, 502, 509, 577
Proselytes 84
Psychology 110, 298, 529, 555
Psychology of Jesus 428, 449f
Purity 235f, 368f, 378

Q 39, 42, 44, 74, 109, 249
Quirinius 206
Qumran 79–80, 82–83, 94, 102, 112, 128, 137, 154, 159-160, 162, 164, 188, 215, 236, 245, 254f, 278, 300, 338f, 342f, 374
Quest of Jesus *see* Intention
Quest, Third xxii

Rationalism 279, 300
Rebirth 144-145, 149
Redemption, ransom 470f, 526, 528-30, 535
Repentance 74, 82-83, 84, 85, 148, 194, 240f, 325f, 380, 404-6, 448
Restoration of Israel xxii, 147-151, 158-194, 239f, 245f, 248f, 255, 271, 279, 492, 530f, 590
Resurrection, General 2, 3, 6, 19, 190, 571f
Resurrection, Jesus' 1-69, 110, 143, 308, 416f, 475-8, 581f, 593f
Revelation 114
Revolution 103f, 209f, 251, 363f
Roads 203, 225
Roman Government in Judaea 204-6, 222f, 310, 359, 489f, 536f, 539f, 544f
Rome 37, 202, 313, 495, 579f

Sabbath 211f, 217, 370-2, 375-7, 445, 492
Sacrifices 148, 507, 524f, 528-30

Sadducees   11, 43, 82, 190, 358, 364, 367, 391
Salome   45
Salvation   78-79, 133, 115, 144, 163-164, 171, 180, 193, 294f
Samaria-Samaritans   145, 149-151, 155, 307
Samuel   98
Sanhedrin   25, 144, 489-91, 525, 538-542
Satan   109-131, 160, 162, 186, 297-305, 342f, 431, 433f, 457f, 471-3, 534, 601
Science   279-282, 295f
Schooling, Jesus   213
Scribes   213, 307, 423
Scriptures   213f
Scrolls   47-49
Sea of Galilee   202, 303, 410, 413, 418
Second coming   xiii, 43-44, 63-64, 493-9, 585-97
Secret, Messianic   301-3, 495
Sepphoris   203f, 210, 302
Sermon on the Mount   246, 249-61, 429f
Servant of the Lord   96-98, 115, 123, 131, 157ff, 183, 253-9, 347, 404, 430, 434, 446, 475f, 522f, 527f, 531
Sex   400
Shammai   25, 214, 384
Sheep   239f
Shepherd   239f, 411f
Signs   293, 297, 360-2, 402, 419, 424, 426, 455, 477, 532, *see also* Miracles
Silvanus, Silas   32, 42
Simon ben Kosiba   364
Simon of Cyrene   554
Simon Magus   8
Simon the Zealot   400
Sin   88-90, 102, 114, 131, 220f, 331f, 529, 581
Sinai   111, 113, 180, 464

Sinners   233-5, 237-9, 369f, 400, 492
Slaves   244
Socio-economic conditions in Israel   200-211
Socrates   4, 533
Sodom   440
Solomon   117
Son of God   92, 101, 122-124, 131, 133, 135, 180, 417, 511-14, 548, 573f
Son of Man   44, 169-170, 184-185, 198-199, 255f, 348-51, 375, 403, 428, 441f, 473, 475, 541f, 575, 585-590
Spirit, Holy   81, 90, 92, 97-98, 133, 144, 149, 156, 171, 183, 193, 299, 402, 575f
Spirits, evil   *see* Demons
Spiritual experience   13f
Spiritual kingdom   xxii, 167-168, 466f
Spread of Christianity   37
Stephen   544
Stoning   491, 545
Suffering   118-120, 277f, 251f, 335
Suffering, disciples'   256-9, 429, 474f
Suffering, Jesus'   428-434, 441f, 467-78
Suffering, Messianic   277f
Synagogue   157f, 201, 211-16, 223, 301, 304, 368

Tabernacles, Feast of   359f, 444-6, 460-462, 502
Tabgha   201
Talmud   83
Targums   77, 94f, 102, 187
Tax Collectors   234f, 237f, 400, 492
Taxation   204-6, 234
Teacher   253, 260, 261f, 320-56, 412
Temple   127-131, 143ff, 146-148, 154, 173, 181-183, 205, 444f, 501, 506-14, 573

Temple, cleansing of 136, 143–144, 145–149, 506–8
Temple, destruction of 37, 508, 540, 583f (*see also* Fall of Jerusalem)
Temple tax 506f, 204, 371
Temptation 108–131, 165, 179, 298, 534f, 557
Theft of Jesus' body 54
Theophilus 50, 228
Theudas 310
Thomas 62, 484, 575
Tiberias 202, 210, 235, 407, 412,
Tiberius 409, 436
Tomb, empty 6, 7, 19–23, 45–46
Tradition 213f, 235f, 378f
Transfiguration 432–4, 447
Trial, Jesus' 537–553
Twelve, The 29, 247–9, (*see also* Disciples)

Varus 302
Via Maris 225

Violence xviii
Visions 25–27
Vows 379f

Way, The 24, 31
Wealth 492 (*see also* Possessions)
Wedding 142–143, 147, 149, 241f
Wilderness xviii, 108–133, 156, 420
Wine 142–143, 147, 149
Wisdom 374
Witnesses 18, 23–30, 45–46, 60, 65, 109, 157, 282, 326, 540, 550
Women 18, 46–48, 51, 56, 58, 399, 543f, 294, 382–5
Word of God 352f
World 2, 3, 131–133, 346
Worship 118, 131–133, 145, 148, 149

Zacchaeus 492, 598, 239
Zealots 363
Zechariah's Song 39